ISBN 978-1-5284-8428-2
PIBN 10145331

READINGS IN
VOCATIONAL GUIDANCE

EDITED BY

MEYER BLOOMFIELD
DIRECTOR OF THE VOCATION BUREAU OF BOSTON

GINN AND COMPANY
BOSTON · NEW YORK · CHICAGO · LONDON
ATLANTA · DALLAS · COLUMBUS · SAN FRANCISCO

The Athenæum Press

GINN AND COMPANY · PRO-
PRIETORS · BOSTON · U.S.A.

TO
A. LINCOLN FILENE

PREFACE

A new literature has come into being within the present decade. Indeed just seven years have passed since Professor Frank Parsons gave the closing years of his life to the Vocation Bureau of the Civic Service House in Boston.

From that beginning the vocational-guidance movement and its literature have grown apace, in definiteness, in insight, and in service. To be sure, the aims of vocational guidance are nothing new in either educational statement or practice. The starting of youth aright in life work is one of the oldest of human interests. Not for centuries later did this interest receive so complete an expression as in the practices of the more enlightened medieval guilds of England and Germany.

Before the close of the nineteenth century, however, youth in quest of a life-career was regaled with the familiar literature of the "How to Succeed" type, which naïvely reflected the uncritical individualism of an age that is gone. That type of vocational monitor is still a frequent apparition, amidst the realistic productions of a wiser outlook on life.

What is vocational guidance? Briefly it is organized common sense used to help each individual make the most of his abilities and opportunities.

Vocational guidance aims to make both school and occupation help boys and girls to discover and develop their powers for service, through school programs in charge of specially trained vocational counselors in schools and employment programs in charge of specially trained employment supervisors in the occupations. Vocational guidance is not a scheme of finding jobs; of forcing vocational decisions upon children; of naïvely adjusting human "pegs" to "holes"; or of narrowing the range of service open to the fit. In a word, it is clear that through thoughtful study of the problems of life work and its choice and through creative sympathy real help may be given, where help is now wanting, to thousands of perplexed youths groping through the complex conditions and demands of the twentieth century.

About half of America's school children quit school for work before they have even finished the grades of the elementary school. These children usually decide to leave of their own accord; they alone make the momentous decisions as to why and when they will leave school, what job they will go into, and how soon they will quit one job for another. Home, school, and employer are of little influence in these grave decisions so vital to the future of these children and our citizenship. Thousands drift aimlessly through school, through work, and through life. Where so many work-beginners seek jobs rather than opportunities for a life work, there can be no foundation for a right attitude toward work.

Pleas for interest in work, loyalty, esprit de corps, training, and efficiency fall on barren ground. The best proof of wasteful drift in work may be found in the large numbers of places held by children during their early working years, and in the excessive turn-over of the working force of the average establishment. This frequent change in employees, this human "turnover," is waste to the child during the decisive years of adolescence, waste to his family, to his employer, and to society.

Obviously the situation just described is not only costly and wasteful, it is needless and in large part preventable. To allow it to go on in the vain hope that somehow boys and girls will eventually find themselves rightly located in the work of the world, is to shut one's eyes to the obvious. Such a situation in the twentieth century is wholly at variance with its conservation spirit.

The main problem, then, is to bridge the gap between school and the after-school life of our future workers and citizens. The solution of this problem means making school life more interesting and purposeful, and working life more educative and productive.

As the result of the vocational-guidance movement, there is now a country-wide endeavor to help children make their start in life with purpose, preparation, and insight. Hundreds of schools and philanthropic agencies are either carrying on vocational-guidance projects or planning to do so.

Nearly a score of colleges, universities, and other institutions are conducting special or part-time courses in vocational guidance. The first college course given in this subject was that at the Harvard University Summer School in 1911 by the Vocation Bureau.

There is plentiful testimony showing that, as a result of the vocational-guidance movement, fathers and mothers now turn to the schools as never before for advice and help concerning their children's future. The abilities, the interests, faults, and promising tendencies in the children are topics of grave discussion between parent and teacher or principal, the viewpoint being not only that of present school requirements but also that of the probable careers of the children. School programs, and even commencement-day programs, have begun to show how schools are facing the challenging world, which is soon to claim the productive years of these children.

Already teachers, on their own initiative and with an expenditure of much time and energy, have gone into the homes of their pupils and have sought to get first-hand knowledge of the industrial environment. If our schools are to have any guiding relation to life (and all educational reform clamors for this relation), teachers must be given every incentive to touch in such personal ways the realities of the lives which their pupils will experience.

The material of the present volume, as contrasted with the earlier " success " order of books, embraces some of the more significant vocational-guidance utterances in terms of the twentieth-century spirit. The citations have been arranged with a view to developing the subject of vocational guidance in a logical and comprehensive fashion. Much more might have been included, had not the limits of this volume, already of fair proportions, necessitated a reluctant setting aside of much valuable material. The volume has been prepared with the hope that it may stimulate the reader to pursue the study of vocational guidance itself, and to follow it also in related fields of economics, psychology, education, and social service.

Thanks are due to the authors and publishers named in the table of contents for generous permission to use their contributions.

MEYER BLOOMFIELD

VOCATION BUREAU, BOSTON

CONTENTS

ix

READINGS IN VOCATIONAL GUIDANCE

A
GENERAL DESCRIPTION

OF ALL

T R A D E S,

DIGESTED IN

Alphabetical Order:

BY WHICH

Parents, Guardians, and Trustees, may, with greater Eafe and Certainty, make choice of Trades agreeable to the Capacity, Education, Inclination, Strength, and Fortune of the Youth under their Care.

CONTAINING,

I. How many Branches each is divided into.
II. How far populous, or neceffary.
III. Which they require moft, Learning, Art, or Labour.
IV. What is commonly given with an Apprentice to each.
V. Hours of Working, and other Cuftoms ufual among them.
VI. Their Wages, and how much may be earned by, or is commonly given to, Journey-men.
VII. What Money is neceffary to fet up a Perfon in each.
VIII. Which are incorporated Companies, with the Time of their Incorporation, Livery-fine, Situation of their Hall, Court-day, Defcription of their Arms, Mottos, &c.

To which is Prefixed,

ESSAY on Divinity, Law, and Physic.

L O N D O N:

Printed for T. Waller, at the *Crown* and *Mitre*, oppofite *Fetter-lane, Fleet-ftreet.* M DCC XLVII.

TITLE-PAGE OF A FORERUNNER IN VOCATIONAL GUIDANCE

This and the two following facsimiles are reproduced from a "contemporary ancestor" in vocational guidance, in the Astor Library collection of the New York Public Library

PREFACE.

*T*HE *Pains and Time spent in compiling this little Book were greater than at first can be conceived, but which will more fully appear on the Perusal, by the great Variety of Matters occurring, which were to be obtained by* Personal Enquiries only : *How well executed, and of what Advantage they may be, the Public will know by Time and Experience.*

It may be truly said, that the greatest Part of this Work is entirely new.

The Uses of it pretty well appear by the Title, which, I doubt not in the least, will answer the chief End proposed, that of giving Parents, Guardians, *and* Trustees, *as well as the* Youths. *themselves, intended for* Trades *and* Business, *not only a general Description of almost all* Handicrafts, Trades, *and* Employs *in Vogue, but also such Particulars of them. as will enable both the one and the other to form a tolerable Judgment which of them all may be most agreeable, and best answer their Purpose.*

And, pray now, what Step in Life is of greater Consequence, than the well placing-out your Offspring in Business? Does not their future Well-doing very much depend upon this? How many hopeful Youths have been ruined, by being put to Trades, *or* Callings, *either improper for them, or they unfit for? But now, 'tis presumed, the splitting on that Rock may, in a great Measure, be prevented: Therefore, 'tis hoped, our Endeavours will meet with Approbation.*

The

PREFACE.

The Matters relating to the several City Companies, *we apprehend, will be found not only useful, but entertaining, they being no where digested in so full, yet concise and methodical a Manner: Nay, indeed, the Whole, being reduced into* Order of Alphabet, *must render the Inspection of any Particular, at all times, as ready as possible: And to be able to compare one* Trade or Business *with another, and instantly to see the vast Differences between such Variety of them, must be no less amusing and instructive: In short, jointly or separately, it may be taken as an* historical Abridgment of Mechanic and Mercantile Affairs.

Now there remains only for me to request the candid Reader, *that, upon his meeting with here and there some little things, that may not exactly tally with his Knowledge or Judgment, he will not immediately condemn the Whole, or major Part, which he knows nothing of: But consider how many different Persons must have been consulted, to gain so much Intelligence as is herein communicated; and add to this the Oddness and Variety of Men's Tempers, on being asked three or four civil Questions, the answering which was no Trouble, nor could be any Detriment; yet some were shy, others jealous; some testy, others sour; nay, some quite angry, thinking one was come as a Spy to steal the Secrets of their Trade: And, besides all this, several of the same* Trade or Business *were met with, who gave very different Accounts.*

Therefore, if any intelligent Persons will, on finding any thing material amiss, or omitted, be so good as to minute it down, and send it to the Bookseller, it shall be carefully corrected or inserted, and the Favour gratefully acknowledged, in our next Edition.

The AUTHOR.

AN

READINGS IN VOCATIONAL GUIDANCE

PART I. THE VIEWPOINT OF VOCATIONAL GUIDANCE

THE VALUE DURING EDUCATION OF THE LIFE-CAREER MOTIVE

By Charles W. Eliot, President Emeritus of Harvard University

(An Address delivered to the National Education Association, Boston, 1910)

The teaching profession nowadays fully recognizes the fact that only those processes of education are successful which procure the active interest and coöperation of the minds and wills subjected to them. During early school life the intelligent teacher tries in every way to rouse and maintain the interest of the pupil in the subjects of study, and endeavors to select studies for the individual pupil which are likely to hold his interest. For many children this animating and selective task on the part of the teacher is a difficult one; and for the great majority of American children of from twelve to sixteen years of age the schools fail to perform it. Hence, multitudes of American children, taking no interest in their school work, or seeing no connection between their studies and the means of later earning a good livelihood, drop out of school far too early of their own accord, or at least offer no effective resistance to the desire of unwise parents that they stop study and go to work. Moreover, from lack of interest they acquire while in school a listless way of working. Again, interest in their studies is not universal among that small proportion of American children who go on into a secondary school ; and in every college a perceptible proportion of the students exhibit a languid interest, or no interest, in their studies, and therefore bring little to pass during the very precious years of college life.

There are, however, certain regions in the total field of American education in which the internal motive of interest in the work comes into full play, with the most admirable results. In general, professional students in the United States exhibit keen interest in their studies, work hard, advance rapidly, and avail themselves of their opportunities to gain knowledge and skill to the utmost limit of their strength and capacity, no matter whether the profession for which they are preparing be divinity, law, medicine, architecture, engineering, forestry, teaching, business, or corporation service. In secondary education the high schools of commerce and mechanic arts have a decided advantage as regards motive power within the pupil over the ordinary high schools. The industrial schools, trade schools, continuation schools, evening and summer schools, business colleges, and Y.M.C.A. classes in secular subjects show a large proportion of strongly interested pupils. The part-time schools which some of the great corporations, like the General Electric Company, the New York Central Railroad, the Grand Trunk Railway, the Ludlow Manufacturing Associates, the Yale and Towne Manufacturing Company, and the International Harvester Company have been conducting for a few years past have no difficulty in interesting their pupils in those academic subjects which make part of their general shop instruction. When one goes through the shops and schoolrooms of Hampton Institute, where hundreds of negroes and scores of Indians are under instruction, or through the working-rooms of the Tuskegee Institute, thronged with negroes of all shades, one is struck with the eager application to the work in hand which is exhibited by the students. One sees no loafing or inattention, or uninterested work. Everyone, whether bright or dull, seems to be doing his best, and to be doing it with hearty good will. What is the motive power in the mind and will of the pupil or student in all these various successful educational institutions? It is the motive of the life-career.

A professional student has chosen his life-career. A pupil in a commercial high school or a mechanic-arts high school has made a primary decision with regard to his life-career; he has determined the first direction of his preparatory work, although later he may come to branchings of the way where a new decision will be needed. The apprentice in a railroad shop or an electric works has in like manner decided on one kind of a life-career, and is bent on pursuing it to advantage. The journeyman who has chosen one of the fundamental trades enlists in a public or endowed evening school or a Y.M.C.A. class with the purpose of improving himself in his trade or art, and believes that good work in the school will increase his earning capacity. The negro or Indian student at Hampton sees clearly that the studies and labors of the place will make him a better farmer, or a carpenter, mason, or wheelwright with good earning capacity; and he has decided to fit himself as well as he possibly can for some one of these gainful occupations. The apprenticeship method in education, though slow and liable to great abuses, produced for many centuries highly skilled workmen, who acquired all the accumulated skill of preceding generations and transmitted it with additions to the next. When, under the factory system, apprenticeship almost disappeared, it turned out that a successful method of education on a large scale had been well-nigh lost. Its success was due to the continuous play of the motive of the life-career. The intelligent leaders of American industries are now trying to recover the apprenticeship system with the modifications made necessary by the factory system. The students in a university summer school, a business college, or a technical school are, as a rule, persons who have chosen their calling, and believe that by taking appropriate additional instruction they can further themselves in that calling.

Of the pupils or students in all these educational institutions which give full play to the motive of the life-career, from the lowest industrial evening school to the highest professional school, that delightful thing can be said which Mr. Shrigley, President of the Williamson Free School of Mechanical Trades near Philadelphia, said in 1908 about trade schools:

The young men who are being trained in a properly conducted school of that type show great interest in their work, and are so enthusiastically devoted to it that their progress is wonderfully rapid and gratifying.

Indeed, on account of this enthusiasm and rapid progress among the students or pupils of such institutions, earnest teachers always enjoy working in them, and teachers who work both in schools where the life-career motive is recognized, and in those schools where it is not, invariably find the first sort of school more interesting and inspiring than the second.

We ought not to be surprised that schools which avail themselves of this strong motive get the best work from their pupils, and therefore do the best work for the community. All of us adults do our best work in the world under the impulsion of the life-career motive. Indeed, the hope and purpose of improving quality, or quantity, or both in our daily work, with the incidental improvement of the livelihood, form the strongest inducements we adults have for steady, productive labor ; and the results of labors so motived are not necessarily mercenary, or in any way unworthy of an intelligent and humane person. There is nothing low or mean about these motives, and they lead on the people who are swayed by them to greater serviceableness and greater happiness — to greater serviceableness, because the power and scope of individual productiveness are thereby increased ; to greater happiness, because achievement will become more frequent and more considerable, and to old and young alike happiness in work comes through achievement.

We come here upon the ancient controversy between pure and applied science, cultural and technical subjects in education, idealism and utilitarianism, and on the old distinction between living and earning a living. The immense increase in knowledge during the past hundred years and the innumerable new applications of knowledge for the benefit of mankind ought long ago to have persuaded us that a greatly enlarged definition of culture and of the cultivated man was indispensable. We also need to discard forever the notion that there is something vulgar or degraded about the useful and the serviceable. After all is said to the discredit of " bread and butter " motives, it is no moral or philosophical objection to a discovery or a field of knowledge that it has useful applications. Even in the realms of the beautiful, fitness for some human use enhances or contributes to beauty, or is an important element in it. A ripening field of grass or grain billowing in the summer wind is not less beautiful because it promises welcome food for man or beast. The apple blossoms are not less beautiful because apples will later be developed from them. The root of landscape beauty is adaptation to the delight and service of man. The useful invention of a Tungsten filament for an electric lamp is no less worthy or dignified than the apparently useless discovery attributed to Thales, that a piece of amber rubbed with a bit of silk would attract a light body delicately suspended by a fine thread. Moreover, the mental capacity involved in the invention of the Tungsten filament is, to say the least, just as strong as the capacity which Thales exhibited in his amber experiment. The student who masters the Tungsten-filament facts in their connection is just as worthily occupied as the student who makes himself acquainted with the exploit of Thales, although the observation on amber was innocent of applications to human welfare for two thousand years. Again, there is nothing inherently selfish or low-minded about hard mental work done in order to improve one's chances of earning a good livelihood, whether in overalls or apron, or in street clothes. Indeed, the earning of a good livelihood, whether by man or woman, is, as a rule, an altruistic performance in high degree — at least after twenty-five years of age, and often before that limit. The conception that useless knowledge is purer and loftier than useful belongs with the feudal system and with that conception of religion which makes it to consist largely of ceremonial, detaches it from ordinary human life, and regards it as in great part an other-world interest. American society has pretty well got over the feudal idea that a gentleman can have no other occupation than that of the soldier, the priest, or the landowner, and is beginning to understand that religion is primarily a matter of loving serviceableness in this world. It is high time that our teachers and leaders of the people understood that every civilized human being gets the larger part of his life training in the occupation through which he earns his livelihood, and that his schooling in youth should invariably be directed to prepare him in the best way for the best permanent occupation of which he is capable. In other words, the motive of the life-career should be brought into play as early and fully as possible.

It is obvious, however, that the early recognition and selection of the best life work for every child is a difficult matter. Let us next consider, therefore, first, the natural helps in performing this great function of the home and the school, and secondly, the precautions which can be taken in indeterminate cases. There are numerous cases in which an occupation is naturally transmitted from parents to children, or from one generation, in a broad sense, to another. Thus, in an agricultural region, or in a town of one industry or two or three industries, it is altogether probable that large groups of children will follow the occupations of their parents. Again, among the children in a given school there will always be a fair proportion whose natural gifts and tendencies become obvious to the observant teacher who watches them for years. Such children should be turned toward appropriate occupations by the teacher in consultation with the parents. There will also be a small proportion of children who know their own minds by the time they are fourteen years old. They too should be helped to the life work which attracts them. Finally, in every community and every school there will be a considerable number of children who can be fairly prepared for any one of several occupations, though not, perhaps, for the highest success in any one. To some one of these sets or classes the great majority of children in any community will be found to belong.

It is wise, if family circumstances permit, to postpone the actual training for a specific trade or occupation till at least the sixteenth year, because in most cases the body is not sufficiently developed before that age to undertake the real work of a trade. Most boys are not fitted for apprenticeship or a trade school until they are sixteen, and in general seventeen is a better age at which to begin. Children who must leave school at fourteen because of home conditions should be required to attend continuation schools or part-time schools; but to this end new legislation and the coöperation of mercantile establishments are necessary.

If, then, the motive of the life-career cannot be brought into full play before sixteen years of age, what precautions ought to be taken to maintain the interest of pupils in school studies up to that time, and to give them a training which will not only increase their mental power and their capacity for rational enjoyment but also their earn-ing capacity in a variety of occupations? In the first place, instruc-tion in every subject taught at school should be accompanied to the utmost extent possible by concrete illustration and fresh, current exemplification. Real shop problems should be used to illustrate the theoretical principles of geometry, mechanics, chemistry, and physics. This sort of illustration is available not only in mathe-matics and elementary science but also in languages, literature, and history. Secondly, much attention — much more than is now given — should be paid in every elementary and secondary school to the training of the eye, ear, and hand, for the reason, among others, that well-trained powers of sight, hearing, and touch are of high value in any life occupation. Thirdly, the elements of the arts applicable in ordinary households and in various trades or callings ought to be carefully taught in all schools, public, endowed, or private, such as drawing and designing, domestic science and art and home economics, carpentry and joinery, and, in rural com-munities, agriculture. Rural schools have an advantage here over urban schools, because agriculture has become such an admirable subject of school instruction since successful farming came to involve acquaintance with plant-breeding, animal-breeding, and a variety of crops, animals, manures, motors, and machines. For children between the ages of twelve and sixteen it is particularly important to provide various forms of training which they can see will be of use to them in after life. The provision of well-graded courses of that nature, with constant concrete illustration of every mental process or problem, will go far to hold the interest of the children in their school work, and prevent premature withdrawals or diminish the number of them.

The next question is — and it is a grave one — Who is going to guide the inexperienced child to a wise preliminary choice of the life-career? The answer must be, The parents and the teacher, but mainly the teacher. The parents and the teacher together ought to be easily able, in the first place, to give the right direction to that small proportion of children whose education clearly ought to be prolonged through the secondary school and the college because of good parts or favorable circumstances, and to that other small proportion whose natural bent is strong. These two sorts of children, however, together make but a small minority; the great majority show no decided bent, and seem about equally fit for any one of several callings, so that some authority must make a tentative sorting and an experimental assignment. Moreover, since the circumstances of the parents unfortunately determine for a large proportion of all children an early discontinuance of systematic education, the selective function of the teacher will at the best have serious limitations. Democratic society has as yet found no remedy for this undesirable abridgment of school life. The profession of teaching must recognize this fact and cope with it, so far as possible. At present we are permitting the great majority of American children to go out into the world as unskilled laborers, without having chosen any trade or other occupation requiring skill, and without having felt in their school work the motive of the life-career. This is an evil which is not to be cured by additional legislation merely. It must be cured by serious modifications of the programs of American elementary and secondary schools, by the acceptance on the part of teachers and school authorities of the function of guiding children into appropriate life work, and by providing new kinds of instruction and new organizations like continuation schools and trade schools. When Benjamin Franklin's father thought it was time for the boy to choose a trade, he took Benjamin about the town and showed him men at work in all the trades then practiced in Boston, and it was only after this comparative survey that Benjamin decided to be a printer. A very skillful printer he became by the time he was eighteen years old. American schools should perform this office for all pupils who ask for such guidance.

If this guiding and selecting function for the public schools looks difficult, we may get encouragement from the fact that it is by no means untried in the wide world of education. Germany, France, Switzerland, and Belgium can all show this thing actually done. Do you say, " True, but those countries are not so free industrially and socially as ours is. Their institutions, or their industrial conditions, or their family habits give them means of directing children into trades which we do not possess." It is well that we do not possess any means of compulsion, for success and happiness in life depend on the individual's following a congenial calling. It is highly inexpedient, as well as unjust, to force any child or youth into a trade which does not attract him, for in it he will be both inefficient and unhappy.

Many interesting experiments in this direction are already started in different parts of the United States, and most educational authorities are taking a keen, though sometimes uninstructed, interest in the general problem of vocational training. It will doubtless occur to many minds that an early choice of a trade or occupation may turn out to be an unwise one. Such mistakes, if soon discovered, will not be very serious under American industrial and social conditions, which are more mobile than those which prevail in Europe, so that an early mistaken choice of the calling can be more easily rectified here than it can be in the old countries. Moreover, a good training for any one trade will always contain many elements which are applicable in another trade; and if the motive of the life-career has been in good play, the animated mental and manual work done by the pupil will have been in some fair measure profitable toward the ultimate career.

When all available means have been used to discover the best vocation for each child and to direct him to it, there will remain in the mass of children who are approaching the end of their school life numerous indeterminate cases which afford no clue to the best calling — at least at the age at which choice urgently needs to be made. What policy should a well-organized school system follow in regard to such children? The first thing to be done is to keep such children interested in their school studies as long as possible, in the hope of preventing them from going to work as unskilled and immature wage earners. To maintain interest it will be expedient to offer in the school a considerable variety of studies, so that each child may have a chance to pursue the studies he most affects, whether chiefly manual, or chiefly mental, whether bookwork or shop work. This involves a school program stated in different groups, or offering options. A program of this sort will provide the best security a school system can furnish for a wise ultimate choice of a calling, for it will enable the undetermined pupil to select the studies to him most congenial. When at a later date he discovers and adopts the trade or occupation for which he is best adapted, it will turn out that by selecting the most congenial studies he will have prepared himself for the congenial trade or calling, because the same natural tendencies which directed him to the selected studies will direct him safely to the ultimate calling. A single uniform course of study prescribed to all offers no such security for pupils who cannot determine their trade or calling at fourteen, fifteen, sixteen, or seventeen years of age. This principle has already been thoroughly worked out with students of college age. Those who do not yet recognize their best calling in life should choose under a free elective system the studies they severally most affect, because those studies will in all probability prove later to have been the appropriate preparation for the calling, when discovered, in which each can best succeed. Both in school and college diversity, not uniformity, of product should be the aim. The fortunate pupil or student is he who early discerns his life-career, and makes his school training or his school and college training an appropriate preparation for it. The vocation once known gives clear guidance to those knowledges and skills which will best contribute to success in it.

Whoever advocates the introduction of concrete illustration and the elements of industrial training into the common schools will at once encounter three objections: (1) there is no time for more subjects; (2) the present amount of instruction in the so-called academic subjects is already inadequate and ought not to be reduced; and (3) instruction in applied science and industrial subjects is costly, and there is no money to pay for it. To meet the first objection, the best way is to increase school time per day and per year. This would now be possible with due regard for the health and vigor of the children, because many of the new subjects call for bodily exercises, and also because improvements already effected in school grounds and buildings make the hours spent in school quite as healthy as those spent at home, healthier indeed under many urban conditions. An extension of school time from twenty-five hours a week to from thirty-three to forty-four hours a week, according to the age of the pupils, would make great improvements possible. In cities and large towns the summer vacation should be much reduced. This lengthening of the weekly school time has already begun in day schools which make much of manual training and industrial teachings, and the vacation schools, summer camps, and summer sessions are making head against the evils of the long vacation. In connection with the increased interest in all school work resulting from the admission of the life-career motive, the increase of school time will meet completely the second of the above objections. There will be no need to reduce the academic or cultural elements of the present high-school programs. It will be possible to give the essentials of the common high-school course and also much manual and industrial instruction. This is not prophecy, but merely the recognition of existing facts. Finally, the third objection — no money — must be met by getting more money, public and private, to spend on schools. Some unobservant and unimaginative people say that it is impossible to increase public expenditure whether for schools or for any other object. The answer to that pessimism is that public expenditure for schools and for many other objects has been greatly increased within the past thirty years, and that almost all citizens hold that school expenditure ought to be increased even though the total expenditures of the community should not rise, because, if judiciously made, it yields a larger and quicker return — material, mental, and moral — than any other expenditure.

Throughout the discussion of the expediency of introducing vocational subjects into American schools, it is important that one fact be kept clearly in mind; namely, that to provide more subjects of instruction does not mean that each individual pupil is necessarily to study more subjects. Thus the city of Munich provides instruction in some sixty trades, but the individual Munich boy or girl learns only one trade. So American schools for children of twelve years and upward must teach many subjects, but each pupil will pursue only that number of subjects which is expedient for him.

To the question where it is most important to introduce industrial training, and to give the motive of the life-career the freest play possible, will not the answer of our profession be well-nigh unanimous — in the public-school system, from the seventh grade to the twelfth grade inclusive? Many other organizations and instrumentalities will share in the good work, but the free public-school system should be the chief field of this great reform. The ample and discriminating report recently published by this association's Committee on the Place of Industries in Public Education exhibits the immense confusion of nomenclature, opinions, plans, and efforts which clouds the subject of industrial education, but out of this confusion emerges one unifying and integrating conception — that of the supreme value of the life-career motive in the lifelong process of education. On being installed as rector of the University of Edinburgh in 1866, Carlyle told the students what "a man is born to, in all epochs. He is born to expend every particle of strength that God Almighty has given him, in doing the work he finds he is fit for; to stand up to it to the last breath of life, and to do his best."

VOCATIONAL GUIDANCE

By President Richard C. Maclaurin of the Massachusetts
Institute of Technology

(An Address delivered at the First National Conference on Vocational
Guidance, Boston, 1910)

It seems to me that this, the first meeting of the National Conference on Vocational Guidance, although there is a total absence
of pomp and circumstance in the gathering, is in Carlyle's phrase
" significant of much." It indicates that an old order is passing
and giving place to a new. The old watchwords, which were so
useful in their days, the watchwords of our fathers and grandfathers,
such as " Breadth," " Freedom," " Liberty," are less frequently
heard in these days. In the political field few people will maintain
to-day that freedom is the mother of all virtue. In the economic
field the old doctrine of *laissez faire* is entirely abandoned. No
economist of repute to-day will try to make you believe that the
best of all possible results to society can be obtained merely by
allowing the free play of competition, by letting every one have
the utmost freedom to fight for his individual interests, without
control or guidance from anywhere. That, in economics, is an
exploded doctrine, exploded by the experience of actual life. And
so in education the old ideal, the noble and splendid ideal of
culture, of breadth, and of the all-rounded man, is, if not abandoned, at least much less prominently presented in the discussion
of educational problems. That in actual practice it has been found
impossible to realize this great ideal is not, of course, surprising.
Few ideals can be realized. The defect of this ideal is that it does
not supply a motive strong enough to be effective for the young
people of the present day. Hence we must turn our attention to
other motives in the hope of finding some that will stand the test
of practical experience. And so we hear everywhere in education

13

to-day talk of the vocational motive; not a new thing, it is true, but one that is being given exceptional prominence. Fortunately, there is less talk to-day than there was earlier, less foolish talk in tones of disparagement of bread and butter studies, as if bread and butter were not excellent things in themselves; rarely despised in actual practice by men of culture and enlightenment. We have to face everywhere in the field of education the problem of fitting men for the actual conditions of the world to-day and to-morrow; we must have an educational device that will make our youth see that to succeed they will have to work seriously; we must have an educational system that will fit them for particular professions. The recognition of this has brought about all over this country and all over the world the establishment of professional schools aimed to fit men for particular professions and having especial regard to the immediate needs of those professions. The success of these professional schools has been remarkable; everywhere they are flourishing to-day, having proved beyond the possibility of doubt that the training they have afforded has been eminently useful. As an unexpected result, they have proved that the introduction of the vocational motive solves a very large part of the problems that are presented in the older forms of education. Look at our educational world in this country to-day; hear all the criticism from men who know and who are really friendly in their attitude toward the institutions of the older type. Hear their criticism of our colleges. Listen to what President Wilson has said of the colleges of to-day: that in many cases the side shows have swallowed up the circus. Listen to similar remarks from prominent educators from New York to San Francisco. Everywhere you hear criticism of education of the older type largely on the ground that the men who are subjected to that form of education do not take their work seriously. Now, no such criticism is possible of our professional schools; in them earnestness and seriousness of purpose is almost all pervading. This, among other things, has suggested to educated men the world over that it may be well to attempt to introduce the vocational motive into all our schools. There have been other forces, social forces, making in the same direction, and now the matter has got well beyond the region of mere discussion, and

presents to-day a great practical problem. It is an immensely difficult problem. How are we to deal with the great mass of young
people who are not going to college nor thinking of entering professional schools as they at present exist; that enormous mass for
whom circumstances, conditions or capacities make any higher
effort absolutely impossible? That is the great problem of vocational education, immensely complex and immensely important.

But vocational education is not the subject we are to discuss
to-night; it is rather vocational guidance. The great question, the
momentous question, What are we to do with our boys? is, like
the poor, ever with us, always a matter of anxious solicitude to
serious parents and daily being answered in the wrong way. That
it should be answered wrongly need give rise to no surprise, for
the problem is intrinsically difficult in the extreme. With those
who have exceptional capacity or exceptionally strong interests,
there is scarcely any problem at all. But these are always infini-
tesimal in number; and the difficulty is to deal successfully with
the great mass of young people. Of course for centuries most
schools have formed something in the nature of a vocational
bureau. Almost every teacher worthy of the name has interested
himself at some time or other in the life work of his students and
helped student or parent in the choice of a calling. At this Institute of Technology it has long been recognized as one of the important functions of the professors and instructors to afford such
guidance. Young men come to us often with somewhat vague
ideas as to their future calling. They have some interest in
science, but have no conception of the enormous variety of
callings to which the scientific training may lead. Even educated
men of experience rarely realize what this variety is. Not one in
a thousand appreciates what an enormous number of openings
there are to a man who really masters even a small field of
science and is alert enough to be conscious of its practical applications. There are literally thousands of such different callings
to-day in the field of applied science, and there will be tens of
thousands in the near future. Under such circumstances guidance
is a necessity. Now at the Institute of Technology the problem is
in some respects unusually simple. We have in the first place to

deal with picked students, and our method of procedure enables us
to watch these students closely for a considerable period of time
and so to form a fairly accurate measure of their capacity and interest before guiding them in any particular direction. Then we
have the very great advantage of having amongst our teachers a
large number of men actively engaged in the practice of their profession and knowing intimately what the real needs of the world
are. But even with these advantages we recognize the problem as
one of great difficulty. And it is evident that the difficulties will
be enormously increased when the selection has to be made earlier
in life for students whose powers are less fully developed and by
men who have less favorable opportunities for wise guidance.

Clearly some guidance there must be, and the question arises
who is to be the guide or who are to be the guides. As far as I
can see, it cannot be any single man or any single body of men.
The pupils alone cannot be satisfactory guides. They, of course,
must take a part — an active and leading part in the choice of their
life work. I sometimes think that the question " What shall we do
with our boys ? " would be better in the form " What shall our boys
do for themselves ? " They, at any rate, have an advantage in knowing their own interests, and no one who has thought of the matter
can fail to see that interest in one's life work or profession is more
than half the battle. But the boys cannot guide themselves wisely
because of their inexperience of the actual conditions of the world.
They do not know and cannot know what it really means to be a
bricklayer or a doctor or a banker, or anything else. Some kind of
assistance from outside they must have. Can the parents guide ?
Here, again, it is obvious that they must take a serious share in
the great work, but alone they are almost sure to be poor guides.
It is common experience that they are too close to their children
to have a proper perspective regarding their capacities and powers.
Apart from this they are unfortunately too often unduly influenced
by what they would like their sons or daughters to be or by their
views as to the relative advantages of different callings for the acquisition of wealth, or power, or social prestige. And if pupil and
parent cannot as a rule make the selection, no more can the teacher,
although he can contribute largely and in many cases can give greater

assistance than any other single person. Strategically, his position is a good one, as he is better placed than almost anyone for sizing up the actual conditions of the individual students. He has opportunities of gauging their powers, capacities, and interests that no one else has, and, of course, it should be capacity and interest more than anything else that determines a man's life work. And yet the teachers do not always make good guides, partly because their circumstances and their mode of living prevent them from having a large enough view of life, although, of course, there are many alert and broad-minded men and women in the profession who can and do perform the work of guidance admirably. If, then, neither pupil nor parent nor teacher alone can guide the students, who is to do it? In my judgment they must all take a part, but their work to be successful must enlist the coöperation of high-minded and public-spirited men in the busy world who are ready to give society the benefit of their experience and aid the rising generation by their suggestions and advice. Such men can help enormously in this great task. And what they might do would doubtless be much facilitated by the establishment of a vocational bureau with a permanent office and properly staffed with men and women whose duties it would be to enlist the sympathy of broad-minded citizens, to keep a record of what they advise and suggest, to find out what are the actual requirements of the various trades and professions, and to study the needs of the community as regards these trades and professions, and generally to form a storehouse of information on vocational guidance. It is by some such combination of effort that the great problem is to be solved, if solved at all. It is not a new problem nor an untried one. It has been attacked in this country in a modest way. It has been similarly attacked in Belgium, France, and other countries in Europe. But no one who looks at the problem and realizes its importance will doubt that the attack to be successful must be far more serious than it has hitherto been and that it must be taken up far more vigorously and helped more constantly by representative men in the community.

Whatever one's views regarding such matters may be, there can be no question of the importance of the right solution of the problem under consideration. Whether we look at the individual or at society the present condition is deplorable. On every hand we meet with the tragedy of failure or of partial failure and see the dissatisfaction and the misery that is brought about by the placing of square pegs in round holes. In these days men who are to amount to anything must be workers in some field, intellectual or manual. If they are to be happy or moderately happy, they must get their pleasure, or the major portion of it, from their work. If they must look elsewhere for such pleasure, they are almost inevitably doomed to dissatisfaction if not misery. It is somewhat surprising that the dissatisfaction is not greater than it actually is when we consider the haphazard methods of choosing callings. And of course it is not merely the individuals that suffer — society as a whole is deeply affected not only through the unhappiness of its members but through their lack of efficiency as workers for the benefit of the community. There is much talk to-day, wise and otherwise, regarding the preservation or conservation of our natural resources. Unquestionably, the waste is enormous, and needless waste is a crime. It seems to me, however, that there are wastes that go on around us daily many times more distressing in their results than the waste of our natural resources that is so much deplored. That is saying a good deal, if you think only for a moment of the waste that goes on in a single city such as that of Boston through unscientific and therefore uneconomic methods of dealing with our problems. It has been estimated that the saving that could easily be effected in this city in the coal bill of its citizens would form a splendid endowment for all the educational institutions in this neighborhood, and there are similar wastes in other fields. There is no waste, however, that is quite so distressing as the waste of human effort that you can see daily in cases where men are engaged in a calling for which they are not fitted. Men everywhere are wearing out their energies and their lives by working in the wrong field and are thereby not only bringing dissatisfaction to themselves but are not serving society to the best of their capacity. If we can do *anything* to diminish such waste, then I say that it is a national duty to take the matter seriously and do *everything* that we can.

THE SOCIAL WASTE OF UNGUIDED PERSONAL ABILITY

By Erville B. Woods, Dartmouth College

(From *The American Journal of Sociology*, November, 1913)

It has been pointed out by a number of writers that the well-known difference between the birth rate of the well-to-do classes and that of the more rapidly multiplying laboring classes is fraught with serious consequences. It is asserted that the upward movement of the able from class to class, and from the country to the city, segregates the brains and the energy, the ambitions and the capacity, of the nation in a section of the population which is dying out by the process of class suicide. Society is thus represented as selecting for extinction its most capable breeds and becoming in consequence an aggregate of increasingly mediocre individuals. One might well suppose from such considerations that the case of modern society is hopeless.

There is the possibility, however, that the machinery of selection does not work with quite the ruthless thoroughness imputed to it. There are a number of considerations which cast doubt upon this assumption. (1) The ability or capacity which leads to success is far from being simple, uniform, or commensurable. It may almost be defined as any variation which proves to be favorable in a given environment. There is probably no variation which would not prove of advantage in some environment. It is because successful people are so indefinitely different among themselves — are so many kinds of variants, in other words — that it is perhaps doubtful whether if they mated exclusively among themselves their offspring would be distinguished particularly from the offspring of the rest of the population. (2) Much ability, many of the valuable variations, are the result not of inheritance but of development and specialization

19

of effort only. The attention of one individual for some reason is drawn off from all other subjects and directed to one task exclusively; that individual succeeds; even ill health, by limiting the number of personal interests, sometimes accomplishes this end; a second individual lavishing attention upon several objects attends with conspicuous success to none. Here is apparently a difference in ability, but hardly a difference likely to be repeated in the following generation. Until exact psychic measurements are further perfected, it is hazardous to estimate the importance of the two sets of causes, hereditary on the one hand, and on the other those connected with economy and concentration of attention. (3) Ability receives its reward only when it is presented with the opportunities of a fairly favorable environment, *its* peculiarly indispensable sort of environment. Naval commanders are not likely to be developed in the Transvaal, nor literary men and artists in the soft-coal fields of western Pennsylvania. For ten men who succeed as investigators, inventors, or diplomatists, there may be and probably are in some communities fifty more who would succeed better under the same circumstances.

In these failures of well-endowed individuals and in the artificial successes of poorly endowed favorites, there may be a crumb of consolation for the social biologist who might rejoice that a few brands escape the burning in which success consumes itself, but to the social economist the waste of social materials involved appears to be a most serious loss in itself.

Professor Lester F. Ward, in his "Applied Sociology," has stated and elaborated this point of view most cogently. Following the way which he has blazed, it should not be difficult to point out certain limitations upon the social selections under discussion.

In the present discussion I shall confine myself to education understood in a broad sense as an agency in the selection of personal ability, for of all the agencies by which individuals may be qualified to play a distinctive rôle in society and one in accordance with their inherited capabilities, education is undoubtedly the greatest.

The imperfect results which our educational system achieves are the result mainly of the undue abbreviation of the period of training for most individuals and of the omission of elements of training of real significance for the purpose of adjusting individuals to social tasks. The crucial question is whether all of those individuals are getting into the running who are capable of putting up the best race, whether those individuals are being inducted into the traditions of science and of industry who are most likely to render those fields the service of large capacities.

The most striking fact which meets the eye from the pages of educational statistics is the abbreviation of the period of instruction for so large a part of the·school population. Only a fraction of those who enter the elementary schools are turned over to the higher schools. The number of those who continue their education does not exhaust the talented part of the population. The handicap imposed by leaving school early consists not merely in being deprived of a vantage ground from which an appropriate vocational choice may be made but also in the fact that such youth are almost certain to drift into inconsequential and totally uneducative tasks such as our society reserves as a heritage for the working boy. Every industry has its "boys' work," and in extremely few cases does such work afford a stimulus to ambitious effort or to personal development.

In the *Report of the Commissioner of Education* for 1909, the enrollment of pupils in the elementary and high schools of 1024 cities and villages of over 4000 population is given by years. The aggregate enrollment of boys and girls in these cities exceeds 4,000,000, so it appears that the returns are sufficiently complete to give them a high degree of significance.

The enrollment of boys is largest in the second grade, and drops gradually until about the fifth grade, where the enrollment is 80 per cent of what it was in the second. In the sixth, however, it has dropped to about 66 per cent, in the seventh to slightly more than 50 per cent, and in the eighth to less than 40 per cent of the enrollment in the second grade. The four years of high school show in terms of the same standard, respectively, one fourth, one sixth, one tenth, one fourteenth. In other words, making no correction for the somewhat smaller number of boys in the population at the high-school age, only one in 14 of those enrolled in the second grade reaches the fourth year of high school.

In the analysis of population according to age found in the census of 1900, the number of boys in the United States of age seven was 904,428, which may be represented by 100 per cent, and may stand roughly for those of about first-grade or second-grade age. (The variation in the total population from one year to the next is not great enough to affect the purpose for which the figures are used.) It will be found that the number of boys of age fourteen constitute nearly 87 per cent of those of age seven; boys of age sixteen constitute 83.6 per cent of the number at age seven. It may be assumed that the age distribution for the United States (between the ages seven and sixteen) would not be found seriously erroneous for the 1024 cities and villages reporting school enrollment.

With this assumption we find that between the second and eighth grades the enrollment falls from 100 to 38.6 per cent, while between the seventh and sixteenth years the number of boys in the population decreases only from 100 to 83.6 per cent. It may therefore be inferred that in these thousand cities and villages less than half the boys who live to a sufficient age are found enrolled in the eighth grade. More than half of them drop out in some earlier grade.

This leads to a point which has received fairly general recognition, that many times the youth who persists to the end of the grammar-school course or even through the high school finds himself even then in possession of no specific knowledge, skill, discernment, or qualification adequate to the selection or the accomplishment of the tasks to which he must presently address himself. A whole series of educational reforms are competing at the present time upon the basis of this general criticism. I shall refer briefly to but one of them — vocational counsel as a part of the education of the boy.

At this point I wish simply to enforce the conviction that the educational net fails by far of catching and holding all whom it is desirable, for the sake of the social good, to drag to the surface.

The explanation of the facts already noted lies mainly outside of the schoolroom. Ward has pointed out that among the really important factors conditioning individual success is " a social position such as is capable of producing a sense of self-respect, dignity, and reserve power which alone can inspire confidence in one's worth and in one's right to enter the lists for the great prizes of life." He quotes approvingly Professor Cooley's remark that " a man can hardly fix his ambition upon a literary career when he is perfectly unaware, as millions are, that such a thing as a literary career exists." Nothing is more likely to prevent the selection and elevation of able characters than that a considerable section of the population should for one reason or another regard·themselves as " counted out " of the running for positions of honor and responsibility. While this is a mental attitude less common in a democracy than in monarchical and definitely stratified societies, yet it is liable to be fostered increasingly among us in proportion as our population is gathered in industrial centers where the family as a whole, not its male head, becomes the unit of economic support, and children in consequence are early sent to work. Whatever the fluidity of American society forty or sixty or eighty years ago, industrial America in the twentieth century is not assured, by any mechanism of selection now in operation, of the automatic detection and utilization of the abilities with which its citizens may be endowed.

It must not be forgotten that ambition is a relative, not an absolute, matter, and that the horizon of the average youth is limited by the radius of the " vocational imagination " possessed by members of his family and social group. The cue to the explanation of success lies in part in ·the self-classification of individuals. We try to live up to what we suppose we are, just as the imaginary kings and queens who are sometimes met with give themselves the airs appropriate to their station. It is not only a question of what individuals are *able* to do, but also of what they are "*put up*" to do by the stimulation and suggestion of their social environment. If one were once accustomed to it, it might not prove so much more difficult to think with the prince in terms of provinces, or with the astronomer in terms of solar systems, than it is to wrestle with the exigencies of the cobbler's bench or with the daily problems of the locksmith or the tinker.

With a view to throwing a little light if possible upon the·influences which shape the ambitions and plans of boys, at about the age when one half of them have brought their formal education·to a close, a simple statistical inquiry was undertaken at the end of 1910, made possible by the courteous coöperation of the public-school authorities of the city of St. Paul. Boys in the seventh and eighth grades of eighteen of the larger public schools, 1076 boys in all, wrote answers to the following questions : " Do you expect to go to high school ? " "What is your father's exact occupation ? " "What occupation or work do you think you would like best to work at all your life ? " " Why do you think you would like this occupation ? "

In the replies to these questions there is material for a rough sort of reconstruction in statistical terms of a part of the social environment surrounding these thousand boys. To understand a state of mind is as important as to understand a purely objective state of facts. While the results are in terms of expectations and preferences and will change materially in many cases during the next few years, it is believed that they throw light upon the working of the mind of the boy early in the period when vocational and career-making choices begin to be made. The replies of these boys reflect such factors as family ambition, degree of economic independence of parents, intelligence of parents, and, in general, varying outlooks upon the possibilities which life affords.

In spite of the difficulties in the way of a satisfactory classification of occupations, it has seemed feasible to classify the boys according to the occupational groups to which the father belongs. For this purpose eight classes have been made use of : the first group is the professional and includes such occupations as lawyer, physician, architect, musician, civil engineer, etc. This group numbers 54 cases. The second group is the mercantile and is composed of proprietors of businesses, superintendents, traveling salesmen, managers, and all the better-paid commercial, industrial, and official positions of a nonmanual character. It is a large group (358 cases), and membership in it implies bearing a certain business or administrative responsibility as well as what some imagine to be a kind of clean-handed respectability. The third and fourth groups are small (63 and 66 respectively) and consist of those following subordinate clerical and petty mercantile occupations respectively. The type of the former is the clerk in an office and of the latter the clerk in a store. Both groups are nonmanual. The fifth group consists of the skilled manual workers. This group again is a large one, numbering 298 cases, and the type is the man following a skilled trade, such as the carpenter, plumber, machinist, etc. The sixth group numbers 111 and includes the unskilled or slightly skilled manual occupations, such as laborers, teamsters, street-sweepers, waiters, porters, etc. The seventh group, which is almost negligible, is made up of 14 cases where the father follows some agricultural occupation. The eighth group consists of all cases not assignable to one of the first seven, and is therefore of no special significance.

Without going into further details, I may state briefly the character of the answers to the question, " Do you expect to go to high school ? " Of the boys from the professional class 94 per cent replied in the affirmative ; of the mercantile class, 86 per cent ; of the clerical, 74 per cent ; of the petty mercantile, 67 per cent ; of the artisan class, 61 per cent ; of the laborer class, 54 per cent.

We may therefore conclude that for boys who reach the seventh and eighth grades (taking no account of those who fall out in the earlier years) the probability of entrance upon a secondary-school education is proportional to membership in the leading occupational groups roughly in the ratio of 94, 86, 74, 67, 61, 54, respectively, as we pass from the nonmanual to the manual occupations.

Inasmuch as it is exceedingly improbable that boys of superior ability predominate in the nonmanual classes in the proportion indicated, it is evident that here is one source of the leakage of ability, one way in which society does not get a chance to subject all of its sons to such further sifting and grading as is involved in the revelations of aptitude and potency made during a high-school course.

The answers to the questions relating to the occupations which the boy thinks he would like to pursue for life, together with his reasons, are interesting. In all, 990 boys expressed preference for some sort of work. Of these, 111 chose each their father's identical occupation, or about 11 per cent. Professional occupations were chosen by 59 per cent of the boys whose fathers were professional men. Of the mercantile class 35 per cent chose professional occupations. Of the clerical and petty mercantile classes 30 and 26 per cent chose professional occupations respectively. Of the artisan class 21 per cent and of the laborer class 16 per cent chose such occupations. Mercantile employments were chosen most largely by those whose fathers were so engaged. Skilled manual occupations were preferred by 9 per cent of the sons of professional men, 15 per cent of the sons of merchants, 18 per cent of the sons of petty merchants, 21 per cent of the sons of clerical employees, and 38 per cent of the sons of skilled artisans.

VOCATIONAL PREFERENCES OF BOYS WHOSE FATHERS'
OCCUPATIONS WERE AS FOLLOWS

Sons' Preference	Profes-sional Percent-age	Mercan-tile Percent-age	Petty Mercan-tile Percent-age	Clerical Percent-age	Artisan Percent-age	Laborer Percent-age	Agricul-ture Percent-age
Professional . .	59	35	26	30	21	16	7
Mercantile . .	6	25	11	16	5	13	7
Petty mercantile .	0	1	5	3	1	2	7
Clerical	6	8	18	16	19	20	14
Artisan	9	15	18	21	38	25	29
Laborer . . .	0	1	0	0	1	3	0
Agriculture . .	9	6	3	8	5	4	29
Other	11	9	19	6	10	17	7
	100	100	100	100	100	100	100

While the cases in which the fathers are professional men are but 5 per cent of the whole number of cases, the cases where sons wished to be professional men are 28 per cent, or $5\frac{1}{2}$ times as many. Fathers who were in the mercantile class constitute 33 per cent, sons choosing mercantile occupations constitute 14 per cent, or less than half as many; clerical positions were filled by fathers in 6 per cent of the cases, but chosen by 14 per cent of the boys. Fathers in the artisan class were 28 per cent, the boys choosing to be artisans 24 per cent. Fathers in unskilled manual occupations were 10 per cent of the whole, boys choosing such were 1 per cent. Fathers in agricultural pursuits were 1 per cent, sons choosing agricultural pursuits were 6 per cent.

There is evident in these figures a considerable tendency to choose occupations in the same general order of vocation as that in which the father is employed; thus three fifths of the sons of professional men wish to be professional men, one fourth of the sons of merchants wish to be merchants, two fifths of the sons of artisans wish to be artisans. A still more pronounced tendency, however, is to choose occupations of a more remunerative or intellectual and less manual sort than those followed by the father. Thus 35 per cent of the boys from the mercantile class want to be professional men; 37 per cent of the boys from the petty mercantile class wish to be merchants or professional men; 49 per cent of the boys from the clerical class want to enter the professional or mercantile classes; and 46 per cent of the sons of artisans wish to follow nonmanual or clean-handed occupations, while 76 per cent of the sons of unskilled laborers wish to be artisans or to follow the nonmanual occupations. These figures illustrate very clearly the relativity of vocational ambitions. These statements of preference are conditioned by the vocational viewpoint established by the occupation of the father.

When we turn to specific occupations preferred by the 990 boys, the results indicate that the adventurous, the out-of-doors, the mechanical or electrical, and the supposedly profitable professions and crafts, the clean-handed office positions, and the occupations involving travel are strong favorites. The list of occupations preferred by ten or more boys is found on page 28.

This is the way in which the vocational horizon impresses the average St. Paul boy in the seventh and eighth grades. That the emphasis is as far as possible from that placed by the actual demand for workers is not at all surprising when the fact is considered that these boys have probably never received a half-hour's formal instruction in their lives with regard to vocational matters, and particularly with reference to the preparation and qualifications requisite for the various tasks to which they vaguely aspire.

We teach our youth about the characteristics of geographical regions, the properties of numbers, and the peculiarities of

OCCUPATIONS PREFERRED

Civil, electrical, mechanical, and mining engineer	139
Office clerk, bookkeeper, and stenographer	113
Machinist and mechanic	77
Lawyer	69
Agricultural pursuits	59
Engineer (locomotive principally)	56
Merchant and business man	55
Electrician	42
Architect and draftsman	36
Traveling salesman	34
Carpenter and cabinetmaker	30
Physician	27
Artistic or musical pursuit	21
Store clerk	19
Plumber and steam fitter	17
Printer	13
Surveyor	12
Banking	12
Real estate	11
Druggist	10
Scattering	138
Total reporting preference	990

language. As they go on with their studies we teach them the characteristics of chemical elements and compounds, the physical properties of bodies, the texture and mechanism of organic structures, both vegetable and animal, and their young minds unfold in the presence of a world richer and more complicated than they had ever dreamed. But about the qualities of men demanded by the world's work, about the rôle played by tact, by ability to meet men, by differing traits and tendencies of mind, as related to individual success in specific present-day tasks, we teach little. That the demands of one profession or craft are radically different from those of another, that the application of individual endowment to its appropriate task is a tremendously difficult thing, they learn only in the wasteful school of experience.

If we turn from aspirations to the actual "choice," so called, of occupations by American youth, we find still less of the rational and more of the accidental. As Mr. Everett W. Lord of the

National Child Labor Committee (*Proceedings*, 1910, pp. 80–81) has put it : "Boys find themselves in their vocations as the result of custom, heredity, propinquity, or accident far oftener than through deliberate and conscious choice." Geographical and industrial conditions, for example, cut out the work of whole communities of people from birth, almost without option on their part, as Dr. Peter Roberts has shown so clearly of the anthracite coal communities.

A year or so ago Mr. Lord sent out "several hundred letters to people engaged in various occupations, asking them to answer certain questions. . . . Among the answers to the question, 'Why did you choose your present occupation ?' were such as, 'Because that was what the other boys were doing,' 'Because I happened to get a job at that trade,' 'Because that was the principal line of work near my home'" (ibid. p. 79).

After a time quite a number of people who have entered occupations haphazard stumble out of work to which they are ill-adapted, and somehow stumble into other work for which they are better fitted. Multitudes of other individuals, I am forced to believe, succeed just well enough at some ill-chosen task to be held to it until readjustment has become difficult or impossible.

The man who is fortunate enough to hit it in selecting or being put into a vocation succeeds if he has good abilities. The other man of equal or greater abilities, just as industrious, self-controlled, or sagacious, who does not strike that happy confluence of circumstances which makes his efforts bear conspicuous fruit, plods along, tasting most of the pleasures of life in the pursuit of activities outside of his trade or business — activities or interests, whether domestic, religious, fraternal, or recreational, which engage as great capacities as the successful man devotes to the conspicuous and interesting problems of his daily work.

After this somewhat extended although imperfect statement of one phase of the problem of dormant ability, it is unnecessary to do more than point out the very great significance of the movement started by the late Professor Frank Parsons of Boston and by educators in several sections of the country looking toward the provision of scientific vocational advice for young people as a part of their formal preparation for life.

In conclusion, the following paragraphs may serve to summarize the points which have been emphasized :

1. Society is suffering less from the race suicide of the capable than from the nonutilization of the capacities of the well endowed.

2. One half of our male population is not carried far enough by our educational system even to see, much less understand, the vocational opportunities afforded by modern life.

3. Of those boys who reach the last years of the elementary school very unequal selection is made, due to the poverty, lack of foresight and outlook, entailed by a narrow and difficult social environment.

4. In their preference for occupations boys are guided by whim, contagious admiration, and ambition divorced from sound reason oftener than by a perceived compatibility between personal traits and the requirements of tasks.

5. In the actual selection of occupations not even whimsical preferences are allowed to guide in very many cases, but rather the first remunerative opening in the local industrial mechanism determines the career of the boy quite irrespective of taste or aptitude.

6. From these causes there results an indefinitely great waste of abilities which remain in some cases undiscovered and in others misapplied.

7. While equality of opportunity cannot be provided by any mere change in educational methods, yet as a step in the direction of diffusing the opportunity of intelligent vocational outlook, every boy before leaving the elementary school should be given an accurate idea of the nature of the principal kinds of human work, the qualities demanded by them, the preparation required, the rewards offered, the advantages and the opportunities for usefulness which they afford. He should, moreover, be taught the rudiments of self-appraisal from the vocational point of view and should have the benefit of counsel with a professional vocational counselor who is thoroughly informed with regard to the industrial opportunities of the community and the means of entrance thereupon.

8. And last : Better vocational adjustments will link the real interests and energies of the spirit with productive tasks instead of allowing them to be turned to merely recreational activities, which in the cramped monotony of industrial communities so often verge upon the unsocial and the criminal. Thus new energy legitimately released will increase the material conditions of happiness, and make men better neighbors and members of society as well.

THE WASTEFUL RECRUITING OF TRADES AND OCCUPATIONS

By N. B. Dearle

(From " Industrial Training," published by P. S. King & Son, London)

The occupations so far considered all have a natural excess of boys, and fail to give employment after boyhood is over to a larger or smaller proportion of them. In the third phase of the problem, this surplus is produced by other causes. The question of wasteful recruiting will be considered mainly in connection with the skilled trades, where its importance is greatest, but it is also found in many others. In such trades learners are taken in the ordinary way, and the nature of the employment does not in itself require an excess, yet more will enter many of them than they can permanently retain, and what is more, they will have to do so if a sufficient number of competent men is to be provided. This surplus, therefore, is brought about by the failure of a good many either to learn their trade at all or to learn it properly, and they thus grow up without proper command of any occupation. Hence this is caused by failure to learn where the opportunity to do so exists, and not, as in the two previous cases, by the lack of that opportunity.

Some failures, indeed, there must always be in every trade, and so wasteful recruiting does not consist in their existence, but in the fact that they are far more numerous than can be accounted for by the sprinkling of lazy or incompetent boys who are found everywhere. In short, wasteful recruiting implies the spoiling of much good material, and that boys start to learn a trade — sometimes with the fairest prospects — and fall out by the way. Hence, even after allowing for necessary wastage, the production of a given number of competent workmen requires the taking of a considerably larger number of boys; and so many skilled trades have a reserve of boy labor. It is, nevertheless, the extent of this rather than its mere existence, that constitutes the problem.

As thus defined, wasteful recruiting falls into two classes: either a boy fails altogether to learn his trade, or he grows up an incompetent or inferior workman; and in either case larger numbers enter it than can find full employment later. The matter may now be considered in detail.

First there is direct *misplacement* or the putting of boys into unsuitable trades or situations — either into the wrong trade or into the wrong shop in the right one. Both mistakes are common; and as regards the former, parents are not seldom to blame, less for want of interest in their children than for want of thought and care. The first thing that offers or that occurs to them is too often taken without reference to the boy's tastes or abilities, and others try to put their sons into positions that are beyond their capacity. Often, again, nothing is done until they have actually left school, and then work has to be found in a hurry; and sometimes the thing is left entirely to chance.

Moreover, considerable difficulties face even the most thoughtful. Good openings are scarce, and some of them appear to be unpromising; whilst a boy often does not know his own mind, or may not be specially suited to anything in particular. There is great danger, too, in his remaining idle, and to this parents are quite alive. "There are so many boys after jobs," said one mother, "that we thought he had better take the first he could get." Finally, the right job is hard to find, and neither parent nor boy knows how to find it, and, till recently, there has been little organization to help them to do so. Anyhow, whatever the cause, the effect is the same. Going to the wrong trade, the boy fails to master it and either has to leave it altogether or content himself with irregular employment.

Even in a suitable trade much the same result follows from choice of the wrong type of shop. If it does inferior work or lacks capacity to teach, or, still more, if it neglects to do so, a boy may come out of his time little better off than when he entered it. Here, too, parents are, or have been till recently, very badly off for expert advice; but, on the whole, this danger is not quite so great as the first. Being suited by the trade and possessing the capacity to learn, the lads only need to get the chance, and the abler of them make one for themselves by moving away to other firms.

For these and other reasons, therefore, it is quite a common thing for a boy to leave one trade for another, as a result of causes which sometimes are and sometimes are not under his control. The change may come soon, or it may come late, but sooner or later it does come. The chance way in which he obtained his job often ties him to it less strictly than if he had been more carefully and formally engaged. So he goes to it for a few months, for a year, perhaps for two, and learns a little. Then he gets tired of the work, or thinks he is not learning quickly enough, or has a row with somebody, or, in some cases, merely wants a change, and off he goes. After this he may get another job in the same trade, he may start in a different one, or he may take purely unskilled work ; and it is not unusual for a youth to nibble at several trades in this way with spells of boy labor sandwiched in between them.

Moreover, change from one trade to another is sometimes the only alternative to long periods of unemployment. Where there are marked seasonal variations, as in pianoforte manufacture, or where the work of individual firms comes in rushes, boys are sometimes treated much as the men are, and are dismissed as soon as things fall slack, though many firms try to avoid this. This forces them into other jobs, — skilled or unskilled, — and some do not return with the busy season and indeed soon contract the habit of wandering about and sticking at nothing. Again, a long spell of unemployment may have a similar effect, and so, for one reason or another, many leave the employment which they started to learn, or, if they do not, work at it so irregularly as to become inferior workmen.

Further, there are the results of defective training, and more especially those connected with the casual picking-up of a trade. Though not unknown, these are as a rule least serious under the more definite forms of regular service. They are more considerable under its other types and in the case of following-up, and probably most serious under migration. To a few of the abler boys, indeed, the latter may give as good a training as, and larger earnings during its course than, more regular methods, discontinuity in the work being in their case compensated for by its greater variety. But for the great majority its dangers outweigh its advantages. They are peculiarly liable to unemployment, as they are compelled to move about from firm to firm. They are left too much to their own devices, and not being recognized learners, it is no man's business to teach them; whilst fear of cheap labor may set their fellow workmen against them. Many leave the trade, and still more, without dropping out altogether, grow up incompetent or only partially taught. " I object to a boy learning as an improver," one foreman said, " because he picks his trade, so to speak, in the gutter."

To learn properly by migration, the improver has to choose carefully the kind of shops he goes to and regulate the time he stays in each; but many stay too long at inferior work, or select a new place mainly with a view to what they can earn. Further, being paid as workers not as learners, they have to be kept on what is most profitable to their employers; and, particularly when paid piecework, are liable to acquire wrong methods by turning out inferior stuff rapidly and in a slipshod way. The necessary changes of job, again, create the habit of continually changing, and lead to loss of capacity to stick steadily to anything.

Finally, the attraction of immediate high earnings causes some to neglect to learn their business thoroughly. Finding employers offering good money, especially when trade is brisk, they fail to see the need for further improvement. Thus between 1895 and 1900 foremen stonemasons in London were putting on almost any one who could handle a chisel, and young men were always changing firms to increase their wages. Only when depression came did they realize their shortcomings, too late to remedy them. In silversmithing, again, young fellows may quickly become worth 25s. to 30s. a week at a particular kind of work, at which they will stick and never learn more.

For even when a youth is at pains to learn, the power to earn comparatively high wages may make him think that he knows more than he does, or that having learnt one section of a trade well he has learnt sufficient. And if some of the more thoughtful boys fall into this error, others simply learn a part of the business and then sacrifice everything to earning as much as possible. Indeed, some instructors in the trade schools are so alive to this danger as to fear even the payment of such good rates. Here the result is less frequently the generally inferior workman than the man who can do only certain parts of a trade. As the most serious, therefore, the case of migration has been described in detail; but much that has been said will apply also, though in a lesser degree, to the various forms of regular service, since these check, but do not always nor altogether prevent, the creation of a reserve of boy labor.

Further, there is often waste in connection with those unskilled jobs about an industry, which can and sometimes do give a chance to learn it. For owing to incapacity or bad behavior or failure to stick to their work, boys allow chances to go begging, and what might be the making of a few boys merely provides a succession of temporary jobs, which lead to nothing, for a much larger number. Again, irregular employment of improvers often creates a casual reserve of them, and in certain cases individual employers find it to their advantage to overstock their business with younger workers.

The same phenomenon is also present in the case of unskilled boy labor, where it is largely a by-product of blind-alley employment. In the skilled trades far more boys enter than learn, not because excessive numbers are engaged, though in some trades this cause also operates to a certain extent, but because so many fail to learn; and, as a result, a reserve of boy labor has to grow up to insure a sufficient supply of men in the future. The chief elements in this reserve may now be briefly summarized as follows: to begin with, there are those who have been wrongly placed from the very first; secondly, those who have started in a suitable trade but failed to stick to it; and, thirdly, those who have failed to learn it fully. It is comprised not only of youths who drop out before or after reaching manhood, but of many of those who stay in a trade as irregular or low-paid workers;[1] and whilst the share contributed by each single cause may not be large, the total reserve

[1] Because, as will be described later, more of such men are required for a given output than if they were well taught. Hence a reserve of boys sufficient to produce this greater number is required.

is often considerable. Its size varies from trade to trade. Where methods of teaching are well regulated, as in printing, it is small ; where the most haphazard ones prevail, it is decidedly large, and it frequently reaches appreciable dimensions.

Moreover, this reserve is not simply an ordinary reserve of casual labor, similar to that which occupies so prominent a place in the case of men. Such a one is sometimes found, arising partly out of the irregular employment of improvers and others and partly from the irregularity of the lads themselves. Still, taking the skilled trades as a whole, it is not important. The real reserve of boy labor is an educational one, and is composed of those who are seeking education and training and not of those who are waiting for employment.

A comparison of the two reserves of adult and juvenile labor will perhaps most clearly explain my meaning. The former may be described as follows : Different firms in a trade employ a number of men which varies from day to day, whilst each of them tends to be busy and slack on different days. If, therefore, as is usually the case, they do not get their less regular workers from a common source, each firm attempts to attach to itself a supply of men sufficient and even more than sufficient for its maximum requirements. Hence the number seeking work is often greater than can find employment even on the busiest day, and some are unemployed more frequently than they are employed. For instance, suppose ten firms require each a number of men that varies from 50 to 100, then if each gets its own absolutely independently of the others, they will have altogether 1000 men in attendance on them, " either working or waiting for work " ; and as their busiest and slackest days never correspond, the whole number is never working on any one day. If, on the contrary, all the men were drawn from a single center, both the maximum and minimum number would fall between these two extremes, being say 800 and 600 men respectively. Consequently, on the busiest day there is work only for 800, but under existing conditions the full 1000 are required. With careful organization, therefore, 200 of them could be dispensed with, but as things are, with each individual employer getting his own separate supply, they are necessary to enable all the work to be carried out. In practice, indeed, there is nearly always some interchange of labor between different firms, though not nearly as much as there might be, and so the reserve of labor is still considerable; but if the work were properly organized, this reserve would become a surplus for which outlets would have to be found elsewhere.

Similarly, in recruiting a trade a certain number of boys are required to keep it up and to allow for any necessary increase in it, and also for wastage by death and in other ways. Now a reserve of boy labor is found when, in order to recruit it, more than the requisite number have to enter it. Under normal conditions, therefore, each trade tends to take enough learners to provide an adequate supply of workmen in the next generation; and the actual number of boys necessary for this purpose corresponds to the men actually employed on the busiest day in the previous illustration. This represents also the total capacity of a trade to absorb them, and varies from one to another according to its rate of growth, the expectation of life of its members, and so on.

Now if the methods of training and organization were perfect, just this number would be required, with a small allowance for deaths and unavoidable cases of failure. Actually under present conditions more and sometimes many more boys have to enter the trade, since otherwise sufficient journeymen will not be obtained. The cause of these numerous failures has already been described, and their number will be in proportion to the efficiency of methods of training. As with casual adult labor, therefore, the additional boys are a reserve and not a surplus, since under present conditions their attempted entry is necessary, and more have to try to learn the trade than could find regular employment at it if all succeeded, just as more casual laborers have to be seeking work than could possibly find it on any one day.

This may perhaps be made clearer by a hypothetical illustration. A trade requires so many learners to keep up its supply of journeymen. Say, for instance, that the number is 105, and that, allowing for natural wastage,[1] 100 of them become journeymen. But a

1 By this I mean such wastage as is caused by death, illness, accident, emigration, and other unavoidable causes of failure.

considerable proportion may fail to learn or to learn properly, and either leave the trade early, fail to find employment as men, or only obtain it when business is brisk and better men are not available. Instead of 100 journeymen, therefore, the trade has only 100 less these failures. If, for instance, there are 20 of them, then the 105 learners only make 80 instead of 100 journeymen, and to get the latter number, something like 130 learners will be needed. These figures are given purely by way of illustration, and the size of the reserve can seldom be so large as this. Often, however, it is considerable ; and so long as it continues to be required, there must, even in the skilled trades, be a special problem of boy labor, and entry into one of them will be no necessary guarantee against growing up without an occupation.

Compared with the reserve of adult labor, indeed, this juvenile one is small. For one reason, the proportion of failures is more or less limited. Employers are not so careful to provide a reserve of boys as of men, simply waiting till the need arises. Then if those they have taken do not prove sufficient, more are engaged or provincial workers are got in. Nevertheless, the reserve of boy labor is both a real and considerable one, and until the causes of wasteful recruiting are removed, the necessity of taking sufficient boys for all emergencies will continue, and those who fail to learn will have to be replaced. So long, therefore, as our methods of recruiting produce a large proportion of failures, the number of boys required to enter a trade will be permanently in excess of the number that can get full employment at it. That is to say, modern conditions bring into the skilled branches of a trade more boys than can find that full employment in it as men, defining it for this purpose as such continuity of work as the general conditions of the trade, including its seasonal and other fluctuations, will permit.

The same result, therefore, is reached as in ordinary blind-alley employments. Each alike leaves a boy stranded in early manhood without full command of a definite occupation, and the only resource left either to the mechanic or the laborer is casual or low-paid work either within or without his trade. The trouble, however, is not so much that existing methods of recruiting cause more boys to enter a trade than it can permanently absorb. This is but a part of the evil, and, if they could be made to leave it before it is too late, but a small part. Indeed some boys only find the right trade after sampling two or three others. The chief trouble, on the contrary, is either that they stay too long in trades to which they are unsuited — until, that is, it is too late to find another — or that they never stick to any but continually chop and change and so learn nothing.

In conclusion, the elements of which this reserve of boy labor is composed may be shortly described. First there are those who drop out altogether from their various trades. Some do so after one or two years, and others nearer the time when they reach manhood, whilst yet others are forced out by stress of competition after they have reached it; and further, there is a stream of boys continually entering and leaving them. Secondly, some who are able to continue in a trade after reaching manhood have such an inadequate knowledge of it as to form a fringe of casual workers whom it is only worth an employer's while to employ during busy times, or for a few days a week as odd men; and either lack of ability, failure to stick properly to the work, or the desire for immediate high earnings, may produce this result.

Thirdly, instead of a smaller body of fully trained mechanics being regularly employed, a larger number who are partially trained are engaged for parts of the year only. This is sometimes the fate of the overspecialized workman. In various trades different prodncts are in brisk demand at different periods of the year, and trade is busy in one article and slack in another. Hence a man who can only make one thing well is kept during its busy season, but as another comes into demand, someone else, who is equally specialized, is taken on to make it, whilst an all-round man would simply be shifted from one job to another and employed continuously. In short, the work is in this case spread out among a larger number of workmen who are employed regularly for a large part of the year but unemployed for the rest — four men, say, work for nine months each instead of three men for the whole twelve.

Fourthly, wasteful recruiting sometimes produces in a trade a class of low-paid but regularly employed workmen. Setting aside those who can only do certain of the roughest kinds of work, like the men who are paid about 4d. an hour to paper up furniture previous to its going to the polishers, there are others who can do a job throughout, but their output is so poor in quantity or quality that they only get and are only worth inferior wages. Thus, in cabinetmaking or upholstery the labor cost of an article is estimated, and a man is paid according to the time he takes to make it.[1] Hence, where each man's output is small, more men are needed to get a given amount of work done, and the reserve of labor takes this form.

Moreover, the growth of these classes of workers not only creates a reserve directly, but indirectly also by its effect on the methods of employment. Often, both in London and elsewhere, the choice between the regular employment of fully competent men and the less regular employment of those who are not is largely a question of supply. In most trades both methods are open to the employer, who may be in a position either to regularize his work and keep good men steadily occupied, or to casualize it; and which is the more profitable process may be determined by the quality of the labor available. If business is brisk and there is an adequate supply of good men, regularization is likely. Where, however, wasteful recruiting provides a large reserve of inferior or not fully competent hands, especially if this is accompanied by some shortage of really good men, casualization follows for the purpose of making the most profitable use of the labor supply. As a result both the reserve of labor and its irregular training tend to increase and perpetuate themselves.

To sum up, therefore, the reserve of boy labor is not confined to those who, in the course of learning it, are compelled to leave a trade. It is composed in part of them, and partly consists of the greater number of men who are required to do the work when they are not properly trained. Its size must not be exaggerated, but when all its elements are added together it constitutes in many trades a problem of considerable gravity.

---

[1] Say, for instance, the labor cost of upholstering a certain kind of chair is estimated at 10s., then a man who will undertake to do it in ten hours will be paid 1s. per hour, in twelve hours 10d., in fifteen hours 8d., in twenty hours 6d., and so on.

One special point remains to be considered. It has been stated that when a boy drops out of a trade, another has to be taken to fill his place, and similar allowance has to be made in order to provide a sufficient number of those who are only fit for casual or irregular work. This is the usual course of events, though, in rare cases, an insufficient supply of fresh labor may cause a shortage of it. Taking the country as a whole, this view holds good, but in London the provincial influx complicates the matter. Instead of engaging other boys to replace those who fail, London employers frequently get in men from elsewhere, many of them indeed relying mainly on provincials, and take very few learners; but it is only the source of supply that is altered, and neither the waste nor the reserve of boys is appreciably diminished, though the number of good openings may be. Moreover, the causes that produce this waste still further increase this preference for, and reliance on, provincial workmen, and reduce the opportunities for advancement of the London boy.

The causes and results of wasteful recruiting have been treated mainly in relation to the skilled trades, but are also at work upon unskilled boy labor, though here they are perhaps best regarded as an incident of blind-alley employment. In the former these causes include defective methods of teaching, wrong selection of a trade, restlessness, and lack of steadiness. In the latter there is little or no teaching, little or nothing to look forward to, and both responsibility and foresight are at a minimum. Employers complain that they cannot keep their boy laborers, and this " obscures from them the fact that they are using a greater number than can be employed in their trade as men." Continual movement from firm to firm creates a reserve of labor in the group of blind alleys, taken as a whole, and also involves many lads in longer or shorter spells of unemployment, whilst some employers have difficulty in getting boys. Now many boys' jobs are themselves steady and regular, and a smaller number might quite well suffice to do the work of them; but as it is, a reserve inevitably grows up.

THE LARGER EDUCATIONAL BEARINGS OF
VOCATIONAL GUIDANCE

By George Herbert Mead, Professor of Philosophy, The
University of Chicago, Chicago, Illinois

(An Address delivered at the Third National Conference on Vocational
Guidance, Grand Rapids, Michigan, 1913)

The school is an institution fashioned as other institutions. It has its roots in the past. It has held its own in the midst of contentions and against hostile forces by being what it is. It has been conscious of its value for society because of its past and has found its courage and self-respect in its accomplishments. Especially the public schools of a democracy such as ours have had need of a strong hold upon its traditions. Our democracy has been suspicious of the standards of a learning and a literary art that belong to an upper class, and of the standard of an efficiency that arose out of a bureaucratic government.

Our school system has had its own practical traditions; and where it has added to its earlier meager curriculum, the addition has been frequently without any controlling principle. We have been very proud of our American common public school, but we have never been quite clear what our schools have done for us, nor from just what standpoint we should criticize them. They have been the bulwark of our liberties, but we have been very generally unwilling that they should undertake more than the drill in the three R's. When we have overloaded their curricula, and the cry has arisen against the "fads and frills," there has been no definite conception of what they should do by which we can test the demands of rival educational theories.

To a large extent the educational policy of most of our large cities has represented a fluctuating compromise between forces that

43

have been by no means all educational forces. This situation is common to our popular education and to our popular government. We know that they are precious institutions, but we treat them with a great deal of good-humored ridicule. They are the palladia of our liberties, but concretely we have not wished to have to take them too seriously. The school-teacher and the politician have been standing subjects for the wit of humorous papers.

But a change has come about in our attitude toward our governmental institutions. It is a great deal clearer to us what these institutions should and can do. We may not be any clearer as to the fundamental theories of government, but the community now knows that popular government is itself our most precious treasure and it is becoming aware that this precious institution can be called upon to do certain specific things.

Industrial education and vocational guidance mark the points at which our public schools are making such contact with actual life that the community may intelligently criticize the schools and control them in something like the same sense that it may control the management of technical departments of our governing bodies.

Fruitful contact implies primarily that the community shall be able to pass in certain respects intelligent criticism upon the school, criticism which the school authorities will themselves seek and of which they will be able to make profitable use. This implies further that the school life reaches back into the home and the community of which the home is a part and out into the occupations which the children enter when they leave the school. Lack of such intelligence and such connection between the school and the life of the community is evidenced in a type of criticism with which we are familiar. These criticisms gather mainly about the lack of drill in the three R's. Spelling, number work, and English, we are told, are slovenly; the graduates of neither the grades nor the high schools can write a fairly respectable letter; the commonest words are misspelled; the English is atrocious; the ability to cast up a simple column of figures is lamentably absent; and yet the children are so possessed with a sense of their own competence that they can not be corrected nor taught in the offices where they are employed. The cry arises at once that the curriculum is stuffed with comparatively useless subjects while the weightier matters of essential importance for vocations are neglected.

The school authorities are compelled to bear the onslaught of this irresponsible criticism. Their critics hark back to the good old years when the simpler courses of study and the sturdier discipline of the rod brought forth the results so lacking in our degenerate days. They continue thus to criticize, though actual proof from the tests of the schools of our grandfathers clearly indicates that the children came out of these more Spartan institutions less well-equipped even in the three R's than are the graduates of our own grades. These attacks upon the schools are recurrent. Each year when the employer of boys and girls loses control of the irritation caused by youthful incompetence he is apt to pour out his wrath on the institutions from whose hands he receives his employees.

Unfortunately the relation between the school and the occupation has been so slight that the comment and criticism called out by the child's failure to fit into the machinery of the office, the shop, or the factory has little value beyond the registration of friction and of the need of adjustment. It is not illuminating comment and criticism. The teacher naturally resents the implication that the child's entire education should consist in drills in spelling, penmanship, and figuring, flanked by stenography, typewriting, and cataloguing. If the child's employer is to have and express an opinion upon the child's school training, that opinion must be more enlightened and more improved by interest in the child's entire welfare. The teachers, failing to find such all-round judgment in members of the community who employ the graduates of our public schools, naturally come to regard themselves as the only competent judges of what the school training should be.

Fortunately this gap between the community and the school has been bridged at a number of points. The schools have undertaken a certain amount of vocational training, and upon strictly vocational training the comment and criticism of those representing these specific vocations is felt to be pertinent. It has been even in some degree sought by the school itself. Out of this interplay have arisen various departments of vocational training, such as technical high schools and commercial high schools. In touch with these schools the business and technical men have formed advisory boards for consultation with the teaching and administrative forces of the school, both as to curriculum and as to the actual conduct of the training itself, and the teacher, on the other hand, has on occasion followed the child in his first entrance into work, at times guarding the child's interests and himself getting concrete material for the subject matter of the schoolroom work. The commercial high schools in Boston and in Cleveland and the technical schools in a number of our cities are illustrations of institutions in which the occupational training already present in the school has not only been improved by this technical outside interest and coöperation, but in which the vocational training has become more educative and cultural than it was when it lacked this outer stimulus to efficiency.

The inference from this is that what we have lacked in the community's complaints against school training has been a larger and more fruitful contact between the school training and the social situation for which the child is trained.

No one will assume that such instances as these solve all the many problems of education which, old and rising in novel forms, face the teachers and administrators of our great public-school systems. A very large number of our school children are not and cannot be oriented toward such specific occupations that their training can be made frankly vocational, and we would be turning our backs upon the best educational traditions if we should separate those who graduate from the grades or the high schools into shops and offices from those who will continue their scholastic training or who have no specific vocations before them. A democratic education must hold together the boys and girls of the whole community; it must give them the common education that all should receive, so diversifying its work that the needs of each group may be met within the institution whose care and generous ideals shall permeate the specialized courses, while the more academic schooling may be vivified by the vocational motive that gives needed impulse to a study which may be otherwise unmeaning or even deadening.

Vocational training came into the American school system somewhat tardily, but it has at last passed the door. It is true that it still remains a question whether in the immediate future it will be frankly recognized as an integral part of our public-school work under a single direction, or whether, under a separate direction, it is to be kept outside the organized system of public education.

However this question may be answered in the immediate future, I cannot believe that eventually it will be possible to keep separate two sides of the training of children which in material and method supplement each other — as theory and practice, as material and interpretation, as technique and application.

There is a further powerful argument against the separation of vocational training from academic training in the public school, and that is that vocational training has made the contact with the community conditions under which this education is to be used and has thus brought itself into a normal situation within which it must be checked and tested by its results. It is just this contact which our public-school training for life has hitherto lacked. In so far as vocational training and public schooling can become a part of the same educational process, just so far will the benefits of this close functional relation between the children's training and the life of the community pass over to all parts of the preparation of our children for life. I know of no answer that can be made to this argument except one which must maintain that vocational training may not be educational, and that the more academic subjects of the school curriculum have no organic place in the curriculum of vocational training — contentions which the best vocational training in this country and in Europe abundantly disproves.

It is to the other phase of this contact of the school with the community to which I wish to direct especial attention, the answering phase of vocational guidance. I hope, however, it has been sufficiently emphasized that vocational training and vocational guidance are normally linked together. Through these two doors the community gains admittance to the school.

Perhaps the most striking evidence that the community through vocational guidance is able to coöperate healthfully with the school and exercise a legitimate criticism in the process is found in the fact that the school more or less unwittingly has been itself a vocational guide, has been determining what occupations many of the children who leave school shall enter, and the further fact that this unwitting guidance and direction, just because it has been largely unintentional, has been in no small degree unfortunate for the children. In so far as the school has fitted its pupils to enter one occupation rather than another, just so far it is guiding them to this vocation.

If the school had in the past as deliberately trained the children in the mechanical arts, had centered its study of history as diligently around the growth of industry, had studied the industries in the community as earnestly as it has trained them in the arts of the office and the counter, as it has organized its study of history about literature and politics, as it has studied the careers of its successful politicians, warriors, and literary men, it would unquestionably have been guiding them toward the mechanical occupations. But the school has uncritically accepted the general attitude of the community that each child should take advantage of the unequaled opportunities that America has offered of getting up in the world ; and the uncritical assumption back of this attitude has been that the upward path lay away from the labor of the hands and led toward the labor of the wits, and that these were trained by the uses of language and mental arithmetic. Success has generally meant achievement in business, in politics, or in one of the professions ; and the schools, apart from the generalities found in its reading books or heard from its rostra concerning the nobility of labor and the beauties of the simple life, have unconsciously adjusted themselves to those callings in which lay the opportunities for the successful man. The training in these branches has not been extensive, but it used to be the boast of our American society that the grounding of the three R's gained in the common school was all that was needed for the energetic man ; that he had much better get the rest of his vocational training in business or politics than in the school ; while the professional man must gain his technique in professional training schools.

While the curricula of both the elementary and the secondary schools have been immensely enriched, especially in those subjects which are termed cultural, the trend of the training has continued to be toward business, politics, or further preparation for college or professional study. It has followed very naturally from this that the children find themselves directed toward office work, and that when training is offered in mechanical arts side by side with the technique of office work the training for the white-collar jobs is the more attractive. The schools growing up in the traditions of the American community have been guiding the children toward a certain type of vocation.

We have referred to positive guidance. There is a negative guidance, which is the more serious, because it arises from a lack of vocational training or direction. In the schools of the country at large between 40 and 50 per cent of the children in the elementary schools are eliminated before they have finished the grades — that is, before they have acquired a common-school education. It is the judgment of those who have studied these children that they are not able to retain even the meager acquirements of the lower grades. They are less capable readers and writers of English and less capable figurers in the years after they have left school than they were in the school itself. They constitute an inconsiderable fraction of those who attend the night schools. They have not that minimum of education which our common-school system, with the compulsory attendance regulations, contemplates. They are not fitted for any but the unskilled vocations; and our community, in leaving the schools with their predominantly academic curricula, their direction toward only one type of vocation, and the inadequate laws governing school attendance, is much more effectively guiding these unfortunate graduates of the fourth, fifth, and sixth grades toward the unskilled occupations than any system of vocational training could guide its graduates into the skilled trades.

It is impossible for the community to avoid the task of guidance. If it is not undertaken consciously and with adequate forethought, the schools, from the very nature of school training, its adaptation or lack of adaptation to the occupations of the community, its success or failure, will determine in large degree what doors shall be open or closed to those who leave school. The aptitudes and ambitions gained in school and from the surrounding neighborhoods shape the children's possible careers.

This guidance must be incomplete even when the school system frankly recognizes its duty toward vocational training. It is through

the door of the vocational guidance and training that the school
enters into immediate concrete contact with the homes and neighborhoods from which the children come, as well as with the industries into which they enter, and the meaning for the school of
this contact is not exhausted when it undertakes various types
of training in the industrial and household arts. The destination
of the particular child cannot be left to his own immature judgment or whim ; nor is the teacher alone a competent judge ; nor
can the decision be safely left to the parents alone — in whose
hands it might seem to be most safely left.

The experience in vocational guidance in England and in this
country is conclusive upon this point. The parent, the social worker
who so frequently must help parents to interpret their social situation, the teacher, and someone who understands the labor market
for children and the character of the occupations, especially what
they have to offer the employees in the future, must get together
if the best possible chance is to be offered the child. This is
especially true if the child leaves school with but little training
and faces a market for only unskilled labor. To find that opening
which carries with it some training in skill, some future beyond
the minimum wage, which avoids the blind alleys and the many
pitfalls that child labor so abundantly provides, to find this opening
for the immature child who goes out to work for the community
under the least satisfactory conditions, is surely the common duty of
the school and of the community. And it is an individual task that
has a new character with each child. It cannot be undertaken or
carried out in a wholesale manner. No child should leave school to
go to work without the benefit of all the guidance which those who
have reared and taught and are about to employ him can give. The
meagerness of the training which we can give the majority of our
children emphasizes this duty. It is further emphasized by the
value for society of the human material with which we are dealing.

But in our interest in the particular child we must not overlook
the immense value which such interest should have for the school
itself. It is the process by which the institution of the school
passes from its fixed dogmatic stage into that of a working institution that has come to consciousness and can test its methods

and presuppositions by its results. For in this task of guiding the individual child into his occupation, the school faces its own accomplishment tested by the most important value which society possesses, its future citizen. The standpoint for the judgment of the school and all its works is inevitably given in the conscientious attempt to guide the particular child into the best occupation he can find in view of his training and background.

It is upon this phase of vocational guidance that I wish to insist — its value for the school. Its importance for the individual child is too evident to need argument or rhetoric. The obligation of the community that employs the child; that too often exploits him; that turns him loose upon the streets at the age of fourteen and refuses him any employment with a future until he is sixteen; that invests great sums in an education which half the time it does not carry to the point of adequate return either to the child or to the community — the obligation of this community to reach out its hand to the child and guide him to the most favorable opening is also evident enough; the only difficulty is to find the corporate bodies of the community upon whom this obligation can be fastened. To a very large extent this sense of responsibility has come home only to the social worker whose interest in the child and his family has made his individual case real and pressing. Even the employer has come to realize in some cases the value of vocational guidance to the business that employs the child. The teachers who inevitably feel a genuine interest in their pupils will, if they are able, extend this interest to these most crucial moments in the child's career — when he seeks his first job. Beyond this human interest there is the import to the school of this first test of the child's training. The test, of course, is that of the whole educational process and it affords ground to criticize the age at which the child comes to school, the whole training given in the school, the age of leaving school, the forms of occupation these factors prescribe for the child, and the care of the child after he has left the schoolhouse up to the time of the completion of his training for his occupation.

It is not too much to say that our schools are still in one respect medieval. They assume more or less consciously that they are called upon to indoctrinate their pupils, and that the doctrine which they have to instill — whether it be that of language, number, history, literature, or elementary science — is guaranteed as subject matter for instruction by its own truth, by its traditional position in the school curriculum, and finally by its relation to the rest of the ideas, points of view, artistic products, historical monuments, which together make up what we call our culture. These tests of subject matter in instruction may be fairly called internal and do not carry the judgment of the pedagogue out of the schoolhouse. The subject matter is determined, then, in a real sense by authority, and it follows that when the results of the training are disappointing, the pedagogue feels that he is secure within his institution and can calmly pass the charge of inefficient training on to other social agents and conditions. No one will question the legitimacy of these tests if they are recognized as organic parts of the larger test of the working of the child's school training when brought up against its use in practice.

The medieval character of the school is shown in the separation of the institution, which has the doctrines of education intrusted to it, from the other training processes in which the intellectual content is at a minimum and the practical facility is at a maximum. In the real sense the doctrine which the school inculcates should be continually tried out in the social experience of the child — there should be a play back and forth between formal training and the child's actual conduct. Until this is brought about the school will continue to be in some degree medieval and scholastic; but every fresh contact with the situation of the child who has been imbibing the doctrine and now must make use of his training in his social world outside is of immense value in enabling us to bring the child's training as a whole a little nearer the normal education of the citizen to be. No small part of this criticism must fall upon industries which are willing to exploit children, in some sense enticed from the school by the promise of a paltry wage, and upon the inadequate training regulations of the governments of our school districts.

After all, the school is the self-conscious expression of the community in child training; it is the rational, intentional institution;

and however essential the activity of outside agencies are in direction and training of children, the school should be the central and organizing agency. It can, however, become such a central and organizing agency only as it abandons its medieval position of giving a body of doctrines and techniques which find their justification in themselves rather than in their value in conduct, at home, in the neighborhood, and in the vocations.

Such a testing of the doctrine and technique of school training is not to be taken in any narrow sense. In the first place, it is the final good of the child rather than his immediate wage that must be considered; in the second place, we all realize that many of the values that accrue to the child from the school training are intangible and can be stated with difficulty, if at all, in terms of his success in a trade or an office. What I am pleading for is the recognition that it is in relation to his vocation that all the child has acquired should be regarded, even if some of the acquirements are intangible and cannot be weighed in the coarser scales of wage and advancement. In a word, it must be through the child's vocation that he can get to the positions in which these very intangible results of schooling will have their season of flowering and fruiting. Unless a child can get into life he cannot have it, no matter how well he may be prepared to appreciate much that is fine therein. The school may not concentrate its efforts upon values to be realized later unless it sees doors open through which the child can reach the uplands of life. It is the whole life of the child that the school must envisage, but it must conceive of it as growing out of the child's first beginnings in the world after he leaves school. Unless the school helps the child effectively into the larger fields, it is in vain that it has given him their chart.

Now it is at least consonant with the traditions of American schooling to assume that culture and training form a whole, and that the higher values grow out of the immediate necessities; to assume that in the immediate experience of the child there are found the opportunities for development of what the school has to inculcate. It is not only possible, but pedagogically correct, to give a child the history of his country from the standpoint of the industries into which he must enter; to follow the line of the child's vocational interest in organizing his course of study, with the full recognition that such a vocation has its essential relations to all that the child has to learn. Even from the point of view of the subject matter of the curriculum, the school can profit by making its standpoint vocational guidance, the guidance of the child becoming the guiding principle of the curriculum. The illustration has been taken largely from the case of the children who go direct from an incomplete elementary schooling into the shop, factory, or office ; but it must be remembered that the same principle holds, whatsoever the vocation of the child may be, and it is even true that the child may well profit in his elementary and perhaps secondary training if he looks toward some vocation whose outline he can discern better than the profession which he may later follow. Trade training when adequately given is sound education even for those who will not be tradesmen.

But it is the still broader outlook that I would insist upon for the school. Not only should the school conceive of its subject matter and method from the standpoint of the success and failure of the children when they leave school ; it should be humanized and socialized more completely by keeping the human fortunes of its children perpetually before it, and by continually questioning its own material and method when its graduates stumble and fall before the obstacles that confront them when they leave the schoolhouse. It should be so organically related to the other agencies that regard the success and failure of children — the home, the social workers, the employment agencies, the employers and their various plants, the higher schools into which some of its pupils will pass, and the whole community into which as citizens it will send its students — that the contacts which vocational guidance brings with it will be largely sought and intelligently used for purposes of criticism and interpretation.

To sum up, vocational guidance means testing the whole training given the child, both within and without the school. It is the point of contact with the outer world from which to criticize both this training and the occupations into which society admits the children whom it has partly educated. The healthful relation of the school to the community, and especially to the other agencies that train our children, depends upon the school making the stand-point of vocational guidance a dominant one in its whole organization.

In accepting this standpoint the school will abandon the medieval position and will come into full human relationship with homes, neighborhoods, occupations, and all the agencies that are bound up with the development of the rising generation. In accepting the challenge of formulating the education of the child on terms of the uses to which he will put it, the school should abandon nothing of the higher values of which it conceives itself to be the carrier, but should recognize its task to be the statement of these values in terms of the child's own experience.

In vocational guidance the school finds its supreme task as the conscious educational institution of a democracy.

In endeavoring to formulate the larger meaning of vocational guidance for the school, I seem to have gone away from the immediate concrete and often meager undertaking of the vocational guidance with which we are familiar; but acquaintance with intensive studies of the schooling and occupations of children in a poverty-stricken industrial section of Chicago has convinced me that the task of following up the boys and girls who, with incomplete schooling, search after wretched jobs, brings out with terrible force the necessity of regarding and judging our whole process of child training from the standpoint of the vocations into which we are unconsciously driving them. The children are worth so much more than the occupations to which we dedicate very many of them, and, after all, the school is the one institution which can express this value of the children in terms of the preparation it gives them for life; hence it can speak with authority to society as to the occupations into which the children may enter. It is at this meeting point of training and occupation that the school can criticize its own achievements and at the same time the life into which the children are to enter. It seems to me of supreme importance both to the children's training and to their vocations that both should be formulated in terms of vocational guidance.

THE INDUSTRIAL FACTOR IN EDUCATION

By Ernest N. Henderson, Professor of Psychology and Education,
Adelphi College, Brooklyn, New York

(From the Report of Committee on the Place of Industries in Public Education
to the National Council of Education, July, 1910)

According to the plan of the committee the purpose of this chapter is to discuss "the psychological and social need for constructive handwork and for industries as a 'subject' in school." The aim will be to analyze and to state as compactly as possible the various phases of this need as it displays itself in the child growing up through the school to maturity. The discussion will assume the results of preceding reports as to the importance of industries as a cultural force and will leave for later discussion the history of the theory of industrial education.

It seems, however, almost necessary to preface a discussion of the psychological need for any subject in the school by a comparison of the part psychology has in the past played in the determination of the work of education with the function assigned to it by schoolmen to-day. The great educational reformers, Rousseau, Pestalozzi, Herbart, and Froebel were convinced that the fundamental need in education was that it should be based on a sound psychology. So thoroughly were they possessed with this point of view that they looked to psychology to determine not only the method but also the aim of education. The problem of the schoolmaster they conceived to be a development of that which is potential within the child. In this attitude they were protesting against an endeavor to enforce upon him a number of disagreeable tasks more or less remotely connected with the business of life. Even Herbart, with his emphasis on the importance of the external process of instruction, agreed that the aim of education is "the harmonious development of all the powers," or, according to his phraseology, the development of "many-sided interest." Education according to this view aims at personal culture, at realizing the self, at bringing to light the possibilities that God implanted in the child; these are all methods of stating the purpose of education which leave to the psychologist the problem of determining its specific character. For who but he whose study concerns the nature of the mind can be expected to know its potentialities?

The theory that psychology should determine not only the method but also the aim of instruction possessed the minds of the earlier advocates of manual training in the United States. Among the important characteristics of the child is the fact that he has a body and is capable of doing an enormous number of things with it. Moreover, he is intensely interested in doing many of these things. For a long time the physical activities are rather more in evidence than the mental ones, and all of the instincts point toward them. Soon the instinct of constructiveness appears, fashioning the form of many games. The teacher, alert to the potentialities of the child, marks the power and the instinct to use the hand, and cultivates it to insure that perfectly developed man toward whom his task is conceived to direct itself.

With the progress of time the ideal of personal culture has been largely modified or replaced by that of efficiency. According to this aim education concerns itself with preparing for life rather than in cultivating all the powers of the child. The study of what man has to do, particularly the study of the social organization into which he must fit, has come to be conceived as the proper method of determining the purpose of education. On this basis the mere fact that a child possesses a capacity is no reason that the school should aim to develop it. On the contrary, many capacities, since they bear no relation to social life as at present constituted, may well be suffered to atrophy. If there is to be education in constructive work, it must be because there is a social rather than a psychological need for it.

Such a need is not, however, far to seek. The growth of industry in modern times has been such as to place it at the very front among the interests of communities and of nations. Science, for many ages merely the pursuit of a learned leisure, has been harnessed and put to work. It has concerned itself with the tasks intrusted to the servile classes. It has relieved their labor of some of its severest strains, has elevated its character, making it more intelligent, and has created the need of a broader intellectual training as a preparation for nearly all the vocations than was required a century ago. If education is to prepare for life, it must begin by preparing to make a livelihood, and the vocations of the vast majority of those whom a democratic society would educate involve forms of handwork and industry in which the school can give an extensive training. Such training is becoming increasingly necessary because of changes in the industrial life that tend to check or to destroy the apprentice system, and because this life is continually becoming more complicated and difficult to understand without specially directed study. Thus the school is being forced to take up vocational training in a great variety of occupations hitherto prepared for adequately in other ways, for the negative reason that the other ways are disappearing and the positive one that it alone is capable of furnishing a training suited to modern needs.

It is evident, therefore, that from the standpoint of aiming to prepare its pupils for efficient living the modern school is more and more compelled to take into account both constructive work and the study of industry as a fundamentally important group of subjects. There is a social need for such work. But in the endeavor to fit it into the course of study difficulties arise. Since the work is commonly recognized as vocational, many parents see no need of it for children who are not expected to pursue the callings to which it is supposed to lead. This is especially true of the constructive work, the survival of "manual training." It finds difficulty in making its way into the earlier part of the curriculum, which is necessarily the same for all. To effect this entrance and to maintain its ground, it has been compelled to assume generalized forms that seem to constitute integral parts in the culture of everyone. Moreover, it has been tempted to defend these forms not on account of their somewhat remote utility, but rather on the ground of the older psychological arguments of discipline and all-round development. If these arguments are, as seems inevitable, to be abandoned, it is evident that the elementary school must find and teach that phase of industrial life that is suited to children and useful for all, and cease to rely on the cultivation through manual training of such general powers as accuracy, moral rectitude, co-ordination of eye and brain and hand, etc.

Many considerations conspire to make wise the postponement of the more purely vocational part of constructive work and the study of industry until at least the dawn of adolescence. It is specialized work, and to introduce such training early seems bad for at least three reasons : (1) It encourages differentiation before the child has revealed himself to others or has discovered his own tastes and aptitudes. (2) It initiates specialization before a child has obtained the general foundations of his culture, and while he is still imma-ture. Many declare that this leads to prematuration and to arrested development. (3) It tries to teach children what can be learned effectively only by older persons and especially under the pressure of practical need. This results in a waste of time.

The problem of constructive work and of the study of industry has thus very quickly resolved itself into one of determining on the one hand the elements of general culture and on the other those of specialization that these subjects involve. This analysis completed, the two factors can be assigned to different parts of the school program. The special training can well be postponed until the work of the elementary school has been finished. The general culture would need to be properly correlated with the age of the pupils and the general arrangement of studies in the school. Herein the issue comes to involve questions of the psychological needs of childhood.

Before taking up these questions, however, let us note a little more carefully the nature of that general social need at the behest of which the studies in question should be introduced into the ele-mentary school. It is evident that their general utility is not iden-tical with what it has been in the past. With the development of industry into more and more elaborate organizations of highly specialized activities, the all-round manual skill so important in both men and women a generation ago is ceasing to be an espe-cially valuable source of efficiency. On the other hand, economic interdependence is becoming greater, and it is growing increasingly important for each to know many things in order to keep his activities socially and vocationally in efficient coöperation with the activities of others in different walks of life. The substitution of economic interdependence for economic independence has made it necessary for each, if he be not to descend into the position of a mere tool of the social machine to be taken up or laid aside at the will of those who use him, to understand the relation of his vocation to others well enough to exert a controlling influence in reference to its status and its development. He must be able not only to readjust himself to changes in his vocation, but to assist in the work of readjusting his vocation to the varying conditions of community life. To do this he needs a general knowledge of many vocations. The world of industry in general becomes of importance to him as well as his own specialty.

It is to the task of laying the foundations for a general knowledge of industrial life that the elementary school must address itself. In this work mere manual training becomes subordinated to the study of industry, as a method rather than an aim of instruction. The group of subjects becomes an introduction to a fundamental phase of economic life and serves a utility quite as definite as that of instruction in the three R's or in geography. Culture having this general aim may well continue after the study of specific vocations has begun. The more effectively it is mastered the more surely, we may suppose, will the trained man be master of his vocation rather than its slave.

Whatever may be the factors in industrial intelligence, it is evident that one is a knowledge of the general facts of economic and industrial life such as enables the individual to see clearly the relation of his own vocation thereto. Upon such knowledge is founded sound judgment as to the rights and duties of each craft as well as of its possibilities and necessities.

We turn now to the psychological problem — the problem of adjusting constructive work and the study of industry to the nature of the child. It may be said of both, and especially of the former, that nature has left the schoolmaster little to do. Children inherit so great an interest in such activity that it, so far from needing aid in order to be made enjoyable, constitutes one of the most effective means of arousing interest in any subject that can be taught through its assistance. Those educational reformers who have striven to reorganize education, making it more interesting and more in accord with the nature of the child, have usually been pronounced advocates of constructive work. We may distinguish between two general uses for which it has been employed : (*a*) to give motive for school work otherwise meaningless and uninteresting, and (*b*) to render more positive and lasting the results of instruction.

As a means of motivation constructive work possesses the following advantages : (1) It appeals to the love of activity, especially physical activity so prominent in children. To younger children the mere making of things seems worth while apart from any uses to which the product may be put. (2) It appeals to the primitive interest in the concrete, that which represents processes and results easily apprehended by both sight and touch and the muscular sense. In such material young children are absorbed, and it is astonishing how little general meaning or value is necessary to insure their interest, provided the material with which they are working be of this tangible character. (3) Constructive work connects itself with occupations and products the utility of which is seen illustrated in the everyday life about the child. Indeed, they are among the first utilities to be grasped by the child's mind.

When we turn to the value of constructive work as a means of strengthening the results of instruction we distinguish two fundamental advantages : (1) It furnishes one of the easiest and most effective ways of applying the principle that learning should, or, as the "functional" psychology puts it, *must* be by doing. (2) It teaches through the application of principles to a sort of practice more nearly similar to that of the life situations in which these principles are expected to function than is that of much of the school.

The newer psychology takes the ground that we do not attend, do not discriminate, and so are not conscious, except when this is necessary to bring about readjustment between reactions and stimuli. Learning is always connected with the reorganization of our modes of behavior. Apart from constructive work the school presents only one form of physical activity of great importance.

This is that of language, either oral or written, and the great aim of such activity is to come into adjustment with certain standard words, notably those of the teacher. Now while such activity must always remain one of the most fruitful occasions for learning, inasmuch as nothing can vie with the social situation in offering emergencies for readjustment, it is exceedingly valuable not to be limited in school doing and learning to this sort of thing. The addition of the endeavor to manipulate materials supplies a characteristically different sort of emergency. In adjusting himself to other minds the child is dealing with persons who are continually by their own efforts furthering or hindering his endeavors. In either event the condition of dependence is emphasized. The child is led to consider success or failure to be a matter of the point of view of others; and this point of view may be, and all too frequently is, dependent upon circumstance and mood, inaccurate, uncertain, transitory, unjust, or absurdly compliant and easy rather than fixed, true, and inevitable. The methods of dealing with minds vary from cajolery and domineering to persuasion and the appeal to the sense of right. In any case they differ greatly from the dealing with mere physical materials, where there is one law, the mastery of which is the only method of securing results, and where the child can have no thought except that of simple direct control. It is an unquestionable addition to the resources of the child that he has accustomed himself to deal intelligently with physical materials as well as with human minds.

Moreover much that is learned in the school is intended to be applied not in the control of men but in the manipulation of material. In that event constructive work in the school offers the only method by which the principles can there be applied as they would be in life. That they should get this sort of school application is fundamentally important. Facts learned in order to be recited are, by a simple principle of recall, not apt to be remembered where the circumstances and the emergencies are so vastly different as in the case of school questioning on the one hand and a workshop on the other. The more nearly the school environment corresponds to that of life in general, the more likely it is that the ideas learned in the former will be applied in the latter.

The identity of principle is not sufficient with most minds to overcome the effect of diversity in all other associations, and the mind recalls many things, but not that far-away bit of school learning which is the one thing useful. It may therefore safely be said that whatever is to be applied to problems in construction should be learned wherever possible in connection with such problems.

Very much the same analysis that has been made of the psychological need for constructive work in the school applies to the study of industry. In fact it deals with that phase of life to aid in the study of which constructive work finds its principal use. Connecting itself with interest in and imitation of the simpler forms of adult life, it leads gradually to a desire to participate in the work of the world. It is to be hoped that the constructive work and the study of industry in the elementary school will ultimately be of such a character that when the pupil reaches the age at which the activities of adult life make their appeal, he will be able to make a wise choice in reference to them and be already advanced in an appreciable measure toward the goal of his special vocation.

It is especially in connection with relating school work to the realities of life that the study of industry becomes important. The public in a democratic and commercial and industrial community are apt to find reality rather more in such work than in science and art, literature and philosophy. The children of such a public are prone to discover in the study of industry something that connects the systematic, and especially the formal, work of the school with the real problems of life. Under these conditions the school finds this study a means of putting motive into many contributory studies and of securing such a setting for its teaching as will make likely its application at least to the utilitarian pursuits of life.

The problem of motive becomes especially difficult in the later years of the elementary school. Children at this time pass, so far as regards their outlook upon life, into a distinctly different phase of development. We can bring this out by describing the earlier phases. The young child is a creature of impulse and of imagination, absorbed in doing or thinking that which is immediately suggested to him. Reflection is gradually forced upon him. The period from eight to twelve is a critical age, an age of rivalry in games, of the felt presence of social criticism and coercion in reference to all the physical and mental activities that the child puts forth. Under this pressure he becomes reflective. He subjects imagination to standards, the standards of social acceptability, of truth, of propriety. Such standards vary with individuals and social groups. The teacher does not always agree with the parents, much less with the man on the street. Among the children groups arise on the basis of difference in ideals. Later on the adolescent discovers that among these warring views of life he must choose one for himself to be his own. He arrives at the age of independence and becomes himself the critic, declaring his freedom from coercion.

It is at this age that the rate of elimination of pupils from school becomes portentous. The reasons that cause children to leave school are very numerous, but unquestionably a very large proportion, at least a majority, give up because they cannot feel that it will repay the sacrifice of effort or expense or both that it involves. Other reasons are for the most part contributory. This one is fundamental. There are two classes of children to whom school work does not seem worth while. One of these consists of pupils who can and do get on well in the school but find the activities on the outside more interesting and profitable. The other is composed of pupils who do not prosper in the school. Such children naturally grow discontented. No one can be expected to regard as worth while for him that which he is incapable of doing. Moreover, in such a competitive atmosphere as a school merely to pass means practically to fail.

Now it is evident that just as constructive work may offer the motives of activity and the making of concrete things to younger children, so to older ones it, especially when combined with a study of industry, will seem worth while to many of both these two classes of the ordinarily eliminated. For those who fail in the older studies of the school, the constructive work may offer a field for success. For both classes it should constitute the main part of the later school program. As an integral part of the preparation for life, it deserves a place proportionate to the number of those who need such preparation and the amount of such preparation it is possible and desirable to give.

We have reached again, from the standpoint of the study of th: developing nature of the child, the issue of specialized vocational training. It is evident that the general training of the earlier years of the elementary school should be what is deemed necessary to all and what introduces those who are to specialize in some form of industry to their work of specific preparation. We have not, however, as yet considered sufficiently the problem of the initial steps in differentiation or specialization. This problem is in our democratic system one among the most difficult and important that we face. It is a question whether the problem of determining what the vocation of the man shall be is not more difficult and exacting than that of preparing him for what has been chosen. The European systems of education, which have not been burdened to such an extent as our own with the ideals of a democracy, have found it easy to ingraft vocational instruction upon an elementary system intended only for those destined by birth to some form of industry. In our boasted continuous ladder of schools, where the elementary school leads into the high school and the high school into the college, the introduction of special training in industry has not been so simple. It means differentiation. It has seemed like cutting off from the children who took it the opportunity for such careers as were limited largely to those who had completed the higher course. We have felt that education shall give to all an equal chance to attain any distinction in life. Hence we have clung to a system associated with the training of leaders, even though such a system may be poorly enough adapted to the education of anyone else.

It is likely that we shall find our way out through a change in our conception of leadership on the one hand and a discovery that our time-honored method of training any sort of a leader needs extensive modification, if not revolution, on the other. It is not, however, the purpose of this chapter to discuss these changes. We may confine ourselves to the crying need for a system of education that shall provide training adequate, in the first place, to enable a fairly intelligent choice of a calling to be made and, in the second place, to prepare for whatever may be selected. We are fully alive to the need for the second of these advances. It is doubtful whether

our educational leaders have been in general adequately impressed
with the need for a system of school work the primary purpose of
which should be to enable the pupil to find himself, and the teacher
to give to him intelligent advice on the matter.

From the point of view of the development of the child, the age
at which this process of experimentation toward a calling should
be definitely initiated corresponds fairly well with the beginning of
the seventh school year. Its external symptom is the high rate of
elimination from school at that time, and its internal sign is the
unrest, the questioning of values, the beginnings of " storm and
stress " that characterize the commencement of the age of independence, of adolescence. It would seem that at this time the
secondary phase of education should begin.

There has been in our country some trouble in defining just
what secondary education is. The demarcation between it and the
elementary school on the one hand and higher education on the
other has been one of years and of studies rather than of general
function. There has been no clear reason except custom and a
felt convenience for having secondary education begin and end
where it does. It is possible, however, to distinguish three well-
marked functions of education, which might be assigned to elementary, secondary, and higher education, respectively, without
much destructive readjustment of our present system. Elementary
education concerns the essentials and the fundamentals. It is the
education that precedes any attempt at differentiation. With the
development of the child up into the age where such differentiation becomes necessary an epoch of experimentation sets in. The
main purpose of the education of this period should be to afford
an adequate basis of experience for the choice of a specialty and
to guide the process of selection. Such education we may call
secondary. When once it has been determined as well as is practically possible what the child should do, the time for higher education, that is, for the special preparation for a vocation, has
appeared.

On this plan we should not have a system in which, while elementary education is supposed to be for all, secondary education
is only for a few, and higher education for the very few; but each

phase of the work would find representation in the education of all or most pupils. At the beginning of the seventh grade the work of experimentation might well begin. A large number of children have by this time demonstrated their unfitness for what might be called a professional career. For them the severer studies, involving the power of mind to grasp and utilize the abstract ideas and processes involved in mathematics, science, language, etc., are not profitable. They should be given experimental work along the line of industrial training supplemented by concrete cultural work in literature, civics, geography, and science, such as adapts them for the duties of citizenship and social life. We may tentatively suggest that two years of such work would put these children in the position of making an intelligent choice of a vocational school in which to complete their education.

At the beginning of the seventh school year those whose mental traits make it desirable might enter schools where the older type of secondary work is prominent. But we might expect that continually new revelations will be made in regard to the talents and tastes of such pupils, and that little by little those who are unable to do the work that leads to the higher professions will be selected out to enter vocational schools that prepare primarily for intermediate positions in industry, commerce, the civil service, etc. The period of secondary education would, on the theory proposed, extend until the choice of a vocation has been made on the basis of sufficient experience. The knowledge necessary to make such a choice is of necessity more extensive, the more advanced the vocation. Properly speaking, the secondary school would include the present liberal college course.

The characteristic feature of the secondary school on this theory. is the emphasis upon experimentation and selection. In such a school the experimental subject would be especially prominent. This may be defined as a subject studied primarily for the sake of finding the extent of its appeal to the powers and interests of the student. Experimental studies therefore should not be elective but prescribed, for their function is to compel, as it were, the student to explore the field of human thought and endeavor adequately before he is permitted to settle upon his peculiar specialty.

An adequate range of experimentation would involve the secondary but by no means unimportant gain of a broad outlook upon life. Thus the student will be getting his liberal culture to a great extent while he is engaged in the process of selecting his vocation. The study of industry and constructive work would thus constitute factors not only in the elementary but also in the secondary education of every student. All children would have enough of them to know and to do the things that they concern in so far as they enter into the life of all. Every student should have enough more such study to enable him, no matter what his calling may be, to understand and to sympathize and coöperate with those whose life work lies in these fields. The process of differentiation initiated by the completion of the elementary course would still leave to all some further work along such lines both for experimentation and culture. We may assume that when the experimental work has been completed the needs of culture will have been in most cases fairly well satisfied.

The current usage assigns vocational schools of the trade-school or technical-school type to secondary rather than to higher education, where they would be placed according to the classification just suggested. This arises historically because such work is usually taken in lieu of the secondary training of the older sort. The classification made in the preceding discussion aims to provide a basis for the determination of the character and function of constructive work and the study of industry as we go from the age of elementary education on into that of experimentation toward a vocation and further into that of specialized preparation for the one selected.

PROBLEMS OF VOCATIONAL GUIDANCE

By Superintendent F. E. Spaulding, Minneapolis

(An Address delivered to the Department of Superintendence, Cincinnati, Ohio, 1915)

More completely than any other single movement, vocational guidance must take for its function the *conservation of human resources*. This movement enters this limitless field of effort, not as a distinctly new agency; it seeks rather to differentiate itself from old agencies — the school, the home, the occupation — by clarifying, coördinating, and rendering more effective the efforts of these agencies whose function is also some phase of human betterment.

The vocational-guidance movement seeks the coöperation of these numerous other agencies, and must depend for its efficiency largely upon securing such coöperation. Out of the problems of these other agencies, rather than *de novo*, the vocational-guidance movement is formulating its problems and thus defining its field. Merely to state a half dozen of these problems as they seem now to be taking shape — with no attempt to suggest their solution farther than their statement may suggest it — is all that the limits of this paper will permit.

The first problem of vocational guidance seeking to conserve human resources is to know the existence of those resources, their extent and number, and to gain and exercise some measure of control over them. Hence the vocational-guidance department of every school system should be responsible for an accurate and always up-to-date census of all the children and youth of the community, covering the ages from four or five to at least eighteen, better twenty-one, years. Furthermore, within these years, the vocational-guidance department should exercise legal control over the children and youth of the community — first respecting their schooling, later respecting their employment, or combined employment and schooling. Hence the issuance of all school-exemption and employment certificates should be under the control of this department and should be so systematized that the department may know at all times, and control in accordance with law, the whereabouts and employment of every youth of the community.

The second great problem of vocational guidance concerns types of schools and school curricula. While the vocational-guidance department must not be charged with the full responsibility of determining what types of schools shall be maintained, what subjects shall be taught, in a given community, this department must render invaluable assistance in determining these matters. For it is the function of this department to know more completely, more extensively, than any other the two great factors which must determine the scope and character of schools and programs of study — on the one hand, the children and youth to be educated, their capacities and needs, and, on the other, the needs of society, the opportunities that society affords for worthy service.

The vocational-guidance department should become a great repository of knowledge, always up to date and significant, of these two great factors in every community — the children and the work of the community. To secure this knowledge the vocational-guidance department should stimulate and assist the study of children throughout the schools — every teacher should have a part in this study, which should materially influence her attitude and work; at least the larger generalizations from these studies in the schools should be formulated and made available for quick reference in the vocational-guidance department. Equally should this department stimulate and take part in frequent industrial, commercial, occupational, surveys of the community, and the significant findings of such surveys should be always available in intelligible form in the office of the department.

But no vocational-guidance department should serve merely as a repository of such knowledge as this. Its knowledge should, indeed, be available for the use of all who may seek it; but the department itself must be at least one of the prime interpreters of this knowledge. When it is a question of the adjustment and the constant readjustment of schools and of school programs to the changing needs of the children and of the community, it may well fall to the vocational-guidance department to take the initiative in bringing about the necessary adjustments.

One important feature that the vocational-guidance department must help to introduce in some effective way into the school program of every community is a study of the rich and varied possibilities of service that not only the local community but the world affords. Such studies must be made not only informing but inspiring, to the end that youth may not merely know of the existence of opportunities for service, but that youthful desire for activity, for self-expression, may be aroused and directed into worthy channels.

Vocational guidance may well formulate for itself a third problem, that of the moral effect of the school on the child. I refer not especially to the conscious and intentional efforts of the school to train the character as well as the intellect — most schools are fully alive to the importance of such character training as a means of vocational preparation ; I refer rather to the continuous, unavoidable, yet rarely appreciated effect of the conditions imposed upon the pupil through the organization, administration, and conduct of the school and of the school work. The character effects growing silently and inevitably out of these fundamental conditions are probably more important than those resulting from conscious and intentional efforts of instructors. They are of all kinds, beneficial and detrimental, measured in terms of their contribution to the realization of each individual's possibilities.

Demanding especial attention from the standpoint of vocational guidance are those conditions which develop in a large percentage of pupils — and usually in the very ones most needing vocational guidance — feelings of personal unfitness and discouragement, habits of failure. Those who know industrial conditions to which young workers are subject, rightly deplore the prevalence of the blind-alley job, the frequent changes from one job to another, the repeated failures to get a sure footing anywhere, for out of these conditions graduate that most pitiable class — the unemployables. It is high time for us to realize that many children in our schools are subject to like conditions — blind-alley studies, repeated and continuous failure, whose character effects are inevitably the same as those resulting from like conditions in industry.

The vocational-guidance movement should help to bring from the industrial world to the school the impressive lesson that the conservation of human resources, in general and in the individual, depends upon success — the habit of success, the feeling of self-confidence that grows out of habitual success. No one wants to fail — least of all the youth whose normal condition is that of confidence and hope; the school must learn to adapt its work and requirements to the natural desire to succeed, so that the entire school life of every pupil may be a series of successes, to the end that — however meager the intellectual accomplishment — the habit of success may be formed. Without this fixed habit of success any young person is poorly prepared to face the discouraging conditions so prevalent in the world of industry. The young person entering industry with the habit of failure developed in school has already made several grades toward graduation into the class of unemployables.

The fourth, and the immediate, problem of vocational guidance is the individual. Vocational guidance must see that the individual learns to appreciate his own capacities and possibilities; that he informs himself concerning the opportunities for worthy service that the world offers; that he prepares himself as adequately as time and conditions permit to apply his powers to the rendering of the highest service of which he is, or may become, capable; that he learns to concentrate his thought, his energy and ambition, to this end of large and worthy service. This problem, like most other problems of vocational guidance, is not one for the vocational-guidance expert or counselor alone; it is a problem that must enlist the thought and effort of everyone, especially teachers and parents, who has any responsibility for the development and success of the child and youth.

The fifth problem of vocational guidance demands extensive knowledge of opportunities for service, especially in the immediate community, but also in the world at large. Such knowledge must not be confined to industrial and commercial occupations — service in the professions, any opportunity for worthy service, great or small, is the concern of vocational guidance. This knowledge must be intimate as well as extensive. It must embrace essential conditions of each distinct occupation — the general character of the occupation from the standpoint of social and civic welfare; the extent of the demand for service in that occupation; preparation necessary; steps, conditions, and limitations of progress; health and other conditions with their effects on workers; seasons and hours of work; wages and other advantages. In short, a well-equipped vocational-guidance department should have at its command such practical analyses of every important organized form of service as were worked out so admirably for certain typical industries in the Richmond Survey. Obviously, the gathering of such knowledge and keeping it always up to date, as is necessary, is an immense undertaking. Here, again, the coöperation of many agencies — industrial, commercial, professional, civic, social, and educational — must be enlisted.

The sixth and culminating problem of vocational guidance has to do with the successful transition of children and youth from the favorable conditions of healthful growth, and of practical education, which the schools must provide, into different but also favorable conditions for continued growth that occupations must be brought to afford. I state this final problem advisedly, with at least some realization of the prodigious responsibility imposed on vocational guidance — the responsibility of influencing the conditions of industry in favor of human welfare.

To accomplish this undertaking in any considerable measure is unquestionably beyond the unaided power of any vocational-guidance movement that is likely soon to develop. But fortunately many organized agencies, public and private, are already engaged in this same undertaking. I refer, of course, to all those agencies whose object is the banishment of human exploitation, the elevation of human welfare above mere industrial and commercial profit — those agencies that are already doing much to shorten the long hours, to improve the working conditions, and to increase the pay of wage earners. It is the function and the unparalleled opportunity of vocational guidance to coöperate with all such agencies, to coördinate their efforts and to concentrate them all to the fullest conservation of human resources.

That the motives of vocational guidance may be above question, this movement should be supported at public expense just as the public-school system is supported. Any distinct organization for the purpose of stimulating, directing, and making more effective the vocational-guidance movement should be a part, a department, of the public-school system. The ideal of vocational guidance is but an elevation and extension of the educational ideal for which the school exists. Vocational guidance seeks the largest realization of the possibilities of every child and youth, measured in terms of worthy service; vocational guidance seeks this not through the school alone but through the upbuilding influences that work and life beyond the school ought to afford every human being.

THE SCHOOLS AND VOCATIONAL GUIDANCE

By John V. Brennan, Superintendent of Schools,
Ironwood, Michigan

(From *The American Schoolmaster*, September, 1914)

A vocational guide is one who helps other people to find themselves. Vocational guidance is the science of this self-discovery. Since the inception of time directive forces have been at work, sometimes under one name, sometimes under another, but more frequently under no name at all. Sometimes one institution was the special agency through which they worked, sometimes another, and yet again no particular agency was visibly active. But consciously or otherwise these forces have been at work molding and shaping human lives and human activities. At present they have come into definite consciousness in the United States, and the schools are to be the active agents in their administration.

Just now there is some difference of opinion as to the scope and direction which vocational guidance is to assume. There are those who contend that vocational guidance has to do with problems purely educational and social rather than industrial, and that industry is only a portion of the human vocation; while others contend that vocational guidance is concerned chiefly with industry. Without entering into a discussion of the merits of either case, let us say that for the present, at least, vocational guidance is to be specially concerned with industry. Vocational guidance of the purely educational and social type has long been an unconscious function of the school. The industrial type of guidance is a new function in American education, and because it is new special interest will center round it until its problems are solved. While we recognize that vocational guidance has to do with self-discovery and direction along all useful lines; that education must aim higher than the bread line; that the utilitarian view is but one phase of the question ; yet any scheme of education which disregards or minimizes the problems of making a living will prove a disappointment and must ultimately be abandoned. And moreover, whatever the theory, the schools in the United States will have to do in the future with the question of industrial training in its relationship. to adequate food, shelter, and clothing.

Because ours is a democracy in which every person may aspire to leadership, and because the rapid increase in population has made leadership more difficult to attain, the demand for economic efficiency has made vocational guidance one of the leading educational questions of the hour. Did we live in India, China, or many of the European countries, our occupations would be determined for us, for the caste system would force us to follow the occupations of our fathers. We would have little choice in the matter, for our social and economic status would be predetermined to such an extent as to preclude any such question as vocational guidance. But because we live in a democracy, no function of which savors of caste or tradition and because economic conditions compel us to give heed to efficiency, we have the problem of vocational guidance. In the United States sons do not pretend to follow the occupations of their fathers ; in fact, in many instances the occupation of the father acts as an antidote against the son's following the same calling. So thoroughly is independence and individualism intrenched and interwoven into our social and governmental fabric that the son feels he is not doing his duty by himself, his community, his state, or his nation, unless he sets up for himself an individual standard of life distinct and apart from that set up by his father. It is this independence of spirit which has made American democracy a success.

An examination of the leading professions of the city of Chicago, and this is apparently true of other places, reveals the fact that 70 per cent of all people engaged in the leading professions were born and reared on the farm. The relationship between the farm and the professions, as far as similarity of work is concerned, is remote if not almost antipodal. Only in point of perseverance and application is there any connection between the two. From the dairy, the hayfield, the ax, and the plow to the laboratory, the bench, the counting house, and the engineering department is a tremendous vocational distance. In fact, so great is the distance that little if any of the technique of the one enters into the technique of the other. The only relationship possible to claim is that of ability to work and to continue working. As far as any conscious effort at vocational guidance on the part of anyone is concerned, there has been absolutely none. The boy on the farm has worked out his own plans and purposes practically unaided. The only vocational guide with which he has been familiar is the everlasting job which has met him at every turn. He has tried himself out on the farm job until he has seen no chance for emancipation from manual toil and no adequate remuneration for labor expended unless he seeks other avenues than those which lead to the farm. Hard work has been his sole vocational guide, and with this as a companion he has been compelled to sit down and consider seriously and alone the question of what he shall do in order to escape the irksomeness of his job. He has been compelled to choose and plan with himself and for himself, and then to be responsible to himself for the chance which he takes and the results which follow. Perhaps in the last analysis this is the best type of vocational guidance, but viewed from the modern meaning of the term there is little if any of vocational guidance in the process.

Not until the United States has become more densely populated and the opportunity for individual choice and leadership more limited has the question of vocational guidance, as at present understood, come into the foreground. Efficiency has come to be talked of. This is simply another way of stating that more people must be fed, clothed, and housed from the same natural resources or the human race must go hungry. It is a sound economic principle, applicable alike to individuals and to nations, that if a man consume more than he produce someone else must labor to make good the deficiency or want and ultimate ruin will follow.

Democracy has been called upon to feed its multitudes, and while the fitting and refitting of the human product according to free individual choice has hitherto meant great progress, yet it is equally true that such process has been wasteful and expensive. The United States has come to the point where it must give heed to the elimination of waste if its people are to be fed, clothed, and given shelter. We have set squarely before us the problem of preserving individual initiative and independence while at the same time providing competence for the individual and for the multitude. Haphazard choice, with its failures, waste, and turnings back, can no longer be disregarded or allowed to go unchecked. Suitability of occupation is the basis of individual and national success. How to secure the suitability of occupation with a fair degree of certainty, while preserving to the individual the right and the opportunity to aspire, has called into being the problem of vocational guidance.

Nor is vocational guidance a matter for the male population only. There are at present in the United States about 2,500,000 women engaged in gainful occupations other than homemaking, and while ultimately 90 per cent of all women are destined to become homemakers, yet the time between their entrance to the industries as wage earners and that of assuming the home duties is gradually lengthening. Nor is there any likelihood that the wage-earning period will not continue to lengthen or the number of women engaging in industrial pursuits continue to increase. Economic efficiency and the welfare of the race demand that women find the work for which they are best suited during this special wage-earning period, hence the necessity for careful vocational guidance on the part of those charged with the responsibility.

For the first time in the history of the United States, the nation has consciously set itself to the task of saving time and material by helping the individual to find himself occupationally with the least possible amount of refitting. Moreover, economic pressure is compelling specialization. The ideal toward which we are striving is that each person shall become socially and economically competent without waste of time or readjustment of occupation, and while this ideal will never be reached, yet we shall constantly come nearer to it. The United States, as a nation, cannot permit the drain resulting from haphazard occupational preparation on the part of its citizenship to continue. Economic pressure compels this change. Democracy has always relied upon education for its support and perpetuation, and as education is primarily the function of the school the question of vocational guidance has come to be a school problem. Fundamentally, the problem of the school is the problem of democracy. How to preserve to the individual his right to aspire, to make of himself what he will, and at the same time find himself early, accurately, and with certainty, is the problem of vocational guidance. Other agencies than the school are concerned with this question, but for the present at least, and probably for a considerable time to come, the problem will be primarily one for the school.

Democracy to-day has called upon the school to solve one of the most difficult problems of all times, namely, how to preserve individualism with a high standard of community efficiency; in other words, how to keep alive in the breasts of the youth of this country the ambition to venture, to experiment, and to attain, while at the same time directing him along certain definite paths best suited to his aptitudes and talents. The youth must preserve his respect for social and occupational tradition, while at the same time adapting himself to the newer economic conditions which compel an early choice and a certainty of action. Heretofore our economic resources have been so great that individuals could be lavish in their ventures and try-outs without national or even great individual discomfort. The United States has been prodigal in its material resources as well as in its men, — new nations are always such, — and the fact that much was wasted brought little or no discomfort because the source of supply was seemingly unlimited. In the past, if a boy chose a wrong calling, or made no choice at all, our wealth of opportunity and abundance of resources furnished him a fair chance of getting a living. He could afford to transplant himself several times, because natural conditions were so favorable that transplanting was easy and rarely completely destructive. But it is not so to-day. This free individual lavish process, while developing men of wonderful leadership and making for marvelous progress, has yet resulted in enormous waste, and, judged from the standpoint of general future efficiency, the price exacted has been altogether disproportionate and exorbitant.

The concrete question now is, How shall the schools set to work to solve the problem of efficiency and progress? That is,

How shall the schools preserve the best of the past, utilize and adapt it to the present, and transmit it unimpaired to the future? Somehow or other the school must help the individual to find himself early in life so that the greatest possible section of life may be devoted to efficient service. This is by no means easy. No task which imposes upon an outside agency the burden of compelling an individual to make a choice when no conscious choice exists within the individual himself is an easy one. It is, however, not impossible. To begin with, the school will have to admit, as society has always admitted, that a certain portion of waste is inevitable whatever the process employed. That there will still be individuals who must go to the economic junk heap is a foregone conclusion. If society believes that the school can do what no other organization has ever been able to do, it is doomed to disappointment. However, society has a right to demand that the school shall do the best of which it is capable, and that it shall be held accountable for any negligence, however small or insignificant this negligence may appear to be.

The school can and will make good in this newer problem of modern efficiency. And in order to do so it will have to furnish means whereby the young people of this country may have an opportunity to try themselves out along various lines at such a time as experiment is least expensive and most valuable. The school may have to press into service the industries outside of the schoolroom, but the directing of this service will have to remain in the school. The hand of the schoolmaster must guide education. Any other agency will consciously or unconsciously exploit it to its own ends.

No person, however versed or expert in the knowledge of occupations, can ever tell with certainty what every individual is best fitted to do. All he can do is to know well the characteristics of the individual, together with the world into which he is to go, and then give him such advice and guidance as he has at his command together with an opportunity to try himself out along the lines suggested before definitely deciding on his life work. This will mean trained experts on the one hand and fields for experiment on the other, and both of these at such a time as the mind and hand of the individual are plastic and pliable. This experimental stage will probably come somewhere between the ages of twelve and sixteen. During these years the schools must provide special fields of training so that the individual may have an opportunity to find to which particular work or calling he is best suited, and all this under the observation of experts trained along vocational lines.

At present not all teachers, by any means, are fitted to give this expert advice; nor will they ever be. Vocational guidance is a work for those fitted by nature, training, and judgment to interpret the present with reference to the future and to see in the child the possibilities and aptitudes of the man. That the schools will eventually furnish such expert advice is beyond question. Education has always been and always will be a matter for the schools, no matter by what name such education may be called.

Vocational guidance requires close observation on the part of the guide. There are two classes which are easy to distinguish. They present little or no problem to the expert. They are those, on the one hand, who seem to know almost from infancy what they are fitted to do. Their characteristics are so marked that they are certain of themselves almost to an infinite degree; they are at the extreme end of the efficient economic line. The other class, equally distinguishable, numbers within itself those who are born "short." They are to be the hewers of wood and the drawers of water. They are doomed to bear the burdens of mankind, and no amount of training can ever raise them above the plane of humble toil and mediocrity of circumstance. They belong to the frayed end of the social and economic line. Fortunately their number is not great, but small as it is there is no immediate possibility of its elimination.

Vocational guidance is concerned with neither of these classes, as they guide themselves. Vocational guidance is concerned with the great multitude between these extremes — the multitude filled with possibilities known to be, yet undiscovered; the multitude which is destined to do the great bulk of the world's work; the multitude upon which democracy has rested and must always rest; the multitude whose name is the "average man."

The school is making a magnificent beginning in the matter of vocational guidance. It is meeting the problem squarely and with intelligence. It is cognizant that much is to be learned and that many of the paths are untried and untrod. It is making haste slowly, deliberately, calculating every step. It will not fail. It is conscious of the greatness and the nobility of the task. Its face is turned upward and to the future, but its feet are planted firmly on the earth. It will guide the youth of the land by placing at their disposal the advice and judgment of those older, wiser, and more experienced than they. The schools will not shirk their responsibility. They will assume the burdens cheerfully and with optimism, confident that the problem, new though it be, is capable of solution. They will make the youth efficient by giving him an opportunity to find himself and then compelling him to do so, or to admit to himself his own failure. They will preserve to democracy individual aspiration. They will make the individual efficient, and hence the multitude of individuals efficient, thus preserving and perpetuating the fundamentals of democracy — freedom of choice with something worthy to choose.

VOCATIONAL GUIDANCE IN THE BOSTON SCHOOLS

By Stratton D. Brooks, President of the University of Oklahoma; Formerly Superintendent of Public Schools, Boston, Massachusetts

(An Address delivered at the First National Conference on Vocational Guidance, Boston, November, 1910)

At the outset I wish to distinguish between vocational placement and vocational guidance. By vocational placement I mean fitting a job to the attainments that a boy now has. By vocational guidance I mean fitting a boy to a job that he will at some future time be able to fill, if he follows the course of instruction outlined by his vocational adviser. Vocational placement finds a job now better fitted to the boy's present attainments than he would otherwise be likely to find. Vocational guidance fits the boy for a better job in the future by training the boy along the lines of his greatest aptitudes and opportunities. Both consider the boy's abilities; one for the purpose of making the best possible present use of them; the other with a view to giving them additional development, in order to secure in the future a still greater use of them. It is this latter phase of vocational guidance that is discussed here.

Educational methods and educational machinery are being overhauled in the light of a new purpose; namely, the more specific preparation of pupils for particular vocations in life. The most important immediate effect of the movement for industrial education has been to move forward suddenly the time of choice, and it is this necessity to choose early a definite career that renders desirable a consideration of vocational direction.

The schools of the past have presented the same type of education for all pupils, and vocational direction consisted mainly in advising a boy to take or not to take additional education. But

83

under the new conditions vocational direction will not only be concerned with advising a boy to take additional education, but with deciding what particular kind of additional education he should take in order to be of greatest service to himself and to the community.

Formerly, a teacher might with a clear conscience advise a boy to take a high-school course or go to college even to prepare for medicine or law, for the education offered in high school or college was so general in character and so wide of application that, whatever the boy's future vocation, he was almost sure to succeed better in it because of his extended training. Furthermore, the final entry into the medical school or the law school came at so late a date that any change of interest or error in the estimate of the boy's ability had time to show itself. But he who in these days of special education advises a boy to enter some particular trade and selects for him a course of study restricted to the practical elements of that trade may not give advice lightly, for the possibilities of error are increased a hundredfold, while the possibilities of correcting an error, if made, are almost nonexistent.

The new element in the situation and the one that causes the chief difficulty, because of the establishment of specific industrial schools, is that the avowed purpose of industrial education is to prepare for a specific end, and in order to be valuable and effective to that end it must be restrictive in nature. Cultural education is criticized because, though good, it is not good for anything particular, while industrial education is praised because it is not only good, but good for something. When considered from the point of view of vocational advice, however, the chief trouble is that industrial education, though good for something, is only good for some *one* thing, and in proportion as it succeeds, it limits for the boy or girl who received it the possibility of success in any other line of endeavor. He who enters upon a successful industrial training, especially of the lower and more specific type, becomes by that very education less fitted for entrance upon a different work. In case events show that the boy is not qualified for the work selected, there is little opportunity to correct the error. To advise a boy to take up a restrictive educational course is a matter requiring much graver consideration than to advise him to take a nonrestrictive course, and vocational direction, therefore, attains an importance that it has not hitherto had.

The chief motto of vocational direction in the past has been, " Aim at the highest." There are those who call our present educational system a failure on the ground that we have attempted to educate every boy to become a president of the United States. But the man who should seriously criticize the school for stating as its aim the education of presidents would fail to recognize that the statement is but the embodiment of the general principle that every boy shall have the incentive and the opportunity to reach the highest development of which he is capable. It will be unfortunate indeed when American education ceases to encourage everyone to take active part in democratic citizenship and to feel honored by the opportunity to render public service. It is undoubtedly true that intellectual superiority has received greater recognition in the schools than mechanical skill; but it is also true that the same difference has existed in the world at large, and that it will probably continue to exist.

To-day we face a new situation. The demand for more skillful workmen is upon us, and the people are asking the schools to solve the question. What I want to keep clearly in mind, however, is that this ought not to be a demand for a *substitute* education but for a *supplementary* education; that the error of the school in the past in pointing every pupil toward academic callings would be even worse repeated, if it should now attempt to place every boy in a mechanical trade.

There is less danger to society from men who have aimed high and failed because of their own lack of ability than there is from able and ambitious men who writhe under an apparently unjust discrimination of society that gives greater rewards to other men naturally no more richly endowed.

But whether we favor or disapprove, it seems evident that industrial education will go forward and that in the larger cities, at least, separate schools will undoubtedly be established, wherein each class of pupils may receive whatever type of elementary industrial instruction the combined wisdom of the citizens, the school committee, and the teachers determine to be best suited to the purpose in hand. The introduction of separate schools will bring upon the American people a new and serious problem; namely, the necessity of an early choice of a vocation. Reliable information and competent advice must be furnished, both to children and to adults, showing what vocations are open to children, what conditions prevail in each, and what the rewards of success may be.

In view of these needs, we have been endeavoring in Boston to establish vocational direction on a satisfactory foundation. I wish to state briefly what has been attempted.

Boston is fortunate in having a group of liberal-minded men and women through whose generosity the Vocation Bureau has been established and maintained. The Boston School Committee has invited the coöperation of the Vocation Bureau and the director of this Bureau has worked hand in hand with the Vocational Direction Committee of the Public Schools — a committee appointed by the superintendent and consisting of masters and submasters in the Boston schools. Among the many activities of the Vocation Bureau, I mention three : First, the investigation of conditions in the trades and businesses of Boston. The Bureau has undertaken to prepare material for the use of pupils, parents, and vocational counselors that will furnish the best available information with reference to the vocational opportunities that exist in Boston. Second, the Vocation Bureau is conducting in one of the public-school buildings a school for vocational counselors wherein teachers and others who are interested in this important work may prepare themselves for the better performance of their important tasks. Third, the Vocation Bureau has brought about a coöperation of effort whereby various organizations have undertaken to perform needed services without duplication of effort.

An important part of the question of vocational selection is the amount of interest and attention that parents must give. To this problem of arousing an interest in parents, the Home and School Association has agreed to devote especial attention. By means of discussions before the Parents' Associations of which it is composed, this society will be able to do much to create a widespread and intelligent interest in the problem.

It is necessary also that accurate information be gathered with reference to the specific instruction offered in day and evening schools both public and private. The Women's Municipal League has undertaken to collect this information and to set it forth definitely and concisely in the form of printed charts.

To the work of giving vocational advice to girls who have left school, the Girls' Trade Education League will give special attention.

In the schools themselves many things have been done at the suggestion of the Committee on Vocational Direction, chief among which is the appointment in each high school and elementary school of one or more vocational counselors. These counselors have been selected by the principals with reference to their interest in the work of vocational direction, their skill in determining the abilities and possibilities of the children, and their willingness to devote extra time to acquiring information and perfecting themselves for the successful performance of their duties. Meetings of these counselors have been held for the purpose of discussing the problems of vocational direction and considering how best to minimize its dangers and increase its beneficial results. Most of them are now taking a course of instruction arranged by the Vocation Bureau wherein they may be even more efficiently prepared for the work of directing pupils wisely. As an illustration of the work of these vocational counselors the following will serve:

Last June twice as many elementary-school graduates as could be admitted elected the High School of Commerce and the High School of Practical Arts. Hitherto when similar conditions have arisen it has been necessary to choose the half that could be admitted either by lot or on the basis of scholarship. This year the existence of the vocational counselors rendered possible a different and a better procedure. The principal of each elementary school was sent a list of the boys in his school who had applied for admission to the High School of Commerce, with the statement that only half could be admitted. The request was made that the vocational counselor of the school select that half. The principal of the High School of Commerce met the vocational counselors, explained the special work done in that school, and outlined the qualities that a boy must possess in order to succeed therein. The vocational counselors then approached the question of choosing the boys to be admitted, having, on the one hand, some knowledge of the special qualities needed in that particular school and, on the other hand, a knowledge of the tastes and aptitudes of the boy as shown by his work in the elementary school. The boys chosen by the vocational counselors were then admitted. A similar course was pursued with girls for the High School of Practical Arts, and it is hoped that this process of selection has brought into these schools a higher percentage of pupils fitted to do the work therein than could have been secured by either of the methods previously pursued.

Somewhat different and less difficult than the problem of selecting a school is the work done in specific vocational schools, as illustrated in the High School of Commerce and the Trade School for Girls.

Since the High School of Commerce was organized in 1906 systematic instruction has been given with reference to existing business opportunities and the possibilities of each. Carefully prepared courses of lectures, based on accurate investigations of conditions in Boston and elsewhere, have been presented each year. The whole atmosphere of the school has been permeated with the idea of choosing wisely some particular business. The purpose of the school is not only to fit the boy for a commercial career, but to find that particular commercial career in which he gives promise of the greatest progress. In order to assist in the process of fitting each boy to his business a system of summer apprenticeship has been established. Prior to the summer vacation in 1909, and again in 1910, the School Committee appointed a man to have charge of the work of finding employment for the high-school boys during the summer in the business houses of the city. The business men have coöperated heartily in the plan. They agree to give the boys the best possible chance to obtain a knowledge of the business and demonstrate their own fitness or unfitness for it. In particular, they agree not to hire the boy after school opens in September, even though he has shown special aptitude for the work in hand. By this means the business men have a sympathetic understanding of the aims of the school, the school appreciates more thoroughly the demands made upon the boys who enter business, and the boys obtain some insight into the relation of their school tasks to their life work.

In the Trade School for Girls provision is made for a *vocational assistant* for each hundred girls. The school teaches certain trade's, and the vocational assistant is charged with the duty of investigating conditions existing in these trades, in order to enable the school to adapt its course to the exact needs of business and to provide accurate and up-to-date information available for use of parents and pupils.

It is the business of the vocational assistant to secure positions for graduates, and in this sense she conducts an employment bureau, but with the important difference that she knows both the conditions in the trade and the qualifications of the particular girls, and therefore endeavors not merely to find a place for the girl, but a place where she will succeed. The work of the vocational assistant, however, but begins with finding a place for the girl. It is success that counts, and the vocational assistant is to keep track of her girls, know which ones succeed, and more especially which ones fail, and why they fail ; to find for those who fail other places better suited to their abilities, or perchance advise them to return to school until they reach a degree of proficiency that will enable them to retain a position once obtained.

On the moral side also the vocational assistant will have great effect. Before the girl leaves school, it is hoped that such a mutual relation of confidence and friendship will be established that any girl who finds herself at work in a shop or factory where conditions are improper will report promptly to the vocational assistant, with the result that the girl will be placed in another position, and that no more girls will be sent to the shop or factory complained of until conditions are improved. When perchance a girl is placed in a position in which she cannot advance or from which she is discharged, the vocational assistant should be on hand to encourage and assist, to tide the girl over immediate difficulty, and to find some other work wherein there is greater prospect of earning a living wage.

In both of these schools it will be observed that the problem is that of selecting a particular business or trade within a comparatively limited range from which the pupil, by entering the school, has elected to choose. Much broader and far more difficult is the task of selecting the school to which a boy or girl should go, or the calling that he should enter on leaving a school that has given him only general preparation. It is in this field that vocational direction will be most necessary.

To secure information that is accurate is comparatively easy, but to give advice that is wise with reference to selecting a life calling is most difficult. He who gives advice must know not only the relative advantages of the different trades, businesses, and professions, but also the specific requirements for success in each. To determine what callings give greatest financial returns and to advise all pupils to seek those callings would be to ignore the element that will make advice valuable ; namely, the careful consideration of the tastes, tendencies, and abilities of the pupils, in order that each pupil may be advised to select a calling in which the requirements for success are such that he may have reasonable expectation of meeting them. The vocational adviser must know business, to be sure, but he has much greater need to know boys.

It is evident that a vast amount of scientific investigation must be made before any form of vocational advice can have any substantial and reliable scientific foundation. Outside of such elements as courtesy, tact, perseverance, courage, honesty, and the like, the factors that are really essential in any single business are as yet undetermined. The extent to which success in each calling depends upon the strength or accuracy of muscular reaction, upon the pertinacity and rapidity of mental associations, or upon any one of a dozen other lines of mental and motor activity, still waits solution in the laboratory of the experimental psychologist. More difficult still is the determination of the exact qualifications of each particular boy ; impossible, in fact, under any system of investigation that now exists or is likely to exist under conditions that will be readily applicable to thousands of children annually. When to these difficulties is added that of determining now with a boy in the adolescent period of rapid and turbulent change what will be his dominant, permanent characteristics when he has reached manhood, it becomes clear that even under the most careful guidance, the giving of vocational advice must still remain in the realm of the uncertain and problematical.

To give advice as to selection of a life work must remain for the most part an appreciative art rather than an exact science. It will depend upon those attitudes of mind that are appreciative and interpretative, rather than upon those which are analytical and scientific. Both the parent and the expert vocational adviser are likely to be in error; the parent because he is too near the life of the boy, knows him too intimately, loves him too well, and is too strongly prejudiced in his favor and too prone to exaggerate both his minor faults and his minor virtues, to enable him to judge with all wisdom as to the present condition or future promise of his child; the psychological expert because he is too far from the child, too unacquainted with his attitudes of mind, his reactions under the stress and irritations of life conditions, too remote to receive the shy confidences of a fleeting moment when the child lifts but for a second the veil that covers many latent possibilities. Between the parent and the expert adviser, however, is the teacher, who possesses or should possess some of the characteristics of each. I do not mean that there is little use for expert vocational advice, but merely to emphasize that its greatest work must be done by utilizing as its agents those who now furnish, and who will continue to furnish, ideals, incentives, and directions to a majority of all the pupils in school.

VOCATIONAL GUIDANCE AND PUBLIC EDUCATION

By Paul H. Hanus, Professor of Education, Harvard University

(From *The School Review*, January, 1911)

At the First National Conference on Vocational Guidance held in Boston under the joint auspices of the Boston Vocation Bureau and the Boston Chamber of Commerce on November 15 and 16, 1910, several hundred persons were in attendance. Forty-five cities sent delegates, including cities as widely separated as New York, Baltimore, Pittsburgh, Chicago, and Grand Rapids. It is apparent that the problems of systematic vocational guidance are attracting the attention their importance deserves.

These problems are, of course, not new. But organization for systematic attention to them is very recent. It has been stimulated by and is naturally associated with three important contemporary tendencies in public education. These tendencies are really only different phases of one comprehensive movement for approximating more closely our democratic ideal of individual welfare and social progress. They are the safeguarding and promotion of bodily health and vigor by an important extension of the work of the departments of school hygiene and physical training in our schools; the progressive establishment of public vocational schools of elementary and secondary grade, that is, of vocational schools other than professional schools, for increasing the efficiency of all who work in industry, agriculture, or commerce; and a widespread effort to make the nonvocational schools we already have, of every grade and kind, more vital — that is, to make the pupil's school life so significant a part of his whole life that it shall be and remain a guiding force, no matter at what point his school life must close.

It is clear that with these tendencies well established in the schools the question of vocational guidance is a pressing question.

Where these tendencies are not yet marked, vocational guidance is equally essential, for there the pupil is likely to be quite helpless when he makes the transition from school to vocation — a momentous transition indeed. This transition cannot be safe unless the choice of the pupil's life-career is deliberate. Even then mistakes will be made, but we may expect that they will be small in number and importance as compared with the mistakes of random choice or mere "job-hunting."

A wise choice of a calling demands accessible opportunities of satisfactory preparation for it, adaptation of personality and capacity to it, and a knowledge of the conditions of employment and of the prospective rewards, material, spiritual, and social, of satisfactory work in it. These are problems of vocational guidance. How much depends on their satisfactory solution for each ambitious youth, both for himself and for society, need not be dwelt upon. What we must deplore now is the absence of such guidance for the great majority of each generation, and the fact that until quite recently we have been unconscious of our duty in this respect; or at least that we have not endeavored to equip ourselves satisfactorily to discharge that duty.

Who the wisest vocation counselors may be, in the end, we cannot now say. Perhaps the parents, made conscious by their own vocational guidance in youth of its significance and importance, and more responsive to their whole duty to their children in this respect than most of them have been in the past; perhaps the employers of children and youth, also rendered more responsive to the permanent welfare of their employees than many of them now are, and knowing better than anyone else the advantages and the limitations of the employment they offer, and the disadvantages to themselves of the present haphazard choice of their employees; perhaps the teachers, always solicitous for the future of their charges and rendered by some training for this work more competent to cope with the difficult problems of vocational guidance than most of them now feel themselves to be; perhaps a body of vocational counselors specially trained for the purpose — a body of men and women each of whom knows equally well the children and youth whom they counsel and a group of employments open to them;

perhaps all of these together. But, whoever may be the wisest counselors in the end, it is clear that we cannot wait to make a beginning. There is too much at stake. Our present duty is plain, namely, to seek to give to all these prospective and present counselors — for they have been and they will continue to be vocational advisers — the best available equipment for their responsibilities. This is one of our most important tasks, and one of the most difficult.

It is clear that much preparation is needed by those on whom the duty of vocational guidance may fall. Information must be had of the young people themselves, their physical condition, their capacity, their ambitions, the opportunities and circumstances of their lives ; similarly, information is needed about occupations, their advantages and disadvantages in view of the natural and acquired equipment for them possessed by prospective workers, the kind of preparation required for them, and the extent and quality of the available preparation for a progressive career in them, and what success in them means. To gather this information and make it available for use will require time and effort. And to give satisfactory guidance by properly trained persons to the great body of young people whose life work is now almost inevitably determined by chance will require an army of devoted workers.

Of course, preparation for the transition from school life to life work must be gradual. That transition must be seen from afar by the pupil. Vocational guidance cannot be safely deferred until the pupil is on the threshold of the world's work. A satisfactory vocation must be a goal toward which his thoughts and ambitions have been directed during the entire period of his tutelage. But the school must not prematurely narrow the pupil's outlook or his educational opportunities.

Up to about fourteen years of age, by statute, in all progressive countries, all children must go to school. But when they are fourteen years old most of them must face the problem of *how to make a living*. For some time they have been asking, "What am I to be ? " At this moment, general or incidental vocational information is no longer adequate. It is accordingly a culminating period for specific vocational guidance. The counselor is not to tell the pupil now, or at any time, what vocation to enter. It is his duty to make sure that whatever vocation the pupil enters, he enters it deliberately, and with as full a knowledge of all that this step means as can be obtained. The counselor does not prescribe a vocation which the pupil takes. The pupil chooses his vocation after full consideration of all the factors and consequences of his choice. Nevertheless, the time for choice has come, and the issues must be met.

One important duty of all the advisers of youth is to bring home to all who can be brought to see it the enormous value of more education for every capable pupil, no matter when he leaves school — and no matter whether the chief purpose of the school he attends is to teach him how to live or how to make a living. One valuable result of satisfactory vocational counseling ought therefore to be to lengthen the period of education for all but the incurably dull or the permanently unambitious.

During the entire high-school period vocational insight and aims still require attention; but another culminating period for specific vocational guidance comes at the close of the pupil's secondary-school career, when all but a small percentage of those who remained in school four years after leaving the elementary school must begin to earn their living. Beyond the school, in the college, the need of vocational guidance is by no means at an end.

All this means that throughout his entire educational career the pupil's vocational insight and vocational purposes should be progressively developed. Each pupil's attention should be directed to a vocation to which he may reasonably aspire; that is, every pupil should be led gradually to realize that a suitable vocation, accessible to him and adapted to him, is indispensable to a useful and happy life. As he approaches the end of his school career, whatever his age may be, he should come to see that his vocation will be not only the means of satisfying his personal wants and ambitions, but because it is the chief means of establishing significant relations between himself and his fellow men, it is also the source of such public service as he is capable of and may be called upon to render. And about the time he must leave school or college he ought to have an answer to the questions, How can I best realize my ambitions? What vocation ought I to choose?

THE UNIVERSITY AND VOCATIONAL GUIDANCE

By Professor E. L. Thorndike, Professor of Educational
Psychology, Columbia University

(An Address delivered at the Alumni Conference at Teachers College, 1913)

Of every hundred pupils who entered school, say twenty years
ago, over thirty left school before completing the sixth grade. And
for these thirty out of a hundred (these half-million children in all
each year) the school did nothing when it let them go, and practically nothing at all afterwards. Even if a pupil had reached the
high school, he was still allowed to drift away and drop out, with
no more care than the pirates of traditional storybooks gave to their
marooned captives. Whether we consider the hundred thousand
boys and girls who drop out of high school in the first year, or the
two thirds of the graduates of elementary schools who go no farther,
in either case we find the school ship sailing away, leaving the
castaways to steer their course without chart or compass.

Until lately, not one person in a thousand felt any duty to inter-
pose between the requirements of industry on the one hand and
the hopes and fears of the child and his parents on the other. It
was thought that giving a child an education was enough. To help
him to use it, and to use his inborn capacities as well, by guiding his
choice of a vocation and supervising his contracts with employers,
would have been thought, I suppose, too paternalistic, or too soci-
alistic, or too much of a usurpation of the duties of the family, or
too much of an infringement on the rights of the individual, if,
indeed, twenty years ago anybody had thought of the matter at all.

To-day the duty is felt. Children will not be left to decide what
employments they will work at in the world as ignorantly and care-
lessly as they decide what neckties they will wear. Vocational
guidance will be given by private philanthropic or commercial
bureaus if it is not given by the public's own schools.

I shall not spend your time in proving what most of you know, and the rest will very soon find out, if you confer with the morally and intellectually progressive men and women in any community ; namely, that the children now in our schools are going to have some form of vocational guidance. The only questions profitable for us here to discuss are, Who shall give this guidance, and What sort of guidance shall it be ?

In both of these questions we all have a great and real interest. The answers to them which I shall try to defend are (1) that the public should give this guidance through the school as its agent delegated with full power, and (2) that the guidance given should be based on the most exact and comprehensive and conscientious investigations that the best men procurable can possibly make.

We should, of course, all be glad to see charitable organizations undertake this work of diagnosing the capacities and interests of individual children and of guiding their vocational choices, as a matter of benevolence. Or, we should be glad to see employers undertake it as a matter of business enterprise, or duty, or both. It is a useful work for either of them, or for the family, or for the church. But the better way is for the community to undertake it as a matter of public policy and social justice. For even the wisest charitable organizations cannot do it adequately. It is not the poor, the incompetent, the dependent — the group with which charitable associations most easily come in contact — whose vocational guidance is a matter of prime importance. The employers, humane though they be, will by habit tend to emphasize only the suitability of a given child for a given job ; whereas, the greater view of the problem is to make sure of the suitability of a given job for the child. It is also unfortunately the case with employers that they, and charitable organizations as well, will at present be suspected (whether justly or unjustly I am not prepared to say) of using the institutions for their selfish interests. Further, as we have again and again been convinced in the course of the last decade, the management of business and industry seems to be now our most pressing and important public concern. So the vocational guidance of children seems to be a public rather than a private duty.

The school, I think, should be the public's delegate in the matter, first, for the sake of economy, and, second, for the sake of safety. It is more economical for the school to diagnose a pupil's capacities and interests, because (1) a large part of the information needed must be got from the school records, the pupil's teachers, and his classmates, in any case, and (2) the school system provides a single convenient source to which any employer can at any time apply for information about any child educated in the community. Further, the school provides a convenient clearing-house for the transmission of such information from one community to another where the child moves. Finally, as I could show if time permitted, the testing of children's fitness for various vocations can be enormously facilitated by giving many of the tests to whole classes at once, with the aid of regular school attitude and discipline.

It is safer for the school, rather than some other agency, to diagnose a pupil's capacities and interests and guide his vocational choices, because the teachers and supervisory officers of schools and colleges will be quicker to detect charlatanism in the men and women doing this particular work than philanthropic workers, clergymen, or regular employers would be ; and because the same man will be less likely to indulge in questionable methods, to claim too much for his diagnosis and guidance, or to advance himself at the expense of his work if he works in a school or university than if he works isolatedly in some special and private bureau of vocational guidance.

Schools, colleges, and universities have many faults, but from intellectual carelessness, tawdry self-advertisement, and from the debasement of knowledge or skill for profit they are relatively free. The great danger to the man who gives vocational guidance is that he shall become a pretentious charlatan. For him to work amongst scholarly men and women is the best means for him to reduce that tendency — his greatest danger.

I may seem to have neglected somewhat the need of knowledge of the industries as compared with the knowledge of interest and capacity of the child. The school certainly cannot give adequate vocational guidance unless it knows the nature of the industries, the services that each important variety of productive labor consists of, and the opportunities and hardships that attend it. But, as I could make clearer, if time permitted, it is far more practicable for school officers charged with the work of vocational guidance to learn once for all about a few hundred vocations than for the officers of charitable or business organizations to learn annually about a million boys and a million girls.

The diagnoses and recommendations made must be made from scientific knowledge, and the problems of individual diagnosis and guidance must be subjected to investigation by the best talent procurable, for many reasons. Three of these I will mention : First, it would be folly to change the present arrangement whereby the boy or girl follows interest as far as he can, and the employer follows the habits of choice that he thinks, from his experience in the past, have been successful, as far as he can, and both experiment until a status more or less satisfactory is reached — unless we can tell with surety as we go along in our new experiment whether we are changing it for the better. It would be folly, because a failure now would set back the whole work of rationalizing and humanizing the employment of labor for perhaps a generation.

Secondly, although a very moderate use of common sense and organization of present knowledge seems fairly sure to eliminate many wastes, such as the aimless trial by a girl of each opportunity presented by a " Girl wanted " sign, or the study of medicine by a seventeen-year-old boy who detests and fails in all the natural sciences and manual arts but earns a hundred dollars a month by the organization of the sale of the *Saturday Evening Post* — these easy negative economies in fitting men to positions are not the main issue. The main issue is not the mere provision of persons to supply the common sense and ordinary knowledge which many children and certain parents lack, but the provision of knowledge of the requirements of each vocation, on the one hand, and of the early symptoms of various features of intellect, character, and skill, on the other, whereby we can give advice as much beyond that of the most sagacious adviser to-day as his is beyond the casual judgment of the average parent.

It is also the case that common sense and sagacity are effective in exact proportion to the knowledge of facts and principles which elaborate and scientific study supplies. Not all the common sense in the world could alone have kept the plague out of Europe, or yellow fever out of Panama for the last six years. Common sense is needed, but it would not have been serviceable alone.

Further still, exact and scientific study which I am recommending in the case of vocational guidance will give results whereby even a mediocre person in this field can do excellent work. A gifted man can give excellent advice now, but we need a set of facts and principles whereby a thousand men and women will, fifteen years from now, be able to advise children and employers. The progress of medical science has been such that the stupidest graduate of our medical school this year will give better medical advice than Hippocrates or Galen ever did. Through the knowledge of the science of human nature and its work in the industries, professions, and trades, the average graduate of Teachers College in 1950 ought to be able to give better advice to a high-school boy about the choice of an occupation than Solomon, Socrates, and Benjamin Franklin all together could give.

This I myself regard as settled. But I presume that, for the sake of those present who have not kept track of certain recent very special work in educational psychology, I should justify this hope of what we may be able to do in the future by showing that we can do something even now.

As an illustration, I choose the very practical case of prophesying how long a pupil will continue in high school. Dr. Van Denburg compiled certain information — and if I make any mistake in my figures, he is here to refute them — obtained from each of a thousand pupils entering the public high schools of New York City, in the month of February, 1906, and then kept track of the length of time that each continued in the high school. First, let us consider the significance of the pupils' answers to the following questions obtained upon the entrance of each pupil into the high school :

1. "Do you intend to complete the high-school course ? "
2. "What do you intend to do for a living ? "

There is a third reason why vocational guidance should depend upon scientific investigations of its problems, and why expert knowledge by him who is to be the school's officer in this activity is necessary. This third reason is, that this new officer of the school, who does this work, mediating as he will between the employer and the employed, will very soon become important in connection with many other relations between the capitalist and the laborer. This new school officer — this " vocational guider " — will advise boys and girls not to enter certain industries or certain trades, or even not to enter certain individual factories or shops. He will do this on moral, or hygienic, or economic grounds. Where the men and women responsible for that trade, or that individual establishment, are selfish or unwise, or both, they will attack him. And he will have no protection from attack so safe as the public respect, which, say, to-day the expert in medicine at the head of the Rockefeller Institute has. If the men and women in question are humane, or wise, or both, they will ask him to suggest means of improving the conditions in the industry. And nothing will so surely provide him with knowledge of what facts and which persons can be relied on in such ameliorative work as will an established body of rigorously demonstrated facts about industries which will serve as means to satisfying and improving human wants. This is only one sample of many ways in which this school officer will be led or forced to play a part in the conflicts between the employer and the employee — and these conflicts in spite of our hopes will not disappear with the next generation — and also in their coöperations, which he should be able greatly to encourage. He may use whatever shrewdness, diplomacy, and political skill he has, but no amount of these will do the peculiar work which the sincere, unvarnished assertion of a person known to be an expert to the effect that a certain thing is so, that this is the best way, and that such-and-such are the reasons, will do for him.

The scientific study of fitting the individual differences of human beings to differences in the work of the world — in the industries and professions — should lead, then, to the study of the whole work of man as a worker, and it should bring, at least in my opinion, a far better understanding than we now have of the defects in our arrangements for productive labor, and of their remedies.

For these reasons, then, it seems to me sure that it is not practical to plan vocational guidance as merely a group of purified and somewhat humanized employment agencies. A thousand such, useful as they may be, would not have the practical value of one first-class institute for the study of human capacities for productive labor and of the especial demands which modern industry makes ; or, rather, their practical services would be multiplied by it enormously. A thousand nurses, working each a lifetime, could not have done the work that has been done in preventing the spread of typhoid and yellow fever by the discoveries of four or five men in a single decade ; and these discoveries will live on long after all the nurses are dead. We should all welcome the establishment of a little dispensary for reliable drugs in every county, but what would that service be, relatively, to the discovery of the antitoxin for diphtheria and membranous croup, or of the means of detecting the typhoid bacillus in milk and water, or the discovery of preventive inoculation against typhoid ?

The only practical sort of vocational guidance, it seems to me, is the sort that provides not only for palliative treatment as we go along, in the present, but also for the discovery of preventive treatment ; not only for the use of what little we know about industries and human capacities, but for the steady and, if possible, the rapid advancement of knowledge about them.

These are a few of the simpler reasons for my hope that vocational guidance may become a regular service of the school to the public and that it may be as scientific in applying psychology, sociology, and economics as modern bridge-building, animal-breeding, and preventive medicine are in applying physics, biology, and bacteriology.

My half hour is overrun, and my message is still incomplete. But, incomplete as it is, it will perhaps lead some of you to share my hope that vocational guidance will become the work of the public-school system in America ; that it may be given by specially trained men and women in accord with broad and accurate knowledge of the world's work and the intellectual and moral capacities of its individual workers ; and that Teachers College may have a share in the discovery of this knowledge and in the training of these men and these women to use it. Let those of us who cherish this hope work to fulfill it.

SUGGESTIONS TOWARD A TENABLE THEORY
OF VOCATIONAL GUIDANCE

By H. D. Kitson, Associate in Psychology, University of Chicago

(From *Manual Training and Vocational Education*, January, 1915)

The concept of vocational guidance has been rapidly developing during the past few years. With amazing rapidity it has been forcing itself upon the attention of all classes of society — upon a misfitted and dissatisfied public who sees in it a possible solution of its individual vocational problems, upon industry which sees in it possible amelioration of numerous economic ills, and upon education which sees in it a means for the fulfillment of its highest responsibility, the fitting of the individual to cope with his environment. In view of the popularity which has favored this movement and of the claims which are being advanced in its name, it is fitting that the concept be examined as to its validity, so that if any part of it be found untenable, a new and more promising hypothesis may be adopted before great mischief is wrought.

Considering vocational guidance as a part of the work of the public school, all agree that its first function is to give vocational information. Its thorough application requires that information be given about a vast number of occupations. Young people must learn what the world is doing before they can decide what part they should play in the world's work. Furthermore, facts should be widely disseminated about the commoner occupations in order that choice may be based upon knowledge, not upon mere guess. This informative function is acknowledged by all to be a legitimate phase of vocational guidance, and to be a necessity for all effective education.

The other phase of vocational guidance which is generally recognized is its individual aspect. Its aim is frequently stated in the words of the old saw, "to keep round pegs out of square holes." It tacitly assumes that every individual is either round or square ; that he is fitted for one kind of work in preference to anything else. It assumes a native capacity present in unchangeable degree. In order to discover this native capacity it is generally held that the individual must submit to a series of tests, psychological and physiological, and on the basis of the results, together with such sociological and economic data as may be relevant, it will be possible to give positive advice as to the right vocation to enter. This fairly represents the prevailing notion about vocational guidance. The idea has been widely exploited and has been made the basis of some rather extravagant promises. Already there is noticeable a tendency toward commercialization of the public interest in the matter, and vocational "prescriptions," compounded in most unscientific fashion, are being furnished for considerations varying from two to twenty-five dollars. Sad to say, the public listens eagerly to the promises of this pseudoscientific vocational guidance, and naturally demands of scientists and educators that they fulfill these promises.

OBJECTIONS TO CURRENT CONCEPTION

A careful examination of the prevailing notion about vocational guidance shows that it is open to serious objections which must be pointed out and overcome if real progress is to be made. In the first place, much misunderstanding about the use of psychological tests will have to be corrected. Popular fancy regards a single one-hour test as probably sufficient to indicate vocational aptitude. Any plan, however, that involves single measurements of mental capacity is bound to meet with difficulties. Power of achievement varies from day to day according to changes in weather, physiological and emotional conditions. This fact vitiates the reliability of single measurements, and any system of psychological tests that claims validity must make allowance for it. It does not constitute an insurmountable obstacle, however, as with sufficient research it will probably be possible to devise a method whereby this can be allowed for. Nevertheless it should be kept in mind as a possible source of error.

But even with the errors due to chance samplings eliminated, there is a further difficulty in depending upon single measurements; namely, failure to measure susceptibility to improvement. It cannot be ascertained from results of a single test, to what extent an individual is capable of profiting by practice. Not only is the individual susceptible to improvement beyond the limits of his first attainment in any task, but also the degrees of improvability vary among individuals as much as do the measures of initial performance. If experimental psychology has demonstrated any one thing clearly, it is that individuals vary enormously in capacity for training, and the arrangement of a series of first measures does not bear a constant ratio to measures in successive trials. This is evidenced in widely different kinds of mental activity, from simple acts such as the discrimination between two tones, to complex acts such as typewriting. It is evident, then, that any system of testing that is to be reliable must be far more elaborate than is popularly supposed. It must provide for measurement of capacity for improvement as well as ability in initial performance.

No matter how highly refined a system of testing might be evolved, it is obvious that an individual could be tested for ability in only a few lines. There might be many occupations wherein he could reach a high degree of proficiency if he were brought in touch with them. How futile it is, then, to postulate a fixity and determinateness of fitness for this or that occupation.

Again, such postulate is open to the criticism that assails any doctrine involving a search for "types." The uselessness of the "type" as a scientific concept has been repeatedly demonstrated by experiment, and as a vocational concept it falls down completely before the simple circumstance that many persons can be trained to do well a number of things.

In any group of individuals whose abilities are arranged according to the normal curve of distribution there are a few persons at the upper extreme who fall readily into the group of geniuses; and the line of their probable success is quite plainly marked. There are a correspondingly small number of persons at the lower extreme whose deficiencies are so apparent that their vocational possibilities fall within a rather limited range. Between these extremes, however, are a large number (approximately 50 per cent) who could be trained to do a large number of things equally well. Besides possessing the capacity for achievement in various lines of endeavor, these individuals also possess varying interests and tastes.

INTEREST NOT A RELIABLE GUIDE

Some vocational guidance proceeds on the assumption that interest should be the guiding factor in determining a career. Such a criterion is very unreliable, as it happens that many individuals of this intermediate group have several interests. These interests are often conflicting and of equal strength. If they were not, the individual would be able to make a choice without the aid of a voca-. tional counselor. These persons who have varied interests and who cluster about the central tendency in amount of ability constitute the most difficult subjects for vocational guidance. In attempting to guide them, the vocational counselor must eschew all pretensions to absolute power to select, and, above all, must remain keenly alive to the limitations of tests. As time goes on and education applies itself more and more vigorously to the preparation of the child for the best possible future, the truth of Professor James's observation becomes increasingly apparent : " However closely psychical changes may conform to law, it is safe to say that individual histories and biographies will never be written in advance no matter how ' evolved ' psychology may become." [1]

Aside from the technical difficulties involved in the current notion of vocational guidance, there are considerations of philosophical import that demand its revision. It holds the fatalistic implication that in the grand cosmic scheme there is but one task that can be satisfactorily accomplished by a single person. It implies that if one finds his niche, success is assured. It further implies that the failures made by " misfits " are due solely to the fact that they did not find the right avenue for their talents. This theory, while embracing the conception of a beautifully well-ordered and harmonious universe, leaves out of account the factor of personal volition. It tacitly assumes that if the methods of science be

[1] James, Principles of Psychology, Vol. II, p. 576.

sufficiently refined, one will be able to foretell with practical certainty what will be the destiny of an individual. Such a program is feasible in astronomy where the course of fixed and soulless stars is concerned, but in the realm of human endeavor it is not likely to be of much value as a working hypothesis.

There is a final consideration that will have weight with all who are not inalienably committed to a mechanistic conception of the universe. The current doctrine fails to make allowance for contingencies beyond the control of the individual. It displays a cocksureness of the future that is at variance with facts. Circumstances arise in the life of everyone which, even with the utmost care, could not have been provided for. Whether one attributes these to "chance" or to "the divinity that shapes our ends," they are a part of the universe and must be reckoned with. The individual is not unalterably fixed in his environment, neither is society cast in an unchangeable mold. Both are in a state of dynamic interplay, and many changes are bound to occur which human intelligence cannot predict.

VOCATIONAL GUIDANCE AS ADVICE ONLY

In view of the serious objections to which the current doctrine of vocational guidance is subject, it seems wise to seek an amendment — some aim that is possible of attainment and that does not depend for serviceableness upon a subversion of facts. At this early stage of development, discretion dictates that the work of vocational guidance be regarded as of purely *monitory* value. That is, it should pretend to do nothing further than to marshal facts and to point out possibilities of attainment in giving advice. Given one or more vocational preferences, a wealth of detailed information about occupations, and a highly refined system of tests, one should only counsel as follows: "If you enter this particular vocation you will be hampered in this or that respect, and you will have this or that factor in your favor. If you have sufficient determination you can probably rise above the handicaps and attain to some degree of success in the calling. Science cannot place a tag on you that will guarantee a safe journey over the road of least resistance to a goal of gratified ambition and unalloyed success."

Such an ideal, while not possessing the dramatic possibilities of the more picturesque " pigeonhole " point of view, nevertheless seems more becoming as a working hypothesis. In the first place, it recognizes the fact that the individual and society are dynamic, not static. Second, it calls for nothing not within the realm of possibilities. It is quite possible to conceive of a development of technic that will enable one to give pointed advice without postulating any mysterious prescience. Third, one who follows such an ideal will be free from the suspicion of charlatanism which can certainly be urged against those who, in order to tickle the ears of a credulous public, would make promises beyond the power of science to fulfill. Fourth, this more modest ideal is free from the errors of a fatalistic philosophy. It postulates no hypothetical "best way." It simply takes facts as it finds them and draws conclusions *based on facts alone.* One is forced to conclude that the former will never lead to a scientific vocational guidance, while the latter observes the precautions demanded by scientific method.

A further advantage which enhances the attractiveness of this monitory type of vocational guidance is that it relieves one individual from responsibility for another's success or failure. A man of scientific mind revolts from the task of issuing ultimate fiats regarding the future such as are popularly demanded. Advice he will gladly give. Scientific measurements he will cheerfully make. Interpretation of these measurements is his bounden duty. Further than this he cannot go, and society should not ask more.

In the light of the conclusions that follow upon the premises of the current conception of vocational guidance, its untenability is readily apparent. This does not mean, however, that educators and others should lessen their zeal in this direction. Instead, the adoption of this monitory conception should accelerate the progress of true vocational guidance. It is thoroughly in accord with the requirements of scientific method and entirely within the realm of possibilities. Positively stated, monitory vocational guidance has for its ideal the granting to every individual of the chance to attain his highest efficiency under the best conditions it is humanly possible to provide. Education can have no worthier aim, and the best efforts of the future can accomplish no more than this.

NECESSITY OF PROFESSIONAL TRAINING FOR VOCATIONAL COUNSELING

By Frederick G. Bonser, Director Industrial Arts, Teachers
College, Columbia University

(An Address delivered at the Third National Conference on Vocational
Guidance, Grand Rapids, Michigan, 1913)

Reduced to its lowest terms, the chief work of the vocational
counselor is to deal with individual persons who are in need of
help in choosing a life-career. There are, however, factors involved in doing this which make it expedient and necessary for
him also to be no less a counselor for the vocations themselves on
the one side and for the schools on the other. Of course, there is
the great problem of the floating population, the vocational tramps,
who need help periodically in getting jobs ; but aid given them is
essentially in the nature of the employment agent's work. His
problem is to know opportunities for immediate employment and
to connect the given job with a man who can do it. He gives no
advice, counsel, or information save only that necessary to provide
the employer with his man, the man with his job. The work of
the counselor, however, is concerned much more with the choice
of permanent life work. He is therefore dealing with a problem
that is fundamental both from the standpoint of the individual
seeking his place in the world's work and of the social world for
which his work is to be done.

Whether one who assumes responsibility for such counsel should
have professional training may be best answered by noting the
elements of specific work which he is to do and the qualifications
required to do it. Upon the efficacy of his counsel depends the
weal or woe of many individuals and the consequent well-being
or misfortune of the society these individuals serve.

Among the qualifications which seem to me to be necessary for successful counseling, I shall note specifically four which are inclusive of many minor elements. These are information, experience, appropriate personality, and capacity for constructive research.

The information definitely needed is of two types — that of the vocational world and that of people. It is manifestly impossible for any one person to know the details of all of the several thousand different kinds of work by which people maintain a livelihood, but it is possible to know something of each of the relatively small number of groups of vocations into which these may be classified on the basis of fundamental activities involved. First of all, there is the grouping into the five large divisions, the professional, the commercial, the agricultural, the industrial, and the household. Within each field are subdivisions rather well defined in some particulars. In turn, each of these subgroups is divisible into specific phases of work, making a total of several thousand different kinds of occupation. There are, however, many overlappings in these occupations from the standpoint of the activities and qualities required for efficient service. As a matter of fact, we know little that is of fundamental character in the classification of qualities for vocational success, or of the activities that are fundamental in the vocations themselves. Viewed from this one standpoint the hit-or-miss, leap-in-the-dark quality of advice given by a counselor who does not even know the little now known and who has not the training and capacity for further discovery is quite apparent. The fundamental activities involved in the larger groups of vocations and their more important subdivisions the vocational counselor should know as the analytical chemist knows the elements, the families of elements, and the compounds of these elements and families of elements.

The counselor must know not only the more fundamental activities involved in these various fields and the personal qualifications required to conduct them, but he must also know the conditions of the occupations as they exist from time to time. The relationship between present and probable supply and demand, the relative wages, and the changes in methods, devices, and organization affecting the workers must all be more or less at his immediate command. Illustrations may be drawn readily from the fields of farming, commercial work, and manufacture to show that new inventions are constantly supplanting whole groups of workers, leaving them out of employment and unable to derive any help whatever from a technical training which may have been developed only through a long and devoted period. A current illustration of this is clearly evident in the commercial field. Stenographers have been in great demand, and means for preparing them have developed in response under both private and public auspices. If a young man or woman seems well adapted to this field, nothing is easier than to advise attendance upon a school appropriately fitting for such work, assuming that such a school exists. But a disturbing factor immediately appears when it is learned that the dictaphone has begun an invasion of this field which points toward the early elimination of the stenographers from perhaps one third to one half of the offices in which they have heretofore been indispensable.

A knowledge of the initial wages in the various occupations is entirely inadequate for the purposes of the counselor. Possibilities for training, advancement, and increase in wages are altogether of more significance than are initial wages. There are hundreds of jobs that offer wages alluringly high for boys in their early teens, 16, 18, or even 20 cents an hour ; but there is nothing in the work save the easily attained maximum of the 20 cents an hour. The end of the "blind alley" is reached. When manhood overtakes the worker in such a calling, he either morosely submits to a life sentence of dulling, monotonous drudgery with all that this implies, or he changes to some other occupation, rarely finding one with much more chance of growth or advancement than the first. Dissatisfaction leads him again to change, and the probability is strong that he will soon become a permanent member of the class of "job floaters" or "hoboes." All such occupations the counselor must know.

The counselor must likewise know in which vocations the capital for success lies primarily in manual skill, and in which it is chiefly a matter of vocational intelligence. In the transition from handicraft methods of manufacture to factory and machine production a whole generation of schoolmasters and not a few tradespeople have made the error of prescribing an effective method of training for an outgrown method of production without realizing that it was fundamentally defective in meeting the conditions for which they were presumably preparing. We all thank God and progress that the day of handicraft production has been supplanted by methods far more efficient, just as log cabins, kerosene lamps, hand-reaping machinery, and "prairie schooners" have been supplanted by inventions a hundredfold or a thousandfold more efficient. But the work of a thousand manual-training teachers in this country, fondly supposing themselves to be vocational trainers for present-day industry, shows how the factory system with its division of labor, its machine processes, and its applied science has entirely escaped them. If these and the authorities employing them have been so oblivious to conditions in the real world of industry, it behooves us to have a care that those counseling young people about to enter such callings should be alive to the world's work as it actually must be done by those taking up its problems. I count it a travesty upon our schools and a tragedy for our boys and girls that a number of large hardware dealers in New York, who conduct supply houses for the whole country, carry a large stock of goods no longer used at all in the trades, but carried to meet the steady or even increasing demand of the manual-training departments and schools of the country.

The vocational counselor must also know people. In addition to the usual meaning which would attach to this statement, I mean that he must know how to use all of the means whereby he may be able to help the candidate to discover his vocational aptitudes and capacities and make the adjustment between these and the work appropriate for him. He must be able to make appropriate use of the tests and devices discovered by psychological research in the finding of individual differences and abilities ; he must know the bearing upon the problem of race and national peculiarities, traditions, prejudices, and characteristics ; he must know the influence of home and social settings and of previous experiences in determining motives, ambitions, and ideals ; and he must know how to interpret those more or less elusive and intangible qualities that go to make up the thing we call personality. Thus to know people requires at least three factors : An intimate knowledge of the methods and values of making records and tests, together with their interpretation ; a large background of experience in observing young people and workers in their work, in their homes, and in their social life ; and a high degree of common sense or the ability to take the results of common observation and experience and from these to deduce quickly a valid judgment. This resulting judgment will seem to the casual observer a matter of intuition, but it is rather only the product of much knowledge, training, and experience reduced to terms by the instant and almost unconscious application of the expert.

Besides this crystalized experience, the counselor must be characterized by tact, decision, and unbounded human sympathy. He is to give advice, not orders. The candidate is to act as a free person, following counsel because of the appeal it makes to his ambition and sense of worth, not because of any sense of compulsion.

As a final qualification, I would add that of capacity for constructive research. Since human life, and notably vocational life, is in a state of constant change, the vocational counselor must be capable of making or of directing such lines of research and investigation as will insure his progressive familiarity with those changes to which adjustments of workers must be made. Furthermore, in our present state of poverty of knowledge relative to questions of fundamental importance in the classification of vocations and of the means for determining vocational aptitudes, the counselor will have the pressing problem of initiating means of inquiry which will help to supply this much-needed information.

The relation of the counselor to the schools is of paramount importance. The needed changes revealed by his work must be wrought through the schools. When he looks at the conditions and needs of vocational life on the one hand and at the pitiable emptiness of the schools with reference to these needs on the other, his spirit must indeed be courageous and heroic, or it will shrink from a task that looks almost insuperable. Besides his own experiences, he reads in one of the most recent studies of the vocations entered by children between 14 and 16, based upon 4386 St. Louis cases, that about 90 per cent entered unskilled occupations ; about 7 per cent, low-grade skilled occupations; and less than 3 per cent, high-grade skilled occupations ; that over 70 per cent of these children entered occupations demanding merely fetching and carrying — "blind alleys" in almost every case. Turning to the Massachusetts study of 1906, the New York study of 1911–1912, the Cincinnati studies still in progress, the Philadelphia study of 1912–1913, and to any others available, he finds this condition approximately true for the country at large. He reads that Charles H. Ludington, of the Curtis Publishing Co., Philadelphia, recently stated that :

Seventy-five applicants were interviewed for a recent vacancy in our typist force. At least 50 were obviously unfitted, and about 25 were tested before one competent worker was secured. To fill the position of correspondent, it is necessary for the Curtis Publishing Co. to interview from 10 to 50 persons; to find a stenographer, 15 to 25 ; a typist, 25 to 50 ; a high-grade clerk, 20 to 25 ; an ordinary clerk, 10 to 15. Whenever it is necessary to secure operators for our office appliances, which are generally used throughout the commercial world, we are obliged in 90 per cent of the cases to train them ourselves.

From these conditions in the vocations the counselor looks back to the schools. What are they doing about it all ? Armies of children are dropping out, largely because the work makes no appeal of appreciable worth to them or their parents ; occupations offering opportunity for growth and progress will not have them until they are 16. Counseling 100 children to enter vocations that will take but 3 is as foolish as it is vain ; counseling them to go back to the schools from which they came is almost as foolish and usually quite as vain. To counsel the child to make the most of the occupation possible as a temporary measure and to take up part-time school work for entrance into an occupation that is more desirable when adequate maturity is reached appeals to the counselor as the most hopeful solution. But here arises the stone wall of ancient tradition, manned by the guns of academic schoolmasters and political boards of education, backed by a quiescent public opinion. The counselor realizes that in most communities there are no schools, there is no school work which his honest conscience will permit him to advise as meeting the need. How long must this army of ambitious, capable boys and girls be allowed to go to the scrap heap of adult inefficiency, disappointment, and too often of pauperism and crime? How long must this army of tens of thousands ask for the bread of real, present-day life, of opportunity to prepare for gaining an adequate, respectable, and efficient living and citizenship, and be given the stones of academic gymnastics?

It is my faith that the vocational counselor, properly trained, will become the great force for bridging this gap between the vocational world and the schools. Timely, tactful, and, most of all, intelligent appeals to employers and school people (boards of education, superintendents, and teachers), revelation to them of facts, needs, and plans, should certainly be one of the most effective and far-reaching duties of the vocational counselor. To be sure, his immediate problem is partly an emergency problem — to do all that he possibly can to meet the specific needs of the individual candidates whom he is trying to aid. But if his work does not reach far enough into the vocational world, on the one hand, and into the schools on the other, to better conditions in both, to bring them closer together, and largely to remove the causes producing the emergency, then his efforts are just so much short of adequate success.

Can the vocational counselor achieve the success for which his position is established without professional training? In considering the problems of the counselor and the means and qualifications for meeting these problems, it seems to me that professional training is implied as essential at every point. His work is not a matter of a card-filing cabinet nor of the mere memory of facts. It is a work requiring trained judgment, intelligence trained to see the crucial point in a mass of complex data, a broad and intensive grasp of many complex social and psychological situations, and rigid training in the accurate interpretation of facts, conditions, and human qualities. Efficiency in these activities does not come by intuition alone nor by casual experience alone. Although every day's work of the counselor will be an asset in the work of the days following, training in every phase of the problem for which provision can be made will aid in eliminating waste from the beginning. It will save many a worker who would probably be wrecked on the rocks of misdirection. The problem comprehends the well-being of individuals, of vocations, of the school, and of society at large. For this significant work let us have men and women of the best possible professional training, that their efficiency may be in proportion to their responsibilities.

PART II. THE FOUNDATIONS OF VOCATIONAL GUIDANCE

BRIEFS OF PAPERS ON VOCATIONAL GUIDANCE

(Read at the meeting of the Boston Masters' Association, Tuesday, November 12, 1912)

I. FROM THE VIEWPOINT OF ITS APPLICATION TO GIRLS IN ELEMENTARY SCHOOLS

By Eleanor M. Colleton, Hancock District

Subject of Investigation in Hancock and Dillaway Schools

(*a*) Graduates of June, 1911.

(*b*) Girls fourteen years of age or over who left between September, 1911, and June, 1912.

Purpose of Investigation

(*a*)

1. How many of the graduates continued to attend school?
2. What schools?
3. What vocational intent entered into their decision to attend a given school?
4. How many persevered to the end of the school year in attendance?
5. How many left school during the year and why?
6. How many of the graduates went to work after graduation? Kind of work?
7. How many remained at home and why?

(*b*)

1. The reason or reasons for leaving school, special reference being made to the number who left school to go to work and to what extent actual poverty of the family was the cause?

2. The occupation entered and why?

(*a*) How obtained? Vocational plan?

(*b*) Wages?

(*c*) Length of employment?

(*d*) Changes of employment?

(*e*) Causes for change?

(*f*) Chances for advancement?

Number in Groups studied

Hancock School:

(*a*) 71
(*b*) 105   176

Dillaway School:

(*a*) 101
(*b*) 54   155

Total   331

Study of Graduates

	GRADUATED	ENTERED HIGH	LEFT HIGH SINCE	STILL IN HIGH
Dillaway	101	65	8	57
Hancock	71	37	7	30

Vocations desired by Graduates

The majority of the Hancock graduates who entered high school had a plan more or less definite to enter some form of commercial life, while the plans of the graduates of the Dillaway School were more varied, comprising plans to be teachers, private secretaries, telephone operators, nurses, sewing teachers, dressmakers, as well as stenographers and bookkeepers.

Girls who went to Work and their Opportunities

There was little or no difference in the occupations open to the girls who graduated and those who left before graduating. The principal places open to them were in the department stores as bundle girls at $2.50 to $3.50 ; in the factories at $3 to $4 ; in stores as salesgirls at $5 ; in tailors' shops at $2.50 to $3.50.

'Needless to state, after the first glamour of working has worn off, the girls tire and leave such work, or the season becomes dull and they are laid off temporarily or permanently, according as they seem more or less desirable to their employers.

Reasons for leaving School

The proportion of girls forced by financial circumstances to leave school was comparatively small. Being backward in their grades, dislike of school, desire for a change, desire to be with friends who were working, were principal reasons.

Parents' Attitude toward Vocational Guidance

On our cards there was no item to be filled out in regard to parents' comments on the results of training in the elementary schools. Nevertheless, there have been certain observations made so repeatedly that I state them here.

1. A comment as to the inability of the girls to write well-phrased, correctly spelled letters when there was personal or family need.

2. A comment as to the inaccuracy shown in anything calling for mathematical knowledge, as exemplified when parents requested help of girls in adjusting accounts with stores, insurance agents, etc.

3. A criticism of the lack of practical value of sewing as it is taught in the schools. This was a lament, a wail of many. " I don't expect the girl to learn the dressmaking trade, but if she were only taught to use a pattern, how much she could help me with the younger children's clothes and what a saving it would be." " If the girl could only do some by herself without waiting for the teacher to tell her what to do next, what a help she would be to me.

She has brought home a garment which she says she made, but when I have given her cloth to do the same at home she can do nothing."

Parents' Knowledge of Vocational Opportunities

It was most pathetic to see how little the parents knew of the real industrial conditions and of what educational and vocational opportunities, entirely within their reach, existed in Boston. This was true in far, far larger extent of the parents of girls who left school in the grades than of those who graduated. This was due doubtless to the fact that the graduating classes have been given talks along these lines and, even if the parents did not attend conferences given by schools and associations, they have gleaned some knowledge from the girls when they did not have personal knowledge.

Deductions

My experience has been that the vast majority of the parents of the girls in the study just completed knew nothing except what they had obtained through the school as to the various high schools and their specialties — the Trade and Industrial Schools — the necessity of extra training and preparation to enter any occupation in which there were chances for advancement. The attitude of the parents when visited in the homes made it appear only too clear that practically all would welcome such guidance and avail themselves of it.

What should the girl do when she is fourteen years?

What is open for her to do according to her physical and mental indications, tastes, and desires?

What schools or courses must prepare her?

What are her obstacles?

Do girl and parent know the future of most girls who enter industrial life without further preparation than the elementary-school training, unless, perhaps, they enter an establishment which is in coöperation with a continuation school?

What are the local recreation centers, settlement house, etc., which can safely be recommended to mothers as places to which their girls may turn for recreation, which is as necessary for youth as food and clothing?

What are the evening vocational advantages of schools and classes locally situated, likewise of those situated throughout the city, to which a girl may have access with profit to herself?

What are the reactions of individual occupations or industries which make or unmake a girl for future good womanhood, physical and moral?

This is what vocational guidance means, and is, to my mind, a work the elementary school should take up and at once.

II. FROM THE VIEWPOINT OF ITS APPLICATION TO BOYS IN ELEMENTARY SCHOOLS

By William T. Miller, Agassiz District

Let me explain briefly just what I conceive to be the real purpose and aim of the vocational-guidance movement. Misconceptions as to the real meaning of guidance have brought much unjust and adverse criticism on the movement. In its only defensible sense vocational guidance as a school activity means leading the boy (and parent) to study his own ability and desires, and to weigh the requirements, opportunities, and rewards of various occupations, all with the aim that he may sometime choose, freely and wisely, some line of work suitable to his inclinations and aptitudes. It does not mean dictating the kind of occupation a boy shall enter or arbitrarily placing him in a job. That would be vocational compulsion and would destroy the initiative on which much of a boy's success depends. It is not even hoped that the elementary-school graduate will be able by means of guidance to select his life work. The fourteen-year or sixteen-year old boy is too young, except in rare cases, to choose a life-career; but he is not too young to begin to think about the need of sometime choosing a permanent calling and to get some ideas about his own traits and real desires. He can also choose more intelligently between different jobs as they may offer themselves to him and begin to prepare himself for a future decision that will be wiser and more permanent than if he had never thought of the meaning of vocational choice. Such teaching will help to give the boy a more serious view of life, and the thought of some future use will give a stronger motive for study and for the development of general good character. Another common misconception is that vocational guidance will tend to drive the boy out of school by encouraging him to go to work. True guidance will have just the opposite effect, by emphasizing the value of training in all occupations, and suggesting the definite schools and courses that will prepare for given vocational desires. A third great concern of the vocational-guidance movement is the boys who leave to go to work. Instead of being set adrift as they now are, they should be followed up, records kept of their progress, advice and encouragement given when necessary, and a constant effort made to promote the educational improvement of those who must work early in life.

I studied

1. Number, ages, grades of boys leaving school to work.
2. Reasons for leaving.
3. Extent to which any vocational choice was manifested.
4. Earnings and kinds of work done.
5. Causes of success and failure.
6. Educational needs.
7. Possibility and limit of vocational guidance as school activity.

You will perhaps be more interested in general conclusions than specific details. My investigation was made in the Wendell Phillips and Agassiz Districts, giving a geographical, racial, and industrial contrast. My figures will be totals from these two schools combined, unless otherwise mentioned. It included boys leaving to work during 1911 and 1912 and the graduates of 1911.

Taking the whole number of boys fourteen years of age or over who were in school during the year, I found of 522 who were eligible to get certificates, 112, or 21 per cent, did go to work during the year, representing over one-fifth loss from the schools by premature leaving. Of the graduates of 1911, 28 per cent went into work and 7 per cent left high school to work during the year. Only 60 per cent finished first-year high school.

As to ages of leaving, 62 per cent left between fourteen and fifteen and 44 per cent before fourteen and a half ; 62 per cent left at or below sixth grade and 25 per cent in fifth and lower ; 16 boys left in seventh or lower above age of sixteen.

Reasons for leaving School

A careful study of family income and expenditures was made and I feel that I got reasonably close to the real conditions.

In cases of doubt the benefit was given to the family, so that I am certain that there is no exaggeration in these percentages for two districts :

Left on account of necessity . . . . 30 per cent
Left on account of desire for profit . . . . . . 10 per cent
Dissatisfied with school . . . . 35 per cent
Preference for work, and in case of graduating not
    going to high school . . . . 25 per cent

Necessity . . . . 17 per cent
Profit . . . . 18 per cent
Preference for work . . . . 65 per cent

A considerable number of nongraduates leave to give their whole time to selling papers, distinctly a bad practice. In the cases of graduates there is much less of this and more entrance into skilled trades. The average time in a position for the nongraduate was seven weeks, for a graduate eighteen weeks, showing greater shifting among the nongraduates. The nongraduates going to work averaged 3.55 per cent in first position, the graduates averaged 4.11 per cent. The average wage during eleven months for all nongraduates was $4.26, for graduates $4.64, and most of the graduates had some prospects of advancement.

The work of the counselors with the graduating class should consist generally of individual private interviews with the pupils, with a view to getting at their vocational ideas and encouraging them to think about the problem seriously. As a necessary prelude some talks should be given to the class on the fundamental meaning of vocation and the elements involved in any choice. As

part of the English work a theme on choosing a vocation will stimulate thought on the matter. The different types of high schools
will of course demand some of the counselors' attention. As far
as possible the counselor should find an opportunity, by special
invitation, to talk with the parents of the pupils, so as to get their
knowledge of the boy's characteristics, desires, and limitations.

At present the counselors seldom take any notice of the boys
leaving to work without graduating. If the counselor can get a
free hour a week he can interview some of these cases. A school
regulation can be made, that to get a working certificate a boy must
apply at least one week ahead. Then a definite day each week may
be set aside as the only time when certificate applications will be
made out. On this day those wishing to leave can tell their stories to
the counselor. They should be required to have one parent with them.
Much good might be done at such interviews and possible means suggested to prolong the boy's school life. Advice can then be given
as to schools suited to the boy's needs, and a postcard can be supplied to the boy on which he is to report two weeks after he has left
as to whether he is still at work and has entered evening school.

I realize that all these things demand time and energy, and we
can't do all of them. But we can all do something, and at least
can preach at every opportunity the wholesome doctrine that
"blessed is he who has found his work and does it," and that the
"boy who works and learns is the man who succeeds and earns."

III. A PLAN FOR VOCATIONAL INSTRUCTION ON
A SMALL SCALE

By Laura F. Wentworth, High School of Practical Arts

    I. General outline of methods of procedure.
        1. Course for teachers.
           To train them so that they may in turn give a
        2. Course for pupils.
           The reports of the children at home will cause a
           demand for
        3. Course for parents.

II. Number of people required to conduct this work.
    1. One person to plan courses and provide speakers.
    2. Two vocational counselors in each elementary and high school *and* the master.

III. Detailed plan of courses mentioned above.
    1. Course for teachers (two meetings a month).
        a. Subjects treated in course.
            (1) Vocations open to boys and girls.
                (*a*) Advantages.
                (*b*) Disadvantages.
                (*c*) Location of specific firms.
            (2) Schools (public and private) which fit for vocations discussed.
            (3) How and where to obtain a working certificate.
            (4) How to apply for a position.
                (*a*) In person.
                (*b*) By letter.
            (5) What an employer expects of an employee.
        b. Talks from time to time on :
            (1) Literature on vocational subjects.
            (2) Meetings to be held in or near Boston dealing with vocational problems.
            (3) Work in other cities in United States and other countries along the vocational line.
            (4) Recreational opportunities in different districts of city.
        c. Visits by groups to the industries and schools discussed.
        d. At least one exhibition at the Bijou Dream of the moving pictures illustrating industries, etc.
    2. Course for pupils (in individual schools once a week).
        a. The groups of children.

        (1) All below eighth grade who are thirteen years or over.

        (2) The graduating class.

        (3) In high schools — graduating class (and those in other classes who indicate intention of leaving).

b. Nature of work with children.

        (1) Train pupils to know themselves in regard to

            (*a*) Characteristics of importance to success: Punctuality, interest, responsibility, etc.

            (*b*) Personal appearance as necessary to success: Neatness, cleanness, etc.

        (2) Reproduction of talks on vocations.

        (3) Reproduction of talks on schools fitting for these.

        (4) Visits to industries and schools.

        (5) How to obtain a working certificate.

            (*a*) A placard should be hung in every schoolroom where children are over thirteen years, telling three things required to obtain working certificate and where to obtain this certificate.

            (*b*) The children should also be shown samples of birth certificate, employer's ticket, and school-attendance record, and working certificate so that they will know what to expect when asking for same.

        (6) How to apply for position.

            (*a*) In person.

            (*b*) By letter.

(7) What employer expects of employee.

(8) Talks on health and danger in industrial world.

(9) In some districts arrangements can be made with local moving-picture theaters to show films illustrating various industries, etc.

(10) Suggestions as to recreations, etc. Settlement houses, recreation centers.

3. Course for parents.

    a. Circular letter to parents of all children over thirteen years of age emphasizing:

       (1) Desirability of a skilled trade with low wages at the outset rather than a fair beginning wage with no prospect of advancement.

       (2) Desirability of future training in some special school.

       (3) Necessity for care of child's health.

       (4) Necessity for watching the recreation of child.

Speakers to be furnished by Central Office if desired

    b. Talks (in evenings at school buildings) on vocations.

    c. Talks on schools training for these vocations.

    d. Talks on how to obtain working certificate.

    e. Talks on health and danger in industry.

    f. Talks on different forms of recreation offered.

    g. Utilizing moving-picture theaters in districts for showing industries, etc.

In the foregoing courses the burden of the work comes on the vocational counselors, who should be allowed a sufficient amount of free time to carry on the talks.

Vocational Guidance in High School

The work in vocational guidance in High School of Practical Arts resolves itself into five definite lines :

I. Helping girls to choose industrial course. By talks to girls and circular letter to parents.
    1. According to natural ability.
    2. According to work intend to do on graduating.

II. Home visiting.

III. Giving talks to girls in fourth year.
    1. About higher schools.
    2. About occupation allied to those taught.
    3. About trade conditions.

IV. Placing girls.
    1. Graduates. Higher schools and trade schools.
    2. Undergraduates who drop out. Trade schools.
    3. Undergraduates out of school hours. Trade schools.

V. Following up graduates.
    1. By system of reporting by mail.
    2. By visits to employers.
    3. By alumnæ association.   .

Summary

The work of the vocational assistant is one of adjustment.

1. Of girls to right course in school.
2. Of girls to right course after leaving school.
3. Of home to school and school to business life.

VOCATIONAL GUIDANCE IN CINCINNATI

By Frank P. Goodwin

(An Address before the Ohio State High School Teachers' Association at Columbus, Ohio, December 29, 1913)

In response to a demand caused by changed industrial conditions, vocational education has become an important part of our public-school system; our high-school courses are, in a great measure, organized in accordance with the vocational idea, and vocational or prevocational education for children who will not go to high school will soon become an essential part of the work of our educational system. This introduction of vocational courses, combined with the complexity of modern vocational life, has forced upon us the necessity of attempting some direction of students in their choice of a life-career and in their preparation for the same.

As a result, the vocational-guidance movement, beginning almost simultaneously in at least two Eastern cities, has spread throughout the United States; and to-day numerous city school systems are attempting work of this character or are studying it with a view to its adoption. It has been introduced into about twenty elementary schools of Cincinnati and has undergone a considerable development in one Cincinnati high school.

The movement had not advanced far in Cincinnati before our teachers realized that vocational guidance should be an educational process, and that the life-career motive should be used as a means for prolonging the period of school life.

With us as in most city school systems it presents two distinct problems, differentiated by two classes of pupils:

1. The elementary-school child who will not go to high school.

2. The student who takes or expects to take a high-school course.

The latter group will include both eighth-grade and high-school children.

In regard to the former group, there is a general agreement among those who have investigated the subject that but little can be done for those pupils, except as prevocational training, manual in character, is introduced into the elementary school. This has been substantiated by the Chicago City Club Survey, under the direction of Professor Mead; by the New York Survey, under Miss Barrows; and by the Cincinnati Work Certificate Office, under Mrs. Woolley. Numerous cities, including Cincinnati, acting upon this idea, have established schools of this character. Already we have made a beginning in eight schools, but it remains to work out a plan of analysis and guidance for these children.

The second problem, that of the child who expects to take a high-school course, is easier of approach, and perhaps much easier of solution. It is to this phase of vocational guidance that this paper is chiefly devoted. In this work, we are endeavoring to have the child select his high-school course on the basis of the life-career motive, and to use that motive as the impelling purpose which will keep him in school until graduation if possible. This supposes that he will endeavor to select that high-school course for which he is best adapted, and which will be of greatest value in the preparation for the vocation of his choice. It does not necessarily follow, however, that the eighth-grade child's choice of a high-school course or his choice of a vocation will be final. In fact, the whole high-school period is distinctly a formative one, and the child should be permitted to change his vocational motive and also his high-school course as often as good reason can be shown for such change. But this must not be understood to encourage vacillation or indecision. The importance of such a principle of selection is apparent when we consider that the child has nine high-school courses based in a considerable degree upon the vocational idea from which to select.

The activities connected with this work in the eighth grade and in the high school present the three phases which are general to the problem.

1. A study of the personal characteristics of each pupil.

2. A study on the part of the pupil of the opportunities and conditions of a variety of vocations.

3. The adaptation of the school work to the vocational needs of the pupil and of the community.

STUDY OF THE INDIVIDUAL

The study of the personal element should begin with the eighth grade and continue throughout the high-school course. It should be done in a systematic manner, but not without that sympathetic interest characteristic of the true teacher. The plan is to schedule and record on guidance record cards those general characteristics which influence the vocational success or failure of the individual. The schedule for the eighth grade is as follows :

VOCATIONAL RECORD CARD . EIGHTH GRADE

    Name   School

  . Date of birth   ·   Nationality ·

    Parent's name   Residence

1. Health and physical characteristics (from the physician) ; height, weight; sense organs : eyes, ears.

2. Powers of observation : good, medium, poor.

3. Memory : good, medium, poor.

4. Attention : good, medium, poor.

5. Association : rapid mental coördination, medium rate of coördination, slow mental coördination.

6. Type of activity : deliberate, impulsive, neither.

7. Intellectual ability : good, medium, poor.

8. Manual ability (domestic-science or manual-training teacher) : good, medium, poor.

9. Social leadership : well developed, moderate, absent (a follower).

10. Perseverance : good, medium, poor.

11. Habits of promptness : good, medium, poor.

12. Studies : preferences, successes, dislikes, failures.

13. Vocation of parents.

14. Which high-school course ?

15. What vocation has the child in mind ?

The schedule for the high school varies but little from the above.

In recording these judgments concerning the student, the type of observation, attention, memory, manual activity, etc. should be indicated. For example, a person may have a good memory for verse but a poor memory for music; another may have a poor verbal memory but a good memory for a logically arranged group of facts; an artisan may be a good carpenter but have no aptitude for the fine work required of a manufacturing jeweler.

In this study of the personal element and the recording of the same, we have a kind of child study, the value of which will be limited by the size of the class, the opportunity to study the individual pupil, and the ability of the teacher to read and analyze character.

Teachers disagree as to the desirability of using the record card, the claim being made that it will be of little value except in the hands of a trained psychologist. It has been suggested also that the schedule herein presented is too general to be of much value. Such criticisms should receive careful consideration, but we believe that teachers should begin to make a more careful study of the mental and physical characteristics of children than heretofore and that at present only a few teachers are prepared to make a more detailed analysis than is herein indicated. Furthermore, we believe that the best way to develop a more careful study of the characteristics of children on the part of the teacher is by the use of a schedule of this character. The record card herein presented is the result of much discussion among a group of Cincinnati teachers, but its present form is due for the most part to valuable suggestions from Mrs. Helen T. Woolley and Dean Herman Schneider. But whether a record card be used or not, it suggests a kind of work that should be in progress in every schoolroom.

Knowledge of some of the characteristics included in this schedule may be acquired in the classroom, but the teacher who relies entirely on that will know all too little about her pupils. Every other opportunity for a study of their characteristics should be embraced. For example, from seeing the children on the playground she may learn more about who have ability for leadership; and perhaps other characteristics not shown in the more formal intercourse of the schoolroom will present themselves. Consultation with the manual-training teacher also is desirable, as he has a peculiar opportunity to know children on the manual as well as on the mental side. Furthermore, pupils may show characteristics in the more informal conduct of the manual-training room which are not noticeable under the conditions of the regular classroom.

Of not less importance in this connection is a personal acquaintance with the parents on the part of the teacher and conferences with them in regard to the characteristics of their children. Although not always possible, it would be well if every teacher could be personally acquainted with the parents of every child under her direction. Opportunity for this may be very greatly increased by a parents' organization in connection with the vocational-guidance work. The meetings of such an organization would give opportunity to discuss the selection of high-school courses of study together with vocational questions, while here teachers might meet parents and discuss the characteristics and welfare of the individual pupil.

The course in vocations should be closely related to the occupational needs of the community and to the individual interests of the children of the class. The first topics discussed should be determined by the interests which the children already have. They will furnish much of the information themselves. This would be supplemented by personal investigation on the part of the teacher, by having experts in various vocations address the pupils, by reading, by industrial excursions, and particularly in so far as possible by reports based upon careful investigation. Out of this work the child should develop a life-career motive on which to base his choice of high-school work.

It is needless to say that the eighth-grade teacher should be well informed as to the details and purposes of the various high-school courses and that she should be able to advise as to the educational and vocational value of each. When such work is definitely established in the eighth grade and children select their high-school courses on the basis of the life-career motive, we believe that a smaller percentage of mistakes will occur and that the proportion of failures in the first year of high school will materially decrease.

If this guidance work is to succeed in a large high school, the organization must be such as to permit a continuation of the careful study of the personal characteristics of each pupil begun in the eighth grade; and in so far as possible, this work, especially in the first year, should be in the hands of teachers who will exercise towards their pupils an intelligent and sympathetic helpfulness.

EMPHASIS UPON LIFE-CAREER MOTIVE

But that phase of vocational guidance in the high school which is most in evidence is the systematic effort to keep the life-career motive before the students throughout the four years of high-school life and to give them information which will assist in the choice of a vocation. In the first and second years the most important duty will be to follow up the failures and to use, along with other incentives, the life-career motive as an important influence in getting pupils to do a better grade of work. This should be under the direction of the group advisers. As introductory to following up carefully the individual pupil who is likely to fail, the first-year students should be given a talk which will include ideas such as are indicated in the following outline:

Why are you in high school?

Why did you select the particular course in which you are working?

Why do you need a high-school education? (Cultural, citizenship, vocational.)

Have you determined what work you will do as a life-career? If not, why not? Think this over; talk about it with your parents and others.

If you have determined what your life work is to be, how do you expect the school work to help you prepare for it?

Are you in the high-school course that will best help you to prepare for the vocation of your choice? Perhaps you cannot answer this now. If necessary, you should be given all year in which to decide. If you can show good reason for a change, you should be permitted to make it at the beginning of another year or perhaps sooner.

Autumn examinations are over. Some of you have failed. Why? Were you prepared? Have you done your duty? If you are to blame, what is the difficulty?

Do you lack earnestness of purpose and determination?

Do you fail to see clearly the influence of your school work on your future career?

The person who is prepared is the one who succeeds. You are forming habits that will make for success or failure. Personal conferences will be held between you and some teacher to determine the cause of failure and, if possible, prevent a recurrence of it. Take advantage of every opportunity to get personal assistance from your teachers when it is needed.

STUDIES OF OCCUPATIONS

For the second year, a series of lectures is presented on the various vocations. The first talk of this series, for which the following may serve as a brief outline, relates to the choice of a vocation :

Some of you entered high school last year with the purpose of preparing for a definite career. Some perhaps had no such purpose then, but you may have now. Some have shown a more or less definite purpose by selecting courses that are vocational in character.

Each of the nine courses has vocational value for particular vocations. For example: The prospective physician should get as much natural science as possible; the boy who would become an engineer needs to take all we offer in mathematics, with physics and chemistry added. Some girls, appreciating that every woman, married or single, may become a home-maker, have elected the domestic science course; some of you have not yet selected a life-career. It is important that you should do so and make your school work a preparation for it. It is not necessary, however, that selection be made at once. The entire high-school period may be used, if necessary, by boys and girls to find that for which they are best fitted; but decision should not be put off longer than necessary. In high school we give a variety of studies and furnish opportunities for a variety of experiences that should help you to find yourself.

The choice may have been made already; if it be a good one, adhere to it. There may be good reasons to change; if so, do it soon. For those who have not decided and for those who are uncertain, we are about to present series of talks and other exercises. For those whose decision has been made, the talks and exercises will furnish a fund of valuable information and perhaps some new light as to what is necessary for success in any occupation.

Further explain to the pupils that these talks will relate to conditions and opportunities of employment in different vocations, to the personal elements of success, and to the adaptability of the individual to the vocation of his choice.

Tell them that under the personal element we shall consider what elements of character and personal habits are necessary for success. Say to them, " From the standpoint of adaptability you need to answer the question, Have you the particular qualifications which are necessary for success in the vocation of your choice ? " Lead them to see that in selecting a life-career it is necessary to investigate the vocational opportunities that are open and the qualifications of the individual for entering the vocation of his choice. Show that a choice should depend upon the answers to the questions : Can I earn a fair living in the vocation of my choice ? Will I be happy in the job ? Will I be able to render some social service ?

Finally say, " After making such a selection, either tentative or permanent, it is then your business to make your school work a preparation for your life work. This preparation includes the acquirement of as much knowledge and experience as you can get which will fit you for the work, the formation of habits which will make for success, and the development of a correct attitude of mind toward your work and toward those whom you are serving."

Some of these vocational talks are given by representatives of the various occupations ; some are given by teachers. Some are given to all second-year pupils, while others are given to the students of a particular department. For example, students in the commercial department will be given talks on the vocational opportunities and conditions in stenography, accountancy, advertising, business management. Students in the industrial department will be given talks on the building trades, the machinist trade, heating and ventilating, jewelry manufacture, etc.

In this connection we should also notice that the vocationalizing of our high-school courses furnishes much greater opportunity for guidance than would be possible otherwise. With nine courses, each having vocational value for certain occupations and with considerable flexibility of program and courses, we are better able to learn the characteristics of the individual student and to meet his needs than would be otherwise possible. In Cincinnati we have about reached the limit in this direction under present college-entrance requirements.

TALKS ON HIGHER EDUCATION

In the third year we are giving our students a series of lectures on higher education, including such topics as the following :

(1) Who shall go to college ? Why ? Who should not go to college ? Why ?

(2) What our local university offers.

(3) Ohio State University ; typical of state institutions of learning, compare with Michigan, Illinois, Wisconsin.

(4) Great Eastern universities.

(5) Schools of engineering: Cincinnati, Purdue, Case, Cornell, Massachusetts Institute of Technology.

(6) The best schools for the social sciences: Harvard, Columbia, Chicago, Wisconsin.

(7) Agricultural education.

(8) Great schools of medicine, law, theology, journalism.

(9) Women's colleges.

(10) Vocational schools other than colleges and universities.

(11) The cost: earning one's way through college.

Perhaps the English department has a superior opportunity to keep before the students of the high school the life-career motive and to assist in giving them information that will be of value in the choice of a career. This has been worked out in the Central High School, Grand Rapids, under the direction of the principal, Jesse B. Davis. In discussing this phase of the work, Mr. Davis says:

Vocational guidance is or should be a process of drawing out from the pupil knowledge of himself, of opening his eyes to see the wide field of opportunity that is before him, and of developing in him the elements of character that make for successful life. It is thus a problem of self-development and not a matter of mere information or the giving of advice. Following out this theory, we have selected in the high school the department of English for the purpose of experiment. In this subject we reach every pupil and at the same time offer the students subjects for composition that are of real interest to them and about which they have some ideas of their own.

During the past year we have been experimenting with this in the Woodward High School with a sufficient degree of success to believe in it.

The following topics (already published), for which we are under obligation to the Grand Rapids High School, will suggest the character of the work:

First Year

1. My health.
2. My habits.
3. My likes and dislikes.
4. A self estimate.
5. (Franklin, etc.) at my age.
6. My opportunities compared with those of (Lincoln).

1. The kind of employment that I can get now.
2. Child labor.
3. Wages of those leaving school at the eighth grade compared with the wages of high-school graduates.
4. Why I have chosen my vocation.
5. My plan for entering the vocation of my choice.

THIRD YEAR

1. What are business habits?
2. What kind of an employee does the business man want?
3. What elements of character are demanded by my vocation?
4. Does my vocation impose upon me any duty or obligation?

FOURTH YEAR

1. My avocation.
2. What is public spirit?
3. Why be honest in business?
4. Should business interfere with public welfare?
5. The right use of money.

It will be seen that the first-year themes are autobiographical or biographical in character; the second-year themes relate to the world's work; the third year to the choice of a vocation and the elements of success; the fourth year to the relation of the individual to society.

In regard to the composition work herein outlined, Mr. Davis further says: "These suggested themes are merely types to show the aim of the work. Teachers who are in sympathy with the plan will readily work out their own ideas. The pupils themselves will also suggest many profitable studies. The one thought of preparation for life and life's work through the chosen vocation should be the dominating purpose underlying the whole scheme."

In connection with this work there is considerable opportunity for the English teacher to direct the voluntary reading of the students to subjects of a vocational character. We have begun the collection of a vocational-guidance library and contemplate a considerable extension of the work within the present school year.

GIVING INDIVIDUAL ADVICE A FINAL STEP

If possible, the senior year should be the time for final consideration of the choice of a vocation on the part of those who are still undecided. In this connection private consultation between the student and some person selected to be his counselor will ·be of great value. This is about the most delicate and distinctly personal work that the counselor of high-school students is called upon to do.

It requires all the knowledge that can be obtained relating to the personal characteristics of the individual, to the characteristics necessary for success in particular vocations, to the probable needs for further vocational training, and to the opportunities for success and the conditions of employment in the vocations which the student has under consideration. The knowledge and guidance gained by the student through lectures and the composition work in the previous year should now have an immediate practical value. That there is need for this is shown by a perusal of the papers recently written by the members of the senior class of Woodward High School, 1913, on " My Plan for a Career." This class had received no such instruction and not more than one third of them had made a definite choice of a career. Those who had made a choice may be divided into three classes :

1. The student who has made a definite choice, has a good reason for his choice, and who has a fair chance of realizing success.

2. The student who has made a choice which may be good, but about which he manifestly needs counsel owing to a lack of knowledge of the vocation of his choice and owing to a lack of understanding of his own qualifications for the same. The largest number belong to this class.

3. The student who has manifestly made an unwise choice and needs to be told of it.

MODIFICATION OF COURSES OF STUDY

The third element of vocational guidance — the adaptation of school courses to the vocational needs of the pupils — began before vocational guidance as a movement was in evidence, but the introduction of vocational guidance as an organized part of the school program is producing a valuable reaction in the acceleration of the development of vocational education. In Cincinnati, as in several other cities, the elementary-school teachers are considering the differentiation of seventh- and eighth-grade work to meet the needs of pupils going into (1) industry, (2) commercial work, and (3) high school. A committee of the Cincinnati High School Teachers' Association is preparing a report on the adaptation of academic subjects to the vocational needs of the student, and the subject of vocational education is receiving more serious and more widespread consideration than ever before. As one indication of this we call attention to the fact that the business men of Cincinnati have become so interested in the movement that the Chamber of Commerce is preparing to begin an industrial and vocational survey of the city for the purpose of obtaining information on which to base a further extension of our system of vocational education and to assist in the work of vocational guidance.

As this paper relates for the most part to vocational guidance in the high school, let us in conclusion sum up the conditions which make for successful vocational guidance in a large high school:

1. The appointment of a director with time for supervision.

2. A school organization which will permit of the close personal contact of each pupil with at least one teacher of the right type.

3. The exercise of an intelligent and sympathetic helpfulness on the part of the teacher.

4. A logical analysis of the personal characteristics of each pupil.

5. An understanding of the relation of the school work to the life-career motive.

6. The adaptation of school work to the vocational needs of the community.

CONSTANT AND VARIABLE OCCUPATIONS AND THEIR BEARING ON PROBLEMS OF VOCATIONAL EDUCATION

By Leonard P. Ayres, Russell Sage Foundation

(From the Russell Sage Foundation publications)

It is commonly claimed that systems of vocational education should be primarily designed to train children to enter the local industries. But when we study industries and occupations in a number of localities, we find that some of the ways by which men and women earn their livings are common to all of them, while others engage many workers in some places and few or none in other places. From the viewpoint of vocational education this seems an important consideration. If there are certain occupations which offer opportunities for employment to a considerable number of workers everywhere, we ought to know which those occupations are. Such occupations which we find everywhere engaging the services of considerable and fairly constant proportions of the workers may perhaps properly be termed "constant occupations" and by contrast those which are not of this character may be termed "variable occupations."

In connection with other studies of problems affecting vocational education the Division of Education of the Sage Foundation has recently conducted a brief study to determine which occupations may fairly be termed constant occupations and the degree in which they are entitled to this classification. The study seems to demonstrate that the classification is a valid one. The constant occupations are in the main those which are necessary to maintain the many branches of that enlarged municipal housekeeping which must go on wherever large numbers of people live together in one place. For example, house painting must be carried

141

on in the city where the house is, while paint may be manufactured anywhere. Thus house painting is a constant occupation, but the manufacture of paint is a variable one. Similarly the baking of bread must be carried on by each community, but crackers can be baked somewhere else and brought to the city. Shoe repairing must be carried on in the city where the shoes are worn, but the shoe manufacturing of the entire country may be confined to a few cities. Similarly the occupations of the butcher and the baker are constant occupations because they are everywhere represented by considerable numbers of people; while the work of the candle-stick-maker is a variable occupation.

The inquiry conducted by the Foundation consisted of an analysis of the occupational data published by the Twelfth Census for cities of more than 50,000 population. A study was made of the data concerning the number of people engaged in each of 140 separate occupations in each of these cities. As a result it was found that there are 20 occupations which are constant in the sense that the number of men workers in each is everywhere at least equal to one for each thousand people in the population.

It was discovered, for example, that among men workers the occupation of being a barber is the most constant of all occupations. Throughout our cities there are almost invariably three barbers for each thousand people in the general population, and this remains true almost regardless of the varying social or commercial characteristics of the different cities. Thus if anyone had been conversant with this fact and had known ahead of time that Gary, Indiana, would be a city of 40,000 population, he might have predicted with almost certain accuracy that there would be in that city 120 barbers, not many more and not many less.

In conducting the study an arbitrary criterion was adopted whereby occupations were considered constant if they were represented in every city without exception by at least one worker for every thousand people in the population. For each of the 140 occupations ratios were worked out for each of the 78 cities, so as to find the city having the lowest proportion of all, the city midway between the lowest and the highest, and the city having the highest proportion of workers in each given occupation. This

TABLE 1. NUMBER OF MEN WORKERS AMONG EACH 10,000 OF POPULATION IN EACH OF 20 CONSTANT OCCUPATIONS IN CITIES HAVING RESPECTIVELY THE LOWEST, MEDIAN, AND HIGHEST PROPORTIONS OF WORKERS IN EACH OF THE OCCUPATIONS. THE CITIES ARE THOSE OF OVER 50,000 POPULATION IN 1900. THE OCCUPATIONS INCLUDE ALL IN WHICH THE NUMBER OF WORKERS IS IN EVERY CITY MORE THAN 10 FOR EACH 10,000 OF POPULATION, AND THEY ARE LISTED IN THE DESCENDING ORDER OF THE PROPORTION OF WORKERS IN THE AVERAGE (MEDIAN) CITIES

OCCUPATION	LOWEST CITY		MEDIAN CITY		HIGHEST CITY	
	City	Workers per 10,000 pop.	City	Workers per 10,000 pop.	City	Workers per 10,000 pop.
Laborers · · · ·	Lynn, Mass.	138	Syracuse, N.Y.	373	Seattle, Wsh.	801
...nts, retail ·	Scranton, Pa.	83	...lle, Ky.	146	Los ...s, Cal.	230
Clks · · ·	Lawrence, Ms.	56	C...n, N.J.	146	Washington, D.C.	413
Draymen · · ·	Harrisburg, Pa.	69	Bridgeport, Conn.	124	...s, Tenn.	236
Salesmen · ·	...n, Del.	57	Albany, N.Y.	118	Somerville, Ms.	234
...rs · ·	Cincinnati, O.	68	Paterson, N.J.	113	Seattle, Wash.	233
Steam R.R. men ·	New Bedford, Mass.	22	Salt Lake City, Utah	109	Harrisburg, Pa.	493
Machinists · ·	Duluth, Minn.	24	New ...d, Mass.	79	...h, N.J.	349
...rs · ·	...gh, Pa.	37	St. Paul, Minn.	66	...n, O.	99
Bookkeepers · ·	...ll, Mass.	20	Col...bus, O.	59	Omaha, Nb.	99
...rs · ·	Manchester, N.H.	12	Col...bus, O.	56	Seattle, Wash.	238
Engineers · ·	Atlanta, Ga.	25	New ...k, N.Y.	48	...l, Minn.	164
...rs · ·	Fall ...er, Ms.	14	...isville, Ky.	40	Washington, D.C.	102
Blcksmiths · ·	New ...k, N.Y.	21	Bridgeport, Ct.	36	...n, Del.	65
Masons · ·	San ...o, Cal.	15	Cleveland, O.	35	St. Jph, Mo.	63
Barbers · ·	Fall ...er, Ms.	21	Oakland, Cal.	29	...as Cty, Mo.	43
...rrs · ·	New ...a, La.	13	Lowell, Ms.	29	...ty, N.Y.	55
S...t R.R. men ·	...er, N.H.	12	Col...bus, O.	26	St. Louis, Mo.	59
Shoemakers · ·	Des ...s, Ia.	11	Springfield, Mass.	23	Lynn, Mass.	922
Bakers · · ·	...as Cty, Kan.	10	St. Joseph, Mo.	22	Hoboken, N.J.	37

TABLE 2. NUMBER OF WOMEN WORKERS AMONG EACH 10,000 OF POPULATION IN EACH OF SEVEN CONSTANT OCCUPATIONS IN CITIES OF OVER 50,000 POPULATION IN 1900

OCCUPATION	LOWEST CITY		MEDIAN CITY		HIGHEST CITY	
	City	Workers per 10,000 pop.	City	Workers per 10,000 pop.	City	Workers per 10,000 pop.
Servants	Fall River, Mass.	98	Detroit, Mich.	244	Memphis, Tenn.	519
Dressmakers	Kansas City, Kans.	40	Portland, Maine	87	Charleston, S.C.	175
Teachers	Kansas City, Kans.	29	Lynn, Mass.	47	Des Moines, Iowa.	83
Saleswomen	Manchester, N.H.	19	Harrisburg, Pa.	43	Boston, Mass.	92
Laundresses	Lawrence, Mass.	27	Chicago, Ill.	39	Savannah, Ga.	588
Nurses	Fall River, Mass.	13	Somerville, Mass.	26	Atlanta, Ga.	85
Housekeepers	San Antonio, Texas	10	Bridgeport, Conn.	21	Lowell, Mass.	46

process showed that there are 20 constant occupations among men workers as listed in Table 1.

In a similar way the analysis of the data for women wage earners showed that there are 7 constant occupations among women. These are shown in Table 2, in which all of the conditions are the same as stated in the title of Table 1.

It is almost certain that if these data were brought entirely up to date one occupation would be added to each of these lists. The one added to the list of constant occupations among the men would be that of the chauffeur, and the one added to the list of women's occupations would be the stenographer-typewriter. These occupations, together with the 20 occupations for men and 7 for women that have been listed, may be termed constant occupations in the sense that in every city, without exception, they engage the services of more than one person for each thousand people in the population. In the aggregate they include more than one half of the people engaged in gainful occupations in these cities.

FORTY-ONE LESS CONSTANT OCCUPATIONS

An inspection of the list of occupations that we have termed constant will suffice to show that many trades, businesses, and professions which are represented in every city have not been included. For example, such common occupations as those of the physician, clergyman, lawyer, journalist, and milliner have not been listed. This is because, while these and other occupations are everywhere represented, they are not invariably found in a large enough proportion so that their workers number at least one in every thousand of population. If, however, we reduce our lower limit so as to include all occupations employing more than one in 10,000 of the population in every city, we shall add some 31 occupations to our list among the men workers and 10 more for the women workers. These 31 less constant occupations among the men are listed in Table 3, in the descending order of the proportion of workers in the average (median) city. In a similar way the 10 less constant occupations among women are listed in Table 4.

TABLE 3. NUMBER OF MEN WORKERS AMONG EACH 10,000 OF POPULATION IN EACH OF 31 OCCUPATIONS IN CITIES HAVING RESPECTIVELY THE LOWEST, MEDIAN, AND HIGHEST PROPORTIONS OF WORKERS IN EACH OF THE OCCUPATIONS. THE CITIES ARE THOSE OF OVER 50,000 POPULATION IN 1900. THE OCCUPATIONS INCLUDE ALL IN WHICH THE NUMBER OF WORKERS IS IN EVERY CITY MORE THAN ONE BUT LESS THAN TEN FOR EACH 10,000 OF POPULATION AND THEY ARE LISTED IN THE DESCENDING ORDER OF THE PROPORTION OF WORKERS IN THE AVERAGE (MEDIAN) CITIES

Occupation	Lowest City — City	Workers per 10,000 pop.	Median City — City	Workers per 10,000 pop.	Highest City — City	Workers per 10,000 pop.
Iron …	San Antonio, Tex.	9	Rochester, N.Y.	51	…g, Pa.	389
…	Fall River, Mass.	4	Louisville, Ky.	29	…lis, …	99
…	Elizabeth, N.J.	9	Reading, Pa.	28	…, N.Y.	165
…	Portland, Maine	4	Evansville, Ind.	26	St. …h, Mo.	116
…	Lynn, Mass.	8	Somerville, Mass.	22	…	50
…	Hoboken, N.J.	8	Minneapolis, Minn.	22	Seattle, Wash.	58
Lawyers	Fall River, Mass.	4	Utica, N.Y.	20	…s Angeles, Cal.	69
Laborers (agri.)	Wilkes-Barre, Pa.	6	Utica, N.Y.	19	…re, Md.	50
…	Manchester, N.H.	5	New York, N.Y.	18	…n, D.C.	48
…	Fall River, Mass.	3	Utica, N.Y.	17	… Little, Ky.	47
…	Charleston, S.C.	7	Cincinnati, Ohio	16	…, Ms.	137
…	Fall River, Mass.	2	Buffalo, N.Y.	16	…s, Ms.	48
…	Hoboken, N.J.	5	Omaha, Neb.	14	…	29
…	Trenton, N.J.	6	Trenton, N.J.	13	Cambridge, Ms.	29
Merchants,	New Orleans, La.	3	Fall River, Mass.	13	…ds City, Mo.	41
…	Elizabeth, N.J.	2	Cambridge, Mass.	13	…ville, Ind.	46
… (gov.)	Troy, N.Y.	6	St. Paul, Minn.	12	Washington, D.C.	32
… (civil)	Kansas City, Kans.	5	Charleston, S.C.	11	Portland, Ore.	25
…	Manchester, N.H.	4	St. Paul, Minn.	11	Seattle, Wash.	45
…	Scranton, Pa.	3	Richmond, Va.	11	…d, Ge.	92
…	Trenton, N.J.	3	Des Moines, Iowa	11	…s Angeles, Cal.	51
…	Elizabeth, N.J.	3	Philadelphia, Pa.	11	Cambridge, Ms.	20
…	Jersey City, N.J.	6	Wilmington, Del.	10	Cambridge, Ms.	30
…	Duluth, Minn.	2	Springfield, Mass.	9	Baltimore, Md.	11
…	Manchester, N.H.	2	Peoria, Ill.	9	St. Joseph, Mo.	18
…	Memphis, Tenn.	2	Memphis, Tenn.	7	Portland, Ore.	29
Journalists	Providence, R.I.	3	Peoria, Ill.	6	Washington, D.C.	14
…	Milwaukee, Wis.	2	Nashville, Tenn.	5	San …	18
…	Jersey City, N.J.	2	Trenton, N.J.	5	Oakland, Cal.	16
Photographers	Charleston, S.C.	1	St. Louis, Mo.	5	…s …, Cal.	11
			Manchester, N.H.	5		

TABLE 4. NUMBER OF WOMEN WORKERS AMONG EACH 10,000 OF POPULATION IN EACH OF TEN OCCUPATIONS IN CITIES OF OVER 50,000 POPULATION IN 1900

Occupation	Lowest City		Median City		Highest City	
	City	Workers per 10,000 pop.	City	Workers per 10,000 pop.	City	Workers per 10,000 pop.
Stenographers	Fall River, Mass.	5	Louisville, Ky.	63	Omaha, Neb.	73
Seamstresses	Fall River, Mass.	4	Detroit, Mich.	32	St. Joseph, Mo.	200
Clerks	San Antonio, Tex.	7	Hoboken, N.J.	24	Washington, D.C.	168
Bookkeepers	San Antonio, Tex.	4	Newark, N.J.	22	Boston, Mass.	64
Milliners	San Antonio, Tex.	8	Columbus, Ohio	19	St. Joseph, Mo.	38
Boarding-house keepers	Jersey City, N.J.	5	Salt Lake City, Utah	15	Savannah, Ga.	39
Musicians	Paterson, N.J.	4	Harrisburg, Pa.	11	Los Angeles, Cal.	28
Merchants, retail	St. Joseph, Mo.	3	Milwaukee, Wis.	9	Wilmington, Del.	24
Laborers	Somerville, Mass.	2	Cambridge, Mass.	6	Kansas City, Kans.	36
Telephone operators	Fall River, Mass.	2	Cincinnati, Ohio	5	Grand Rapids, Mich.	16

OCCUPATIONS THAT ARE EQUALLY CONSTANT

If we consider merely the figures that have been presented in these four tables, we shall note some curious and interesting facts concerning the relative importance of different occupations, as shown by the number of workers employed. For example, it will be noted in Table 3 that hucksters and physicians are represented by precisely the same proportion of workers in the cities where they are least frequent, the median cities, and the cities in which they have the largest representation. The same thing is true of clergymen and sextons, for whom the data will be found in the same table.

CITIES HAVING LOWEST AND HIGHEST PROPORTIONS OF WORKERS IN MANY OCCUPATIONS

We have noted that in the main the occupations that we have listed even as "less constant" are those occupations which are necessary to carry on the different branches of that enlarged municipal housekeeping which must be conducted wherever large numbers of people live together in communities. In other words, these are the occupations that are necessary for the maintenance of community life. Nevertheless the proportion of workers engaged in any of these occupations is largely influenced by the social and economic characteristics of the city in which they work. Thus we find that in cities where the economic stress of earning a livelihood is great many occupations have few representatives, whereas in cities that are economically more fortunate these occupations are well represented. Among the seventy-eight cities for which conditions were studied, Fall River, Massachusetts, and Manchester, New Hampshire, best represent the conditions that exist where the strain of earning a living is severe, while conditions in cities of the opposite sort are represented by Los Angeles and Washington.

In each of the following twelve occupations the city of Fall River has a smaller proportion of workers than any other city of more than 50,000 population in the entire country:

Commercial travelers	Nurses	Printers
Tinsmiths	Seamstresses	Servants
Electricians	Lawyers	Stenographers
Barbers	Bank officials	Telephone operators

In a similar way we find the city of Manchester with a lower proportion of workers than any other of the cities in six occupations as follows:

Messengers	Civil engineers
Confectioners	Waiters
Street-railroad men	Saleswomen

In contrast with Fall River and Manchester are Los Angeles and Washington. In Los Angeles we find six occupations employing a larger proportion of the population than is found in any city elsewhere. These occupations are the following:

Physicians	Agricultural laborers
Bankers and brokers	Photographers
Retail merchants	Musicians

Six occupations are found more numerously represented in Washington than in any other city. They are the following:

Messengers	Journalists
Government officials	Men clerks and copyists
Printers	Women clerks

The nature of the occupations so numerously represented in Washington indicates that the cause is to be found rather in the fact that the general business of the city consists of work pertaining to the activities of national government than in any extreme economic condition such as is found in Fall River or in Los Angeles.

SIGNIFICANCE OF CONSTANT OCCUPATIONS FOR VOCATIONAL EDUCATION

The facts that have been reviewed do not constitute a guide for the formulation of courses of vocational education. They do, however, throw additional light on some characteristics of occupations employing in the aggregate a considerable majority of all the wage earners in our larger cities. All such information is useful in helping secure a better fact-basis for our thinking and acting with respect to the problems of vocational education and vocational guidance. These data are presented as a contribution toward that end.

SOME CONDITIONS AFFECTING PROBLEMS OF INDUSTRIAL EDUCATION IN SEVENTY-EIGHT AMERICAN SCHOOL SYSTEMS

By LEONARD P. AYRES, RUSSELL SAGE FOUNDATION

(From the Russell Sage Foundation publications)

During the closing weeks of the school year 1912–1913 the Division of Education of the Sage Foundation undertook an investigation in coöperation with the superintendents of schools of some 78 American city school systems. The study included all of the cities of between 25,000 and 200,000 population which were not so suburban in character as to be in reality subsidiaries of larger cities and in which the school authorities were able to coöperate. The object of the investigation was to gather facts concerning the boys in these cities who had reached the limit of the compulsory-attendance period and the fathers of these boys. The purpose of this study was to secure a more definite fact-basis for thought and action in the field of industrial education. Data for girls were not included for the reason that thirteen-year-old girls are in the main distributed through the same grades as are thirteen-year-old boys, and the occupations of their fathers are in the long run identical with those of the fathers of the boys. Hence the study would have produced the same results if data for girls had been included and would have entailed nearly twice as much work.

In each case the results were secured for all the thirteen-year-old boys in the public schools of these cities at the date when the facts were gathered. The aggregate number of cases studied was 22,027. The facsimile on page 151 shows the type of card used to gather the original data.

These cards were supplied by the Division of Education of the Foundation. The data were gathered by the local school authorities, and the results were tabulated by the Foundation. In cities having separate schools for white and colored children, the data were gathered for the white boys and their fathers only.

THIRTEEN-YEAR-OLD BOYS IN EVERY GRADE FROM KINDERGARTEN THROUGH HIGH SCHOOL

The first data secured were those showing the school grades of the boys. The tabulation of these figures brought to light two significant facts. The first was that these boys who have reached the limit of the compulsory-attendance period are scattered through the grades from the kindergarten to the senior year in the high school. Although they are all of the same age, they represent every stage of school advancement and are scattered through grades normally representing thirteen years of school progress — one of the kindergarten, eight of the grades, and four of the high school.

MIGRATION — OCCUPATION — PROGRESS STUDY, 1913

RECORD FOR BOYS 13 YEARS OLD (AT LAST BIRTHDAY)

NAME OF BOY_____GRADE_____

WAS HE BORN IN THIS CITY ?_____IN THIS STATE ?_____IN THE U.S. ?_____

WAS HIS FATHER (OR GUARDIAN) BORN IN THIS CITY?_____IN THIS STATE?_____IN U.S. ?_____

WHAT IS HIS FATHER'S (OR GUARDIAN'S) OCCUPATION?_____

_____

(STATE IF POSSIBLE BUSINESS AS WELL AS OCCUPATION, FOR EXAMPLE, "CONDUCTOR ON STREET RAILWAY," "CLERK IN SHOE STORE," "MACHINE OPERATOR IN BOX FACTORY.")

SCHOOL_____TEACHER_____

HALF OF THE BOYS IN SIXTH GRADE OR BELOW

The second significant fact is that one half of them are in the sixth grade or below. Since previous studies of retardation among school children have shown that the children who drop out of school earliest are largely those who are seriously retarded and find themselves in the lower grades at relatively advanced ages, these facts are most important. They indicate that large numbers of these boys may be expected to leave school soon and go to work with an educational preparation so inadequate that they cannot enter the ranks of industry with profit either to themselves or to the community. If we reduce our original figures showing the grade distributions of these 22,027 boys to relative figures indicating conditions among each 10,000 boys, we have the figures shown in Table 1.

TABLE 1. GRADE DISTRIBUTION OF BOYS. RELATIVE FIGURES SHOWING BOYS IN EACH GRADE AMONG EACH 10,000 BOYS

Grade	Boys in each Grade	Boys in and below each Grade
Special and kindergarten	92	92
1	25	117
2	76	193
3	316	509
4	944	1,453
5	1,814	3,267
6	2,493	5,760
7	2,507	8,267
8	1,441	9,708
High school		
I	243	9,951
II	28	9,979
III	15	9,994
IV	6	10,000
Total	10,000	10,000

These figures which show the grades of the children who have reached the limit of the compulsory-attendance period constitute one of the simplest and most significant measures of the efficiency of the city school system in carrying its children through the grades. If, upon reaching the age of thirteen years, a large proportion have nearly or quite completed the elementary course, we know the system is so administered as to insure the completion of a common-school education for a large proportion of the children. If, on the other hand, considerable numbers of children at the end of the

TABLE 2. PER CENT OF BOYS IN AND ABOVE THE SEVENTH GRADE

City	Per Cent of Boys in and above Seventh Grade	City	Per Cent of Boys in and above Seventh Grade
1. Brockton, Mass. . . .	77	40. Madison, Wis. . . .	44
2. Aurora, Ill. (East) . .	73	41. Canton, Ohio	44
3. Kalamazoo, Mich. . .	64	42. Superior, Wis. . . .	44
4. Waterloo, Iowa . . .	63	43. Columbus, Ohio . . .	44
5. Scranton, Pa.	62	44. Reading. Pa.	42
6. Decatur, Ill.	61	45. Harrisburg, Pa. . . .	42
7. Aurora, Ill. (West) . .	60	46. Williamsport, Pa. . .	41
8. Holyoke, Mass. . . .	59	47. Niagara Falls, N.Y. .	40
9. Racine, Wis.	57	48. Albany, N.Y.	40
10. Newport, R.I.	57	49. Hazelton, Pa.	39
11. Mobile, Ala.	57	50. South Bend, Ind. . .	38
12. Amsterdam, N.Y. . .	54	51. Troy, N.Y.	38
13. Rockford, Ill.	54	52. Hamilton, Ohio . . .	38
14. Davenport, Iowa . .· .	54	53. Atlanta, Ga.	37
15. Pittsfield, Mass. . . .	54	54. Pueblo, Colo. (Dist. 1)	36
16. Paterson, N.J.	53	55. Lincoln, Nebr. . . .	36
17. Saginaw, Mich. (West)	52	56. Chattanooga, Tenn. .	36
18. Lancaster, Pa.	52	57. Bay City, Mich. . . .	35
19. Dubuque, Iowa . . .	51	58. New Bedford, Mass. .	34
20. York, Pa.	51	59. Portland, Maine . . .	34
21. Evansville, Ind. . . .	51	60. Manchester, N.H. . .	34
22. Norwich, Conn. . . .	50	61. Fall River, Mass. . .	34
23. Auburn, N.Y.	50	62. Johnstown, Pa. . . .	33
24. Utica, N.Y.	49	63. Nashville, Tenn. . .	33
25. Springfield, Ohio . .	49	64. Youngstown, Ohio . .	33
26. Syracuse, N.Y. . . ͟	49	65. New Britain, Conn. .	33
27. San Diego, Cal. . . .	49	66. Danville, Ill.	32
28. Chicopee, Mass. . . .	49	67. Galveston, Tex. . . .	32
29. Tacoma, Wash. . . .	49	68. Trenton, N.J.	31
30. Meriden, Conn. . . .	49	69. Pueblo, Colo. (Dist. 20)	28
31. Elmira, N.Y.	47	70. Woonsocket, R.I. . .	24
32. Springfield, Mo. . . .	47	71. Richmond, Va. . . .	24
33. Saginaw, Mich. (East) .	46	72. Norfolk, Va.	21
34. Waterbury, Conn. . .	45	73. Lansing, Mich. . . .	21
35. Joliet, Ill.	45	74. Birmingham, Ala. . .	20
36. Council Bluffs, Iowa .	45	75. Columbia, S.C. . . .	18
37. Flint, Mich.	45	76. Charleston, S.C. . .	18
38. Binghamton, N.Y. . .	45	77. Bridgeport, Conn. . .	16
39. South Omaha, Nebr. .	44	78. Portsmouth, Va. . . .	12

compulsory-attendance period are still in the lower grades, we may be sure that most of them will drop out of school without staying to finish the course. According to the conventional standards for measuring retardation, the child who is thirteen years of age is considered to be in his normal grade if he is in the seventh grade or above and to be retarded if he is in the sixth grade or below. If then we compute for each of our 78 cities the per cent of thirteen-year-old boys who are in the seventh grade or above, we have an important index of one phase of the efficiency of their school systems. This comparison shows the results presented in Table 2.

WHAT SOME CITIES HAVE DONE, OTHERS MAY DO

Table 2 impressively illustrated the wide range of conditions in city school systems. At one extreme we have Aurora, Illinois, and Brockton, Massachusetts, with more than 70 per cent of their thirteen-year-old boys in the seventh grade or above, while at the other extreme we find Columbia (South Carolina), Charleston (South Carolina), Bridgeport (Connecticut), and Portsmouth (Virginia) with less than 20 per cent above the seventh grade. The contrast between the cities at the two extremes of the table shows that in Brockton almost 8 boys out of every 10 are within sight of completing the common-school course, while in Portsmouth scarcely more than 1 in 10 shows the same advance. From the point of view of industrial education these conditions are of the greatest importance.

They indicate that in many cities the problem of securing a reasonably complete elementary schooling for all the children is far more pressing than that of instituting specialized industrial training. They show, too, that since this has been accomplished by some of the cities, it may be hopefully undertaken by all.

ONLY ONE FATHER IN SIX NOW LIVES WHERE HE WAS BORN

The data giving the birthplaces of the boys and their fathers show that only about one father in six is now living in the city of his birth and that among the boys only a few more than one half are now living where they were born. These facts are significant because it is often urged that the schools should develop courses of industrial education that will directly prepare the children to enter the local industries. But if present conditions maintain in the future, the great majority of adults are not going to work in the same communities in which they received their schooling.

The facts as to the birthplaces of the boys and their fathers among the 22,027 cases studied are shown in Table 3.

TABLE 3. BIRTHPLACES OF BOYS AND BIRTHPLACES OF THEIR FATHERS

BIRTHPLACE	Boys		Fathers	
	Number	Per cent	Number	Per cent
Same city	12,699	58	3,601	16
Same state but not same city	4,233	19	5,349	24
Other state in United States	3,069	14	4,364	20
Foreign country	2,026	9	8,713	40
Total	22,027	100	22,027	100

This table shows that even among American-born fathers the number now living in the cities where they were born includes only about one in four, while among the boys the proportion is only about three in five. While this is true for the group as a whole, the figures for the different cities show wide variations. The ranges, together with the figures for each city, are shown in Table 4.

INDUSTRIES IN WHICH THE FATHERS WORK

The returns of the investigation showed for each of the fathers the nature of the trade or business in which he was engaged and also what kind of work he was doing in that trade or business. This made possible a double classification of the data, first by industries and second by occupations within the industries.

TABLE 4. PER CENT OF BOYS LIVING IN CITY OF BIRTH AND
PER CENT OF THEIR FATHERS LIVING IN CITY OF BIRTH

CITY	NUMBER OF CASES	PER CENT LIVING IN CITY OF BIRTH	
		Fathers	Boys
Albany, N.Y..	468	39	71
Amsterdam, N.Y.	129	13	64
Atlanta, Ga.	583	14	53
Auburn, N.Y.	101	24	62
Aurora, Ill. (East Side)	100	12	50
Aurora, Ill. (West Side)	57	19	53
Bay City, Mich..	203	13	61
Binghamton, N.Y..	182	14	63
Birmingham, Ala..	451	7	46
Bridgeport, Conn..	704	9	55
Brockton, Mass.	333	11	68
Canton, Ohio	291	16	47
Charleston, S.C.	115	51	71
Chattanooga, Tenn.	103	5	37
Chicopee, Mass.	166	8	51
Columbia, S.C.	58	7	35
Columbus, Ohio	876	15	50
Council Bluffs, Iowa	187	9	56
Danville, Ill.	184	11	39
Davenport, Iowa	280	25	60
Decatur, Ill.	162	13	41
Dubuque, Ill..	98	21	72
Elmira, N.Y.	167	12	56
Evansville, Ind..	277	24	63
Fall River, Mass.	801	13	72
Flint, Mich.	210	8	21
Galveston, Tex..	141	20	69
Hamilton, Ohio	176	20	59
Harrisburg, Pa..	402	19	55
Hazelton, Pa..	161	19	62
Holyoke, Mass..	299	7	61
Johnstown, Pa..	317	26	69
Joliet, Ill.	262	10	63
Kalamazoo, Mich..	184	9	44
Lancaster, Pa.	214	34	64
Lansing, Mich.	164	9	35
Lincoln, Nebr.	178	2	37
Madison, Wis.	140	14	49
Manchester, N.H.	277	11	62
Meriden, Conn..	194	16	70
Mobile, Ala.	198	29	50

TABLE 4. PER CENT OF BOYS LIVING IN CITY OF BIRTH
AND PER CENT OF THEIR FATHERS LIVING IN CITY OF
BIRTH (CONTINUED)

CITY	NUMBER OF CASES	PER CENT LIVING IN CITY OF BIRTH	
		Fathers	Boys
Nashville, Tenn.	396	22	63
New Bedford, Mass.	689	9	52
New Britain, Conn.	248	7	51
Newport, R.I.	145	30	79
Niagara Falls, N.Y.	161	12	47
Norfolk, Va.	296	18	54
Norwich, Conn.	141	21	52
Paterson, N.J.	897	17	68
Pittsfield, Mass.	242	12	42
Portland, Maine	307	17	61
Portsmouth, Va.	101	39	72
Pueblo, Colo. (Dist. 1)	118	1	25
Pueblo, Colo. (Dist. 20)	118	3	39
Racine, Wis.	234	13	60
Reading, Pa.	575	38	72
Richmond, Va.	461	32	71
Rockford, Ill.	315	10	64
San Diego, Cal.	291	1	13
Saginaw, Mich. (East Side)	183	15	60
Saginaw, Mich. (West Side)	130	24	63
Scranton, Pa.	659	23	78
South Bend, Ind.	265	9	47
South Omaha, Nebr.	151	—	48
Springfield, Mo.	94	9	43
Springfield, Ohio	344	13	46
Superior, Wis.	173	1	64
Syracuse, N.Y.	676	20	65
Tacoma, Wash.	415	—	35
Trenton, N.J.	484	19	65
Troy, N.Y.	276	33	78
Utica, N.Y.	427	16	57
Waterbury, Conn.	416	12	63
Waterloo, Iowa (West Side)	59	5	25
Williamsport, Pa.	181	24	65
Woonsocket, R.I.	199	7	50
York, Pa.	333	35	64
Youngstown, Ohio	234	10	48
Total	22,027	16	58

The industrial classification was the one adopted by the United States Census Bureau and included the following five main divisions :

I. Industries of Extraction—Agriculture, Forestry, Mining, etc.

II. Industries of Transformation— Building Trades, Manufacturing, etc.

III. Industries of Transportation and Communication — Railroads, Telegraph, etc.

IV. Industries of Trade — Wholesale and Retail Trade, Real Estate, etc.

V. Service — Government, Professional, Domestic, Personal, etc.

The tabulations showed that the fathers were distributed in these five main industrial divisions as shown in Table 5.

TABLE 5. INDUSTRIAL DISTRIBUTION OF FATHERS

INDUSTRIAL GROUP	FATHERS	
	Number	Per cent
Extraction	754	3.5
Transformation	10,934	51.6
Transportation	2,774	13.1
Trade	4,129	19.5
Service	2,597	12.3
Total . . . . , ...	21,188	100.0
Retired, not stated, or none	839	
Grand total	22,027	

ONLY HALF OF THE FATHERS WORK IN BUILDING TRADES OR MANUFACTURING

One fact, shown in Table 5, is that only about one half of these men are found in the Industries of Transformation which include the building trades and all classes of manufacturing. This is important, because plans for inaugurating systems of vocational education are commonly based on the proposition that a large majority of the young people in our city schools will find their life work in these industries.

Another important fact is that the distribution of these men in these industrial groups is different from the corresponding figures for male workers in the country as a whole or in all American cities. The chief reason for this is that we are here dealing with adult men of sufficient maturity and stability of position in their communities to be fathers of thirteen-year-old boys in the public schools. The group includes no very young or very old men, few recent immigrants, few floaters, and few chronic ne'er-do-wells. It is because of these characteristics that it furnishes facts which seem of unusual significance in the attempt to foresee what sorts of life work the young people now in city schools may be expected to go into.

The variations between the different cities in the proportions of the men engaged in the five industrial classes are so great that each city is characteristically different from all the rest and no one shows even approximately the conditions indicated by the averages for the entire group. The degree to which this is true may be judged from the figures in Table 6. Since there are 78 cities, the fortieth has in each case been taken as the middle one.

TABLE 6. PER CENT OF FATHERS IN EACH INDUSTRIAL GROUP IN CITIES HAVING RESPECTIVELy THE LOWEST, MIDDLE, AND HIGHEST PER CENTS IN EACH GROUP

INDUSTRIAL GROUP	LOWEST		MIDDLE		HIGHEST	
	City	Per cent of fathers in each group	City	Per cent of fathers in each group	City	Per cent of fathers in each group
Extraction . .	Harrisburg	—	Rockford	3	Hazelton	34
Transformation	Galveston	20	Aurora	51	Chicopee	78
Transportation .	New Britain	4	Youngstown	12	Harrisburg	33
Trade	Chicopee	6	Trenton	18	Columbia	45
Service . . .	Chicopee	4	Danville	11	Newport	23

Table 7 gives the percentages of fathers in each industrial group for all of the 78 cities. Where these percentages do not add to 100 per cent, it is because the figures for the group entitled "Retired, not stated, or none," have been omitted.

TABLE 7. PER CENT OF FATHERS IN EACH INDUSTRIAL GROUP

City	Per Cent of Fathers in				
	Extraction	Transformation	Transportation	Trade	Service
Albany, N.Y.	1	38	18	21	16
Amsterdam, N.Y.	5	63	5	16	8
Atlanta, Ga.	1	32	18	32	16
Auburn, N.Y.	3	52	11	20	11
Aurora, Ill. (East Side)	2	63	10	12	8
Aurora, Ill. (West Side)	5	51	9	19	9
Bay City, Mich.	14	42	16	14	12
Binghamton, N.Y.	3	49	19	19	9
Birmingham, Ala.	3	34	20	31	10
Bridgeport, Conn.	2	61	7	18	11
Brockton, Mass.	2	63	7	14	12
Canton, Ohio	2	60	9	17	8
Charleston, S.C.	4	22	23	41	9
Chattanooga, Tenn.	2	32	14	33	17
Chicopee, Mass.	2	78	8	6	4
Columbia, S.C.	3	26	12	45	14
Columbus, Ohio	1	46	15	20	13
Council Bluffs, Iowa	2	36	23	19	14
Danville, Ill.	12	34	18	16	11
Davenport, Iowa	3	42	12	20	19
Decatur, Ill.	10	41	14	17	16
Dubuque, Iowa	7	46	11	20	10
Elmira, N.Y.	5	39	19	21	13
Evansville, Ind.	8	46	9	22	13
Fall River, Mass.	2	59	8	17	12
Flint, Mich.	3	58	14	15	8
Galveston, Tex.	2	20	20	31	22
Hamilton, Ohio	3	55	6	17	12
Harrisburg, Pa.	—	34	33	17	13
Hazelton, Pa.	34	22	13	18	6
Holyoke, Mass.	1	66	6	13	12
Johnstown, Pa.	5	56	10	14	9
Joliet, Ill.	3	53	21	12	9
Kalamazoo, Mich.	5	55	11	17	8
Lancaster, Pa.	2	53	12	22	9
Lansing, Mich.	4	63	7	17	8
Lincoln, Nebr.	1	25	19	31	21
Madison, Wis.	1	43	14	20	19
Manchester, N.H.	3	57	9	17	13
Meriden, Conn.	7	62	7	13	8

TABLE 7. PER CENT OF FATHERS IN EACH INDUSTRIAL
GROUP (CONTINUED)

CITY	Per Cent of Fathers in				
	Extraction	Transformation	Transportation	Trade	Service
Mobile, Ala.	3	26	23	31	13
Nashville, Tenn.	1	37	17	26	15
New Bedford, Mass.	4	61	5	14	13
New Britain, Conn.	3	67	4	19	6
Newport, R.I.	11	33	11	19	23
Niagara Falls, N.Y.	1	61	9	11	14
Norfolk, Va.	2	31	17	33	14
Norwich, Conn.	6	55	9	19	11
Paterson, N.J.	—	66	8	14	10
Pittsfield, Mass.	6	58	8	16	8
Portland, Maine	1	38	18	25	12
Portsmouth, Va.	—	56	8	27	10
Pueblo, Colo. (Dist. 1)	4	37	18	23	16
Pueblo, Colo. (Dist. 20)	3	54	21	11	9
Racine, Wis.	2	65	11	12	7
Reading, Pa.	1	57	14	14	10
Richmond, Va.	1	45	18	21	13
Rockford, Ill.	3	71	8	12	6
San Diego, Cal.	6	38	9	21	21
Saginaw, Mich. (East Side) . . .	7	43	15	22	9
Saginaw, Mich. (West Side) . . .	14	48	15	15	7
Scranton, Pa.	25	28	13	17	11
South Bend, Ind.	1	58	13	18	10
South Omaha, Nebr.	—	47	11	13	9
Springfield, Mo.	5	37	14	27	16
Springfield, Ohio	3	51	7	14	13
Superior, Wis.	2	34	17	30	13
Syracuse, N.Y.	1	52	11	21	13
Tacoma, Wash.	3	45	16	18	13
Trenton, N.J.	1	58	11	18	11
Troy, N.Y.	2	49	12	20	14
Utica, N.Y.	2	50	12	20	10
Waterbury, Conn.	1	64	8	12	12
Waterloo, Iowa (West Side) . . .	3	49	12	25	7
Williamsport, Pa.	2	51	18	13	10
Woonsocket, R.I.	1	61	8	15	13
York, Pa.	1	55	13	15	10
Youngstown, Ohio.	—	62	12	13	10

OCCUPATIONS OF FATHERS

The occupational classification of these workers was made under six heads, of which the first three relate to occupations primarily manual in nature, while the remaining three groups are primarily mental.

TABLE 8. OCCUPATIONAL DISTRIBUTION OF FATHERS

OCCUPATIONAL GROUP	FATHERS	
	Number	Per cent
Manual		
Unskilled laborers	785	3.7
Semiskilled laborers and machine operatives	4,621	21.8
Artisans and foremen	8,490	40.1
Total manual	13,896	65.6
Mental		
Clerks and salesmen	1,883	8.9
Managers, superintendents, and proprietors	4,562	21.6
Professional and financial workers	847	3.9
Total mental	7,292	34.4
Total manual and mental	21,188	100.0
Retired, not stated, or none	839	
Grand total	22,027	

ONE THIRD IN HEAD WORK; TWO THIRDS IN HAND WORK

Three significant facts are brought to light by the figures of Table 5. The first is that more of these men are in professional work than there are engaged in unskilled labor. The second is that the group of managers, superintendents, and proprietors is practically as large as that made up of semiskilled laborers. The third is that the mental workers constitute more than one third of all the workers.

In the occupational distribution, as in the industrial one, we find the greatest variation in the conditions in the different cities. Table 9 shows the range in percentages and here again the fortieth city in the list is in each case taken as the middle city.

TABLE 9. PER CENT OF FATHERS IN EACH OCCUPATIONAL
GROUP IN CITIES HAVING RESPECTIVELY THE LOWEST,
MIDDLE, AND HIGHEST PER CENTS IN EACH GROUP

OCCUPATIONAL GROUP	LOWEST		MIDDLE		HIGHEST	
	City	Per cent of fathers in each group	City	Per cent of fathers in each group	City	Per cent of fathers in each group
Manual						
Unskilled . .	Charleston	—	Lancaster	6	S. Omaha	26
Semiskilled .	Mobile	3	Albany	18	Brockton	51
Artisans and foremen .	Columbia	14	New Britain	40	Meriden	56
Mental						
Clerks . . .	Chicopee	2	Pueblo	9	Columbia	28
Managers and proprietors	Chicopee	7	Aurora	21	Charleston	45
Professional .	Trenton	1	Lancaster	4	Springfield, Mo.	10

Table 10 gives the percentages of fathers in each occupation group for each of the 78 cities. As before, where the figures for any city do not add to 100 per cent, it is because data for the "retired, not stated, or none" group have been omitted.

MORE FOREIGN BORN IN MANUAL WORK; MORE AMERICANS IN MENTAL WORK

The records showed that 40 per cent of the fathers were born in foreign countries. A tabulation of their occupational records was made to see how they differed from those of the American-born fathers. The results are presented in Table 11, which shows the number in each occupational group among each 1000 fathers among the foreign and American born.

The results show that the foreign born are relatively more numerous among the manual workers, and the Americans among the mental ones. Nevertheless, the disproportion is not so great as many would perhaps have expected.

TABLE 10. PER CENT OF FATHERS IN EACH OCCUPATIONAL GROUP

| | Per Cent of Fathers in | | | | | |
| | Manual occupation | | | Mental occupation | | |
City	Unskilled laborers	Semi-skilled laborers and machine operatives	Artisans and foremen	Clerks and salesmen	Managers, superintendents, and proprietors	Professional and financial workers
Albany, N.Y.	6	18	39	11	22	3
Amsterdam, N.Y.	6	34	30	8	17	3
Atlanta, Ga.	—	9	33	14	36	7
Auburn, N.Y.	4	11	46	6	26	6
Aurora, Ill. (East Side)	3	12	54	6	16	8
Aurora, Ill. (West Side)	5	11	46	12	21	2
Bay City, Mich.	6	25	41	8	15	5
Binghamton, N.Y.	5	19	40	12	20	4
Birmingham, Ala.	2	5	39	15	32	6
Bridgeport, Ct.	4	27	41	9	18	2
Brockton, Mass.	3	51	22	5	17	2
Canton, Ohio	6	23	41	7	20	3
Charleston, S.C.	—	9	23	19	45	4
Chattanooga, Tenn.	3	6	32	17	35	8
Chicopee, Mass.	6	29	54	2	7	2
Columbia, S.C.	2	14	14	28	36	7
Columbus, Ohio	8	16	37	11	22	5
Council Bluffs, Iowa	5	20	40	8	24	2
Danville, Ill.	10	12	47	8	19	5
Davenport, Iowa	4	17	36	11	26	3
Decatur, Ill.	4	9	48	9	22	6
Dubuque, Iowa	4	21	27	5	37	6
Elmira, N.Y.	6	15	41	13	21	5
Evansville, Ind.	4	13	47	9	21	5
Fall River, Mass.	7	46	22	6	15	2
Flint, Mich.	3	24	47	7	16	3
Galveston, Tex.	8	12	28	20	26	5
Hamilton, Ohio	10	12	43	6	23	4
Harrisburg, Pa.	6	22	40	12	17	3
Hazelton, Pa.	7	10	52	8	21	2
Holyoke, Mass.	3	35	35	9	14	4
Johnstown, Pa.	15	18	40	7	16	4
Joliet, Ill.	7	24	45	5	16	3
Kalamazoo, Mich.	7	23	32	11	23	3
Lancaster, Pa.	6	21	37	10	23	4
Lansing, Mich.	5	25	34	6	26	4
Lincoln, Nebr.	5	11	34	20	23	7
Madison, Wis.	6	16	41	9	20	8
Manchester, N.H.	4	36	32	9	14	5
Meriden, Conn.	3	17	56	5	17	2

TABLE 10. PER CENT OF FATHERS IN EACH OCCUPATIONAL
GROUP (CONTINUED)

CITY	PER CENT OF FATHERS IN					
	Manual occupation			Mental occupation		
	Unskilled laborers	Semi-skilled laborers and machine oper-atives	Artisans and foremen	Clerks and salesmen	Managers, superin-tendents, and pro-prietors	Profes-sional and financial workers
Mobile, Ala.	—	3	29	16	40	9
Nashville, Tenn.	1	10	38	18	25	9
New Bedford, Mass. . .	5	45	26	6	12	3
New Britain, Conn. . .	5	27	40	6	19	3
Newport, R.I.	6	12	38	4	33	8
Niagara Falls, N.Y. . . .	11	26	39	5	16	4
Norfolk, Va.	1	6	36	14	36	5
Norwich, Conn.	1	23	39	6	26	5
Paterson, N.J.	3	39	31	6	18	3
Pittsfield, Mass.	7	24	36	7	23	3
Portland, Maine	5	11	41	13	26	4
Portsmouth, Va.	1	11	52	8	26	3
Pueblo, Colo. (Dist. 1). .	6	14	38	9	27	6
Pueblo, Colo. (Dist. 20) .	14	23	40	4	16	2
Racine, Wis.	6	22	44	5	19	3
Reading, Pa.	9	17	47	7	17	2
Richmond, Va.	3	8	45	11	27	5
Rockford, Ill.	3	16	54	8	16	3
San Diego, Cal.	5	8	33	10	32	9
Saginaw, Mich. (East) . .	4	19	43	20	19	1
Saginaw, Mich. (West) .	5	29	38	10	16	2
Scranton, Pa.	9	16	46	9	16	3
South Bend, Ind.	3	23	40	9	22	3
South Omaha, Nebr. . .	26	13	35	5	17	3
Springfield, Mo.	3	10	40	14	23	10
Springfield, Ohio	17	9	43	6	20	5
Superior, Wis.	13	14	38	7	25	2
Syracuse, N.Y.	8	19	42	11	16	4
Tacoma, Wash.	7	15	41	8	24	4
Trenton, N.J.	7	27	37	7	21	1
Troy, N.Y.	7	24	38	10	20	2
Utica, N.Y.	11	21	34	7	24	3
Waterbury, Conn. . . .	4	19	55	8	14	1
Waterloo, Iowa (West) .	9	10	32	12	29	9
Williamsport, Pa. . . .	11	24	37	8	17	4
Woonsocket, R.I. . . .	7	40	30	7	15	1
York, Pa.	8	15	48	9	15	4
Youngstown, Ohio . . .	9	18	47	9	13	4

TABLE 11. OCCUPATIONAL DISTRIBUTION OF AMERICAN- AND
FOREIGN-BORN FATHERS. RELATIVE FIGURES PER 1000 IN
EACH NATIVITY GROUP   •

OCCUPATIONAL GROUP	FATHERS	
	American	Foreign
Manual		
Unskilled laborers	41	88
Semiskilled laborers and machine operatives	169	278
Artisans and foremen	398	374
Total manual	608	740
Mental		
Clerks and salesmen	113	60
Managers, superintendents, and proprietors	228	180
Professional and financial workers	51	20
Total mental	392	260
Grand total	1000	1000

OCCUPATIONS IN DIFFERENT INDUSTRIES

The original returns showed the occupations of the fathers in
many hundreds of industries, and in order to tabulate them the
data were consolidated under some 35 industrial groupings, following the plan adopted by the office of the United States Census.
The distribution of the men by occupational classes in each of
these industrial groups is shown in Table 12, which gives the original data in some detail, and again in Table 13, in which the same
facts are presented in relative figures on the basis of a total of
10,000 after omitting those classified as "retired, not stated, or
none." In these tables the first three columns refer to the occupations we have termed manual, while the next three are those we
have called mental. In the list of 35 industrial groupings those
numbered from 1 to 6 are industries of extraction, numbers 7 to
20 are those of transformation, numbers 21 to 26 are industries
of transportation, and numbers 27 to 31 are those of trade.
Those numbered from 32 to 35 come under the general caption
of service.

TABLE 12. INDUSTRIAL AND OCCUPATIONAL DISTRIBUTION
OF 22,027 FATHERS

	Fathers in							
	Manual occupations			Mental occupations			Retired, not stated, or none	
Industrial Group	Unskilled laborers	Semiskilled machine operatives	Artisans and foremen	Clerks and salesmen	Managers, superintendents, and proprietors	Professional and financial workers		Total
1. Agriculture	38	13	7	—	286	1	15	360
2. Forestry	—	—	—	—	—	2	—	2
3. Animal husbandry . .	1	15	12	—	7	1	—	36.
4. Mining	20	11	297	6	15	2	—	351
5. Quarrying	2	4	3	—	2	—	—	11
6. Salt, oil, and natural gas	4	1	—	—	4	—	—	9
7. Building trades	23	29	1807	2	368	24	1	2254
8. Chemicals and allied products	12	16	21	4	21	3	—	77
9. Clay, glass, and stone .	26	77	141	4	30	1	—	279
10. Clothing	1	66	272	4	41	2	—	386
11. Food and kindred products	14	59	272	12	47	—	—	404
12. Iron and steel and their products	166	459	1928	47	125	8	1	2734
13. Leather and its finished products	2	169	179	6	21	—	—	377
14. Liquors and beverages .	10	34	41	6	18	—	—	109
15. Lumber and its remanufacture	17	123	250	14	46	9	1	460
16. Metals and metal products other than iron and steel	7	68	203	3	18	3	—	302
17. Paper	9	88	27	8	14	—	—	146
18. Printing and bookbinding	—	7	158	19	33	25	—	242
19. Textiles	28	1042	159	25	48	4	—	1306
20. Miscellaneous industries	63	394	1121	66	180	37	—	1861
21. Water transportation .	10	28	47	5	26	—	—	116
22. Road, street, and bridge transportation . . .	40	898	153	12	95	9	—	1207
23. Transportation by railroad	71	294	612	118	94	2	—	1191

TABLE 12. INDUSTRIAL AND OCCUPATIONAL DISTRIBUTION
OF 22,027 FATHERS (CONTINUED)

| INDUSTRIAL GROUP | FATHERS IN | | | | | | | TOTAL |
| | Manual occupations | | | Mental occupations | | | Retired, not stated, or none | |
	Unskilled laborers	Semiskilled laborers and machine operatives	Artisans and foremen	Clerks and salesmen	Managers, superintendents, and proprietors	Professional and financial workers		
24. Express companies . .	—	5	4	18	1	—	—	28
25. Post, telegraph, and telephone	2	53	39	109	29	—	—	232
26. Other persons in transportation	—	—	—	—	—	—	—	—
27. Banking and brokerage	1	4	1	25	56	13	—	100
28. Insurance and real estate	—	—	1	12	353	1	—	367
29. Wholesale trade . . .	22	30	31	481	226	5	1	796
30. Retail trade	24	26	42	766	1941	13	5	2817
31. Other persons in trade .	11	3	6	13	19	3	—	55
32. Public administration .	137	88	81	51	46	56	—	459
33. Public defense and maintenance of law and order	1	219	218	19	41	22	—	520
34. Professional service . .	—	6	6	6	15	596	2	631
35. Domestic and personal service	23	292	351	22	296	5	1	990
36. Retired, not stated, or none	520	9	9	126	10	1	137	812
Total.	1305	4630	8499	2009	4572	848	164	22,027

MORE WORKERS IN RETAIL TRADE THAN IN ANY OTHER GROUP

An inspection of the totals in Table 13 shows that a large proportion of the workers are found in a small number of industrial groups. If we rank the industrial groups according to the number of workers in each, we shall find that two industrial groups include more than one fourth of all these men, six include more than one half of them, and fourteen include more than three fourths.

TABLE 13. INDUSTRIAL AND OCCUPATIONAL DISTRIBUTION OF 21,188 FATHERS.
RELATIVE FIGURES ON THE BASIS OF 10,000 AFTER OMITTING THOSE CLASSI-
FIED AS "RETIRED, NOT STATED, OR NONE"

| INDUSTRIAL GROUP | FATHERS IN | | | | | | TOTAL |
| | Manual occupations | | | Mental occupations | | | |
	Unskilled laborers	Semiskilled laborers and machine operatives	Artisans and foremen	Clerks and salesmen	Managers, superintendents, and proprietors	Professional and financial workers	
1. Agriculture	18	6	4	—	135	—	163
2. Forestry	—	—	—	—	—	—	—
3. Animal husbandry	—	7	6	·—	4	—	17
4. Mining	10	5	140	3	7	1	166
5. Quarrying	1	2	1	—	1	—	5
6. Salt, oil, and natural gas	2	—	—	—	2	—	4
7. Building trades	11	14	853	1	174	11	1064
8. Chemicals and allied products	5	8	10	2	10	1	36
9. Clay, glass, and stone	12	37	67	2	14	—	132
10. Clothing	—	31	128	2	20	1	182
11. Food and kindred products	7	28	128	6	22	—	191
12. Iron and steel and their products	78	217	910	22	59	4	1290
13. Leather and its finished products	1	80	84	3	10	—	178
14. Liquors and beverages	5	16	20	3	8	—	52
15. Lumber and its remanufacture	8	58	118	7	22	4	217
16. Metals and metal products other than iron and steel	4	32	96	1	9	1	143
17. Paper	4	41	13	4	7	—	69
18. Printing and bookbinding	—	3	74	9	16	12	114
19. Textiles	13	491	75	12	23	2	616
20. Miscellaneous industries	30	186	529	31	85	17	878
21. Water transportation	5	13	22	2	12	—	54
22. Road, street, and bridge transportation	19	424	72	6	45	4	570
23. Transportation by railroad	34	139	289	56	44	1	563
24. Express companies	—	2	2	9	—	—	13
25. Post, telegraph, and telephone	1	25	18	51	14	—	109
26. Other persons in transportation	—	—	—	—	—	—	—
27. Banking and brokerage	—	2	—	12	27	6	47
28. Insurance and real estate	—	—	—	6	167	—	173
29. Wholesale trade	11	14	15	227	107	2	376
30. Retail trade	11	12	20	362	916	6	1327
31. Other persons in trade	5	1	3	6	9	1	25
32. Public administration	65	42	38	24	22	26	217
33. Public defense and maintenance of law and order	—	104	103	9	19	10	245
34. Professional service	—	3	3	3	7	281	297
35. Domestic and personal service	11	138	166	10	140	2	467
Total	371	2181	4007	891	2157	393	10,000

These facts are shown in Table 14, from which the group entitled "Miscellaneous Industries" has been omitted on account of its indefinite character.

TABLE 14. FOURTEEN INDUSTRIAL GROUPS RANKED IN ORDER OF NUMBER OF FATHERS IN EACH. RELATIVE FIGURES ON BASIS OF 10,000. DERIVED FROM TABLE 13

INDUSTRIAL GROUP	FATHERS IN EACH GROUP	FATHERS IN EACH GROUP AND PRECEDING GROUPS
1. Retail trade	1327	1327
2. Iron and steel and their products	1290	2617
3. Building trades	1064	3681
4. Textiles	616	4297
5. Road, street, and bridge transportation	570	4867
6. Transportation by railroad	563	5430
7. Domestic and personal service	467	5897
8. Wholesale trade	376	6273
9. Professional service	297	6570
10. Public defense and maintenance of law and order .	245	6815
11. Lumber and its manufacture	217	7032
12. Public administration	217	7249
13. Food and kindred products	191	7440
14. Clothing	182	7622

By examining the totals in the last column of Table 14, it will be noted that the first two industries include 2617 out of each 10,000 fathers, or more than one quarter of them, the first six 5430, or more than half of them, and the whole fourteen industries 7622, or more than three fourths of them.

SUMMARY

1. The investigation included 22,027 thirteen-year-old boys in 78 city school systems and the fathers of the boys.

2. The boys were scattered through all the grades of the course from the kindergarten to the last year in the high school.

3. One half of the boys were in the sixth grade or below. They need a common-school education more than they need specialized industrial training.

4. In some cities nearly eight boys in ten were in the seventh grade or above, while in others only about one boy in ten was in the seventh grade or above. What some cities have accomplished, others may hopefully strive for.

5. Only one father in six was born in the city where he now lives, and only a few more than one half of the boys were born where they now live. This has an important bearing on the proposition that the schools should shape their courses with the predominant aim of preparing the children to enter the local industries.

6. Only about one half of the fathers are engaged in industries of the building trades and manufacturing.

7. More of the fathers are engaged in the professions than are in unskilled labor.

8. Mental workers constitute more than one third of all the workers. This fact, and the two preceding ones, indicate the inaccuracy of the common generalization, to the effect that only one child in ten in our public schools will find his life work in an intellectual occupation while the other nine are destined to do hand work.

9. Foreign-born fathers are relatively more numerous among the manual workers and Americans among the mental workers, but the disproportion is not very great.

10. A large proportion of the workers are engaged in a small number of industrial groups. The most numerous single group is retail trade, and in this group more than one half are proprietors.

THE VOCATIONAL INTERESTS, STUDY HABITS, AND AMUSEMENTS OF THE PUPILS IN CERTAIN HIGH SCHOOLS IN IOWA

By Irving King, State University of Iowa

(From *The School Review*, March, 1914)

Various studies have recently been made of different character-istics of the young people attending public high schools. One of the best is the well-known study of j. K. Van Denburg, which pre-sents various characteristics of 1000 pupils who entered the New York high schools at the same time, with a view to discovering the sort of pupils who are eliminated. From a somewhat different point of view, V. L. Mangun recently studied the character of pupils in attendance upon the short courses provided by some of the Minnesota high schools.[1]

The present writer has recently collected some data regarding Iowa high-school pupils. In part, the information is similar to Van Denburg's and in part goes farther. Moreover, it is not con-fined to entering classes but includes practically the entire student body of the four schools studied. No attempt, however, has been made thus far to connect this information with the subsequent records of these pupils.

The first query made by the writer was as to the occupations of the fathers of these Iowa high-school pupils. The following Table (I) presents the information obtained, together with Van Denburg's figures for the 1000 New York high-school pupils.

The figures for these two widely separated localities present many striking similarities, — for example, in the case of trade and manufacture and artisans, — and in most cases the differences which are noted may be easily explained. It is not surprising, for instance,

---

[1] "A Study of the Eliminated," *Winona Normal Bulletin*, November, 1913.

to find the agricultural class well represented in the Iowa schools. Some of the other differences, such as those seen in the number of city and federal employees, those doing personal service, and those in the printing trades, suggest that the distribution of men in the various vocations is slightly different in these smaller Western cities from that in New York. But the fact that the children of men in professional work are found more than two and one half times as frequently in these schools as in New York indicates that the schools in this section are even more democratic than in the East. The professional classes, quite as much as the humbler types of workers, see in the public high school a suitable place for the education of their children.

TABLE I. THE FATHERS' VOCATIONS OF 1112 PUPILS IN THE IOWA CITY, OTTUMWA, AND DUBUQUE HIGH SCHOOLS, 1913, COMPARED WITH THOSE OF 1000 HIGH-SCHOOL PUPILS IN NEW YORK CITY

	Iowa	New York		Iowa	New York
Agriculture	151	—	Clerical	30	52
Trade and manufacturing .	268	227	City and federal employees	40	61
Artisans	156	150	Personal service	18	41
Middlemen and office work-			Printing trades	10	35
ers	92	106	Unclassified	51	36
Transportation	75	46	Blank	63	89
Professional	93	36	Retired	17	13
Semiprofessional	19	36	Dead	40	76

The high-school pupils' vocational intentions throw much interesting light upon the pupils themselves and probably have much to do, as Van Denburg found, with their persistence and success in their high-school work. The variety of occupations mentioned reveals to some extent the breadth of outlook of these high-school youths. Van Denburg found forty different types of work mentioned by boys and twenty-one by the girls. The 1109 pupils in Iowa mention an even larger number of vocations. This may be largely due to the fact that the answers were taken from the upper-class pupils as well as from those just entering. It may also indicate a slightly wider range of outlook among the boys and girls of central parts of the country.

The following table (II) presents the data from New York and from Iowa in parallel columns for comparison. The larger number of different occupations mentioned by the Iowa children and the smaller percentage who have no plans as to their future work are the significant points to note from this table.

TABLE II. VOCATIONAL CHOICES OF 1109 PUPILS IN THE THREE IOWA HIGH SCHOOLS

	IOWA	NEW YORK
Different occupations chosen by all	71	—
Different occupations chosen by boys	54	40
Different occupations chosen by girls	30	21
Different occupations chosen by 2 per cent or more of the boys	15	9
Different occupations chosen by 2 per cent or more of the girls	10	7
Undecided or blank, boys	23 per cent	41 per cent
Undecided or blank, girls	23 per cent	51 per cent

Table III enumerates the different vocations chosen by five or more pupils of either sex with numbers of New York pupils who also chose these vocations. Here again the general tendency is the same. Teaching stands easily first with the girls in both the East and the West, and engineering is likewise the favorite with the boys. Van Denburg accounts for the large choice of engineering in New York by the striking examples of great engineering enterprises which the boys see on every hand — the great bridges, tunnels, subways, railway terminals, and lofty steel buildings. But an even larger number of Iowa boys have an interest in engineering — boys who can at best only have read about these modern engineering wonders. Does this not indicate that there is something inherently attractive to boy-nature in the engineering pursuits? Among the vocations mentioned by considerable numbers of Iowa girls but apparently not at all by New York girls are nursing and domestic science. Law and business are apparently about equally attractive to both groups of boys; but the Iowa boys far exceed those of New York in their interest in medicine, and naturally also in farming.

TABLE III. VOCATIONS CHOSEN BY FIVE OR MORE PUPILS OF EITHER SEX, IN THREE LARGER IOWA HIGH SCHOOLS

	Iowa		New York	
	Boys	Girls	Boys	Girls
Teaching	13	261	11	168
Engineering	94	—	78	—
Stenography and bookkeeping	16	85	4	55
Law	32	—	24	2
Farming	34	—	1	—
Nursing	—	24	—	—
Medicine	30	3	7	1
Business	33	4	36	4
Music	—	23	1	19
Dentistry	8	—	2	—
Pharmacy	8	—	3	1
Salesman	16	—	2	—
Mechanic	8	—	—	—
Army or navy	8	—	3	—
Labor	5	—	—	—
Domestic science	—	22	—	—
Housekeeping	—	8	—	2
Librarian	—	12	—	3
Physical training	1	6	1	1
Civil service	5	1	—	—
Office work	6	5	—	2
Architecture	6	—	7	—
Millinery	—	6	—	2

Table V shows how much alike the choices of the two groups are, for only three vocations are mentioned by more than 2 per cent of the New York children which are *not also* chosen by more than 2 per cent of the Iowa pupils.

Van Denburg found a close relationship between the high-school student's estimate of the *value* of high-school work and the length of his stay in high school. For instance, only 47 per cent of those 1000 children stated that they regarded a high-school education

TABLE IV. DISTRIBUTION OF VOCATIONAL CHOICES IN THREE SMALL HIGH SCHOOLS

(The narrow range as compared with that of the larger schools is significant.)

	LISBON		WEST BRANCH		GRANITE FALLS, MINN.		TOTALS	
	Boys	Girls	Boys	Girls	Boys	Girls	Boys	Girls
Teacher	1	18	—	12	1	39	2	69
Farmer	6	—	14	—	15	—	35	—
Engineer	4	—	3	—	10	—	17	—
Nurse	—	2	—	—	—	4	—	6
Merchant	1	—	—	—	2	—	3	—
Mechanic	3	—	—	—	1	—	4	—
Bookkeeper . . .	—	—	1	—	—	5	1	5
Stenographer . . .	—	—	—	1	—	4	—	5
Scattering	2	1	1	4	9	11	12	16
Undecided	2	13	2	18	9	5	13	36
Total							87	137

TABLE V. VOCATIONS MENTIONED BY 2 PER CENT OR MORE NEW YORK HIGH-SCHOOL STUDENTS, BUT MENTIONED BY LESS THAN 2 PER CENT IOWA HIGH-SCHOOL STUDENTS

	Boys	Girls
Electrician	9	—
Designer	—	6
Dressmaker	—	7

as necessary for their purposes in life; the rest answered that it was not necessary or that they were uncertain as to its value. In following the high-school histories of these pupils Van Denburg found that the expectancy of staying in and completing the course was much higher with those answering "yes" to both questions than with those answering "no" or "undecided."

The following are the exact figures:

50 per cent of the boys who answer "yes" stay two years.
50 per cent of the girls who answer "yes" stay three years.
50 per cent of the boys and girls who answer "no" do not stay one year.

TABLE VI. IOWA PUPILS' ESTIMATES OF THE VALUE OF
HIGH-SCHOOL AND COLLEGE WORK

		YES	No	UNCERTAIN	TOTALS	PERCENTAGE YES
Are four years in high school necessary for your purpose?	Boys	354	93	87	534	66
	Girls	336	113	84	533	63
Do you intend to spend four years in high school?	Boys	470	44	34	548	85
	Girls	534	47	33	614	87
Is a college education necessary for your purpose?	Boys	337	113	87	537	63
	Girls	297	206	114	617	48

In Table VII are presented some figures as to studies in which the students of four large Iowa high schools were most interested, least interested, and the ones in which failures were reported. It was thought in gathering this information that there might be some relation between a student's school interests, his vocational preference, and perhaps even his intention to remain in high school for the entire course. We were not able to detect any such relationships from the data as they came to us but the figures by themselves are of some significance.

The difference between boys and girls in regard to English, Latin, and German is especially interesting. Several questions arise in one's mind. For example: Is the girls' preference for these subjects due to the fact that the intrinsic quality of the subjects makes more of an appeal to the girl-mind than to the boy-mind, or does the fact that these subjects are taught by women mean that they tend to be presented in ways better suited to arouse the girls' interest than the boys'? Both of these factors probably have their influence. On the other hand, boys surpass girls in their interest in mathematics, history, and physical sciences, judged both by positive preference and by the much smaller numbers of boys who select these subjects as those in which they are least interested. From the small numbers of each sex who mention commercial subjects, manual training, and domestic science as most interesting we should judge either that they are not largely elected or are not taught, thus far, so as to make a very definite appeal to children of high-school age. Whether one or both of these conditions be true, it indicates that these so-called practical and semivocational subjects do not thus far awaken the interest in the pupils of these cities that the older and better standardized subjects are able to do.

TABLE VII.[1] STUDIES IN WHICH THE HIGH-SCHOOL STUDENTS OF IOWA CITY, DUBUQUE, BURLINGTON, AND OTTUMWA ARE:

		MOST INTERESTED	LEAST INTERESTED	FAILURES REPORTED
English	Boys	179	146	54
	Girls	321	118	44
Latin	Boys	64	106	87
	Girls	154	86	53
German	Boys	69	65	79
	Girls	192	78	50
Mathematics	Boys	286	120	143
	Girls	237	296	148
History	Boys	158	88	48
	Girls	153	160	53
Physical science	Boys	137	26	11
	Girls	89	46	17
Biology	Boys	31	19	4
	Girls	38	13	2
Commercial	Boys	70	10	9
	Girls	63	4	6
Manual training	Boys	55	5	1
	Girls	2	6	—
Domestic science	Girls	64	10	4

As to failures, the various mathematical subjects easily outrank all others. This may be due to less efficient teaching, to too great difficulty in the subjects, or to too little willingness of large numbers of high-school pupils to overcome the difficulties that they present.

[1] In the preceding tables data are given from three schools. In this and the following tables four schools are reported.

In connection with these figures regarding failures, which are based solely upon the pupils' own reports and which therefore are subject to more or less error (probably in most cases in the pupils' favor), the following data are of interest. It is a comparison of the failures and successes by subjects from the official records of over 1000 pupils in 23 successive classes in the Iowa City High School.

From Table VIII, covering an eleven-year period for a single high school, it appears from the failures recorded that algebra ranks first in difficulty, Latin is second, and geometry a close third. While no percentages can be computed from Table VIII for exact comparison with the data in Table VII, there is a striking similarity in the relative difficulty of subjects as there presented.

TABLE VIII. THE NUMBER OF PASSING GRADES MADE IN VARIOUS SUBJECTS BY 1042 PUPILS IN 23 SUCCESSIVE CLASSES IN THE IOWA CITY HIGH SCHOOL

	PASSING GRADES	FAILURES	PERCENTAGE OF FAILURES
English including literature	4541	544	11
Algebra	2140	498	19
Geometry	1506	253	14
History and civics	3163	397	11
Latin	2693	468	15
German	1271	87	6
Commercial work	644	45	8
Physical sciences	1189	111	9
Biological sciences	1013	82	8
Manual training	678	32	5

The questionnaire which yielded the data given above for the four Iowa high schools also asked for a report from each student as to the approximate number of hours spent in study outside of school hours. Practically all high-school officials agree in thinking that some outside study is both desirable and necessary, unless there is special opportunity provided by the school for supervised study during school hours, and this notwithstanding the arguments recently presented in certain popular magazines against home study.

These pupils were asked to check the following estimates, which most nearly represented the amount of time spent per week in home study :

0–4, 5–8, 9–12, 13–16, 17–20

Table IX gives the answers of 1431 pupils of four schools. Here, as in the answers to the previous questions, there is doubtless more or less inaccuracy, with the probabilities lying on the side of an over- rather than an under-estimate. The correspondence in the times given by the students of the different schools is very striking, and indicates that in spite of errors in individual cases these estimates represent fairly the distribution of Iowa high-school pupils as to the amount of time spent in home study. Five to eight hours of home study per week is the most common report. Whether this is enough time for the average pupil, each high-school principal

TABLE IX. HOURS OF STUDY PER WEEK OUTSIDE OF SCHOOL
(FOUR IOWA HIGH SCHOOLS)

	0–4		5–8		9–12		13–16		17–20	
	Boys	Girls	Boys	Girls	Boys	Girls	Boys	Girls	Boys	Girls
Dubuque . . .	13	18	123	100	27	48	10	14	2	3
Iowa City . . .	21	20	91	115	50	69	11	30	8	3
Ottumwa . . .	8	13	96	118	42	88	11	27	1	6
Burlington . . .	17	20	51	77	23	32	4	15	2	4
Totals	59	71	361	410	142	237	36	86	13	16

must judge for himself. It is, at any rate, of some importance in dealing with the high-school situation to know the actual distribution of our pupils in this matter of home study. It was thought that there might be some relation between success in studies and amount of home study. The reports of 244 Burlington pupils in the tenth, eleventh, and twelfth grades were studied with this question in mind, but there was no clear relationship apparent from the data furnished by the students. The results were as follows :

TABLE X

Hours per Week in Home Study	Percentage failing One or More Times	Percentage failing Two or More Times
0– 4	56	33
5– 8	45	29
9–12	54	36
13–16	17	17
17–20	0	0

While there is no clear relationship in terms of mere failures, there is, no doubt, a relationship in terms of the quality of work done if we but had its measure in actual grades. This is a point upon which we must for the present defer a definite answer.

The pupils in these four Iowa schools reported themselves as spending entire evenings per week at home, as follows:

TABLE XI. ENTIRE EVENINGS PER WEEK SPENT AT HOME AS REPORTED BY PUPILS OF FOUR LARGE IOWA HIGH SCHOOLS

	Evenings																Total	
	7		6		5		4		3		2		1		0			
	Boys	Girls	Boys	Girls	Boys	Girls	Boys	Girls	Boys	Girls	Boys	Girls	Boys	Girls	Boys	Girls	Boys	Girls
Iowa City	12	34	17	24	39	53	30	50	43	25	23	11	6	1	11	4	—	—
Dubuque	6	19	13	18	28	42	40	59	43	30	27	6	10	1	7	0	—	—
Burlington	5	10	6	14	31	45	35	53	19	12	15	2	3	0	4	2	—	—
Ottumwa	7	14	9	36	24	78	38	94	40	37	19	7	4	1	9	0	—	—
Totals	30	77	45	92	122	218	143	256	145	104	84	26	23	3	31	6	623	782
Percentages	8		9		24		28		18		8		2		3		—	

SIMILAR REPORT FROM TWO SMALL SCHOOLS

	Evenings																Total	
	7		6		5		4		3		2		1		0			
	Boys	Girls	Boys	Girls	Boys	Girls	Boys	Girls	Boys	Girls	Boys	Girls	Boys	Girls	Boys	Girls	Boys	Girls
West Branch	—	1	5	8	8	8	2	7	4	4	1	—	—	—	3	5	23	33
Lisbon	4	3	2	5	4	7	2	5	1	7	3	5	1	1	4	2	21	35
	4	4	7	13	12	15	4	12	5	11	4	5	1	1	7	7	44	68

It will be seen from the table that the boys most commonly report three and four evenings out of the week at home and the girls four and five. Not many of us will feel that this report is altogether auspicious for the good of the high-school pupils. When the number of evenings per week spent at home falls below five on the average, one cannot help but feel that home life and home influences are playing too little part in the lives of these adolescents. Fifty-nine per cent spend four evenings or less at home.

In order to see what relation might exist between success in school and evenings at home the answers of the entire 1400 pupils were reëxamined and the number of failures reported by them was distributed according to the entire evenings per week which they report themselves as spending at home. Tables XII and XIII give the results of this inquiry.

Pupils reported as spending 4–7 entire evenings per week at home average 55 failures per hundred pupils.

Pupils reported as spending 0–3 evenings per week at home average 135 failures per hundred pupils.

TABLE XII. CORRELATION BETWEEN NUMBER OF PUPILS FAILING ONE OR MORE TIMES IN STUDIES AND ENTIRE EVENINGS SPENT AT HOME PER WEEK

| | | EVENINGS | | | | | | | |
		7	6	5	4	3	2	1	0
Iowa City . . .	No. of cases . .	46	42	86	80	68	34	7	15
	Percentage failing	14	36	27	28	50	64	70	74
Dubuque . . .	No. of cases . .	25	39	81	99	73	35	11	7
	Percentage failing	12	20	30	34	50	46	55	86
Burlington . . .	No. of cases . .	15	28	66	78	31	17	3	6
	Percentage failing	47	20	47	48	58	65	100	67
Ottumwa . . .	No. of cases . .	21	46	102	132	77	26	5	9
	Percentage failing	48	37	36	47	51	51	60	45

A recent study of 380 delinquent pupils in the Minneapolis high schools [1] revealed the fact that 46 per cent of them confessed

[1] W. W. Hobbs, "An Inquiry into the Cause of Student Delinquency in the Minneapolis High Schools," *School Review*, November, 1912.

TABLE XIII. DISTRIBUTION OF NUMBER OF FAILURES PER
HUNDRED PUPILS ACCORDING TO EVENINGS AT HOME

	Entire Evenings at Home							
	7	6	5	4	3	2	1	0
No. of failures per 100 pupils —								
Iowa City	20	48	53	59	89	86	114	153
Dubuque	24	23	51	55	100	117	72	157
Burlington . ·	80	31	98	105	180	206	300	166
Ottumwa	76	69	51	93	100	104	120	90
Averages	50	43	58	78	116	128	152	145

that they were "out" the larger share of evenings in a week. No
data were there collected as to the home-staying habits of the pupils
whose school work was up to grade, but in the light of the returns
from the Iowa high schools it is fair to assume that there was a
direct relation between the delinquency of those Minneapolis pupils
and the little time they spent at home.

The preceding information regarding these 1400 pupils in the
four Iowa high schools relates more or less directly to their school
work and school interests. It is interesting to know, in connection
with this, something of what these pupils are doing aside from their
school work, whether they help at home, whether they earn money
or not, and the extent of their participation in certain forms of
amusement.

The following table (XIV) gives the answers to the question,
Do you have work at home? The data are given separately for
each city in order to show how far there is any uniformity in this
particular.

The fact that the girls slightly exceed the boys in helping with
home work is natural in view of the sort of work that is usually
available for children in city homes. It is encouraging for those
who believe that children should learn to participate in home
duties to note the large percentage of these pupils who report
such participation. In the above-mentioned study of 380 delinquent pupils in the Minneapolis high schools it was found that the
number who reported home work of any kind was much less than

TABLE XIV. DO YOU HAVE WORK AT HOME?

	Yes		No	
	Boys	Girls	Boys	Girls
Iowa City	156	197	33	32
Dubuque	140	143	24	34
Burlington	87	142	10	20
Ottumwa	154	242	7	16
	537	724	74	102
	Yes, 88	per cent	No, 12	per cent
Grand total				1426

this. Whether, however, there is any general connection between lack of home work and delinquency is a subject demanding further investigation before it can be definitely answered. It is natural to suppose that a complete absence of all responsibility at home might lead to an excess of outside activities which would interfere materially with school success. The only data from which we can infer school standing of these Iowa pupils are the number of semester failures reported by each pupil, and there was no apparent relation between these failures and home work or lack of it.

The distribution of time spent at home work by these pupils was given by them as follows:

TABLE XV. TIME PER DAY SPENT BY IOWA HIGH-SCHOOL PUPILS AT HOME WORK

0		Less than 1 Hour		1–2 Hours		3–4 Hours		5–6 Hours	
Boys	Girls	Boys	Girls	Boys	Girls	Boys	Girls	Boys	Girls
74	102	51	69	263	343	67	113	46	54

The question next arises, Do any of these pupils, who do not work at home, have work of some sort outside of home? Some of these do, but it happens quite as frequently that they do no work of any kind, while those who report home work also quite as often report that they work outside also. In answer to the question,

Do you earn money outside of school? the following data were secured: Yes: boys, 426; girls, 192; No: boys, 205; girls, 665; 68 per cent of the boys and 22 per cent of the girls reporting that they earn money in one way or another outside of school.

It is of some interest to know the kinds of work mentioned by these pupils. This information is given in Tables XVI and XVII.

The considerable variety of work which high-school pupils in these cities find to do is significant. While a number of these employments would have to be classed as " juvenile occupations " and as not leading anywhere in particular, a " juvenile occupation " is not altogether to be condemned in these cases. When a boy or girl is in school, such a type of work, even though it does not lead directly to any future vocation, is a steadying influence upon the youngster, serving to give a little experience in personal responsibility and in the practical side of life. The experience of earning money for oneself, even in a temporary employment, is a preparation for future work that is decidedly worth while.

TABLE XVI. KINDS OF WORK FOR WHICH MONEY IS EARNED.
MENTIONED BY TWO OR MORE PUPILS

Clerking	92	Usher	4
Odd jobs	70	Picture show	4
Helping at home	48	Printing	3
Delivering papers	44	Reporting	3
Farming	19	Telephone office	3
Music teaching	16	Elevator boy	3
Vacation work	15	Automobile and motor and cycle	
Music and singing	14	repairs	3
Collecting	12	Distributing ads	3
Delivery boy	11	In bank	3
Shop and office	10	Tailor	3
Caring for furnace	10	Engineering gang	2
Factory, mill, etc.	10	Painter	2
Canvassing	9	Hunting	2
Office attendant	9	Fancy work	2
Chauffeur	8	Railroad office	2
Photography	8	Newspaper office	2
Artist	6	Sheet metal	2
Poultry	6	Mechanic	2
Waiter	5	Baking	2
Barber	5	Y.M.C.A.	2
Janitor	5	Salesman	2

TABLE XVII. KINDS OF WORK MENTIONED BY ONE PUPIL ONLY

Reading gas meters	Fishing
Millinery	Delivering eggs
Staying with neighbors nights	Mowing lawns
Checking	Pumping church organ
Making pennants	Plumbing
Selling cream	Garage
Selling milk	Window-trimming
Typewriting	Sewing
Dentist's office	Pantatorium
Selling peanuts	Messenger
Running a boat	Greenhouse
Soda fountain	Engineer
Electrical work	Artist's model
Helping neighbors	Carpentry
Auto sales	Library work
Substitute teacher	

TABLE XVIII. DIFFERENT KINDS OF WORK MENTIONED BY
BOYS AND GIRLS

	Boys	Girls	Combined
Iowa City	—	—	37
Dubuque	36	6	39
Ottumwa	36	17	44
Burlington	23	15	35

It is hardly to be expected that many high-school pupils, with the best part of their day given up to school work, should find much time outside to spend in preparing for any particular vocation. And yet out of the 618 who report themselves as earning money, 36, or nearly 6 per cent, are doing outside work more or less directly related to what they are planning to do when they leave school. Table XIX shows just what these employments are.

In view, however, of the present interest in vocational education, the question may be raised whether the conditions here shown are as favorable for high-school boys and girls as they should be. Should not the school and the community attempt to provide more opportunity for these pupils to get work which will minister more directly to their vocational interests ? As long as the school studies

TABLE XIX. CORRELATION BETWEEN OUTSIDE WORK FOR PAY
AND VOCATIONAL INTENTIONS

Collection	1	Bank	2
Office work	1	Manufacturing and artisan	2
Teaching	1	Engineering	2
Domestic science and art	4	Auto repair	1
Clerking	2	Tailoring	1
Teaching music	6	Dentist's office	1
Singing and music	4	Railroad office	1
Farming	4	Artists	2
Salesmanship	1		

pursued by these pupils are so largely of the purely "liberal" or cultural type there can, of course, be little relationship between school work itself and work outside. Furthermore, it must be recognized that many types of vocational interest, such as engineering, law, medicine, or teaching, could not usually find any opportunity for expression during the school years. But there are also many interests which might find expression while the pupil is in school. To bring about such a connection, the school on its part would have to give more attention to cultivating the vocational interests of its pupils. With no special effort on the part of the school to cultivate such an intelligent insight into the diverse opportunities of the modern world, the range of interests already possessed by these Iowa pupils is comparatively limited, as we saw above in Table III. If the school would undertake to enlighten its pupils systematically as to vocational opportunities, and if it would also provide more vocational studies and give more attention to the practical relationships involved in the ordinary studies, the pupil would be provided with a better basis on which to go out into his community and choose his work.

But the community also should do something, perhaps under the leadership of the school. The modern community should be led to take a more direct interest in the future of its children than is expressed in simply providing them with school opportunities. People engaged in different lines of work should feel a responsibility for providing ways for boys and girls who are inclined in various directions to gain a little experience in the work that interests them while they are going to school.

The industrial schools have already begun to work out and apply various schemes of part-time employment in the trades for their pupils, but what we have in mind here is a more general and less intensive application of the idea. Not that the boy in the ordinary high school who wishes to work shall be employed in some trade — for example, in alternate weeks — but rather that opportunities shall be carefully developed in every community whereby many such boys and even girls shall gain some slight contact with different vocations in their outside work. Such contact should give the youngster not merely a chance to make a little money but also an insight into, and a practical appreciation of, the requirements of the vocation he wishes later to follow.

As to the social and recreational interests of these 1400 Iowa high-school pupils, Table XX summarizes the returns as to the number of parties, moving-picture shows, and theaters per month which they report themselves as attending. The reports from different cities are fairly uniform.

TABLE XX

PARTIES PER MONTH ATTENDED BY IOWA HIGH-SCHOOL PUPILS

	NONE OR LESS THAN 1		1		2		3		4		5		6		7		8 OR MORE	
	Boys	Girls	Boys	Girls	Boys	Girls	Boys	Girls	Boys	Girls	Boys	Girls	Boys	Girls	Boys	Girls	Boys	Girls
	196	161	117	199	128	216	56	94	36	58	22	31	10	23	2	2	9	4
Percentage .	26		23		25		11		8		4		2		0.3		1	

About 48 per cent attend 1–2 parties per month.
About 26 per cent attend more than 2 parties per month.
About 26 per cent attend none or less than 1 party per month.

MOVING–PICTURE SHOWS PER MONTH

0		1–3		4–6		7–9		10–15		16 OR MORE	
Boys	Girls	Boys	Girls	Boys	Girls	Boys	Girls	Boys	Girls	Boys	Girls
91	176	153	265	185	197	57	63	71	64	53	43

THEATERS ATTENDED PER MONTH

NONE OR LESS THAN 1		1		2		3		4		5		6		7		8 OR MORE	
Boys	Girls	Boys	Girls	Boys	Girls	Boys	Girls	Boys	Girls	Boys	Girls	Boys	Girls	Boys	Girls	Boys	Girls
109	230	15	134	101	138	58	61	75	85	23	19	26	19	9	4	30	16

As in the case of preceding tables, the reader will have to interpret these figures for himself. Possibly no one of these diversions, by itself, is indulged in by large numbers to excess, but taken together they represent a considerable expenditure of time in at least three forms of amusement. In most cases the pupil who goes to few or no parties does not indulge in the other forms of amusement. The general tendency is for all to be represented in about the same proportion in the pupils who do participate at all. These figures will be taken by some as a proof of the statement often made that it is not the school work as such which is injurious to the health of the ordinary adolescent but that he suffers most from the multiplicity of his *outside* interests.

AN INQUIRY INTO VOCATIONAL AIMS OF HIGH-SCHOOL PUPILS

By Miss Bessie D. Davis, of the Somerville High School

(From a tentative report to the superintendent of schools, Somerville, Mass., and to the Vocation Bureau of Boston)

QUESTIONNAIRE FOR HIGH-SCHOOL PUPILS

Name　　　　Age　　Yrs.　　Mos.　　Class　　Room

1. Do you expect to complete a course of four years in the high school?
2. If not, how many years do you expect to stay?
3. If you do not expect to remain four years, what is the reason:—
    (*a*) Financial conditions?
    (*b*) Lack of success in school work?
    (*c*) Desire to go to work?
    (*d*) Loss of interest?
4. Please underline the course which you are now taking:
    (*a*) General; (*b*) College Preparatory; (*c*) Manual Arts; (*d*) Commercial; (*e*) two-year Commercial.
5. What led you to choose this course —
    (*a*) Advice of parents, teachers, friends?
    (*b*) Success of others?
    (*c*) Belief in your personal qualifications and ability for the work of this course?
6. Do you know what studies are included in this course —
    (*a*) In the first year?
    (*b*) In the second year?
    (*c*) In the third year?
    (*d*) In the fourth year?
7. What qualifications do you think you have for the work of this course?
8. What line of work do you intend to follow after you leave high school?
9. What do you understand to be the requirements of this work?
10. How have you ascertained these requirements?
11. Is this the work which you really desire to do?

12. What have your parents advised?

13. To what extent, if any, have possible financial benefits influenced your choice?

14. If this is not the work which you really desire to do, why are you not preparing to follow your personal choice?

15. What service to the community are you planning to render through your vocation?

EXTRA

A. For College-Preparatory pupils
  1. For what college are you preparing?
  2. Why have you chosen this college?
  3. What are its requirements?

B. For Scientific, Normal School, Normal Art School, etc., Preparatory pupils
  1. For what school are you preparing?
  2. Why have you chosen this school?
  3. What are its requirements?

NOTE. Please answer questions in full where space is given; otherwise, as briefly as possible. The purpose of this inquiry is to help in the conduct of the school rather than to be inquisitive concerning the personal affairs of the pupils. Please answer frankly. Replies will be considered confidential.

REPORT UPON QUESTIONNAIRE

A printed copy of this questionnaire was, without warning, given each pupil of the upper three classes one morning last February. One period, about forty-five minutes, was allowed for the answering of the questions. No attempt was made to have absent pupils answer them later. The same plan was followed a week or so later in an afternoon session with first-year pupils.

The present report is based on only 1226 of these papers. It has been impossible to complete it; some 528 yet remain. These 1226 include, however, every year and every course and are, therefore, enough from which to draw conclusions. No attempt has been made to reduce all the answers to tables and schedules. The writer prefers to give summaries or actual quotations which give real insight into the pupil's mind and heart.

For the first two questions, however, a table seems most illuminating :

QUESTION NO. 1

Years	Number of pupils	Average age	Yes	No	?
1913	188	18.27	184	0	2
1914	240	17.29	233	1	5
1915 A-B	394	16.55	361	16	5
1916 A-B	230	15.36	187	32	7
1917 A	174	14.72	137	29	6
	1226		1102	78	25

QUESTION NO. 2

Years	−1	1 yr.	1-2	2	2-3	3	4	?
1913				2				3
1914						2	5	1
1915 A-B		1	1	11		3	1	1
1916 A-B		2	3	23	3	1		4
1917 A	1	3	3	20	1			
	1	6	7	54	6	6	6	9

It is evident that there is less certainty in the minds of first- and
second-year pupils regarding the length of stay in the school. The
large number of two-year statements is doubtless due to the fact
that most of these pupils belong to the two-year Commercial class.
The reasons given for less than four years' stay fall under the
respective headings as follows :

	a	b	c	d	OTHER REASONS
1913					
1914	1	1	2	2	4 — to prepare at Exeter Academy
1915 A-B	1	2	4	1	4 — three to other schools; one moved away
1916 A-B	9	3	8	1	6 — five to other schools or business
1917 A	10	0	9	2	5 — four to other schools; one, " account of
	21	6	23	6	19 knowledge "

Financial conditions and desire to go to work are evidently the
chief reasons.

Of the 1226 pupils 154 are in the General Course; 489 in the College Preparatory, which includes Normal and Scientific pupils also; 29 in the Manual Arts Course, which is new and not well understood; 480 in the Commercial Course; 56 in the two-year Commercial, and 1 special student. In the senior and the junior classes more are in the College divisions; in the sophomore and the freshman classes the Commercial Course predominates.

It is in the reasons for choice of these courses that special interest lies; and in the changes of course. Of the latter, 11 were mentioned. Several of these are worth mentioning:

1. Started in (*b*). Changed to (*a*) — due to poor marks and death of father.

2. Changed to (*a*) because he had not definite plan at first.

3. Changed from (*a*) to (*b*) at the beginning of the fourth year, etc. That they and others needed guidance is shown by such reasons for choice as these:

1. " Chosen at random."

2. (*d*) " Mostly because there was nothing I really wanted, and I had to take something."

3. (*a*) " Did not intend to go to college or take business course."

4. (*d*) " Did n't know what else to take."

In view of these answers, one is not surprised to find that of 1157 answers to question 6, only 426 indicate knowledge of the work of the four years; 145 of three years; 272 of two years; and 275 of the first year. The first- and the second-year pupils know little about the years ahead; no wonder they make serious errors in choice.

Their ideas of their qualifications for the course taken range from " None " or " I 'm sure I don't know " to statements of personal factors, special abilities or interests, etc. Among the most interesting are these:

" Ability to do mathematics better than many girls."

" A brain and ability to study until I get what I want."

" Willingness to work hard."

" Ambition, honesty, common sense, good health, etc."

The occupations to be followed later cover much ground. I have divided them into four groups for comparison:

1. Commercial, including bookkeeping, stenography, etc.

2. Future study, including college, normal school, etc.; professional and semiprofessional work, including medicine, law, music, art, etc., and trades. Of the 1226 only 11 indicated desire to engage in the work of trades. Many already know what profession they purpose to engage in, and many plan to go into commercial life — 172 as stenographers, 36 as bookkeepers, and 56 in office work.

Knowledge of the requirements of these occupations is limited. Personal factors are named in much the same way as in answer to question 7. Business factors — ability to work; appreciate the value of time; willingness to do what is required and more if necessary — are mentioned. Special demands are spoken of in very few instances; viz. apprenticeship or special training. Is it any wonder that lacking information concerning employments, one says later, " There is nothing to take to be a nurse "; and another, that he made a mistake in taking the wrong course and cannot, therefore, prepare for the vocation he desires?

Information has been gained from many sources: people, reading, inquiry, experience, observation, and thought. One suggested examining and checking off subjects already taken. And one, bewildered, asked for advice. His case was followed up with care.

In the majority of cases pupils are doing the work they really wish to do. Answers to question 14 show that financial conditions and family objections are the chief obstacles. But I also find as reasons :

" I made a mistake in taking the wrong course."

" I could n't change my course."

" I do not want to carry out the course."

" No personal ability for any line of work."

These are the people likely to become discouraged and leave school.

That parents know too little about the school, and play too small a part in the child's choice of work there, is indicated by the next group of answers :

	Agree	Disagree	Nothing	Own Choice	General Advice
1913	127	10	7	16	6
1914	145	25	13	24	1
1915 A-B . . .	287	27	8	17	
1916 A-B . . .	130	18	7	5	3
1917 A	111	15	4	5	12
	800	95	39	67	22

Unfortunately too many of the first group may be like the case of one pupil, who said parental advice was, " Think and decide ; then let me know to approve or disapprove." One has reason to believe that such is often the case, because so many say that they made their own choice. As one puts it, " They have given a good deal of advice, but let me be guided by my own wishes." Another says : " Nothing. I chose this work of my own accord. I am putting myself through school." Still another says, " No advice to give." And a boy whose longing for ornithology has not yet been met by information or help, wrote concerning parents' advice, " Nothing. Absolutely nothing." His mother died only a few years ago.

Financial benefits have much to do with choices. Two hundred eighty three say frankly that it did. One says that he has a brother going to college. Another, " Must support parents." " Family need support ; father is not living." " College graduates obtain better paying positions." " Want to earn money for a musical career." " Most money in it for me." " I shall have to work my way if I go to college." " If I really knew what I should like to become, I should go to college ; but I think that it would be a waste of time to do something that I do not know anything about." Can anyone with sympathetic spirit and understanding heart fail to respond to the appeal in this statement ? The opening is there ; one needs only to follow up the boy, and he is appreciative and grateful.

Service to the community was to many a new idea. Twenty admitted that they had no thought about it, and fifty-eight did not know what they could do. Some cared little for others. One said, " None. I am going to look after myself first." " None. I expect to be a peaceful citizen," answered another. . .

Many, however, showed much thought and understanding of what service might mean. I grouped the answers under the headings : through work, social help, as a citizen, through character, all possible. Some were, like the last, mentioned vaguely. Others were very specific. Here are several typical replies :

" Hope to be instrumental in alleviating suffering caused by cancer."

" Aid city government."

" Be a credit to S——." (Somerville.)

" The better I am educated, the more I can do for the community."

" To better conditions where I live."

" To lay out better cities."

" Design public buildings so that they will last."

" Defend innocent men and women who are accused of crime."

" Help unfortunate people."

And with unintentional humor, and perhaps sad comment on what he has heard and read, " Justify wrong." To awaken the minds of *all* pupils to the idea of " noblesse oblige " is surely the duty of any school.

Of these pupils many are going to colleges and other higher institutions. Harvard, Tufts, and Massachusetts Institute of Technology attract the larger number of boys ; Radcliffe, Wellesley, Simmons, Salem Normal School, and Boston Normal Art School, of the girls.

Answers with regard to choosing college, etc., and requirements, were fewer in number. Only 357 answered the former and 282 the latter. Location, standard of scholarship and instruction courses offered, time required, reputation, experience and recommendations of others, type of graduates, cost of tuition, etc., all are mentioned in some way or other. It is, however, plain that information is general and limited. Knowledge of requirements seems to be still less. Perhaps many, like one, "leave it to the principal " or keep "a book of requirements at home," etc. Apparently they little realize that requirements differ as do colleges.

It is rather encouraging to find some opposition on the part of the parents, which must arouse the pupil. Some parents urge the choice of definite instead of indefinite or drifting attitude ; some have such radically different choices as music, *not* stenography, or private school instead of office work. Even parents disagree, and we find father wanting his boy to be a surveyor, and mother choosing for him a business course.

Not, however, until grammar-school masters and teachers work more closely with high-school masters and teachers, and both groups work with pupils and parents, can the needs indicated in these papers be met. Every master of a grammar school should visit the high schools of his city, study their work, and be ready with coöperation of the high-school teachers to give such information as will help pupils to choose carefully courses which will look far ahead. Then in the high school there should be flexibility enough to permit of readjustments. There is no reason why those in the wrong course by mistake must stay there. Finally, the high school must give to the pupils, whether they ask it or not, definite, clear, simple information regarding the work they may do in the world. Not until all this is adequately done will the gap between high school and grammar school, on the one hand, and high school and after life, on the other, be bridged.

RECOMMENDATIONS

A

I. That in the high school one or two teachers be officially designated Vocational Counselors, with time allowed for vocational guidance among the pupils. If possible, one of these counselors should be a man.

II. That a committee of five or more teachers be appointed to work with these counselors in such ways as the latter may find necessary and advisable.

III. That a group of citizens, men and women of recognized character, experience, and standing in profession, business, and trade, be invited to coöperate with counselors and committee by allowing themselves to be interviewed by such boys and girls as the aforesaid counselors may deem it necessary to send to them for information or advice.

IV. That by means of talks, books read, compositions, etc., *all* pupils be given at least a general idea of occupations and their requirements.

V. That the questionnaire papers of last year be at once used in " follow up " work among the pupils. Special attention should be given papers marked or starred.

VI. That advisers endeavor at once to make sure that pupils have read the entire course of study, understand what is offered through-out the four years, and have reasonable basis for choice of course.

VII. That effort be made to have pupils going to higher institutions obtain and read carefully the catalogue, etc., of the school or the college which they plan to enter, find out as much as possible about the requirements and the life of that and other schools and colleges, and choose with some thought and reason.

VIII. That, if possible, information be obtained and given pupils, especially those of third or fourth year, concerning scholarships, loans, etc., offered by state, clubs, societies, colleges, etc. to first-year students in colleges and kindred institutions.

IX. That pupils obviously unfitted for the work of any course be transferred *as soon as possible* to the course to which they may be found by teachers and counselors to be adapted.

X. That through meetings or personal conferences (possibly through the formation of a Parents' Association) greater coöperation be brought about between high-school teachers and parents, and high-school teachers and grammar-school masters and teachers.

XI. That in ethics, in conferences with advisers, in class work, or through some other means, greater emphasis be placed on personal service as the ultimate goal to be sought, whatever the life work chosen and the return due for the education received.

B

I. That the Superintendent make a request, equivalent to demand, that *every* grammar-school master visit, while it is in session, the high school and acquaint himself or herself with the course of study and the requirements of the school.

II. That the grammar-school masters and assistants be required early in the year to study their pupils, find out what they plan to do at the end of their grammar-school course, and seek to help them choose carefully and wisely school and course of study or occupation, using all possible effort to prevent their choice of work for which they are plainly not fitted.

III. That, as the Superintendent suggested last year, meetings of parents and graduating classes of grammar schools be held at intervals during the year in the respective schools, such meetings to be addressed by heads of departments or those in charge of the various courses in high school and vocational schools.

C

I. That in all schools effort be made to find out when and why pupils leave school, and to keep in touch with them after they have left.

II. That pupils be required if possible, as in Boston, to give teacher or Vocational Counselor one week's notice of intention to leave.

III. That through conference between parent and teacher, and pupil and teacher, effort be made to keep the pupil in school if possible.

IV. That pupils be sent for employment certificates only after careful investigation of the merits and the needs of their respective cases.

SHALL ELECTIVE COURSES BE ESTABLISHED IN THE SEVENTH AND EIGHTH GRADES OF THE ELEMENTARY SCHOOL?

By District Superintendent I. E. Goldwasser, Manhattan, New York

(From *The Psychological Clinic*, January 15, 1914)

Table XLI of the Fourteenth Annual Report of the City Superintendent of Schools to the Board of Education of the City of New York presents the following figures:

REGISTER BEFORE PROMOTION, JUNE 30, 1912

1A	40,489
1B	49,740
2A	40,327
2B	45,986
3A	40,336
3B	43,131
4A	39,568
4B	41,224
5A	37,329
5B	36,783
6A	33,237
6B	32,245
7A	28,875
7B	25,718
8A	22,250
8B	21,169
Total 1A–8B	578,407

In computing registers for the spring terms of the year, it has been found that the totals for B classes in the various grades are larger than those for the A classes. This is due to the fact that the admission into the 1A classes in September of each year is greater than that in February. The weather conditions are somewhat responsible for this situation, parents being reluctant to have their children begin their attendance at school in the midst of winter. Furthermore, the old tradition that the year begins in September is also a factor tending to make the 1A registers larger in the September term than in the February term. Thus the register in 1A before promotion, January 31, 1912, was 60,962, while that on June 30, 1912, as already noted, was 40,489. As a result of this, A registers are larger in the fall term and smaller in the spring term in all the grades.

Despite this fact, the 5B register is less than the 5A register for the spring term of 1912; and similar conditions obtain in the case of the 5th, 7th, and 8th years. In addition, it should be noted that the 6A register is 7252 less than the 1A register, while that of 8B is 12,068 less. It is fair to assume that of a given register in 6A classes at any specified time about one third will leave school without graduation.

There is nothing novel about this inference from the data. It cannot, however, too frequently be brought before the notice of those interested in the schools, that under the present forms of organization and administration we are not able to hold children in the schools even to the end of the elementary course.

Economic stress cannot be cited as the cause of this great reduction. No one who has interviewed the boys and girls applying for an employment certificate can fail to have become convinced that most of these children leave not because there is a real need for their going to work, but because the remaining years of the course do not offer features which bind them closely to school. It is not that work is necessary but rather that school is not attractive.

In order to determine why the course of study seems not to hold within itself the features that make the school a vital thing to the pupils, it is not necessary to take the subjects individually and show wherein they have become narrowed by reason of traditional influences still operative in our school system. It might, of course, be shown that the course in English history in the seventh year, by reason of the lack of preparedness of the teacher, the vast scope of the subject matter, and the immaturity of the pupils, can never be made to enter into the real thinking experience of the children. We might refer to the 7A review of the United States and the 8B general review in geography and point out that this constant re-presentation of old material is uninteresting. Or the 8A course in geography might be cited as a curious relic of the old interest in science as an academic subject.

In a similar way, the course in grammar could be analyzed so as to show wherein it demands a power of discrimination and logical thinking beyond the average child of the elementary school in so cosmopolitan a city as ours. Again, the selection of masterpieces for literary study might be criticized on the ground that it does not properly provide for a vital point of contact between the emotional life of the pupils and the spirit of the selection.

All these criticisms have been made, and with authority. In fact earnest efforts are now being made to revise the various courses of study so as to rid them of the burdens of the centuries and make them adequately representative of the demands of our times. Our board of education and our superintendents have been at work at this problem for several years, and notable reforms have already been accomplished. Others are promised for the immediate future.

But even if an ideal situation is created in each of the subjects, the fact will still remain that the course of study will be essentially academic. Book knowledge will still be emphasized. General culture, of the sort that one attributes to the well-read or well-informed man, will still be the distinguishing mark of the pupil who has mastered such courses. And the unfortunate fact will still confront us, so serious in its implications that its import is truly tragic, that the general fitness which we attempt to secure really means specific unfitness.

Take if you will the ordinary graduate of an elementary school. What is he fit for? Has he an equipment that will make him ready to take up with even a reasonable degree of efficiency any occupation other than that of a clerk or an office assistant whose work is unskilled? His manual training has been with wood as the only material and with no machines. Her sewing has been by hand or on a foot-driven sewing-machine. Entering any shop or factory, such a graduate is no better, save in general intelligence, than an absolutely untrained beginner. The seventh and eighth years of the course have given no preparation that would serve as a recompense for the extra time spent in the school. Why, then, should a pupil stay? The lure of the diploma, as a cachet of culture, is not strong enough to hold one third of the pupils. That fact is attested by the figures in our possession. And as an offset to the diploma, there is the larger pay envelope of the pupil who left in the seventh year and in a year or so has become economically more valuable to his employer than is the inexperienced graduate.

Even this, however, serious as it is, does not give us a true picture of the gravity of the situation. The inflexibility of the course, essentially academic — a book course — would seem to imply a homogeneity of interests in the pupils. There is no material offered on which a variety of tastes can be tested. We have no way of discovering aptitudes of pupils. Excellence in history and geography may be discovered. But what assurance have we that we are not neglecting some extraordinary power in another direction? Eventually, such power must find expression. But the waste of tentative effort before a final form for activity is discovered is bound to be tremendous. Nor is it with extraordinary ability alone that we are concerned. How about the pupil who may be just a little above the average in some trade, who would find happiness in self-expression, but who is doomed to discontent because he was never given a chance to discover himself until it was too late?

Opinions may differ as to whether we can develop efficiency in any trade by training pupils in the seventh and eighth years of the course. There may be debate as to whether children of thirteen are old enough or mature enough to select their life occupation. But what argument can be advanced against giving them an acquaintance with many different kinds of activity — commercial, industrial, and the like — so that their choice of a vocation shall be made *not in spite of their ignorance of all, but because of an*

actual, if limited, experience of work in each of the vocations?
Let them learn and know the different trades, so that, knowing, they shall be able later to exercise a free choice. Let us
eliminate, as far as we can, the accidental determination of a
life pursuit.

If our seventh and eighth years were converted into an experimental period, pupils would soon come to find value in these final
years of the course. And if, when the choice had been carefully
made, an added year were given to the elementary schools, so that
a pupil might receive simple training in his work, we should be
producing efficient graduates, with choices rationally made and
with an equipment that would increase their wage-earning power.
In short, we should be laying the foundations for happiness and
competency. Incidentally, we should be holding a greater number
of pupils for a longer period in our schools.

Is there the variety of demand that is presupposed by our statement of the needs of the situation? Is it true that pupils in our
seventh and eighth years have decided preferences for pursuits,
for which no training whatever is given in our elementary schools?
In order to determine this a study was made of 2552 boys and
girls in the seventh and eighth years of Public School 62, Intermediate. This school receives pupils from the 6B classes of seven
neighboring schools. Almost all the children are Jewish. Each
child was told to write a letter to the principal of the school,
covering these points:

1. What do you intend to do when you go out into life?
2. Why do you make this selection?
3. If you could begin at once to prepare for this pursuit what
would you like to take up?

The idea was to secure a statement of

1. Choice.
2. Reasons.
3. Pupils' ideas of content of courses.

Before any attempt is made to present the results of this study,
one fact must be made clear. The mere choice of a certain vocation on the part of the pupil should not mean that such vocation

is necessarily to be followed by him. Guidance is more important than choice. The selections here indicated were made under conditions which made it impossible for children to have discovered themselves. They were judging relative values, as will be seen, not in terms of their own powers but largely in terms of the degrees of desirability of the work they intended to engage in. The point to bear in mind, however, is that with a thoroughgoing academic course wishes, at all events, have already been registered in their minds.

In order to make the choice more intelligent the words "academic," "industrial," and "commercial" were used and carefully explained to all the pupils.

TABLE 1. CHOICE OF VOCATIONS

	ACADEMIC	INDUSTRIAL	COMMERCIAL	TOTALS
Boys	396	273	440	1109
Girls	376	326	741	1443
	772	599	1181	2552

Assuming that we had a perfect academic course, we should then be supplying the needs of 772 out of 2552 pupils, 30 per cent. In this particular section of the city there are many "business schools" which turn out, as from a hopper, stenographers and bookkeepers, often with one year's training or less. Such schools meet the needs of 46 per cent of the pupils. The remaining 24 per cent of the pupils wish industrial work, and the only agency in the seventh and eighth years, outside of the Vocational Schools for Boys and for Girls (where carfare is a deterrent factor), is the course in woodwork and hand sewing, with a little training in sewing on a foot-driven machine.

What are the considerations that influence pupils in their choice of a vocation? What is the occupation they wish to follow, preparation for which involves study in the courses indicated?

The second of these investigations is extremely interesting as affording an insight into the definiteness of the selection made by pupils.

TABLE 2

Among the 396 boys selecting an academic course these ambitions are to be noted:

Architect	4
Astronomer	2
Artist	2
Chemist	3
Civil engineer	19
Civil service	16
Doctor	65
Electrical engineer	2
Forester	1
Lawyer	76
Literary man	4
Musician	4
Optometrist	1
Orator	1
Pharmacist	19
Philosopher	1
Rabbi	1
Surgeon	2
Teacher	45
Veterinary Surgeon	1
Total	269

The remaining 127 will be accounted for in another way.

TABLE 3

Among the 376 girls selecting an academic course these ambitions are to be noted:

Teacher	220
Physician	12
Nurse	10
Dentist	2
Music teacher	6
Librarian	17
Teacher of athletics	2
Lawyer	16
Author	5
Artist	3
Teacher of drawing	2
Pharmacist	2
Musician	2
Total	299

The remaining 77 will be accounted for in another way.

TABLE 4

Among the 273 boys selecting an industrial course these ambitions are to be noted:

Carpenter	23
Electrician	20
Civil engineer	64
Machinist	10
Plumber	8
Printer	12
Telegrapher	5
Designer	6
Surveyor	4
Diamond setter	1
Farmer	4
Mechanician	4
Letter carrier	1
Post-office clerk	1
Artist	11
Builder	4
Machine designer	1
Factory owner	1
Furniture maker	1
Inventor	1
Tailor	1
Teacher of manual training	2
Wool manufacturer	1
Engineer	6
Automobile industry	1
Pattern making	2
Cloak and suit cutter	2
Mechanical engineer	1
Electrical engineer	5
Jeweler	1
Chauffeur	2
Forester	2
Bookbinder	3
Cabinetmaker	10
Motion-picture operator	1
Mining engineer	1
Ironworker	1
Total	224

The remaining 49 will be accounted for in another way.

TABLE 5

Among the 326 girls selecting an industrial course the following ambitions are to be noted:

Dressmaker	143
Milliner	75
Milliner and dressmaker	22
Designer	34
Teacher of cooking	2
Photographer	1
Nurse	3
Artist	4
Embroiderer	9
Embroidery designer	1
Librarian	6
Total	300

The remaining 26 will be accounted for in another way.

TABLE 6

Among the 460 boys selecting a commercial course the following ambitions are to be noted:

Grocer	1
Florist	1
Jeweler	1
Salesman	81
Traveling salesman	82
Bookkeeper	186
Stenographer	69
Office clerk	6
Bartender	1
Reporter	1
Public accountant	2
Banker	3
Typewriter	4
Letter carrier	2
Post-office clerk	2
Bank clerk	7
Shipping clerk	3
Foreman	1
Wholesale dry goods	1
Jewelry business	1
Commissioner of deeds	1
Telegrapher	1
Stenographer, typewriter, and bookkeeper	1
Broker	1
To know how to pay workmen	1
Total	460

TABLE 7

Among the 741 girls selecting a commercial course the following ambitions are to be noted:

Bookkeeper	262
Saleswoman	25
Typewriter	30
Stenographer	39
Bookkeeper, typewriter, and stenographer	51
Cashier	2
Office assistant	6
Bank clerk	1
Bookkeeper and typewriter	22
Bookkeeper and stenographer	4
Stenographer and typewriter	97
Buyer	7
Clerk	1
Composer	1
Traveling saleswoman	1
Total	559

The remaining 182 will be accounted for in another way.

Were the courses of various kinds given to the children of the seventh and eighth years, it is probable that choices would be entirely different. Moreover, were the teachers afforded an opportunity to observe children at work in the various courses, they would be able to add to their original judgment of aptitude the results of their observation and so might make intelligent suggestions to influence choice. For it is to be noted that with a definite aim in view, children have selected the wrong course.

In some instances the choice indicated clearly that the child had made a selection and still was entirely wrong in conception as to the nature of the course.

This was true in the following cases:

	ACADEMIC	INDUSTRIAL	COMMERCIAL
Boys	4	3	6
Girls	0	0	0

In some cases the choice was made and no aim at all was stated:

	ACADEMIC	INDUSTRIAL	COMMERCIAL
Boys	0	0	0
Girls	4		14

The mere fact of personal preference sufficed as a reason in many cases:

	ACADEMIC	INDUSTRIAL	COMMERCIAL
Boys	1	1	0
Girls	46	20	128

The wish of parents was frequently cited as the only reason for the choice. The numbers are:

	ACADEMIC	INDUSTRIAL	COMMERCIAL
Boys	11	11	21
Girls	9	6	22

A general liking for the content of the course was occasionally cited as a reason:

	ACADEMIC	INDUSTRIAL	COMMERCIAL
Boys	30	14	0
Girls	19	7	

In some cases the selection was based on the child's aptitude for such phases of the work as had already been taken up in the regular course:

	ACADEMIC	INDUSTRIAL	COMMERCIAL
Boys	0	0	2
Girls	0	6	3

The desire to help parents in their work was cited as a reason:

	ACADEMIC	INDUSTRIAL	COMMERCIAL
Boys	0	1	1
Girls	0		2

Miscellaneous reasons were given as follows:

	ACADEMIC		INDUSTRIAL		COMMERCIAL	
	B	G	B	G	B	G
To lead a useful life	1	1	—	—	—	1
Course is short	—	—	—	—	5	5
Desire to be happy	—	—	—	—	—	1
Because of health	—	—	—	—	—	1
Work is easy	—	—	1	—	18	1
Salary is good	2	—	9	—	1	1
Course is practical	—	—	2	—	3	—
Step to higher work	—	—	—	1	1	—
Postpones need of final choice	1	—	—	—	—	—

An interesting study was made of what the pupils should like to have the various courses include.

ACADEMIC COURSE

	Boys	Girls
Mathematics	102	240
Grammar	2	
Spelling	9	
Latin	50	89
Music	3	15
Current events	1	
How to overcome obstacles in life	1	
How to use surgical instruments	1	
Drawing	14	
French	179	1
Chemistry	19	
German	45	1
Modern languages	43	63
English	72	254
Spanish	18	
History	32	56
Geography	33	1
Reading	2	1
Medicine	25	
Biology	7	
Civics	5	
Law	31	
Hygiene	16	2
Physiology	1	
Penmanship	6	
Contracts	2	
Botany	5	
Greek	15	
Astronomy	1	
Art	1	
Italian	5	
Russian	1	
Debating	2	
Science	2	

INDUSTRIAL COURSE

	Boys
Surveying	2
Plumbing	2
Languages	5
Arithmetic	113
Grammar	1

INDUSTRIAL COURSE (Continued)

Agriculture 1
Botany 2
Penmanship 8
Latin 5
German 17
French 19
Geography 23
History 6
Spanish 7
English 56
Salesmanship 3
Art 2
Electricity 13
Carpentry 11
Machine work 10
Mechanical drawing 22
Free-hand drawing 15
Woodwork 24
Science 22
Designing 5
Printing 3
Astronomy 1
Architecture 2
Bookbinding 1
Foundry work 2
Metal work 1
Tailoring 1
Wood-turning 3
Geometry 4
Engineering 2
Algebra 1
Painting 1
Greek 1
Polish 1
Russian 1
Turkish 1
Spelling 5
Reading 1

COMMERCIAL COURSE

English 137
Mathematics 172
Penmanship 81
Geography 38
Commercial law 2

History	12
Science	2
Drawing	3
German	16
Letter writing	10
Geometry	1
Designing	1
French	33
Spanish	20
Buying	5
Salesmanship	31
Physics	1
Botany	1
Italian	2
Dutch	1
Languages	12
Bookkeeping	59
Typewriting	35
Stenography	65
Algebra	1
Designing	2
Spelling	13

A similar study of the content of commercial and industrial courses as judged by girls has not been tabulated, owing to circumstances which lead us to question the value of the data.

It is interesting to note how definite is the demand. There is little or no suggestion of basic preparation, of a training larger than the need of the occupation itself. An ordinary trade school or a private business school will give the narrow work desired by these pupils. It requires a larger view of social and economic needs to build upon these desires of the children a broad, fundamental preparedness making for greater efficiency in any particular vocation. How can this be done in a school of the type of Public School 62, Manhattan?

It may be well to make clear at the outset that an intermediate school offers many opportunities for organization which do not exist in the regular grades of an elementary school. The number of pupils in the seventh and eighth years is much larger; in this school almost 3000 pupils are enrolled in the last two years of the course. There are three shops, three kitchens, two sewing rooms, a typewriting room, two science rooms, and one laboratory. There is space for the equipment of special rooms for the various industries as they are taught.

The following plan of organization is suggested :

1. Secure from the principals of 6B schools a detailed statement of the special aptitudes and weaknesses of pupils entering the intermediate school. Classify new admissions on the basis of these reports so as to secure a certain degree of homogeneity in the composition of each class.

2. Institute tests of a general nature in the 7A grade, to determine general intelligence, manual skill, power of judgment in practical situations, etc. Tabulate all such findings for future reference. Münsterberg tests or others of a similar nature may be used to furnish a basis for teachers' judgments.

3. Beginning with the 7A grade and extending through the 8A grade, courses should be established in electric wiring, sheet-metal work, wood-turning, leather work, etc. for boys, and in dressmaking, millinery, embroidering, machine work, etc. for girls. Each course should extend over a period of nine weeks, thus affording a series of six courses. All pupils should be required to take each course in turn. Time schedules should be so arranged that at least eight hours a week may be devoted to the special courses. No attempt should be made to do more than acquaint the pupil with the fundamental simple processes underlying the various occupations.

4. Every pupil should be carefully observed while at work and a detailed record kept of his or her proficiency in the course. The work should be so planned as to make data available with regard to general adaptability, rather than to give skill in the occupation as such.

5. During the 8A grades, conferences should be held between parent, pupil, and teacher, the results of the tests and the records of the course should be carefully examined, and the pupil should be directed into the course for which he appears to be suited and in which all conditions combine to make it probable that he will become efficient.

It is in the 8B grades that the special training should begin. Small groups should be formed for each course. Intricate processes cannot be taught nor can work of a heavy nature be undertaken. One of the objects sought in the studies of the Vocation Bureau of Boston is stated thus: "To analyze the relation of aptitudes, interests, and habits to modern industrial demands, and thus lay an adequate foundation for a system of training regardful of social as well as economic needs." Whatever training is given should be along lines determined by some such study as this. The courses should be checked up constantly by the results of occupational investigations and must be organized with an ever-present ideal of sympathetic vocational guidance.

Pupils who wish to enter a classical high school with the idea of graduating should be enrolled at the beginning of the 8B grade in classes organized for such pupils. Special attention should be given to technical grammar, to the fundamental principles underlying arithmetical operations, to oral English with particular reference to the technique of correct speech, to penmanship, to the mechanics of written language, spelling, punctuation, etc. and to teaching pupils how to study.

Pupils who intend to complete the full course in a commercial high school should be enrolled at the beginning of the 8B grade in classes organized for such pupils. Special attention should be given to correct oral English, as regards both the technique of speech and freedom from foreign idioms; to letter writing; to study of business forms; to an explanation of the principles underlying the various kinds of business to which arithmetic applications are made, such as commission, discount, insurance, etc.; to commercial geography and to modes of manufacture.

Pupils who intend to complete the full course in a manual-training trade high school should be enrolled at the beginning of the 8B grade in classes organized for such pupils. Special attention should be given to correct oral English, as regards both the technique of speech and freedom from foreign idioms; to mechanical and free-hand drawing; to the fundamental arithmetical operations; to simple constructional geometry; to elementary algebra; to science; to modes of manufacture in the various industries; to shop work.

Girls who intend to complete the full course in a technical high school should be enrolled at the beginning of the 8B grade in classes organized for such pupils. Special attention should be given to sewing (hand and machine), embroidering, with applications to dressmaking and millinery; to cooking and a study of food values; to home making in general. For the last-named work, use should be made of the model flat built for this specific purpose.

This will leave a large number of pupils who, under ordinary circumstances, would leave school at the end of the eighth year, or when they had attended a half year or more at a high school. During the year and a half, from the beginning of the 7A grade, the aptitudes of these pupils have been tested at the different occupational activities carried on; their general intelligence and their special powers have been carefully noted. A study should also have been made of their home conditions, the needs of the family, etc. The principal or competent teachers should have held interviews with the parents with a view to arriving at some knowledge of the pupil's aims and those of his family. The "vocational guide" should proceed to suggest what line of work the pupil should take up.

If there is still uncertainty as to what the ultimate choice is to be, the academic course should be recommended. For those intending to enter business the commercial course should be urged, while the industrial course should be recommended to those who wish to enter one of the trades.

The term in these courses should be one and a half years. In this way, for pupils who ordinarily would leave school at the end of the eighth year, we shall be adding a year to their school career, giving them a quality and a degree of preparation which will soon convince parents that the extra time spent in school is more than compensated for by the increased efficiency — yes, and the increased earning power of the child who has this more extended preparation. It may be urged that parents will not be able to afford to keep their children at school for the longer period. This may very well be true. Still it must be borne in mind that where legislation has prolonged the compulsory school-attendance period, parents have found the means to support their children at school. When the grade at which pupils may apply for employment certificates was made 7A instead of 5B, parents resigned themselves to the inevitable and adapted themselves to the situation as best they could. Under the plan set forth, however, the force which compels the longer stay in school is not exercised by a law but by the self-interest of pupil and parent. Is it not reasonable to expect that once the work has justified itself, parents will be more than willing to have their children remain in school for the extra year?

Many graduates from our elementary schools enter a business school for a training of a half year. The commercial course which is here suggested will keep many pupils in the school, and the city will for the first time be meeting a need which has for many years been clearly expressed by the people of the community.

The records show that large numbers of the pupils who enter our high schools from the elementary school stay in the secondary institutions for a year or so and then drop out. A certain percentage of this "mortality" has been rightly attributed to the inflexible course of study, to poor teaching, to the unpreparedness of the pupil for independent study. But all the discharges cannot be traced to any one of these causes or to any combination of them. In many cases parents are so situated that they can afford to keep the boy or girl at school for one year, but no longer. Under the present system the only place for such pupils to go to is the high school. They are not really a part of the student body; they cause an unhealthy condition as regards size of classes in the first two terms; they call for large and expensive buildings; they create problems of management, of organization, of discipline, of supervision, which inevitably reduce the efficiency of the school. The pupils who have come to the high school for the purpose of completing the entire course are to a certain extent neglected because of the great number of transients on the register.

If the ninth year which is here recommended were adopted, such pupils would not clog and clutter up the administrative and supervisory channels of our high schools. They would not be sent out into the world with such inadequate equipment as must necessarily result from a truncated course. For they all have had one fourth of some subjects, one third of others, one half of still others. Their work ends nowhere. They have no general culture; they have no special training. In the ninth year, however, they will receive a complete course. True, they cannot get as much training as would be theirs were they to complete the entire course in an academic, a manual training, or a commercial high school. But they will be far more efficient than the derelict high-school student who leaves at the end of one year, who does not know what he wants to do, or who, if he does know, cannot do it because he has had no training for it.

The planning of the work for such courses calls for much careful thought and systematic preparation. A body of opinion should first be gathered from men of affairs representing different outlooks, different occupations, etc. This may be considered the norm by which to test any course that may be evolved by educators. In every case the course should be adapted to the community, and due regard should be had for the kind of pupils the course is intended to serve.

There may be some doubt whether a purely academic course should find a place in a ninth-year school, the aim of which is to increase vocational efficiency. As a matter of fact, this course is intended merely to relieve the situation as it exists in our classical high schools to-day. Arrangements should be made whereby pupils may be transferred from the academic course to either the industrial or the commercial, as soon as the more special demand makes itself felt.

The academic course should include literature, current history, business conditions, business arithmetic, science, civics, music, and physical training. If possible there should be work in ethics through organized activities involving personal, civic, and social service.

The commercial course should include business English, office practice, business arithmetic, commercial geography, and bookkeeping.

The industrial course should cover for boys and for girls a complete course in the occupation, the training to extend over the full year and a half. In no course should work in English, oral and written, and in civics, be omitted.

The details of these courses must be worked out with the greatest care. Much preparatory work has already been done. Analyses have been made of some of the industries, and the processes have been reduced to their simplest elements. We are coming to understand better the principles that must govern the elimination of nonessentials from the traditional academic and commercial courses. All this, however, is a matter of time. The experiments will be tentative, and there must always be the frankest kind of self-criticism. But in work of this kind lies what seems to be a constructive attempt to meet one phase of the problem of elementary-school education in its relation to the efficiency of the individual and the progress of the state.

CHARTING CHILDHOOD IN CINCINNATI

By Helen Thompson Woolley, Bureau of Vocational Guidance,
Child Labor Department, Public Schools of Cincinnati

(From *The Survey*, August 9, 1913)

When a pharmacist compounds a prescription he knows what effect the various elements have on each other. He can analyze them even after they have interacted with the juices of the human system. When a manufacturer starts a piece of raw material on the road toward a finished product, he can account for the smallest change, the minutest process. But when a child starts on the bleak road which leads from one deadening occupation to another, who can chart his path or gauge the forces that mold and shape his future life?

To do this very thing is becoming one of the paramount purposes of educators. The task is enlisting the interest of all who desire a saner conservation of childhood. The boy and girl who leave school untrained, adolescent, groping, are more and more seen to be the rawest of raw materials. Society's obligation to do its utmost that this material may increase in beauty and efficiency is no longer thought to cease when the school door closes.

One of the most comprehensive attempts to find out just what industry means to children is being made in Cincinnati. This attempt was made possible by the passage three years ago of a unique child-labor law which, for the first time in history, gave to one office sufficient authority over the working children of a community to permit a many-sided study of a large group of them. While this study has not been completed, some absorbing discoveries can be forecasted, entailing some equally absorbing reflections on current educational movements. For example, we are making a special investigation of 800 school children, as a result of which we hope to be able to compare the rate of development, mental and physical, of those in industry and those in school. It will then be possible to say what is the effect of industry on children who enter it at fourteen.

But let us look for a moment at the workings of the law itself. During the school year from September 1, 1909, to September 1, 1910, 3348 children between the ages of fourteen and sixteen took out certificates permitting them to work in Cincinnati. The following year the number dropped to 2800, and in 1911–1912 the number of beginning child laborers went down to 2366. This was a direct result of the child-labor law. The first drop was due chiefly to the raising of the educational requirement from mere ability to read and write to the completion of the fifth grade in school. The second was the effect of establishing the compulsory continuation school for children who had not completed the eighth grade.

The exemption of eighth-grade children from the continuation school put a sort of cash value on the completion of the eighth grade which held many in school. The percentage of those who had completed the eighth grade rose from 13 per cent in 1910–1911 to 19 per cent in 1911–1912. Provisions compelling employers to return certificates and report on the children, as well as allowing workers to attend continuation school for four hours a week, tended to reduce the number of positions open to children under sixteen, since some employers preferred to dispense with juvenile labor rather than conform to those requirements. We have no measure of the importance of the last factor.

Our project represents an interesting form of private coöperation with the public-school system. The investigation is being conducted by the Schmidlapp Bureau through the work-certificate office, which ordinarily performs the function of issuing work certificates. This office is a subdivision of the office of the superintendent of schools, and the investigation would not have been possible without the constant support of both the former superintendent, Frank B. Dyer, and the present one, Randall J. Condon. All of the financial burden of the investigation, except office room and the supplies used in issuing the certificates, is met by a group of private citizens.[1]

1 The investigation was planned and the funds collected by Miss Edith Campbell of the Schmidlapp Bureau and E. N. Clopper of the National Child Labor Committee. The

By assuming the responsibility of issuing work certificates, those conducting the investigation secured complete control of the material for research. By a unique provision of the law, employers are required to return certificates to the issuing office and children to have the certificates reissued each time there is a change of position. The certificate office is thereby given a measure of supervision over working children up to the age of sixteen and is enabled to enforce the regulations about the kinds of work permitted children as well as those concerning the hours of employment.

The work of the bureau is therefore divided into two parts : first, that of issuing certificates and keeping records of all working children, and, second, that of investigating intensively a large group of working children.

Every child who applies for a work certificate must present four credentials : first, a satisfactory health record from a physician of the Board of Health ; second, a legal birth record proving that he is at least fourteen years of age ; third, a school record showing that he has completed at least the fifth grade ; and fourth, a contract signed by his future employer. By the time a child has been sent back three or four times, as is often necessary to secure all four records in proper form, the process of taking out a work certificate becomes a far more serious ordeal than in the days of old.

When certificates are issued, all children who have not completed the eighth grade — and these constitute eight tenths of the total — must be assigned to a continuation school. Notice of the assignment is sent to both the school and the employer. The time required by the continuation school is four hours a week, and each employer has an opportunity, when he signs the child's contract, to indicate the school and hours which he prefers. If he expresses no preference the office makes the assignment.

Schmidlapp Bureau, through the generosity of J. G. Schmidlapp, bears one half of the expense. The other contributors are W. H. Alms, L. A. Ault, Mrs. Thomas J. Emery, Edward Senior, John B. Scarborough, Sidney Pritz, James N. Gamble, Harry Levy, Omer T. Glenn.

The staff consists of Helen Thompson Woolley, director, Charlotte Rust Fischer, Rose E. Rankins, and William A. Spencer, laboratory investigators ; M. Louise Boswell, home visitor ; Annis E. Alden, issuer of certificates, and Emma Day, assistant in the certificate office. Since the above was written Mr. Spencer has resigned and his place has been taken by E. S. Jones.

But this does not end the formalities. The law requires that upon the termination of employment the certificate must be returned by mail to the issuing office, accompanied by a statement as to when and why the child left. The question of enforcing this requirement will be discussed later. When a child takes another position he must present to the office a contract signed by his new employer. The certificate is then reissued on a form like the original one and mailed to the employer. The child is again assigned to a continuation school, and both school and employer are notified. A full record of all these proceedings, except the assignment to a continuation school, is kept. In addition to these necessary records, the office is noting also wages and the children's reasons for changes of position. A second card of employment is made out for each child and placed in a file classified by employers, so that the office has an industrial history not only of each child but also of each employer in so far as his dealings with child labor are concerned.

The two provisions of the law which are difficult of enforcement are the one which states that no child under sixteen shall work without a certificate, and the one which forbids children under sixteen and girls under eighteen to work more than eight hours a day.

The first difficulty breaks up into two distinct problems. The first is how to prevent children from taking an initial position without a certificate ; the second, how to prevent those who have already had a certificate from taking another position without a reissuing of the certificate.

Close coöperation with the schools is our method of dealing with the first problem. Of course some children, on first coming to the city, may not be sent to school at all. The difficulty here is the general one of enforcing the compulsory education law. We deal with them as we deal with all who take employment without a certificate and rely on the factory inspector. This is our only recourse, but Cincinnati is fortunate in having a factory inspector who understands the certificate system and who coöperates by sending to the office all children for whom the employers cannot show certificates. Nearly all employers of large numbers of children are now scrupulous about demanding certificates. It is only occasional and inexperienced ones who take children without them. We believe that the number of those who evade the law is small. During the last year the factory inspector has found only six children working without certificates, though the same inspector in previous years has found hundreds.

To prevent children who have legally held one position from taking a second without reissuing the certificate is a different problem. The key to this situation is the requirement of the return of the certificate by the employer to our office. In a majority of cases this is done. Sometimes the child informs the office that he has left, and sometimes our first notice of the change is when the child comes in for a second position. Several times we have verified long series of employment records and have found that by one or another of these checks we have kept records of over 90 per cent of the changes in positions.

More difficult still is the enforcement of the eight-hour day for children. When each certificate is issued the employer is notified of the legal number of hours. The children themselves are asked about their working hours and reports of violations are sent at once to the factory inspector. From its file of employers the office can give the factory inspector a list of all the children under sixteen employed by any firm which is reported for violation of hours. This information is of great value in making investigations and in securing evidence.

While there are other devices by which we minimize violation of law, I have indicated enough to show how effectively such a measure may be administered. The best evidence of what its enforcement means to the childhood of Cincinnati is to be had, of course, in the figures quoted at the outset of this article. These show the tremendous drop since the law went into effect in the number of immature youths going untrained into factory and workshop.

I have said that 2366 children between 14 and 16 took out work certificates last year. A careful classification has been made of these, showing the type and location of the schools from which the children came, their age, school grade, and the kind of work in which they are now engaged. Cincinnati, like other cities, has both public and church schools. Forty-three per cent of the total were from church schools and 57 per cent from public. While the exact enrollment of the church schools is not given out, it is known that the enrollment of the public schools is about three times that of the other. The proportion, therefore, of those leaving the church schools is more than twice that of those leaving the public schools. Over 34 per cent of those leaving the public schools are fifteen years of age, while only 18 per cent of those leaving the church schools are that old. But in spite of the fact that the children from the church schools are younger, more of them are in the higher grades. This is due in part to the fact that the public school is losing chiefly its retarded children, while the church school, which sends into industry twice as large a proportion of its children, is losing both retarded and normal children. Differences in methods of grading children may also be a factor. A comparison of the retardation of children who leave the public schools to go to work with that of the children who remain in school shows that twice as large a proportion of working children are retarded as of school children.

The occupations entered by the children can be grouped as follows : factories, 33 per cent (19 per cent shoe, 4 per cent paper box, 2 per cent candy, and 8 per cent miscellaneous factories) ; errand boys and girls, 22.5 per cent (5 per cent public messenger service and 17.5 per cent private business houses) ; department stores, 15.5 per cent ; tailoring and sewing trades, 8.7 per cent ; helping parents at home, 6.8 per cent ; and the remaining 13.5 per cent scattered among many occupations.

Very little of the work represented has any value as trade education. Each child in the shoe factory performs from one to three of the 150 or more operations necessary in making a shoe. They lace shoes, ink edges, or wet soles. The girls in tailor shops pull bastings or baste one kind of seam. The messenger-service and errand-boy positions are notoriously blind-alley occupations. The department stores use these young children for inside errands and for wrapping packages. A few of them may have a chance to become saleswomen if they are fitted for it, but in Cincinnati saleswomen are paid such low wages that the occupation can scarcely be classed as skilled.

It is a safe statement that only a very small percentage of children who work from fourteen to sixteen years make any real gain in general industrial efficiency.

The wages paid to a group of over 2000 children are graphically represented in a chart. The wages represent what was paid at the start, in each of the first five positions, provided that many were held. The median wage for girls is $3 and for boys $3.75 a week. There is a sex difference in wages throughout. In their first positions as well as in subsequent ones, girls receive about 75 cents a week less than boys. The charts also show that both boys and girls better themselves in wages by mere change of position. There is a larger proportion of children at the lower wage in first positions. With subsequent positions the proportion at the lower wage decreases and the proportion in the higher wage increases. Other statistics, not yet published, show that the increase in earnings obtained by changes of position is greater than that obtained by sticking to one job for a year. The point is an interesting one to bring to the attention of employers when they complain about the instability of child labor.

The eight hundred boys and girls of whom we are making a special study were fourteen years old when they left school to begin work. All of them were entering some industry, not merely helping at home. All were native-born white children. Except for these characteristics the children were taken at random, as fast as our office force would permit. We feel sure that the series adequately represents the whole group.

The scope of the investigation includes a study of the mental and physical development of children in industry as compared with children of corresponding age and grade who stay in school. We are visiting and comparing the homes of both working children and school children. We are studying in detail the industrial life of the working children. Finally, we are investigating the industries themselves in which the children engage.

It has already been pointed out that we hope to be able to compare the rate of mental and physical development of children in industry with that of children in school. We can also study the children who do not succeed industrially and find out whether their failure is to be attributed to the children themselves, to the home, to the school, or to the industry. By discovering what relation there is, if any, between a child's mental and physical tests and his success or failure in various kinds of industry, we can throw some light on the problem of vocational guidance. Although Münsterberg and others have made scientific beginnings in determining vocational guidance by the psychological laboratory,

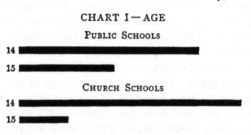

CHART I — AGE

PUBLIC SCHOOLS

14
15

CHURCH SCHOOLS

14
15

ratory, no one knows just how useful this means will eventually prove. Such a correlation as we can make between the record in tests and the industrial record will help to decide the question. A set of norms that can be used in any group as a basis of diagnosis is being established, and this will be of great importance if the laboratory method proves useful.

Meanwhile all the records we are collecting about the industrial experiences of the children themselves — the kind of work open to them, their earnings, increases of pay, the amount of unemployment among them, their reasons for changes of position, and their attitude toward work and school — will be indispensable in deciding upon a program of industrial education or of vocational guidance. A study of the industries is equally

CHART II — GRADE

PUBLIC SCHOOLS   CHURCH SCHOOLS

5   5
6   6
7   7
8   8
9+10   9+10

necessary in both these problems. The information about industries may be cast in the form of bulletins for the use of teachers and parents.

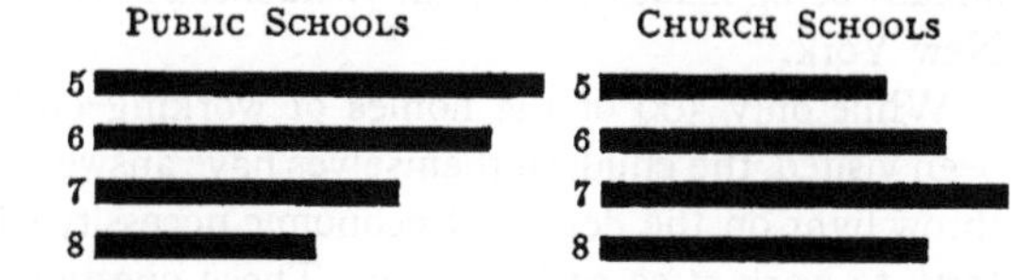

Mental and physical examinations have now been made of all the 800 children at the time they started to work. Seven hundred of

them have been retested at the end of the first year of work and
200 at the end of the second year. A group of school children
has been selected to conform in grade to the working children and
400 of them have been tested. Only the first series of tests with
working children has been evaluated and tabulated. The outcome
shows that the tests will furnish a reliable basis of comparison. In
all of the mental tests the children from the higher grades did
better than those from the lower in spite of the fact that they were
all of the same age. In other words, tests showed a high degree
of correlation with school grade. The tests then are almost or quite
as efficient in classifying children according to mental ability as is
the school, and we can feel confident that comparisons between
school children and working children made by this means will yield
reliable results.

The belief that girls develop mentally more rapidly than boys is
confirmed by the tests. At fourteen, the girls are superior to the
boys in all the mental tests. Physically they are superior in height
and weight and in coördination, but the boys are superior in strength
and rapidity of movement.

When the series of psychological tests is published in detail with
careful directions both for giving them and for evaluating the results, a set of norms will be furnished for fourteen-year-old children
which can be used for many purposes. One of the most interesting
will be the comparison in mental development of older delinquents
with normal fourteen-year-old children — an application which is
already being made by Dr. Jean Weidensall at Bedford Reformatory,
New York.

While only 300 of the homes of working children have as yet
been visited, the children themselves have answered questions which
throw light on the degree of economic necessity which drives them
forth to work at so early an age. These questions have to do with
the family and home life, occupations of parents, number of children, number of rooms occupied by the family, presence of lodgers,
disposition of the children's earnings and attitude toward work
and school.

Under the direction of the National Child Labor Committee,
all the records bearing on the economic status of the families have

been studied. After inadequate records had been rejected, there remained a group of 650 families about whom it seemed possible to
draw conclusions as to economic necessity. The question which we
tried to answer with regard to each family was whether the child's
earnings were essential to maintain the family without assistance
from outside. And the outcome was similar to that of the government investigation and to those of Massachusetts and New York.
Only 27 per cent of the families were believed to require the earnings of the children, while 73 per cent had apparently no such
economic need. This is one more proof that necessity is not the
most potent force behind child labor.

The other face of the picture is that the majority of children
declared that they were tired of school and anxious to go to work.
The parents were sometimes equally ready to have children work,
sometimes indiffer-
ent, and sometimes
merely overruled by
the child's eager-
ness. We found
very few cases, if
any, in which the
child who wished
to stay in school and whose parents could have afforded to let
him was forced by them to go to work. Even after trying it, the
children continue to prefer work to school.

CHART III — RETARDATION

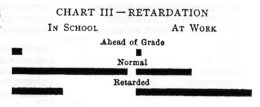

We now have a full industrial history covering a year or more
for 700 working children. In a tabulation of 474 of these histories,
it was discovered that the median weekly wage for girls for the year
is $3 and for boys $3.75. Of the industries employing children in
considerable numbers, the department store paid the lowest wage
to both boys and girls. Here, as in most communities, the highest
wage was paid to boys by the most injurious occupation — the
public messenger service. Shoe factories paid the next best wage
to boys and the best wage of all to girls.

The amount of unemployment among working children has been
a matter of frequent comment. With regard to this group of children, 50 per cent of the girls and 60 per cent of the boys were

employed for the entire 52 weeks of the year. Only one tenth of the boys were unemployed for twelve weeks or more out of the year, while one tenth of the girls were unemployed one half the time or more. Thirty eight per cent of the boys and 45 per cent of the girls had held but one position during the year, while 4 per cent of the boys and 3 per cent of the girls had held more than four

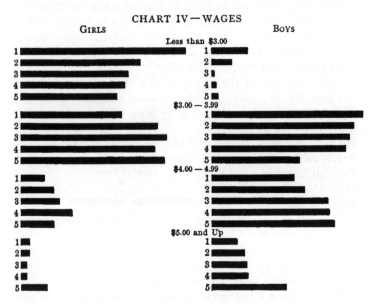

CHART IV — WAGES

positions. The median number of positions during the year for both boys and girls was two.

Each time a child changes his position the office makes a record of his reason for the change. A study of the reasons assigned in 700 cases showed that 41 per cent were included under economic reasons. In 60 per cent of these the child had voluntarily left because the pay was low or because a better position was offered him or because he wanted to learn a trade. In the remaining cases the employer had either laid the child off or reduced his earnings because of slack season. The next largest group of reasons, 20 per cent, was that of dissatisfaction on the part of the child for reasons other than economic, such as work too dirty, workroom too noisy, could not bear the smell of paste, fellow employees too rough, afraid of lead poisoning, foreman cross and "hollered" at him, or unjustly charged with spoiled materials. Physical reasons, such as illness or work which proved to be too hard physically, account for 11 per cent of the changes. The same proportion is due to failures on the part of the child, which the children themselves report almost as frequently as the employers. Disagreement either with foremen or with fellow employees and incompetence make up most of this group. Reasons connected with the home comprise 9 per cent of the whole number and conflicts with the child-labor law the remaining 8 per cent.

I want to discuss now two of the applications to educational problems which some of these facts bear. The first deals with the placement bureau for children under sixteen as part of a program for vocational guidance in the public schools. Sometimes the term "vocational guidance" is taken to mean little more than a well-conducted placement bureau. The facts we have presented seem to me to throw serious doubt upon the wisdom of allowing the public school to undertake the placing in industry of children under sixteen. There is no work open to them worth advising them to take. If the schools take over placement work, it may have the effect of legalizing and perpetuating a condition which it ought to be opposing; that is, allowing children under sixteen to leave school for work. If the school could lend all its energies to readjusting its system of instruction to meet the needs of the children who are now leaving, and thus hold them in school, it would be rendering a far greater service than it could in finding for them jobs which, at best, are of no real advantage to the child.

The placement bureau, it may be said, has the virtue of bringing the schools into immediate contact with the industries — but continuation schools do it even better. The placement bureau is also one means of investigating the conditions in industry, but it is not the only means, and may have dangers inherent in it. No placement bureau which deals with large numbers of children under sixteen can avoid putting many of them in thoroughly undesirable positions, provided it places them at all. It seems much more

pernicious for the public school to place a child in an injurious occupation than for the child to place himself. The influence which
can be brought to bear on the industries themselves through such
a bureau is necessarily small, because child labor is not essential
to most industries.

The second application I wish to make deals with a problem also
previously discussed in *The Survey* — the question as to whether
vocational and industrial schools shall be organized from within our
present school system and kept in organic relation with it, or shall
be organized under a separate board made up not from the leaders
of education but from the leaders in industry. I would like to ask
this question : Have the dealings of industry with children in the
past been such as to warrant the state in turning over the training
of the children destined for industry to the forces of industry itself ?
The report I have given shows the status of children under one of
the best child-labor laws in the country, well enforced. There is
very little suggestion of an educational attitude on the part of industry towards the children.[1] The undoubted educational possibilities of the industries are left undeveloped, and it is exceedingly
rare to have an interest in the development of the children prom-
incnt in the mind of the employer. This is a state of mind which
is quite understandable. With the best intentions the employer
can scarcely avoid viewing the educational problem first from the
standpoint of the welfare of the industry. He wants more efficient workmen, first of all because the industry would profit by
them. In his mind the welfare of the worker must be a secondary
result of the success of the industry, and he has scant patience
with anyone who suggests molding the industry to fit the needs
of the workers.

Now there is undoubtedly a sense in which the welfare of the
worker is secondary to the success of the industry. It is an obvious
enough fact that the industry must be successful enough to exist,
or the worker cannot earn his living by it. But when the scale
which measures the success of the industry is solely the profits of

---

[1] The continuation schools for machine-shop apprentices and for printers' apprentices in
Cincinnati, which were started by the industries, are important exceptions to this statement,
though they apply only to children over sixteen years of age.

the employer it ceases to be true that the welfare of the industry and that of the worker must be the same.

It makes a very great difference, then, whether those who mold the system of industrial education in this country have as their immediate object the development of industries in which the workers are first of all parts of the machine, or the development of well-rounded, intelligent citizens, who shall possess specific industrial ability as one phase of their training. The habit of mind of the educator would lead him to take the latter attitude, and that of the leader of industry the former.

But the plan would be objectionable even if industry were so socialized that its leaders could be expected to view the problem of industrial education first from the standpoint of the development of the individual child. It would mean a sharp separation at a comparatively early age of the children destined for industry from those destined for academic and professional careers. The decision would inevitably be made rather on the basis of the economic status of the family than on that of the child's fitness. The plan would lead us directly towards class distinctions of a thoroughly undemocratic sort. As John Dewey has declared: "Those who believe in the continued separate existence of what they are pleased to call the lower classes or the laboring classes, would naturally rejoice to have schools in which those classes would be segregated. And some employers of labor would doubtless rejoice to have schools, supported by public taxation, supply them with additional food for their mills. All others should be united against every proposition, in whatever form advanced, to separate training of employees from training for citizenship, training of intelligence and character from training for narrow industrial efficiency." [1]

1 See *The Survey* of March 22, 1913, p. 870.

WORK, WAGES, AND SCHOOLING OF EIGHT HUNDRED IOWA BOYS IN RELATION TO THE PROBLEMS OF VOCATIONAL GUIDANCE

By Ervin E. Lewis, Associate Professor of Education

(Published by the University, Iowa City, Iowa)

SCOPE OF THE INVESTIGATION

The original intention in this investigation was to interview 1000 boys of Iowa, from sixteen to twenty years of age, who had not completed a course in a high school, and to secure from each an accurate statement of his vocational progress since leaving school. The investigators were instructed to go directly to the boys, to explain briefly to them the purpose of the investigation, and to ask for their coöperation. A printed card containing the following questions was formulated and placed in the hands of the investigators. All of the questions were to be answered by each boy.

What is the boy's name?
What is his present age (nearest birthday), and address?
What grade does he say he was in at the time he left school?
What was his age at that time?
What is the name and location of the school he last attended?
What was his reason (or reasons) for leaving school?
How long after leaving school was he idle before he secured work?
How many different jobs has he been in since leaving school?
For each job he has been in, answer the following questions:
 Kind of job;
 Kind of business;
 How he found the job;
 ·How long he was in it;
 His average weekly wages;
  (*a*) When he started the job, and
  (*b*) When he left it;

234

The length of time idle between jobs;
The reason for changing jobs;
What trade if any does the boy now desire to prepare for?

About 900 boys in Des Moines and 100 boys in Sioux City were interviewed by the investigators. Nearly 20 per cent of them were reached on holidays and during the evenings in pool halls and on the street. Returns from about 80 per cent were secured during working hours through the coöperation of employers, more than 200 of whom were interviewed. Only two employers regarded the investigators with suspicion and refused to allow the boys in their establishments to be interviewed. Reliable data were received from more than 800 boys. The remaining cases are excluded from this report, because the replies were not complete.

The investigators are aware that one cannot depend too much upon the memory of boys of these ages. The errors are larger and more numerous than desired. On the other hand, the selection is one of pure chance and the errors to some extent counterbalance each other. Although the data are not so reliable as desired, they are at all events approximate and certainly are better than any other data at present available upon the same subject.

AGE OF THE BOYS AT THE TIME OF THE INVESTIGATION

Of the boys whose ages were known 1 was twelve years old at the time of the investigation, 2 were thirteen years old, 17 were fourteen years old, 58 were fifteen years old, 101 were sixteen years old, 139 were seventeen years old, 126 were eighteen years old, 131 were nineteen years old, 93 were twenty years old, 89 were twenty-one years old, 61 were twenty-two years old, and 1 was twenty-four years old. These figures show that 507 boys, or 60 per cent of those investigated, were from sixteen to nineteen years of age. No effort was made on the part of the investigators to select boys below sixteen or boys above twenty. On the other hand, they were definitely instructed to secure as many cases as possible of boys from sixteen to nineteen years of age. All of the boys lived when interviewed either in Sioux City or Des Moines. However, they had not always lived in these places, as is shown by a study of the location of the schools which they last attended.

LOCATION OF THE SCHOOLS WHICH THE BOYS LAST ATTENDED

More than 40 per cent of the boys came from schools located outside of the city in which they were living when interviewed.

Four hundred and fifty-five (52 per cent) came from 62 different schools located in Des Moines; 150 (17 per cent) came from schools located in 107 cities and towns in Iowa outside of Des Moines and Sioux City; 117 (13 per cent) came from 27 different states other than Iowa; 41 (nearly 5 per cent) came from 8 different foreign countries. The remaining boys came from schools located in or near Sioux City.

These facts are rather significant to those interested in training boys for the various vocations. If these figures are accurate, *40 per cent of the boys at work in the various pursuits receive their training in schools located outside of the cities in which they are working.* Boys trained in the various vocations in the public schools of a city would come in competition with boys coming into the city from other cities and states of the country. In other words, the city would not be able to train all of the boys for any kind of pursuit without a compulsory system of continuation school attendance, which would operate across not only the boys leaving the schools of that city but also across the boys leaving schools located in other cities and coming to that city.

AGE AND GRADE AT WHICH THE BOYS LEFT SCHOOL

Each boy was questioned as to the grade he was in at the time he left school. While the answers received in this way are not so reliable as may be desired, they are sufficient to indicate the general tendency of boys of this class. It would be much better to get their records from the schools which they left, but this was impossible, inasmuch as many of them left schools located outside of Des Moines and Sioux City.

From our data it may be seen that relatively few of the boys leave school before they are fourteen years old and before they have finished the fifth grade. Table No. 1 gives the data for the entire group. Three boys left school while in the first grade; one of these boys was six years old, one fifteen, and one sixteen. Only 64 boys left school before completing the fifth grade. Thirty-eight per cent left school before finishing the seventh grade and 61 per cent before finishing the eighth grade. The present child-labor law in Iowa requires that children must be fourteen years of age before they may legally quit school. According to this table 103 of the 826 boys studied were under fourteen. However, the reader should

TABLE NO. I. THE AGE AT WHICH THE BOYS LEFT SCHOOL

Leaving Age	Grade Left								High School				Totals
	1st	2d	3d	4th	5th	6th	7th	8th	1st	2d	3d	4th	
6	1												1
7					1								1
8													
9					1								1
10		1	1	3									5
11			1	1	1	1		1		1			6
12			1	2	9	3	2						17
13				5	6	20	18	21	1				71
14				8	14	37	45	76	15	3			198
15	1			3	7	33	40	68	35	20	4		211
16	1			1	2	15	17	59	26	23	11		155
17					1	6	9	36	17	11	11	9	100
18					1		3	11	5	8	10	10	48
19							1	1	1	2	2	3	10
20								1					1
21													
22											1		1
Totals	3	2	22	37	121	136	276	100	69	38	22		826

remember that the majority of the boys had, at the time of the investigation, been out of school more than three years, and the child-labor law was not so well enforced three years ago as at the present time. Furthermore, upon checking the records of these boys we find that nearly 90 per cent of the violations of the age-requirement are made by boys coming to the two cities studied from other cities in the state and from other states in the Union. These boys leave schools located in small towns and migrate to large cities where they carry on a more or less precarious existence, avoiding further school attendance.

It is apparent from these figures that *workers in juvenile occupations come largely from the sixth, seventh, and eighth grades of the public schools.* It is also evident that most of them leave school at about the time when they are fourteen, fifteen, or sixteen years of age.

THE VARIOUS REASONS THE BOYS STATE FOR LEAVING SCHOOL

To determine exactly the reason or reasons why a boy leaves school is very difficult. Some argue that boys leave school because they have to work and earn, while others argue that they are dissatisfied with the kind of schooling that is offered them. In interviewing the boys an attempt was made to find out the reasons that they give for leaving school.

Case No. 457 said: " I came here from England at the age of eleven. I started in school in Des Moines, where they put me in the fourth grade. I found the work in the fourth grade too easy and asked to be promoted, but they refused to promote me, and so I left school and went to work."

Case No. 165 gives quite another reason. He says: " I completed the eighth grade in the country school where my folks lived. There was no high school within twelve miles. If there had been, I am sure I would have gone to school. I went to work for my father in a freight depot and have been working ever since."

Case No. 570 related as his experience the following: " I did not like school as I wanted to do tool work or follow some commercial line. And as soon as I became fourteen years of age I quit and took a three months' course in a business college. I was in the sixth grade when I left school, but that did not seem to make any difference to the business college."

Case No. 782 suffered from stuttering and said: " I felt neglected and very frequently ashamed, as the children laughed at me. However, I could have continued in school, and probably would have, if an attractive position as a clerk had not been offered me at the time."

The above reasons for leaving school are somewhat exceptional, but they show something of the variety of motives actuating boys at the time of leaving school. A tabulation of all the reasons includes the following:

I. Necessity

" Had to work " 128
" Sickness or death of parents " 40
" Earnings necessary to family support " 43
" Self-support necessary " 33
" Help needed at home " 16
" To earn money for education of self or relative " . . 1
" Father insisted that he quit " 1

II. Child dissatisfied with school

" Tired of school " 81
" Disliked school life " 104
" Disliked teacher " 26
" Disliked study or some particular subject " 15
" School work too hard; could not learn " 20
" Not promoted; failed " 17
" Expelled or had trouble " 20
" Too big for class " 2
" Had enough school " 8
" Irregular attendance " 3

III. Preference for work

" Preferred work to school " 116
" Wanted spending money " 29
" Wanted to earn money " 9

IV. Other causes

" Wanted to learn trade or business " 23
" Moved away or came to America " 26
" Wanted to travel " 6
" Had completed school course; no other school near " . 5
" Ran away from home " 4
" Ill health " 24
" Wanted to go to business college " 3
" Trouble in the family " 9
" Father thought I was too old " 2
" Liked tool work " 2
" No particular reason; just left " 1

The thirty-odd reasons given in the preceding list are reducible to three:

1. Either the earnings of the boys are necessary, or their help is desired to support the family. This probably accounts for one third of the withdrawals.

2. The second large factor is the boys' dissatisfaction with school. When they reach the age of fourteen many of them seem to be in an indifferent frame of mind toward further schooling. The routine of the schoolroom is too coercive to their growing sense of independence. They think they ought to be allowed to do about as they desire, and too frequently their parents agree with them. No general theory fits every case, and probably no child leaves school for any one reason; his reason for leaving is a complex of causes, no one of which is in itself sufficient to explain his withdrawal. *If we could go behind these figures, we would probably find that the chief reason for dropping out of school can be traced directly to a lack of parental control and interest. Many parents seem to be in an indifferent frame of mind about their children's schooling after the children have reached the legal age.* Frequently parents of foreign children sacrifice the future education of the children to the immediate wants of the family. A feeling is common among such parents that the child should be put to work at the earliest possible moment and his earnings be turned into the family income. They are disposed to cut short the child's school days for entirely insufficient causes.

3. The third general cause for boys' leaving school is not so much necessity or dissatisfaction as it is their preference for work. They want spending money, or, more serious still, they want to do something " worth while "; something big physically or materially that appeals to their growing sense of power. Furthermore they do not think that schooling is of financial value to them. They look upon it as a lazy boy's occupation. Case No. 537 said: " Schooling does not help a fellow make money. I have to make my own living and I cannot afford to go to school." In Case No. 461 the father told the boy: " There is no money in going to school. You had better get to work." About 20 per cent of the boys left for some one of these reasons.

In a few cases the family moves or the boy is sick for a few days, or he desires to travel. Occasionally there is trouble in the family, as in the case of one boy whose stepfather continually punished him for insufficient reasons. A few of the boys do not like the social life of the high school, especially children from the poor and foreign classes. One boy said, "The high school is for the rich people and not for poor boys." Apparently these social factors do not account for many of the withdrawals.

HOW LONG ARE THE BOYS IDLE IMMEDIATELY AFTER LEAVING SCHOOL

A few of the boys after leaving school remain idle for some time before going to work. In order to find out just how much time is wasted in this way, the investigators were instructed to ask each boy to state the length of time he was idle between leaving school and securing his first job. Of the boys who gave satisfactory answers to the questions 634 said they went to work immediately; 115 were idle less than one month; 25 from one to two months; 11 from two to three months; 10 from three to four months; 4 from four to five months; 8 from five to six months; 14 from six months to one year; 6 between one and one and a half years; and 2 for two years and over.

From these figures it will be seen that about *75 per cent of the boys went to work immediately*. Of the remaining 25 per cent over half of them were idle less than one month. One reason why children are idle so little between leaving school and taking their first job is probably that they have the job before they leave school, and that induces them to quit. If the boy is fourteen years of age, has little spending money, and no one at home to insist upon his going to school, it is pretty hard for him to resist a lucrative blind-alley job.

HOW THE BOYS FIND THEIR JOBS

Another of the questions asked each boy was, " How did you find your job?" An answer was secured for each job they had had since leaving school. The purpose of the question was to discover how much assistance they received in finding positions, and from what sources. The usual method of "selling" one's labor is to hawk it from door to door. A common method of securing employees is to put out a sign that hawkers may apply for work. Usually in this country the burden of finding employment falls upon the individual. The cities and states of America do not have well-organized systems of employment bureaus for the purpose of adjusting either juvenile or adult laborer to employer. The boys as they leave school to go to work are for the most part thrown upon their own resources, as is shown by the results of this investigation. More than 85 per cent of the jobs were found by the boys' hawking for them. The remaining jobs were found in the following way :

92 by answering an advertisement
57 through assistance of parents
55 through assistance of friends
1 through teacher in public school
1 by being asked by an employer

Apparently the teacher does not attempt to assist these boys in securing work. Nor are their friends, relatives, and parents of very great assistance. The majority of the boys find work for themselves. It seemed not to be considered the business of any social agency other than the public school accurately to inform such boys concerning the occupations open to them. No literature is handed them concerning desirable vocations, and apparently no advice is offered them regarding unskilled, semiskilled, or highly skilled employments. They are not told about the "blind-alley" jobs. No one looks after them systematically, following them from the door of the schoolroom into the jobs which necessity or choice causes them to accept. They find their own jobs and take the jobs that they can find quickly. These boys studied are therefore fair examples of what happens in the absence of vocational guidance. What might have happened if careful vocational guidance and supervision had been provided can only be inferred. It is safe to guess that the percentage of those entering and remaining in un-. skilled and low-grade skilled occupations would have been greatly decreased, and also that the "fetching and carrying" occupations — in which the chief duty is to wait upon the casual needs of others—would have been avoided to a much greater degree. Some-one might study an equal number of children leaving schools of a city where vocational guidance is provided and contrast the two groups. Such a contrast would measure, to some degree at least, the kind and value of the guidance offered. It would then be possible to know how much a city could afford to spend in instituting such guidance. At present we have a feeling that guidance is valuable, but are unable to say to what degree.

NUMBER OF BOYS WHO HAVE COMPLETED ONE OR MORE JOBS SINCE LEAVING SCHOOL

A careful study was made of the number of boys who had concluded one or more jobs since leaving school. A job was considered "concluded" if the boy had entered and left it. A typical working record of one or two of the boys may be of interest at this point.

Case No. 51 was last in the eighth grade, and was fifteen years old at the time he left school. He started to work in a brickyard at $6 a week, and at the end of one year was getting $9 a week. He left the job because he thought it was "too hard." Within one week he found work in a hosiery mill, where he stayed for two years, starting at $4 a week and receiving at the end of two years $12 a week. He gave as his reason for leaving the job, "tired of it." He then secured work on the fair grounds for four months at $10 a week, but the job "came to an end" and he went to work as a helper in a tin shop, where he remained for five months, getting $7 a week. He left it "to learn a trade," and started in assisting a brick mason at $6 a week. At the end of the year he was getting $14 a week, but was unhappy and left it "for no very good reason; just because he wanted a change," and went back to work on the fair grounds for $7 a week and board. At the time of the investigation he was a tender to a brick mason at $12 a week, and said he desired to become a brick mason. He is now twenty years old, and has had in all seven different jobs in five years.

A study of all the cases gives the following results :

228 boys had concluded 1 job since leaving school
214 boys had concluded 2 jobs since leaving school
169 boys had concluded 3 jobs since leaving school
94 boys had concluded 4 jobs since leaving school
58 boys had concluded 5 jobs since leaving school
31 boys had concluded 6 jobs since leaving school
19 boys had concluded 7 jobs since leaving school

11 boys had concluded 8 jobs since leaving school
13 boys had concluded 9 jobs since leaving school

Two boys had concluded as many as 12 jobs each. These boys belonged to that shiftless class that is continually moving from place to place and job to job in search of excitement. *The average boy passes through 3 jobs in two years*. Such figures emphasize the instability of juvenile occupations. The boys do not remain in one occupation for a very long period of time. *The work that they are in is unsatisfactory and does not succeed in holding them.*

LENGTH OF TIME THE BOYS SPENT IN THE JOBS

A few of the boys had spent over three years on a job. No job is included in these figures which was not concluded at the time of the investigation. A complete analysis is shown as follows:

In 17 jobs the boys spent less than 1 month
In 37 jobs the boys spent between 1 and 2 months
In 105 jobs the boys spent between 2 and 3 months
In 138 jobs the boys spent between 3 and 4 months
In 133 jobs the boys spent between 4 and 5 months
In 102 jobs the boys spent between 5 and 6 months
In 147 jobs the boys spent between 6 and 7 months
In 90 jobs the boys spent between 7 and 8 months
In 69 jobs the boys spent between 8 and 9 months
In 85 jobs the boys spent between 9 and 10 months
In 69 jobs the boys spent between 10 and 11 months
In 25 jobs the boys spent between 11 and 12 months
In 222 jobs the boys spent between 1 and $1\frac{1}{2}$ years
In 110 jobs the boys spent between $1\frac{1}{2}$ and 2 years
. In 68 jobs the boys spent between 2 and $2\frac{1}{4}$ years
In 25 jobs the boys spent between $2\frac{1}{2}$ and 3 years
In 27 jobs the boys spent between 3 and $3\frac{1}{4}$ years
In 3 jobs the boys spent between $3\frac{1}{4}$ and 4 years
In 30 jobs the boys spent between 4 years and over

Of the total number investigated, 218 had not concluded their first job at the time of the investigation and therefore are not included in the above figures. The average length of the time for a job is shown to be less than over a year. The boys seem to shift a great deal. Some of the reasons for changes are given in the following section.

REASONS THE BOYS GIVE FOR CHANGING JOBS

It is impossible to state the exact number of boys leaving jobs for any particular reason. Some of them "wanted better pay," or "to find a better job." Others "did not like the work they were in and wanted a change." Another boy said he "wanted inside work." About 20 per cent of them "lost their jobs"; 15 per cent found their jobs "too hard"; a few, perhaps 7 per cent, were forced to leave the work they were in because "the business failed." One boy was working at night and left it because he "wanted day work." Another boy who was working on a punching press in a machine shop was injured slightly and, after recovering, did not go back.

Reasons that are given many times are: "laid off," "was let out," "found the work too hard," "got fired," "had trouble," "did not like it," "moved away," or "came to America."

Reasons that occur rarely are: "little chance for improvement," "no future," "wanted to learn a trade," "was advanced or promoted," "left the work because it was n't steady."

The one striking note through all these reasons is the desire on the part of the boys for better wages. *They seem to think more of an increase in salary than they do of an advancement in skill.* For this they are not entirely to blame, as they receive little or no advice to the contrary. In their minds the boy who is getting the best wages is the most successful boy. Their idea of success is expressed in financial terms. In a later section more definite evidence is given for this conclusion.

THE BEGINNING WAGES OF THE BOYS

One of the most interesting parts of the study pertains to the wages received by the boys when they begin work. The facts are as follows:

    4 boys received nothing a week
    7 boys received $1 a week
   22 boys received $2 a week
   87 boys received $3 a week
  128 boys received $4 a week

124 boys received $5 a week
111 boys received $6 a week
94 boys received $7 a week
64 boys received $8 a week
47 boys received $9 a week
54 boys received $10 a week
6 boys received $11 a week
40 boys received $12 a week
4 boys received $13 a week
6 boys received $14 a week
22 boys received $15 a week
5 boys received $16 a week
2 boys received $17 a week
7 boys received $18 a week
2 boys received $19 a week
1 boy received $20 a week

The range is from nothing to $20 a week. The average is about $5.50 a week. *There are as many who received $5.50 or less a week as there are boys who receive more than $5.50 a week.* If we leave out of consideration the first and last 25 per cent of the boys, we find that the middle 50 per cent received a weekly wage of from $4.50 to $7.

The boys working in coal mines are of special interest. This includes 37 boys. Their average age on beginning work was found to be fourteen years and six months. Their beginning wages were $12 a week. However, some of the boys received as low as $6, and others as high as $20 a week. One boy worked for three weeks in this occupation, while another stayed in it for eleven years. The reasons the boys give for leaving coal mining are interesting. Four " got hurt "; in the case of three the " parents objected "; four said they " did n't like it "; one " got fired "; three " wanted to learn a trade."

The Mine Workers' Union has had a great deal to do with the elimination of boys from mining occupations. Practically no boys under sixteen are now used to drive mules. The number of trapper boys has been greatly reduced by many of the miners' adopting overhead systems of ventilation that make trapdoors unnecessary. The fact that the mine operators must assume all risk for boys under sixteen has also tended toward their elimination.

CORRELATIONS BETWEEN LEAVING GRADE AND BEGINNING WAGE

The question is sometimes asked, Do the boys who leave an advanced grade receive a higher beginning wage than those who leave a lower grade of the public school? This question is answered by the figures in Table No. II. The wages and grade were known for 812 cases.

TABLE NO. II. CORRELATION BETWEEN LEAVING GRADE AND BEGINNING WAGE

Average Weekly Wage	Grade								High School				Total
	1st	2d	3d	4th	5th	6th	7th	8th	1st	2d	3d	4th	
$1.00 and under					1	4	1						6
$1.01 to $2.00		1	1	1	5	1	4		4	1			18
$2.01 to $3.00			4	6	14	15	26		6	4	2		77
$3.01 to $4.00	1		4	10	30	19	36		13	6	2		121
$4.01 to $5.00			2	3	17	25	45		11	9	5	1	118
$5.01 to $6.00	1		1	3	18	19	37		15	11	2	3	110
$6.01 to $7.00		1	3	6	6	24	30		8	8	6		92
$7.01 to $8.00	1		2	1	8	8	18		10	6	1	7	62
$8.01 to $9.00					4	8	19		10	2	4	2	49
$9.01 to $10.00				2	7	1	27		11	6	5	1	60
$10.01 to $11.00				1	1	2	1		1				6
$11.01 to $12.00			1	1	1	5	17		5	7	3	2	42
$12.01 to $13.00				1						4			5
$13.01 to $14.00				1		1	2		1				5
$14.01 to $15.00		1	1	1	3	1	7		2	2	2	1	21
$15.01 to $16.00				1		1			1	2	1		6
$16.01 to $17.00							2						2
$17.01 to $18.00				1		·	2			3		1	7
$18.01 to $19.00						1				1			2
$19.01 to $20.00							1	1	1				3
Totals	3	3	23	37	118	131	275		98	73	33	18	812

Not enough boys left grades below the fifth to make our figures worth while. The average (median) wages of the boys leaving each grade above the fourth were as follows:

$4.25 a week for those leaving the 5th grade
$4.50 a week for those leaving the 6th grade
$5.20 a week for those leaving the 7th grade

$5.60 a week for those leaving the 8th grade

$6.00 a week for those leaving the 1st year high school

$6.60 a week for those leaving the 2d year high school

$7.60 a week for those leaving the 3d year high school

$7.50 a week for those leaving the 4th year high school

If one argues that schooling alone is the reason for any increase in wage, he may conclude on the basis of these figures that the average boy leaving the junior or senior year of high school gets about $1 more a week than the average boy leaving the freshman or sophomore year, and that the average boy leaving the freshman or sophomore year gets about $1 more than the boy leaving the sixth, seventh, or eighth grade. This assumption is probably wrong. *We cannot be sure that the increase in amount of schooling is the real reason for the increase in wage.* Age probably is a much more important factor than grade in determining the beginning wage. In fact, by comparing the beginning wage of seventeen-year-old boys who leave one grade with seventeen-year-old boys who leave another grade we find a very slight increase.

All of the boys who were seventeen years old when they left school were studied to see if those who left advanced grades received higher wages than those who left lower grades. The average wage for each group of seventeen-year-old boys was as follows :

4 boys leaving the 6th grade averaged $6

9 boys leaving the 7th grade averaged $6

38 boys leaving the 8th grade averaged $8

14 boys leaving the 9th grade averaged $8

13 boys leaving the 10th grade averaged $7

14 boys leaving the 11th grade averaged $6.50

4 boys leaving the 12th grade averaged $7

Boys of the same age leaving different grades get about the same beginning wages.

CORRELATION BETWEEN LEAVING AGE AND BEGINNING WAGE

The correlation between the age at which these boys left school and the average weekly wage which they received when they began is set forth in Table No. III.

TABLE NO. III. CORRELATION BETWEEN LEAVING AGE AND BEGINNING WAGE

Beginning Wage	Ages																	Total
	6	7	8	9	10	11	12	13	14	15	16	17	18	19	20	21	22	
$1.00 and under						1		1	3			1						6
$1.01 to $2.00					1	1	2	11	2			1						18
$2.01 to $3.00		1			2		2	20	15	17	11	5	2	1				76
$3.01 to $4.00	1				1	1	3	12	50	30	14	7	1					120
$4.01 to $5.00						1	2	12	29	42	22	5	5					118
$5.01 to $6.00							1	5	26	36	26	13	4					111
$6.01 to $7.00					1	1	2	7	25	22	19	9	7					93
$7.01 to $8.00						1	1	3	8	17	15	9	5	2	1			62
$8.01 to $9.00							4	3	7	12	6	13	3	1				49
$9.01 to $10.00							1	2	8	9	21	9	8	2				60
$10.01 to $11.00								1	2	1	1	1						6
$11.01 to $12.00									4	8	14	9	6					41
$12.01 to $13.00										1		4	2					7
$13.01 to $14.00								2	1		1		1					5
$14.01 to $15.00						1		1	3	4	3	8	1			1		22
$15.01 to $16.00									1	2	2							5
$16.01 to $17.00											1			1				2
$17.01 to $18.00								1	1	1	1	1	1	1				7
$18.01 to $19.00										1			1					2
$19.01 to $20.00										3								3
Totals	1	1			6	4	18	71	192	211	157	93	49	7	2	1		813

Table No. III should be read as follows:

> One six-year-old boy received from $3 to $4
> One seven-year-old boy received from $2 to $3, etc.

Very few boys went to work before they were fourteen years of age, and very few received less than $2 a week. In fact there are so few cases of boys under twelve years of age that comparisons are hardly reliable. The same is true of boys more than nineteen years of age. But between the ages of twelve and eighteen sufficient cases are available to justify comparison.

The correlations between leaving ages and beginning wages are as follows:

> $4.10 a week for boys 13 years of age
> $4.90 a week for boys 14 years of age
> $4.30 a week for boys 15 years of age
> $5.25 a week for boys 16 years of age
> $7.60 a week for boys 17 years of age
> $8.80 a week for boys 18 years of age

According to these figures the older the boy when he begins work the higher his wage. Between boys thirteen, fourteen, and fifteen years of age there is little difference. But after the fifteenth year there is a remarkable increase; $1 a week from fifteen to sixteen, nearly $1.50 from sixteen to seventeen, and more than $1 from seventeen to eighteen.

The amount of wages received by boys thirteen, fourteen, and fifteen years of age would hardly justify their withdrawal from school. The report of the United States government claims that at least $2 a week is necessary for the self-maintenance of a person more than ten years of age. Using this figure as a minimum standard, it will be seen that the thirteen-year-old boys are making about twice as much as is absolutely necessary for existence. However, the figures in the government report are considered by many economists as very low. It would certainly be difficult for a Des Moines or Sioux City boy to live and save if receiving the minimum weekly wage above indicated.

CORRELATION BETWEEN WAGES AND YEARS OF EXPERIENCE

Additional data upon the question raised in the preceding section are furnished by a study of the relationship that exists between the increase in weekly wages and years of experience. One would naturally expect a boy who has been out of school three years to get a higher wage than a boy who has been out of school one year, a boy who has been out of school five years a higher wage than a boy who has been out of school two years. Just how much experience counts is, however, a much more difficult question to answer. In Table No. IV the figures across the top refer to years of experience, such as one year, two years, three years, four years, etc. By "years of experience" is meant that the boy had been out of school and at work at least one year, two years, three years, etc. The figures down the left-hand side of the page refer to the average weekly wages received during the year. For example, 5 boys had been out of school one year and had received an average weekly wage of from $1.01

to $2 a week ; 11 boys had been out of school one year and had received an average wage of from $2 to $3 a week, etc., for the remainder of the table.

TABLE NO. IV. CORRELATION BETWEEN WAGES AND YEARS OF EXPERIENCE

Average Weekly Wages	Years of Experience															Totals
	1	2	3	4	5	6	7	8	9	10	11	12	13	14	15	
$1.00 and under																
$1.01 to $2.00	5	2			1											8
$2.01 to $3.00	11	7	2										1			21
$3.01 to $4.00	37	13	2	2	2	1	1									58
$4.01 to $5.00	36	23	1	3	1			1								65
$5.01 to $6.00	26	19	16	4	2											67
$6.01 to $7.00	16	30	12	7	4	1	2		1	1						74
$7.01 to $8.00	15	20	14	20	6	3	1		2							81
$8.01 to $9.00	13	26	21	10	9	2	3	4		1						89
$9.01 to $10.00	7	5	6	3	4	2	2									29
$10.01 to $11.00	8	16	18	16	14	13	3	1	1	1	1					92
$11.01 to $12.00	2	3	1	3	6	1	3				1				1	21
$12.01 to $13.00	2	4	5	4	5	4	2	1								27
$13.01 to $14.00	8	10	6	16	12	10	3	3	2	1		1				72
$14.01 to $15.00	2	3	1	4	1	2	1	2								16
$15.01 to $16.00	1		2	4	3	1	1									12
$16.01 to $17.00	2	3	2	5	8	5	1	2	2	3						33
$17.01 to $18.00	1	1		1		1	1									5
$18.01 to $19.00	2	3	2	3	3	4	2	1	1	1						22
$19.01 to $20.00				3		1										4
$20.01 to $21.00			1			1	2									4
$21.01 to $22.00								1				1				2
$22.01 to $23.00			1			1				1						3
$23.01 to $24.00					1		2	1								4
$24.01 to $25.00						1										1
$25.01 to $26.00					2				1							3
$26.01 to $27.00					1	1										2
$27.01 to $28.00																
$28.01 to $29.00				1									•			1
$29.01 to $30.00																
$30.01 to $31.00																
$31.01 to $32.00																
$32.01 to $33.00						1										1
$33.01 to $34.00																
$34.01 to $35.00																
$35.01 to $36.00																
$36.01 to $37.00		1														1
Totals	194	188	113	110	86	55	30	15	12	9	2	3			1	818

From Table No. IV we may draw the following conclusions with regard to the financial value of different years of experience. The weekly wages received are as follows :

$5.30 a week during the 1st year of experience
$6.05 a week during the 2d year of experience
$8.50 a week during the 3d year of experience
$10.33 a week during the 4th year of experience
$10.00 a week during the 5th year of experience
$11.00 a week during the 6th year of experience
$11.66 a week during the 7th year of experience
$14.30 a week during the 8th year of experience
$14.50 a week during the 9th year of experience

That *experience is the chief factor in determining the wages of these boys is very evident.* The boys with two years of experience received almost $1 more than those with one year experience, while those with three years of experience received over $3 more per week. Those with four years of experience have doubled their wages. They do not reach a level until about the eighth or ninth year of experience, and are then receiving over $14 a week and are more than twenty-one years of age.

It would be interesting to compare these figures with figures on an equal number of cases of boys graduating from high school, but such figures are not at present available. How much more money high-school graduates in Iowa would receive at the end of six or nine years of experience can only be inferred. Perhaps many of the conclusions with regard to the value of school training which in the last few years we have been telling high-school and grammar-school boys are not as accurate as we have thought. Before we can present to boys the actual facts, further careful study must be made along these lines.

AVERAGE ANNUAL INCREASE IN WAGES PER YEARS OF EXPERIENCE

In order to find out just how rapidly the boys increased in wages over their initial wage a study was made of their average annual increase. For example, Case No. 204 had been out of school five years. He received a wage of $3.50 to start with and was getting a wage of $10 at the time of the investigation, which was after five years of experience. That is, he had increased $6.50

in five years, which would give him an average annual increase of $1.30 a week. He would appear in Table No. V under column marked five years, and opposite the left-hand column marked $1.01 to $1.50. The other cases were studied in the same way.

TABLE NO. V. AVERAGE ANNUAL INCREASE IN WAGES FOR YEARS OF EXPERIENCE

Average Increase in Weekly Wages	Number of Years of Experience																Totals
	-1	1	2	3	4	5	6	7	8	9	10	11	12	13	14	15	
No increase	13	29	16	4	4	6	1			1							74
Under 50 cents	2	5	11	9	10	8	6	6	3	1							61
$0.51 to $1.00	4	38	12	22	17	9	9	3	5	1	4			1	1	1	127
$1.01 to $1.50	1	19	25	18	21	9	10	4	1	1	5						114
$1.51 to $2.00	5	23	28	18	12	11	10	4	3	4	1						119
$2.01 to $2.50	1	11	14	5	7	10	6	4	1								59
$2.51 to $3.00	1	18	11	7	7	2	3										49
$3.01 to $3.50		2	8	2	9	3											24
$3.51 to $4.00	3	5	3	6	4	3	2										26
$4.01 to $4.50		6	2			2											10
$4.51 to $5.00	1	6	1	1						1							10
$5.01 to $6.00	3	2	1														6
$6.01 to $7.00		2	1														3
$7.01 to $8.00		5															5
$8.01 to $9.00						1											1
$9.01 to $10.00		1															1
$10.01 to $11.00		1		1			1										3
$11.01 to $12.00	1																1
Totals	35	172	134	93	81	64	48	21	13	8	11			1	1	1	683

From the foregoing table it may be seen that 74 cases had not made any annual increase in wages. The others had increased in wages from less than 50 cents to $12 a week. The boys average an increase of a little less than $2 a week for each year out up to and including the ninth year. This would seem to be a fairly good rate of progress. The cases from which no data could be secured are not included in this table.

THE DIFFERENT OCCUPATIONS IN WHICH THE BOYS WERE ENGAGED

It is very difficult to determine the exact number of different lines of work in which these boys were engaged. In fact there is no standard to follow in determining what is and what is not an occupation. A boy may be working at carpentry work in making brooms in a broom factory, or he may be working at carpentry work in a cabinetmaker's shop. In the first case he would be apt to call himself a "scraper," and in the second a carpenter's helper. The same thing occurs in many different lines of work. It becomes necessary, therefore, to group the occupations, and that has been done in this section. The occupations are then studied with regard to their popularity among boy workers. For example, as will be seen in the lists which follow, 59 different boys worked at one time or another in occupations which are listed under the heading "printers." For convenience in considering the pursuits that boys are likely to get into, the list has been divided. In the first list occur all the occupations in which at least 10 of the boys had at some time worked. In the second list, all occupations in which less than 10 boys at any time worked.

THE THIRTY-THREE MOST POPULAR PURSUITS AMONG IOWA BOYS

Helpers and general workers	376
Drivers (delivery, transfer, teamsters, etc.)	256
Clerks (shipping, stock, sales, etc.)	233
Errand and messenger boys	157
Farm hands (gardeners, dairymen, etc.)	130
Wrappers and packers	79
Apprentices (all occupations)	69
Printers (pressman, type and linotype, etc.)	59
Office boys	57
Bill posters and peddlers	49
Porters, pages, hall and bell boys	48
Hosiery-mill operatives	39
R.R. hands (brakeman, section, freight, etc.)	25
Elevator boys	22
Cement workers (mixers, feeders, carriers, etc.)	22
Electrical workers (wiring, lineman, switchboard, etc.)	21
Water boys	21
Bookkeepers, stenographers, and timekeepers	21
Drafters and engravers	20
Machinists	20
Waiters	20
Agents and collectors	18
Tailors	18
Cutters (glass, shoe, paper, etc.)	15
Soda-fountain boys	15
Painters and decorators	14
Cigar makers	14

Labelers and letter addressers 11
Pressers (clothes) 11
Bootblacks 11
Checkers, sorters, and ticket takers 11
Miners 11
Cash boys 10

THE SEVENTY-EIGHT OCCUPATIONS NOT SO POPULAR

Butchers	9	Icemen	2
Factory workers (n.o.s.)	9	Actors	2
Foremen and managers	9	Cashiers	2
Telegraphers	8	Brick- and tile-dressers	2
Musicians (playing, singing, tuning)	8	Blacksmiths	2
Sign painters, stencilers, and markers	8	Bookbinders	2
Chauffeurs	8	Wipers	2
Box-factory workers	7	Furriers	2
Bottle washers	7	Fruit pickers	2
Tinners	6	Pattern makers	2
Molders	6	Boiler makers	2
Firemen (fire department and engine)	6	Barbers	2
Pin setter and ball racker	6	Floorwalker	1
Candy makers and mixers	5	Picture framer	1
Polishers	5	Syrup maker	1
Upholsterers	5	Shearer	1
Journeymen	5	Corn husker	1
Optical workers (mounting and grinding)	4	Paperer	1
Janitors	4	Oiler	1
Cooks	4	Boatman	1
Horsetraders and hostlers	4	Coal shoveler	1
Bakers	4	Stonecutter	1
Carpenters	4	Vulcanizer	1
Solicitors	3	Bar tender	1
Weavers (rug and basket)	3	Sailor	1
Contractors	3	Ranger	1
Inspectors	3	Coat maker	1
Bottlers	3	Tramp	1
Riveters	3	Button maker	1
Caddies, guides, jockeys	3	Glazier	1
Bricklayers	3	Art-glass cementer	1
Fowl pickers	3	Glove trimmer	1
Lathe workers	3	Florist	1
Mail clerks	3	Dye setter	1
Lumbermen	3	Toy maker	1
Tool makers	3	Harness maker	1
Operators (motion pictures)	2	Reporter	1
Engineers (R.R.)	2	Steam fitter	1

Relatively few of the pursuits in the above list are skilled, though in many of them there is some opportunity for advancement. A rough estimate would seem to indicate that from 75 to 80 per cent of the boys were engaged in unskilled or semiskilled pursuits. By unskilled and semiskilled pursuits is here meant a pursuit in which the operations to be performed are relatively few in number, simple in character, and for the most part uncoördinated with operations which precede and follow. Most of these operations can be easily and quickly learned, and the grade of ability and the responsibility required is relatively low.

It may be concluded from these figures that the most common method followed by boys in learning a vocation is a "trial and success" method. They go to work and try this or that pursuit to see whether or not they are suited to it or it is suited to them.

It may be contended that this is a very wasteful method, and undoubtedly the contention can be supported by considerable evidence. On the other hand, as the present system of industry is organized no adequate substitute has as yet been provided. Nor is it proved that vocational education as introduced in other cities in this country provides a totally adequate substitute.

CORRELATION BETWEEN PREVIOUS WORK AND FUTURE AMBITION

The last question that the investigators were instructed to ask of each boy concerned the boy's ambition. It was expected that many of them would be satisfied with the line of work in which they were or had been engaged, while others would desire to enter other pursuits. In this connection special cases may be interesting.

Case No. 11 began work as a clerk at $8 a week, and after five years of experience was a clerk receiving $11 a week. He had no desire to change his occupation at the time of the investigation.

Case No. 18, on the other hand, began as a coal digger at $14 a week and left it to enter an automobile shop at a lower weekly wage, $6, where the opportunity for advancement was much greater and the work of a more skilled character. He expressed himself when interviewed as ambitious to become an expert mechanic.

Case No. 55 left the eighth grade and began work at the age of fifteen as cook at $12.50 a week, and continued in the same position and at the same wage for five years. During that time he completed a course in a correspondence school in draftsmanship with the intention of becoming a draftsman.

Case No. 117 came to Des Moines from Missouri. While in Missouri he finished the first grade of the public school when he was six years old. His father then took him out of school and put him out to work on a farm, where for seven years he labored for his board and lodging and spending money. When he was thirteen years old he came to Des Moines and became a coal digger at $12 a week. He remained in this occupation for three years, and at the end of that time became a cattle helper in the stockyard at $6 per week and board. After fifteen years of experience he is now a truck-farm driver receiving $9 per week and board. He can read and write poorly and has no ambition for any particular pursuit.

The above cases exhibit the variety of vocational experience through which boys pass. According to our data of the entire group of boys studied, 628 (75 per cent) had an ambition and 216 (25 per cent) had no preference for any particular occupation; that is, they were satisfied with what they were doing or at least could not, at the time of the investigation, state anything that they would rather do.

A boy was considered as having an ambition if he expressed a desire to prepare for and enter any particular occupation. A boy whose ambition for the future was along exactly the same line of work as that in which he had been engaged for the majority of the time since leaving school was classed in the group whose previous work and future ambition correlated almost perfectly. In this group must be placed 35 per cent of the 628 boys having an ambition.

A boy who had been engaged but a very small portion of his time since leaving school in a line which corresponded with his ambition was classed in the group whose previous work and future ambition correlated but slightly. This group includes 23 per cent of the ambitious boys.

The work of a boy was classed as not correlating with his ambition when he desired to enter a pursuit in which he had had absolutely no experience. This group includes 255 cases, 42 per cent of those having an ambition.

FINANCIAL PROGRESS IN RELATION TO FUTURE AMBITION

The records of the boys who had an ambition were studied with regard to whether or not they had made financial progress since leaving school. By financial progress is here meant any increase no matter how slight in weekly wages. The increase is considered without regard to the age of the boy or the amount of experience which he had received.

Of the 628 boys who had a definite ambition 501 (79 per cent) had made some financial progress since leaving school and 21 per cent had failed to make any financial progress. Of the 210 boys who had no definite ambition 188 (82 per cent) had made financial progress and 18 per cent had failed to make any financial progress. There is practically no difference between these two groups with respect to this point. On the other hand, 93 per cent of the ambitious boys whose previous work correlated almost perfectly with their future ambition have made financial progress, while only about 75 per cent of the boys whose previous work and future ambition correlated but slightly or not at all have made financial progress. From these figures it appears that *proportionally more boys who are working along lines in which they desire to continue are financially successful than those whose ambitions lie outside of the field of their previous work.*

FINANCIAL PROGRESS IN RELATION TO PROGRESS TOWARD SKILL

A comparative study of the ambitious and the unambitious groups was made to determine the financial progress and the relative amount of progress which the two groups had made toward skill. It was recognized that there are two ways of making progress toward skill: first, by changing from an unskilled occupation, as that of office or messenger boy, to a more skilled occupation, as that of clerk or apprentice; second, by making progress in skill while remaining in a given occupation, as in printing. In this study the latter was determined by a consideration of the time spent in the occupation and the increase of wages shown, as well as by the character of the occupation itself.

In general two groups were easily distinguishable, one making noted progress toward skill and one not making any progress. After some deliberation it was decided that credit would be given for noted progress toward skill only in case the record showed continuous employment for three years or more in one trade or position ; for example, three years as a bricklayer or machinist, etc. About 17 per cent of the boys with an ambition had made noted progress toward skill. Only 12 per cent of the group without an ambition had made noted progress toward skill.

Credit for no progress toward skill was given to errand boys, day laborers, farm workers, or helpers in any trade, factory positions, or business for less than one year. Approximately 63 per cent of the boys without an ambition and only 45 per cent of the ambitious boys fall in this group.

All others, including doubtful cases, were placed in the group showing little progress toward skill. This group includes 25 per cent of the unambitious and 38 per cent of the ambitious boys.

TABLE NO. VI

PROGRESS IN SKILL AND FINANCIAL PROGRESS	BOYS HAVING NO AMBITION		BOYS HAVING AN AMBITION	
	Number of cases	Per cent of cases	Number of cases	Per cent of cases
NOTABLE PROGRESS IN SKILL	27	12	106	17
(1) Financial progress	27	100	104	99
(2) No financial progress	0		2	1
LITTLE PROGRESS IN SKILL	54	25	238	38
(1) Financial progress	46	85	211	88
(2) No financial progress	8	15	27	12
NO PROGRESS IN SKILL	135	63	284	45
(1) Financial progress	100	74	202	71
(2) No financial progress	35	26	82	29

Table No. VI contains the data for the three groups. From this table it is evident that *a larger number of boys with an ambition make progress toward skill than do boys without an ambition, and at the same time they make about the same financial progress.*

THE DIFFERENT OCCUPATIONS FOR WHICH THE BOYS DESIRED TO PREPARE

The names of the different occupations for which the ambitious boys desired to prepare follow. They are distributed under nine headings as given by the United States census of occupations, 1910. The figures which precede the names indicate the number of boys desiring to follow the particular line.

I. Agriculture, forestry, and animal husbandry:

Only 28 of the boys desired to follow agricultural pursuits. The number is suprisingly small, when we remember that 130 of the boys had worked at various times in agricultural occupations. Apparently the back-to-the-farm movement has not affected these boys to any great extent.

II. Extraction of minerals:

Only 2 of the boys expressed themselves as desiring to be coal miners. When we remember that 38 boys had had experience along this line these figures would seem to indicate that mining is not an occupation for which boys are very anxious to prepare.

III. Manufacturing and mechanical industries and pursuits:

There were 325 boys who desired to enter lines listed under this heading. The most common lines are as follows:

65 Machinists	8 Bricklayers
50 Printers	5 Painters and paper hangers
29 Carpenters	4 Bakers
20 Electrical engineers	4 Blacksmiths
20 Mechanics	5 Jewelers
19 Electricians	3 Boiler makers
16 Civil engineers	3 Saddlers
13 Plumbers	3 Broom makers
10 Candy makers	2 Masons

2 Lithographers

2 Tinners

2 Bookbinders

1 Contractor

1 Furniture man

1 Molder

1 Tool maker

1 Bottler

1 Sheet-metal worker

1 Weaver

1 Locomotive fireman

1 Expert tuner

1 Vulcanizer

1 Tenter

1 Upholsterer

Apparently the boys are more interested in manufacturing and mechanical pursuits than in agricultural and mining industries. One result as shown in these figures is the tendency away from many of the occupations in which the boys have had considerable preliminary experience. While 376 boys had some experience as general workers none gave this as their ambition. The same is true of errand boys, drivers, messenger boys, wrappers, and packers. The boys seemed to realize that many of their early occupations are typical blind alleys. While more than 75 per cent of them were or had been employed in unskilled lines, over 60 per cent desired to leave such lines for more skilled trades. Only 200 had had experience along manufacturing lines, although, as already shown, 325 desired such experience.

IV. Transportation:

Only 45 boys desired to follow lines that are listed under this heading. The list is as follows:

15 Telegraphers

7 Locomotive engineers

4 Chauffeurs

4 Mail clerks

4 Railroad officials

2 Railroad dispatchers

2 Mail carriers

3 Messengers

2 Brakemen

1 Switchman

1 Fireman

About an equal number of boys had had experience along these lines. With the exception of the messengers these workers may be considered skilled employees. It is significant that for the most part those who had experience in skilled lines desired to remain in the same.

V. Trade and commerce:

One hundred nineteen boys desired to enter lines that are listed by the United States census as concerned with trading and commerce. They are as follows:

38 Business men	12 Optical business
12 Clerks and agents	9 Auto business
9 Grocerymen	1 Decorator
7 Pharmacists	1 Cigarette business
2 Hardware business	1 Window trimmer
2 Bankers	1 Tailor
3 Cutters	1 Newsboy
1 China store	1 Butcher
1 Cigar maker	

About the same number of boys had had experience along these lines, though most of them in minor positions, such as office boys, wrappers, messengers, etc. Commercial pursuits appear to succeed in holding children who had some preliminary experience in the same.

VI. Professional service:

Fifty-three boys desired to enter lines that are listed under the heading Professional Service. They are distributed as follows:

6 Musicians	2 Teachers
7 Newspaper work	2 Actors
4 Physicians	2 Veterinary surgeons
4 Lawyers	2 Dentists
3 Draftsmen	2 Civil service
2 Advertising artists	1 Chemist
1 Artist	1 Author
1 Minister	1 Photo engraver
1 Violinist	1 Photographer
1 Journalist	1 Vaudeville
3 Architects	1 Reporter
3 Sign painters	1 Cartoonist

Very few of the boys had had any experience in professional pursuits. That so many of them desired such experience is significant. It is another indication of the inability of juvenile occupations to hold their workers. The boys realize as they grow older that the skilled trades and professions offer them better opportunities for vocational supremacy.

VII. Domestic and personal service:

3 Bootblacks	1 Cook
3 Barbers	1 Restaurant
3 Hotel owners	1 Hospital work
2 Clothes pressers	1 Laundry
2 Pool-hall business	

Only 16 boys were ambitious to follow domestic and personal pursuits. Over 75 had had experience along these lines. Apparently domestic and personal service is not primarily attractive to growing boys.

VIII. Clerical occupations:

Clerking is not an attractive occupation to many of these boys. Only 26 were ambitious along this line. Their ambitions varied as follows:

15 Bookkeepers	6 Stenographers
3 Office work	2 Stockroom in store

It is very difficult to classify the remaining boys in any of the foregoing groups. Three of them desired to go to college. One wanted to enter the navy, one to operate a moving-picture machine, one to be a prize fighter, and one an aviator.

CONCLUSIONS

The chief facts brought out by this study may be summarized briefly :

1. More than 40 per cent of the boys leave schools located in cities other than the one in which they are now living. This means that if these boys were to receive vocational education for the various pursuits which they enter, it would be necessary for them to receive it before coming to Des Moines and Sioux City. A compulsory system of continuation-school attendance might succeed in reaching most of these boys.

2. Workers in juvenile occupations are recruited largely from the sixth, seventh, and eighth grades of the public schools and at about the time when the children are fourteen, fifteen, and sixteen years of age.

3. Boys leave school for a great variety of reasons. The three most commonly offered are "necessity," "dissatisfaction with school," and "preference for work." However, lack of parental control and interest is probably the chief cause.

4. About 75 per cent of the boys go to work immediately, and only a very small percentage are idle more than a month after leaving school. This would indicate that there are plenty of opportunities for boys who want to work.

5. Over 85 per cent of the jobs which these boys entered were secured by the boys themselves with little or no assistance. For the most part, teachers do not attempt to assist them in securing employment. The boys as they leave school are thrown on their own resources. Vocational guidance would probably be of great value to most of these boys.

6. On the average a boy passes through three jobs in two years. It is evident from this that the work that the boys are in is unsatisfactory and does not succeed in holding them.

7. The boys give a great variety of reasons for quitting jobs. Their chief reason seems to be a desire for better wages. They think more of an increase in salary than they do of an advancement in skill.

8. The beginning wages of boys is about $5.50 a week. This includes boys of different ages. The range is from nothing to $20 a week. Fifty per cent of the boys receive a beginning weekly wage of from $4.50 to $7. This would seem fair wages for inexperienced boys of these ages.

9. Boys of the same age receive about the same beginning wage regardless of the number of years of schooling which they have had. Age is probably a much more important factor than grade of schooling in determining the beginning wage.

10. Boys eighteen years of age receive nearly twice the weekly wage of boys fourteen years old when they leave school. Between boys thirteen, fourteen, and fifteen years of age is little difference, but after the fifteenth year there is a very remarkable increase — $1 per week from fifteen to sixteen, nearly $1.50 from sixteen to seventeen, and over $1 from seventeen to eighteen.

11. Experience is the chief factor in determining the wages of boys. Boys with four years of experience double their wages, and they do not reach a level until about the eighth or ninth year of experience, at which time they are receiving over $14 a week and are over twenty-one years of age.

12. Boys are engaged in over 111 different occupations. However, 33 of these occupations include about 70 per cent of the workers. The most popular occupations are typical blind alleys; for example, helpers and general workers, drivers, errand messenger boys, wrappers and packers, etc.

13. A rough estimate indicates that from 75 per cent to 80 per cent of the boys are engaged in unskilled or semiskilled pursuits.

14. The most common method followed by boys in learning a vocation is a "trial and success" method. They try this and that pursuit to see whether they are suited to it or it is suited to them. While no elaborate system of vocational schools would entirely eliminate this method of learning vocations, it might succeed in reducing and eliminating some of the waste resulting from the present system.

15. Of the 846 boys studied, 628 (75 per cent) had at the time of the investigation a definite ambition. That is, they desired to prepare for and enter a particular occupation.

16. Of the group having an ambition, 35 per cent were ambitious along lines of work in which they already had had most of their vocational experience.

17. In the case of about 23 per cent of the ambitious boys there was but a very slight correlation between their previous work and their ambitions.

18. In the case of 42 per cent of those having an ambition there was absolutely no correlation between their previous work and their ambition.

19. Proportionally, more boys who are working along lines in which they desire to continue are financially successful than those whose ambitions lie outside of the fields of their previous work.

20. A larger number of boys with an ambition make some progress toward skill than do boys without an ambition. By progress toward skill is here meant advancing toward a skilled pursuit by

changing occupations or by advancing in skill while remaining in an occupation, as in printing. From these figures it would seem that ambitious boys are more successful than unambitious boys, measured either in terms of skill or in amount of weekly wages.

21. Fewer than 20 per cent of the boys who had had experience in agricultural pursuits desired to remain in the same. Apparently the back-to-the-farm movement has not affected these boys to any great degree.

22. Mining is not an occupation for which boys desire to prepare. Only 2 of the 38 boys who had had experience along this line desired to continue in it.

23. Manufacturing and mechanical industries and pursuits attract more than 50 per cent of the boys. This is true in spite of the fact that less than 40 per cent had had experience along these lines. The boys want to be machinists, printers, carpenters, electricians, mechanics, plumbers, and engineers. They are also greatly interested in commercial pursuits. In all, 119 boys desired to follow such lines. A very few are interested in professional services, domestic and personal service, and clerical occupations.

A STUDY OF THE VOCATIONAL GUIDANCE OF GRAMMAR-SCHOOL PUPILS

By Ellen M. Greany

(From *Educational Administration and Supervision*, March, 1915)

That the average grammar-school graduate of a generation ago should have a life-career motive was unthinkable alike to parents and to educators. There was, of course, the rare musical genius, and the mathematical prodigy, whose abilities it was clearly advantageous to foster, but for the normal child, who exhibited no marked talents, why consider a matter so remote as a life-career? It could be decided upon at the close of his high-school course, or, if he were going· on to college, let the decision be put off still longer. If he belonged to the great army of those to whom leaving the grammar school meant going to work, then he must find a job. Very likely he was too young to begin to learn a trade. Nobody had ever analyzed with him seriously his capabilities or his limitations, nor had he ever received any systematic or ·definite information concerning the industrial opportunities about him. To go to work did not necessarily mean to take up a permanent occupation. It merely meant to get a job. If he differentiated among jobs at all, it was probable that he had a vague hope that the one which fell to his lot should not be too strenuous or too poorly paid.

But the growth of the vocational-guidance movement, and the increasing specialization of our secondary school and college courses, have called the attention of those interested in child welfare to the tremendous waste of human talent and economic productivity which is traceable to the lack of an early-conceived life motive.

The philosophy which underlies the vocational-guidance movement may be briefly stated as follows:

There is marked variety in inborn gifts.

The greatest happiness and the highest efficiency result from the exercise of native talents in the right environment.

For the great masses of men, life is organized around work. "Nothing," says Marshall, "influences a man so much as the work he does, unless it be his religion."

Such a philosophy focuses attention upon the seriousness of the blind-alley trades. It points out the significance of a study of occupational classification. It emphasizes the importance of wide vocational information. It wants education and industry to bring out the best in every individual. It calls upon the individual for self-analysis. It is vitally interested in equality of opportunity and diffusion of education. It is directed against every form of maladjustment, and its goal is well-rounded, fully developed manhood and womanhood.

If we accept the premises of vocational guidance, we must be deeply concerned with the job which the child takes when he leaves the grammar school. But the higher school which his classmate chooses is of no less interest to us. Our high schools and the courses which they offer are yearly becoming more highly specialized. The "general course" is rapidly becoming obsolete. One must know, when he enters the high school, whether he is headed for college, or the normal school, or a business career, or stenography, or mechanical work, or what not. This means that he must know his tastes and capabilities and the general requirements of the work which he hopes to do. Otherwise multitudes of our boys and girls will continue, as they have in the past, to choose their high school for such trivial reasons as "because so and so is going there," "because it has a good track team," "because they say the lessons are easy," etc. Our high schools will continue to cope unsuccessfully with misfits. The boy who would have been interested and proficient in the industrial work of the Mechanic Arts High School will be found struggling unsuccessfully with the business courses of the High School of Commerce. The girl who would have made a capable and artistic milliner will be a dull and unsatisfactory member of the class in stenography. Both children will very likely drop out of the high school in a few months and join the 30 per cent of our first-year high-school pupils who annually recruit the ranks of untrained juvenile workers.

It seems, therefore, that the closing year of the grammar-school course is the most advantageous time for the boy or girl to decide upon a life-career. But the real initiative in the choice must come from the child himself. There arises the tremendously vital question, Has the child of age and capacity to graduate from our grammar schools any permanent interest ? Is he capable of visualizing his occupational future ? Can he be helped to study himself, to study the occupations about him, and thus be led to an intelligent, discriminating choice ? Is it possible to reduce the theory of vocational guidance to a practical working program, so that it shall be less vague to the teacher and more valuable to the pupil ?

In the hope of getting some reliable answers to the above questions an investigation was made in five graduating classes of four Massachusetts city schools in 1913. The purpose of the investigation was outlined as follows :

1. To discover whether there exists in the minds of certain groups of eighth-grade elementary-school pupils the vision of a vocation.

2. To find how this vocational vision has been acquired, what is known of the avenues of entrance to the chosen career, the characteristics necessary to success in it, its limitations, and its rewards.

3. To show increased tenacity of purpose or the awakening and development of a visualized vocational purpose, as brought about through a course of systematic, expository instruction in vocational and educational opportunities.

The procedure of the investigation was as follows :

Five eighth-grade classes were selected, where the heredity, environmental influence, economic conditions, social standing, and probable ideals of the pupils appeared to be somewhat similar. These classes were two in the Hugh O'Brien School of Roxbury, and one each in the Kelly and Houghton schools of Cambridge and the Bingham School of Somerville. There were 42 boys and 45 girls in the first-named school and a total of 34 boys and 57 girls in the three other classes. During the last week of March and the first week of April, 1913, all five classes were given a forty-minute preliminary test. After a brief explanation to the children, telling them that this was not a school examination but merely an inquiry which was made by people who were interested in them, the following questions were put, one at a time, on the blackboard.

1. How do you intend to earn your living when you are all through going to school?

2. How do your parents wish you to earn your living?
3. (a) Have you any relatives or friends who are interested in how you are going to earn your living?
   (b) If so, what do they wish you to do?
4. (a) Why have you decided to earn your living in this way?
   (b) Did you make your choice from something you have read?
   (c) Do you know anyone who does the kind of work you have chosen?
5. (a) What education do you need to fit yourself for the kind of work you intend to do?
   (b) How much longer will you have to go to school?
   (c) If you need to go to the high school, which is the best one to go to?
6. How much will it cost your parents to fit you for the kind of work you are going to do?
7. What kind of a boy (or girl) would be most successful in the kind of work you are going to do?
8. (a) Do you expect to work very hard?
   (b) Is it a healthful occupation?
   (c) How many hours a day do you expect to work?
9. How much pay do you expect to get each week of the first year that you work?
10. (a) What chance do you think there is to get more pay as you grow older?
    (b) What is the highest pay you can probably ever get?

A series of fifteen lessons was then planned for the children of the Hugh O'Brien School who had taken the preliminary test. The other three classes were to remain uninstructed. The first three lessons were given to boys and girls together, the remaining twelve were given to them separately. The subjects of the lessons were as follows :

Lesson 1. General Classification of Occupations.
Lesson 2. Opportunities for Boys and Girls from 14 to 16 years old.
Lesson 3. Opportunities for Boys and Girls from 16 to 20 years old.
Lesson 4. The Doctor (Boys). The Teacher (Girls).
Lesson 5. Civil Service (Boys). The Stenographer (Girls).
Lesson 6. The Printer (Boys). The Telephone Operator (Girls).
Lesson 7. The Building Trades (Boys). The Trained Nurse (Girls).
Lesson 8. The Business Man (Boys). The Dressmaker (Girls), The Milliner (Girls).
Lesson 9. The Machinist (Boys). The Saleswoman (Girls).

The aim of the first lesson was to give the children a general survey of occupations and thus call their attention to the many varieties of work from which it may be possible for a youth to choose. As the working opportunities for children and adults necessarily differ, it was thought well to make the second and third lessons a survey of the occupations usually open to those in adolescence. An attempt was made to select for the remaining lessons occupations not only representative of the different groups given in the general classification, but also those concerning which fairly reliable information was accessible, and which appeared to be within the realm of the interests and possible future choice of the children. As only nine lessons could be given to the boys and girls before the close of school, the choice of subjects was, of course, further limited.

The lessons were given on nine successive Tuesday mornings, beginning on April 15 and ending on June 10. They were forty minutes in length and followed these outlines:

LESSON 1

Kinds of work.
I. Brain and hand workers.
    1. Professional workers.
    2. Public-service workers.
       (a) Officials of the federal government.
          Officials of the state government.
          Officials of the county government.
          Officials of the city government.
          Officials of the town government.
       (b) Officials of the army and navy.
    3. Managerial and commercial workers.
    4. Personal-service workers.
II. Hand and brain workers.
    1. Skilled workers.
    2. Semiskilled workers.
    3. Unskilled workers.

This outline was filled out by the pupils, aided by the questions and suggestions of the teacher.

LESSON 2

1. General opportunities for boys and girls from 14 to 16 years old.
2. Reasons why these opportunities are so few.
3. Reasons why some employers are willing to take children between 14 and 16 years old.
4. General health conditions in these occupations.
    1. Compared with school conditions.
    2. Dangerous occupations.

5. Beginning wage.
6. Future prospects.
   (*a*) As to wage.
   (*b*) As to increase of skill.
   (*c*) As to mental growth.

LESSON 3

1. Opportunities between 14–16 } compared.
   Opportunities between 16–20 } compared.
2. Reasons why 16–20 opportunities are greater.
3. Amount and kind of education needed for the various groups of occupations given in the general classification.

Lists of industries in the neighborhood of the Hugh O'Brien School discovered and reported by the children. (Not directly related to the subject of the lesson.)

Lessons 4–9 were developed according to the following topics :

1. The Occupation.
2. General Characteristics needed for Success in this Occupation.
3. Education needed.
4. Age of Entrance to the Occupation.
5. Time it takes for Training.
6. Cost of Training.
7. Chance to get Training in Boston.
8. Wages and Demand for Workers.
   (*a*) Beginning Wage.
   (*b*) Average Adult Wage.
9. Health Conditions.
   (*a*) Hours.
   (*b*) Strain.
10. Is it a Seasonal Occupation?
11. Chance for Promotion.
12. Value to Society.
13. Relative Desirability.

The last topic was not added until Lesson 6, when the preceding lessons had established some definite data which might be used for profitable comparison.

On the day following the teaching the children had thirty minutes to write what they remembered of what had been talked over in the lessons. No assistance and no topics were given them, the object being to test the reaction rather than to get a finished composition.

The synopsis which follows records the resultant reaction on the matter presented in the last twelve lessons.

PERCENTAGE OF REACTION ON TOPICS TREATED IN LESSONS

Boys' Lessons

	4 The doctor	5 Civil service	6 The printer	7 Building trades	8 The business man	9 The machinist
				Per cent		
1. The occupation and sub. div. . .	48.7	78.5	81.3	100.	48.7	36.8
2. Characteristics	100.	64.2	72.	63.4	90.2	60.5
3. Education needed	70.7	85.7	60.4	58.5	87.8	68.3
4. Age of entrance	65.8	54.9	48.9	24.3	31.7	60.5
5. Time it takes to learn	49.8	9.5	34.8	34.1	7.3	50.
6. Cost of learning	7.3	2.3	16.3	11.5	2.4	15.7
7. Chance in Boston	95.1	9.5	34.8	36.5	51.2	71.
8. Wages	34.1	33.3	67.4	82.9	46.3	81.5
9. Health condition	0	14.2	55.8	75.5	41.4	65.7
10. Seasonal	0	9.5	27.9	48.7	41.4	18.3
11. Chance for promotion	39.	28.5	34.8	39.	46.3	44.7
12. Value to society	70.7	21.4	39.5	41.4	14.6	50.
13. Relative desirability	—	—	16.3	41.4	58.5	42.1

Girls' Lessons

	4 The teacher	5 The stenographer	6 The telephone operator	7 The nurse	8 The dressmaker	9 Milliner The saleswoman
				Per cent		
1. The occupation and sub. div. . .	77.5	66.6	80.4	85.	88.3	88.3
2. Characteristics	100.	89.5	95.6	100.	100.	100.
3. Education needed	62.5	58.3	78.2	84.7	83.7	86.
4. Age of entrance	50.	52.	69.5	63.	62.7	76.7
5. Time it takes to learn	66.6	33.3	80.	73.9	67.4	27.8
6. Cost of learning	8.3	58.3	91.3	58.6	18.6	39.5
7. Chance in Boston	91.6	91.6	65.2	30.4	90.6	25.5
8. Wages	62.5	93.7	80.4	89.1	88.3	100.
9. Health condition	33.3	64.5	76.	76.	55.8	76.7
10. Seasonal	0	10.4	26.	23.9	53.4	46.5
11. Chance for promotion	6.2	58.3	71.7	71.7	62.7	81.3
12. Value to society	50.	18.7	36.9	50.	18.6	30.2
13. Relative desirability	—	—	50.	67.4	62.7	69.7

As the percentages indicate, the reports were, on the whole, very satisfactory. They gave abundant evidence that the subject matter is within the scope of the interest and understanding of eighth-grade pupils.

In the last school week of June both the instructed and the uninstructed classes were given the same test as in March, with the addition of the following question:

11. (a) Have you thought over any occupation and then decided not to take it up?
(b) What are the reasons why you decided not to take it up?

After the completion of this test the results of both this and the March test were carefully examined. The following table indicates the general classes of occupations into which the children's choice fell:

MARCH

	Instructed						Uninstructed					
			—No.—		—%—				—No.—		—%—	
	No.	%	B	G	B	G	No.	%	B	G	B	G
Professions	12	13.8	5	7	5.8	8.1	15	16.5	6	9	6.7	9.9
Teachers	8	9.2	1	7	1.1	8.1	8	8.8	0	8	.0	8.8
Civil service	1	1.1	1	0	1.1	0	4	4.4	4	0	4.4	0
Business	5	5.8	4	1	4.6	1.1	6	6.6	4	2	4.4	2.2
Commercial	19	21.9	2	17	2.3	19.5	27	29.7	2	25	2.2	27.4
Stenographers	12	13.8	0	12	0	13.8	9	9.9	0	9	0	9.9
Bookkeepers	4	4.6	0	4	0	4.6	6	6.6	0	6	0	6.7
Trades	18	20.6	13	5	14.9	5.8	13	14.2	11	2	12.0	2.2
D. K. (don't know)	27	31.0	14	13	16.1	14.9	12	13.2	4	8	4.4	8.8
Miscellaneous	5	5.8	3	2	3.4	2.3	14	15.4	3	11	3.3	12.0
Army	1	1.1	1	0	1.1	0	0	0	0	0	0	0
Dancer	0	0	0	0	0	0	1	1.1	0	0	0	1.1
Farmer	0	0	0	0	0	0	1	1.1	1	0	1.1	0
Hairdresser	0	0	0	0	0	0	0	0	0	0	0	0
Musicians	1	1.1	1	0	1.1	0	3	3.3	2	1	2.2	1.1
Music teacher	0	0	0	0	0	0	4	4.4	0	4	0	4.4
Nurse	0	0	0	0	0	0	1	1.1	0	1	0	1.1
Private sec'y	0	0	0	0	0	0	0	0	0	0	0	0
Proofreader	0	0	0	0	0	0	1	1.1	0	1	0	1.1
Sailor	1	1.1	1	0	1.1	0	0	0	0	0	0	0
Tel. operator	2	2.3	0	2	0	2.3	3	3.3	0	3	0	3.3
Totals	87	100.0	42	45	48.2	51.7	91	100.0	34	57	37.4	62.6

JUNE

	Instructed						Uninstructed					
	No.	%	B	G	B	G	No.	%	B	G	B	G
Professions . . .	14	16.1	5	9	5.8	10.3	6	6.7	2	4	2.2	4.4
Teachers . . .	10	11.6	1	9	1.1	10.3	4	4.4	0	4	0	4.4
Civil service . .	1	1.1	1	0	1.0	0	2	2.2	2	0	2.2	0
Business	11	12.6	10	1	11.6	1.1	5	5.4	3	2	3.3	2.2
Commercial . .	21	24.1	1	20	1.1	23.0	28	30.7	1	27	1.1	29.6
Stenographers .	14	16.1	0	14	0	16.1	12	13.2	0	12	0	13.2
Bookkeepers .	4	4.6	0	4	0	4.6	6	6.7	0	6	0	6.6
Trades	27	31.0	20	7	22.9	8.1	13	14.2	11	2	12.0	2.2
D. K. (don't know)	7	8.0	3	4	3.4	4.6	22	24.2	14	8	15.4	8.8
Miscellaneous . .	6	6.9	2	4	2.3	4.6	15	16.5	1	14	1·	15.4
Army	0	0	0	0	0	0	0	0	0	0	·ö	0
Dancer . . .	0	0	0	0	0	0	0	0	0	0	0	0
Farmer . . .	0	0	0	0	0	0	0	0	0	0	0	0
Hairdresser . .	0	0	0	0	0	0	1	1.1	0	1	0	1.1
Musicians . .	1	1.1	1	0	1.1	0	2	2.2	1	1	1.1	1.1
Music teacher .	0	0	0	0	0	0	5	5.4	0	5	0	5.4
Nurse	3	3.4	0	3	0	3.4	1	1.1	0	1	0	1.1
Private sec'y .	0	0	0	0	0	0	2	2.2	0	2	0	2.2
Proofreader . .	0	0	0	0	0	0	1	1.1	0	1	0	1.1
Sailor	1	1.1	1	0	1.1	0	0	0	0	0	0	0
Tel. operator .	1	1.1	0	1	0	1.1	3	3.3	0	3	0	3.3
Totals . .	87	100.0	42	45	48.2	51.8	91	99.8	34	57	37.4	62.6

A glance at the list of occupations chosen by the two groups in March shows that the percentages of those whose choice lay in the professions, business, commercial work, and trade were approximately even enough to indicate that the vocational desires of these children were fairly similar, and hence to warrant the confidence that the groups had not been unwisely chosen for comparison.

It will also be noted that in the March test 31 per cent of those to be instructed answered that they did not know what their future occupation was to be. Thirteen and two-tenths per cent of the group which was not to be instructed gave the same answer. In the June test the percentage of "don't knows" in the first group diminished to 8 and, rather singularly, rose to 22 in the second group.

A further comparison of the results of the tests points out that there is for the instructed classes in June a slight growth in the number of those who proposed to enter the professions and commercial work and a relatively large increase in the number of those who chose business and trades. Seventy and one-tenth per cent of the instructed children gave as their chosen occupations those which had been the subjects of lessons in school. In the uninstructed group we find a slight increase in the number of those who chose commercial work and a relatively large decline among those who chose professions. The number of those choosing business and the trades remained about the same.

Question 2 brought out the information in the March test that 42.5 per cent of the children to be instructed and 18.7 per cent of the parallel group did not know how their parents wished them to earn their living. The figures changed in June to 15 per cent and 22 per cent respectively. It is not to be inferred, however, that the parents were altogether uninterested. It is rather that, in the usual fashion of the juvenile American, the child made the choice and the parent did not, as a rule, oppose it, for 39.2 per cent of the first group and 69.2 per cent of the second said in March that their choice was unhampered by the parents. In June 58.6 per cent and 54.9 per cent gave a similar answer.

To question 3 (a), " Have you any relatives or friends who are interested in how you are going to earn your living?" 69.7 per cent and 44 per cent replied that their relatives were not interested. The figures given in June were 52.9 per cent and 50.5 per cent.

To question 4 (a), "Why have you decided to earn your living in this way?" 38 per cent of the first group and 11 per cent of the second replied in March that they did not know. In June 5.7 per cent and 28.6 per cent gave the same answer.

Question 4 (b), "Did you make your choice from something you have read?" brought affirmative answers as follows:

──Instructed──		──Uninstructed──	
March	June	March	June
5.7	8.0	7.7	4.4

Question 4 (c), "Do you know anyone who does the kind of work you have chosen?" received the following percentages of affirmative replies:

──Instructed──		──Uninstructed──	
March	June	March	June
41.4	71.3	73.6	57.1

In June 38 per cent of the instructed children made the un-
solicited reply that they had chosen an occupation because they
decided that they liked it when they had talked it over in school.

The answers to question 5 (*a*), "What education do you need
to fit yourself for the kind of work you intend to do?" (*b*) "How
much longer will you have to go to school?" (*c*) "If you need
to go to the high school, which is the best one to go to?" divided
themselves as follows:

┌──Instructed──┐		┌──Uninstructed──┐	
March	June	March	June
Wrong idea of the education necessary:			
11.5%	5.7%	6.6%	8.8%
Right idea of the education necessary:			
49.5%	80.5%	51.6%	46.1%
Did not know what education is necessary:			
6.9%	4.6%	20.9%	12.1%
Thought no more education needed:			
1.1%	1.1%	7.7%	8.8%
Made no choice of occupation:			
31.1%	8.1%	13.2%	24.2%

Question 6, "How much will it cost your parents to fit you for
the kind of work you are going to do?" was evidently interpreted
quite generally by the children as referring to the cost of the
necessary education. The answers were these:

┌──Instructed──┐		┌──Uninstructed──┐	
March	June	March	June
"Don't know" the cost:			
57.4%	14.9%	40.6%	40.6%
Will cost nothing:			
2.3%	54%	14.3%	17.6%
Reasonable estimate of the cost:			
5.8%	18.4%	13.2%	11%
Unreasonable estimate of the cost:			
3.4%	4.6%	18.7%	6.6%
Made no choice of occupation:			
31.3%	8.1%	13.2%	24.2%

Question 7 asked, "What kind of a boy (or girl) would be most
successful in the kind of work you are going to do?" The sum
total of the qualities enumerated in March by the classes to be

instructed was nineteen; the parallel group gave twenty. Only two qualities were agreed upon by more than 10 per cent of the first group; they were "intelligent," given by 10.3 per cent, and "smart," given by 14.9 per cent; 27.5 per cent of the children who were to remain uninstructed wrote "application," 25.2 per cent "honest" and 17.6 per cent "neat and clean." In June also these same qualities were the ones most frequently cited, but the percentages diminished to 16.5 per cent, 22 per cent, and 9.9 per cent respectively. In the June answers of the instructed group "education" was given as a desirable quality by 18.5 per cent, "good sight and hearing" by 16.1 per cent, "health and strength" by 32.1 per cent, "intelligence" by 19.5 per cent, "neat and cleān" by 28.7 per cent, "quick" by 42.5 per cent, and "smart" by 22.9 per cent.

To question 8 (a), "Do you expect to work very hard?" the answers were as follows:

Instructed		Uninstructed	
March	June	March	June
"Don't know":			
11.5%	8.1%	6.6%	13.2%
"Expect to work hard":			
24.1%	36.7%	39.5%	23.1%
"Do not expect to work hard":			
33.3%	47.1%	40.7%	39.5%

In March 64.3 per cent of the group to be instructed answered to (b), "Is it a healthful occupation?" "Yes," but gave no reason for the reply. In June all but 21.8 per cent gave reasons why they considered the occupation healthful. In the uninstructed classes 83.5 per cent in March and 71.4 per cent in June said the occupation was healthful, but failed to tell why.

Question 8 (c) asked "How many hours a day do you expect to work?" The answers were these:

	Instructed		Uninstructed	
	March	June	March	June
"Don't know" the hours	14.9%	4.6%	8.8%	12.1%
Reasonable estimate	45.9%	81.6%	70.3%	59.3%
Unreasonable estimate	8.1%	5.7%	7.7%	4.4%

The answers to question 9, "How much pay do you expect to get each week of the first year that you work?" distributed themselves as follows:

	Instructed March	Instructed June	Uninstructed March	Uninstructed June
"Don't know" the wages	19.5%	5.7%	16.5%	23.1%
Reasonable estimate	25.3%	65.5%	37.4%	28.5%
Unreasonable estimate	24.1%	20.7%	32.9%	24.2%

Question 10 (a), "What chance do you think there is to get more pay as you grow older?" aimed to bring out the children's ideas of the opportunity for promotion in their chosen occupations. The answers divided readily into the following groups:

	Instructed March	Instructed June	Uninstructed March	Uninstructed June
"I don't know"	17.2%	8.1%	28.6%	29.7%
"A good chance"	17.2%	14.8%	8.8%	16.4%
"A fair chance"	34.5%	66.7%	49.4%	29.7%
"No chance"	—	2.3%	—	—

Question 10 (b), "What is the highest pay you can probably ever get?" brought answers as follows:

	Instructed March	Instructed June	Uninstructed March	Uninstructed June
"I don't know"	18.4%	10.3%	26.4%	29.7%
Reasonable estimate	41.3%	62.1%	41.7%	32.9%
Unreasonable estimate	9.2%	19.5%	18.7%	13.2%

The question numbered 11 (a), which was given in the June test only, "Have you thought over any occupation and then decided not to take it up?" received the following replies:

	Instructed	Uninstructed
Thought over and rejected no occupation	23.0%	54.9%
Thought over and rejected one occupation	25.3%	40.7%
Thought over and rejected two occupations	19.5%	2.2%
Thought over and rejected three occupations	9.2%	—
Thought over and rejected four occupations	8.1%	—
Thought over and rejected five occupations	3.4%	2.2%
Thought over no occupation and held to first choice	11.5%	42.8%

The answers to question 11 (*b*), "What are the reasons why you decided not to take it up?" distributed themselves thus:

	Instructed	Uninstructed
Intelligent reasons given by	67.8%	15.4%
Unintelligent reasons given by	13.8%	7.7%
No reason given by	6.9%	34.1%
Thought over no occupation, but held to first choice .	11.5%	42.8%

That the instructed classes show in June a substantial growth in intelligence regarding occupations in general, and their own vocational futures in particular, there can be no doubt. There is indication of an awakened vocational vision in some, in others tenacity of purpose. There is evidence that practically all have been helped in some degree to a better understanding of the qualifications which the worker must bring to his task, the conditions which are peculiar to it, the education which will best train for it, the elements which make for success in it, and its comparative desirability. This is the more significant when the meagerness of the time spent in actual instruction is taken into account. The uninstructed classes indicate, in general, a deterioration rather than a growth of interest and intelligence in their vocational aims. While growth without instruction was hardly to be looked for, deterioration is not difficult to explain to those who are familiar with the conditions which are likely to obtain in graduating classes during the last days of a school year.

A general description of the instructed children and a brief account of some of the experiences of the teacher who conducted the investigation may be of interest.

The children live in a district in Roxbury, where most of the houses are flats. The majority are of Irish or Irish-American parentage. There are perhaps eight per cent Jews and Italians. The fathers are teamsters, motormen, carpenters, ironworkers, laborers, piano-factory employees, etc. The children come to school clean and neatly dressed. They are of the average capacity that might be expected from such environment; it is to be doubted if an expert would select from among them any that are either supernormal or subnormal. With a few exceptions, there seems to have been evidenced among them no very great interest in books or reading and no very pronounced aptitudes.

Throughout the series of lessons on occupations they displayed much interest. Many showed an unexpected knowledge of hours, wages, health conditions, and the desirable and undesirable features of certain kinds of work. The active part taken in the lessons by the older and commonly considered duller children was especially noticeable.

In June, 1914, the year following the graduation from grammar school of these pupils, a questionnaire was sent to each child who had taken the March and June tests. These are the questions asked of the children who were at school :

1. Do you remember answering some questions last year about the kind of work you would like to do when you were through going to school?

2. What occupation did you then say you were going to take up?

3. Have you changed your mind about the kind of work you would like to do?

4. If you have changed your mind, what do you now think you would like to do?

5. If you have changed your mind, what were your reasons for doing so?

6. What school are you attending now?

7. What courses are you taking?

8. Do you think that what you are studying now will help you in the work you have chosen?

The first five above questions were also asked of the children who had gone to work, and the following questions were added :

6. Give the names and addresses of the places where you have worked.

7. Where are you working now?

8. What kind of work do you do?

9. Do you like your work?

10. What pay did you get at first?

11. What pay do you get now ?

12. What are the chances for promotion?

13. Do you go to evening school?

14. How do you think what you are learning there will help you with your work?

Answers were received from seventy-six of the instructed children and from sixty-three of the uninstructed. As fifteen of the first group were children who had failed of graduation and were still in the grammar school, it was thought well not to include them in the comparisons which follow.

To question 1, "Do you remember answering some questions last year about the kind of work you would like to do when you were through going to school?" all but one, an instructed girl, replied in the affirmative. Eighty-five and two-tenths per cent of the instructed children and 82.5 per cent of the uninstructed answered correctly question 2, "What occupation did you then say you were going to take up?"

The percentages of those going into the different groups of occupations and the various changes may be seen in the following table:

MARCH, 1913

PERCENTAGES OF THOSE GOING INTO	Instructed						Uninstructed					
	No.	%	B	G	B	G	No.	%	B	G	B	G
Professions . . .	10	16.4	5	5	8.2	8.2	12	19.0	4	8	6.3	12.7
Teachers . . .	6	9.8	1	5	1.6	8.2	8	12.7	0	8	0	12.7
Civil service . .	1	1.6	1	0	1.6	0	3	4.8	3	0	4.8	0
Business	3	4.9	3	0	4.9	0	3	4.8	2	1	3.2	1.6
Commercial . .	16	26.2	2	14	3.3	22.9	21	33.3	1	20	1.6	31.7
Stenographers .	9	14.8	0	9	0	14.8	8	12.7	0	8	0	12.7
Bookkeepers .	4	6.5	1	3	1.6	5.9	5	7.9	0	5	0	7.9
Trades	11	18.0	8	3	13.1	4.9	7	11.1	7	0	11.1	0
Don't know . . .	17	27.9	8	9	13.1	14.8	10	15.9	4	6	6.4	9.5
Miscellaneous . .	3	4.9	1	2	1.6	3.3	7	11.1	0	7	0	11.1
Nurse	0	0	0	0	0	0	1	1.6	0	1		1.6
Tel. operator .	2	3.3	0	2	0	3.3	1	1.6	0	1		1.6
Proofreader . .	0	0	0	0	0	0	1	1.6	0	1		1.6
Soldier . . .	1	1.6	1	0	1.6	0	0	0	0	0		0
Hairdresser . .	0	0	0	0	0	0	0	0	0	0		0
Music teacher . .	0	0	0	0	0	0	3	4.8	0	3		4.8
Private sec'y .	0	0	0	0	0	0	0	0	0	0		0
Factory . . .	0	0	0	0	0	0	0	0	0	0		0
Dancer . . .	0	0	0	0	0	0	0	0	0	0		0
Mov. pict. actress	0	0	0	0	0	0	1	1.6	0	1		1.6
Artist	0	0	0	0	0	0	0	0	0	0	8	0

JUNE, 1913

PERCENTAGES OF THOSE GOING INTO	Instructed						Uninstructed					
	No.	%	B	G	B	G	No.	%	B	G	B	G
Professions . . .	13	21.3	5	8	8.2	13.2	4	6.4	0	4	0	6.4
Teachers . . .	9	14.8	1	8	1.6	13.2	4	6.4	0	4	0	6.4
Civil service . .	1	1.6	1	0	1.6	0	1	1.6	1	0	1.6	0
Business	9	14.8	8	1	13.2	1.6	4	6.4	2	2	3.2	3.2

	No.	%	B	G	B	G	No.	%	B	G	B	G
Commercial . .	16	26.2	0	16	0	26.2	23	36.5	2	21	3.2	33.3
Stenographers .	10	16.4	0	10	0	15.4	10	15.9	0	10	0	15.9
Bookkeepers .	4	6.5	0	4	0	6.5	5	7.9	0	5	0	7.9
Trades . . .	16	26.2	12	4	19.7	6.5	9	14.3	8	1	12.7	1.6
Don't know . . .	4	6.6	2	2	3.3	3.3	12	19.0	8	4	12.7	6.3
Miscellaneous . .	2	3.2	0	2	0	3.2	10	15.9	0	10	0	15.9
Nurse	1	1.6	0	1	0	1.6	1	1.6	0	1	0	1.6
Tel. operator .	1	1.6	0	1	0	1.6	1	1.6	0	1	0	1.6
Proofreader . .	0	0	0	0	0	0	1	1.6	0	1	0	1.6
Soldier . . .	0	0	0	0	0	0	1	1.6	0	1	0	1.6
Hairdresser . .	0	0	0	0	0	0	4	6.4	0	4	0	6.4
Music teacher .	0	0	0	0	0	0	0	0	0	0	0	0
Private sec'y .	0	0	0	0	0	0	2	3.2	0	2	0	3.2
Factory . . .	0	0	0	0	0	0	0	0	0	0	0	0
Dancer . . .	0	0	0	0	0	0	0	0	0	0	0	0
Mov. pict. actress	0	0	0	0	0	0	0	0	0	0	0	0
Artist	0	0	0	0	0	0	0	0	0	0	0	0

JULY, 1914

PERCENTAGES OF THOSE GOING INTO	Instructed						Uninstructed					
	No.	%	B	G	B	G	No.	%	B	G	B	G
Professions . . .	10	16.4	3	7	4.9	11.5	5	7.9	2	3	3.1	4.8
Teachers . . .	8	13.1	1	7	1.6	11.5	3	4.8	0	3	0	4.8
Civil service . .	2	3.2	2	0	3.2	0	3	4.8	3	0	4.8	0
Business	10	16.4	9	1	14.8	1.6	3	4.8	1	2	1.6	3.2
Commercial . .	18	29.5	2	16	3.3	26.2	30	47.6	2	28	3.2	44.4
Stenographers .	10	16.4	0	10	0	16.4	15	23.8	2	13	3.2	20.6
Bookkeepers .	8	13.1	2	6	3.2	9.9	11	17.5	0	11	0	17.5
Trades . . .	18	29.5	11	7	18.0	11.5	12	19.1	11	1	17.5	1.6
Don't know . . .	1	1.6	1	0	1.6	0	2	3.2	1	1	1.6	1.6
Miscellaneous . .	2	3.2	0	2	0	3	8	12.6	1	7	1.6	11.0
Nurse	0		0	0			1	1.6	0	1	0	1.6
Tel. operator .	0		0	0			1	1.6	0	1	0	1.6
Proofreader . .	0		0	0			0	0	0	0	0	0
Soldier . . .	0		0	0			0	0	0	0	0	0
Hairdresser . .	0		0	0			0	0	0	0	0	0
Music teacher .	0		0	0			0	0	0	0	0	0
Private sec'y .	0		0	0			1	1.6	0	1	0	1.6
Factory . . .	1	1	0	1		1	2	3.2	0	2	0	3.2
Dancer . . .	0		0	0			2	3.2	0	2	0	3.2
Mov. pict. actress	1	1.8	0	1		1.8	0	0	0	0	0	0
Artist	0	0	0	0	8	0	1	1.6	1	0	1	1.6

There were found to be sixty-one different kinds of work selected by the instructed classes and sixty-three kinds by the uninstructed. Twenty-four and five-tenths per cent of the first group and 23.8 per cent of the second held to the occupation which they had given as their choice in the first test. Of all the children who were questioned, only one, a girl of the uninstructed group, replied to all three queries regarding her choice of occupation that she had not decided. Seventy-two and one-tenth per cent of the instructed children gave as their chosen occupations those which had been studied in the school lessons. Seventy-five and four-tenths per cent of the instructed group and 60.3 per cent of the uninstructed held to the occupation which they had said in the preceding test it was their intention to take up. Of the first group whose occupational choice had changed, 9.8 per cent had evidently forgotten what occupation they had given in June, 1913, as their preference. Of the uninstructed, there were 22.2 per cent who had also apparently no correct recollection of their previous written choice.

Six and five-tenths per cent of the instructed children and 14.2 per cent of the uninstructed children gave no reason in answer to question 6, " If you have changed your mind, what were your reasons for doing so ? " The following are the changes of occupation in the instructed group and the reasons which they gave :

No. 18. Girl changed from cooking teacher to stenographer. Reason : " Because I had not fully decided what I was going to do."

No. 21. Boy changed from civil engineer to lawyer. Reason : " I think I will like it better. My brother has changed, and I desire to be the same as he."

No. 35. Boy who gave as his choice " civil engineer " and is now an errand boy in a printing office and would like to be a printer. Reason : " My father died, and I could not go to school any longer."

No. 47. Girl changed from stenography to school-teacher. Reason : " I thought a position as a school-teacher was much better than a position as a stenographer."

No. 51. Girl changed from teacher to secretary. Reason : " My parents thought I would have a better chance if I should take up this work."

No. 53. Girl changed from telephone operator to dressmaker. Reason : " It is too long to wait to be a telephone operator, as I am only 14 and you have to wait to be 17."

No. 56. Girl changed from stenographer to salesgirl. Reason : " I like it better than going to school."

No. 68. Boy changed from cabinetmaker to " I do not know." Reason : " I was advised."

No. 88. Boy who gave as his choice " machinist " is now " delivering orders on a peddling wagon," and " would like to get an office position and work myself up to a bookkeeper or some- thing better." Reason for change : " When I left school I had to take the first thing that came along to help my mother along."

No. 89. Boy changed from soldier to electrician. Reason : " Because then I had wrong ideas of what army life was ; now I know better."

The following are the changes and the reasons given by the uninstructed group :

No. 153. Boy changed from traveling salesman to chauffeur. Reason : " More money."

No. 156. Girl changed from stenographer to trained nurse. Reason : " I would rather do something to help others and that war has appealed to me."

No. 164. Girl changed from music teacher to typewriter or stenographer. Reason : " I like typewriting so I thought I would be a typewriter, and if I like stenography, I might be a stenographer."

No. 172. Boy changed from grocery business to automobile painting. Reason : " Did n't like business."

No. 179. Boy changed from electrical work to " I would like to get a job in an automobile place learn how to repair and run a car." Reason : " Because automobiling is the becoming thing, to repair and run cars."

No. 181. Girl changed from music teacher to dressmaker. Reason : " I have gone to a school where I have learned dress- making and have liked it better than music."

No. 185. Girl changed from typewriter to factory work. Reason : " A lady spoke for me in the Edison Light and I am waiting to receive word from them."

No. 207. Girl changed from school-teacher to bookkeeper. Reason : " I thought that there would be a better chance for promotion and for higher wages."

No. 215. Boy now working in a dental laboratory changed from " some office work " to " be skilled in teeth which is a trade under the name of Mechanical Dentistry." Reason : " I wanted to learn *this* trade."

No. 224. Girl now working as cashier in a dry-goods store changed from bookkeeper to " undecided." Reason : " Did n't care for school."

No. 232. Boy changed from bookkeeper to engineer. Reason : " I think it is better."

No. 244. Girl changed from teacher to " I would like to work in a department store." Reason : " Because I knew I could not afford to go to school all that time."

No. 252. Girl changed from music teacher to stenographer. Reason : " I have n't changed my mine."

No. 265. Girl changed from stenographer to bookkeeper. Reason : " I liked it better."

No. 268. Boy changed from machinist to printer. Reason : " I had to take both machine-shop work and printing, and I liked the printing best."

No. 275. Girl changed from teaching to commercial work. Reason : " Decided not to teach."

The answers to questions 6 and 7, " What school are you attending now ? " and " What courses are you taking ? " brought out the information that 72.1 per cent of the instructed and 65.1 per cent of the uninstructed group were attending some high school. All of the first group were on the school road which will lead most directly to their chosen occupation. Three and two-tenths per cent of the uninstructed were not headed in the best way educationally.

It was found that 27.9 per cent of the instructed children and 36.5 per cent of the uninstructed were at work in June, 1914. Of these, 13.1 per cent and 9.5 per cent were engaged in occupations which would help to fit them for the kind of work which they had indicated they were eventually to take up. Eight and two-tenths per cent of the first group and 22.3 per cent of the second were not engaged in occupations which would train them in any direct sense for the life work which they had chosen. The remaining 6.6 per cent of the first group and 6.3 per cent of the second were classified as doubtful cases.

The classes with whom the investigation was conducted are typical of many thousands of groups of children throughout our land. The conclusions which the study warrants are therefore widely applicable. There are sufficient data to indicate that children about to be graduated from our grammar schools are deeply interested in the work of the world. The vast majority of them are evidently capable of visualizing for themselves an occupational future. They lack neither comprehension nor vision. What they do lack is definite, systematic, expository instruction in vocational opportunity, and inspiration and direction as how to discover their own talents and limitations. Clearly the way to place opportunity to do this before the great masses of our children is to give occupational study a definite place on our seventh- and eighth-grade grammar-school program. The objection that we have no reliable information to give is rapidly losing weight. Such studies as those which are now being made in Buffalo, Dr. Ayres's very recent valuable classification of constant occupations under the Russell Sage Foundation, the Chicago, Minneapolis, Cincinnati, and Cleveland studies, the contributions of the Boston Vocation Bureau and of the Women's Industrial Union, furnish ample material for the foundation of a grammar-school course in occupational study. The elementary school can render no more valuable service to society than to take this means of awakening in the minds of its graduates a life-career motive.

VOCATIONAL GUIDANCE

(Extracts from the Report of the Committee on High Schools and Training Schools, Board of Education, New York, 1914)

No problem that is before the public-school system deserves more careful consideration than that of vocational guidance. In order to ascertain definite facts based upon scientific opinions, your subcommittee based its hearings upon the following questions:

(1) What is the definition of vocational guidance, its nature and purpose?

(2) Into what employments or types of work do the boys and girls of our high schools enter, either upon dropping from school or upon graduation?

(3) How adequate are the present high-school courses in relation to the employment into which boys and girls enter?

(4) At what period of the school work should vocational guidance be begun?

(5) What is the relation of vocational guidance to elementary schools?

(6) What are to be the methods of discovering the capacity and aptitudes of school children?

(7) What methods and agencies exist for the purpose of aiding vocational guidance through further training?

(8) What agencies exist for the distribution of school children with a view to their securing the training made necessary through vocational guidance?

(9) What methods shall be pursued to prevent the possible exploitation of children?

(10) What is the value and effect of vocational scholarships?

(11) What shall be the relation of vocational guidance to employment agencies?

Wherefore, as far as may be possible, a similar order will be followed in presenting our report.

(1) *What is the definition of vocational guidance, its nature and purpose?*

According to the new Standard Dictionary a vocation is "any occupation or pursuit for which one qualifies one's self, or to which one devotes one's time or life; a calling." The exact adaptation of this definition is not wholly possible in the light of present educational tendencies.

In the twenty-fifth annual report of the United States Commissioner of Labor, it is stated that vocational guidance does not mean selecting a pursuit for a child nor finding a place for him. It means rather leading him and his parents to consider the matter themselves, to study the child's tastes and possibilities, to decide for what he is best fitted, and to take definite steps toward securing for him the necessary preparation or training.

The Vocational Guidance Association of New York City presents, as its definition : " Vocational guidance is the selection of the means for giving each boy and girl the training and the opportunity for doing that work for which each is best fitted by ability and inclination."

The aim of vocational guidance is to secure an increase in efficiency in the various occupations, together with an elimination of the social wastage due to the maladjustment of workers in unsuitable occupations ; to decrease the number of inadequately prepared workers ; and to lessen unemployment in so far as it may be due to a failure of the schools to supply the types of workers who are in demand. The aim of vocational guidance, however, should hold in the forefront the necessity of a broad culture, together with a diversified industrial experience, as the fundamental basis of preparing school children for life.

In order to accomplish the preparation of school children three steps are essential :

(1) A vocational survey is a prerequisite which involves a study of industries to ascertain what specific abilities and training are needed in each of them, together with the industrial opportunities which they afford and the fundamental processes which may possess an educational value.

(2) Vocational analysis must be considered in so far as it involves the capacities, characteristics, and familiar tendencies of children, that there may be an adequate personal basis in guiding the education of the children.

(3) Vocational education to such a degree as will provide for a readjustment of school work that will enrich the curriculum or offer new courses such as may be shown to be necessary as a result of the vocational survey.

Vocational guidance can only be of service in so far as it is based upon a practical study of industrial life. In the language of Professor Mead, of The University of Chicago:

It is at the meeting point of training and occupation that the school can criticize its own achievements, and at the same time the life into which the children are to enter. It seems to me of supreme importance, both to the children's training and to their own vocations, that they should both be formulated in terms of vocational guidance. [Again,] In vocational guidance the school finds its supreme task as the conscious educational institution of a democracy.

The direct training of a child for a particular calling may not necessarily advance the best interests of the boy or girl and may, to some extent, interfere with his future development. Industry itself provides in many lines opportunities for direct education within the trade. The general attitude of employers, however, is that boys and girls should receive in school particular preparation for their particular employments, which is obviously impracticable as well as undesirable. Vocational guidance must be considered essentially from the standpoint of the standards of an educational system, and the expenditure of all moneys for vocational guidance should be viewed in the light of its educational return.

The clash between the view of the manufacturer and that of the educator is well illustrated in the words of Mr. George Elwell:

It is not the aim of the manufacturer to provide opportunity for more industrial education for his workers. As a manufacturer I desire that the boy who goes into the shop should learn one process and be content to stick to that to the end. Of course, as president of the board of education I have to proclaim higher ideals.

Vocational guidance from the educator's standpoint must not concede too much to the employer. In the words of Mr. Lovejoy:

Business assumes that its jobs are fixed and eternal, and it demands of education that the latter fit the children to the jobs. A proper rejoinder on the part of educators would be, "Here are our children; what kind of industry have you to offer?"

Let us insist that the child's future usefulness, not the present balance sheet, shall be the measure of the success of this guidance into vocations, and let us resist every scheme to make the labor of your children a makeshift to maintain themselves or their families.

At the present time the entire subject of vocational guidance is in its incipient stage, and the final policies cannot be adopted for many years to come. The views that are laid down in the Hanus Report deserve consideration, and we find in the " Report as a Whole " :

Public education should direct each pupil's attention to a vocation to which he may reasonably aspire; that is, every pupil should be led gradually to realize that a suitable vocation, accessible to him and adapted to him, is indispensable to a useful and happy life. As he approaches the end of his school career, whatever his age may be, he should come to see that his vocation will be not only the means of satisfying his personal wants and ambitions, but because it is the chief means of establishing significant relations between himself and his fellow men, it is also the source of such public service as he is capable of and may be called upon to render. Public education should therefore provide for the development of vocational purpose based on vocational enlightenment (vocational guidance); and should offer each pupil appropriate training for the vocation of his choice.

Strengthening this, Professor Hanus continues:

It may not be out of place here to emphasize once more that vocational guidance does not mean merely helping boys and girls to find work, but to find the kind of work they are best fitted by nature and training to do well. It does not mean prescribing a vocation; it does mean bringing to bear on the choice of a vocation organized information and organized common sense. It should therefore not only tend to bring about a better adjustment of the boy to his work, but also point the way to more education for more efficient work.

Vocational guidance and vocational education are closely interrelated, and the guiding of education so that it may have a vocational bearing is probably one of the most important phases of vocational guidance. The function of vocational guidance is not to train for a job, but to afford the education necessary for the efficient fulfillment of the work in life, giving equal stress to the educational values which are to be derived from industry and to those derived from the liberal professions. Until very recently it would have been possible to say that the trend of public elementary-school education was to guide into law, medicine, or the ministry. What may be borrowed from industry remains to be demonstrated, but, as Dr. Leonard P. Ayres has wisely pointed out, vocational guidance " must be prepared to challenge each industry whether or not any given occupation holds out the promise to the future worker that it may justly ask the coöperation of the public schools. . . .

Vocational guidance and vocational education are in reality merely symptoms of a world-wide movement for bringing education into vital touch with the needs and requirements of the problems of real life. I believe that future history will show that they were the beginning of the most fundamental revolution in education since the Renaissance."

In brief, vocational guidance should be an educational plan sufficiently elastic and flexible to afford the opportunity to school children to find themselves in terms of their vocational aptitudes. It should seek to devise means for securing broad information regarding the numerous groups of industries, together with the underlying processes available for the children, and to ascertain, in so far as may be possible, the aptitudes and characteristics of school children with a view to giving them suggestions how to develop their innate powers. In addition, it should offer advice as to the places wherein educational advantages may be secured in order to foster the types of training best adapted to the needs of individual children.

(2) *Into what employments or types of work do the boys and girls of our high schools enter, either upon dropping from school or upon graduation?*

There is a distinct lack of definite information regarding the nature of employments or types of work into which the boys and girls of our high schools enter, either upon dropping from school or upon graduating.

In the words of Chatfield, in the last report of the Permanent Census Board:

Probably the most significant statistics yet published by this Board were those concerning the occupations of 132,000 children registered in this office. The casual nature of this employment and its lack of opportunity for training and development again emphasized the need for changes in elementary education which would give greater promise of a fair measure of economic independence to the average individual than is now the case.

The fact that the types of occupations are not highly remunerative and require comparatively little skill, or indeed are "blind-alley" occupations, is emphasized by the statements of Mr. Chatfield

The statistics concerning workers 14-18 years of age gathered by the Permanent Census Board likewise emphasize the necessity for more complete and detailed information if the vocational problem is to be attacked in any comprehensive way. It is true that these statistics do not include the whole body of workers between these ages. Many parents, fearing that information given concerning working children would be used to their detriment, withheld the facts desired concerning such children. In the various classifications represented, however, 131,972 children are employed, and there is no reason to suppose that the character or proportions of these classifications would be greatly changed by the addition of the number not enumerated. The 131,972 workers are almost equally divided as to sex and age — 66,620 being boys and 65,252 girls. Between 14 and 16 years of age there are 23,864 boys and 24,215 girls; between 16 and 18 years, 42,756 are boys and 41,057 are girls, this last group being nearly twice as numerous as that made up of the most mature pupils. The occupations most numerously represented are shown in the table:

	14-16		16-18		Total		Grand Total
	Boys	Girls	Boys	Girls	Boys	Girls	
Housework	1	8693	1	9583	2	18,276	18,278
Errand boys and girls . .	6366	661	6163	561	12,529	1,222	13,751
Clerks	2122	795	7023	2191	9,145	2,986	12,131
Office boys and girls . . .	3551	667	4442	1109	7,993	1,776	9,769
Helpers	1807	577	3144	793	4,951	1,370	6,321
Machine operators . . .	367	1236	859	2380	1,226	3,616	4,842
Packers and wrappers . .	331	1453	727	2106	1,058	3,559	4,617
Idle	1793	34	2053	73	3,846	107	3,953
Stenographers and typists	115	563	471	2681	586	3,244	3,830
Salesmen and saleswomen	201	605	1088	1823	1,289	2,428	3,717
Not known	877	471	1440	898	2,317	1,369	3,616
Messengers	1117	156	1358	79	2,475	235	2,780
Stock boys and girls . . .	364	388	1003	863	1,367	1,251	2,618
Bookkeepers	107	222	717	1142	824	1,364	2,188
Dressmakers	—	605	2	1384	2	1,989	1,991
Seamstresses	—	587	—	1105	—	1,692	1,692
Feather workers	13	551	32	1050	45	1,601	1,646
Shirt and waist workers .	33	421	90	919	123	1,340	1,463
Millinery	6	436	11	984	17	1,420	1,437
Wagon boys	433	—	920	—	1,353	—	1,353
Telephone operators . .	59	223	161	844	220	1,067	1,287
Outer-clothing workers .	57	228	204	645	261	873	1,134
Paper-box makers	73	354	192	495	265	849	1,114
Drivers	251	—	853	—	1,103	—	1,103
Printers	278	9	751	36	1,029	45	1,074
Tailors	159	88	613	178	772	266	1,038
							108,744

While it would no doubt be difficult to classify these occupations strictly as skilled, partly skilled, or unskilled, it is plainly evident that with a few notable exceptions no highly remunerative occupations are represented and very few indeed which would provide a competence in the future or the skill and experience that make the taking up of more skilled work natural and easy. Rather will be noticed the prevalence of "blind-alley" occupations, such as errand boys and girls, office boys and girls, packers and wrappers, messengers, stock boys and girls, wagon boys, telephone operators, paper-box makers, drivers, and without doubt a large proportion of those included in such occupations as housework, clerks, salesmen and saleswomen, and others.

That the problem of vocational guidance as far as occupation is concerned is not acute in all high schools is evidenced by the statements of Mr. Denbigh and Mr. Larkins:

MORRIS HIGH SCHOOL

In January, 1911, of 141 graduates, 120 went to higher institutions
In June, 1911, of 211 graduates, 152 went to higher institutions
In January, 1912, of 154 graduates, 93 went to higher institutions
In June, 1912, of 253 graduates, 184 went to higher institutions
In June, 1913, of 183 graduates, 107 went to higher institutions

The children who drop out earlier than that undoubtedly go into positions where unskilled work only can be procured. We cannot place those with any certainty, — the unskilled and the children who have not graduated, — which, of course, bears out the statement made here to-night, that we ought to keep those children just as long as we can; but that does not touch the statement that there are vast numbers of children who must leave and who ought to be taken care of.

In the Manual Training High School in 1911 there were graduated 237 graduates, of which 197 went to higher institutions. The following year, with a few more students graduated, there were between 45 and 55 who did not go to some higher institutions.

There is a great deal of scattered material on the subject of employments entered into by boys and girls who leave school between the ages of fourteen and sixteen. The collection and correlation of such facts represent one of the basic needs of our educational system. Some striking figures are evidenced in the report of Miss Mary Van Kleeck, of the Russell Sage Foundation, who made a study of 13,000 girls attending the evening schools.

One thousand seven hundred of these 13,000 had attended high schools in the city. Of these in professional service, 72.2 per cent were high-school graduates; in manufacturing and mechanical pursuits .2 of 1 per cent were high-school graduates. Among the factory girls a majority — 55.1 per cent — left school while in the fifth, sixth, and seventh grades, while in trade and transportation a large proportion, 75.8 per cent, finished the elementary course. In office work and department stores 27.8 per cent went to high school, only 2.1 per cent graduating, however. We find that the girl who leaves school in the fifth, sixth, or seventh grade will go into some manufacturing or mechanical pursuit and that there is a very big difference as to the particular form of manufacturing or mechanical pursuit that the girl is likely to achieve success at. Girls who leave school earliest and have gone the least distance in school go into such occupations as paper-box manufacturing, button making, candy manufacturing, and that kind of work, whereas girls who go further in school go into dressmaking, etc.

There is little information at hand to show whether high-school graduates take the skilled work and elementary-school pupils the unskilled work, but it is obvious that the jobs first available for children are most likely to be in unskilled labor.

In the language of Meyer Bloomfield:

It is as true in Germany as in England and here that the jobs that amount to nothing pay the highest wages and attract the most children. The problem of boys and girls in unskilled callings is hardly even considered, despite the vast system of continuation schools.

The experience of Mrs. de Fremery at the Wadleigh High School leads her to state:

As far as I have been able to judge, there is very little difference in the type of occupation into which the high school and the elementary school students go. While they go in large numbers from the high schools into the unskilled trades, a great many of them go into department stores; they have a tendency to go into unskilled office positions rather than into the factories.

Considering the nature of occupations into which boys and girls go from our elementary and high schools, it is apparent that the type of vocational guidance that is required is the type that will keep them in school for a longer period of time, as well as the type of instruction that will prepare them for something else besides "blind-alley" occupations. The fault, however, does not lie entirely within the educational system. Industry itself is partly at fault, and under the present form of organization it does not discriminate sufficiently between the graduates of high schools and of elementary schools, particularly as regards the monetary value of the services rendered, nor, indeed, are employers able to state the characteristics or general training which is essential for their industries, because each employer is considering his own particular establishment and endeavoring to secure workers for particular processes.

(3) *How adequate are the present high-school courses in relation to the employment into which boys and girls enter?*

It is difficult to estimate the exact relation between the high-school courses in our commercial and technical high schools and the actual field of occupation into which their graduates go. There is a serious feeling that our high schools do not necessarily supply a sufficient variety of courses to give adequate opportunity for the secondary education of the various types of children who attend them. There has been an unfortunate tendency to differentiate children into those destined for professional work and business work and manual work. This policy fails to recognize the universality of education and differentiates phases of education as though they possessed little value in common. This attitude does not serve as a proper basis for the establishment of high-school courses.

At the Wadleigh High School Mrs. de Fremery states:

I find that one third of the girls leaving give as their reason for leaving that they took up special courses elsewhere, which indicates that the work that they found in that school was distinctly inadequate; one third said that they would probably take up other courses, and one third said that they would stay at home.

It would seem to be of the utmost educational value to have a careful study made of the social return given by graduates of our various types of high schools. The high mortality would suggest that probably there is too great narrowness in the courses provided or that we are clinging to a traditional view of education that is interfering with educational progress in terms of the needs of our public-school children. Widely variant courses may be essential in order to permit of vocational guidance in its broadest educational meaning.

(4) *At what period of the school work should vocational guidance be begun?*

Vocational guidance is generally considered as a function of the high school. It is obvious, however, that the sanest view of vocational guidance demands that it be considered not as a specific duty of the high school but as a fundamental motive of the entire educational system. In evidence of this we may call your attention to a series of authoritative views.

Associate Superintendent Shallow thinks vocational guidance should be begun in the upper grades of the elementary schools.

In the Hanus Report on " Intermediate Schools " we find this statement :

By reason of the number of children in the intermediate schools who are approaching a time when they must choose a pursuit, and who need advice that they may choose wisely, and by reason of the number of teachers having to deal only with such children, the intermediate school affords the best possible opportunity to experiment and to develop systematic vocational guidance.

Professor Leonard comments :

It seems to me vocational guidance should be part of the elementary-school curriculum from the very first grade. Granting that the work of vocational guidance is to be begun in the high-school period, the teacher then must have information relative to the pupil from the very time he entered school.

Mr. Gruenberg advocates that vocational guidance should be begun in the school work early enough (1) to enable the pupil to acquire a sufficiently broad basis of information for making a wise vocational choice, and (2) to enable the teacher to acquire a sufficiently intimate knowledge of the pupil to give him competent counsel in the making of choice of further study.

Inasmuch as most of the children between fourteen and sixteen years of age are in the elementary schools, this work should begin in these schools — at least a year or two before the children reach the working-certificate age.

Frishberg expresses his views as follows :

I suppose if we went into that question very broadly we ought to say that vocational guidance really ought to commence in the kindergarten. It is our intention not to tell a boy you are fit for this or that particular thing, but to give him an opportunity to work at different things and different kinds of work, and let the boy find himself first. I think if that opportunity were given to a boy in the seventh year it would help to reduce that so-called mortality in the first and second year of high school. To come down to the definite year for the beginning of that work, the sixth or seventh year I would recommend as the commencement of the so-called vocational guidance.

Associate Superintendent Straubenmüller, who has given very much thought to this subject, expresses his views in this way:

I do not believe that the establishment of vocational courses in the elementary schools will be a remedy for preventing children from leaving school at fourteen to any greater degree than manual training did. I do not believe that mechanics can be made out of children who have not sufficient intelligence or sufficient will power to secure an ordinary school education. I do not believe that over-age children in the grades are by reason of that fact handminded and should be preferred in industrial courses to children of normal age. I do believe that the main object of vocational courses in the elementary schools should be to assist children in selecting their life work, and to give them some industrial or business intelligence.

Professor Bonser, of Teachers College, of the Vocational Guidance Association, indicates that vocational guidance should be a factor promoting the entire school system:

It begins in the kindergarten and continues through the whole elementary-school system so that boys may intelligently choose when they have an opportunity or when they must leave school. A boy or girl who goes to a place because he or she must go to work is usually absolutely without any basis of choice whatsoever.

Mrs. Woolley, of Cincinnati, who has had a wide experience with this subject, asserts that most educators are agreed that differentiation should begin at about twelve years or at the end of the sixth grade. She would, therefore, introduce vocational guidance at this point.

At the last conference on vocational guidance at Grand Rapids many of the speakers considered it important to point out that it is too late to attempt vocational guidance as the child is about to leave the school.

Mr. Henry Hatch, principal of the Thorp School in Chicago, at the same conference pointed out that, if we wait until after the sixth grade, we leave out more than one half of the pupils and those who most need guidance. Mr. Jesse B. Davis, principal of the Central High School of Grand Rapids, said that they had started the work in the high school, but as a result of their experience they now begin vocational guidance in the seventh grade. He believed, however, that something could be done before this grade to broaden the experience of the children.

In the Davis Report we find the following suggestive quotations:

> We recommend also for every pupil in the general course, as soon as properly equipped teachers can be found to give it, a course in civics and vocational guidance.
>
> We recommend . . . that the principals of the schools be authorized to discover the real needs of both boys and girls and to establish special courses that are required to meet them.

In the Final Report of the School Inquiry Committee, in discussing the working aims of the schools, we read that " The school should induct the child into industrial and economic life far enough so that his education will serve as a vocational aid. ' It should make the child feel that there is a suitable vocation open to him to which he may aspire.' As a separate responsibility of the school this duty does not become separate and permanent until toward the end of the high-school course. It should always be a part of the three duties of the school stated above to keep the facts of industrial and economic life prominent, and they will have their place as a matter of course, if the work of the school is made sufficiently concrete."

In Cincinnati there is a movement on foot to try some vocational-guidance work in connection with the prevocational school pupils who will not go to high school and who are behind in the grades.

The United States Commissioner of Labor, in 1910, wrote:

> One large aim in vocational guidance is to develop the methods and material by which the public schools may help fit their individual graduates for the work they are likely to do, and in this effort to use all the spiritual, economic, educational, and other agencies which may coöperate to bring about the most complete information and the best suggestions.

Considering the views of the quoted authorities, it is the belief of your committee that vocational guidance is not essentially a high-school function. If vocational guidance be regarded as an educational measure, its value should be extended to all children attending the public schools in so far as may be possible. This means that vocational guidance should be begun in the elementary schools. In our interpretation of the term, this does not mean that special teachers should be assigned to consider the vocational tendencies of the children, but it means that the work in the elementary schools should be considered with relation to the commercial, industrial, and professional lines of work into which children must necessarily go.

In its last analysis we believe vocational guidance is valueless unless it serves to keep children in school for a longer period of years than is possible at the present time. We believe it highly desirable to consider the curriculum of the elementary schools with a view to adapting it and enriching it so as to give a larger number of children an opportunity to discover themselves or at least evidence some aptitudes which may be of further service in assisting teachers to give the guidance so essential for their further educational development.

In the words of Professor Hanus:

> Vocational guidance does not mean merely helping boys and girls to find work, but to find the kind of work they are best fitted by nature and training to do well. It does not mean prescribing a vocation; it does mean bringing to bear on the choice of a vocation organized information and organized common sense.

In our opinion such an adaptation of the curriculum would mean not so much a change in courses of study as modifications in the syllabuses, materials, and methods of presentation. A considerable amount of information can be given to the pupils concerning the various trades which may be open to them, so that the children themselves may be guided into a consideration of the question of life-careers. To make this point of view more apparent we present herewith some concrete examples of how the elementary-school curriculum might be enriched in the light of its value for vocational guidance. These have been especially prepared for this report by Professor Bonser and Mr. Gruenberg.

The Elementary-School Curriculum and Vocational Guidance

By F. G. Bonser

If the common subjects of study are rich in material relating to present-day life activities, the regular school work will contribute much that is basic for vocational choice. Illustrations of such material in mathematics, geography, history, and civics will show possibilities.

Mathematics. Studies in the money values of education yield excellent material. A comparison of the wages of skilled and unskilled workers in the five principal branches of the building trades, taken from a report of the Bureau of Commerce and Labor, shows these results: The average wage for this country of skilled workers is $22.27 a week; for the unskilled, $10.45. In the five leading machine trades, the average for the skilled workers is $17.70 a week; for the unskilled, $9.69. What would training in a vocational school for three or four years, lifting the worker from the unskilled group to the skilled group, cost in money? How much would this be worth as an investment? What would be the difference in income for a year resulting from such training? How would the standards of living of the two groups compare?

A boy may start at sixteen years of age at $3 a week in a shop and work up to $16.50 a week at twenty-five years of age; he may also enter a trade school at sixteen, go for three years, and expect, on the basis of results from trade-school graduates, to receive $22.50 a week at twenty-five years of age. It has been estimated that every day a boy spends in the trade school was worth $10 to him in money value. Similar figures are available for girls. Using the available facts, find whether these estimates are true.

The study of a number of the more common occupations as to cost and income, unemployment, seasonal characters of work, is valuable material in giving arithmetical practice as well as in developing good common sense in choosing an occupation. Compare the work of different occupations in such items of cost and income as stock and depreciation, heat, light, rent, ice, insurance, pay roll, advertising, delivery, losses or waste, bad sales, cartage and express, conventions, books and periodicals, taxes, telephone, incidentals, total expenses, sales or salary per year, per-cent profits, and net income. Facts may be gotten that are approximately correct from the community. Out of these will come such questions as: What occupations require most and least education? most and least investment? most responsibility? longest hours of work? What are the wages or salaries in each and how rapidly do these advance? What are the limits of advancement? Which offer greatest rewards for honest, efficient effort? In which is there largest opportunity for social service? In which occupations is there most unemployment? Why were there over 15,000 business failures in 1913? Why do we see failures here in New York in almost every block several times a year? In how far would the right kind of education prevent most of these failures? What would such education cost? And various other questions which bring out facts of importance in making vocational choices.

Problems in the economics of living, — values and costs of food, rent, clothing, health, insurance, and entertainment, — if made concrete, have very significant values in relationship to choice of occupation. A realization of the cost of living under varying standards and the means necessary to attain the higher standards is important. The proportions of income to be spent for rent, for food, for clothing, and for other purposes is a problem worth attention. The need of thinking in terms of per cents is very essential. Buying soap at six bars for a quarter rather than one bar at a time at five cents saves less than a cent a bar, yet it does save 20 per cent. Twenty per cent on a wage of $40 a month is $8 — nearly $100 a year. If both men and women could be so trained in school in the economics of buying that they would always think in terms of per cents, it would profoundly affect their standards of living for the better.

Through the grades from fifth to eighth, practically all problems in mathematics might well come from the daily problems of business, industry, and household and general expenses. These, with sufficient drill work in processes, would be eminently valuable in furnishing information basic to intelligent vocational choices.

Geography. The study of the sources of the materials of industry, the centers of production and manufacture, of markets, of the causes of all of these, and of their effects upon the occupations of men have indirect but significant value in arousing interest and developing intelligence about occupations and their opportunities. Through the studies of the occupations in different regions and centers of the world, and the modifications of these in response to environing conditions, the relative attractiveness, economic and social, of many is brought out. The conditions of labor in the various countries and centers of production and manufacture, the wages, the stability of the occupations, the migrations of laborers, and the connection of all of these with the products used in our own community or sent by us to these other communities will give a wider and more intelligent interest in the occupations studied. The sources of materials used in a single dinner, including food, china, glass, silver and other metal wares, linen, and dining-room furniture, would lead us to industrial and commercial centers in nearly all parts of the world. To trace these products to their source, study their methods of production, and consider other problems, economic and social, would make the geography have a vital relationship to each boy and girl. Similarly, tracing the materials of one's clothing or household furnishings, of building materials, or of other activities about us would bring him into intimate contact with every place and people in the world worth knowing and would enable him to see why they were of importance. Tracing the products sent from New York for one day to their ultimate markets would further build up this feeling of interdependence and relationship and dignify the occupations producing these exports.

If the work of the sixth, seventh, and eighth grades in geography were centered about the problems of industry and commerce of vital importance to the people of New York City, it would be highly valuable in developing intelligent attitudes toward occupations, and would omit little of geography worth knowing from any standpoint.

History. The study of the evolution of industry, commerce, and the occupations in general is possible in such a way as to give much intelligent understanding of present-day vocations. Every occupation has its heroes, its discoveries, and its romances, some of which are as fascinating as military history. The information of these evolutions, together with the economic and social consequences growing out of them, is really more fundamental and valuable than is most of the knowledge of political events usually taught in history.

Some of the suggestive fields of history which might well be taught in the upper grades are the following:

The evolution of the textile and clothing industries — primitive spinning and weaving; textiles and methods of production among the Greeks and Romans; tapestries and tapestry weaving; colonial looms and textiles; the industrial revolution and the textile industries — Whitney, Cartwright, Kay, Hargreaves, Arkwright, and Jacquard; the guilds and the textile industries; the sewing machine and the inventions of Howe, Singer, and Wilson; present-day power-driven sewing machines; Goodyear and the rubber industry; and the status of the textile and clothing industries of to-day as the product of all these centuries of development.

The metal- and wood-working industries offer much of interest.' From Tubal Cain to Bessemer is a long and interesting story. Period furniture is rich in historic relationships. The development of power machinery with the stories of Watt, Stephenson, Fulton, Parsons, Stevens, Ericsson, Langley, Wright Brothers, Edison, and other inventors in the fields of transportation and communication are all of interest and may be directly connected with present-day problems of one's own community.

Palissy, Wood, Wedgwood, and others, together with Greek, Italian, French, Delft, Dresden, and English pottery, constitute another field. In brief, every field of commerce and industry is rich in historic material, the study of which may lead to the discovery of latent interest and aptitudes and provide information helpful in vocational selection. This kind of historic study by no means excludes the important parts of political history, but rather furnishes an intelligent background for them.

Civics. In the study of the history of industry, with its changes from hand production to factory production by machine processes, the need for civic regulation can easily be traced. Many of the most important problems of civic life have to do with the conditions of industrial production and distribution. Among these are the conditions of hazardous industries, the enforcement of laws relative to sanitation of the working places and homes of the workers, fire protection, factory laws and inspection relative to child labor, hours of labor, organizations of laborers and of employers, standards of purity of products, of pensions and insurance, and of employers' liability and workmen's compensation in case of accident. The theory of collective bargaining, the legal rights of workingmen, and the laws pertaining to education are all of importance. The general public problems of taxation and the expenditure of taxes, the conditions of tenements and of streets and other public places, of banking privileges and security from usury in borrowing, and how to secure protection in all forms against exploitation are questions of immediate importance to the worker. The actual conditions, the laws relative to them, and the means for improving present laws or for enforcing them, all have definite bearings upon the choice of vocation and upon the civic efficiency of the worker. Problems of this type constitute a civics of appreciable worth to the boy and girl. Formal recitation of the skeletal facts of civic organization are of almost no consequence in awakening civic interest or developing civic power. Civic problems taken in direct relationship to the topics in history, industrial arts, geography, or out of the happenings of the day, develop an interest in the situations and conditions out of which the problems arise. They acquaint children with the conditions by which the various vocations are surrounded. They bring out aspects of the relative desirability of many occupations.

The mathematics, geography, history, and civics here suggested should all be closely related to the study of the industrial and commercial arts. Many of the problems in each field can be approached most naturally through the study of the industries or occupations themselves — those relating to food, clothing, shelter, utensils, and so on. The basis for vocational choice thus developed is at the same time a beginning in the most efficient kind of vocational training and education.

SUGGESTIONS AS TO VOCATIONAL OUTLOOK, ETC.

By B. C. Gruenberg

Geography:

What people have to do to keep alive, to make themselves comfortable.

How obtaining the necessities is dependent upon climatic and other external conditions.

What kinds of supplies are easily obtained in tropical countries; what kinds are more easily obtained in temperate regions.

What kind of work is necessary to get the various kinds of raw material that people use.

The kinds of work that are necessary to convert the raw materials into usable articles.

The conditions that lead to the rise and development of trade and commerce. The function of commerce in relation to meeting human wants.

Division of labor within a country; within a branch of industry or a major line of occupations.

The mutual interdependence of peoples in different regions of the earth for raw materials and other supplies.

What we get from country A, B, C, etc. What we return to the various countries. The kinds of work that are done to produce the major groups of commodities.

How people live in different parts of the country; how the mode of life depends upon natural conditions and upon occupational conditions.

History:

All historical study in elementary schools and in high schools should center upon the evolution of people's ways of living rather than upon the political forms and conflicts.

The young children are instinctively in sympathy with primitive modes of life; and long before we can think of giving them historical instruction they love to hear of the Indians and their tent life, of hunting and fishing, and fighting wild animals.

The evolution of civilization is one side a development of institutions and ideals and an accumulation of spiritual treasures. On another side, however, it is the development of man's mastery of the forces of nature. This mastery shows itself in man's economic activities. Growing out of the study of geography should come the study of this evolution of man's control through work.

The problems in history would then be such as these:

How people lived and how they supplied their wants at the time of the Crusades; what improvements in the modes of life and in the modes of getting a living from nature arose during the succeeding centuries.

What economic improvements made possible the releasing of men's time for the pursuit of philosophy or the fine arts?

How widely were the successive gains distributed; that is, what portion of the population profited by each of the great epochal achievements in the practical arts?

The great contributors to the arts of peace, the heroes of navigation, of scientific discovery, of practical inventiveness, should receive increased attention.

Changing conditions as to hours of labor, as to housing, municipal affairs, transportation, communication, education, amusements, recreation, etc., should be connected with increasing efficiency of labor and improving organization of the political side of life in relation to industry, etc.

Civics:

The growth of urban populations in recent times can be connected directly with the "industrial revolution."

The problems of city life can be developed from two major sources:

(1) People living close together must avoid stepping upon each other's toes. This has always been true.

(2) Modern ways of producing and distributing commodities raise new problems calling for community or civic solution rather than individual treatment.

Much of the present-day teaching in civics has to do with factors arising out of (1); the great need is for clear recognition of the second aspect and for increasing emphasis thereon.

Regulations of industry, municipal, state, and federal. Why the "right of contract" has been considered so important; and why other considerations often conflict with this supposed right.

Examples from the regulation of hours of labor; the relation of these regulations to the health of the population.

Regulation of industries with respect to pollution of streams; pollution of the atmosphere.

Examples of traffic regulations from conditions in the immediate neighborhood.

Why regulations of the labor of women and children must be differentiated from the general regulations.

Prohibitions of specific industries; for example, the manufacture of white-phosphorus matches.

Safety devices in various kinds of shops and factories, required by law. The inclosure of wheels, belts, saws, and other moving parts.

Fire regulations in relation to industrial conditions.

Public regulation of docks and waterfront activities.

Health regulations for factories, etc., through departments of health.

Compulsory insurance as a social function, arising from the nature of certain occupations and from the relations of the workers to employers, etc.

Exercise in percentage; multiplication; extensions, etc.:

Given a table showing the percentage distribution of family incomes, in rent, food, clothing, etc.

How much does the Smith family spend upon each of these items, the yearly income being calculated from the following data:

> Weekly wages . . . .
> Weeks employed during the year . . . .

How much rent is paid for your home? How much is that per room?

How does your family income compare with that of the Smith family?

From a table supplied, find out in what occupations a man would be able to maintain a family in a home which costs $20 per month; $25 per month, etc.

What would be the average expenditure for food each week for a family supported by a man working at trade A; trade B; trade C, etc.

It would be feasible to make a schedule of family consumption and then have children figure how much food is allowed by various levels of income.

Girls can figure how much they can save on home sewing: so many hours of work, plus so much material. Compare with cost of ready-made garments of same grade. Does it pay to make this garment at home? What kind of work does it pay to make at home? What kinds of goods does it pay better to buy ready-made?

Family budgets and individual budgets, to determine the minimum wage upon which a living of a specified level can be maintained.

From statistical tables, to determine ratios of wages to capital invested in different industries (indicating relative proportion of skilled and unskilled or low-wage and high-wage workers).

Amount of capital invested in industries A, B, C, etc., in each of a series of years — indicating the growth or shrinkage of an industry. Number of men employed in each industry for a period of years. Number of men, women, and children, and percentages, in each of the industries. Changes in the proportions of men and women and children, during a period of years, to show the trend and modification of opportunities.

(5) *What is the relation of vocational guidance to elementary schools?*

If the curriculum of the elementary school could be adapted by this process of content enrichment, the practical phases of vocational guidance would be manifest during the elementary-school period. It is true, of course, that courses of study must present fluidity. They should not be fixed for any particular space of time, but should be modified according to the changes in the economic conditions of the times they are serving and according to the nature of the school population. From the standpoint of guidance the elementary-school curriculum must possess vision; in a sense, it must foresee industrial, commercial, and professional possibilities of the future so that its graduates may be prepared for them. This view is partially supported in the Final Report on School Inquiry, wherein the place of education in modern life is thus referred to:

Any educational standards must be regarded at present as provisional and temporary. The public school is an instrument of social development. Its existence testifies to the fact that the present economic and social order is not final. If education were subordinated to the present economic order, its influence would become the more deadly as it became more scientific and compelling. It is therefore clear that the secondary school should not aim to determine a child's vocation definitely or to fit him for a certain calling. The various agencies of general society and higher education can do that. The elementary school should facilitate and simplify the process of economic selection, and should act as a transmitter between human supply and industrial demand.

A committee of the National Education Association has formulated a similar view :

It is to be hoped that the constructive .work and the study of industry in the elementary school will ultimately be of such a character that when the pupil reaches the age at which the activities of adult life make their appeal he will be able to make a wise choice in reference to them, and be already advanced in an appreciable measure toward the goal of his special vocation.

With this interpretation vocational guidance does not become a special function of a particular official, but is virtually a by-product of the educational system. In the language of Mr. Lovejoy, "The whole school curriculum should be shot through with industrial interpretation instead of merely having a single vocational counsellor."

For those children who are to complete the elementary schools, the first large problem presents itself in their deflection to the high school supplying the courses for which they are physically and mentally best adapted. A wise distribution of the elementary-school graduates to the high schools will simplify the difficult problem of vocational guidance during the secondary-school period. Under the present system it may hardly be said that the basis of distribution is on a scientific basis. The immense mortality of the first two years of high school attests in part that the children have not found themselves.

Obviously, the ordinary teacher in the elementary schools or any ordinary individual does not possess sufficient information regarding vocations to be of great value in vocational guidance. To remedy this defect it would appear wise to consider the educational and psychological bases of vocational guidance as they appear in individuals, with a view to supplying instruction in this direction in our training schools. Such instruction could be afforded without the sacrifice of any really valuable subjects in the training school. If, in addition to this, training schools would lay more stress upon the concrete problems that are available for teaching in elementary schools, the present deficiency of elementary-school teachers might be corrected.

Mrs. Woolley at Grand Rapids called attention to the fact that an adequate school system should possess the facilities for training all children for any reasonable demands in the way of an occupation. The most obvious demand upon the school she finds to be that for increased variety of instruction, for more teachers, and for more kinds of teachers. Hence the practical problem as to what kinds of training should be introduced into the schools as a start must bring out the need for information about the educational facts of the community and information about the occupational opportunities. Moreover, the schools should offer a sufficient variety of work to test out the capacities of the pupils.

(6) *What are to be the methods of discovering the capacity and aptitudes of school children?*

That there are many difficulties in any extensive plan in vocational guidance has been expressed by many persons. In the words of Mr. Tildsley,

It seems to me it is both impossible and undesirable to do any extensive vocational direction in the elementary schools; I am rather inclined to believe it is almost impossible to do very much of it in high school.

In order to successfully undertake vocational guidance there must be some methods of discovering the capacities and aptitudes of school children. There have been seven, more or less, plans or methods proposed or in use for discovering the abilities of school children:

    (1) Direct study by pupils of information about occupations or of occupations through visits, etc.

    (2) Psychological tests.

    (3) Examination of physical characteristics, known or assumed to be correlated with mental and moral qualities.

    (4) Questionnaires.

    (5) Study of pupils by the teachers.

    (6) Varied school work.

    (7) Employment supervision.

(1) While a certain measure of information may be derived by visitation of industrial organizations and by direct study at these times, the most fundamental thing to be remembered is that a good education is essential in the elementary schools. The 40,000 children who come out of our schools yearly would be greatly

helped if the study of industries merely gave them the important information as to the types of trades they should not enter. Great advantages would result from pointing out the "blind-alley" trades. The difference between juvenile employments and those which possess a future of significance to adults should receive most careful attention. By the study of occupations, it would be possible to drive home the necessity of continuing to study, if perchance economic stress forces children into "blind-alley" occupations, with a view to fitting themselves for forsaking such occupations at the earliest possible moment. If it were possible to discover the aptitudes demanded in various occupations, vocational guidance would be simplified. As has been well said by Dr. Ayres:

> If we are to know what are the methods of discovering the capacities and aptitudes of children, we must know what are the aptitudes needed in the occupation, and, secondly, in what measure this applicant possesses those aptitudes. It has been suggested just now that we must know what an employer wants. Unfortunately the employer does not know. You can ask him if you will, but just what specific abilities he needs in a boy he does not know. Even with the employer employing people to work at machines he does not know what he wants them to be, except that they must be skillful, honest, energetic.

Apparently many of the aptitudes will be evidenced by interest in various occupations, by imitative construction, or by an enhanced desire for further study of some of the occupations examined. Mr. Tildsley criticizes the elementary schools not alone because no aptitudes are developed, but because the power of thinking has not been fostered. In his words:

> It is perfectly right to say that the average elementary-school boy does not know how to work, and I suppose the colleges say the very same thing of our high-school graduates. The fundamental difficulty is that the boy has no aptitude to do any kind of work. I believe that the fault, after all, is in the methods of training; that, instead of devising some system of analysis by the pupil or somebody else, we ought to pay attention to improving the methods in the elementary and high schools. Our boys and girls come to the high school without the power of thinking a thing out for themselves, and they largely go out from the high school without that power.

(2) The psychological tests thus far have been suggestive of possibilities, but have not produced significant results. Thus far it is safe to assert that the psychological tests can be regarded

as of very little consequence in the field of vocational guidance. Mrs. Woolley has been doing some excellent work with psychological tests as the basis of classifying the abilities of children. She has experienced the greatest difficulty in the way of developing these tests for the purpose of vocational guidance because of our general ignorance as to the requirements of the various occupations. The fundamental difficulty lies in the fact that few employers or managers are capable of analyzing their own industries or of indicating what type of employees they require for particular jobs.

(3) Insufficient investigation has been made of the correlation of physical characteristics with mental and moral qualities. Outside of the claims of phrenologists that they are able to determine characteristics and aptitudes through cranial topography, few individuals have given much thought to the subject. Similarly, the claims of physiognomists have not been verified through scientific study. Impressions as to character derived from personal observation and contact may be of service in individual cases, but as a general method for determining aptitudes it has little scientific value.

(4) The use of questionnaires has been tried in places, as indeed have questionnaires for self-analysis. Mr. Charles Perrine stated to your subcommittee: "I believe it would be a very simple matter for us to have in every school in this city questions answered by each teacher from the fifth year on — not fool questions — and I believe it would pay to ship them on with the children when they get a transfer, the object being that the principal, on graduation of the boy or when he leaves school, can guide him."

If it were possible to have a continuous record of school children bearing the annotations of all their teachers, possibly some benefit might accrue by the end of the elementary-school period. It is doubtful, however, whether this plan is practical, though it would be a valuable experiment in the direction of determining the ability of teachers to gain some idea of the aptitudes of children from their interest, activity, and results in the various subjects of the elementary-school curriculum.

Self-analysis appears to be undesirable, because even during the high-school periods most pupils are too young to carry on an honest, scientific, and correct self-analysis though they have been trained in the psychological methods of introspection.

(5) The direct study of pupils by the teachers may possess some value, although it is difficult to estimate this in the absence of adequate data. That some high-school principals believe that it is impossible for high-school teachers to determine these aptitudes is evident from the statement of Mr. Tildsley:

> I do not believe that any considerable amount of vocational direction is possible in the high schools, because no one of us is capable of measuring the aptitudes of boys. I have been meeting boys for the last twenty years and I have associated with them very intimately, and I must say it is impossible for me to decide what profession or calling they are suited for. All I feel I can do is to warn the boy against certain occupations. I think if I find a boy has no aptitude for science I have a right to say to him, " Don't be a physician." In other words, all we can do in the high schools is to warn boys against occupations for which they are unsuited, but we cannot in any way guide them into the occupations to which they are to go, boys change so.

Where schools are organized upon a departmental basis, as in the high schools, it obviously becomes more difficult for teachers to learn anything of the aptitudes of their children except in so far as they may be related to the special branches taught by the departmental teachers. This condition does not obtain in most of the elementary schools, and consequently the ordinary teacher in the elementary school is probably as capable of judging aptitudes as the special teacher of particular subjects.

(6) In so far as vocational guidance demands the self-discovery of aptitudes, it is evident that there is great necessity of having a greater variety in school work. In the language of Dr. Straubenmüller: "When you talk about vocational guidance based upon certain experiences in various trades it means teaching the children some of the processes of these trades in order to give them a knowledge of the trades. Now, the great difficulty is to find what are the processes." If, however, it is possible to demonstrate some of the essential processes, it might be possible to incorporate them in the elementary-school training during the period of the seventh and eighth grades, where differentiated courses have now been instituted for purposes of experiment. The experimental

value of differentiated courses, well chosen on the basis of industrial needs and educational processes, cannot be overestimated.

If school work could be varied in method, possibly a great advantage might be demonstrated for practical vocational guidance. This view is well expressed in the words of Mr. Tildsley:

> If in our elementary and high schools we would substitute problem methods (let the problems be simple in the earlier grades) by which a pupil would be given some little task to do by himself, something which he would have to think about, we would have done more to solve the problem of vocational guidance than in any other way. With the course of study that we have, the substitution of the problem method and the requirement of some thinking on the part of the pupil for the present system of memorizing would produce pupils who could go into almost any line of work and do it successfully.

The reconstruction of the educational content of some of our courses could be secured without the sacrifice of any essential values. It is well to bear in mind the statement of Mr. Leonard

> The things that are interesting from the standpoint of vocational guidance are the people, what the people do, what the human problems are. That involves not eliminating any of those things, but reconstructing in the way of an addition, relative to occupations, relative to nationalities, immigration, the tenement industry, the fire system, and all that sort of thing which can be presented from the first grade to the last; the work of the police and fire departments, the work of New York City's administration, rather than things which deal more largely with physical facts. Aside from that kind of reconstruction, which is rather an addition, rather an enlargement, there must be an enlargement of the various units.

In order to keep pace with the constant changes in industrial life, school work should possess adaptability. To quote Miss Barrows:

> This power of adaptability must be based upon general training rather than specialized training, because you cannot adapt if you have only one thing from which to adapt. The teaching of the simple process rather than special trades is the practical end.

The late Mr. Sheppard struck a keynote of the problem by stating the need of real training and not the mere giving of information. The actual training should possess potential power. Children may learn to adapt themselves to the various complexities of the life into which they are to enter. This power must be based, however, upon fundamental training all through the school system.

Professor Lough has indicated one of the difficulties in determining the variations essential in school work in that it is first necessary to find out what is required in an industry. This must precede any complete plan that contemplates devising methods, for determining the aptitudes necessary for our special occupations. In his opinion, it might be possible to classify our vocations not with regard to the practice of or the names applied to the vocations, but with regard to some fundamental aptitudes. He has wisely commented :

> One of the things that we can do in our school work very easily is to make it possible for a person to go from one general field of training into another without a great loss of time. A student going from the Commercial High School in this city will find something of a blind alley if he tries teaching. He cannot get into the Teachers' Training School in New York City and train himself, from the Commercial High School.

(7) The supervision of employment based upon a system of placement with a follow-up plan provides a means of learning the aptitudes demanded in industry, but during the period of trial many mistakes would undoubtedly result. This plan has a distinct value, though this cannot be definitely fixed at the present time.

At the Grand Rapids conference Professor S. P. Breckinridge, of The University of Chicago, called attention to the value of placement work as a means of discovering the aptitudes of children. She insisted, however, that in all work of this character the interests and welfare of the child should be constantly in the mind of those responsible for the supervision. Vocational counselors are necessary for placement work as at present organized. Experienced counselors are not available even though they might be more valuable than teachers interested in the subject of placement who lack the practical knowledge of industrial life. The true value of employment supervision, as reported by Gruenberg, was stated by her as follows : "Through employment supervision one would get information not only about the children, their needs, their capacities, but also about the industries." She quoted with approval Mrs. Sidney Webb: "You go to the man at the head; he talks well, but he does not know the work. You must get at the workers to find out actual conditions."

On the other hand, the professional educational counselor is a makeshift and up to the present time has not demonstrated his value in throwing light upon the aptitudes of children as related to the business world. Puffer has again stated that

In certain ways, to be sure, the professional vocational guide has an advantage even over the teacher. He is supposed to have the better technical equipment, and he devotes himself more or less exclusively to this single field. But such vocational counselors are, unfortunately, few; and not one parent in a thousand ever thinks of seeking their advice. Moreover, they commonly see their clients too late, after they have finished their schooling and have lost opportunities that would have been to their advantage or have acquired habits that tend to their detriment. Even with all the elaborate and accurate modern technique for diagnosing a youth's equipment, the professional counselor is always a partial stranger, who deals with his subject under somewhat artificial conditions.

(7) *What methods and agencies exist for the purpose of aiding vocational guidance through further training?*

In order to give vocational guidance even for the purpose of securing a proper distribution of elementary-school children in the high schools there should be the opportunity for children to come in contact with specially selected literature on occupations. There would be little cost in having a reference table containing books on vocations with an index to magazine articles on separate vocations for the use of inquiring boys and girls. In the language of Meyer Bloomfield:

The main purpose of a series of pamphlets dealing with vocations for boys and girls should be to equip the schools with facts now lacking, showing that the specializations of business and industry are such as to make the leaving school on the part of fourteen-year-old children a most wasteful and unprofitable step. In the next place, such booklets must show parents and children that the occupations in which young people can amount to anything are those which require some kind of preparation, some preliminary apprenticeship, best obtained in school.

Booklets on occupations, therefore, intended for guidance, are valuable only to the extent of their appeal to motives which prolong school life, which help send the children into further training opportunities. In pointing out what is ahead for the young worker, and the training required in order to enter a promising employment, such studies should help reduce the drifting and tragic self-experimentation of a multitude of young wage earners.

The mere giving of information and advice is insufficient. There must be offered opportunity for further training based upon the aptitudes demonstrated and the advice given. The public schools, therefore, should have at their command facilities and resources for any legitimate vocational training that a child may wish to pursue. This does not require the installation of such training in all the public schools; it does mean, however, that the schools through the principals or other authorized persons should be able to give definite information as to the places where further training may be secured in specific vocations. There appears to be a great need for a bureau of information. As was well stated by Miss Anna E. McAuliffe:

Latent power cannot be estimated and for that reason vocational guidance must establish bureaus of information rather than bureaus of assignment. We may give any available information as to the nature of certain employments, the ratio of supply and demand, the rate of wages, the necessary qualifications. And here I feel constrained to say that this task ought not to be placed on teachers.

There is every indication that there is a need for the establishment of a new social-service agency. More information must be secured with reference to juvenile employment. Present agencies interested in vocational guidance, vocational training, vocational analysis, and placement should be brought into a coöperating commission for the purposes of studying the practical methods which may be devised for extending vocational guidance through further training.

(8) *What agencies exist for the distribution of school children with a view to their securing the training made necessary through vocational guidance?*

There is a dearth of agencies for the distribution of school children in a vocational direction based upon an educational ideal. Vocational counselors have been employed in many cities of the United States for the purpose of guiding children in so far as information and opportunity permit it. The school has not been equal nor indeed has it attempted to be equal to the task of distributing school children with a view to securing further training. Greater stress, unfortunately, has been placed upon the supplying of an occupation. Employment organizations, employment secretaries, employment offices, represent agencies which may secure occupations leading in one way or another to some possible further training in specific occupations. If manufacturers possessed the same interest in the training of children that they do in securing them as workers, a new agency might be devised in coöperation with employers with a view to furthering vocational guidance through occupation. In this relation the continuation school possesses some merits, but here again is a problem which requires careful study in connection with the schools of New York City. Plans which might be successful in Cincinnati, Fitchburg, Rochester, or Gloversville might fail when introduced into the New York City system.

The greatest educational use of agencies for the distribution of school children should be to return them to the schools for further training. In Chicago the vocational advisers have succeeded in inducing a very large percentage of children who apply for work certificates to go back to school if only to complete the course.

In the record of the Vocation Bureau of Boston, 1914, we learn:

One of the principal provisions in the arrangements between the School Committee and the Vocation Bureau was for a group of teachers to be known as vocational counselors, to be appointed by their respective principals and to represent every school in Boston. Over one hundred teachers were so appointed three years ago, and they have been meeting throughout the school year to consider the educational opportunities of the city, the vocational problems of the children, and to confer with employers and others who have been invited to the sessions. The work of the vocational counselors has been a labor of love.

In order to appreciate the value of the school counselors we desire to call attention to Circular Number 10, 1913, of the Superintendent of Schools of Boston. This circular was issued after the School Committee had voted to establish a vocational-guidance department.

Boston Public Schools,
Superintendent's Office,
February 12, 1913

To the Principals of Schools and Districts :

In order to make the work in vocational instruction uniform it seems desirable to have the counselors all over the city chosen as follows:

Two from each elementary-school building containing a graduating class.

One from each building containing grades above the fourth but below the eighth.

Two from each high school.

The plan, which will be outlined later, will consist of (1) work with the graduates and (2) with those who drop out before the graduation; hence it will be wise to have the counselor who is to deal with the graduates an eighth-grade teacher, while the other counselors may be teachers of lower grades.

Realizing the high character of service which has been given by the present group of vocational counselors, it is hoped that so far as possible they may be retained, and that in choosing additional counselors the principals will bear in mind the fact that it is essential to the success of our undertaking to have only those who are keenly interested and willing to give of their time and strength. Aside from the counselors, all principals are urged to attend the meetings whenever possible and to coöperate in every way possible.

For 1914, important plans looking to an effective enlargement of the counseling service have been adopted.

From the standpoint of child welfare the success of any plan for distributing school children depends upon the retention of a greater number of children in educational work. The success is not to be measured in terms of the number of jobs which are secured. From the standpoint of working through the employers, little help can be expected at the present time. Even the late apprenticeship system has so largely disappeared that it affords little help in the solution of vocational training. Another difficulty in the way of a rational distribution of school children lies in the fact that we have insufficient information as to what are the skilled and unskilled occupations. Therefore we are unprepared to suggest the types of training which should be secured.

In *Bulletin No. 4* of the United States Bureau of Education (1914) Meyer Bloomfield makes an important and suggestive statement. In view of the failure of evening-school classes to answer this question in this country and England, his statement may be regarded as applicable to the New York City situation.

The most immediate problem with respect to these children is not an extension of evening training facilities so much as it is a thoroughgoing scheme of protection; not the acquisition of manual skill, as it is the conservation of their physical and moral vitality. Industry holds out diminishing educative possibilities. In the majority of occupations, indeed, there is no place for apprenticeship. Yet service to an individual or a group of individuals is none the less valuable because it fails to solve the problems of a multitude.

(9) *What methods shall be pursued to prevent the possible exploitation of children?*

In order to prevent the exploitation of children many methods have been suggested. It is not likely that the school can reform industry, but if the educational system is to formulate any plan for linking itself up with industry, it should be able to impress upon employers that its greatest concern is in the educational development of the juvenile employees. The spirit of the late apprenticeship system may possibly be revived. Employers must receive through proper channels information as to their responsibilities for the training of those who, through economic stress, are forced into employment. Some plan of practical coöperation with employers should be devised wherein a shortened work day or some other concession may be made by employers for the purpose of furthering the educational development of their employees.

Bloomfield again states :

Sooner than many people realize, the schools will be required definitely to perform some of the functions which have hitherto been distributed among such agencies as the home and shop. To accomplish this the schools must undergo changes, as they have already changed in response to other social demands made upon them for a generation past. Comprehensive vocational assistance through specially trained teachers and others must become a part of the new machinery of service — service which should begin in the elementary grades and continue at least to the period of young manhood and womanhood.

The question of parents in the whole plan of vocational guidance has not been dwelt upon. It seems patent that parental coöperation must be secured in order to lessen exploitation. Parental coöperation is also necessary in any effective plan of vocational guidance. That this is not a local problem is obvious. Parents exercise too little influence upon intelligent vocational direction. Any plan to prevent exploitation must involve some measures designed to awaken a greater sense of responsibility on the part of parents. This can be done through an organized effort to bring the school into closer relation with the parents of the children during the entire period of school life.

Some placement may tend to facilitate exploitation. In the language of the United States Commissioner of Labor:

A considerable work is done in placing students who are ready or obliged to leave school, although both teachers and committee look upon this as a somewhat subsidiary branch of the work. It is, they say, but a comparatively small number who need help of this kind. For the larger number it is not so much that they need help in securing employment as that they need advice in wisely selecting their work and oversight in working out their vocational aims.

This is essential to lessen exploitation.

In school training stress should be placed upon those occupations which are likely to yield a decent and respectable living during the adult years. While the economic wage should not be the only determining factor, it is a reasonable assumption that skilled work requiring more advanced training is likely to have a higher schedule.

In considering methods to prevent exploitation, Mr. Lovejoy urges the following:

In the first place, to increase the public-school attendance age to sixteen years.

2. Provide for the return of the child between jobs who does get along in his employment and who receives a certificate for employment. This will do away with the problem of truancy and unemployment.

3. Have teachers and parents trained to distinguish between vocation and a job before we undertake any kind of placement work.

That effective work in this line can be secured by the coöperation of schools and employers is supported by the view of Mr. Tildsley.

I believe in the long run the schools will accomplish the best results through placement work. When you place a boy with a manufacturer and the manufacturer reports, you then have the proper method for statistics because it is based on actual facts. It seems to me the chief value of the placement work is the recognition of the schools themselves by the employers of our boys and girls; the interest of these people would be aroused in our schools by the fact that they take our boys and girls directly from the schools. That can only be brought when the employers in New York City are willing to take a more intelligent interest in the schools than they do at present.

On the other hand, there are many who believe that placement work virtually serves to exploit children. To illustrate, we may quote the views of Miss Barrows, as follows:

There are about 40,000 children between fourteen and sixteen years of age who leave elementary school and go to work every year. It is desirable for these children if it means that they are going to advance in their efficiency and in their wage-earning power and in education. The point is, Do they? They will if they get the kind of jobs that will give them that kind of advancement. Children between fourteen and sixteen years of age cannot get those jobs in New York City. The placement bureau in the school system for elementary-school children is simply systematizing, unconsciously, the exploitation of those children. I should think there certainly would be a place for a placement bureau for graduates of technical high schools.

The problem of having a placement bureau for graduates of technical schools is a separate problem and will be considered separately.

There is one vital question which forces itself upon our minds. If the educational system makes specific efforts to induct children into industrial life, does it not assume a moral responsibility in assisting the children to secure specific jobs? At one of the conferences the chairman asked the following question:

If we can grant for the time being that it has given more assistance to the boys in getting them specific jobs, does not the school stand sponsor when it says, " There is a job for you"?

The reply of Mr. Tildsley was, " To a large extent."

This view seemed to have general support. It therefore becomes apparent that the responsibility of the Board of Education for vocational guidance demands most careful consideration so that it may not be accused of assisting in the exploitation of school children.

(10) *What is the value and effect of vocational scholarships?*

Among the numerous devices for securing rational vocational guidance, the plan of vocational scholarship deserves the most serious consideration. Undoubtedly the selection of children obliged to leave school for economic reasons and the paying to their families of a weekly wage such as $3 a week presents a practical solution of the problem of retaining children in school for a longer period of time.

The success of the Committee on Vocational Scholarship of the Henry Street Settlement, as presented by its secretary, Miss Brown, is most commendable and suggestive. On this basis of vocational scholarship children who otherwise would have entered into unskilled industry were given two additional years of schooling along definite trade lines. The committee maintains no special employment bureaus, but the children with this additional training readily secure positions through normal channels. While this plan may be regarded as expensive and its adoption therefore impractical at the present time by this school system, the principle involved warrants thoughtful study.

Regarding education as a social asset, the social worth of the children thus aided by vocational scholarships far exceeds the money involved. The estimation of education in terms of social values and results may at some time have an appealing force to the community. It is far cheaper to pay $250 for the special training of particularly gifted children whose limitations are only those of poverty than to permit their potential values to the community to be sacrificed through a lack of civic interest or public appreciation. The development of one inventor, one painter, one mechanical genius, and one writer represents a social asset that far overshadows the incidental loss of a few hundred dollars for further education. In fact, vocational scholarships represent educational investments whose values are readily ascertained and whose dividends go to society in general.

The economic advantage of educational scholarships is supported by the figures of the Massachusetts Commission on Industrial Education, which indicated that the child who goes directly into a trade after leaving a grammar school is capable of earning less than $400 at eighteen years of age, while the child who has attended a trade school after leaving the grammar school may earn $550. Throughout life the trained child is capable of adding to his economic resources to a much larger extent than is the child whose educational opportunities have been limited. The underlying principle of vocational scholarships is worth emulation. While the Board of Education may not feel at liberty at the present time to advise an appropriation for the purpose of establishing vocational scholarships, it is desirable for it to express its belief in the substance of the doctrine and invite the philanthropic-minded to coöperate with it in extending the opportunity of vocational scholarships to specially selected children who would otherwise be forced to leave the public-school system.

(11) *What shall be the relation of vocational guidance to employment agencies?*

According to the laws of the state of New York, Chapter 700, 1910, the term "employment agency" means and includes the business of conducting, as owner, agent, manager, contractor, subcontractor or in any other capacity, an intelligence office, domestic and commercial employment agency, theatrical employment agency, general employment bureau, shipping agency, nurses' registry or any other agency or office for the purpose of procuring or attempting to procure help or employment or engagements for persons seeking employment or engagements or for the registration of persons seeking such help, employment or engagement, or for giving information as to where and of whom such help, employment or engagement may be procured, where a fee or other valuable consideration is exacted, or attempted to be collected for such services, whether such business is conducted in a building or on the street or elsewhere.

The present conception of vocational guidance, in laying special stress upon placement, virtually places the school system in the position of an employment agency, though, to be sure, no fees are charged. It is exceedingly doubtful whether the school should be regarded in the nature of an employment agency, even though inducting children into life be part of the problem of education. The actual steps leading to employment are not distinctively those of the school system. There are very many other agencies which must be brought into such a scheme for placing children in actual positions. The whole scheme of placement involves the relation of vocational guidance to employment agencies. The most recent expression of thoughtful views as to the relation of schools to employment agencies is afforded in some quotations from the report of Meyer Bloomfield on "The School and the Start in Life," United States Bureau of Education, *Bulletin No. 4,* 1914:

Any scheme of vocational service which does not in some way come in direct contact with the problems connected with the actual start in life of youth is in danger of finding itself an unreal undertaking, busied with lifeless abstractions regarding shadowy beings, instead of men, women, and children.

Workers in the fields of vocational education and guidance, therefore, whether they be in vocational schools, labor exchanges, advisory committees, or vocational-guidance enterprises, are expected to face their task from two standpoints when helping young people to a start in life. They are forced, necessarily, to deal with the working world as they find it, and they are equally obligated to illumine their work with an ideal of what ought to be the conditions. A knowledge of existing conditions is the foundation of the daily personal service which a vocational agency is called upon to render; but without the corrective of a social vision any vocational scheme, whatever may be its immediate practical benefits, can hardly be regarded as an important instrument of human conservation.

Vocational service — both guidance and training are here included — is an instrument for talent saving, and for interpreting school life in terms of career building.

The question arises as to whether the public-school system would best undertake alone to deal with the start in vocation or leave it to other agencies, while reserving for itself the task of providing for needs which arise in the course of employment, such as further training opportunities. It is submitted that the schools will have to concern themselves, actively and dominantly, with every phase of the vocational start in life. Is the average school system ready to undertake this new and enormously difficult business? It is not. Indeed, so little is it prepared to do this work at the present time that hasty undertaking of it would probably indicate a lack of understanding. It is doubtful, in the first place, if a school department can alone effectively organize the labor market for young workers. On the whole, experience seems to support the proposition that the school system is not the most suitable agency to attempt the organization of the labor market for the young, and the correlative proposition, that the carrying on of juvenile employment agencies without control over them by the school is not in the best interests of the children.

The public school must remember the fact that it is primarily an educational institution with social aims. What a century of child-welfare effort and experience has taught the friends of working children, the schools can, least of all, afford to ignore. More than any other institution, the school must stand for a high minimum of protection for all children. It is not to the credit of our schools that, on the whole, they have been unaware of a situation which many an employer has known for some time, and this is, the economic uselessness of children from fourteen to sixteen. Schools have sometimes been willing to plunge into small or large employment schemes as if full-time work were the right thing for growing children.

There are three distinct aspects of the problem of adolescent employment: the educational, economic, and social. Through extension of vocational-training opportunities, and especially through the provision for prevocational schools, which, when their purposes are better understood, will become self-discovery schools, and as such afford young people and their teachers a most important basis for vocational guidance, the schools are beginning to deal with the first of the three aspects named.

The greatest difficulty in dealing with the boy who is about to leave school for work lies in the fact that he regards himself as a worker who has outgrown the learner. Not until disastrous experience has overtaken many of these children do they begin to realize how much a learning attitude would have meant in building a career. A large part of this difficulty is due to leaving the question of the boy's future unconsidered until school-leaving time.

We need to write into the law establishing labor offices that a juvenile department shall be managed by a central executive committee appointed by the school system, which committee shall be made up of school people, employers, social workers, and employees, to advise as to the school vocational guidance and training activities on the one hand, and manage the occupational research and placement supervision activities of the labor bureau on the other. This committee should be empowered, through health officers and other trained specialists, to study children; to take them out of work places, if need be; and through scientific investigations to list occupations from the viewpoint of opportunity as well as their manifold reactions on the worker. Children under sixteen are to be under training, part time at least, and until the public is ready to care for their entire fourteen- to sixteen-year period.

Contemplating this point of view, one must consider the opinions of some of the workers in this city who have given thought to this phase of the matter. In some schools there is coöperation between the vocational-guidance counselor and some existing employment agency. In sharing the responsibility with the employment agency, it is desirable to have connection with an agency that investigates employments to a sufficient extent to safeguard prospective employees.

Dr. Rowe's experience leads him to say:

I think the advisory work as to what work to take up in life, what field should be covered, should really belong to the school, but if you have a well-organized and equipped bureau, such as the Alliance Employment Bureau is, it would be very desirable to use its services as we have. Our results seem to indicate that it should be continued.

Mr. Weaver draws attention to the experience of cities where coöperation placement has been instituted to some extent. In his words,

This placement work for the schools is done under the supervision of the Board of Trade, and they coöperate directly with the schools, so that the schools make their prescriptions and send those to the general placement agency of the city, which is managed by the Board of Trade, and as far as Liverpool and Edinburgh are concerned the educational authorities have a special department maintained for that purpose, just for the handling of young people. So that while the school makes the prescription and gives the advice, the carrying out or filling of that prescription, as it were, is done through this general public, legally authorized placement agency for the city.

In a recent Report of Public Employment Exchanges issued by the City Club, we learn :

The function of the Wisconsin Industrial Commission includes doing " all in its power to bring together employers seeking employees and working people seeking employment." It is also to "aid in inducing minors to undertake promising skilled employments." The offices have attempted to guide boys into the less crowded and better-paying positions, but recommend that a vocational bureau be established to pay special attention to the needs of juvenile applicants.

These further quotations from the same report give more light upon the relation which is felt to exist between schools and employment agencies :

In Edinburgh, for instance, a division of work has been arrived at by the labor exchange and the school board by which the latter furnishes the advice and the former finds the situations, an officer of the labor exchange occupying a room in the school-board building to facilitate the interchange of information.

In discussing the functions and methods of the German public employment bureaus, the Munich Municipal Exchange has been chosen, as it is said by Mr. W. H. Beveridge to be fairly illustrative of the German exchanges (W. H. Beveridge, " Unemployment, a Problem of Industry," pp. 239 seq.).

The objects of the Munich office are (1) to put employers and employees (especially those engaged in industry, commerce, or domestic service, casual labor, and apprentices) into communication, with a view to employment ; and (2) to supply as far as possible information on all questions concerning workmen and conditions of the employment.

There is a special section for apprentices. Boys and girls in elementary schools are told of the exchange a few months before they leave, and they are given time off to visit it and are encouraged to register. As a result most of them have completed all arrangements for work before they leave school.

The exchange finds places outside of the city and even outside of Germany. In 1906 about 10,000 out of a total of 50,000 positions found were " externals." Workmen sent to places over 25 km. (15 miles) distance are allowed, on presentation of a certificate from the exchange, to ride on the state railways for half price.

That this employment exchange is recognized as being of serious importance is evidenced by the fact that in Germany the Social Democrats in their municipal platforms are demanding municipal vocational bureaus ; these are intended to serve the schools, which have no economic outlook, and the labor bureaus, which have no educational contact. As stated by Mr. Bloomfield at the Grand Rapids Conference, to quote from Mr. Gruenberg's report :

These bureaus should bridge the gap between the school and the job on the one hand, and between the elementary school and the continuation school on the other. There have already been established parents' consultation hours. They use statistical materials gathered for various purposes and have applied them to the problems of occupational adjustment. The information is made available to parents, teacher, employers, and workers.

Mr. Brumbaugh, in advocating the appointment of a director of vocational education, referred to one phase of the work as follows :

The school can also place this director of vocational education in such a relation to the outgoing child as to advise him concerning the best possible relation to his wage-earning career. This is the function usually referred to as the bureau of vocational guidance. The individual who supervises vocational education in the schools is best fitted to advise the child on leaving school concerning the type of activity he should undertake. The two places, therefore, really resolve themselves into one, and the office for which I am asking would conserve both these important functions.

Philadelphia certainly needs, for its thousand of outgoing boys and girls, some wise person, skilled in the industrials, in intimate relation with the great manufacturing establishments of the city, and thoroughly familiar with the educational career of the child, to advise each outgoing individual pupil just how best to link himself with the industries of the city.

The form of organization in Philadelphia has been the establishment of a Vocational Bureau whose purpose, according to the statement of the City Superintendent, would be to know —

(1) The capabilities and aptitudes of the pupils at the time they leave school;
(2) The form of training they have had in school;
(3) The types of industrial occupations promising the largest return for good to the individual. This carries with it

(*a*) A knowledge of the several employers of labor, to the end that only those who endeavor to deal fairly and helpfully by their employees should be allowed to receive the assistance of the bureau;

(*b*) Such utilization of (the school system's) agents and the service of accredited volunteer organizations willing to coöperate, as to visit the employees certified by the bureau at their homes and, by counsel and admonition, give them such an ordered and studious life as to make possible for them at the beginning of their wage-earning careers to live modestly, morally, and economically; thus securing to the employer an increasingly desirable worker and to society an increasingly desirable citizen.

Apparently the main work of vocational guidance must be done previous to the contact with the employment agencies. The school system itself should not constitute itself a mere employment agency. The dearth of information regarding industries and the various positions thereof is such as to make it impossible for effective and thorough placement on the part of the teacher. Some plan must be devised whereby the responsibilities of the school will be defined and methods of coöperation between the schools and some type of employment agency be developed. Probably the best results will accrue from the organization of a new type of vocational service bureau such as that suggested by Mr. Bloomfield.

It is unnecessary at this time to describe in detail the systems of coöperation existent in England, Scotland, and Germany, but suffice it to say that numerous plans are being tried in these countries which merit careful study before any scheme of organization is evolved. It is sufficient at this time to call attention to a quotation from a circular of the Board of Education in London with reference to the exercise of powers under the Education (Choice of Employment) Act, 1910:

In the opinion of the board it is of the first importance that in urban areas and, where possible, in county areas, local education authorities should take the opportunity afforded by the act of initiating such work where it is not at present carried on, of coördinating and organizing the existing voluntary agencies in a single coherent scheme, and of linking the whole with the work of the juvenile departments of labor exchanges in such a way that the moral and educational influences, which naturally center round elementary schools and continuation schools, should play their proper part in the transition from school life to the life of adult employment.

PLACEMENT

Unfortunately, in the minds of many vocational guidance is summed up in the single word " placement." This idea is totally erroneous. Placement or the placing of children in vocational work for which wages are to be received has been given too much attention. Placement is the last phase of vocational guidance entitled to consideration. As the most evident thing which could be done, it has received more than its warranted consideration without regard to its relations to the entire problem. The main thought in the minds of many dealing with vocational guidance is that placement is the end and aim of vocational guidance. This view falls far short of the truth. Placement should be relegated to its proper place in the scheme of vocational guidance and not be permitted to dominate the field of thought.

In our own public-school system there has been considerable work done by teachers in our high schools in the interests of placement. Before discussing the nature of placement, it is well to consider the well-intentioned efforts on the part of the many volunteer teachers who have endeavored to follow out principles of placement in so far as they were able in the light of their training, general education, knowledge of industries, and sympathy with the children. In order to ascertain the status of placement in the high schools of our cities, the following letter was written to the principals of the high schools:

DEAR SIR:

The Committee on High and Training Schools is investigating the subject of vocational guidance and desires the following information regarding placement work, if any is being attempted in your school:

1. Who are placement teachers?

2. Do they keep written records?

3. How many children do they place each year?

4. Do they aim to place all children or are they interested in placing only the brightest or more promising children?

5. Is there any discrimination in placement work with regard to color?

6. Is there any follow-up system to ascertain whether children retain the positions in which they have been placed?

7. If children fail to retain the first position in which they are placed, does the placement worker seek to secure another position for them?

8. Are there any available figures to indicate the success or failure of your placement work? If so, of what nature?

Thanking you for the courtesy of an early reply,

Yours sincerely
IRA S. WILE

A tabulation of the responses to each question, with the exception of number one, is as follows:

Do they keep written records?

Curtis High School: Yes
Eastern District: No
Manual Training: No
Washington Irving: Yes
High School of Commerce: First detailed record now simpler. Special study
Newtown: No system
Richmond Hill: No
Jamaica High: No
Commercial: Yes
Bushwick: Yes
Bryant: Yes
Wadleigh: Yes
Stuyvesant: No answer
Boys': Yes; time required to get it in shape to present it
Far Rockaway: Card index
Flushing: No
Vocational School for Boys: Yes
Girls': Occasional record
Bay Ridge: No
Manhattan Trade: Careful records

How many children do they place each year?

Curtis: 25 or more
Eastern District: No idea
Manual Training: 12 on an average
Washington Irving: 182
Commerce: 100 to 150
Newtown: 40
Richmond Hill: 10 or 12
Jamaica
Commercial: 300 and 400; 200 graduates, rest boys compelled to drop out
Bushwick: 15
Bryant: Average 50
Wadleigh: 4

Stuyvesant: 60
Boys'
Far Rockaway: 12 to 20
Flushing
Vocational School for boys
Girls': Approximately 12
Bay Ridge
Manhattan Trade: All who complete course and need assistance

Do they aim to place all children or are they interested in placing only the brightest or most promising children ?

Curtis: All worthy
Eastern District: Any pupil he can
Manual Training: Any worthy
Washington Irving: All who apply
Commerce: All who apply. Better and more promising far exceed the supply
Newtown: Preference to poor but deserving students
Richmond Hill: All; no discrimination
Jamaica: Recommend all, but brightest are speedily placed
Commercial: Preference to most worthy
Bushwick: Preference to those obliged to leave school. No recommendations to those without satisfactory records
Bryant: All who apply
Wadleigh: No discrimination
Stuyvesant
Boys': No discrimination
Far Rockaway: No discrimination
Flushing
Vocational School for Boys
Girls': Does not aim to place all nor those most promising
Bay Ridge
Manhattan Trade

Is there any discrimination in placement work with regard to color?

Curtis: No
Eastern District: No
Manual Training: No
Washington Irving: No. Most take dressmaking, no difficulty in placing them. Only 1 or 2 take commercial course and they have been placed
Commerce: No
Newtown: No
Richmond Hill: No
Jamaica
Commercial: No, negligible number. (Jews discriminated against. 40 to 50 per cent in school. Can't place as soon or as well as Gentiles. Inquiries of Jewish firms contain the requirement " must be Christian ")

Bushwick: No
Bryant: No
Wadleigh: No
Stuyvesant: No
Boys': None applied
Far Rockaway: No
Flushing
Vocational School for Boys: Difficulty in placing them
Girls': No color line
Bay Ridge: No
Manhattan Trade School: No, but trade discrimination very strong. Difficulty in placing them

Is there any follow-up system to ascertain whether children retain the positions in which they have been placed?

Curtis: Yes
Eastern District: No
Manual Training: No
Washington Irving: Yes
Commerce: Not comprehensive
Newtown: No
Richmond Hill: No formal system
Jamaica
Commercial: Yes
Bushwick: Yes
Bryant: Yes
Wadleigh: Yes, operate hereafter
Stuyvesant
Boys': Pupils requested to notify if position is not suited, and employers if pupils do not make good
Far Rockaway: Yes
Flushing
Vocational School for Boys
Girls': No
Manhattan Trade

If children fail to retain the first position in which they are placed, does the placement worker seek to secure another position for them ?

Curtis: Attempt is made
Eastern District: If possible
Manual Training: Yes
Washington Irving: Yes
Commerce: Yes
Newtown
Richmond Hill: Yes

Jamaica
Commercial: Yes. Until seventy times seven
Bushwick: Yes, if fault is not directly the pupil's
Bryant: Yes, if fault is not directly the pupil's
Wadleigh: If possible
Stuyvesant
Boys': Yes, if fault is not pupil's
Far Rockaway: Yes
Flushing
Vocational School for Boys
Girls': Yes
Bay Ridge
Manhattan Trade

Are there any available figures to indicate the success or failure of your placement work? If so, of what nature?
Curtis: Few figures
Eastern District: No
Manual Training: No
Washington Irving
Commerce: No
Newtown: Failures, less than 10 per cent; success, none
Richmond Hill: No
Jamaica
Commercial
Bushwick: No
Bryant: Yes; records kept open for inspection
Wadleigh
Stuyvesant
Boys': Yes, but considerable time required to get them in presentable shape
Far Rockaway: Yes
Flushing
Vocational School for Boys
Girls': No
Bay Ridge: No
Manhattan Trade

From a consideration of the figures above presented there are a number of objections which may be raised against placement as at present conducted.

I

The scheme of placement as at present organized is essentially undemocratic. All children desiring positions cannot be placed, nor indeed can opportunities be found for them. The school becomes a party to discriminations for which industry is responsible. There are discriminations because of religion, because of color, because of differences in mental power. There are discriminations because of economic stress which requires some children to leave high schools previous to graduation. If placement be organized on the theory that it is part of the function of a school system to introduce children into vocational employment, equal opportunity should be afforded to all children. The school should not be obliged to be selective in its action.

If placement is a school function, it should be work carried on in the interests of the school children and not in behalf of the employers. That discriminations are made in favor of boys and girls who are bright in school work and evidence their competence in this way is evident; for example, from the answer of Mr. Tildsley to the following question of the chairman:

Taking the two boys side by side, the competent and the incompetent, don't you think the incompetent requires placement help more than the competent?

In answer to this Mr. Tildsley stated:

He does require placement help more than the competent, but I believe the school system does a service to the employer by furnishing him the more competent. It is our duty to the employer to furnish him wherever possible a competent helper.

They should place all they can, but they only will place the most competent. Any placement agency will find it easier to find an employer for a competent boy; the competent boy will deserve more.

The same answer indicates a feeling that placement is in the interests of the employer rather than of the boy. This is also accentuated by the statement of Mr. Raynor:

The employer has a perfect right to insist upon having such employees as he wishes, even though his wishes may be fanatical.

In answer to the question of the chairman, " What would you do with regard to the placement of incompetents who leave the high school?" Mr. Tildsley made the following statement:

I would not place an incompetent. I do not believe that social efficiency requires the placement of incompetents until the competents are placed. I think if the boys find that they cannot obtain a place because they are incompetent most of them would make a greater effort to be competent.

The Employment Committee of the High School Teachers' Association of New York City deems its functions to be as follows :

To collect information regarding opportunities for profitable and permanent employment for the graduates of the high schools of New York City.

To advise graduates and other students of these schools in regard to the selection of suitable vocations.

To assist pupils who are partly or wholly dependent upon their own effort for their support to secure employment during vacations.

To prepare, for the use of employers, lists of suitable persons by the aid of which help may be selected.

Here again one sees that the view of placement assumed is that of finding a job largely with a view to satisfying employers. While it may be a fanciful analogy, it would not be unfair to state that, if the proper vocation for girls is marriage and the maintenance of a home, it is a legitimate function for high schools to conduct a matrimonial agency. If equal opportunity is to be given to all children to secure positions, then all children should have an equal opportunity for placement and the selection by the school of the child should have as a correlative proposition the selection of the job for the child. At the present time it is largely a case of finding a child for the job.

II

Placement work is distinctly, as at present conducted, uneducational. The present tendency apparently is to find jobs and not vocations ; an immediate position, not a life's work. The stress is placed upon monetary returns and not upon the educational training which may be possible. This is evidenced by the statements of Mr. Hartwell :

I would like to hand to the chairman a little statement of what I got up in regard to the pupils who in fourteen months have earned $47,000 while they have been in school. . . . It makes little difference whether boys change from one job to another. I am sure many of the pupils are better by changing. I want to help just as many boys and girls as possible while I am in this system, and we have proved by statistics that in this one school the boys and girls have earned $47,000 in fourteen months.

In answer to the question of the chairman, " What has been the educational benefit, considering this matter as a problem for an educational institution ? " Mr. Hartwell answered, " To earn is to learn."

It must be remembered that even with superior training and capability, it often becomes necessary for individuals to enter into occupations with low wage returns in order to become familiar with the details of work which are essential to ability to command the higher wage. For the schools to consider positions in terms of the immediate monetary returns constitutes a failure to place a proper value upon the educational training which is to be secured through industrial life.

While it is true that there are many boys in high schools who cannot remain to graduate and still would need assistance through placement, to maintain the precedent of placing nongraduates would lead many graduates of elementary schools to enter high schools simply because of the advantage of securing this type of assistance. Such a condition of affairs would lead to increased congestion of our high schools during the first year, with an increased mortality during the first two years. There are many who do not entertain this idea of the function of placement, whose views may be stated in the words of Mr. Gruenberg :

But the idea embodied in this proposition is that the public schools are to hold on to the child until he is fit to do something in particular and not simply until he feels he must go to work. The question of placement, however, is a systematic procedure of our machinery, so that there will be some preparation for placement as they leave the grammar schools, and most of those who leave the grammar school are not prepared for definite placement ; they are prepared for guidance in finding the kind of work in which they are likely to succeed.

The question still remains whether the schools can place 40,000, 20,000, or 10,000 children every year in jobs that have educational opportunities without establishing some form of part-time or continuation school. As investigations have shown that there are not a lot of jobs, placement comes to be of special advantage to those who are already so fortunate as to have the additional education that high schools give, or the individual endowments that enable them to carry a job and continue their education at the same time.

I wish to call attention also to the fact that the Commercial High School students who have gone to the higher positions open in the business world are students who are graduates of the vocational school. They are not students who have to leave because they want a job right away. If work is good for the child, I should claim that work under the supervision of school people is more wholesome than work under the supervision of the foreman who treats children not as social assets but as industrial instruments. The question resolves itself into this : To what extent is placement work educational ? Changing jobs is educational, but drifting is not educational; it is demoralizing. It is just as demoralizing for a boy to go into four or five jobs a year, none of which leads to anything, as to sit in school and learn nothing.

In regard to the Manhattan Trade School for Girls, the 15th Annual Report of the City Superintendent contains the following statement :

Since the school has found a year of training to be the minimum with which it can recommend girls for placement in the trades for which it trains, it would be obviously unfair to place them with less, and would encourage them to leave school before completing their course. The knowledge that the school will endeavor to find positions for girls at the end of their year has placed a premium on achieving the standards set by the school, and raised the tone of the entire school work.

Recognizing the difference of placement work in a technical trade school and in the ordinary high school, it is only fair to consider what educational values are believed to exist in placement as organized at the Manhattan Trade School.

From an educational point of view the work of the placement department is of great importance. Its effect on the school's training may be summarized as follows :

a. It enables the school to keep in constant touch with the supply and demand of workers in various trades, and with opportunities for advancement.

b. It serves as a continual check upon the methods used in training girls for trades. Criticism from employers and girls' reports of weak places in their preparation are of the greatest value in keeping the school out of ruts and up to date.

c. It gives a perfectly definite purpose and aim to the school work, and saves it from going off into all kinds of by-paths. It is a perpetual measuring rod for gauging the school's efficiency.

d. It makes discipline a matter of little significance, and gives every girl a motive and interest in reaching the goal for which she is striving.

It must be remembered that thorough placement work as organized at the Manhattan Trade School involves a follow-up system which keeps track of the girls placed, with a view to assisting them to make further progress in industrial life. This is apparent from the following paragraph :

After a girl is thus started the real work of the placement department begins, which is the " follow-up " of all students, to see that they have the right opportunity to progress. As most occupations for girls are seasonal and girls are frequently " laid off," the first placement is not usually sufficient. Without some guidance young girls are too apt to look at the immediate wage return rather than the chance for future advancement, and it is therefore of great importance the school keep in close touch with its girls, ready to give help and advice until they are well started and have sufficient maturity and experience to take entire care of themselves.

To establish throughout the city placement work with a follow-up system would be exceedingly expensive, and it is unproved thus far that the results attained warrant the consideration of such expenditures. From a practical point of view it is exceedingly doubtful whether placement workers in all the high schools would be able to continue a follow-up system, considering the large number of graduates going into industry each year. If, indeed, placement of nongraduates were to be considered, it would be absolutely impossible for 20 placement workers at $1100 to $1400 per annum to do the placement work and the follow-up work with any degree of thoroughness or success. They would be swamped by numbers within three years.

It is true that placement is valuable as a means of securing industrial information which is necessary as a basis for determining the kind and character of industrial education. While it is doubtful if placement work should be carried on directly by the schools, undoubtedly great benefits would result if the schools were to have some voice in placement work. At the present time placement work is generally regarded as an acute or emergency problem. It is designed to find a job. As a matter of fact, it should be considered as a part of vocational direction, leading to further industrial training that will enable boys and girls to escape becoming misfits in industrial life. It is probable that greater educational returns could be secured through enabling children to find themselves in industrial life. In the language of Miss McAuliffe,

There really is nothing in the world which brings the growing boy down to his own level like a search for a position. And there is nothing, I believe, that goes so far toward making a man of him. The boy who secures his position without looking for it loses a great and valuable experience.

It does not seem, therefore, that placement as at present conducted possesses any particular educational basis, but represents an endeavor on the part of placement workers to enter into the economic sphere for which they have had insufficient training.

III

If the schools are to place children in industry, it immediately becomes apparent that the school assumes in a measure responsibility for the job provided. With our lack of information regarding industrial life, it is hardly fitting that teachers should assume responsibility of this character. The employer secures the advantage of all the information which teachers possess about the children, but the children do not receive a similar advantage regarding the nature of the positions into which they are placed. The school has no authority nor, indeed, information warranting an assumption of authority to guarantee positions for children, nor does it seem right that the school system should place children without a full explanation of the physical and moral hazards which may be inherent in the position provided.

The school owes its first responsibility to children in so far as it is an educational institution. The responsibility to employers is satisfied when the schools provide adequate education to prepare children for industrial, commercial, or professional life. The real responsibility is to prevent exploitation and to provide functional training.

Mr. Bloomfield suggests that

It is not the business of a public school, nor of any other agency which purports to be social in its aim, to lean in the direction of employment. Whatever the bias, it should be in favor of the child. The employer belongs in the scheme of vocational guidance only so far as his employment is or may be made advantageous to the young worker and to the community. Only so far as he socializes the conditions of his occupation is he entitled to the coöperation of social and educational agencies.

The school responsibility should be considered rather ; the necessity of keeping children in school rather than aiming to get them into industrial life. Miss Kate M. Turner stated this most clearly in the following words :

It seems to me that we are on rather dangerous ground. The last speaker spoke of finding jobs for boys and girls. Now, that is just what we are going to do, and that is what we must not do. It is not going to give us any satisfaction to get jobs for boys and girls; the thing that we must keep in our mind is what this boy and girl has come into this world to do. . .

The responsibility that is felt toward the employer at the present time is emphasized by the statement of Mr. Tildsley:

It seems to me that, while it is somebody's function to revolutionize the industrial system, I hardly think it is the function of the Board of Education; it does not lay within its power. Now, the placement work advocated by some one on the part of the schools is that we should have certain persons in our schools who should have time to get in touch with as many employers of industry as possible and assure those employers that we can furnish them with boys and girls who have certain characteristics that we know about and that we can send them those boys and girls with a certain warrant.

A very vital question of school function arises when one considers how frequently the same child should be afforded the assistance of a placement worker. If the school may place a child once, as a matter of principle may he place the child a second time if he fails to secure success in his first position? If he fails in a second position, shall the school place him a third time? If it may place him a third time, when shall it refuse to place him? In answer to the question of the chairman, " I should like to have an answer to the question as to how many jobs the high schools should find for children and for how many years should such services be continued," Miss Strachan gave the following answer:

I should say that the high school should get jobs or positions for pupils just as often as the high school can in response to requests from those pupils, unless the pupil so placed made a record that the high school could not tolerate, was dishonest or unfaithful or lazy or something of that sort, but if the boy or girl had left through simply not getting along, not being satisfied with the place or the employer, then I think the school should help the child again.

For how long a period of time should such service be rendered?

I do not like limits of any kind.

Mr. Denbigh expresses himself as follows:

It seems to me that we are surely better fitted to guide these children into work that is better fitted for them than the work they would find at random for themselves. As for the number of times we should place a boy, we should place him just as often as we can better his condition, if he came back to us, until he is twenty-one. I was fortunate to find a place for one of our boys of twenty-eight, but I do not think the school's business is to undertake to do that, but until the boy or girl should reach the age of twenty-one we should place them just as often as we can.

If at Mr. Denbigh's suggestion it were possible to place a child until he reached the age of twenty-one, manifest discrimination would exist in favor of the younger graduates of high schools as opposed to the older graduates in so far as the years of service of the placement worker are concerned. An extreme view is given by the representative of the Commercial High School, who would place children "until seventy times seven."

If frequency of placement is to be the practice, virtually the school is to maintain an employment agency. This cannot be regarded by itself as a function of an educational system. Public moneys are not to be diverted from strictly educational projects for the purpose of maintaining an employment agency; nor is it reasonable for public moneys to be diverted for a selected group of high-school graduates, or even high-school nongraduates, if placement is distinctly a function of an educational system. It is probably true that there should be some coöperation between the educational system and other agencies whose actual aim it is to secure employment for individuals desiring it. This complicated matter deserves thorough study and should be considered by a committee of the Board of Education, together with representatives from the Chamber of Commerce, the Labor Union, representatives of the teachers of elementary and high schools, and other existing organizations interested in juvenile employment and vocational guidance.

IV

At the present time there is insufficient information on the part of teachers in our public schools to warrant the expenditure of public money for the purpose of extending placement work in our high schools. The placement workers, diligent as they may be and conscientious as are their efforts, do not possess sufficient knowledge of occupations or industries to warrant them in assuming the responsibility of the work they have undertaken. Mr. Gill has urged as follows:

The parents to-day do not know as much about industry as the placement teacher can know and ought to know, and so I think the work ought to be done in the school because it is more efficiently carried on by the school than if carried on in the home, and so long as that condition remains as it is to-day, the school is not doing its duty to society unless it does that work.

While it is true that parents have insufficient knowledge regarding all industries to be effective in either vocational guidance or placement, it is doubtful whether the schools would represent a great improvement over the present plan if placement were to become a school function. In the language of Professor Bonser,

Placement, as I see it, is not a term for vocational guidance at all. It is simply taking persons who want jobs and getting jobs for them. What information do these placement people have by which to determine what a boy or girl is best fitted for? It is taking the best jobs that can be got.

This view is partially supported by the opinion of Mr. Prosser:

No vocational counselor, however competent and however devoted, will be able to deal with most children at fourteen years of age unless he knows more about their tasks and ability than the fact that they have made this or that per cent in spelling, reading, arithmetic, geography, history, and other public-school subjects. Such a record may determine whether or not the child is destined for high school and for college; it does not at all reveal the other tendencies and capabilities of most pupils.

The by-law of the Board of Education, Section 81a, states as follows :

To be eligible for license as placement and investigation assistant in high schools, the applicant must have the following qualification: three years' satisfactory experience in placement and industrial work, together with a general education satisfactory to the Board of Examiners.

It is obvious from the wording of this by-law that very little effort has been made to establish qualifications for placement and investigation assistants that would insure their reliability or efficiency. On the basis of this by-law, it would be possible to burden our high schools with persons totally unqualified to attempt the serious performance of placement work.

From the figures presented by Mr. Denbigh and Mr. Larkins, it is evident that placement work as at present conducted is not really essential in all high schools. There are many who feel that placement work in public schools should be carried on only in connection with graduates of high schools in technical and trade courses. Possibly, for the purposes of study and investigation, it might be desirable to test out the efficiency of one or two placement workers. At the present time there is one at the Manhattan

Trade School and one at the Washington Irving High School. It is undesirable for the Board of Education to appoint any further placement and investigation assistants until a thorough analysis has been made of the value and efficiency of the work undertaken by these two individuals. It would be a short-sighted policy to burden the educational system with a number of placement workers until complete data are in evidence attesting their value to the community and particularly to the children for whom their service is intended.

At the present time it is impossible to place elementary-school graduates, and yet one cannot but agree with Frishberg: " I think we agree that the boy or girl who can reach high school is far more able to help himself or herself than the boy or girl who leaves school before sixteen."

If placement is to be construed as a principle of education, in terms of social advantage, it is evident that it should be made available to the largest possible group of children. This would require that the subject of placement in the elementary schools be carefully considered. It seems quite possible that placement in the elementary schools might serve to decrease the attendance at high schools. On the other hand, it is more probable that investigations of industry as related to placement would show the necessity for greater differentiation in the courses of the seventh and eighth grades of the elementary schools, together with an extension of vocational schools or the introduction of continuation schools. Education for placement deserves no greater consideration than education for leisure or avocation. The function of education is to prepare for life, and, while vocation is an essential part of life, it is not all of life.

Vocational analysis

If it be granted for the sake of argument that placement should be installed as a feature of the school system, the question of vocational analysis is of the utmost importance. From what has been said before, it is apparent that there is insufficient information as to what is demanded by industry of its, workers. There are no rules or regulations or definite procedures for determining the aptitudes of children so as to give them effective guidance.

Vocational training

If placement is an end and aim in itself, it would become necessary to reconstruct our educational plans so as to have the courses of training lead up to placement. At the present time vocational training has no fixed position. We are not wholly certain of the value of our vocational schools. They are probably doing excellent work, in so far as is possible with the comparative lack of information upon which they were created. It would be unwise to extend vocational training until some definite information is available to indicate the lines along which vocational education should be given.

Vocational-education survey

Lack of information regarding vocational guidance appears to be the most definite fact one can reveal. In the report on Commercial Education of the School Inquiry are found the following recommendations :

A temporary special commission to consist of commercial teachers temporarily relieved of their ordinary duties, to investigate with the help of business conditions in relation to commercial education; and to lay the foundation for coöperative relations between commercial courses and schools and commercial houses.

What is needed is a clear definition of the aims, scope, and methods of training actually required for business careers as seen by business men who have seriously brought their minds to bear on this problem, and the gradual development of instruction that will provide this training by the schools. . . . Commerce, like industry, must recognize its responsibility to the thousands of young lives devoted to its service.

In the report on vocational schools it is recommended "that the occupations into which children go as soon as the law permits them to go to work be studied in order that the proper continuation-school and coöperative-school instruction be wisely planned; that a comprehensive survey be made showing the number of boys and girls in different occupations, and the nature of these occupations; and that continuation schools, . . . and to a limited extent, at least, coöperative schools too, in the energizing occupations be established as soon as possible."

The Vocational Guidance Survey has stated that "it is useless to attempt to guide children into vocations before we have more information. No existing organization has adequate information at present about the demand for workers or the opportunities for and conditions of work and training in the twenty largest industries, not to mention the numerous minor ones."

Mr. Chatfield in the last report of the Permanent Census Board stresses the same thought:

It is becoming more and more clearly recognized, however, that movements for vocational training and vocational guidance are dependent upon the classification and collection of information concerning industry itself. The teaching of children cannot be adapted to manufacturing, industry, and commerce until, in a variety of specialized trades and industries, processes and variations of processes are known, the part performed by persons and the part played by machinery is analyzed, and until the growth and decline of various lines of business have been made a matter of systematic record and rendered available for the use of school administrators.

THE OCCUPATIONS OF COLLEGE GRADUATES AS INFLUENCED BY THE UNDERGRADUATE COURSE

By Dean Frederick P. Keppel, Columbia College, New York

(From the *Educational Review*, December, 1910)

The college course is to-day receiving at least its share of discussion on the part both of professionals and amateurs. In these discussions references to the relations of the college to the life work of the men who graduate from it are constant, but specific information as to the nature of that relation is not so easily found. In fact, it is pretty hard to come upon at all. It occurred to me, therefore, that some definite data as to how the college men of the present time themselves regard this relation might be of service. Accordingly I sent a letter of inquiry to the members of the classes of 1908–1910 of a typical independent college, Dartmouth, and a typical university college, Columbia. What I wanted to find out was, of course, just what influence the college course had exerted on each man's choice of a life-career. I knew, however, from experience that a direct inquiry upon this point would be likely to force the answer, and I therefore endeavored to get the information, so to speak, between the lines from the answers to the following inquiries:

Have you come to a fairly definite decision as to what your life work is to be?

Nature of work.

Was the decision reached before entering college?

If after entering, was it in the freshman, sophomore year, junior or senior year, or after graduation?

If you can conveniently do so, state in a few words the reason for your decision.

If you have changed one fairly definite plan for another, kindly indicate the time of change and the reason for it.

346

In all, 800 inquiries may be assumed to have reached their destination, and up to the present 519 replies have been received. I have not endeavored to round up the men who have not replied; for even the clinical material of educational inquiry possesses as individuals some rights of privacy, and, considering my own record in such matters, it is not for me to complain if the "inclosed postage stamp" has been used for another and, to the recipient, more useful purpose.

The addresses of the men who failed to reply have been checked up roughly. The number who are apparently in university professional schools or in teaching positions make it clear that we may safely draw our conclusions as to the general conditions from the replies that have been received, provided we remember that the proportion of men still in doubt as to their future work is naturally greater in the case of men who did not reply than in that of those who did.

The first thing which the replies show is that the young college man of say twenty-three is pretty sure to possess a definite idea as to what he is going to do with his life. Only 26 men replied that they had come to no definite decision as yet. Of the 493 who had made up their minds, 216 had done so before going to college, and had not changed since. Forty-three did not make up their minds until after graduation. For those who decided while in college, the junior year seems to be the critical period, 87 men reporting that the decision was reached in that year, as against 20 in the freshman, 38 in the sophomore, and 63 in the senior year. One reason for this may well be that, considering the present age for college entrance, a student's twenty-first birthday is likely to fall in his junior year. Thirty-two men did not specifically indicate in their replies the time when their decision was reached.

The actual choices of career affect our inquiry only secondarily, but they are interesting as showing the professional trend in a college such as Columbia, where a college student may elect professional work for the Bachelor's degree. Indeed, a similar influence is seen from the opportunities open to the Dartmouth undergraduate in the Thayer, the Tuck, and the Medical schools.

Agriculture and forestry 15
Architecture 4
Business 107
Engineering 45
Financial 36
Letters (including journalism, etc.) 17
Law 96
Manufacturing 28
Medicine 32
Ministry 20
Public service 20
Teaching and research 66
Unclassified . . . . _7_
493

We have now some general idea as to what about 500 young college men are actually planning to do with their lives. Let us see their reasons for these plans, and in particular just what their college experience has had to do with the matter. Not all of them who replied gave any reason at all, and, as is natural, a number of those who did, gave more than one reason. In checking up the answers, therefore, I have apportioned these pro rata, so that the answers represent not only whole "votes," but one-half and one-third votes.

More than half the reasons are not very illuminating — which is, in part at least, the penalty one pays for deliberate failure to "beg the answer" in the form of question. Of these vague replies 84 were to the effect that the work was likely to be congenial; 57, that the calling chosen was one for which the man seemed best fitted; in 23 cases it was apparently the path of least resistance. The more definite factors, when given, are interesting. The 35 votes for an opportunity for service and the 24 for a career with wide opportunities are promising signs, for which the college may fairly take some credit. We shall see in a moment that the college had better take all the credit it can. The 16 decisions for an outdoor life, most of them from men who are preparing for forestry, is an interesting sign of the times. Only 23 men confessed to choosing their work chiefly for the financial reward immediate or prospective, and several of these had others depending upon them. Nineteen men chose some particular calling as a permanent occupation, because they liked the sample of it they got in summer employment; 27 were decided by the opening up of some specific opportunity; and 52 by the example of parents or other relatives.

In the great majority of cases the college was not mentioned at all as a factor in the student's choice. Indeed, several men, guessing the main object of the inquiry, made it a point to write that their college career had had nothing to do with their plans for the future. Of the men who had made no change in their program, 29 referred specifically to the college courses as influencing their decision — and one only of these confessed to having asked and taken the advice of his professors.

Eighty-seven men changed their plans during the college course. The comparatively small number of these changes (only 16 per cent of the total number replying) is, I think, significant, as is also the large proportion of changes which apparently came from causes lying outside of the program. In 40 of the 70 cases where specific reason for the change is given, no mention is made of the student's college career. Some men were turned by a specific business opportunity; an early marriage caused one man to give up the study of medicine and take a teaching position; others changed for reasons of health, family affairs, and the like. Five changes were due to indirect college influence; for example, a call to the ministry resulting from a student's visit to Northfield, a change from medicine to law due to success in college debating. Sixteen men changed their plan because they *disliked* the sample they received in college of the work required in the calling of their first choice; a biological course, for example, turned more than one prospective doctor into a lawyer, and, particularly at Columbia, the chance to offer professional work toward the college degree gave several undergraduates all they desired of law, medicine, or architecture. (It must not be forgotten, by the way, that the men with whom we are dealing are not the lame ducks of college life; they had at least entered the senior class with good standing, or they would not have received an inquiry.) Only 25 men changed their plans because of the irresistible attraction of some college subject. Perhaps the most interesting reply received was from a man who had intended to be an engineer but who became greatly interested in an elementary-law course. He cast about for some occupation which would enable him to serve both masters, and he has found what he wanted in patent law.

No conception can be given in a brief article of the interest of the individual replies as *documents humaines.* One man used the blank to preach a Christian Science sermon. Another explained how acquaintance with Jack London had turned him to the task of improving the social order. Another, who had planned to be an artist, found his æsthetic taste atrophied after four years of undergraduate life. One man gave up his plans to be a teacher because the college instructor impressed him as singularly remote from the real things of life. Another, whose triple ambition was to lead a life that was at once spiritual, active, and practically useful, has, after considering the law and ministry, decided upon Y.M.C.A. work. A manufacturer, in moments of depression, thought of becoming a professional musician. We have, on the one hand, him who decided upon the law as a career at the age of five and, on the other, the man who gave up its study because of the difficulty attending the practice of law by an honest man. One man considered for a long time the rival attractions of chair making and teaching, and finally decided upon the latter. On the whole, the most interesting replies are those from men who, like the patent lawyer of whom I spoke, have thought out their own line and then followed it, even if it led off the beaten path, and of these there are a considerable number.

I have cited these random examples largely in the hope that men in other colleges may be led to make inquiries along the same lines. Unless I am greatly mistaken, the actual relationship of the college to the student in this matter of life work, as it is indicated from the replies received by me, differs considerably from the off-hand opinion on the subject now held by most men engaged in college teaching. It seems to me further that the question has sufficient practical importance in these days, when we are beginning to realize that an American college is not a German university, to justify a study of five thousand cases instead of five hundred.

If my information is typical, a very large proportion of boys before entering college have decided upon a very definite scheme of life from which they are not likely to change. The question arises, therefore, whether the colleges are using intelligently the lever which this places in their hands. A competent instructor or dean, having ascertained the boy's ambition, ought to be able to focus his interest, according to the type of boy with whom he is dealing, either in the subjects which form a broad foundation for his work or in those which lead directly toward it.

The references to the influence of what are generally known as undergraduate activities are scattering, but there are enough of them to furnish one more argument for paying attention to these as integral parts of the educational equipment of the college. A faculty ought not to be satisfied when it has devised machinery to prevent abuses. It ought not to limit itself to keeping some boys out of these activities, for there are at least as many boys who ought to be led into them.

Finally, knowledge that a student has not yet made up his mind as to what he will do, or that he is thinking of changing a program previously formed, is of no small importance. Here is an actual hinge in the armor of "remoteness" for the college to attack in making its endeavor to establish a real personal influence with the student. It is startling to read between the lines in so many cases that a student had no expectation whatever that the faculty could or would be of any help to him. I do not mean that an undergraduate should be pestered with suggestions and advice, but the college certainly can fairly be expected to have a little more to do with his decision upon so vital a matter than appears to be the case at present. I am confident that many a student, particularly in the great middle class of men, conspicuous neither for brilliancy nor for delinquency and therefore too often left wholly to their own devices, would welcome a sympathetic and intelligent interest on the part of the college in his future career.

PRACTICAL ARTS AND VOCATIONAL GUIDANCE

By C. A. Prosser, Secretary National Society for the
Promotion of Industrial Education

(From the *Manual Training Magazine*, February, 1913)

In spite of all the other excellent things which our public-school system does for childhood, most boys and girls leave the portals of the schoolhouse to enter all kinds of wage-earning occupations not only untrained but undirected as to what they ought to do in life.

More than 6,000,000 boys and girls between fourteen and eighteen years of age are employed in various ways in this country. This does not include the additional army of children in some of the Southern states leaving school at the tender age of twelve. During the present year at least 2,000,000 more childish wage-earners, upon reaching the age of fourteen, will enter the ranks of industry. More than seven out of ten of this multitude did not finish the work of the elementary school. More than three out of four of them did not reach the eighth year of the schools, and more than one out of two, the seventh year. Almost half of them had not completed the fifth-grade work. Great numbers of them were barely able to meet the test for illiteracy necessary in order to secure working certificates, which in most of the states is a test on the work of the fourth grade.

These children not only entered life deficient in the elementary-school education which our day regards as being necessary to the civic intelligence and the vocational efficiency of everyone, but practically all of them had been trained by a formalized process in the things of the books alone, which gave them no opportunity to find what they would like to do and what they were best able to do in life. Practically all of them went to work without proper vocational guidance and direction. All of them found the doors of most of the skilled and desirable industries closed to them until they should become sixteen years of age.

Since they must work somewhere, most of these childish wage earners find their way largely by accident into low-grade skilled or unskilled occupations — the great child-employing industries and enterprises which are always wide open at the bottom to receive young workers but closed at the top so far as permanent desirable employment is concerned. Here, because their work lacks purpose and hope, they drift about from one position to another, changing in some states, it is said, from one unskilled position to another on an average once every four months. The resulting moral degradation to the child and the tremendous cost to the employer, due to this indifferent, unstable, fluctuating service, cannot be estimated. For most of these children the years from fourteen to sixteen. spent in wage earning in store and shop and factory are wasted years, since they find themselves at sixteen in the same position as at fourteen — starting life without any adequate preparation for wage earning. Their menial, monotonous, more or less automatic work not only gives no skill which will be useful to them in after years but also arrests rather than develops intelligence and ambition.

Out of the great army of children who leave the schools at fourteen to go to work, and get from those schools no further attention, come the ne'er-do-wells, the loafers, the tramps, gamblers, prostitutes, and criminals for whose care the state spends more money in penal and correctional work than it would have cost to have prevented, through proper vocational guidance and training, many of them from becoming a burden and menace to society.

In the absence of any work in the elementary schools which discovers the taste and ability of children, many pupils, after receiving the graded-school diploma, elect the high school when it does not give the training which is best suited to their needs and to the kind of work they are to do in the world. They do this largely because they have not found themselves and have not come to realize either the kind of work which they are destined to do or the kind of training which would best prepare them for it.

SOME CHOICE INEVITABLE

All boys and girls are, in the neighborhood of fourteen years of age, required to make a choice of some kind. They decide first of all whether they are to attend school or go to work. If they are to attend school, they must decide what kind of school they are to enter. As vocational schools, or departments, are established to meet the needs of those who are not destined for business and professional careers, every pupil ought, as the results of his previous training, to be in a position at fourteen years of age to make an intelligent choice of the occupation which he desires to follow or the kind of training which he wishes. This can only be done by some system of instruction, in the upper grades of the elementary schools, which will test pupils out by other things in addition to arithmetic, spelling, reading, writing, and other traditional subjects of a general education.

The results of our failure through the schools to properly direct and train all the children of all the people for useful service are unmistakable. Misfits in all vocations confront us everywhere. Many workers are inefficient because they are not adapted to the work they are doing, and some because they have not been properly prepared for it. This lack of efficiency constitutes a permanent handicap not only to the worker but to the calling which he follows. It means lessened wage, uncertain employment, failure of promotion, economic struggle, waste in the use of material, poor workmanship, reduced output, and the lowering of the standards of skill and workmanship of American industries.

We talk much to-day of the necessity of conserving our natural resources. Let us not forget that the richest asset which this country possesses is the practical and constructive ability of the children who sit in our schoolhouses to-day, who are to be the workers and the leaders in industry of the future, and whose talent and aptitude, whatever it may be, can only be uncovered by some system of training within the schools that will give it a chance for expression. Every consideration requires that every worker should have a chance to discover and to develop to the full all his possibilities, both for the good of himself and for the welfare of the social order. It is idle for us to talk much about conserving our natural resources, until we have, by a system of vocational guidance and training, developed a type of intelligent skilled workmen in shop and home and farm who will so deal with the products of our soil and our mines as to eliminate waste and transform them into products of higher and still higher value.

Above all, we must in some way secure a better adjustment of every worker to the calling in which he can work most successfully, in order that he may have the joy that comes from a sense of achievement, and experience the uplift that blesses every man who finds himself employed at a task in which he is interested and at which he is able to render a service creditable to himself and beneficial to his fellows.

Vocational guidance and vocational education are necessary in meeting the problem of fitting the great mass of our people for useful employment, each as the handmaiden of the other and each as indispensable to the success of the other. This paper will confine its attention largely to the question of how vocational guidance may be best given boys and girls at fourteen years of age.

Two things are necessary in any successful program of vocational guidance: a greater knowledge of the child than we have thus far obtained through the work of the schools, and the close coöperation of other agencies with the schoolmaster in the attempt to give advice and counsel to the child as to his choice of a life work.

No vocational counselor, however competent and however devoted, will be able to deal with most children at fourteen years of age unless he knows more about their tasks and ability than the fact that they have made this or that per cent in spelling, reading, arithmetic, geography, history, and other public-school subjects. Such a record may determine whether or not the child is destined for high school and for college; it does not at all reveal the other tendencies and capabilities of most pupils. It is equally true that the vocational counselor must learn, if he would be successful, how to secure in some way the active, helpful coöperation of laymen, drawn from many different walks and occupations of life, who will be able to give him and those children with whom he deals the benefit of the experience which they have had, and serve as big brothers and big sisters in the task of helping the adolescent boy and girl to find themselves.

IMPORTANCE OF ELEMENTARY-SCHOOL PERIOD

The greater knowledge of the child which we need to have in order to give vocational direction is only to be obtained by some system of training within the schools between twelve and fourteen years of age which shall help us to find out what they would like to do and what they are best able to do.

Under the comparatively simple and primitive conditions of farm and village life of an earlier day the experiences the child went through in his environment on the farm and in the village uncovered his interests and his ability largely without the aid of the schoolroom. The little red schoolhouse on the hill still tested him in the things of the book; his environment tested him in the things of life.

The boy came in contact with a round of activities which were distinctively educative to him in the practical affairs of life. He followed the plow while his father sowed. On rainy days he tinkered with the farm machinery in the barn. When he was not able to repair it, he took it to the village hard by and helped, in a humble way, the artisan there to do his work. In the village he came into rather intimate contact with the work of the blacksmith, the wheelwright, the saddler, the carpenter, the shoemaker, and all the other skilled trades which the community afforded.

Out of this experience with the realities of things, certain undoubted benefits came to the boy. The experiences he went through were distinctively educational to him. He learned to do many things by doing. He touched the realities which in themselves gave insight and power. There can be no doubt but that the success which the little red schoolhouse was able to obtain with its short term of school, its inadequate facilities, its poor teachers (measured by our modern standards), was largely due to the fact that the pupils came to the school with a background of life experience, and a knowledge of the things which the book only photographed and symbolized, which inspired them in a short time and under unfavorable conditions to master the things of the book.

This experience was distinctly socializing. The boy came in an elementary way to understand the trials and difficulties and achievements, workmanship, and ideals of the artisan. No matter what he became in after life, — the judge on the bench, a lawyer at the bar, a doctor driving lonely roads at night, a teacher in the schoolroom, an artisan following one of the trades which his community needed, — he carried into his life work a sympathetic understanding and appreciation of the work of his fellows that rendered him measurably more capable in his own and bound him and them together in a bond of appreciation and understanding.

Out of this work came a very sensible vocational guidance. The father and the boy and the neighborhood came to know what the boy was interested in and where his largest success would be made. With the doors of the trades opening up before him at the close of his elementary schooling, he was able to choose and to follow in content and with success the work for which he was best fitted.

It should be said by the way of passing that this elementary experience, during his childhood days, with the tools and processes of different occupations, particularly the one in which he became interested, gave him considerable elementary preparation and understanding of the work which he was to follow, and was a distinct benefit to him in mastering it in a more serious and thoroughgoing way when he came to his adolescent years.

It seems clear to all of us that under the conditions of modern life the opportunity of the boy to secure such real experience outside the school has, to a very great extent at least, disappeared. Trades have become factoryized. Large-scale production has not only taken the ownership of tools from the worker, but it has harnessed him as a machine-hand to one machine under the shop roof where he may serve all his days in carrying on one process, making one small part of the finished output of the establishment. Seldom, if ever, does the boy of tender years have an opportunity to get beyond the factory gate to even witness the work which is being carried on beyond it.

Children have become herded together in great cities; the population is becoming more and more urban; children live huddled together in apartment houses; even playgrounds are difficult to secure. The school term has been lengthened from four months to ten, and the pupils are being crammed and saturated with the things of the book, which at best are only photographs or summations of the life experience denied most of them. Of course, children do have life experience, but it is the experience of the superficial observer of the rapidly changing phenomena around them, and not the kind with which in former days they had an opportunity to come into intimate contact and in which they were able to participate actively with brain and with hand.

All the arguments that are being used to-day to show the necessity of vocational direction and guidance for children facing the complexities of our modern industrial and commercial life point at the same time to the need of securing for children in some way the kind of life experience, before they become fourteen years of age, which will give some basis upon which they and those guiding and directing them may deal intelligently with the problem of placing them in proper schools, in giving them proper training, and in placing them in the callings of life for which they are best suited.

THE SCHOOL MUST FURNISH REAL LIFE EXPERIENCE

If it be submitted that practical experience with the realities of things is a necessary part of the training of the child between twelve and fourteen years of age, and if it be admitted further that under modern conditions it is not possible for the child to secure this training as he should in his environment outside the school, then the duty and responsibility rests upon the school, as the agent of the state for the welfare of childhood, to give it under the school roof.

There is a sense in which it may be truthfully said that to a very great extent in the past the result of the training of the elementary school, and of the high school as well, has been to select by elimination, closing the door from time to time, by a system of tests and examinations, against all those who were not able to respond successfully to the kind of studies that were being offered in the

schools and to the demand upon the capacity of the child in dealing with abstractions. More and more, in our theory of the American public-school system, we are swinging around to the idea that
it is to be the mission of the schools in the future to select and
to adjust boys and girls for life by having them undergo varied
experiences in order to uncover their varied tastes and aptitudes
and to direct and to train them in the avenues for which they
display the most capacity.

Such a program as this would require a differentiation of the
course of study for pupils between twelve and fourteen years of
age. The amount of difference in the course of study for different
kinds of pupils in any given school system would of course depend
upon the size of the city, the extent of its resources, the size of
the building, the number of different groups of pupils dealt with,
and the size of each group.

POSSIBILITIES OF THE ELEMENTARY SCHOOL

In a city of 50,000 people the usual elementary school might
well offer for the seventh and eighth years a high-school preparatory course, a commercial course, a household arts course for girls,
and a practical arts course for boys. All the pupils from these
different groups could well take, in the same classes if necessary, the same work in English, history, civics, music, drawing,
penmanship, physical training, which would occupy at least half
of a lengthened day in the schoolroom. They would separate
from each other for different work in the lines in which they
were being tested.

Pupils in the high-school preparatory course, who were in it
because it was already determined that they were to go to high
school and to college, could take courses in elementary algebra and
in a foreign language. The elementary algebra would be as good,
or better, training to meet the demands of the high school as any
other course. The foreign language could be taken up at a time
when the child was better prepared to deal with it. It is a well-
known fact that one of the great difficulties in the teaching of foreign languages in the high schools is that pupils take them at a
time when the language instinct is at an ebb rather than at the flow.

Pupils taking the commercial course would be those who were going out to commercial life at fourteen, or going into the commercial department of the regular high school, or going out to the private commercial college, or intending after the regular high-school course to fit themselves to enter business life. These should take, in the differentiated work between twelve and fourteen, rich courses in the keeping of simple accounts, commercial arithmetic, commercial geography, and probably should be given some elementary experience in handling a typewriter. Such commercial arithmetic and geography is just as good as any which the schools have ever offered, and, because it appeals to the interests of these pupils, is better than any other.

Girls taking the course in household arts between twelve and fourteen would be girls who were going out to the factory to spend, on the average, six years before taking up home-making in their homes, or who were going to the high school for a year or two and then going home to await marriage, or who expect to take the household-arts training offered by the regular high school. These should have rich courses, in a lengthened day, in cooking, with the "how" and "why" of the work; sewing and hat trimming, with the "how" and the "why"; sanitation and hygiene of the home; household decoration; and some little elementary experience in the problem of the care of the sick.

Boys wanting the training in practical arts would be boys who at fourteen were going to make a choice of some wage-earning occupation, or who were going to enter some industrial or trade school, or who were going to take the manual-training work in a regular high school or enter a technical high school. These should have rich courses in the practical arts, with the "how" and the "why" of the process given whenever possible, industrial arithmetic, industrial geography, and elementary drawing closely related to the work which they were doing in the shop.

The high school claims that what it wants is trained minds rather than any particular content or book experience leading up to its work. If this be true, then any one of these courses is as good a preparation, at least for the general course in the high school, as any other course of instruction. Pupils taking any one of these courses, who decide after graduating from the elementary school that they wished to attend the regular high school, would be in as good a position as any other pupils to take its work. So far as the door of opportunity leading out to the regular high school, they would not be injured, to say the least, by the kind of elementary-school experience which they had received.

Nor is there any reason why, between the ages of twelve and fourteen, a flexible arrangement of the school program should not permit the pupils in any one of these courses to receive some experience in some of the other courses as a test of their interest and their capacity.

It goes almost without saying that after such an experience in the upper grades of the elementary school, boys and girls, upon graduating, would be in a position to face either some calling or further schooling much better prepared to make an intelligent choice of what they should do than they can be under the present school régime, under which most of them know only that they have or have not been able to respond successfully to the tests which have been set up in the academic work.

Where courses in the practical arts and in the household arts were offered in the seventh and eighth years of the work, the administration should be so flexible as to permit boys and girls twelve years of age, who were retarded in their work so that they had not reached the seventh year of the course, to receive the benefit of the instruction irrespective of the question of where they might be located in the graded schools. This training in the practical arts would probably be of more benefit to this kind of boys and girls than to any other. Practically all of them will leave school at fourteen years of age or seek to enter an industrial school. They must make a choice of some wage-earning occupation. They need perhaps most of all to have such experience between twelve and fourteen years of age as will help them, when they reach the period of compulsory education, to make an intelligent choice of an occupation. Every experience goes to show that these retarded boys and girls who were not able to measure up to the things of the book are able to learn by doing. When they are taught such subjects as spelling and arithmetic in connection with the work which they are doing with their hands, they are able to grasp them much better because they are being taught on the basis of the actual experience which they are receiving.

CONTENT OF WORK IN PRACTICAL ARTS FOR BOYS

This paper will from this point direct its attention entirely to the question of training in the practical arts for boys between twelve and fourteen years of age. If this training in the practical arts is to help boys to find themselves, in order that at fourteen they may make an intelligent choice of their work for the future, it must be varied. A course in woodworking, excellent as it may be, only reveals whether or not the boy responds to it with his interest and aptitude. A course in metal working alone will determine only whether or not he is adapted to that work. A course in printing alone shows whether or not he has any tendency toward the printer's trade. What we need is not a course in woodworking or a course in metal working, but an organization of training in the practical arts during the seventh and eighth years which will include experiences drawn from many different fields of employment, such as woodworking, metal working, electrical working, printing, bookbinding, leather working, clay working, and gardening. These should not be known as courses at all, but should consist of a series of jobs, projects, enterprises, tasks — call them what you will — taken some from one field and some from another. The progress of the boy through the school in a given year should be stated in terms of a series of experiences, some of them in wood, some in metal, some in printing, some in electrical work, etc.

The boy should follow these as a series of carefully graduated experiences, each one being taken up when, as the result of his previous training, he is able to deal with it. The work might be arranged so that he gave his time in the shop for a certain period — a month or so — to wood, then to metal, then to electrical work, then to printing, etc. It is believed, however, that the best results would be secured by having him assigned jobs from different fields rather indiscriminately, a job in metal working following one in wood, a job in electrical work following one in printing. These shop tasks he should follow individually rather than as a member of a group.

There is no reason why all the pupils in the class should be working upon the same kind of a job at the same time, nor that they should be working upon different jobs from the same field of industry the same moment.

A course of training in the practical arts like that described above would require a varied rather than an extensive equipment. Instead of duplicating tools and machines so as to provide every pupil with a carpenter's bench, every pupil with a case of type, every pupil with a lathe, every pupil with a doorbell and battery, just a few pieces of equipment necessary in order to give the boy experience in any occupation would be necessary, the pupils being taught individually and being shifted about so as to permit the varied equipment of the shop to keep them all busy at different tasks. The total cost of the equipment necessary to do this would certainly not be any more, and would probably be less, than that of the present method of duplicating pieces in order to teach pupils by the group method.

Some cities have some of their ward or elementary-school buildings located near each other. Where this is true, it would be possible to secure varied experience in different practical arts for boys by having each one of these buildings devote its attention to arts or lines of employment different from that to which each of the other buildings gave its attention. By shifting the pupil for a portion of his day or year from one building to another, these buildings through coöperation could secure training in various activities for the boys.

PROBLEMS CONFRONTING THE TEACHER

If the interest and capacity of the boy is to be properly tested, the experience which he receives in the school shop should be made as *real* as possible. This means that the instructor in charge of the work should have at least some elementary knowledge of the industry dealt with. For the purpose of this prevocational training he need not be a journeyman or master of the calling, but he should have a sufficient contact with it to be able to bring some of its atmosphere into the schoolroom. There are probably some excellent instructors in manual training for boys in this country to-day who are women, but the burden of proof rests upon him who proposes a woman as teacher of the practical arts for boys to show that she has had such experience and possesses such ability as to render her an exception to the general presumption that the teachers of this work should be men.

The work should be carried on as nearly like the actual shop as possible; otherwise the experience lacks reality. This does not at all mean that in the instruction an attempt should be made to reach shop standards of workmanship. In the earlier days, boys had an opportunity to tinker in an elementary way at different occupations. The work was valuable to them not because shop standards were reached but because they had an opportunity through it to find out whether they responded to it. The aim of the work should not be large skill but life experience. Ideals of workmanship for the boys in the shop are good and to some extent necessary, but they should not be approached through refined work on a few limited tasks to the point of defeating the larger aim of helping the boy to find himself.

At the best it will be impossible for the school to make this work in practical arts so real as to present to the child the work as it is carried on in the industry. Every place where the local community has the work which is being done in the school carried on in a shop or factory, arrangements should be made to have the boy visit the establishment and secure an opportunity, under favorable conditions, to see grown men carrying on the work on a large scale which he is attempting to do as a boy would do it under the school roof. In this way the manufacturing establishments, shops, and farms of the community would be made to coöperate with the school in bringing the boy into contact with the work of the world so that he might choose from it that which he is best adapted to pursue.

ACTIVITY MUST HAVE PRACTICAL OUTCOME

Pupils should be taught individually rather than by the group method. The work should be put on a productive rather than on an exercise basis. The shop should make useful things to be utilized by the school or by the school system. Every experience goes to show that boys are much more interested in making things which are to be used in the school system, and through which the boys are conscious of the fact that they are contributing something that is useful, than they are in making a taboret for sister's parlor. Somewhere in the course there should be work done by the boy that smacks of the time element and approach of the shop outside. Where pupils make parts of things, all should get an experience sometime of making parts and assembling those parts into the finished product.

The experience which the boy undergoes in the shop should be made educative for him. He should do there something more than merely use his hands. On every job which he performs every opportunity should be utilized for whatever drawing, arithmetic, spelling, and even composition work will enable him to do the job better and to gain power in the use of related academic work.

NECESSARY MODIFICATION OF MANUAL TRAINING

Such a program would not be a difficult or complicated one were it not so totally at variance with the present practice of the schools. The large results to be obtained from the work justify its introduction, though a more flexible administration of both academic and manual-training work in the seventh and eighth years would be necessary. It seems certain that to carry out such a program more time would have to be given for manual training, or training in the practical arts, than at present. This might be secured by the substitution of such work for other required subjects. It would probably be best secured by lengthening the school day. Advocates of the lengthened school day point out that if pupils gave half their time to actual work with their hands, rather than close attention to books, a longer school day would not only not be burdensome but beneficial to them physically as well as otherwise. It is certain that if we are to accomplish anything worth while in working with the hands with children between twelve and fourteen years of age, we must give more time to the work in the program than the average of fifteen or twenty minutes per day which in most cases is allotted the practical work, thereby giving it the same importance in the curriculum as music and spelling. We need wider experience and training for the instructors. Woodworking and metal working have been the only lines of training for which they have been prepared in our schools. They need not only preparation for different lines of work in the schools but a wider and more intimate contact with other lines of industry. In order to attract desirable teachers to the work, who will be willing to make such preparation and secure such experience, there should be more salary for the capable. Above all, there needs to be in all quarters a greater recognition of the place and the value of training in the practical arts in the elementary schools, both for its educative benefit to the pupils and as an indispensable part of any successful attempt to give proper vocational guidance to the adolescent.

It is not denied that the program set out above raises some problems new in character, doubtless some that are difficult of solution from the administrative standpoint, which cannot be discussed in detail here. I have attempted to formulate some of these questions as follows :

SOME QUESTIONS FOR SOLUTION

1. Should all children of twelve to fourteen years be required to take some training in the practical arts?

2. What difference in amount and kind should be made in the training as between those strongest in book work and those strongest in manual work?

3. Should this training in the practical arts be restricted to those who have reached the seventh grade at twelve years of age or should all children, even if they are retarded in their work, who need the work be given it?

4. How much experience in an industry or occupation should an instructor have in order to teach it as a part of prevocational training in the practical arts?

5. What changes should be made in the preparation of teachers of manual training in the practical arts as now given, in order to fit them properly to carry on such training as shall serve effectually as a part of a program of prevocational guidance and education?

6. How many teachers of practical arts in the upper grades of the elementary schools secure necessary experience in lines of industry or occupations with which they are expected to deal?

7. What should be the time allotment for training in the practical arts?

8. What are the kinds or types of jobs or experiences or enterprises from each of the practical arts, such as gardening, metal working, woodworking, · electrical working, printing, bookbinding, cement working, clay working, that the schools should give?

9. To what extent should the school add to the list of practical arts others carried on by the local community?

10. How can the instructors in the practical arts aid in giving proper vocational guidance and direction to the pupils?

11. What should the school authorities do with the output of the work in the practical arts?

12. What are the working programs for such training in the practical arts, for those twelve to fourteen years of age, which seem best for typical or representative school units in cities and towns of varied and given populations?

13. Should the school day be lengthened in order to give the training, or can it be given in the present school day by substituting it for some work now required?

14. If proper time allotment is secured by substitution, in place of what other work should it be offered?

15. To what extent should this school training in the practical arts be supplemented by visits to places in the community where they are being practiced commercially?

16. To what extent should the job or enterprise be used as the means, or center, or core of instruction of the boy in related arithmetic, drawing, English, geography, civics, etc.?

17. What would be the best equipment for a two-year course of training in the practical arts, for a group of twenty boys, in which the jobs or experiences of the pupil were drawn from a number of different occupations or employments?

18. From what practical arts should the experiences be drawn for a course of training as a basis for the vocational guidance of girls, and what would be the best equipment for such a course in meeting the needs of a group of twenty girls?

19. To what extent, by coöperation between different elementary-school buildings each equipped to give work in only one or two practical arts, could pupils be interchanged for a part of the day so as to give them varied experience in activities drawn from a number of different arts?

20. How may we best impress school authorities with the great educative as well as social and economic value of the right kind of work in the practical arts, for children twelve to fourteen years of age, so that it may cease to be a mere appetizer for academic activities and be given its proper place and opportunity in the work of the school?

SELECTING YOUNG MEN FOR PARTICULAR JOBS

By Herman Schneider, Dean of the College of Engineering, University of Cincinnati

(From the *American Machinist*, April 10, 1913)

Several years ago two young men appeared at my office to apply for admission to the coöperative course. Although they came together, they were not mutually acquainted, one being from Kansas and the other from Ohio. They were of the same physical build; they had the same facial characteristics; their scholarship records were equally good; and both said they felt an impulse toward mechanical engineering. Both looked like good material. The conversation disclosed no radical or even slight differences in their personalities. They gave promise of being a good " pair " and consequently were sent to the same machine shop.

In due process of events a coördinator from the engineering college called at the machine shop. The foreman said Kansas was satisfactory, but Ohio didn't get into the work. Each time the coördinator called, the foreman reported Kansas as most satisfactory and Ohio as more and more unsatisfactory. In a month Kansas was turning out his work with the ease, sureness, and dexterity of an old hand, while Ohio was getting a case of nerves, spoiling work, and developing fatigue. The superintendent asked us to try Ohio elsewhere, but we decided for a number of reasons to continue him in the shop a little longer.

In the university, however, Kansas was soon reported to my office as utterly hopeless. His scholastic grades were almost zero in all his subjects. He gave no reactions at all in class and laboratory work. His teachers said he was stupid. But Ohio came to his school work with avidity. He was mentally keen and seemed to delight in his work.

Kansas grew nervous over his school work, Ohio thrived on it. Kansas at school was tired out at 10.30 each morning; Ohio got better as the hours went by. Kansas longed for the rest which shop work gave him; Ohio longed for the rest which school work gave him. Careful tests and conference showed conclusively that Kansas broke under mental work, mental responsibility, and self-directed and diversified manual work, but that he expanded in spirit, health, and satisfaction under repetitive shop processes which were planned for him. Similar tests and conferences showed that Ohio broke under the strain of directed repetitive processes, and to a lesser degree under self-directed and diversified manual work, but that he thrived when given mental problems and responsibility.

We have lost track of Kansas, but Ohio is happy and successful in commercial life.

There comes to mind another young man, who called one morning and presented a splendid scholarship record from a rigorous high school. He was a most attractive youngster — sturdy, clear eyed, and cheerful, but he had not the faintest idea what he wanted to do for a life work. The whole world looked good to him, but no lead I made could discover any particular bent. He smilingly offered to try anything, and finally offered to try everything we had so as to arrive at something by process of elimination.

We started him at foundry work. He did n't like it, so he went cheerfully from one type of work to another for two years, always working hard and faithfully, but without satisfaction, either to himself or to his employers. His school work was excellent except in technical courses. All this time we were taking account of his talents. Certain characteristics began to stand out, and one day the question was put to him bluntly, "Blank, how would you like to be a librarian?" His response might possibly be called a grateful, unanimous yell. So he is now making progress in a library school.

Cases similar in kind but highly dissimilar in detail to those cited could be given by the dozen. We have found, for example, that some young men cannot grow in all their parts in indoor work, and others like it and thrive on it; some must have roving work (such as the railroads furnish), while others are upset by it and are happy only in a settled job; some like to fuss over a little piece of intricate mechanism, while others like a hurly-burly task of big dimensions; some chafe under accurate directions, which eliminate personal initiative, while others produce cheerfully under them; some evade responsibility, while others assume it naturally.

GREATEST EFFICIENCY WHEN WORK IS SATISFACTORY

Now a man is most efficient when his work gives him the greatest satisfaction; when he is doing the thing his Creator intended he should do. Every working man, from the hewer of wood and drawer of water to the research scientist, should get three things out of his work: first, mental and physical development and discipline; second, joy in doing it (or at least satisfaction); and third, a decent living. And the man who has found the job his soul is blindly craving, the job for which he has inborn talents, gets these. But the man whose whole being revolts at his task becomes a captious citizen, an inefficient worker, and a meager earner.

Under present conditions our youth blunder into jobs; the gambling odds against their finding work suited to their temperaments and talents are too high, for there are many types of work and usually but one general type will fit any single individual. There is no method or agency to determine the general type of work for which a youth is talented and to classify the various jobs which fall under this type.

Unfortunately, work has been classified heretofore by the materials used or produced rather than by the characteristics necessary for success in it. Thus, if a boy were successful in wood-shop work, he was told he would make a good carpenter; however, wood turning in a shop and outdoor carpentry are dissimilar types, while wood turning in a shop and metal turning in a shop are similar types. The fact that work is becoming more subdivided and more intensified makes the situation more acute, and the problem becomes a national one. A nation, especially a self-governing nation, many of whose self-governors do not get the three returns mentioned out of their work, is not a stable nation.

Every individual has certain broad characteristics, and every type of work requires certain broad characteristics. The problem then is to state the broad characteristics, to devise a rational method to discover these characteristics (or talents) in individuals, to classify the types of jobs by the talents they require, and to guide the youth with certain talents into the type of job which requires those talents. This is a big problem, but one possible of measurable solution, or, at worst, possible of a solution immeasurably superior to our present haphazard methods.

In seven years of coöperative work at the University of Cincinnati, we have had experience with about five hundred coöperative students. As with the young men, Ohio and Kansas, so with other students, marked characteristics in time stand out. These we have classified, and they now constitute a sort of guide to us in helping students to find themselves. The list is by no means considered as final; future experience will modify it, of course. But it does furnish a rational basis of broad selection.

It is realized also that our work is principally in coöperation with manufacture, construction, and transportation; other broad characteristics would probably be listed if we had similar relations with commerce, law, medicine, and religion. And since the object of this paper is to point out what appears to us as a rational beginning of vocational guidance, criticism of the characteristics given is looked for in hope rather than in fear.

THE MAJOR CHARACTERISTICS

(a) In many occupations physical strength is an essential; for example, in draying, stone masonry, and baggage handling. In others it is not; for example, in bookkeeping, telephone installing, and piano tuning. Mankind ranges from the almost helpless cripple to the physical giant. We therefore have the two characteristics, physical strength and physical weakness.

(b) I have in mind a number of our students who were utter failures at all kinds of work requiring manual dexterity but who maintained uniformly good grades in all their school work. Their efficiency was all head efficiency. There have been a number also who were hopeless in all their university work but whose hands acquired skill easily. Their efficiency was all hand efficiency.

The first type might make good designers, inspectors, executives, or writers, but unlike the second type would drag out hopeless existences as machinists, molders, masons, or piano makers. Of course most of our students possess both efficiencies. Our experience has taught us that some men are mental and some are manual, while some are both.

(c) There is a type of man who wants to get on the same car every morning, get off at the same corner, go to the same shop, ring up at the same clock, stow his lunch in the same locker, go to the same machine, and do the same class of work day after day. Another type of man would go crazy under this routine; he wants to move about, meet new people, see and do new things. The first is settled; the second is roving. The first might make a good man for a shop manufacturing a standard product; the second might make a good railroad man or a good outdoor carpenter.

Recently two of my students were not doing well; both were getting into a condition of unrest. One was in a railroad shop; he complained that every job was different from every other job, that he was sent here and there, that there was no continuity to the work, and that he was getting nervous. The other complained that there was not enough variety to his work, that it was too confining, that he could not move about and do new things all the time, and that he was getting nervous. We gave each the other's place and both are swinging along and learning most satisfactorily.

(d) There are two broad characteristics which are easily discoverable even in first interviews, the indoor and the outdoor. When a blizzard is raging the first type likes to hear the roar of the wind because it heightens his sense of protection indoors and emphasizes the coziness of his fireplace, while the other wants to go out and fight his way against the storm. When the rigors of outdoor railroad and construction work are vividly pictured to these two types of young men, one's eyes will light up and his muscles will get tense; the other will compact himself as if for shelter.

(e) We have found two characteristics which are quickly brought out in practical work but which are not so easily discernible in school work. Some young men naturally assume responsibility; others just as naturally evade it. It is a well-known fact to all superintendents that the most productive workmen often make inefficient foremen, while an inferior producer often makes a good foreman. One man is directive ; the other is dependent.

A drayman for a large jobbing house was promoted to foreman of drays, at a substantial increase in salary, because he was intelligent, honest, sober, accurate in his deliveries, careful to a marked degree of his team and dray, and loyal to his employers. In his new position he worried and grew fretful ; in time he began to fail physically ; finally he asked for his old job, happiness, and efficiency, just about the time his employers had decided that he was incompetent as a foreman.

(f) There are two characteristics which are sometimes confused with those just stated, but which are essentially distinct. For example, we had two students in a large shop working in the planning department ; one was fertile in suggestions, but the other usually put them into effect. The first was original ; the second was directive.

The man who is original may make a good designer, but unless he were also directive he would make a poor superintendent ; he might be a good window dresser but not a department-store manager, a writer but not a publisher, an inventor but not a manufacturer, a reformer but not a mayor. A partnership in which one man is directive and another original is usually successful. Of course one person may possess both characteristics.

Then there is the man who does only what he is told to do and exactly as he is told to do it. He is imitative. He would dress every window like every other window. He might make a successful milk-wagon driver, since he would have a fixed route and a bottle of uniform size to deliver ; but he would probably make an indifferent drayman, since he would not have a fixed route, and originality (or ingenuity) would be needed to load and unload unwieldy boxes and barrels under adverse conditions. He might make a good machine molder, but not a good floor molder ; he would probably be successful and happy at a punch press, but not in a toolroom.

(g) Then there are the two types mentioned before, one of which likes to fuss with an intricate bit of mechanism, while the other wants the task of big dimensions — the watchmaker, the engraver, the inlayer, the painter of miniatures, on the one hand ; the bridge builder, the steel-mill worker, the train dispatcher, the circus man, on the other. One has small scope ; the other large scope.

(*h*) Some men can easily adapt themselves to any environment, while others act the same under almost any circumstances. One takes the local color like a chameleon ; the other is always the same monochrome. One is adaptable, the other self-centered ; one a salesman, the other a statistician.

(*i*) There is a distinct type which thinks and then does, in contrast to which there is the type which does and then thinks. One is deliberate ; the other impulsive. The northern races are usually deliberate, the southern impulsive ; one controls its passions, the other is frequently controlled by them. An army of cool-headed officers and hot-headed soldiers is a highly effective machine, but in the civilian walks of life the impulsive characteristic is negative ; that is to say, there seems to be no occupation in which it is a requisite. There are many vocations, however, in which a man must be deliberate.

(*j*) Our coöperation with a piano-building factory made it necessary to secure men who had a native musical ability — a strong tonal sense. It was found that this was a requisite for success in the higher positions ; hence the music sense is included in this list. Obviously the music sense is necessary to the musician, to the violin maker, and to the piano tuner. It should be noted in passing that this is only one of the characteristics needed for the violin maker. He must also be settled, manually accurate, and indoor. But the piano tuner must be roving.

(*k*) Similarly our coöperation with the chemical industries, particularly the ink and paint industries, showed us the necessity of selecting men who possessed strongly the basic characteristic of color sense. It is obvious that this characteristic is necessary also in other occupations, such as house furnishing, window dressing, painting and decorating, and theatrical staging.

(*l*) We learn quickly that some men have manual accuracy and others manual inaccuracy. Where manual inaccuracy is inherent, it is well-nigh impossible to correct it ; but where accuracy is inherent and the man is inaccurate through habit, the defect can be remedied.

(*m*) Similarly we have the two elements mental accuracy and mental inaccuracy. The former has much the same meaning as the word "logical," and the latter as the word "illogical."

(*n*) Certain men are concentrative mentally; they bring all the light they possess to focus on the subject under consideration; they are mentally centripetal. On the other hand, we find men who are mentally centrifugal and who wander from the subject under consideration or flit from one subject to another; they are diffuse.

(*o*) Some men go to pieces in an emergency; whereas if they were given time to consider the situation they would hold together and act wisely. They possess slow mental coördination. The emergency man must possess rapid mental coördination. The latter is necessary for success in the baseball player, the locomotive engineer, the motorman, the surgeon. The former is usually typical of the philosopher, the jurist, the research scientist.

(*p*) One often hears it said of a man that he has no push, or that he lacks determination, backbone, grit, sand; other men are said to possess these qualities. The first we call static, which means to cause to stand still, and the second dynamic, which means to cause to move. It should be noted that the noisy man is not always a dynamic man — on the contrary, he is frequently static; while the quiet man is very frequently dynamic.

The list then reads:

(*a*) Physical strength
Physical weakness
(*b*) Mental
Manual
(*c*) Settled
Roving
(*d*) Indoor
Outdoor
(*e*) Directive
Dependent
(*f*) Original (creative)
Imitative
(*g*) Small scope
Large scope
(*h*) Adaptable
Self-centered

(*i*) Deliberate
Impulsive
(*j*) Music sense
(*k*) Color sense
(*l*) Manual accuracy
Manual inaccuracy
(*m*) Mental accuracy (logic)
Mental inaccuracy
(*n*) Concentration (mental focus)
Diffusion
(*o*) Rapid mental coördination
Slow mental coördination
(*p*) Dynamic
Static

DANGER IN HASTY JUDGMENT

Experience has warned us against the danger of hasty judgment; for we have found strong characteristics buried deep under the influence of environment, inborn controlling talents held repressed or stunted by acquired habits of life, and sometimes the habit is mistaken for the talent until patient experimenting or some unusual occurrence discovers the hidden ability. Let it be noted at once that while the characteristics are placed in juxtaposition, it does not follow that one may not be, for example, both mental and manual, or both an indoor and an outdoor man; further, one may not possess either characteristic to any marked degree.

It should be noted also that certain moral qualities, such as bravery and honesty, are not given on this list. While these are, of course, very important characteristics, and while certain jobs require them to a high degree, we have felt that the ethical qualities are not essential for the purposes for which this list was devised.

It is again desired to emphasize the fact that this is an empirical list, growing out of the observations of about five hundred young men in industrial work and university work connected with the engineering profession. It is probably too restricted, and may not contain characteristics which are fundamental. For example, we believe that there is another element which is not given and which is not a result of combinations of the elements given. The words "organization sense" have been suggested for it. The idea to be conveyed is something like that of the word "tidy," the natural tendency to keep things in proper and becoming neatness. This characteristic is evidenced in the way men keep their desks, the way they write their reports, and in the general orderliness of affairs within their jurisdiction.

Again, we find among our students two distinct types, one of which does a thing more for the personal satisfaction of doing it than for the immediate or prospective material gain, while the other places the material gain first. One plays the game for the game's sake; the other plays it as a means to a tangible prize. I know a doctor who sacrificed $10,000 a year to be a research scientist;

he is a vocational idealist. I know also a research scientist who gave up a brilliant career to acquire $5000 more a year; he is a vocational materialist.

The type of craftsman to whom pride in his product means more than time or money, and whose soul goes out through his fingers into the thing he makes, is of the first type; the other type makes the thing to sell at the largest profit. It is probable that most men have these two characteristics in about equal measure; that is to say, while they have pride in their product, they do not let this outweigh the commercial necessities. The sincere reformer is a type of the vocational idealist; the practical politician of the vocational materialist.

To the idealist the doing of the thing as well as he can possibly do it is the end; to the materialist the doing of it in such a way as to get the most material return is the end. In extreme cases the vocational idealist will suffer all kinds of privations, and let his family suffer too, rather than be less thorough and better fed. On the other extreme, the vocational materialist will drop any idea which does not pay and take up any which does.

In the fore part of this paper three things were mentioned as necessary results of work: two of them were joy in the doing of it or mental satisfaction, and a good living or physical satisfaction. When mental satisfaction dominates a man's work, he is idealistic; when physical satisfaction predominates, he is materialistic. These should probably be placed in the table of major characteristics.

The psychologist may object that these characteristics are not basic, that they are complex in that they are made up of simpler elements. This is true, but the same objection could be urged by the chemist against the engineer's use of the words "water," "air," "wrought iron," "steel," "brass," "wood," "granite," and "cement." And just as the hydraulic engineer uses "water," so does the shop manager use mental accuracy or originality; neither is concerned with the more refined science of the basic elements of which the substance or the characteristic is composed.

Of course the degree or strength of human characteristics can never be measured as can the strength of material things. The mind of even the lowliest man is too subtle a thing to be catalogued.

Hence the limitations of vocational guidance. I am of the opinion that for the present, vocational guidance can only point out in which types of occupations an individual will in all probability *not* be successful.

CHARACTERISTICS HAVE DIFFERENT MEANINGS

It will be contended, too, that a characteristic, as for example originality, has different meanings to the artist, the shopman, and the department-store manager ; that it depends upon the point of view. So it does, just as the quality of wood means a different thing to the paper maker, the bridge builder, and the furniture maker. But to each in his own field the meaning approaches a fairly well-defined standard.

It must be borne in mind that the results given here have been obtained from young men whose average age is about twenty years. How many of these characteristics are determinable in children from thirteen to sixteen years old I am not prepared to say, since I have had no experience with boys of this age.

While the classification given has been found empirically, the working of the principle of evolution is at once evident. Every distinct people possesses certain characteristics, the result of the thousands and thousands of years of conditions peculiar to it. Thus the Chinese are settled, the Arabs are roving, the Sicilians are impulsive, the Hindus are deliberate, the Japanese are manually accurate, the Persians possess a refined color sense. If a nation has been a roving nation for several thousand years and then a settled nation for several thousand years, some of its present-day representatives will be roving and some settled.

Any individual's characteristics are probably atavistic. If all the age-long impresses of the past were equally transmitted, all brothers would be alike. When an individual does not possess certain characteristics which he might be expected to possess, it is a case of arrested development of these characteristics in that individual. They are probably latent but inhibited, and will appear in his descendants.

EFFECT OF NOISE, FATIGUE, AND ENVIRONMENT ON WORKER

By Herman Schneider, Dean of the College of Engineering, University of Cincinnati

It is only within the past two generations that mankind has worked in masses within walls. For centuries men did individual, self-directed work almost entirely in the open. The change has come, of course, through the development of power devices, and dates from the invention of the steam engine.

In the second place, the industrial worker formerly knew a whole job rather than a part of it; he performed a great variety of functions in the completion of his task instead of endlessly repeating the same operation. The clockmaker made a whole clock, working individually, and the necessity of working out every part's relation to every other part gave the worker a mental stimulus and therefore a higher mental development. The finished product was all. his own — the desire for self-expression which every man has found an outlet through his work; and once having served a thorough apprenticeship he worked largely by self-direction.

Under our present highly organized industrial conditions the making of a clock is subdivided into a large number of operations. Each workman in a clock factory makes piece after piece of the same kind, principally by feeding material into a machine, and why he does it he need not know and usually is not told.

We are putting the brains into the machine and into the management office, and making the workman a purely automatic adjunct. It is unquestionable that much of the present spirit of industrial unrest is nature's protest against work without light, physical and mental.

It is this purely automatic, high-pressure work in closely crowded rooms which is the most ominous feature of modern industrialism, its most serious aspect being the effect upon the mental development. Scientific research has shown us that the monotonous rhythmic repetitions of the machine's motion and the monotonous rhythmic motion of feeding the machine produce a hypnotic, deadening influence on the mind. The lower brain centers, controlling habits, are developed at the expense of the higher thinking centers. As the habit becomes ingrained, the worker becomes more lethargic and automatic, and almost as incapable of independent, intelligent action as the machine itself. Research further shows that the higher centers in the brain of such a worker are in danger of getting into a permanent, inelastic, hopeless set, if a lively stimulus is not supplied.

Further, there is in every individual a desire for self-expression, and if this cannot be had in one's daily work nature will force an outlet for it. It cannot be dammed up very long; and since there is no outlet in the worker's daily task, it must come during his idle hours, and sometimes takes a form which leads to many of our most vexing sociological problems.

The situation, then, sifts down to this: energizing work is decreasing; enervating work is increasing. The physical workers are becoming more and more automatic, with the sure result that their minds are becoming more and more lethargic. The work itself is not character building; on the contrary, it is repressive, and when self-expression comes it is hardly energizing mentally. The real menace lies in the fact that in a self-governing industrial community the minds of the majority are in danger of becoming atrophied, or at best of becoming trifling and superficial, because of lack of continuous exercise in conjunction with the earning of a livelihood. The kind of citizenship that a republic needs cannot be built on sixty hours per week of automatic work. But we cannot reverse our present economic order of things. Automatic work is increasing and will continue to increase for a long time to come. The condition is here, and philosophical discussion will not remove it.

It is evident then that the law of physical labor must be divided into two laws; namely, the law of energizing work, which makes for progress, and the law of enervating work, which makes for retrogression. Nearly all the work still done in the open air, where there is a dependent sequence of operation, involving planning on the part of the worker, is energizing work. Specific examples may be cited in farm work, railroad work, and the building trades. Certain work done indoors, under good conditions of light and air, is also energizing; for example, the work of a toolmaker, a locomotive assembler, and a cabinetmaker. The enervating work has come through the subdivision of labor in factories, so that each worker does one thing over and over in the smallest number of cubic feet of space. This type is recognizable at once in the routine of the garment worker, the punch-press operator, the paper-box maker, the shoe worker, etc.

For the purpose of analyzing work, a scale has been devised in which the most energizing work is at the 100 per-cent point and the most enervating at the zero point. The 100 per-cent work is that of the locomotive engineer. This has been selected because his work has the following elements:

(a) It is done in the open air.

(b) It provides a well-rounded physical development.

(c) The constant improvements in locomotive design and in railroad appliances require continuous mental development.

(d) Mental alertness is constantly required for emergencies.

(e) A comprehensive grasp of the whole interdependent scheme of production (a railroad produces transportation) is essential.

(f) The conditions under which the same run is made are never alike.

(g) The work itself — not lectures or preachments or popular acclaim — breeds in the engineer the highest quality of good citizenship; namely, an instant willingness to sacrifice himself for the lives in the train behind him.

The zero point on the scale, or the most enervating work, is the work of a girl in her formative years in a steam laundry, when the following elements prevail:

(a) Supersaturated, vitiated air.

(b) Standing in a strained position.

(c) The work consisting of feeding one piece after another of the same kind at high speed into a machine.

(d) The hours of work being so long that fatigue poisons accumulate in the blood.

The scale is crude and lacks scientific accuracy. A statement, for example, that the work of a laster in a shoe factory is 40 per cent energizing would be a guess. But the purpose of the scale is not so much to arrive at a percentage as to establish some standard of actual work for the purpose of diagnosis and treatment. Three investigators, analyzing the work of a laster, might classify it as 30 per cent, 40 per cent, and 50 per cent energizing. The difference in their classifications would lead to a closer analysis and hence to a surer treatment.

To take a specific analysis, consider two adjoining weave sheds of a silk mill. Going first to mill A, you find a long room with an aisle down the center, on each side of which are the machines. Between the machines there is ample space for the operative (nearly always a girl) to go up and down tying the broken threads. In the main aisle and adjacent to each machine is a chair. When the girl has finished one round of her machines, she rests for a short period of time, and in this way fatigue is prevented. The two girls of adjoining machines usually time their rounds so that their rests come simultaneously. The noise in the mill is so slight that they can converse without any effort. The light is good, the air is not vitiated, the rest periods are sufficient, and there is no nervous tension from noise or speed. The work is not monotonously automatic, the position of the body is not strained; but, on the contrary, many muscles are lightly brought into play. However, the work itself does not stimulate any mental activity nor develop any of the finer and higher mental qualities. It can be classed as about 70 per cent energizing.

The silk after leaving this mill is sent to mill B, where a number of strands are woven into a single strong strand. Since the silk is strengthened, the machine can be run at a higher speed. On entering mill B you are confronted with a noise so great that talking is entirely out of the question. The layout at mill B is precisely the same as at mill A, except that there are no chairs in the aisle. There are no rests between the rounds which the operator makes of the machines, since the speed does not permit. Talking is utterly impossible because of the noise. This mill is at once diagnosed as the sore spot of the concern. The investigator is enabled to say to the owner : " This is your trouble center ; here is where agitation begins. More operatives leave this mill per year than leave mill A. These workers are suspicious of each other's actions, particularly of the foreman's. They feel that you are their natural enemy. The foreman himself is a grouch. More jarring families, more unkempt back yards are represented here than in mill A, and finally the actual efficiency of this mill is less than in mill A, and the work more strenuous." The work is classified as low as 10 per cent, and yet the only difference between the two mills is in noise, speed, and lack of rest. The noise is a mechanical engineer's problem, possible of solution. The speed and the fatigue are within the owner's control. With these three factors eliminated, the work would go up to 70 per cent energizing ; as much work would be produced under the better conditions, since the force could be kept as intact in mill B as in mill A.

Two doctors of industry would treat mill B in opposite ways. In order to increase the production, one would increase speed, ignore the noise, study the motions to eliminate waste moments, and by the unanswerable argument of figures show you that production must go up. This is the headache-powder method and leads to a constantly broken, shifting, dissatisfied working force. The second doctor would decrease the speed and cut down the noise, insist on carefully determined rest periods, and thereby maintain a sound organization of skilled workers. Equally important, he would raise the general efficiency, and hence the economic efficiency, of the community. Nor would he stop at that, for he would further strive by known methods to introduce additional conditions, so that the work in both mills would be brought to about 80 per cent, which would probably be the limit for this class of work.

It should be noted that where the work is done under conditions which permit the operatives to talk, without interference to their work, the rating is much higher than where such is not the case. When we walk out, habit cells control the action, but we can walk and think at the same time. The same principle holds in automatic occupations. If the motions are not too rhythmic, both of the hand and of the machine, and conversation is permitted and encouraged, the work is not nearly so repressive. In a certain mill, employing girls at strictly automatic work, the employees were placed facing one way, so that one operative looked upon the back of another; between adjacent operatives was a small partition. This mill had to replenish its entire force each year, until the scheme was changed to a round-table plan, which encouraged conversation. After this the losses were normal.

An interesting case of shop psychology is the following: In a certain piano factory a number of girls were employed to assemble the mechanism which transmits the action when the key is struck to the strings. Each girl attached a piece with a limited number of motions, and was paid on the piecework plan. These employees were the most discontented in the firm, and were constantly shifting to other occupations. Various means, such as rest rooms and decorated surroundings, were tried without success. As a last resort, the foreman got a fine big Maltese cat and placed it in the room one morning before the girls arrived. This solved the trouble completely. The cat compelled rest periods, for every now and then it would jump into a girl's lap and take her attention from her work for a few moments, and in this way relieved the tension of the high speed and permitted the elimination of fatigue poisons at irregular but sufficient intervals. Every girl planned at home to bring something in her lunch basket for the cat to eat, whereas attempts to get them interested in the decorating of rooms failed. When girls left this firm and went elsewhere, where there was no cat, they quickly returned. Production increased and peace reigned. The commercializing of a woman's instinct for a cat probably energized the work 10 per cent. It was found also that the introduction of the cat began to arouse an interest in the other betterment plans, which had originally failed. This particular case is worthy of a very careful psychological analysis.

The details just stated are cited not so much to show specific methods of procedure as to emphasize the basic fact that we are, individually and collectively, human units, towns, states, and, as a nation, what our work makes us. We have just pulled out of a thousand-year swamp up to firmer ground, and whether we go higher or begin to slide back depends upon how energizing our work is.

· It is fundamental that mankind must do stimulating work or retrogress. This is the bedrock upon which our constructive programs of education, industry, sociology, of living, must rest. Fortunately we are now far enough away from the thousand-year swamp so that one may safely propose, as a thesis, that only that civilization will prevail whose laws and life conform most nearly to natural law. The spirit of unrest, whether it be evidenced by the spontaneous and seemingly unaccountable strike of automatic workers, the questioning introspection of university faculties; the open defiance of law, or the cry for the doctor of industry, is the headache-giving warning of deeper seated organic trouble.

THE PERMANENCE OF INTERESTS AND THEIR RELATION TO ABILITIES

By Professor Edward L. Thorndike, Teachers College, Columbia University

(From the *Popular Science Monthly*, November, 1912)

There is a wide range of opinion amongst both theorists and practitioners with respect to the importance of the interests of children and young people. These early likes and dislikes, attractions and repulsions, are by some taken to be prime symptoms of what is for the welfare of the individual or even of the species. By others they are discarded as trivial, fickle, products of more or less adventitious· circumstances, meaning little or nothing for the nature or welfare of anyone. It seems therefore desirable to report whatever impersonal estimates of the significance and value of interests one can secure.

I have measured the significance of interests in certain limited particulars, with very definite results, and shall in this article describe these results and the method by which they were obtained and by which anyone can readily verify them.

The particular problems attacked all concerned the *relative* amount or *relative* intensity or *relative* strength of interests *within the same individual*. That is, " greater interest" will always mean the interest which was greater than the others possessed by the same individual; "little interest" will mean little in comparison with the individual's other interests. The question " To what extent is the strength of an interest from ten to fourteen prophetic of the strength which that interest will manifest in adult life ? " will mean " To what extent will it, in adult life, keep the same place in an order of the individual's interests which it had in the order which described his childish preferences ? " Amounts or degrees of ability or capacity will similarly always mean *relative* amounts.

Thus, to say that a person was, during high school, most interested in mathematics and most able at mathematics will mean that the person liked mathematics more than *he* did anything else, and did better at mathematics than *he* did at anything else. The statement will not imply anything about the degree of his interest or ability in comparison with other individuals.

The particular problems attacked are limited further to seven varieties of interests and the corresponding varieties of ability or capacity : namely, mathematics, history, literature, science, music, drawing, and other handwork (this last being defined as " carpentering, sewing, gardening, cooking, carving, etc."). All comparisons or relations of interests and abilities are within this group, so that, for example, the statement that John Doe had interests in the high-school period distributed in the same order of strength as in the elementary-school period will mean that these seven interests had the same order in the two periods.

Such being the meanings of terms and the limitations of the field of inquiry, I have measured :

1. The permanence of interests from the last three years of the elementary-school period to the junior year of college or professional school.

2. The correlation, or correspondence, between interests in a given subject and ability therein at the elementary-school period.

3. The same relation at the high-school period.

4. The same relation toward the end of the college or professional course.

5. The same relation on the whole (this will be explained later).

6. The correlation or correspondence between *interest* in a given subject at the end of the *elementary-school* period (during its last three years) and *ability* in that subject toward the end of the *college* or professional-school period.

The results to be here reported are for one hundred individuals, juniors in Barnard College, Columbia College, and Teachers College. These results are corroborated by a similar but less minute study of two hundred other individuals.

The original measures are the judgments of the hundred individuals themselves concerning the order of their interests in mathematics, history, literature, and the rest, at each of the three periods. Each individual reported in writing in response to the following instructions :

EXPERIMENT 34. (TABLE 1)

Consider your interests in the activities listed below during the last three years of your attendance at the elementary school. Mark (under El. Interest) with a 1 the activity which at that period was to you the most interesting of the seven listed. Mark the one that was next most interesting, 2; and so on.

Record similarly (under H. S. Interest) the order of interest for you during the high-school period. Record similarly (under C. Interest) the order of interest for you now.

Pay no attention at present to the spaces under ability.

Later he reported similarly his judgment as to his relative ability in each of these seven lines of activity in response to the following instructions :

TABLE 1

	IN LAST THREE YEARS OF ELEMENTARY SCHOOL		IN HIGH SCHOOL		IN COLLEGE	
	El. Interest	El. Ability	H. S. Interest	H. S. Ability	C. Interest	C. Ability
Mathematics						
History						
Literature						
Science						
Music						
Drawing						
Other handwork[1] . .						

EXPERIMENT 35

Consider your ability in each of the activities listed in Table 1, as it existed during the last three years of your attendance on the elementary school. Rank the activities from 1 to 7 according to your ability in each, marking that activity in which you had most ability, 1. Record your ranks under the column headed El. Ability in Table 1. Record similarly (under H. S. Ability) the order of ability for you during the high-school period. Record similarly (under C. Ability) the order of ability for you now.

[1] Other handwork means carpentering, sewing, gardening, cooking, carving, etc.

TABLE 2

	In Last Three Years of Elementary School		In High School		In College	
	El. Interest	El. Ability	H. S. Interest	H. S. Ability	C. Interest	C. Ability
Mathematics	3	3	3	2	4	2
History	1	1	4	3	1	1
Literature	2	2	2	1	2	3
Science	4	4	1	4	3	4
Music	5	5	7	5	5	7
Drawing	6	6	5	7	6	5
Other handwork . .	7	7	6	7	7	6

We have, then, for each of the hundred a record such as is shown in the case of one of them in Table 2. These data are obviously subject to certain errors of memory, prejudice, carelessness, and the like, which will later be given due attention. It will be best to consider first what the meaning of the records would be, were each number a perfectly true statement of the relative strength of the interest or ability in question.

Consider, then, this sample record as perfectly true, and compute from it the differences between each subject's position for interest in the last three years of the elementary-school period (column 1) and for the high-school period (column 3).

We have :

Mathematics 0
History 3
Literature 0
Science 3
Music 2
Drawing 1
Other handwork 1
    Sum of the seven differences 10

These facts are repeated in the first column of Table 3.

Computing the other differences as shown in the second and third column of Table 3, we have for this individual the means of answering question 1, concerning the permanence of interests. If

TABLE 3

	I Difference between El. interest rank and H. S. interest rank	II Difference between El. interest rank and C. interest rank	III Difference between H. S. interest rank and C. interest rank
Mathematics	0	1	1
History	3	0	3
Literature	0	0	0
Science	3	1	2
Music	2	0	2
Drawing	1	0	1
Other handwork	1	0	1
Total	10	2	10

the individual had remained unchanged in his interests from any one period to any other, the appropriate seven differences of Table 3 would obviously have been all zeros, and the sum of that column would have been zero. If, on the other hand, he had, from one to another period, changed as completely as possible, the sum of the appropriate column of Table 3 would have been 24 (7–1, 6–2, 5–3, 4–4, 3–5, 2–6, 1–7, giving 24). If the individual's interests had been due to mere caprice, changing their relative strength at random, the sum of any column of Table 3 would approximate 16. For if a 1 is equally likely to become a 1, 2, 3, 4, 5, 6, or 7, and so also of a 2, a 3, a 4, etc., the average result will be 16.[1]

Any quantity below 16 as the sum of a column, then, means some permanence of interests in the individual in question, and the degree of permanence is measured by the divergence from 16 toward 0.

For the permanence from the elementary-school period to the junior year of college or professional school in my hundred individuals this figure is, on the average, 9, three fifths of the individuals showing sums of from 6 to 12 for column 2 of Table 3. This average result of 9 may be expressed as a coefficient of correlation,

[1] 1 becoming 1, 2, 3, 4, 5, 6, 7 gives as differences 0, 1, 2, 3, 4, 5, 6;
2 becoming 1, 2, 3, 4, 5, 6, 7 gives as differences 1, 0, 1, 2, 3, 4, 5;
3 becoming 1, 2, 3, 4, 5, 6, 7 gives as differences 2, 1, 0, 1, 2, 3, 4.
Continuing and dividing the sum of the 49 differences by 49, we get 2⅓ for the average difference by mere chance shifting, and 7 × 2⅓, or 16, as the average sum of a column in Table 3 by mere chance shifting.

or correspondence, such as is in customary use to measure resemblances of various sorts. It is equivalent to a correlation of over .60. This means that a person's interests in the late elementary-school period resemble, in their order and relative strength, the constitution of interests which he will have eight years later to the extent of six tenths of perfect resemblance. For the coefficient of correlation is a magnitude running from — 1.0 (which would be the coefficient if the sum of differences was 24) through 0 (which would correspond to a sum of differences of 16) to + 1.0 (which would correspond to a sum of differences of 0). A sum of differences of 8 means a resemblance greater than half of perfect resemblance, as the reader expert in the mathematics of probability will realize. The sums 12, 10, 8, and 6, in fact, mean coefficients of resemblance or correlation of + .38, + .55, + .71, and + .83 respectively.

The effect which the errors to which the original reports are subject would have in making this obtained degree of permanence too high or too low may now be considered. The chance errors—the mere failures of memory or carelessness in report or inability to distinguish slight differences in the interest of nearly equally interesting subjects — would make the obtained estimate *too low*. Their action would be to change the true sum of differences, whatever it was, toward 16, or the true coefficient of correlation toward zero. The effect of errors of prejudice, on the other hand, might have been toward so distorting memory and observation as to make the order given for interests in the two later periods more like the order given for the elementary-school period than was in truth the case. This would, of course, unduly raise the obtained estimate of permanence, that is, lower the sum of the differences. I do not believe that such tendencies to read present interests into the past, and to leave the order reported for one period unchanged so far as possible, are very strong, there being a contrary tendency to remember and look for *differences*. On the whole, I should expect the effect of the large chance errors in *lowering* the estimate of permanence to nearly or quite counteract whatever balance of prejudice there may be in favor of similarity of interests or projection of present conditions into the past.

A correlation of .6 or .7 seems, then, to be approximately the true degree of resemblance between the relative degree of an interest in a child of from ten to fourteen and in the same person at twenty-one.

Consider now the difference between a subject's rank for interest and its rank for ability at the same period. Using the same sample record (Table 2), and assuming it to be a true record of the order of interests, and computing from it the difference between each subject's position for interest in the elementary-school period (column 1) and its position for ability in the same period (column 2), we have:

Mathematics 0
History 0
Literature 0
Science 0
Music 0
Drawing 0
Other handwork 0

These facts are repeated in the first column of Table 4. Similar facts for this same individual, for the differences between the order for interest and the order for ability in the high-school period and in the college period, are given in the second and third columns of Table 4.

TABLE 4

	I Differences between El. interest and El. ability	II Differences between H. S. interest and H. S. ability	III Differences between C. interest and C. ability
Mathematics	0	1	2
History	0	1	0
Literature	0	1	1
Science	0	3	1
Music	0	2	2
Drawing	0	2	1
Other handwork	0	0	1

If at any period an individual has greatest ability in the subject which is most interesting to him, next greatest ability in the next most interesting subject, and so on, the sum of the seven differences for that period will be zero. If the order of ability was as unlike as possible to the order of interest, this sum would be 24 ; and if the relation between interest and ability was that of mere chance, this sum would be 16. Any quantity below 16 as the sum of a column in Table 4, then, means some positive relation or resemblance between the individual's degrees of interest and his degrees of ability.

For the hundred individuals studied this figure is on the average approximately 5, being practically the same for the elementary-school period, for the high-school period, and for the college period. This average result may be expressed as a coefficient of correlation of .88. Nearly three fourths of the individuals show records between 2 and 8 inclusive — that is, correlations of from .70 to .98.

If, in the case of any individual, we add together the three ranks for each subject in interest at the three periods and do like-wise for its ability ranks, we have measures of the general order of the seven subjects for interest and for ability over the whole period from, say, the age of eleven to the age of twenty-one. Thus, in the sample chosen, the combined ranks give :

	SUM OF RANKS FOR INTEREST, ALL THREE PERIODS	SUM OF RANKS FOR ABILITY, ALL THREE PERIODS
Mathematics	10	. 7
History	6	5
Literature	6	6
Science	8	12
Music	17	17
Drawing	17	18
Other handwork	20	19

Turning these into positions from 1 to 7, we have :

	GENERAL RANK FOR INTEREST	GENERAL RANK FOR ABILITY
Mathematics	4	3
History	$1\frac{1}{2}$	1
Literature	$1\frac{1}{2}$	2
Science	3	4
Music	$5\frac{1}{2}$	5
Drawing	$5\frac{1}{2}$	6
Other handwork	7	7

The differences in the order are, then, 1, $\frac{1}{2}$, $\frac{1}{2}$, 1, $\frac{1}{2}$, $\frac{1}{2}$, and 0, their sum being 4.

I have made the calculation for each of the hundred individuals. On the average this sum of differences is approximately $4\frac{1}{2}$ and corresponds to a coefficient of correlation of .91. The individual whose interests follow his capacities least closely still shows a substantial resemblance (nearly .5). The correlation between an individual's order of subjects for interest and his order for ability is in fact one of the closest of any that are known. A person's relative interests are an extraordinarily accurate symptom of his relative capacities.

The effect of the errors to which the original reports are subject is on the whole probably to make this obtained degree of resemblance between interest and capacity too *low*. Errors due to accident, carelessness, and inability to distinguish or to remember slight differences in interest or in capacity would make the sums of difference in the long run greater — and the degree of resemblance obtained, less — than the true facts would have given. The only sort of error that could make the obtained resemblance *greater* than the true fact would be an error whereby either order was falsified to make it more like the other — notably the possible tendency to rate one's self higher than one should for ability in a subject which one likes. On the whole the resemblance between interest and ability may safely be placed at about .9 of perfect resemblance.

I have computed the resemblance between *interest in the last three years of the elementary* school and *capacity in the college period* as a partial measure of the extent to which early interest could be used as a symptom of adult capacity. The average for the hundred individuals is a coefficient of correlation, or resemblance, of .60.

I have also, for comparison with the last measurement and with the measurement of the resemblance of interest in the late elementary period to interest in the college period, computed the coefficient of correlation, or resemblance, between the order of the seven subjects for *ability* in the elementary and their order for *ability* in the college period, using the records from these same hundred individuals. The average resemblance obtained is six and a half tenths, or slightly closer than that for early and late interest.

These facts unanimously witness to the importance of early interests. They are shown to be far from fickle and evanescent. On the contrary, the order of interests at twenty shows six tenths of perfect resemblance to the order from eleven to fourteen, and has changed therefrom little more than the order of abilities has changed. It would indeed be hard to find any feature of a human being which was a much more permanent fact of his nature than his relative degrees of interest in different lines of thought and action.

Interests are also shown to be symptomatic, to a very great extent, of present and future capacity or ability. Either because one likes what he can do well, or because one gives zeal and effort to what he likes, or because interest and ability are both symptoms of some fundamental feature of the individual's original nature, or because of the combined action of all three of these factors, interest and ability are bound very closely together. The bond is so close that either may be used as a symptom for the other almost as well as for itself.

The importance of these facts for the whole field of practice with respect to early diagnosis, vocational guidance, the work of social secretaries, deans, advisers, and others who direct students' choices of schools, studies, and careers, is obvious. They should be taken account of in such practice until they are verified or modified by data obtained by a better method, and such data should be soon collected. The better method is, of course, to get the measurements of relative interest and of relative ability not from memory but at the time, and not from individuals' reports alone but by objective tests. Such an investigation requires a repeated survey of each individual at three or more periods, say in 1912, 1915, and 1920, and demands skill and pertinacity in keeping track of the hundred or more children and arranging for the second and third series of reports and tests. I hope that some one of my readers will be moved to undertake it.

OPPORTUNITIES IN SCHOOL AND INDUSTRY FOR CHILDREN OF THE STOCKYARDS DISTRICT

By Ernest L. Talbert

(From the Report of an Investigation carried on under the Direction of the Board of The University of Chicago Settlement)

INTRODUCTION: THE PROBLEM, THE METHOD, AND THE NEIGHBORHOOD

THE PROBLEM

What are the industrial opportunities for children, especially those between fourteen and sixteen years of age, in the stockyards district? What are the jobs they secure, their wages, and the chances for advancement? Does the public school adjust them to the economic environment? What is the attitude of parent and child to the school and to the job? What is the relation of the income of the family to the early leaving of school? What is done to bridge the gap between school and work, and to guide the youth to the vocation suited to his capacity and to future usefulness? What may be done?

These are the main topics of inquiry in this study. They relate principally to the immediate situation in the school, the family, and juvenile work, but in their implications they are a part of the wider problem of the moral and civic welfare of the children and of the community. They touch the effect of the work which father and child pursue upon social attitude, the consequences of irregular employment and "blind-alley" jobs. They revive the problem of the function of the public school in an industrial democracy.

THE METHOD

It may be claimed that the present study has the advantage of being focused on a limited area and of proceeding from a social settlement. To know the neighborhood, to have children and parents come to the residents looking for a job, and to be in touch with principals and teachers of the local public schools is to secure points of contact and a coöperation generally denied to the census taker, and the material secured is likely to be more accurate, even if more restricted in scope. Finding a position is to the boy and girl a specific need, which takes away the natural resentment when questions are asked. The union of vocational help and keeping of schedules, therefore, is a way of approach different from that of Miss Susan Kingsbury in her investigation for the Massachusetts Commission on Industrial and Technical Education, and of Miss Rachel Edwards for the St. Louis School of Social Economy. Miss Kingsbury and her assistants secured their valuable data from representative sections of Massachusetts by the usual method of house-to-house canvass and interviews with employers and school officials. Miss Edwards, in like manner, studied the city of St. Louis. Their reports are comprehensive, taking in the whole situation, but suffer from the extension of the field and the necessarily short and slight acquaintance with the persons consulted. An immigrant community, largely depending on the packing houses for employment, in which the University Settlement has for years been a recognized center, presents another problem.

The Settlement, of course, has long been a means of securing employment, so that a kind of historical connection was already established. The extension of this endeavor during the nine months spent in this investigation took the following directions:

1. Coöperation with employers, visits to firms which employ boys and girls, and arrangements by which the employers agreed to notify us of vacancies.

2. Personal letters asking for a conference sent to boys who have left school to go to work.

3. Observation of the tastes and abilities of the children looking for work, advice as to the most desirable occupation, securing of the best place available, and following up the worker so that connection with his work might not be needlessly broken.

4. Preparation of schedules, part to be filled out by the applicant. The schedules included these points: date of leaving school; age; grade; reasons for going to work given by parent and child;

attitude toward school and future occupation ; industrial biography
— wages and treatment by employers ; income of the family ; attendance at night school ; and other evidence of definite interests.

RACIAL ELEMENTS

The people living in the vicinity of the University Settlement
are largely immigrants, comparatively recent, from Russia and
southeastern Europe. The region south of Forty-seventh Street
is considered a desirable residence district, and the Bohemians,
Lithuanians, and Poles who are prospering tend to leave the more
crowded tenements to the north for the use of the recent arrivals.
There is a sprinkling of Irish and German, although the successive waves of immigration — Polish, Bohemian, Lithuanian, and
Slovak — have scattered the older settlers. A count of 904 boys
and girls from the local public schools who received their "working
papers" during the period between June, 1908, and June, 1911,
shows the following percentages, taking the nationality of the father
as a criterion :

	PERCENTAGE
Bohemian	31
Polish	28
Lithuanian	11
German	10
Irish	8
American	8
Miscellaneous	4

The same count suggests the grouping of races about the local
public schools. From the standpoint of number the Seward School
has a majority of Polish, then in order Bohemian, Lithuanian, German, Irish, Slovak, and American. The Hamline School shows a
majority of Bohemian, then in order Polish, Irish, German, and
Lithuanian ; the Hedges School is dominantly Bohemian, while
the Seward branch, closest to the stockyards, contains a large
preponderance of Polish children.

The ratio, of course, does not represent the exact distribution of
races in the district, but it does indicate the large majority of the
foreign children over the "Americanized." Consequently, assimi-
lation is imperfect ; Old-World customs are not yet adjusted to our

traditions. As will be seen later, the child is often in subjection to the patriarchal authority of a parent ignorant of the economic as well as of other resources of America. There is an advantage in dealing with some unusual conditions found in a foreign industrial community, for the low family standards and the fewness of opportunities put the school to its severest test and allow us to see the elements of the problem with greater clearness. However, to anticipate again, the general situation regarding the work of children is not materially different from that proved true of places as remote as England. The problem is not that of race.[1] At first it was thought that a marked difference in the fortunes of children after leaving school would be found to follow racial lines, but except for a slight preference of Bohemian and German parents to. have their children follow trades, the situation is the same for all, as far as nationality is concerned.

SECTION I. THE SITUATION IN THE SCHOOL

A large number of the children in our district attend, at some time, the parochial school. Often they leave, after confirmation, to continue in the public school until they are fourteen years old. The, teachers in the public schools are confronted with the difficulty of harmonizing two courses of study having diverse aims and methods. It is difficult to adjust the ecclesiastical ideal of the Catholic school to the undenominational and civic purpose of the municipal schools, and a part of the dissatisfaction and dropping out of school comes during the critical period when the parish-school child tries to accommodate himself to the public school.

There is excellent teaching in the schools of the stockyards district, and there are capable, enthusiastic principals; there is also some ineffective teaching and failure to keep in contact with the pupil's interests as he approaches adolescence. Judged from the confessions of many administrators in the reports of the National

---

[1] Mr. Ayres reaches the conclusion that in America the schools reach the child of the foreigner more generally than they do the child of the native-born American. Cf. his table showing percentages of children of native parentage as compared with children of foreign parentage in school at the ages five to fourteen. In the United States more white children of native parents are illiterate than is the case with white children of foreign parentage ("Laggards in our Schools," pp. 16, 105, 115).

Education Association, this defect is not confined to one locality. In general the primary grades, influenced by the constructive play activities of the kindergarten, are more successful than the upper grades. Principals and teachers recognize this fact clearly, but the lack of home stimulus, the faulty knowledge of our language and institutions, and the precarious family incomes all conspire to defeat the most heroic attempts to " hold " the pupils after the fifth grade. The excellent Chicago Course of Study, introduced by Superintendent Young, because of its attention to the economic, civic, and historical background of the city and the state, will do much to give breadth of outlook to the growing youth, if well taught by teachers possessing a social and evolutionary perspective ; and the success of the cooking, sewing, and manual-training instruction now offered points to the need of extending such opportunities.[1] Meanwhile, the struggle of those in authority to " raise the standard of scholarship " so as to make it harder for the children to secure work certificates by adding to the reading and writing qualifications now existent is pathetic and useless without the introduction of direct occupational interest from the beginning.[2] As it now is, the " subnormal room " is the best place for boys and girls of active, nonbookish dispositions to find free outlet to the demand for spontaneous expression. The principal of the Hamline School tells the story of a subnormal-room girl who, in the absence of the regular teacher during the passing out of the children, rose to

---

[1] Since this was written, more manual and occupational instruction has been provided in the upper grades of the elementary school. This is commendable. Still, the new courses appear to have the character of the ordinary manual training. What is more desirable is separate vocational courses. There should be teachers conversant with shop methods and discipline. Vocational-training methods ought to be given a fair trial. To add to an already full curriculum a number of occupational subjects taught according to the formal pedagogical methods is clearly an unsatisfactory compromise.

[2] The Illinois law provides that a work certificate may be granted to the child by the school authorities when he reaches the age of fourteen, that until he is sixteen the child shall be either in school or at work, that the period of daily work shall be limited to eight hours, and that dangerous employments shall not be entered.

The glaring defect of the laws regulating juvenile labor is that no efficient machinery is provided by which the child may be kept track of until he is sixteen. He may elude the truant officers entirely. If he leaves a job he retains his working papers. The compulsory-education department does not have a record of his whereabouts. Thousands of boys and girls are thrown out upon the streets each year. There is no educational oversight. The result is demoralizing idleness or entrance into an economic atmosphere peculiarly unsuited to the first requirement of adolescence — free expression under sympathetic supervision.

the occasion and directed the marching with skill. Such executive capacity is likely to be wasted in the case of many when a school system puts a premium upon passive receptivity and "recitation." It is small wonder that boys grow restless and girls impatient to escape a régime in which they can see little present meaning.

To add to the growing proof of the elimination from school as the child grows older, we have the figures prepared from the record of attendance in the Seward School, June 23, 1911 :

ATTENDANCE

Grade	No. of Pupils
Kindergarten	94
First	336
Second	173
Third	111
Fourth	136
Fifth	125
Sixth	61
Seventh	39
Eighth	41

It is clear that after the fifth grade there is a marked decrease. The total number of pupils up to the fifth grade, not including those in the kindergarten, is 756 ; compared with the primary grades, the grammar grades — from the fifth through the eighth — contain only 266 pupils. That is, in the upper grades, where most of the liberalizing forces which exist in the school are brought to bear on the child, there are only about one third as many students to work with, a loss in numbers of 490 pupils.

It is furthermore true that the high school has comparatively little influence on the life of our neighborhood. Yet teacher and principal are practically forced to urge the child to take more advantage of the regular free-school facilities, because of their loyalty to the school system.[1] There are few alternatives to bring before

[1] In this connection a statement made by the eighth-grade teacher of the Seward School, as to the future plans of the graduates, is relevant. She said that eight girls and five boys announced their intention to enter high school, two boys and one girl were looking for work, one boy and one girl were to attend business college, one girl was needed at home to do the housework, one girl was planning to go to the new Technical High School, and three were uncertain. The information at least shows a drift of opinion. The number who actually reach high school will probably be smaller than that given, and the evident desire of the teacher that they should go very likely provoked some of her pupils to promise.

the child, and if there is no handwork nor machine-shop course in
the elementary curriculum it is difficult for the boy to realize the
far-away possibilities of the technical high school. As it is, the
enthusiasm for technical training of the principal and manual-
training teacher of the Seward School influences a considerable
number of the graduates to attend Lake High School, but the
number is small in comparison with the many who require such
training and skill. The solicitor for the "business college" rises
to the emergency, and vividly pictures the prosperity following a
thorough three months' course in his institution.

The principal of the Lake High School corroborates the statement that few boys and girls of the district either start or continue
in high school. The instruction offered in the technical high
schools is closed to a large number of students who drop out of
school before the eighth grade. These children are not given the
kind of instruction answering to their varying needs. The failure
of the high school to reach the handworking groups is strikingly
exhibited in the stockyards district.[1]

GRADES AND AGES OF CHILDREN LEAVING SCHOOL

Grade reached	Number of Pupils	Percentage (Boys and Girls)
1	1	—
2	4	—
3	10	3
4	52	11
5	79	16
6	129	26
7	133	27
8	89	17
Total	497	100

The material for this table comes from the work certificates of
497 cases issued between January 1, 1909, and June 1, 1911, by
the principals of the local schools.

[1] The seven instances of high-school attendance found are representative of the degree
to which the high school attracts and selects. Of the three boys, A was taking the two years'
commercial course, and selling papers to piece out the family income. B, a Polish boy, after
trying errand-boy jobs for two months, was planning to go, although the father's weekly pay

Slightly over one half of the total left school in the sixth and seventh grades, and in most cases their systematic " education " was finished. It cannot be repeated too often that this exodus takes place in the wide-awake, imaginative period of youth. Nearly one third of the number left school before reaching the sixth grade. Of the 17 per cent in the eighth grade, many were not graduated. A few left in order to attend business college.

The figures for the 286 boys and the 211 girls may be given separately :

Boys			Girls		
Grade	Number	Percentage	Grade	Number	Percentage
1	0	—	1	1	—
2 . . :	4	—	2	0	—
3	7	—	3	3	—
4	36	13	4	16	7
5	52	18	5	27	13
6	66	23	6	63	30
7	74	25	7	59	29
8	47	16	8	42	19

Before the seventh grade was reached 59 per cent of the boys had stopped school and 52 per cent of the girls. The number of older boys who come to this country and attend school for a brief period in order to fulfill the educational requirement, explains in part the higher proportion of boys. During the sixth and seventh grades 59 per cent of the girls received their work certificates, as compared with 48 per cent of the boys. A serious situation is seen in the branch Seward School, where in the last two years 35 per cent of the boys stopped in the fifth grade, while the corresponding highest percentage of the girls was 31 per cent for the sixth grade.

was only six to eight dollars. C was the son of a prospering Jewish merchant, was a student by inclination, and bound for the University and one of the learned professions, according to his mother.

One of the girls went to high school for a month, then poverty caused by a strike, in which the father took part, forced the daughter into a gum factory. The family is now in better circumstances, but there is no sign that the girl wishes a return to school or that her mother desires it. B is pursuing the business course ; C, after six months, went to a business college, and was searching for a place when she was visited. The fourth girl belonged to a superior, ambitious family and was studying the classical course preparatory to the normal school and the teaching profession.

Age of Pupils leaving School

The average age of a total of 608 boys and girls receiving work certificates between January 1, 1909, and June 1, 1911, was found to be fourteen years and five months, the average for girls being less than that for boys. Twenty-nine per cent of the 377 boys went to work *as soon as they became fourteen years old.* All those less than fourteen (at the time of the June closing some under fourteen take out their papers) and those not yet fourteen years and one month old are placed in the above class. In some cases the children refuse to stay in school, even though their graduation comes in a week's time ahead. Of the girls, 35 per cent stopped school when they reached fourteen, again showing the inferior level set for girls. The whole situation discloses how firmly and generally a minimum standard upheld by law is responded to by this community.

Reasons for leaving School

There is some value in catching the drift of sentiment as it comes from the lips of parents and children. Their criticism of the school is neither discriminating nor conclusive, yet a successful school system cannot afford to neglect the reaction of its pupils and patrons. To get at the matter, the question was put, Why did A leave school ? The answers give only dominant hearsay evidence, since there is a difference between professed reasons and real ones.

The answers grouped below are from both parent and child. In some cases, several joint reasons were given by the same person. Necessarily, we are led away from the immediate school problem in the classification of replies.

Reasons given

A. The first group relates to the illness either of child or relatives, without special connection with financial difficulties.

Cause	Number of Answers
Father ill	9
Mother ill	8
Other relatives ill	2
Illness of child	8

Four girls and one boy left because of defective eyes or general ill health ; one boy was represented by his mother as needing "rest"; and a woman said that "hot weather is bad for Nick."

B. The second group refers to the economic status of the family. Eight persons were needed to work at home, either in the parent's store or "to tend the baby." One hundred and seventy-one answers specified the need of money as the determining cause, many adding the explanation of idleness, irregular work, and low wages of members of the family.

C. A third group of miscellaneous reasons is not without suggestiveness. Ten boys and girls confessed that being "too big and awkward" made them objects of ridicule. Two girls wanted money for clothes; four said "I was confirmed." One boy complained that he was teased for being a Jew; four were "too old" to go to school (although two of them were but fourteen); a number said "I am fourteen"; one youngster made the proud reply, "I was in the fifth grade"; and others revealed the same assumptions. Four answers gave, "It's the way we do in our family."

D. The fourth group concerns the opinion of the school. The replies are detailed in the loose fashion of the answerers' words.

REASON	NUMBER OF ANSWERS
Did n't like school	36
Did n't learn	18
Did n't like teacher	15
Preferred to work	13
Trouble in school	11
Subjects not interesting	5
"Too bad" in school	3
"Mad at principal"	2
Put back	2
Teacher struck him	1
Teacher advised leaving	1
Quit to learn something useful	3

In all, 330 answers are represented. Out of this number 110 gave a reason bearing negatively on the school, and 171 gave lack of money as the prime cause of leaving school. Miss Edwards found that 202 out of 1085 children in St. Louis gave the economic cause, and she estimates that probably a half of these misrepresented the situation. How far this is true in our district will be considered later.

ATTITUDE OF PARENTS TO THE SCHOOL

While vague in details of criticism, the parents are dissatisfied with the schools. They feel that something is wrong with the teachers and the subjects taught; often they cannot see the practical advantages of " schooling " for their children. Some women complain that the sixth-, seventh-, or eighth-grade teacher does not " understand " their sons and daughters. Irritation is apt to assume a personal cause, and the natural tendency of mothers to take the side of their children leads them to express unreasonable dislike for teachers. Yet there is some real friction. One woman fiercely assailed the manual training and general " girl's work " for her son; what she wanted was more " mental " education. A Bohemian woman used to German methods said that what the schools needed was men teachers. However, more than a half of the parents consulted appreciate the advantage and necessity of a more practical training. Many said that they could have contrived to keep their children in school had *suitable instruction been offered.*

The high school is a remote institution, not connecting with these working people. Parents ask, " What 's the use of sending John to high school ? We don't belong to that bunch." They do see a value in the business college, because the canvassers of commercial schools make periodic visits to parents in order to praise the virtues of " business training." It is hard to convince parents that their children can obtain a proper business training in the two years' commercial course now given in the high school. Parents point to examples of neighbors' children who have become " silly " on attending high school. At the most, a brief stay in high school is associated with a greater chance to get a " clean job," not with greater efficiency.

That 171 answers specified the need of money as the cause of leaving school reveals the ever-present strain of making a living, and it is natural that the attitude to the school should be grounded in the practical. If the family resources are fitful, the child's wage is considered to be necessary, and under these circumstances concrete proof of the school's economic value must be presented before the parents are willing to have their children continue.

This hard-headedness of the parent is reënforced by custom. In reply to the question, Who was responsible for A's leaving school? we have this result :

Responsibility placed on	Number of Cases
Parents and child jointly	106
Both parents	21
Mother	48
Father	37
Boy	48
Girl	22

In 38 per cent of the cases, leaving school was taken as a matter of course by both parent and child; in an equal number of cases the parents, singly or collectively, were the deciding agents, while in 24 per cent of the cases the boys and girls were the active agents. The fixing of responsibility is of course a most complicated problem. Still, we should expect a peasant mother to retain her traditional authority in the family and to demand of her children a contribution to the family income. Parents say that they must have the boy's money, because he will marry soon enough. Thirteen children made the statement that they were forced to leave school, although they liked to go and were not "too poor."

This certainly argues the need of educating parents to the American situation. In their behalf, however, it should be said that a considerable number expressed a wish that their children continue some form of education after leaving the day school. Parents were asked, Do you want A to learn a trade? (whether in school or out was not specified). The parents of 42 girls answered yes, 27 no, and 23 didn't know. Of 108 replies from the parents of boys, 61 were affirmative, 15 were negative, and 32 were uncertain.

The Child's Criticism of the School

Although there is some parental despotism, most of the children are entirely willing to leave school. A part of this feeling is due to childish love of novelty, restlessness, and lack of forethought which would, under the most favorable conditions, be present to some degree. Nevertheless, the variety of answers already listed and the manifest disposition to regard the school as something to be rid of as soon as possible, are evidence of a serious lack of adjustment. It is true that the child cannot analyze the school intelligently. In many cases he says, rather indifferently, " It 's all right," and " I liked it while I was there." It is sometimes said that girls are more contented with school than boys. This was not found to be true in the stockyards. Those girls who gave a distinctly favorable opinion were more enthusiastic than the boys, but of those who showed marked dissatisfaction, 39 per cent were girls. This ratio reveals no decided difference as regards sex, considering the fact that in this matter less than one half of the persons from whom opinions were secured were girls.[1]

One test of the child's real attitude to school may be found in his interest in educational lines of development after he leaves the day school.[2] It is fair to judge the success of a school by its power of arousing interests. Accordingly, the attempt was made to determine the extent to which the boys and girls attended evening school and clubs after going to work. Forty-five girls said point blank that they never had continued or wished to continue in night school or to study or to do " heavy reading," some of them adding that they were "too tired " or spent their extra time in dancing.

[1] More information about the status of boys than of girls was secured. While it is believed that the figures in regard to girls represent the general trend, more data are necessary. A special investigation of girls is now under way, and the results of this study will be more conclusive.

[2] In studying the answers of working boys in night schools and in factories to simple questions about civil government and history, Mr. Ristine discovered the following :

" Very few of the boys could be termed good in this test, not many were even fair, and by far the larger per cent were marked poor or poor minus, which in this table means very close to zero.

" Taking the matter up from the standpoint of the grades, it may be said that the eighth-grade boy has enough knowledge of civil government so that the more important points of the subject will probably clear up in his mind as he gets a little older and reads the newspapers more. The same thing can be said for a very few of the seventh-grade boys. The information of the sixth- and fifth-grade boys is so meager along the lines of civil government and history that it seems doubtful whether they will ever have understanding of what democratic government is.

" It was also a disappointing fact that the boys who were nearing their majority were the very poorest, as a rule, while the younger boys fresh from school were able to answer with much more facility." — " Educational Status of Working Boys of School Age in the City of Chicago," *University of Chicago Dissertations*, pp. 37, 38.

Fifty-seven boys gave similar testimony that their education was finished. One boy said, in answer to the query whether he had gone to night school, " I am able to read," evidently considering the matter settled. Of a total of 180 cases, 22 boys and 8 girls had been to night school. Three girls and 24 boys professed an intention to go. Two boys had gone to Lake High night school for the instruction in drawing, but had left after a few lessons. One boy, after having been told of Lewis Institute, planned to go. Three boys and 1 girl had gone to business college, but were discontented because they had secured no position in commercial work afterward. Several were distributed in settlement clubs, the School of Citizenship, a Turner society, sewing and music classes, and Davis Square[1] activities. A conservative estimate is that one half of the entire number considered their education closed. About 40 had actually attended evening classes, some for a very short time, showing not only a want of interest but also the physical impossibility of profiting much by night instruction after the day's work. The willingness of 27 children to embrace an opportunity for further training indicated partly a real desire in those possessed of unusual ambition, partly a temporary enthusiasm destined soon to give way to indifference.

Leaving aside such drawbacks as unfavorable home conditions, improper food, and the personal dislike of teachers, the elements of the child's opinion of the school may be summed up in two counts. He feels that there is a lack of interest, activity, and appeal to his constructive powers in the present course of study, and he contrasts this situation with the wider world of amusement, freedom, and contact with people. Second, he cannot see the connection between what he is studying and his future job.

The proof of this conclusion is drawn from observation of the schools, the testimony of teachers, and acquaintance with the child and the parent. In many cases the children proudly exhibited their drawing, painting, and needlework to the visitor, lamenting that they had no chance to use their skill in the positions held; many of the older boys confessed that by reason of their early

---

[1] A neighborhood small park center under the management of the South Park Commissioners.

withdrawal they were not fitted for positions suited to their inclinations. The vague dissatisfaction of some of the younger children becomes defined as time shows the defects of their preparation.

One thing that strikes everyone acquainted with the people of our neighborhood is the ignorance both of parent and child regarding the educational opportunities now existing. It was found that a Polish woman did not know that there was a night school in a public school within two blocks of her house, and the boys and girls were not familiar with the art schools and technical schools which offer instruction. It is manifestly one of our first duties to remedy this failure to utilize all the agencies now available. There is a great need of spreading abroad full knowledge of all the present educational resources of Chicago. Perhaps the parent lacks such information more than the child.

SECTION II. THE JOB AND THE FAMILY INCOME

I

VARIETIES OF OCCUPATIONS, WAGES, AND ADVANCEMENT

We shall here concern ourselves with some salient facts regarding the character of juvenile occupations and their possibilities. Before presenting the classified data, several typical experiences of boys and girls in our neighborhood may be narrated.

W left school nearly three years ago, a seventh grader, fourteen years old. He did not know what he wanted to do; just wanted a "job" because he was tired of school. His first place was driving an express wagon at $4 a week. This he kept for six months. Next he nailed boxes at Hammond's packing plant at $7.50 per week. Then he "bottled" for a brewery at $8 a week, holding this position six weeks. W has been idle exactly half the time since he left school, and has earned $452, an average per month of $13.43. When asked, "What can you do?" he replied, "Anything."

S, a Bohemian girl, has been out of school for ten months, quitting at the age of fourteen, in the seventh grade. Her first position was "peeling in a peanut factory," as she phrased it. After two weeks here at $4.50 she left to become a packer in a spice mill at $4 a week, continuing for four months. She has been idle more than half the time. She was dull, and thoroughly tired of the factory. She wanted housework.

J, a Polish boy, secured a place as errand boy in a printing establishment at $5 a week; he stayed one week, then left suddenly, alleging that it was "too hard, too heavy bundles to carry." Next as errand boy in the stockyards he worked four weeks at a wage of $4. Following this he took a place in Donnelley's press in the same capacity of errand boy and for the same pay. He remained here three weeks. He said that he hated all the places he had held and wanted "office work."

Although her mother wanted C to learn dressmaking, she refused and entered a soap factory as "wrapper," the wage being $3.50. After four months at the place she received $5.50, and said that was as much as she could ever earn there. She liked her work because it was "easy," and expressed pleasure that she had stopped school in the sixth grade. Her mother said that C had left school because the father was then out of work.

B, an intelligent and ambitious boy, has worked steadily for two years, first as clerk in Rothschild's department store at $5.50, then in the uniform factory at $6, his present wage. He disliked his work and said that he wanted to do nothing but draw, proudly relating his proficiency and success in having pictures "exhibited" when in the public schools.

R has worked at six different places in the thirteen months he has been employed since leaving school. After spending $75 in tuition at a telegraph operators' school, he failed to find work in this occupation and proceeded to go the rounds of messenger boy, stock boy, tobacco cutter, etc., earning an aggregate sum of $352.57 in twenty-seven months, an average of $19.28 per month for the actual working period, and an average of $9.36 per month for the entire time. The places were all secured by the method of "seeing a sign," "following up ads," and "being told by a friend." A position leading to telegraphy has now been secured for him.

Some representative facts are brought out by each of these cases. W, being large and strong, received fairly good wages because of the heavy man's work he performed, but there was no difference in the length of time of idleness between his various jobs, and he showed a decreasing zeal in looking for work.

S received less money at the second job than at her first place. She is an exception, however, in preferring housework to factory employment.

J is an example of the boy with an ambition for office work without either the necessary training or capacity.

C is well satisfied with her factory job, although the $5.50 maximum wage offers no great future.

B is obviously out of place in a uniform factory, since there is nothing in the work corresponding to his interests and talents.

The last boy cited is a type of those who knock about from one job to another, at last hitting upon a congenial occupation. He had the advantage of special training in a telegraphy school, even though, as he said, the teacher was " bum " and the manager " swindled " him.[1]

Judged from these cases, a few tentative observations may be made. For children not yet sixteen years old, who need unspecialized occupation calling for initiative, interest in processes, and affording the worker a sense of achievement, the character of the successive jobs secured is not encouraging. They are unrelated and noneducative. A boy may quit or be " fired " and suffer no great inconvenience in finding another place, either like the former one or totally different. On the other hand, there may be long intervals of idleness between jobs, the results of which are both unprofitable financially and demoralizing. Nor does such enforced idleness tend to bring the boy back into school ; school no longer receives consideration. Thus we see the boy after he is out of

---

[1] There were other assertions that private commercial schools are giving poor instruction, yet they flourish. The demand for the training persists in spite of the questionable advertising methods of the " colleges."

The employment secretary of a mail-order house employing many boys says that a large number of graduates of business colleges apply for work, that they are often unprepared for office routine, and that the ordinary jobs offered them are, by the boys, considered inferior to what their notions of their own attainments lead them to expect.

school, finding or failing to find suitable employment, with the chances all against his meeting with that line of work for which his tastes or his meager equipment would seem to fit him. The haphazard methods of securing work which the boy is compelled to use can lead to no other consequence.

How Positions are secured

The hit-or-miss way of finding work is proved by the testimony of parent and child. There are two chief methods of finding a place. One is to have the path made easy by the father or mother or other relative "who has a pull" with the boss, and with this method may be included the plan of having "a friend put in a word." The second way is to "hang around" after leaving school or a previous place, looking up "ads," walking the streets in order to catch sight of the "Boy Wanted" signal, or making written and oral application to many establishments. Data on this point show about an equal number of boys and girls using the "assisted" and the "alone" method. It is needless to say that aid in many cases is but nominal, and the places are not invariably superior to those obtained without help. Girls working in a particular factory "speak for" their younger sisters and their acquaintances: on a dark winter morning may be seen groups of girls from a neighborhood entering the street car bound for the same store or factory. The desire of companionship often determines the selection of work, perhaps more with girls than with boys. A company of four girl "chums" came to the Settlement looking for employment, and refused possible individual chances because they wanted to work in one place. The employer has a difficulty here, because when one girl quits the others follow.

In a few instances it was found that the father or the older children obtained desirable places for members of their family, such as opportunities to learn dressmaking, printing, plumbing, and the jewelry business. A large number of the boys in the packing-house district make written application and secure jobs as errand boys in the stockyards. A few resort to private employment agencies, and pay a fee of from one to three dollars on securing a place.

The human side of these situations should not be overlooked. There are boys who stop school the day they are fourteen, intermittently look for work, elude the truancy officer for weeks, and are strenuously defended by their parents. Boys, and girls too, abandon fairly good places without apparent reason and without prospects of another position. A gang of boys in the vicinity of the Settlement have a practice of working until they have accumulated a little money, when they leave their employers without notice, knowing that a place as messenger boy is almost always available. Young girls take their cold lunches down town to spend the day tramping the streets looking for work. Mothers force their children out of the house early in the morning, forbidding them to come home until late at night unless they have found jobs, so strong is the feeling of the immigrant woman that there is no excuse for not working. In two instances a long-continued period of idleness, very likely through no fault of the boys, ended in their banishment from home — to sleep in stables and alleys — and a further lessening of chances to meet the favor of an employer. This is more evidence of the authority of the parent over the economic fortunes of the child, and the general consent that no matter what the conditions are the child must bring in money.

CLASSIFICATION OF KINDS OF JOBS

The following grouping is merely suggestive. It is made from a record of cases coming under the observation of the Settlement during the past year; it has to do with the character of positions held by boys and girls between fourteen and seventeen years of age.

KINDS OF JOBS	NUMBER OF POSITIONS
Factory (box, candy, tin, biscuit, etc.)	252
Errand boy	109
Mercantile establishment	62
Messenger	26
Office	19
Driving wagon	16
Domestic service	15
Working around saloon, grocery, bakery, etc.	15
Farm work	9
Telephone operator	2

Miscellaneous skilled occupations:

	NUMBER OF POSITIONS
Dressmaking	9
Millinery	4
Printer's apprentice	3
Tailor's apprentice	3
Butcher's apprentice	3
Cooper's apprentice	2
Druggist's apprentice	2
Baker's apprentice	2
Plumber's apprentice	2
Tinner's apprentice	1
Carpenter's apprentice	1
Jeweler's apprentice	1
Painter's apprentice	1
Telegraph operator	1
Total of skilled occupations	35
Total of all occupations	560

The classification needs explanation. Under the factory heading are placed those positions which are largely mechanical, which require a short time in learning, little responsibility, and great specialization of processes. This group is composed of jobs in candy, box, tin, hammock, biscuit, gum, canning, and piano establishments, and some operations in clothing, machine, and printing industries.

The errand-boy group is made up chiefly of those boys either in down-town firms or in the packing establishments, whose main work is to deliver packages and messages, and is distinguished both from the private telegraph messenger service and the "office work," which mainly has to do with indoor routine. Mercantile employments comprise the jobs in department and other large stores — cash boys and girls, stock keepers, bundlers, clerks, and addressers. In the "skilled occupation" are included those places which promise to lead to a recognized trade. The farm work represented here in most cases does not mean a serious application to farming — usually temporary chances to do the odd jobs possible for boys on farms of acquaintances. The domestic service of the girls often means short-time positions in families needing some one to assist in taking care of children. In some cases "dressmaking" fails to offer an opportunity to learn a number of the processes involved in needlework.

A few boys and girls in offices, factories, and department stores may rise to places requiring responsibility and skill. Some errand boys have become heads of departments, just as some cash girls have become "buyers." However, it is apparent that the majority of these positions are low in grade and require little preparation and skill. Of these 45 per cent are factory positions ; 34 per cent are in errand, office, and mercantile employments; and those which can be designated as leading to skilled and high-grade occupations are less than 10 per cent of the total. This, moreover, is an exceedingly liberal estimate of the situation. The report of the Massachusetts Commission says that " 33 per cent of the children of this State who begin work between fourteen and sixteen are employed in unskilled industries, and 65 per cent in low-grade industries : thus a little less than 2 per cent are in high-grade industries." [1] It is difficult to fit these boys and girls into Miss Kingsbury's grouping of occupations. In the first, the unskilled, she places those in which there is repetition of a single process, in which knowledge of one part is not essential to that of another. These occupations are no preparation for skilled labor ; in fact they are often a handicap because of the routine. Low-grade skilled industries, the second class, are cleaner ; they require more care, time of learning, and versatility, lead to numerous openings, and command higher wages. Such operations are those centering about power machines, the handwork in the clothing industry, and woodworking in factories. The third group, the high-grade skilled industries, requires several years of preparation or apprenticeship, and implies knowledge of related processes and great skill.

Unless one has a record of children for a number of years, as well as an indication of the future of the particular industries here represented, an accurate grouping cannot be made. Assuming that one half of those in the factory, office, mercantile, and errand classifications and the domestic, telephone, and farm workers can be included under the second class of low-grade skilled industries, we have the following proportion :

	PERCENTAGE
Unskilled occupations	49
Low-grade skilled	44
High-grade skilled	7

[1] Massachusetts Report, p. 31.

This, however, is not a reasonable supposition. The larger number are in the specifically juvenile occupations in which the appeal is made to youthful quickness, delicacy of touch, and easily acquired skill in a few processes. There is little incentive to grow, and no preparation for further work in the respective avenues of employment. These occupations can claim to be nothing else than children's temporary means of earning money.

First Jobs of Girls

The situation with regard to girls is clearly shown by the record of the first positions of 86 girls who left the local schools between fourteen and sixteen years of age.

Kinds of Jobs	Number of Girls
Factory (candy, box, soap, etc.)	52
Department store	9
Printing establishments	7
Dressmaking	6
Domestic service	5
Millinery	2
Tailor's apprentice	2
Helping in grocery	2
Office	1

Wages of Girls

The average beginning wage of the girls included above is $3.61 per week. The following table represents the distribution:

Wages	Number of Persons
Not exceeding $1.00	5
From $1.00 to $2.00	3
From $2.00 to $2.50	4
From $2.50 to $3.00	6
From $3.00 to $3.50	25
From $3.50 to $4.00	14
From $4.00 to $4.50	12
From $4.50 to $5.00	4
From $5.00 to $5.50	9
From $5.50 to $6.00	1
From $6.00 to $6.50	1
From $6.50 to $7.00	1
From $7.00 to $7.50	1

As is evident, the beginning wage of a large number fluctuates between $3 and $4. Girls who make less than $2 a week are either apprentices in millinery and dressmaking or those who find positions in housework or in local stores.

The entire group of girls here considered have been at work for a period ranging from a month to a year and eight months, the greater number having worked about five months. During this time 59 have had only one position, and 27 have had more than one. In the case of those who remained in one place, the average increase of pay up to the time when the girls were interviewed was 18 cents per week. Of those who changed places, the last job averaged a weekly wage of $3.83, slightly above that of those who remained in one place. However, 3 girls received less pay in the last job, 5 earned the same amount, and 19 increased their wages. There is some justification for saying that the girls who change jobs, whether voluntarily or because they are " fired," suffer no decrease in wages ; on the whole, outside of the possible idleness, there seems to be a slight advantage in migrating. There is more shifting of places in the case of boys, however. In following up the boys and girls receiving work certificates, one can count on one person out of four being idle when visited. This ratio is exclusive of those girls who are helping at home. There is no superiority in the character of the last jobs when compared with the first ones. The change from factory to factory does not lead to better opportunities, as the following table indicates.

Those who changed jobs show these differences in positions :

First Jobs		Last Jobs	
Factory	19	Factory	18
Department store	2	Department store	4
Domestic	2	Domestic	3
Grocery	2	Grocery	0
Dressmaking	1	Dressmaking	0
Office	1	Office	5

There is no marked advance. In four instances girls quit to take places in the same line of work elsewhere. In three cases they received more money ; in one case there was no advance.

Relation of Wage to Grade and Age

Of the girls who changed jobs, 14 out of the 19 whose wages *advanced* stopped school and took jobs before they were fifteen years old, and 5 were above fifteen years. Of those whose earning power *decreased*, 2 were fourteen years old and 1 fifteen and seven months. Those whose pay remained the same were all fourteen years of age. As to grades in school of those whose wages *increased*, 2 were in the eighth grade, 1 in the fourth grade, 6 in the seventh grade, and *10* in the *sixth* grade. Of those whose wages diminished, 2 were in the seventh grade and 1 in the fifth grade. Of those not advancing in pay, 1 was in the seventh grade and 4 were in the sixth grade.

In the accompanying table the fortunes of 59 girls who stayed each in one position are shown. The weekly earnings at the time the girls were seen are placed in relation to the age and grade reached on leaving school.

Number of Girls	Wages	Age				Grade					
		14–14½	14½–15	15–15½	15½–16	3	4	5	6	7	8
4 . . .	Not exceeding $1.00	2	2	—	—	—	—	—	1	2	1
1 . . .	From $1.00 to 2.00	1	—	—	—	—	1	—	—	—	—
3 . . .	2.00 to 2.50	1	2	—	—	—	—	1	1	—	1
4 . . .	2.50 to 3.00	1	3	—	—	—	—	1	2	1	—
12 . . .	3.00 to 3.50	8	2	2	—	1	—	2	4	2	3
11 . . .	3.50 to 4.00	6	3	1	1	—	—	1	5	4	1
10 . . .	4.00 to 4.50	10	—	—	—	—	1	3	5	—	1
3 . . .	4.50 to 5.00	1	1	1	—	1	1	—	1	—	—
7 . . .	5.00 to 5.50	2	2	1	2	—	—	2	2	1	2
1 . . .	5.50 to 6.00	1	—	—	—	—	—	—	—	1	—
1 . . .	6.00 to 6.50	—	—	—	1	—	1	—	—	—	—
1 . . .	6.50 to 7.00	1	—	—	—	—	—	1	—	—	—
1 . . .	7.00 to 7.50	—	—	1	—	—	—	—	—	—	1

There is no indication that those leaving school in the higher grades will receive higher wages. The conclusion to be drawn is not that the school is useless or that it is not desirable for all to remain through the eighth grade. In fact, the present elementary school is constructed on the basis of an eight-year course, and its full benefit cannot be had if there is a shorter period of attendance. The "fundamentals," the tools for reaching the world's inheritance, — reading, writing, number, and history, — are essential for all. Mr. Ristine demonstrated the superiority of eighth-grade boys; the tests used were questions in the formal school branches.

The point is, considering the inferior employments open to children, a longer stay in the elementary school does not help financially. Two problems are left open: (1) a reorganization of the school with the occupations as centers of interest, for the sake of the "fundamentals"; (2) a vocational purpose, making a longer attendance obligatory and worth while.

It is true that the highest beginning wages, $7, was secured by an eighth-grade girl, but nine eighth-graders received less than $5.50 and fare no better than the sixth-graders. While the maximum wage was reached by a fifteen-year-old girl, a wage of $6.90, 10 cents a week less, belonged to a fourteen-year-old girl. Size or general dexterity seems to determine wages more than age and grade in school. From the point of view of the occupations open to girls between fourteen and sixteen years, it is manifestly not an economic advantage to continue in school after the minimum age has been reached.

Eight girls of the number included above were studied by Mrs. C. B. McArthur. We may observe the relation between their school record and their industrial careers.

Case 1. School record: absent sixty-eight days during last year; conduct and effort good; average mentality; repeated grades two, four, and six. Industrial record: candy factory, two weeks, $3 per week; printing firm — bindery — $5. Likes the job; chance of making $12 a week.

Case 2. Retarded, absence great. Gum factory, $4.50 per week. Now out of work.

Case 3. Considerable absence; mentality good, but a "repeater." Parisian Novelty Company, $2.50 per week; box factory, $3.50 per week. Satisfied with the place.

Case 4. Average mentality; good effort and conduct. Box factory, $3.50; then housework at $3 per week.

Case 5. Average mentality, conduct poor. Box factory, two months, $3 per week; then fig packer, $4 per week. Likes the "short hours."

Case 6. Restless, unreliable, conduct poor; repeated one grade. Factory, $3 per week; then fig packer, $4 per week.

Case 7. Absence; did n't get along well. Candy factory, $3; then factory, $4 per week.

Case 8. Absence great, conduct fair, average mentality. Office, $3 per week; then at Libby's packing plant. Irregular wages, $4 to $6 per week.

All except Case 8 were fourteen years old; all except Case 7 left school in the sixth grade. The fifteen-year-old girl and the girl leaving school in the fourth grade met the same fortunes as the rest. There does not appear to be any noticeable positive relation between conduct and mentality as judged by conventional school requirements and success or failure in the employment undertaken by the girls.

RELATION OF WORKING PERIOD TO WAGES

Since the working periods of the girls whose records were secured vary greatly, not much can be said on this point. Of 25 girls whose working time was six months, 13 increased in amounts from 50 cents to $2 per week, and 12 received an equal wage at the end of the time. At the end of twenty months 1 girl whose initial pay was $3 per week in a candy factory was receiving $4 a week in a spice mill. Several times a girl doubled her wage in two months, and then continued to work without increase. Of 15 girls at work an average of fourteen months, 7 were receiving no more money at the end of the time than at the beginning, and the highest advance was from $2 to $6. There is not sufficient information to show the ups and downs of the girls who held three or four jobs. These are typical cases:

First Job	Second Job	Third Job	Fourth Job
$2.50	$3.50	—	—
3.00	4.00	—	—
3.50	5.00	$4.00	$3.00
3.50	5.00	2.50	3.50
3.00	1.84	—	—

Altogether it is not, as a general rule, the factor of time and experience in the kinds of occupations open to girls which determines their pay. This would not be undesirable provided the children under sixteen were preparing themselves for a self-maintaining future; the period of apprenticeship could not pretend to be a lucrative one. The matter is serious when a job calling for little skill is succeeded by another job similarly lacking in educational quality, and when there is no relation between previous training and the work to be done.

The main features of the situation as regards girls may be summarized:

1. Most of the jobs secured belong to the low-grade industries.

2. A limit is soon reached in wages.

3. Finding another job is sometimes the only way to secure more pay.

4. The advance is largely a matter of chance, there being no observable economic advantage in leaving school at an age greater than fourteen and a higher grade at school, or in previous experience in other jobs of the character accessible to girls of the neighborhood.

First Jobs of Boys

A grouping of the jobs of 131 boys shows this result:

First Jobs	Number of Boys
Errand boy	51
Factory	26
Messenger	15
Small store — as grocery, bakery, or meat market	10
Mercantile establishments	7
Printing firms	6
Driving wagon	5
Office	3
Tailor's apprentice	2
Baker's apprentice	1
Painter's apprentice	1
Plumber's apprentice	1
Druggist's apprentice	1
Farm	1
Selling papers	1
Total	131

An important feature is that 50 per cent of the boys represented above enter industry in errand and messenger service. The unfavorable character of telegraph-messenger work, with its irregularity, freedom, "tipping," and precocious acquaintance with the dark side of city life, has been sufficiently explained.[1] There is a considerable number of boys who are given odd jobs in groceries, bakeries, and sometimes in saloons. The daily round is often hard, with its early and late hours and constant activity, and there is no factory inspector to enforce conformity to law, as in large establishments. An interesting fact is the liking of many boys for driving wagons, because of the excitement and novelty of traveling about the city. There is great competition for these positions. Some of the printing firms give opportunities for boys to fit themselves for one or more of the printing trades; and the boys listed above as apprentices were confident that they would fit into their respective trades when they were older.[2] Still, under a liberal estimate only twelve of the one hundred and thirty-one boys have any prospects of reaching a skilled occupation.

CHANGES OF JOBS

Fifty-five boys had held more than one place. The chief changes in the nature of the jobs are:

(1) Errand boys number 18 in the first-job column and 12 in the last-job list, and messenger boys decrease from 9 to 3; (2) factory jobs number 15 in the first, 19 in the last column; (3) department-store places increase from 2 to 7, and drivers of wagons from 2 to 6; (4) of the positions, outside of possible good opportunities in factories and stores, which can be called preparatory to first-class occupations, there is a decrease from 6 to 5. How is it with the 27 boys who started in errand and messenger work? Their last jobs are messenger or errand boys, 11; factory, 8; department store, 3; driving wagon, 2; and one each for printing, office work, and jewelry. There is, in these cases, an average time at work of six months, and although the short time does not prove much about the future of the boys, it does show the migration from one errand job to another and the tendency to drift to the factory work as they grow older, and it confirms the

[1] Florence Kelley, Some Ethical Gains through Legislation, pp. 15–26.

[2] One eighth-grade Polish boy, from the vicinity of The University of Chicago Settlement, is in the apprentice school conducted by the Lakeside Press, and is "making good." The director of the school says that Polish and Bohemian boys are the brightest apprentices.

judgment of Mr. Cyril Jackson that "few boys pick up skill after a year or two of errand work." [1]

The number of individuals who are listed as having held but one job is large because some of the boys were followed up only a few weeks after they had procured their work certificates. The proportion of migration from one place to another shown in the 55 who did and the 76 who did not change places is not a true picture of the situation; one must consider the older boys' experience to determine that.

WAGES OF BOYS AND RELATION TO AGE AND GRADE

The average beginning wage of the 55 boys who changed places is $4.27 per week; the average last wage is $4.96. This shows a higher initial wage and a greater increase in practically the same period than is the case with girls. Eleven boys received less money in the last position than in the first, and 8 received the same wage. One half earned a beginning wage of either $4 or $4.50, and 45 came within the $3 to $5 limits.

In this group 12 boys decreased in wages: 7 of these left school between fourteen and fourteen and a half; 4 were between fourteen and a half and fifteen, and 1 was over fifteen, when the working papers were applied for. Of the 8 boys whose wages remained the same, 2 were fifteen years old, 3 less than fourteen and a half, and 3 were fourteen years old when they left school.

Thirty-five boys increased in wages: 1 was over fifteen and a half; 8 were between fifteen and fifteen and a half; 5 were between fourteen and a half and fifteen; and 21 were less than fourteen and a half when they stopped school. Since the average age of leaving school in our district is fourteen years and five months, these results are to be expected; but the fact that the 6 boys getting the highest beginning wages, between $6 and $9, are under fifteen years of age, and the fact that the initial pay of those who received less than $6 is independent of the age reached, tends to strengthen the conclusion reached in studying the histories of girls, that there is no important relation between age and advance in the occupations open to children between the ages of fourteen and sixteen.

[1] *Royal Commission on the Poor Laws and Relief of Distress*, Appendix, Vol. XX, p. 20.

Does the boy who leaves school in an upper grade have an economic advantage over the boy who leaves in a lower grade? Of the 12 boys who decreased in earnings 6 left school in the seventh and eighth grades, and only 10 of the 36 who increased their wages were seventh- and eighth-graders.

On the whole, it is safe to say that a higher grade and a greater age do not guarantee better positions and higher earnings. This conclusion has no reference to any period other than the one under consideration, for when the boy reaches sixteen the case is somewhat different. Legally, he is then allowed to engage in a greater variety of occupations; if he is adaptable, positions of some promise are open to him and all his school training may be used. In the formative period. from fourteen to sixteen, whatever discipline the school has given is of little service in unskilled juvenile occupations.[1]

Boys holding One Position

Since the results are not different when we consider those boys who have had a single job since leaving school, a repetition of the above statements is unnecessary. Two thirds of the seventy-six boys are engaged in messenger, errand, and factory employments. Twenty-four of the group received $4 a week, the average pay of all being $4.42. Some of those who receive the highest pay come from the lowest grades in school. Many of the errand boys are employed in the general offices of the stockyards, in which $4 and $4.50 are the usual beginning wages.

School Progress and Industrial Record

There are not enough cases to correlate adequately the later industrial advance with the record of school progress which was

---

[1] Mr. Ristine studied relative proficiency in simple intellectual tests of boys in night schools and those at work. He found, by means of oral and written questions in mathematics, English, civics, and history, that boys out of school pass examinations inferior to those who are in continuation classes; that eighth-graders are superior to boys quitting in the sixth and seventh grades; that boys in the carpenters' apprentice school, having a "life-career motive," are better in the arithmetic test than those in other evening schools or those at work (Ristine, "Educational Status of Working Boys of School Age in the City of Chicago," *University of Chicago Dissertations*).

compiled by Mrs. McArthur.[1] The following instances, however, are suggestive :

Case 1. School record: average mentality; conduct and effort excellent. After one month's idleness, a job in the Yards, $7.50 a week.

Case 2. Average mentality, good conduct. First job, opening doors in the Yards, $4.50; then idle four months; then a job driving an express wagon at $6.25. Prefers work in machine shop.

Case 3. Graduate of parochial school ; entered fourth grade in the Hamline Public School. Absent 58 days in year, conduct good, mind above the average. Errand boy, 1 week, $5; errand boy, 4 weeks, $4; errand boy, 3 weeks, $4; out of work when seen.

Case 4. Suspended from school, conduct and intelligence poor. Errand boy in the Yards; likes the place.

Case 5. Retarded and frequent absence. Box factory, $5. Parents say that the boss likes their boy.

Case 6. Slow mind, conduct poor, absence. One position since leaving school in a wholesale coffee house, $7; very well satisfied.

Case 7. Parochial school, retarded. Factory and department store, each $2.50; now errand boy, $4.

Case 8. "Repeater" in school. Tinshop, $7; contented because job is "clean, dry, and easy."

Case 9. Lazy and truant. Messenger boy, $5.

Case 10. Repeated grades 2, 3, 4. Effort spasmodic, stubborn, below average mentally. Worked for Western Union several months, then apprenticed to a jeweler. His sister claims that he is making excellent progress.

The plain absence of correlation between school progress and economic progress does not contradict the preceding results.

EXPERIENCE OF OLDER BOYS AND GIRLS

The preceding account does not do justice to some of the aspects of juvenile work. There are boys who have had six jobs in nine months, and girls who have been "fired" for petty offenses or "laid off" after the Christmas season. Not enough has been said of the effect of weeks of loafing between jobs, and the occasional spurts of eagerness to find a place, succeeded by a period of absolute indifference. Moreover, the comparatively short time at work does not reveal the history of the later industrial life in which the outcome of the wasted years is evident. To give some idea of what happens as time goes on, the records of twenty-one — nineteen

[1] This report will appear later.

boys and two girls — in addition to the above list were examined. The time out of school was from one to four years, in each case carrying the biography beyond the age of sixteen. The three points to be noted are the average weekly wage estimated on the basis of the entire time out of school, in order to determine the actual average weekly earnings ; the average time spent in each job ; and the percentage of idleness on the basis of the entire working period.

Case No.	Average Wage	Average Time in each Job	Percentage of Idleness
1 [1]	$2.56	5⅝ months	18
2 [1]	7.50	8 "	—
3	4.50	15½ "	11
4	3.50	7 "	50
5	3.79	10⅔ "	33
6	1.86	2⁷⁄₁₀ "	66
7	4.09	4½ "	21
8	4.74	15½ "	28
9	1.81	3⅔ "	47
10	3.93	4⅔ "	55
11	4.00	7¼ "	52
12	4.21	12 "	25
13	6.15	9 "	11
14	4.77	4⅜ "	22
15	2.50	4½ "	54
16	7.36	4⅔ "	11
17	2.90	2 "	48
18	2.85	5⁸⁄₁₀ "	48
19	6.34	12 "	18
20	5.36	9¼ "	43
21	1.92	2¼ "	52

The purpose of the arrangement of the records above is to present the irregularity in the three columns. As to wages, it is apparent that in but four instances has the average weekly contribution to the family income gone above $5.50. Most of these boys are now eighteen and nineteen years old. The highest wage is received by a girl who stopped school when nearly sixteen and in the eighth grade. In two years she has had three places, the first as telephone operator, and the present job as " saleslady " in a department store

[1] Girls.

at $10 a week. Department store, driving of delivery wagons, and factory places are the most numerous. Many of the boys held temporary jobs in the stockyards.

Four of the twenty-one persons show an average time of holding a job of a year or over; eleven stayed less than six months. *Two thirds of the boys* show an average period in one position *of less than nine months.*

It is not probable that the figures regarding the time of idleness are exceptional. Of the twenty cases in which there was idleness six were *out of work 50 per cent or over* of the entire period out of school. Fifteen were idle *more than a fifth* of the time. Some of the idleness was due to illness, some to the desire of boys to take a vacation between places, some to seasonal occupations and inability to find work.

Idleness of the adult workman means loss of income and the results that attend this economic loss. When, however, opportunity to work again appears, the workman, as a rule, finds that he has not lost his instinct of workmanship or his habits of industry. Under normal conditions this instinct is being developed and these habits are being formed during the adolescent period. While children in these years should have recreation, *idleness* during this period is inevitably attended by a more than economic loss both to the individual and to the community, a loss which can never be entirely made good. It is a legitimate conclusion from this that the community may not safely surrender the training of children during the formative period of their lives to the factory, the store, the saloon, messenger service, or to the business office.

The general public falsely imagines that the fear of police, prison, and scaffold prevent crimes against property, order, person, and life. The value of this fear has been greatly overestimated; at best it restrains; it rarely prevents. The public is never protected until vicious and debasing influences are removed and the life habits of youth are formed in home, school, and industry under public supervision and control. The cheap, superficial, and disappointing method of attempting to prevent crime by punishment actually diverts public attention and thought from those more radical, thorough, and rational means which actually do prevent the rise and development of vicious and criminal habits. The life histories of the youthful murderers who have of late years shocked Chicago are precisely like those of many thousands of others who are being led downward along the same route. The public needs also to be startled by its own neglect of the true causes of disease, weakness, immorality, and brutality.

Subnormal Boys

In the local schools one room is set aside for those children who are unable to progress under ordinary class instruction. The after-school record of ten subnormal boys was secured in order to compare the industrial careers of " normal " and " subnormal " children.

Three boys were found to be absolutely unfit to be trusted with any position of responsibility. They were capable of simple muscular labor and needed the training given in a school for the feeble-minded. One of the defectives succeeded in holding two positions for several months. The remaining six boys were as competent as the " normal " ones. Two German boys belonging to a large family in which the father is a drunkard and the mother shiftless had no difficulty in finding work. The younger became messenger boy down town, and the older boy worked steadily in the stockyards for a year and a half, receiving $1.25 a day. After six weeks of idleness another of the group went to work on a farm. A uniform wage of $6 a week during a period of fifteen months was earned by a Polish boy. He worked successfully in a box factory, in a sawmill, and for the Western Electric Company. Especially noteworthy was the career of an energetic boy who is now driving a sprinkling wagon after a year's alternate work and idleness. He is a handy, steady worker, anxious to learn a trade.

Most of these boys are vigorous and active; they earned an average wage of $5.73 a week, an unusual amount. The high average can be ascribed in part to the circumstance that most of them were over fifteen years old and capable of heavy work. However, it is a significant commentary on the connection between school and job as well as on the character of juvenile employment

that a group of " subnormal " boys should have a degree of success
in the world of industry which compares favorably with that of
those students who are pronounced " normal " by the school.

II

FAMILY INCOME OF WORKING CHILDREN

The 217 boys and girls whose wages were considered in preceding tables were also studied from the standpoint of the incomes of
the respective families represented. The method of Miss Kingsbury in grouping the families was used; that of adding up the
wages of members of the family over sixteen years old and any
other regular means of support; deducting the chief stock expenditures (such as rent, carfare, and lunch); dividing the resulting sum
by the number of members in the family. This gives a rough division representing the amount of money available for each person in ·
the family after fixed expenses are paid: those families in which
the average amount is $3 or over per person per week are put into
Class 1, those whose average is between $3 and $2 per person per
week are placed in Class 2, and those whose average is less than
$2 are put into Class 3.

The estimate of family income is a difficult task, as everyone
who has tried it knows. The result of the estimate was: 37 families
belonged to Class 1, 64 to Class 2, and 116 to Class 3. That is,
53 per cent belonged to families of a very low economic grade
and in which, we may presume, the wages of the children were
absolutely needed; 47 per cent of the families were able to keep
the boys and girls in school, judged by the amount of money
made by the family at the time the child left school.

Of the 217 families represented, 118 gave the economic cause
as determining the leaving of school. Thirty-one of these were
found to be entirely able to send their children to school. Twenty-
nine families, however, said that dislike of school, being 14 years
old, etc., were the reasons, when further inquiry proved that the
income of the family was inadequate. That 54 per cent of the
families gave the economic cause is a difference of result from

the St. Louis investigation, in which 18 per cent is the ratio. Miss Kingsbury says that the class of family seems to have but little to do with the child's dropping out of school, except when the grades below the seventh are considered.[1] Her final estimate is that 76 per cent of the families are capable of giving their children industrial education, if convinced of the necessity.[2]

It is apparent that economic pressure is more in evidence in the stockyards district than is apparently the case in Massachusetts and in St. Louis. This is natural, considering the low grade, unskilled work, and underemployment of many of the men. A comparison of the average family incomes, the wages of the heads of the families, and the monthly rents in the three groups will make the situation of those in Class 3 plainer.

	CLASS 1	CLASS 2	CLASS 3
Average family income	$24.31	$15.60	$9.46
Average wage of head	14.92	11.52	8.46
Average rent	—	14.40	8.56
Average number in family	6.17	6.26	6.50

It should be remembered that the figures are computed on the basis of the actual income at the time the child leaves school to search for work, and the fathers who are out of work at the time the child stops are counted as factors in the average. In Class 1 most of the families are prosperous, some have steady employment, and more than half own their homes. The ownership of homes is in itself no criterion of economic security, for there is no more hard-pressed family than one striving to pay for a home or one subrenting a rundown tenement; nineteen of those in Class 3 owned their homes. Nearly half of the third group, also, derived the whole or a part of their incomes from work in the stockyards.

The meager wages of the male heads of families in this group are further apparent from the fact that 26 of them received less than $6 a week, 44 less than $8 a week, 59 less than $10 a week, and 76 less than $12 a week.

[1] Massachusetts Report, pp. 85, 86. [2] Massachusetts Report, p. 92.

It was thought at first that the precarious condition of Class 3 could be partly ascribed to the larger families, but although there is a slight tendency upward from the first to the third class, the difference is so slight that it is negligible.

The ever-present danger of being "laid off," the seasons of strenuous work followed by complete idleness, and the impossibility of knowing from one week to the other just how many hours were to be "made" were the tales told by scores of men and women ; and under these circumstances the temptation to grasp at the three or four dollars which the boy or girl can earn is almost irresistible.[1] In this neighborhood, therefore, the judgment of Ayres, that "while pupils who leave school very naturally go to work, it is probably comparatively seldom that they are compelled to leave for the purpose of seeking work," is not sustained.[2]

SECTION III. SOME PHASES OF THE PROBLEM OF VOCATIONAL DIRECTION

THE FUTILITY OF VOCATIONAL GUIDANCE FOR THE FOURTEEN-TO-SIXTEEN-YEAR-OLD WORKING CHILD

Little service can be rendered by the vocational adviser if children leave school before the age of sixteen years. Their lack of preparation is against them ; the jobs available are inferior and poorly paid ; the number of applicants is legion ; and boys and girls are lacking in judgment and forethought.

Study of the children and the occupation suited to each of them should be undertaken while they are under the supervision of the school. When they become older they may gain a comprehension of themselves and a sense of the historical and social value of their occupations. Before sixteen, at least, the children's vocation is to grow.

Difficulties and obstacles are the theme of any discussion of vocational guidance in the fourteen-to-sixteen-year period. The

[1] The description of labor conditions in the stockyards written by John R. Commons in 1904 has value still as a general outline, *Quarterly Journal of Economics*, Vol. XIX, pp. 1–32.

[2] Ayres, Laggards in our Schools, p. 100. The statement is made in connection with a table giving reasons for leaving high school, but it characterizes the standpoint of the whole chapter.

obstacles present in the stockyards district are to be viewed from the standpoint of the parent, the child, and the employer. Why the school is the logical means of coping with the situation will then be stated.

I. The Standpoint of the Parent: Ignorance, Cupidity, and Good Intentions

As a rule the parent does not know his own child, has taken little account of his aptitudes, and cannot see the mistake in accepting a job paying fair beginning wages but offering nothing afterward. Sometimes parents seemed entirely unconcerned about what happens to their daughters and sons; some were unable to tell where their children worked. They knew that it was down town, that there was a street car concerned, and that money came in on Saturday night. This ignorance is a symptom of something besides vague geography. If the parent uses the criterion of money to test the desirability of every job, it is no wonder that the child adopts it. We have come across several cases in which the father took an indefinite vacation to celebrate the son's entrance into money-making.[1]

The parent also admires the ".genteel" and poorly paid "inside work." The Lithuanian father is proud that his fourteen-year-old son works in a stockyards office, and the mother thinks that sorting coupons is a ladylike occupation for her daughter. The glitter and cleanliness of the department store tend to obscure its undesirable features for the adolescent.[2]

A deplorable condition already mentioned results from the willingness of parents to allow their sons to leave school and loaf around their groceries or saloons. The boys are indolently waiting until they are older before entering upon a serious program of life. The parents are able to give their children years of preparation, but seemingly do not realize the effect of this period of idleness upon the child. An owner of a cigar factory said that after a

[1] An example of irresponsible oversight of youth is found in the case of a father reeking with whisky, bewailing the degeneracy of boys generally, and his son (who was denounced for smoking cigarettes) particularly.

[2] There were, however, several expressions of the undesirability of department-store, factory, and stockyards jobs from mothers and fathers, as well as from children.

while he was going to send his boy to "college," and a Bohemian shoe-store-keeper explained that he was giving the finishing touches to his son's education, and that quitting school gave his boy more time to play the fiddle.

But the solicitude and desire for the welfare of the child on the part of some of the parents is as marked as their lack of knowledge of the means thereto. More than a half of the parents consulted were in favor of a kind of school training leading to a better kind of position than that for which the present course prepares; the women who scrub floors, "take in washing," and deny themselves in order that their children may continue in school are evidence that in many instances the feeling for better things needs but to be instructed. In scores of families the parents are on the lookout for an opening for the children, and deplore the fact that the trades and the labor unions are closed to them because they have no influence.[1] Fathers who have worked for years in the Yards for constantly diminishing pay realize the disadvantages of unskilled labor, and they desire that their children may have as few handicaps as possible. One who directs the children, therefore, has to fight the prejudice and ignorance of the parents and utilize their good feelings and intentions.

II. The Attitude of the Child to his Job

(a) *Demand for self-expression and growth.* When a boy leaves school, tired of its routine, he demands novelty, excitement, and action. He prefers occupations which afford them. Almost any place may satisfy for a time, but one position soon grows monotonous and the youth demands a change. If the job fails to yield the joy of being an "enterpriser," of seeing some results, he passes on to another. Moving about the city is one of the attractions of messenger and errand boy. Boys often volunteer the information that they care for such employment because it "learns them something about the different parts of the city." It

---

[1] There is much waste in this regard. Employers have asked us to recommend candidates, and suitable persons could not be found easily. Some unions are closed to all except relatives of those in the trade; consequently healthful competition for places is stopped. There is no labor exchange to equalize supply and demand.

is also true that there is more excitement and a feeling of a glowing future in looking for work than in actually holding a tame job. This fact should enable us to look with some lenience on the frequent quitting of places for trivial reasons, although it does not do away with the pedagogical duty to counsel the offender regarding the results of the rolling stone and the rewards of steady industry.[1]

(*b*) *Impersonal relation of children to large industries.* Since there is a constant coming and going of workers in most large establishments, and since the personal relation with the employer is often slight, there is a great temptation for the beginner to feel that he does not "belong" and consequently to stop work on the slightest pretext. One boy complains that his boss "takes his dinner"; that is, compels him to work during the noon hour. An errand boy states that he is not given enough carfare; another stops work because the street-car conductor would not allow him to obstruct the passageway with large bundles. Probably all these grievances could have been adjusted, but the boy rebels against the necessary trouble of bringing the matter before officials with whom there is not much acquaintance, and he suddenly quits. There are other more serious causes of friction, as the several instances of boys under sixteen who were asked to work longer than the legal number of hours. In all these cases the child realizes that he is part of a complex machine and asserts his freedom by leaving it entirely.

The external and impersonal nature of the contact of the boy with the employer is further shown when we consider the uncontrolled

---

[1] The discussion of Bray in his book, "The Town Child," merits the attention of every one interested in vocational direction. The view is that mental and moral changes are taking place in the city child due to the effect of the street, shallow amusement, diversity and shifting of sights and sounds, irregular placing of buildings, the motiveless coming and going of people, the vicissitudes of employment, and other urban phenomena. The features of the "city mind" are lack of continuity, restlessness, superficiality of thought and feeling, undue suggestibility, and failure to appreciate the mystery of human life and the presence of natural law. The slowness and depth of the rural boy, his tranquillity, sense of power, pleasure in the rhythm of the seasons and the quiet beauty of primitive nature, and knowledge of biological sequences ought not to be lost. We should amalgamate the two dispositions, giving the best features of the city to the country and transferring rural advantages to the city.

Some exaggerations of the "mob mind" sociologists are evident in this theory. The elements of truth any observer of city children can verify.

way in which jobs are secured. Sometimes the finer grade of
boy makes a poor appearance when he looks for work, alone.
The aggressive boy of the motor type is apt to draw the attention
of the man who hires, and boys of other types are at a disadvantage. The Minority Report of the English Poor Law Commission
has made it plain that the capacity to do work and the ability to
find work are two distinct processes.[1] The first job of the child
presents an important crisis, and the future disposition to work
and to shoulder responsibility often depend upon the degree to
which the child responds to the demands made upon him in his
first position.

Frequently the boy " happens " to get a job on leaving school,
becomes irritated at what he considers the tyranny of the boss, and
quits, with the seeds of the roving habit thus early sown. Almost
all of a group of boys giving a great deal of annoyance to the
Settlement began their working careers with temporary jobs as
messenger boys. The testimony of the juvenile-court officer in
our district confirms the all-importance of " getting started right."
In most cases " getting started right " is an impossibility for the
juvenile worker.[2]

(c) *Loyalty to family as a cause of entering "blind-alley" jobs.*
A generous desire to help their parents is often the reason why
boys accept fairly lucrative " blind-alley " jobs rather than permanently desirable kinds. To keep the younger children in school
and to pay the rent is a pressing need in comparison with which
the future is insignificant. A boy who had paid his tuition in a
business college left after a few weeks of school to go to work,
without the knowledge of his parents. He brought his two weeks'
pay to his parents, saying that it was his duty to take the place of
his father, who had been laid off. He has not returned to finish

---

[1] Minority Report, Vol. II, pp. 169, 190–193.

[2] The feeling of boys working in an establishment toward the "green" newcomer is
also a hindrance for the timid sort. A good chance of placing a boy was spoiled by the
tricks and jeerings of a group of "hazers" who sent the applicant from one part of the store
to another in his search for the employer until he finally came back to the Settlement, dis-
gusted. Some employers are finding out that there is need of leadership and oversight
of juvenile workers, more than the busy manager of departments can give. Antagonism
and jealousy will crop out, and children especially ought to be guarded from their hurtful
consequences.

the business-college course and is now out of work. Another example may be mentioned. A boy who was given an opportunity to enter a printing establishment, in which there is provision for going to school at the same time that a number of hours a week is spent in paid work during the apprenticeship period, refused to take the place because the beginning wage was smaller than that paid to errand boys. His family needed the additional support.

(d) *False estimates of the desirability and future of jobs.* (1) Boys : Boys are not good critics of their positions nor can we expect them to be. After leaving school many of them start in enthusiastically and continue in a place where there is no possible chance of being assimilated. One bright, industrious boy worked over a year at hard, responsible tasks in a large office without either friendly encouragement or an increase in pay, and he at last realized that his endeavors were being wasted.[1] There is a general opinion that opening and shutting doors is a good job. Boys say they like their jobs because they are easy or clean or pay " good money."

What occupations are preferred by boys ? To determine customary opinion in this regard the children already at work and those looking for employment were questioned. In some instances but a short time had elapsed since the child had commenced to work. Consequently the period is not long enough for the first elation at making money and the feeling of newness to die out; the child's satisfaction may be momentary. On the other hand,. the discontent first felt may give way to liking for a place.

Half of the boys holding messenger, errand, and office jobs expressed satisfaction with their places, a ninth were dissatisfied, and the rest " didn't know," " never thought of it," showing indifference or uncertainty. In addition to the contented ones noted

---

[1] Several boys claim that it is the policy of a few firms to hire young persons for small beginning wages under a pseudo-apprenticeship arrangement. After a year or more of work without increase of pay, they are discharged. This report was not verified, but the boys are confident that they are unjustly treated. It is unfortunate that boys sometimes consider the apprenticeship plan of little account, and that employers are not careful to avoid an erroneous impression, for to destroy a boy's faith in the rewards of steady industry at a time when dreams of future excellence and responsibility are natural is more than stupidity.

above, the occupations for which decided satisfaction was shown were as follows :

Number of Boys satisfied with Jobs	Jobs
11	Factory
6	Apprentices in printing firms
4	Helpers in grocery, bakery, etc.
3	Wagon boys
1 each of	Farm, buying cattle, baker, tailor, painter, druggist, plumber, and jeweler positions

This question was put to boys out of work : What kind of job do you want ?

Number of Boys	Jobs
9	Errand or messenger
7	" Some trade "
3	" Machine shop "
2 each of	Bookkeeper, farm, elevator boy, and cracker factory
1 each of	Running auto, navy, electrician, drawing, butcher, office work, telegrapher, engineer, plumber, " business," driver, and " inside job "

For examples of the differences between the job held and the job wished for, we may cite a wagon boy who is ambitious to become a teacher, a factory boy who looks for a place involving drawing, a cash boy who seeks to be a carpenter, a " tagger " at Armour's packing plant who aims to be an electrician, a messenger boy who wants a place where he can " work with his hands."

The opinions which boys venture are reflections of immature judgment and a narrow field of choice. As children grow older, restlessness and friction are apt to intensify and become articulate; some of the older boys expressing dissatisfaction were hostile to any work except the easiest and best paid. Somewhat less than one fourth of the boys were discontented, a fourth were without an opinion, and a half were satisfied.

Mr. Ristine found a similar incapacity to analyze the relative advantages of positions among older boys. Dissatisfaction was more general, outside of those in desirable trades. He estimates that 60 per cent of the 350 cases wanted "trade or business training." This is not true of the children of this district; as a rule, they do not know clearly what they want or what is best for them. This does not gloss the undefined discontent, the occasional vivid perception by them of their unused capacities, and the necessity of studying and supervising their careers.[1]

(e) *False estimates of the desirability and future of jobs.* (2) Girls: Like the boys and the parents, the girls are often too optimistic of the future, saying, "I'll get a fine job after a while." They refuse chances to learn millinery and dressmaking on account of the smaller wage, and because they think that they will be discharged after the apprenticeship is over.[2] There is less roving and chafing under the burden of uncongenial jobs. In some girls the habit of obedience is so strong that they will do unreasonable "extras" for the employer, such as scrubbing out a factory at the end of the Saturday's work, and unscrupulous employers can make the most of this attitude on the part of both boys and girls. A grievance of one girl was that her employer kept all the girls of a large factory working on Christmas Day.

On the whole, there is less discontent among the girls. Ten only of those employed were decided in their distaste for their work, the jobs held being garment, millinery, office, and factory work. It is significant that twenty-eight girls in candy, box, and net factories said that they had good places and wished no change. The other occupations considered satisfactory, in the order of number of cases, were department store, office, housework, tailors' apprentices, dressmaking, bindery work, and millinery. Of those not working when interviewed, the preferences were for sewing, factory, housework, office employment, and stenography. One fifth of the entire number were uncertain.

Several girls, after trying a few jobs, went back to school, and one was found who planned to take a $25 course in a private

---

[1] Cf. Ristine, op. cit., pp. 44 ff.

[2] A milliner of the neighborhood alleges that it is very difficult to obtain a sufficient number of apprentices for her business, although the prospects held out to them are brighter than the futures of most occupations open to fourteen-year-old girls. A few girls see in housework superior educative advantages, but many prefer the excitement, sociability, and regular hours of the factory or department store. The local stores because of this can hire girls of the neighborhood for $1.75 per week.

dressmaking school; but generally there is little patronage of the commercial institutions in which garment making, hairdressing, and the finer arts are taught.

The conclusion is that working boys and girls are immature in judgment of their jobs, can therefore be exploited by employers, and that vocational oversight can do little positive service in the adolescent period once the child has entered industry. The children should be in school, and the study of the child and the future occupation should be made by the vocational adviser while the adolescent is securing training in the school.

III. Attitude of the Employer: Inefficiency of Juvenile Labor

Many employers question the utility of juvenile labor. Some of the packing establishments dislike to hire boys under sixteen years of age. This is partly due to the advantage of the longer hours of the older boys, partly to a pronounced dissatisfaction with the bother of training the irresponsible children. The criticism of the employer is that the boys are impolite, mischievous, do not apply themselves, are not ambitious, and cannot be depended upon. One employer in the general office of a packing house said that more "mental" schooling and a "code of ethics" were necessary; another believed that the "quality of boy" is much inferior to that of the old days; he complained that 40 per cent of the boys employed during the year either left or did not advance.[1] He preferred eighth-grade or high-school boys. Another employer of a large number of boys in one of the general offices of the stockyards declared that he advises every boy who applies for work to go back to school. The head of another employment department said that "foreign boys" are unclean and rowdy, and recited the

[1] According to the estimate of a man who employs boys in one of the packing establishments, there are over three hundred fifty boys under sixteen employed in errand running and clerical work in the Yards. The annual shifting is therefore considerable. Some of the failure to be assimilated is to be ascribed to childish instability, some to the fact that the undersized boys are not likely to be selected for the work outside the office, much of which requires endurance and weight. Another obvious reason is that the defective training of the boys does not fit many of them to take managerial positions.

According to the testimony of an executive in a mail-order firm employing many boys, the average "life" of a boy is one year. That means a replenishing of the entire juvenile force each year. This executive also said that his business and all industries could be adjusted to the sixteen-year school minimum.

story of an errand boy who on being sent to a prominent official with a message, began his speech with " Say, that there guy down below. . . ." What he demanded of boys was " not so much book knowledge as gumption." A printing-concern manager said that only one out of twelve boys sticks to his job, and that they want an immediate " raise " and the highest pay for the easiest work.

Several employers in the offices of the stockyards said that under existing conditions it is better to take boys of fourteen or even younger and train them for their business. Boys fresh from elementary school are more docile and less " smart-Alecky " than the older boys, and the commercial training in the schools is not practical, according to their opinion. An owner of a box factory declared that he was in favor of industrial education, but that the competitive state of the industry was such that the cheap, mechanical tending of the machine was necessary, and that only those who start in before they are sixteen learn and stay with the business.

What are qualities which employers demand of boys and girls ? The following personal answers of employers will suggest the situation. The requisite qualities for employees in department stores are said to be " neatness, quickness, and loyalty " ; they must also be good " talkers." Employees in candy and box factories are asked to be " bright " and have " quick fingers." Errand boys must be " polite, obedient, resourceful, neat, and clean." Office boys must " write a good hand, take an interest, be steady, and look for advancement."

It is plain that there are two tendencies struggling for supremacy : one is to consider the fourteen-year-old child undesirable material for industry, both in education and mental characteristics ; the other is a disposition to utilize him in the interests of a specialized business, on the theory that the training thus early secured is beneficial and a road to advancement. The latter view is being abandoned in all industries except those to be classed as parasitic.

A word may be added about the employer's relation to girl labor. The testimony of the president of one of the box factories is interesting because the box industry is a low-grade avenue of employment for a number of girls in our neighborhood. This employer says that industrial education would not help him in the least, since the shortening of hours and the increase of age limit are forcing him to introduce machinery to counteract the advancing cost of help. This means that less intelligence is constantly being required. He states that his attitude to his employees is a commercial one, and that "sociological workers" fail to appreciate the employer's side of the problem. The necessity of hiring girls under sixteen comes from the fact that he finds it impossible to get permanent workers unless he can train the younger girls in his factory, since only 20 per cent of the girls over sixteen when they begin to work remain more than two weeks. Girls who have worked from fourteen to sixteen "like the place," are capable, and "stickers" when put on machines.[1]

The women who employ young girls to do "housework" or to care for children complicate the matter. Several times it has happened that well-disposed girls refuse to work longer than a few weeks for the women employers. The girls say they are not fairly treated and that more and more work is constantly thrust upon them, so that they finally were performing in an efficient manner the full duties of a domestic servant, and for a small weekly sum. Certainly this is only a phase of the wider domestic-servant problem; and the old argument that the women use, that they are "taking the girl into their home" and teaching her a fine art, does not remove the narrow and undemocratic character of the relationship.[2] The girls, under these conditions, dislike the care of the house and prefer the definite duties of the factory. In either housework or factory employment of the type represented by the box industry there is an undoubted absence of stimulus and opportunity for promotion, and the employer does not deny the fact.

IV. The School and Vocational Direction

The one point to be insisted upon here is that the institution upon which the solution of the problem of vocational guidance logically rests is the public school. Private organizations may

---

[1] Webb, Industrial Democracy, Vol. II, pp. 749-766, deals with "parasitic" industries; that is, those which cannot afford to pay a living wage.. Cf. Florence Kelley, "Minimum-Wage Boards," *American Journal of Sociology*, November, 1911, for the attitude of the Consumers' League to underpaid occupations.

[2] Cf. Dean, The Worker and the State, chap. iii.

demonstrate the feasibility and helpfulness of limited experiments in this movement, and they may coöperate at all times, but their experiments are preparatory to state or municipal management as a part of the public-school system. The state employment agencies now undertake only a relatively slight control of the immediate stress of employment, and they have had small success because of a lack of thoroughness, perspective, and the social attitude which the public school possesses.

The school is already organized and recognized; its time-honored function — preparation for life — is preserved by the more systematic method of adjusting the child to his work which has been developed in Boston by Professor Parsons and Mr. Bloomfield. The school already connects with the legal machinery of the state, with the family, and to some extent with the professions and the humbler occupations. The present problem is to enlarge the scope of education so as to include the store, the factory, the office, and the shop in the circle of reputable and dignified social agencies.[1]

Vocational guidance will stimulate needed changes in the school curriculum. The responsibility of taking care of the child, of connecting him with the economic world, will contribute toward a change in the method of instruction in the public schools. There is a close relationship between vocational education and vocational guidance. Each should work with the other, the economic world affecting the school curriculum, and the methods and aims of the school refining the methods and aims of industry.

The introduction of vocational guidance as an integral part of the school administration would go far toward increasing the dignity and efficiency of "business" in all its forms. To look upon education as "the method of democracy" and to extend its scope in the way contemplated by a vocational-guidance program, it is

---

[1] Marshall Field's department store is now making provision for definite instruction of the women employees in the art of sales-making. The history and process of manufacture of the articles sold are presented by the most competent persons in each department. This experiment, ably conducted by Miss Collins, has undoubtedly helped to add dignity and significance to commercial transactions. In New England cities a further step has been taken — that of coöperation between school and store — so that children still in school may devote part time to study and practice in this field of employment. Cf. *Bulletin No. 13*, Part I, pp. 6–16, issued by the National Society for the Promotion of Industrial Education; Dean, The Worker and the State, chap. vii.

necessary to view industry as more than a money-making process, and to demand a social attitude which neither the public nor the employer has hitherto exhibited. It implies a reversal of the individualistic notion of allowing free swing to the thousands of children competing for jobs and to short-sighted employers who are willing to profit by juvenile labor. The admirable character of much German instruction, it is true, implies military and feudal stratification of classes, but Germany has embodied an idea which, in some form, must be realized in America — the idea that the occupation is the root of civic virtues, that the employer is an agent of the community, and that all citizens must be given facilities to learn a useful occupation and be helped to find a steady place.[1]

Since the school aims to be a world in miniature, with the same problems and activities there as are found in the larger world; since the school is a converging point of child, home, government, and industry, it is most fitted to cope with the task of guiding the boy and girl to the appropriate occupation. Through its reorganization of the curriculum, through its influence upon the parent, and through the demands it makes upon industry, legal standards, and public sentiment, it can accomplish what no other institution is qualified to attempt.

SECTION IV. SUMMARY AND CONCLUSION; LINES OF BETTERMENT

SUMMARY

The leading items intended to be emphasized in the foregoing discussion are:

1. The district studied is peopled by immigrants of various races; their work is unskilled, and their main source of employment is the stockyards.

2. The testimony of principal, teacher, child, and parent unites in the conclusion that the public school is not meeting the needs of adolescence and adjusting the child to his future work.

---

[1] Cf. Draper, Our Children, Our Schools, and Our Industries, p. 15; Snowden, Industrial Improvement Schools of Württemberg; Kerschensteiner, The Education of German Youth for Citizenship, chap. iv.

3. The great exodus from school comes before the seventh grade and shortly after the child reaches the age of fourteen.

4. The ignorance of parents, the willingness of children, and the pressure of straitened circumstances combine in forcing boys and girls to leave school for work as soon as the law will permit it.

5. Few children from the neighborhood go to high school, trade school, or keep up any form of educational interest after leaving school.

6. Yet the boys and girls have talents and abilities in special directions.

7. The occupations entered are easily learned, mechanical, and devoid of educational value.

8. The kind of jobs secured is much a matter of chance; the migration from place to place does not lead to better opportunities; the pay is small; and the net result is instability of character.

9. A number of "subnormal" boys are as successful in industry as many "normal" boys.

10. There is no marked economic advantage to be gained by a longer stay in school; before the age of sixteen preparation in school does not count, considering the ordinary run of mechanical occupations open to children.

11. Over half of the families from which the working children come have such a low income that the wages of the boy and girl are judged necessary.

12. The experience of older boys and girls shows a small average contribution to the family income, a short average time in each position, and a long average period of idleness. All of these persons stopped school during the fourteen-to-sixteen-year period.

13. Aside from parasitic industries, there is no economic necessity for juvenile labor, according to the testimony of employers.

14. The public school is best adapted to deal with the problem of vocational direction.

WHAT SHOULD BE DONE?

There are three directions of betterment. The first is to improve the organization and scope of the school. The second is to increase the incomes of the families, so as to make school attendance possible. The third is to institute a vocational-guidance program.

I. Reorganization of the School

(a) *Raising the minimum school age.* The least thing that one may ask is that the school be made attractive and profitable for the sixth- and seventh-grade children before they leave school, even if we accept present conditions and a fourteen-year-minimum school age. If industry entails a sacrifice of children, society should bear the burden of giving them a generous training preparatory to their entrance into uneducational employments, a training appealing to constructive powers and imagination. But moral perception has reached a point where it demands a higher standard than the one at present set. The fixing of the compulsory school-attendance law at a sixteen-year minimum seems essential and introductory to all other devices for betterment. Especially in a community like the stockyards in which custom and habit are dominant, a legal standard is quickly conformed to by the people. Such a standard also registers the conviction of those who believe that the school can adjust the new generation to a changing social order most quickly and economically. If, as has been shown, the period between fourteen and sixteen is an economic and moral waste and if, as psychology asserts, the mind and body of the adolescent are injured by fatigue due to mechanical occupations, it is foolish to refuse to extend the period of responsibility to the sixteen-year minimum. The superior standard has a further advantage; it will hasten the reorganization of the existing school system and stimulate inquiry into causes which limit the success of the school.

(b) *Provision for continuation instruction.* Those already at work and those who leave school on reaching the age of sixteen should be provided for. The existing night schools in the local elementary schools are good, but they are dominated by bookish, academic traditions. They must be also practical, definite, informal, with shop and laboratory atmosphere, if they are to draw the children.

Arrangements with employers so that a number of hours could be spent in school during the daytime would be desirable. In this matter we have the experience of Munich for suggestion.[1]

[1] Kerschensteiner, The Education of German Youth for Citizenship, and Lectures on Industrial Education (Commercial Club of Chicago); Hanus, Beginnings in Industrial Education, chap. v.

There should be opportunities in continuation work: (1) for a boy leaving school to review and extend his knowledge along the regular existing lines of day instruction, so that he may be graduated and attend high school if he desires; (2) for a factory or department-store child to study a trade, as carpentry or millinery; and (3) for a boy engaged, for example, in printing, to get a rounded and generous background at school for his daily specialized work.

An indispensable condition of discovering talents and furnishing guidance is that young persons between fourteen and seventeen be kept under systematic discipline.[1] Such training should have an immediate appeal. To repeat, the reasons for the demand to extend the period of preparation and to alter its character are: (1) the present-day schools do not attract and meet the needs of all types of children; (2) occupational training is not given in sufficient degree in the evening classes of the public schools; (3) after the child leaves school the character of his work and associations tends to lessen interest in all forms of "education." In addition to these practical, near-at-hand considerations, there is the argument which Dr. Kerschensteiner urges, that without such attention to youth the civic welfare of the whole community, including the employer, is threatened.[2]

(c) *The reorganization of the day school.* With a sixteen-year minimum the school will have a fair chance. It is not necessary to repeat the details urged by the exponents of industrial education. A starting point already exists in the local schools — the provisions for the backward, subnormal child, and the manual-training and domestic-science instruction.[3]

These are successful, interesting to the child, and demand extension. The reorganization of the spirit and methods of the school so as to center about occupational and concrete problems and processes will proceed from such extension. Considering the fact that the amount of "culture," information, and lasting interests

[1] The Ohio law gives a municipality the right to compel the sending of children to school in continuation classes until they are seventeen years of age.

[2] Ketcham, The Need of Industrial Education from the Manufacturer's Point of View (Winona Technical Institute School of Printing, Indianapolis).

[3] Principal Hill of the Seward School says that the best woodwork he has ever seen was turned out by his students last year, and the success of the domestic-science instruction in the Hamline School is equally decided.

attained by the children is not now alarmingly great, there is no danger of sacrificing literary and cultural accomplishments if the school becomes more of a laboratory and workshop than a place of recitation. One can assume that the doctrine of "formal discipline" to be obtained exclusively by a selected group of subjects is a relic of medievalism. Whatever devices [1] of flexible articulating courses, relative time given to vocational and nonvocational subjects, etc., may be found feasible, it is absolutely essential that the occupations having to do with the home and the basic industries should have a prominent place.[2]

The domestic arts, designing, decorating, work in wood and metal, the elements of industrial history, civics, geography, and the sciences which are involved in solving practical problems of construction and understanding the evolution of society should be preparatory to a possible further specialization in one of the trades, and it may be added that they are valuable and "cultural" on their own account in any future profession or job. The reported success of the schools of Gary, Indiana, in revolving the curriculum around the neighborhood occupations, and the introduction into the schools of Albany, New York, of definite pieces of work in sewing and mending sent in by the residents of the town, are anticipations of what may be worked out to suit local conditions. For a further example of what may be included in elementary instruction, the rich program of a leading vocational school is cited. The list comprises woodwork in its various forms of carpentry, cabinetmaking, turning, use of milling machinery; metal work — shop practice, forging, plumbing, and electric wiring; printing, bookbinding; drawing, — mechanical, free-hand, — industrial design, and making of blue prints; trade mathematics, business letters, commercial law, geography, composition, applied physics and chemistry, and industrial history.

[1] These points are handled in the forthcoming report of Mr. Ernest Wreidt to the City Club of Chicago.

[2] Training in the domestic arts is essential for all girls. A girl may be married or "keep house" for relatives, or she may work at a trade or in a factory where the machine reproduces the household processes on a large scale. In any case she needs skill and knowledge. The domestic occupations, psychologically, were the chief means by which primitive woman developed intelligence, and they are still fundamental, pedagogically. On this matter the argument has been put by Dewey, The School and Society. Cf. Dopp, The Place of Industries in Elementary Education; Mason, Woman's Share in Primitive Industry.

Description of vocational schools for girls, such as the Albany Vocational School and the Manhattan Trade School, must be omitted. The new Lucy L. Flower Technical High School established this year in Chicago is also illustrative of what will come, not only in the technical high schools but also in the elementary schools.

This vocational instruction is not narrow and "utilitarian." It has the merit of giving a sense of achievement, responsibility, and the power of adaptation. If introduced it would keep a larger number in school, and the increased skill and efficiency would very likely tend to raise the economic grade of the future families of those children who receive the training. At all events, so much anxiety, solicitude, and money have been directed toward the well-being of those who are able to pass on to the high school, technical schools, and the university that it is simple justice to provide for the less favored ones who are of some importance in contributing to the wealth of society.[1]

II. An Economic Aspect of Juvenile Labor

Miss Kingsbury found in Massachusetts that twenty-four children out of each one hundred left school because of economic necessity; in the stockyards district 53 per cent of the number of families studied were in poverty. The stress of faulty preparation for civic life and irregular, underpaid labor now falls upon the boys, girls, and men of this neighborhood, most of whom are at present destined to mechanical, unskilled occupations.

It must be asserted that a sixteen-year-minimum school age and provisions for occupational instruction are not sufficient remedies for the conditions under which the immigrants in the stockyards live. Too much emphasis cannot be placed upon the factor of low family income.[2] In some way, whether by following the example of England in selecting several unskilled occupations and

[1] Cf. Person, Industrial Education, pp. 57–58. On other points treated cf. Snedden, The Problem of Vocational Education, especially pp. 32, 71 ff.

[2] Under probable conditions in the near future it is not at all certain that the elimination, through legislation, of all juvenile labor before the age of sixteen would result in an increased wage to adult workers in unskilled industries, if the regulation is left to the automatic action of competition, and if the supply of immigrant labor is not curtailed. As urged above, it is safer to accept the fact that a large number of young persons are bound to pursue

prescribing a minimum wage standard, or by other intelligent means of regulating competition and free initiative, wages of unskilled labor must be raised to correspond with the higher standard set for the education of children. All observant and humane writers deplore the universally precarious state of the unskilled laborer.[1] Social legislation to remedy this grave state of affairs is an experiment worth trying.

III. The Method of Vocational Direction

The contention is that few occupations, and these mostly undesirable, can be entered by the child before he is sixteen years old. At sixteen he is presumed to be better prepared by school discipline, more stable, and more positions are available. During the fourteen-to-sixteen-year period in school the skill of the vocational director is most valuable, for this period is the seedtime of possibilities. There should then be the closest study of the children, the parents, and the fields of employment.

INADEQUACY OF PRIVATE EMPLOYMENT AGENCIES

Private employment agencies are purely for the purpose of placing persons who will pay a fee. They do not study each candidate adequately; their snapshot and commercial character renders them unfit for more than an immediate means of securing work.[2]

nonstimulating employments, that unskilled adult labor, subject to seasonal demand, is required by our methods of production. It is therefore doubly necessary (1) to give broad social perspective to the rising generation, in order to counteract the narrow specialized machine processes; (2) to give generous pay and protection against unemployment to those engaged in undesirable occupations.

The assumption of many educators that vocational training will inevitably lead to higher wages *for all* is not warranted. It will tend to a richer social existence and more pay to some; for the thousands of men and women who must continue in low-grade industries there must be means of giving protection, security, and a decent wage.

[1] Cf. Hobson's article on "Science and Industry" in the volume entitled Science in Public Affairs, especially p. 204. Fetter admits that "the low income of unskilled labor seems to fall short of its social service" (Principles of Economics, p. 379). Webb, English Poor Law Policy, pp. 300-306, states the preventive policies, including the regulation of unemployment and "underemployment," which are advocated by the authors of the Minority Report of the Poor Law Commission; chaps. iv and v of the second volume of the Minority Report, The Public Organization of the Labour Market, are fundamental.

[2] Grace Abbott, "The Chicago Employment Agency and the Immigrant Worker," *American Journal of Sociology*, November, 1908; cf. the excellent description of German and English labor exchanges, and "Recommendations for a National Regulation of Unemployment" in the Minority Report of the Poor Law Commission, chap. v.

The municipal and state agencies are more successful in handling a relatively few grades of work in the case of older men and women. The efficiency of private benevolent organizations is undoubted, but they reach a small number. The next step is to unify and correlate all the forces directed toward a far-sighted placing of the young, and experiments already tried show that this unification is best done under the supervision of the municipality. To manage the problem requires the coöperation of school board, principals, teachers, employers, and parents.

Some Essentials of Vocational Direction

1. The first requisite is a qualified person in each public school who can give sufficient time to this difficult task. Principals and teachers in the local schools have given attention to placing boys and girls, but the pressure of other duties makes it impossible to handle the situations.

2. The vocational adviser should study the advancement, tastes, and changing interests of the growing boys and girls, keep a record of their progress, and if they pass on to higher schools, send the record to the person there having charge of vocational direction. The points useful in making the record and the manner of studying each individual have been detailed by Parsons and Bloomfield as a result of their experience in Boston.[1]

3. The census reports, opportunities in the various occupations open to children, and any material bearing on the wages, treatment, and qualifications of workers in specific lines of work should be studied, and these facts should be written simply and given to the children for reading and study.[2] For instance, it would be a valuable thing if the conditions and future of candy-factory and

---

[1] Bloomfield, Vocational Guidance, chaps. iii–v; Parsons, Choosing a Vocation, chaps. iii–iv.

[2] To keep in touch with schools and firms offering some pay to boys during the apprenticeship or student period is especially valuable. The coöperation of Lewis Institute with machine foundries — the half-time system, the promotion and bonus scheme of the Lakeside Press, and the apprenticeship system of the Santa Fe and Rock Island railroads are extremely interesting to boys from families of limited resources. The chief phases and examples of coöperation between school and store, factory and shop, as well as a good description of the advantages and limitations of apprenticeship systems, are given in Dean, The Worker and the State, chaps. vii–viii.

errand-boy work should be known beforehand by those who prefer to enter these occupations. Similar information regarding various trades and professions should be at hand.

4. Visits made by the older children in order to see the factories, stores, and workshops with a specific purpose in mind would have a like advantage. They would make the children familiar with the places in which they are to work, and each visit could be supplemented by talks given to the older pupils by business men, professional men, and representatives of labor unions. These talks should be concrete, simple, and unbiased.

5. Coöperation with the labor unions, through some district organization by which promising boys are taken in as apprentices, would be exceedingly desirable, but present conditions in organized labor and organized capital render this a delicate undertaking.[1]

6. An important phase of the vocational-direction movement is the attention given to the instruction of the parent. Bulletins in his own language presenting the advantages and disadvantages of the various avenues of employment, the importance of further training for the children, and the schools now available should be sent to each parent. The circular sent to parents of children leaving school by the Edinburgh School Board is reproduced in Bloomfield's book.[2]

7. Not only should vacancies be reported by the employers, but also permanent relations secured by which the progress of the boy may be kept track of; a " follow-up " system is essential.[3]

[1] That is, difficult if worked out on a large scale; the coöperation of the unions with the Young Men's Christian Association technical school and the school for carpenters' apprentices under the direction of the public-school system are indicative of a new tendency. The trade union has a right to protect its members — their wages and the conditions under which the group works. The readjustment must take place along the line of several conflicting interests. For recent statements of the attitude of organized labor there are the official report of the Federation of Labor on industrial education and the speech of Winslow in *Bulletin No. 13*, Part IV, of the National Society for the Promotion of Industrial Education. Cf. Snedden, op. cit., p. 64; Draper, Our Children, Our Schools, and Our Industries, pp. 32, 92, 93; Professor Richards, Report to the New York State Department of Labor (1908); Apprenticeship and Skilled Employment Association, London; Trades for London Boys; Trades for London Girls; Bemis, " Relation of Labor Organizations to the American Boy and to Trade Instruction," *Annals American Academy of Political and Social Science*, Vol. V, pp. 209–241.

[2] Vocational Guidance, pp. 80 ff.

[3] Cf. Greenwood, Juvenile Labour Exchanges and After-Care; Rowntree and Lasker, Unemployment, chap. i.

One need scarcely suggest that the stimulus of having school advancement count directly toward the boy's finding of a job is a motive, not theoretically the highest, perhaps, but very effective.

Many aspects of vocational guidance have not been mentioned. Without a legal authority like that of the factory inspector, many of the facts regarding some industries cannot be secured by the investigators; such information is indispensable and should be accurate and full, not the amount and kind of data which please the good nature of the persons consulted. This demand is based upon the theory that any business is subject to the common good, and that obtaining information regarding the future places of work of the child is just as essential to the success of the public school as setting a standard of entrance into the teaching profession.

More information from all levels of society regarding the many phases of juvenile labor is requisite. Social settlements, children's protective associations, and other agencies should devise a uniform method of keeping such facts as come to them, so that a sufficient body of material may be available upon which to base public opinion and wise legislation. The provision for an investigation of the conditions calling for vocational direction made by the Massachusetts state legislature recently is a precedent which may profitably be followed by Illinois.

THE AMERICAN GIRL IN THE STOCKYARDS DISTRICT

By Louise Montgomery

(Extracts from an Investigation carried on under the Direction of the Board of The University of Chicago Settlement and the Chicago Alumnæ Club of The University of Chicago)

SECTION I. THE EDUCATIONAL STANDARDS OF THE COMMUNITY

1. The Attitude of the Majority

The dominant educational standard of the neighborhood is the minimum legal requirement of the state, accepted with little protest by the majority, for the people as a whole are essentially a law-abiding people. By habit and tradition they bow before the accepted order of things. In the absence of higher ideals 585, or 65 per cent,[1] of the 900 families take advantage of the compulsory age law to fix the limit of the child's schooling. Within this group it is possible to make a loose classification of the controlling influences among the parents who maintain this minimum standard : (a) the peasant belief that education is the privilege of " the upper classes"; (b) the need of money and the ambition to own property ; (c) the failure of the school to meet the practical demands of the working people ; (d) the ecclesiastical ideal of education which must permeate a community that is dominantly Catholic. This classification is not given to represent exclusive boundary lines. It is common to find families both consciously and unconsciously governed by two or more or all of these influences united.

[1] The percentage is higher for the neighborhood as a whole. To secure material for later comparisons in the wage-earning capacity of girls, a search was made for families who had kept their girls in school to complete the elementary course.

(*a*) Among many hard-headed peasants there is the traditional feeling that education is a luxury either for the well-to-do or for those whom some mysterious power has placed above the common people. "You are not a rich American. You need no education beyond the law," was the answer of the Slovak mother to the daughter who wished to remain in school until the end of her course. "My children belong to the working class," said the German father. "Education will spoil them for earning a living with the hands." Polish parents who owned a three-story tenement from which they were collecting sixty dollars a month in rentals placed their fourteen-year-old little girl in a factory at three dollars a week, not because they were pressed for money but because in the natural order of things she was destined to marry a Polish workingman and it would be very unwise to unfit her for that position by giving her "the education of a Yankee." In more than one half of the 585 families this underlying sentiment rises and falls, sometimes carrying all the weight of an authority that has never been questioned, and again overpowered by a sudden comprehension of the equal opportunities open to all classes through the public schools.

(*b*) A number much larger than that in the above group find an actual need of the child's wages to supplement the earnings of the father. Broadly speaking, when the father's wage falls below two dollars a day there is less hope for the extension of the girl's schooling beyond the compulsory age limit, although the neighborhood furnishes heroic examples of parental sacrifices proving many exceptions to the rule. In this group of 585 families there are 125 women widowed, deserted, or with husbands incapacitated for work, who are dependent wholly or in part on the wages of their children, and the wage of 297 men is steadily below two dollars a day.

The ambition of the immigrant to own property in America is one of his most striking characteristics. For it he will make almost unbelievable sacrifices both of his own comfort and of that of his wife and children, since the heavily mortgaged house too often calls for the united wage-earning power of the entire family. "We are building without money," was the reply of the fourteen-year-old girl when asked why she was leaving school before completing the sixth grade. The strength of this feeling is due in part to the natural desire for a home, which in the stockyards district is intensified by a constant fear of reaching an early [1] old age in helpless penury. The possession of a house from which one may draw an income is the highest mark of prosperity, just as the inability to pay one's rent is the lowest degree of poverty. The sacrifice of little girls to this passionate determination to own property may be found in any social group, from the undaunted widow who takes in washing six days of the week and drives her children to any task that will bring in money to meet the payments on the four-room cottage, to the thriving saloon keeper who is landlord over a dozen tenants. Thirty-seven of the 125 women who must live without the help of the wage-earning man, 138 of the 297 men who can never command two dollars a day, and 95 of the remaining 163 are property owners. [2]

(c) The failure of the elementary school to meet the practical needs of an industrial community is recognized by many parents. Although they cannot always define their dissatisfaction, their ultimate demand is that educational processes shall be measured in terms of economic advantage. With the vague notion that the school should bear some relation to the future usefulness of the child, they often look for concrete results that shall bring immediate returns. " Mary left school in the sixth grade and she can bring home just as much money as Helen, who made all that expense for another year to finish the seventh grade " is a characteristic comment given as conclusive proof that an added year in school has no practical value. A German father who had spent fifteen years as an unskilled laborer in the stockyards patiently and laboriously pondered the relative value of different courses offered in the elementary school and finally decided that even girls need a steady job. " Work with the hands is· good," he explained, " and American education does not give it." A prosperous Bohemian who owns three tenement houses has four daughters who bear witness to the power of his authority by bringing home a weekly wage from department store and factory. Each girl was sent out to work at the age of fourteen

1 Before he is forty years of age the stockyards laborer begins to have a fear of being laid off permanently and giving place to younger men. At forty-five he is in the ranks of the old men, with a lowered vitality that lessens his chances of employment in any capacity.

2 The important subject of housing as it affects the family life has been purposely omitted, as this subject will be considered in forthcoming papers.

years because the father firmly believed that, in the absence of vocational training in the schools, there is no other way of getting a mastery of any occupation. In 123, or 21 per cent, of the 585 families the parents expressed a desire for some definite training that should furnish either trade or business opportunities for girls. This is a small number. More than 50 per cent of these same families believe in trade and business training for boys. The skilled workers from the older countries lament the lack of opportunity to learn a trade in the public schools, and willingly give their girls to tailors, dressmakers, and milliners to work for a nominal wage that merely covers the street-car fare, or even pay for places in the sewing trades because they do not know that apprenticeship as they conceive of it does not exist in America. Parents of this type are ready to make sacrifices for their children, and frankly say that the need of money or the desire for larger gains would not stand in the way of continued schooling "of the right kind," as they phrase it.

(d) Among the 900 families 805 feel an obligation to send their children to the parochial school for a part of their training. The feeling arises from a deep religious conviction that conquers even those who recognize the greater practical value of the work of the public school. In many families the confirmation of the child is the triumphant end of his term of schooling, although this religious ceremony may take place at the close of the fourth or fifth grade. "She has finished school" is the simple reply to a challenge of the idle fourteen-year-old girl, or to the suggestion that more training would be advisable, but in the mind of both parents and child this statement relates to the confirmation only.

* * * * * * * * * *

2. The Attitude of the Minority

Apart from the group of parents who from one motive or another accept the compulsory age limit as their educational standard is another group made up of those who look beyond the law. In 315 families one or more of the children had completed the elementary public-school course, and in a few there was an ambition for high school or business college. Often fathers and mothers had a vague notion of putting their children "beyond their parents" and labored to that end with the patient hope that schooling would do it. Just how this was going to be accomplished they could not explain. As a Bohemian laborer of the stockyards expressed it, "People who have learned nothing do the dirty work of the world. I want my children to have a chance at a clean job. That's why I send them to school." At the birth of his first child, a little girl, a Polish carpenter bought an English dictionary and began paying for an encyclopedia on the installment plan, because he meant to educate his children and he knew that "educated people always have books around." A strong conviction that continued schooling would be best for the child sometimes conquered extreme poverty. An Irish mother denied herself sufficient food that she might pay the cost of sending two children to the high school, and it is not uncommon to find women taking in washing to meet the tuition of a six months' course in a business college. We have seen that in the first group of 585 families 422 are struggling with a poverty that makes the wage-earning child a probable necessity. Although the prosperous financial condition of the family is by no means a guaranty of a higher educational standard, broadly speaking again, when the father's wage is above the two-dollar-a-day limit there is less haste in getting the children into temporary occupations and a little more intelligent consideration of their future. In 180, or 57 per cent, of the 315 families the wage or income of the father alone is steadily above two dollars a day. For 92, or 51 per cent, of the 180 families the father's income is above $825 a year; and $825 a year, according to the standards of the neighborhood, is considered a very comfortable living. This emphasis is laid upon the position of the head of the family because in the majority of cases it is his earning power, and not a temporary income from boarders, lodgers, rentals, or the mother's work, that determines when the child shall leave school.

3. The Prevailing Attitude in Regard to the Education of Girls

The educational standards of the foreign home as outlined above influence the future of both boys and girls, but in the stockyards district it is necessary to take into consideration a point of view that affects girls as a separate class. The fundamental idea that the education of the girl is a matter of much less importance than the education of the boy is accepted without question in all of the 900 families. A well-to-do Polish landlord who doubted the advisability of sending his fourteen-year-old daughter to the high school told with pride of the plans he had in mind for the university training of his son, who was then playing in a kindergarten. A kindly and indulgent father, he had no reason for making this distinction except his negative attitude toward the education of women. "If a girl is very smart," said a Lithuanian mother, "it is well to keep her in school, but when she is not so she must make money before the marriage time comes." That marriage is the ultimate goal of the girl admits of no argument in the community. This state requires no special schooling, and it will come early in life. In the families hard pressed by poverty the girl is made to feel that she must earn money enough to make some cash return for her bringing up. In the probable event of an early marriage, prolonging her school time shortens the period of her life when she is paying this debt. However, it does not follow that all girls are neglected. There are subtle influences that may temporarily obscure a fundamental ideal and give the girl a permanent advantage. Among those who completed the elementary-school course 40 possessed an unusual cleverness that enabled them to finish before the age of fourteen. The only daughter or the youngest girl in the family may be given the exceptional chance to extend her school life a year or more into the high school, not always from any definite conviction of the parents in regard to the needs of the girl, but rather as a matter of indulgence. Especially is this true in families where the income is sufficient, $825 a year or more, and there is a desire to protect the girl at home and keep her from the limited field of industry which a few parents now recognize is the only field open to the girl under sixteen years of age. Still the fact remains that in a community of comparatively low educational standards there is an underlying thought which both consciously and unconsciously assigns to the girl a position inferior to that of her brother.

SECTION II. THE LOCAL SCHOOLS

1. PUBLIC AND PAROCHIAL SCHOOLS

The 900 families live within the district boundaries of three public schools,[1] the Hamline, the Hedges, and the Seward. The combined membership of these schools at the close of September, 1912, was 1273 boys and 1222 girls. They are subject to the general course of study outlined for all of the elementary public schools of the city. Cooking and sewing are the only occupational subjects provided for girls, and there are as yet no opportunities for vocational courses.[2] The Lake High School [3] offers the usual studies, with the exception that the course in household arts is omitted, owing to the lack of a sufficient number of girls to form classes in subjects designed to equip the home-maker. At the close of September, 1912, the membership was 459 boys and 307 girls. The one evening school of the neighborhood, which is open four evenings in the week for twenty weeks of the year, offers optional classes in cooking and sewing for girls over fourteen years of age, and provides special instruction for foreigners who wish to learn the English language. It also gives all pupils who did not complete the eighth grade a chance to make up that loss. The total enrollment for the season closing March 13, 1913, was 511 men and boys and 102 women and girls.

[1] The Hamline School contains an open-air room, a dental room, and provides special instruction for subnormal children. The Seward School has two special rooms set apart, one for subnormal children and one for truants and other children who need individual attention.

[2] For the present the elementary industrial course for grades 6, 7, and 8 (adopted June 29, 1911) is offered only on the special permission of the superintendent and in districts where the demand is sufficient to call for four divisions of pupils.

[3] The Lake High School offers special vocational courses for over-age boys from grades 6, 7, and 8 of the elementary schools. Eighty boys were transferred to these courses in September, 1912. No such provision is made for girls. They may be admitted to the Lucy Flower Technical High School, but the distance, which requires car fare, makes this school prohibitive for those whose need is greatest.

Within this same boundary or closely adjacent to it there are nine parochial schools (eight Catholic and one German Lutheran) that draw pupils from the population of these public-school districts. At the close of September, 1912, the total membership[1] was about 5722. No adequate information is on record of the work of the parish schools, of the relative amount of time spent in teaching the English language, nor of the number of subjects which the pupils are required to accept in a foreign tongue. No study of the parochial-school child has been made. In the absence of an exact card system which records the work of the pupil from the beginning to the end of his school life we have no data from which to draw conclusions. There is a constant movement between the public and the parochial school, and the number of years any child spends in each depends upon the family standards. Some ambitious parents appreciate the loss involved in the change and give to the parochial school the minimum time required. To this group may be added many who are too poor to carry the burden of continued tuition. A large number are loyal to the parochial school as an institution and send their children to the public school only after confirmation.

.   .   .   .

2. The Adaptation of the Public School to the Needs of the Girl

The public-school teachers work under a serious handicap. In a community of low educational standards they are dealing largely with children who either have begun or must end their formal education in a parochial school, or at best are obliged to interrupt the public-school course with a year of absence. However, there are three legitimate methods of testing the success of the present school system: (*a*) the attitude of the girl to the school; (*b*) her continued interest in educational opportunities; (*c*) the extent of retardation and elimination.

(*a*) *The attitude of the girl to the school.* To what extent girls would be able to rise above the level of the home under a different

---

[1] The figures for seven of these schools are given in the official *Catholic Directory* for 1912. Membership by sex is not given.

school system cannot at present be estimated. That the school as it stands to-day has too little power in drawing their voluntary attendance is the conclusion based on the combined testimony of teachers, parents, and children. Of 300 girls who left school before completing the elementary course, 195, or 65 per cent, were below the seventh grade. Of the entire number only twelve went unwillingly, forced to do so by the purely commercial attitude of their parents. Two hundred and eighty-eight, or 96 per cent, had a more or less pronounced dislike of school, as shown by their trivial reasons for leaving and by the eagerness with which they welcomed the first opportunity to escape and go to work for a meager wage. Since the possession of an eighth-grade certificate is a matter of pride, it is not surprising to find a larger number among the so-called "graduates" who expressed a cheerful or even an enthusiastic attitude toward the school. There are certain types for whom the everyday life of the school runs smoothly. They are bright and secure their promotions easily ; they are sociable and find friends ; they are tractable and submit to the discipline of a routine which, if sometimes irksome, is on the whole a part of a happy childhood. Of the 200 girls who are now proud of having completed the elementary course, 102, or 51 per cent, liked school. Ninety-eight disliked it and, if they had been allowed to follow their own childish inclinations, would have left at the earliest opportunity. The parents who compelled 98 girls to complete the eighth grade told many a tale of their trials. "Don't talk to me of high school," said a father. "It's been all I'm worth to drive my children through the first school." "My girls won't take education easily," explained the mother of three daughters with unconscious irony, "because they're all so strong they like something to do."

The girl's dislike of school is not grounded in any discriminating analysis of the situation, and her feeling is often exaggerated [1] by the natural restlessness of this period of youth which brings the desire for new fields of endeavor more alluring because remote and untried. To secure some understanding of the attitude of the older

---

[1] One girl threatened to kill herself if she were forced to stay in school, and cheerfully accepted the alternative of rising at six o'clock in the morning to be ready for a position in a tailor shop, where she could earn three dollars a week.

girl who has had her chance to gratify this childish longing, the simple question, " What did you learn in school that has helped you to earn a living ? " was put to 200 working girls of the first group and to 100 of the second group who are between sixteen and twenty-four years of age. One half of the first group replied, " Nothing." The other half gave, in about equal proportion, reading, writing, arithmetic, and " English when it helps you to talk well." One thoughtful girl realized the gist of the matter when she said, " Nothing helps me much because I had so little of it." The vague notion that training of some kind might increase their earning capacity was revealed in a few answers. As one girl sadly put it, " After we get out and try working a couple of years, we find we need something we have n't got. Maybe it 's education. Whatever it is, we don't know how to get it." The 100 girls of the second group, being eighth-grade graduates and engaged largely in commercial work, gave the same list of studies, but emphasized the value of spelling and grammar. An effort was also made to discover whether education meant greater efficiency, joy in work, or any other satisfaction apart from money values. The revelations were pathetic. For the girls who had missed the benefit of the complete course the school was something altogether remote. It had taught them the " fundamentals," reading, writing, and figuring, which all agreed are a necessity in any position. Beyond this service the school was in no way related to the business of living as they had experienced it. The " graduates " invariably gave some credit to school discipline and training, regardless of their feelings at the time when they were a part of it. A few had found pleasure in the mental activity of the high school or the business college. For the greater number a longer period in school meant an opportunity to enter that respectable form of occupation known as " the office job." These positions are held in exaggerated esteem throughout the entire neighborhood and, by giving a certain " upper class " quality to the girls who secure them, add to the value of the conventional requirements of the school.

It is not possible to draw exact conclusions from evidence of this character, yet it has a certain suggestive value. Judged by the personal feelings of girls, there is too little joy in the present formal processes of education. From the testimony of the older girls it is evident that the school leaves but slight impression upon those who fail to receive the benefit of a complete elementary course.

(b) *Continued interest in educational opportunities.* It has been a widely accepted notion in the past that pupils may take advantage of the evening school to compensate in a measure for their failure to secure the needed training of the eight grades. The principal who has had ten years of experience in the evening school of the neighborhood states that few girls care for what he calls "regular class work." One wishes to make a shirt waist, another would like to trim a hat, a third asks for the teacher's help in fitting a skirt, and a few enjoy the sociability of a cooking class. The majority are seeking a pleasant evening, the free use of a sewing machine, and some immediate practical returns for their time, but do not take kindly to technical instruction in any subject. During the past year two girls completed in the evening school the required studies of the elementary course and at the present writing are candidates for the eighth-grade certificate. No other cases are on record. In the first group of 300 girls there are 18 who attended the evening sessions for one season. Only 15 have been willing to spend their evenings at the Settlement in cooking, sewing, or millinery classes. Two ambitious girls paid $50 and $60 respectively for special courses in sewing, one to a private dressmaker and the other to a "college of dressmaking." Of the three girls who went to business college two gave it up before the end of the six months' course because of deficient preparation in English. The third, after spending six months in the college and three months in searching for an opening, surrendered in bitter disappointment and went into a bookbindery, though she innocently insisted that she might have been a stenographer if anyone had been willing to give her a position. This is the record of 38 girls who made the effort to secure systematic training in some form after leaving school. For the remaining 262, when the school granted the work certificate it was equivalent to a dismissal from all active educational interests. It is evident that even the American-born girl of the community cannot make up for a deficient education by taking class instruction after working hours.[1] Yet these girls are not stupid. They are[2] handicapped in many ways. Work from eight to ten hours a day taxes their strength; neither their ambitions nor their special aptitudes and interests have been stimulated to the point of making further attendance at school seem desirable. Moreover, the independent effort expected of those who voluntarily attend special classes is too often beyond their capacity because they have missed the training and discipline they should have received at an earlier age.

In the second group of 200 girls 19 attended the Lake High School for periods ranging from three months to three years. (One remained three years, and six stayed two years.) Twenty-four were in the high school at the time this investigation was in process. Thirty-four went to business college for periods ranging from two months to one year. Five are in business college at the present writing. Five had given one winter to the evening school, but not one had attended the domestic classes at the Settlement. This makes a total of 87 out of 200 in contrast to the 38 out of 300 who tried to take advantage of educational opportunities open to them after leaving the elementary school. This difference in favor of the eighth-grade graduate is due in part to a greater freedom from financial pressure, but in a larger measure to the school training that made a profitable continuation of any line of study possible.

(c) *The extent of retardation and elimination.* The recent conclusion that the instruction given in the eight grades of the elementary school is better fitted to the needs of the girl than to the nature of the boy is based upon Ayres's[3] investigation showing the relative distribution of boys and girls in the grades and the greater percentage of retardation and elimination among boys. He finds

[1] The new compulsory education law of Ohio, in effect May, 1910, recognizes the need of part-time day schools for working children between fourteen and sixteen years of age who have not completed the eighth grade. Evening-school hours may not be accepted as a substitute.

[2] In his study of the educational status of working-boys Mr. Ristine found that "boys of the eighth grade were superior to those of the seventh, as were those of the seventh superior to the sixth" (A Report on Vocational Training in Chicago and in Other Cities by a Committee of the City Club of Chicago, p. 277). As far as the writer knows, no similar tests have been given to girls.   [3] Ayres, Laggards in our Schools, p. 158.

that "retardation among boys in elementary schools is 13 per cent more prevalent than among girls"; also that "the proportion of girls who remain to the final elementary grade is 17 per cent greater than the proportion of boys who remain." Accepting the method of computation used by Ayres, Mr. Wreidt,[1] in his study of the public schools of Chicago, finds that for the city as a whole there is 15 per cent more retardation among boys than among girls, and also that the percentage of girls in the first grade who remain to enter the eighth is 15 per cent greater than the percentage of boys. He accepts Ayres's conclusion that the present school system is "better suited to the needs of the girls than to those of the boys."

This conclusion is not wholly true for the district under consideration. The following tables present retardation and elimination figures[2] for three public schools :

TABLE I. PERCENTAGE OF RETARDED PUPILS AMONG BOYS AND AMONG GIRLS IN THREE LOCAL SCHOOLS

School	Boys	Girls	Difference in Favor of the Girls
Hamline	33.6	23	10.6
Hedges	26.6	21.9	4.7
Seward	34.6	32.8	1.8 .
Average of percentages .	31.6	25.9	5.7

In each school there is more retardation among boys than among girls. Since the average percentage of retardation is 31.6 among

[1] A Report on Vocational Training in Chicago and in Other Cities by a Committee of the City Club of Chicago, pp. 31-32.

[2] Based on the age and grade records of pupils at the time of their first enrollment during the school year 1910-1911. The method of computation is that used by Ayres in presenting the relative amounts of retardation and elimination among boys and girls in fifteen cities. The results differ slightly from those obtained by securing the percentage of retardation and elimination for the three schools together according to the method of computation used above to obtain the percentage for each school separately. The results obtained in computing retardation must vary according to the method employed and the time in the school year at which the statistics are gathered. Ayres has pointed out the difference between figures on record in September and those on record in June even in the same city; also the difference between figures gathered on the basis of total enrollment and those gathered at a given date in the school year.

boys and 25.9 among girls, taking the percentage of retardation among girls as a basis, we find that retardation among boys is 22 per cent greater than among girls.

TABLE II. PERCENTAGE OF BOYS AND GIRLS RETAINED TO THE EIGHTH GRADE IN THREE LOCAL SCHOOLS

SCHOOLS	PERCENTAGE OF BOYS RETAINED TO THE EIGHTH GRADE	PERCENTAGE OF GIRLS RETAINED TO THE EIGHTH GRADE	DIFFERENCE IN FAVOR OF THE BOYS
Hamline	30	27	3
Hedges	35.5	28.1	7.4
Seward	32	23.4	8.6
Average of percentages .	32.5	26.2	6.3

In each school a greater percentage of boys than of girls is retained to the eighth grade, the difference in favor of the boys being 6.3 per cent. Taking the percentage of girls retained to the eighth grade as a basis, we find that the proportion of boys who remain in school to enter the eighth grade is 24 per cent greater than the proportion of girls who remain. These figures show a condition for the three local schools the reverse of that revealed in other investigations in which a higher percentage of retardation is naturally followed by a higher percentage of elimination. Not all of the pupils retained to the eighth grade remain to complete the course. A count was made of the number of children who received eighth-grade certificates from the three schools during a period of six years. From September, 1906, to July, 1912,[1] 249 boys and 213 girls are so recorded. Judged by the extent of retardation, the tendency of the girls of the stockyards district is the same as that of girls everywhere. They are meeting the demands of the American public-school system more easily than their brothers. In spite of this fact,

---

[1] During the same period 14 boys and 2 girls, who had previously graduated from the Seward or the Hamline schools, completed a four-year course at the Lake High School. One boy and one girl, both from the Hamline School, finished the two-year business course. No boy or girl from the Hedges School has completed any course at the Lake High School. No records were secured from the Catholic High School located at Wallace and Forty-fifth streets.

the percentage of elimination among the girls is greater than that found in Chicago as a whole and in other cities of which we have similar records.

It is not possible to push the logic of Ayres to the conclusion that these local schools retain to the eighth grade and also graduate a higher percentage of boys because the work offered is better suited to their needs. The explanation seems to lie in the educational standards of the community, which, as we have seen, regard the education of the boy as a matter of more consequence than the education of the girl.

SECTION III. THE GIRL AS A WAGE-EARNING CHILD

1. THE ATTITUDE OF THE PARENTS

The political and religious conflicts of the older nations have had little influence in determining either the character or the extent of immigration to the stockyards district. With few exceptions, these foreign people came to America with the hope of improving their financial condition. Many brought with them the simple conviction that in the New World there are vast spaces in which may be found unlimited opportunities to work at relatively high wages. It must be remembered also that there is no economic surplus which makes the idle woman possible. From necessity neither women nor children are exempt from labor of some kind, and there is no sentiment in the community that favors their existence as an unproductive class. The ever-present thought of the girl's early marriage renders the careful choice of an occupation unnecessary. As a natural result of this point of view, the immediate money value of any position open to little girls is too often the first consideration, in entire disregard of disastrous effects that may follow in the physical, mental, or moral life of the child. Yet the foreign mothers who appear to accept as a matter of course demoralizing conditions of employment for their daughters are not necessarily brutal in other relations with them. The women are vigorous, hard-headed, and practical, and to them belongs the difficult task of making ends meet. Moreover, they are altogether ignorant of the city outside of their very limited round, for the majority who innocently send their little girls to look for work " down town somewhere " have never done a day's shopping beyond the two or three blocks on Ashland Avenue where the department stores supply all of their needs. Fathers too often have no knowledge of opportunities other than those of the packing industry where they are employed. Many a father who persistently refuses even in the face of poverty to secure a place for his daughter in the " Yards," because he has some understanding of the conditions there, will unwittingly expose her to greater dangers in remote industries of which he knows nothing. Men and women are facing unknown conditions, a strange language, and an unwonted freedom. They look back to their own childhood of early hard labor in the small village or the open field and justify the work of their children in the city factory. It is a complex situation for simple minds, and a confusion of standards is inevitable.

2. The Method of Finding Work

Since parents lack a constructive knowledge of the occupations open to their daughters, the girls are thrown upon their own limited resources. The first information often comes from a neighbor's daughter, who knows the wage of the beginner in the place where she herself is working. With this one fact only as a guide the girl may make an application in person with no thought of her fitness for the place and no knowledge that a vacancy exists. Assistance of this kind from friends or relatives can have no positive value without a point of view which they do not possess. The best employment offices do not care to handle child labor. Boys sometimes resort to them, but little girls, being less daring and more economical, will not promise the first week's wages for the sake of a position which others have found with no expense. The only intelligent assistance has come from a few school-teachers, who have voluntarily followed a limited number of children beyond the door of the schoolhouse, and from the Settlement, which has always made an effort to keep in touch with groups of young people. However, there is another factor to be reckoned with in the problem of supervision. The escape from the discipline of school often brings a sudden recognition of an unaccustomed freedom that may be used without question. Girls have been known to avoid the Settlement for fear of being advised to return to school, or of missing the chance to go to the heart of the city. Untrained girls of this age and type are essentially gregarious, and they blindly follow this instinct. If one finds a place in a factory on the West Side of the city, a dozen others in her block will follow if possible, in spite of the inconvenient distance and an altogether undesirable occupation. The haphazard way of finding work has its attractions and appears to offer wide opportunities. Day after day groups of little girls go the round of one factory after another, pitifully ignorant of a condition that makes the field of industry into which they seek an entrance always overcrowded with applicants of their kind, and feeling only a certain childish wonder and joy in the roar of a great city. Often they spend weeks following the incomplete and misleading advertisements of the newspapers, usually finding that the positions call for girls beyond their years and ability, and it is not impossible to find them walking up and down State Street, leaving a poorly written application for work at the several department stores and even stopping men and women with an eager request for "a job somewhere." In all this there is a pleasurable excitement if it does not last too long and a cheap position results from their wanderings.

In such a manner and with no preparation little girls go from the comparative protection of the school and the home to gain their first experiences as wage earners. The opportunities for indiscretions and follies at the close of many such days of unguided freedom in a large city must not be underestimated.

3. Where the Compulsory Education Law Fails

The first group of 300 girls contains 185 who found immediate occupation. (This does not mean steady employment.) Forty-two were taken out of school by busy mothers who demanded the sacrifice of the fourteen-year-old girl to the care of younger children. The remaining 73 were idle for periods ranging from four months to one year. Their record showed futile and unintelligent efforts to find work, repeated to the point of discouragement and exhaustion but relieved by weeks at home, for not one of the 73 girls thought of returning to school, and not one was compelled to do so. They had taken out their "working papers," and so final is this legal possession of the work certificate that in spite of the failure to secure employment few girls[1] return to school after this certificate has been granted. Although the law calling for the alternative of school in the event of unemployment may be enforced when boys are concerned, it is practically a dead letter for the girls of the district, because they may always put forth the officially honored excuse of being " needed at home," in spite of the fact that this usually means no positive training and many hours of idleness on the street. Omitting the 185 who succeeded in obtaining some kind of temporary position without loss of time after leaving school, there remain 115 for whom the work certificate meant a license to be idle regardless of the fact that they had failed to complete even the seventh grade of the elementary school. The defect lies both in the law and in the lack of machinery for enforcing it. As long as children are allowed the independent possession of their working papers,[2] educational oversight in a large city is impossible.

4. The Family Need

The customary method of considering the entire income of the family at the time when the child leaves school, in order to determine the extent to which the economic pressure is responsible for his leaving, is likely to be misleading when applied to the people of the stockyards district. Many families will show for a period of two or three years an abundant income due entirely to the wages of several children. But it must be remembered that these same children did not grow up with this plenty, nor are they going to remain long at home to add to the common purse. The older son who may be earning ten dollars a week makes larger personal demands as he nears his majority, and resents being asked to contribute what he considers an undue share to the family for no other reason than to prolong the education of a girl. The older daughter, who is more capable of such sacrifices, finds it difficult to surrender

---

[1] One of the truant officers of wide experience says it is impossible to make a successful court case of the girl after she is fourteen years of age. If the mother appears and swears that she needs the child at home, the judge accepts this as "being employed."

[2] The Ohio law recognizes this fact effectively. In case the child is either dismissed or voluntarily withdraws, the employer is obliged to return the work certificate to the superintendent of schools. The return of the certificate at once calls attention to the fact that the child is not employed and must be followed by the truant or other special officer.

her desire for social pleasures to a kind of training for the younger children which she did not herself receive. The small sums a mother may earn by taking in either washing or boarders are often needed to meet some unusual drain upon the family, like sickness or burial expenses. The income derived from rentals is usually applied on the mortgage and does not count in the apparent surplus, for at all times the need of keeping up the payments on a house outweighs the need of keeping a child in school. The following tables present the wage-earning power of the head of the family as the important steady economic factor in the lives of the 500 girls under consideration. For the men here represented there has been little variation in wages during the past eight or ten years except that due to the irregular employment common to the neighborhood. That is, the men who are now recorded at two dollars a day and less have been steadily in the ranks of those who can never command more even when opportunities to work are abundant, and who have never had a year of "full time." Wage earners above this level include the more skilled workmen who have had fairly steady employment. Those considered "successful" can depend upon an income of $825 a year and more. This last group is made up of skilled workmen, foremen, and small merchants (including saloon keepers), who have made financial gains since they came to the neighborhood.

TABLE III. THE ECONOMIC POSITION OF THE HEADS[1] OF FAMILIES WHO ALLOWED THREE HUNDRED GIRLS TO LEAVE SCHOOL BEFORE COMPLETING THE SEVENTH GRADE

NUMBER OF WOMEN[2]

62 . . . . Irregular: $1 a day and less

NUMBER OF MEN

112 . . . . Below $2 a day
24 . . . . $2 a day
47 . . . . $2.01 to $2.60 a day
21 . . . . Successful

1 There is not an exact correspondence between the number of heads of families and the number of girls, since some families furnished more than one girl.

Although no effort was made to study racial characteristics, the following figures showing the nationality of the father given by the 300 girls are suggestive: Poles, 70; Germans, 89; Irish, 51; Bohemians, 43; miscellaneous, 27; Slovaks, 20.

2 The woman's wage is difficult to estimate. The figures do not mean that she never earns above $1 in a given day. When the woman is thrown upon her own resources, her average earnings are usually between $5 and $6 a week.

TABLE IV. THE ECONOMIC POSITION OF THE HEADS[1] OF FAMILIES WHO ALLOWED TWO HUNDRED GIRLS TO COMPLETE EIGHT GRADES

NUMBER OF WOMEN	WAGE
25	Irregular: $1 a day and less

NUMBER OF MEN	
37	Below $2 a day
17	$2 a day
47	$2.01 to $2.60 a day
63	Successful

The contrast needs little comment. If it is necessary for the head of the family to command with a fair degree of regularity over $2 a day in order to keep the children in school, then less than 26 per cent of the first group should be expected to do it. That this wage is one of the important determining factors seems evident from the 58 per cent of the second group who are above the $2-a-day limit. The remaining 42 per cent represent families where ambition conquered poverty, where the mother took on the added burden of a supplementary wage earner, or where the girl was able to complete her course either below or close to the age of fourteen years.

5. Occupations open to Girls under Sixteen Years of Age

The little girls of the stockyards district are found in the factory, the bookbindery, the department store, domestic service, the sewing trades, typewriting and stenography, and occasionally in the laundry. The factory positions are those in which the quick and delicate touch of the girls' fingers are required. These include wrapping or packing all small articles, like soap and toilet preparations, confectionery, chewing gum, crackers, and chipped beef, or tending some of the simpler machines similar to those of a box factory. The bookbindery offers only mechanical work like sorting and folding, or operating a simple machine. The laundry has a few easy positions like shaking out clothes and marking them, but the other handwork, as well as the operation of the machines, requires the strength of the older girls. The department store stands next

[1] The following figures show the nationality of the father given by the 200 girls: German, 61; Bohemians, 58; Irish, 48; Poles, 13; miscellaneous, 20.

to the factory in the list of occupations accessible and considered desirable. Many little girls have a nervous dread of being near a factory machine, and to them the work in the store seems easy and attractive. Here there are places as cash girl, wrapper, assistant in the stock room, or inspector. The girl under sixteen is seldom found in the position of clerk, but she often looks with envy upon the girl behind the counter and clings to her poor little job with the hope of advancement. Domestic service and the sewing trades furnish the ideal opening according to the simpler standards of foreign parents. From their point of view the time-honored household occupations of women may be practiced outside of the home with dignity and a fair remuneration. The American-born girl does not accept this standard. Although the parents sometimes prevail with the younger ones, the positions of the older girls prove that there has been a general tendency to leave domestic service and even the sewing trades to the immigrants. These last occupations are usually regarded as the time-serving of the apprentice who is learning a trade. A partial truth obscures the real situation, which does not admit of any positive training to the child who is "minding a baby" and which often compels girls in a dressmaking establishment to spend months in clipping and pulling basting threads or in delivering packages to customers.[1] The undue importance attached to the office position has been mentioned. This term may be used to dignify any kind of indoor routine in mercantile and other business establishments, from folding circulars and addressing envelopes to typewriting.

It is difficult to classify the above positions either with reference to the relative amount of skill they require or by their opportunities for advancement. With the possible exception of stenography, typewriting, and some requirements of the office position, they represent what is by common consent looked upon as "girls' work." The boy is not found in these positions for three reasons: he scorns the low wage which the little girl endures as her birthright; by

[1] A girl apprenticed to a milliner for one year spent her entire time in delivering hats. A Polish woman gave a tailor $25 to secure for her daughter a year's training in his shop. At the end of six months the girl was still pulling basting threads as a preliminary to the instruction to be given later.

nature he cares less for details and will not do his work with the same niceness and dexterity; and he seldom submits to the "speeding-up process" of the piecework system which is common in factories and upon which the possibility of increased wages usually depends. The greater docility of the girl added to her temporary attitude toward any employment renders her an easy victim. No preparation is exacted for entrance into these occupations, little time is required in learning the simple processes or duties involved, and few of them lead to openings calling for skill beyond that of speed or mechanical dexterity. There are always a limited number who by strength of character, persistency, or the native possession of some unusual ability may rise to positions of responsibility. To what extent the above occupations open such opportunities will be revealed in the records of the older girls.

6. The Relation of Wage and Occupation to Grade

Although the first position a girl secures is so often a matter of accident, the relation of wage and occupation to grade as revealed in the following tables is suggestive.

TABLE V. GIRLS BEGINNING WORK UNDER SIXTEEN YEARS OF AGE, SEVENTH GRADE NOT COMPLETED

Kind of Work	No. of Girls	Beginning Weekly Wage by Occupation											
		$0.50	$1.00	$1.50	$1.75	$2.00	$2.50	$3.00	$3.50	$4.00	$4.50	$5.00	$6.00
Bindery . .	9	—	—	—	1	—	—	2	1	3	1	1	—
Store[1] . .	63	—	—	1	11	—	23	16	9	2	—	1	—
Domestic .	26	—	2	1	—	9	4	6	2	2	—	—	—
Factory . .	108	—	—	1	—	—	1	45	11	38	4	7	1
Laundry . .	5	—	—	—	—	—	—	—	—	1	1	3	—
Millinery . .	5	—	3	1	—	—	1	—	—	—	—	—	—
Office . . .	13	—	—	—	—	—	—	2	1	2	—	7	1
Dressmaking	29	1	—	1	—	4	3	12	3	3	—	2	—
Total . .	258	1	5	5	12	13	32	83	27	51	6	21	2

[1] There is an interesting story, current in the neighborhood, of the morning when a little group of cash girls who had been working for $1.50 a week banded together and refused to continue for less than $2 a week. This juvenile strike was settled by a compromise which placed the wage in that store at $1.75.

TABLE VI. GIRLS BEGINNING WORK UNDER SIXTEEN YEARS OF AGE, EIGHTH GRADE COMPLETED

Kind of Work	No. of Girls	Beginning Weekly Wage by Occupation										
		$1.00	$1.50	$2.00	$2.50	$3.00	$3.50	$4.00	$4.50	$5.00	$6.00	$8.00
Bindery . . .	7	—	—	—	—	—	1	2	1	1	2	—
Store	28	1	—	—	4	8	4	4	2	3	2	—
Domestic . . .	7	—	1	2	1	2	—	1	—	—	—	—
Factory. . . .	6	—	—	—	—	3	1	—	—	2	—	—
Hairdressing . .	1	—	—	1	—	—	—	—	—	—	—	—
Millinery . . .	3	—	1	—	—	2	—	—	—	—	—	—
Office	22	—	—	—	—	1	1	4	2	10	4	—
Dressmaking. .	22	—	—	7	—	14	—	1	—	—	—	—
Stenographer .	9	—	—	—	—	—	—	—	—	3	5	1
Typist	2	—	—	—	—	—	—	—	—	2	—	—
Total. . . .	107	1	2	10	5	30	7	12	5	21	13	1

Including the purely mechanical positions of the bindery and the laundry under the head of factory work, among the girls who did not complete the seventh grade the factory and the department store claim 185, or 71 per cent of the whole number. Sixty-two, or 50 per cent, of those included as factory workers began at a wage below $4 a week. Fifty-five per cent of the department-store girls began at less than $3 a week. The girls in the sewing trades who could begin above $3 are exceptionally clever with the needle. The office position of this group does not mean either typewriting or stenography. The alluring wage of $5 or $6 a week is the highest point ever reached by the girl under sixteen in work of this character. In the total of 258 girls, 178, or nearly 69 per cent, began at a wage below $4 a week. Only 11 per cent were able to begin above that point.

The second table shows the marked tendency which is always found in the eighth-grade girl to get away from factory work and seek employment where she thinks she is holding a position of higher social value. The factory and the department store employ only 38 per cent of the whole number. Fifty-four per cent are in the sewing trades or in office positions. The domestic helper is also represented, due to the influence of the foreign home. In the total of 107 girls, 55, or 51 per cent, began at a wage below $4 a week. Thirty-seven per cent began above that point.

These figures disclose the general trend. Judging solely from the beginning wage, the eighth-grade girls can earn more money. In so far as the apprenticeship and the office may lead to better opportunities than the factory or the store, the greater number have chosen their occupations with more insight.

It is difficult to estimate the actual money value of the girl's labor from beginnings only. The child's lack of judgment and love of novelty lead to frequent changes, and many seasonal and temporary places are open to her. Naturally this child labor is the first to be dispensed with in the dull or slack season of any industry. The small candy packer may be required only seven or eight months of the year, the sewing and the millinery apprentice in the fashionable shop gets her enforced summer vacation, and the important little office girl in a mail-order house is often laid off for a month after the advertising circulars have been sent out. Only the department-store girls and the household helper seem to be in perpetual demand. The following table shows the real money value of 100 of the girls whose beginning wage is given in Table V. These girls were selected from the group because it was possible to follow their ups and downs for a year with a fair degree of accuracy. Moreover, they represent families who embrace the earliest opportunity to send their children to work and keep them employed. The weekly wage is estimated on the basis of the actual amount earned by the girl during the first year after leaving school. To show more clearly the exact contribution to the family income, the amount the girl was obliged to spend each week in street-car fare was deducted.

TABLE VII. AVERAGE WEEKLY CONTRIBUTION TO THE FAMILY INCOME OF ONE HUNDRED GIRLS DURING A WORKING-PERIOD OF ONE YEAR. STREET-CAR FARE IS SUBTRACTED

Age	Number	$1.50	$1.51–$2.00	$2.01–$2.50	$2.51–$3.00	$3.01–$3.50
14–15	91	11	32	32	11	5
15–16	9	—	8	1	—	—
Total . . .	100	11	40	33	11	5

Thirty-three of these children were driven before that family specter, the mortgage on the house.

The suggestion that girls should be legally forbidden to go to work under sixteen years of age brings out the old argument of the family need. It is put forth by thrifty parents and local politicians, by employers who wish an excuse for accepting children, and by charity workers struggling with the family problem of poverty. The school[1] has accepted the argument without questioning its real value, and children have learned to make use of it. The law determines the amount of the widow's pension on the supposition that the fourteen-year-old child is a legitimate wage earner. The ability of the child to add to the family income has been exaggerated and overemphasized. For these paltry sums they have been forced to exchange schooltime and playtime, the natural rights of the child.

7. Some Physical, Mental, and Moral Aspects of the Problem

We have as yet no scientific knowledge of the physical effects of child labor. We have certain recognized standards with reference to night work and the so-called "dangerous occupations," and a widespread public opinion that up to the age of fourteen years children should be allowed to develop their bodies in the freedom of the play activities most natural to them. Of the exact relation between the demands of the industries employing little girls and the actual power of the growing child to meet them without physical deterioration we know nothing with the certainty based upon scientific study. That there are several untabulated bodily injuries which result from their continuous employment in any one of the present occupations open to little girls in the city of Chicago no one who has observed girl labor for any length of time can deny. More than one half of these children who have come under the observation of the writer during the past eight years have been nervous, troubled with headaches, and "tired most of the time." This is a small number and is a record of confessions reluctantly given, for it is a

---

[1] The Fifty-eighth Annual Report of the Board of Education, city of Chicago, for the year ending June 30, 1912, voices the common sentiment and gives the need in the home as a reason for not recommending an amendment to the Compulsory Education Law forbidding the employment of children at fourteen years of age.

significant fact that until the working-girl has suffered to the point where she can no longer conceal it, she will seldom admit poor health. " I am always well. I never lose time from sickness " are the persistent assertions of thin, anæmic-looking little girls. This is a natural attitude resulting from their employment in industries which are usually making heavier demands upon the body than upon the brain, and every girl soon learns that the one thing she must not confess is physical weakness of any kind. That the very evident lack of vitality in many little girls was not due to any serious organic trouble was proved by the number of cases sent to a physician, who merely prescribed "rest" or "a tonic," and by the rapidity with which they recovered if they were so fortunate as to be "laid off" for a few weeks, except in instances of extreme poverty, where the mental anxiety more than offset the recuperative value of a period of leisure. However, there is considerable evidence that the intermittent weeks of enforced idleness are all that save the majority of these girls from an earlier and a more complete physical deterioration than apparently takes place.

This group of girls furnishes no evidence that for them one form of occupation had been better or worse than another as long as they were employed "on steady time," that is, receiving a fixed weekly sum and not the uncertain wage of the pieceworker. The most pernicious side of factory work is the "speeding-up" process which strains every nerve and keeps the worker on a rack of anxiety. Some little girls acquired a premature wisdom as a result of their factory experiences and refused to go beyond a certain fairly comfortable speed limit which they established for themselves when the nature of the occupation permitted it and they were not forced to "keep up with a machine." Some of them found a pleasurable excitement in discovering just how "comfortable" they could be without losing their positions. Girls who held to a more even pace and never revealed their utmost capacity have endured the piecework system with less injury than those who were eager to respond to pressure. As there is often a difference of two or three dollars a week between what she accepts as her limit and what she can do "on a spurt," the temptation to earn more money may be accepted at a frightful cost of nervous energy. Mothers frequently give an additional incentive to increased speed by making their daughters' spending money and even necessary clothing depend entirely upon this extra sum. It is difficult to reach fair conclusions on the subject of piecework. Employers say that girls "don't hurt themselves." Girls testify that they are always in danger of having a cut in the rate of payment for a certain output if the girls who represent the highest speed begin to earn "too much money." When a cut in the rate is made, they are forced to increase their speed or accept a lowered wage. Miss Goldmark concludes that although the system is sound in theory and "works admirably in highly organized trades where collective agreements assure the workers fair, fixed rates, it fails among the most helpless workers, who most need to be protected from overpressure and the inroads of fatigue. With them it almost inevitably breeds a spirit of permanent 'rush' in work, and to that extent it is physiologically dangerous."[1] It is this "rush" that the American temperament cannot endure. Factories that use this system are obliged to draw upon the more enduring vitality of the hardy immigrant.   .

The legal hours of labor are eight daily, but girls who seek the down-town factories and stores must allow at least two hours in addition for street-car rides. As they are obliged to go and return when all cars to and from the stockyards district are overcrowded, the fatigue of standing the greater part of the time must also be included in the day's work. The fact that local department stores can secure cash girls for $1.75 a week is due in part to the number who cannot endure the nervous strain of getting down town and back again. The daily walk and the warm noon meal at home are all health-preserving factors, but as there are comparatively few local opportunities,[2] for the majority this street-car ride on their feet is inevitable. Of the 365 girls who began work under sixteen years of age 310 were obliged to ride distances consuming from two to two and one-half hours daily.

The noneducative character of all occupations open to these children is not the only negative side of the problem. Here again

[1] Josephine Goldmark, Fatigue and Efficiency, p. 84.

[2] Judging from the records at the office of the state factory inspector, the entire packing industry seldom employs at any one time more than 100 girls under sixteen years of age. These positions are usually filled by the foreign girls.

there is no proper basis for exact conclusions in regard to the mental effect of the child's work under the modern conditions of industry. Yet if the tendency is to an overstrain and fatigue detrimental to physical growth, it is not unreasonable to conclude that disastrous results both mental and moral may follow. Girls grow dull with a routine that calls for no exercise of brain power, and the general stupidity of which many employers complain is increased as the months go by. Noise and confusion, the whirl of factory machines, or the distractions of the department store make consecutive thought-processes difficult, and the unconscious reaction from monotonous labor is a desire for excitement in some novel form — the moving-picture show, the forbidden saloon-hall dance, or late hours with companions on the street after the day's work is over. The fifteen-year-old factory girl who gave as her excuse for going to the five-cent theater six nights in the week her need of "something to make me feel rested" is not an exaggerated type but a painful illustration of the lack of nervous balance which is all too common among these children. Whether such an unstable condition is due to purely physical or to mental causes it is often difficult to say, since for many girls there is such a close connection between health and mental attitude. Girls are held to one miserable, distasteful piece of work by fear, discouragement, timidity, or the lack of knowledge of other opportunities. A few have confessed that they thought all the factories down town made candy and there was nothing else for little girls to do except wrapping and packing confectionery. Some who had learned a single simple process in a box factory were unable to adapt themselves to other positions when laid off temporarily. One girl insisted that " pasting labels " was her " trade " and refused to consider anything else. Another said she could work only in the one department store in which she began. She had tried others, but they always made her feel " strange and queer.' Still'another worked a full year in fear of the forewoman who had an " evil eye " that held girls to their work. A different type of girl makes a continuous effort to break through the limitations of her enforced occupation by changing as often as possible. These changes are a means of stimulation which the girl's nature demands. Three girls who were chums and refused to be separated

had worked together in eleven different places during fifteen consecutive months. For them the mere thought of steady employment had grown distasteful. One girl flippantly remarked: "The
new boss may have rēd hair. Anything to change the scenery."
That the search for excitement as an antidote for fatigue and
monotonous labor may be attended by grave moral dangers, no one
can doubt. Girls do not understand this abnormal craving. They
are caught in the meshes of feelings too complex for their untaught
minds to comprehend. Unfortunately both parents fail at this point.
Many endeavor to exercise a strict surveillance that would keep the
working girl at home in the evening " helping mother " as the safest
outlet for any extra energy she may have. The diverse attitude on
the part of parents and children in regard to the way the leisure
time should be filled is one of the greatest causes of family clashing.
Here the girl usually conquers. Those who faithfully hold to a
difficult and uncongenial occupation, bringing home the entire wage
to the family and submitting to an almost patriarchal control in
other matters, will demand a freedom in the use of their evening
hours before which the foreign parents are helpless. " She is a
good girl," said the Polish mother. " She brings home all her
money, but — she goes out where she pleases nights and Sundays,
and we can't follow." Ninety per cent of the parents admitted that
they had little control over their daughters in this matter. Many
fiercely condemned "the American life " which made such insub-
ordination possible. This unnatural position of the little girl, carrying the premature responsibility of the wage earner and asserting
her right to a feverish search for evening pleasures, is forced upon
her at the beginning of the period marked by physical changes,
rapid growth, and the dawn of sex consciousness, when curious
and misunderstood moods are dominant.

8. THE ATTITUDE OF THE EMPLOYER

Interviews with employers revealed two points of view: (1) the
labor of girls under sixteen years of age is of doubtful value to
the employer and is not necessary to the continuation of any industry; (2) unless girls begin to work under sixteen years of
age, they do not get the necessary training that leads to their

advancement, and therefore the number of skilled workers among older girls will be depleted.

The first point of view has four causes : the eight-hour day, the general inefficiency of the girls who apply for work, the introduction of new machinery, and a growing sentiment against the employment of children. One of the common grievances which employers find it difficult to adjust is the difference in hours which causes jealousies and petty disturbances among girls not far below and just above the age of sixteen years. The girl who was sixteen last week will work out her full time cheerfully with seventeen-year-old companions, but will be restless and dissatisfied if associated with a group six months younger having the advantage of an earlier dismissal. A surprising amount of supervision is needed to prevent the fraudulent record of the child's age, for which the employer alone is held responsible when the factory inspector appears. The inefficiency of the untrained mass which is recruited from the ranks of children who leave school below the seventh grade makes them a financial loss to any business or industry during the period required for their training. The amount of shifting adds to the work of the employment department. The superintendent in a large factory using over 300 little girls stated that they expected to register five girls in order to secure one who would feel any responsibility for reappearing to take up the work she had applied for. Even the girls who have finished the eighth grade are childish and cannot be given places of responsibility which the office requires. The introduction of machinery is displacing the need of many a small pair of hands. The inventions for covering, gluing, and labeling in the box factories are comparatively new and are pronounced satisfactory. The machine-dipped chocolate drops look almost as well as those covered by hand and are in greater demand. The clever devices for closing packages with the unfeeling points of a machine almost human in its skill are a monument to inventive genius. One of the largest employers of child labor in the city of Chicago said : " If we could not by law employ the girl under sixteen years, we should find some way to make the machine do her work."

Finally, there appears to be a growing sentiment against the employment of children, in spite of the evidence of the school census taken May 2, 1912, which gives a total of 8923 girls and 8214 boys under sixteen years of age either temporarily or permanently employed in the city of Chicago. A sentiment is a difficult thing to measure in figures until it reaches a definite expression in legislation. Yet the feeling exists, voiced all along the line by the head of the firm, the superintendent, the business manager, and the foreman, often in the face of the actual fact that the practical policy of the business or the industry allowed the use of children. The proposition to exclude the girl from early employment met with a quick response from employers who look at the boy from a different point of view. The frankest words came from the president of a large manufacturing establishment: "As an employer, I can and do make money out of the work of little girls. As a man, I know it would be better for them and for the state if I were forbidden by law to employ them."

The second point of view, that the girl must get her training for business or industrial efficiency by going to work at the earliest age possible, is advanced by employers who find temporary help a convenience and by those who wish the speed and skill that come with the repetition of a single highly specialized process. They are looking for a very limited efficiency, which may be acquired only by practice in the business or industry calling for it, and they know that youth is the golden age of this kind of skill. They do not ask for a longer period in school or for any form of industrial education to fit girls for their positions. " Give us girls who are quick, bright, and healthy, and we will do the training" is their demand. Their further suggestion that the supply of skilled adult workers will be lessened if girls do not receive this early training is without proof.

These advocates of child labor could not fail to refer to the family poverty that apparently can be relieved only by the work of children. Three went so far as to say that they engaged girls under sixteen solely because the families represented were in need. And yet when it came to the final question, no employer would admit that either the business or the industry he represented rested upon so slight a foundation as the labor of little girls. One conclusion at least seems permissible : the premature employment of girls under sixteen years of age is not necessary to the continuation of any business or industry.

THE SCHOOL AND THE WORKING-CHILD

A Plea for Employment Supervision in City Schools

By Sophonisba P. Breckinridge and Edith Abbott, Directors,
Department of Social Investigation

(From a Report to the Chicago Woman's Club, the Chicago Association of
Collegiate Alumnæ, and the Woman's City Club)

While it is generally known that the Illinois law requires that
all children between the ages of seven and fourteen shall attend
school unless excused on the various grounds enumerated in the
statute, many people do not know that on the fourteenth birthday
the child may demand an age and school certificate and go to work,
subject of course to the limitations of the Child Labor Law upon
his hours and time of work and kind of employment, and subject
also to the provision of the Compulsory Education Law that, until
he is sixteen, he must be either at work or in school. Still less,
perhaps, do people know the consequence to the child who is thus
deprived of further schooling on the one hand and made to assume
the heavy burden of responsibility on the other. For to most of
these children leaving school means much more than a loss of
opportunity. It means being placed in the way of great and varied
temptations while the will is weak and the mind not yet intelligent. Work is not always easy to find, and desirable work, which
offers even a small amount of training and awakens ambition and
interest, seems hopelessly scarce.

Every year thousands of children in Chicago take advantage of
the privilege which the law gives them and leave school on the
very day when they reach the age of fourteen and can legally obtain
their working papers. On this day the child is suddenly released
from the discipline of the school and thrown on his own resources
to find a job in any way he can and to become an independent

wage earner making a much-needed contribution to the family income. This sudden transition from school to work must necessarily be a difficult time of readjustment for the child, and the question of the kind of work which is undertaken is one of serious importance. The first job or the first year of work will often have a decisive influence on his whole working life, and may make or mar his character.

There are many important questions which should be considered when a child leaves school to go to work, such as the kind of occupation to which he is best adapted, the industry which holds the best promise for the future, how to find the employer who is "good to boys and girls" and is willing to give them proper training, sympathetic oversight, and a chance for promotion in the shop or factory, and, finally, the critical question of how to find the vacant job which most nearly answers all of these demands. At present the child faces this problem quite alone and unaided, with no broader object in mind than that of an immediate contribution to the family income. His parents may be zealous for his welfare, but they are quite unable to help at this crisis in his life. For the boys and girls who go to work are not the children of intelligent skilled workingmen. Men in skilled trades do not take their children out of school at fourteen, for they know that a boy of that age must wait two years before he can be apprenticed, that the girl of that age is not strong enough to work and not yet able to protect herself, and that the years from fourteen to sixteen are wastefully spent by the child in work. These boys and girls who go to work, then, are children of parents who are either very poor and in urgent need of the small wage which the child may earn, or unintelligent with reference to the importance of further education and therefore not willing to sacrifice their standard of immediate comfort for the child's future; in the majority of cases they are immigrants, frequently unable even to speak our language, almost uniformly ignorant of industrial conditions, and quite unable to advise their children wisely with reference to the beginning of their working lives.

The result is that at the age when children in a well-to-do family are still treated as children and are never allowed to make any important decision about their future careers, the boy or girl in a poor family is turned loose to find work alone. It is obvious that these children are not competent to distinguish the good employer from the bad or the occupation with a future from the "blind-alley" employment that leads nowhere and leaves them stranded at the age of seventeen or eighteen, not merely untrained but demoralized.

At present there is no organized effort made on the part of the community to protect these boys and girls who are leaving the schools every week and starting forth alone, timid and eager, on a discouraging hunt for a first job; no serious effort is being made to prevent the wastage that comes from the child's haphazard choice of a job. The theory has been that the responsibility of the school to the child comes abruptly to an end when he obtains his working papers. Picture the child who is facing the problem of finding work. A boy will usually trudge through the business or factory streets looking for the magic card "Boy Wanted" in the window — in any window, without regard to the character of the work or of the employer; or he follows the more demoralizing habit of loafing about the newspaper offices in a crowd of idle men waiting for the most recent Want Ads to appear. Small wonder that after he gets work he finds it hard to settle down. The young girl who goes forth alone to hunt a job may find much graver perils before her. It is only necessary to recall the success-ful prosecution in 1908 of seventeen men and three women who had built up a profitable business in leading astray young girls in search of work who made use of the department-store waiting rooms to read advertisements in the newspapers and to rest during the intervals between unsuccessful applications for jobs.

The difficulty in finding work means, of course, that a child usu-ally takes the first job that is offered him, without any regard to the industry, occupation, or employer, without any regard to his interest in the work or his fitness for it. His whole future may be decided by the merest chance, and he may take the most temporary kind of job in a most undesirable place, when on the same street a good firm offering permanency and every opportunity of advancement may have been looking for just such a boy or girl. It is, of course, an inevitable result of this careless and accidental hunt for "any kind of job" that temporary jobs are frequently taken and children easily get into casual habits and, in fact, become confirmed "casual laborers" before they are sixteen, shifting from job to job with an interval of unemployment between each.

It is now becoming generally recognized that the result of this neglect of the child by the school and by the community during the critical period between fourteen and sixteen, when the school-boy or schoolgirl suddenly becomes a working "man" or a wage-earning "woman," has far-reaching social consequences — a small army of boys and girls going into the street trades, which are demoralizing, and into occupations and industries which profit by boy or girl labor but have no responsibility to the boy and girl beyond the weekly wage, no care for their health or training.

Attention has already been called to the fact that, although the law gives the child his working papers at fourteen and does not provide for any supervision or protection during the critical years which follow, still the law does not entirely take its hands off. It regulates the hours of labor for children under sixteen; it at the present time excludes them from certain physically dangerous trades and doubtless will soon exclude them from morally danger-ous trades as well. Even more important, perhaps, is the provision of the Compulsory Education Law that boys and girls between fourteen and sixteen shall not be absolutely idle but that they must return to school if they are not at work.

Unfortunately, no adequate machinery for enforcing this provi-sion of the law exists, and the problem of the child between four-teen and sixteen is still a serious one. The Parental School is restricted to the care of boys under fourteen; there is no similar institution for older boys and no provision at all for girls who refuse to go to school. The last report of the Superintendent of Compul-sory Education strongly emphasizes "the necessity for better pro-vision for the correction and care of children between fourteen and sixteen years of age who are beyond parental control and who prefer idleness to school attendance or employment. The only recourse under present conditions against a fourteen-year-old truant who has committed no other offense than truancy, is to charge him with incorrigible or delinquent conduct and ask his commitment to the John Worthy School or St. Charles. The former is a prison school where the worst type of delinquent boys is sent. St. Charles has not sufficient capacity to provide for urgent delinquent cases. It is therefore a question of consistency for one state law to provide for compulsory attendance up to the age of sixteen while another state law—the Parental School Law—provides for truants only between seven and fourteen years, and bars the truant between fourteen and sixteen." [1]

Ever since the year 1905 the Department of Compulsory Education has called attention in every succeeding annual report to the necessity for better means of protecting and disciplining boys between fourteen and sixteen, not merely because they become demoralized themselves but because they encourage smaller boys to become truant and delinquent.[2] As a result of a recent study of the statistics of the Juvenile Court relating to delinquent children, it appeared that the great majority of boys who were brought to court as delinquent were boys who left school to go to work when they were fourteen. After that time they were often out of work as well as out of school and were given special opportunities to become delinquent. More than half of all the delinquent boys brought into court come in at the age of fourteen or in the two years immediately following their withdrawal from school. If the provision in the state law which requires the compulsory school attendance of boys between the ages of fourteen and sixteen who are not working could be rigorously enforced, the number of delinquent boys of these ages would undoubtedly decrease. There is, however, a method, which might be adopted, of meeting this problem, which would be preventive rather than corrective, and that is for the school to assist these boys in finding the right kind of work. It would seem to be wiser for educational authorities to take

[1] Chicago Board of Education, Fifty-seventh Annual Report, "Report of the Superintendent of Schools for the year ending June 30, 1911," p. 56.

[2] See Chicago Board of Education, Fifty-first Annual Report, 1905, in which the following statement appears in the report of the Superintendent of Compulsory Education: "There are many idle boys between the ages of fourteen and sixteen on the streets of Chicago. . . . Many of these boys do not go to work because employers, as a rule, prefer a boy who has attained the age of sixteen years in order that they may have employees whose employment and hours are not regulated by the Child Labor Law. These idle street boys, over compulsory-education age, frequently encourage smaller boys to become truants and delinquents."

steps to help children to get the right kind 'of work, rather than to punish them for being idle.

In this connection we should like to quote from the recent report of the Department of Compulsory Education : [1]

The social waste in a boy's life between fourteen and sixteen often determines his future career and citizenship [writes the Superintendent]. Many employers do not want a juvenile employee under sixteen years of age; they. cannot become apprentices. Principals do not care to have the irregular attendance of the fourteen-to-sixteen-year-old pupil who alternates between school and work so much, seeking employment. These older boys influence younger ones — and herein lies a great handicap to truant officers. It accounts, in a large measure, for the increase in truancy in some districts, although many of the fourteen-to-sixteen-year-old boys are repeatedly taken from the streets, and some remain in school. There is no central juvenile-employment agency, and conditions could be better if one were established, to expedite the employment of boys and girls as soon as possible after they secure their age and school certificates.

It is evident too that if work is recognized by the law as the alternative to school, it should be on the ground that the work will give the child the needed training or preparation for what is to come after. That is, the implication in the law is that either in school or in work will be found the preparation for that later period in the child's life in which the law wholly ceases to exercise control. The problem of adequately protecting children who leave school to go to work has then three important aspects : (1) the question of what opportunities for employment that are educational and disciplinary instead of demoralizing are open to children of fourteen and fifteen ; (2) the question of devising some machinery for ascertaining good vacancies and fitting the right boy or girl into the right job; (3) the development of some method of supervising the boy or girl after a job has been found, in order to ascertain whether the job proves suitable on the one hand, and to see that the child is supported against temptation to change his job frequently on the other. In the solution of this problem we have at once an important duty of the school and a unique opportunity to render a most difficult and delicate service to the child, to the family, and, in the long run, to the community, in saving the health and character of the working-child.

1 Chicago Board of Education, Fifty-seventh Annual Report, " Report of the Superintendent of Schools for the year ending June 30, 1911," p. 56.

EXPERIMENTAL WORK DURING THE YEAR 1910-1911

In the autumn of 1910 this department of the Chicago School of Civics and Philanthropy, supported by a grant from the Russell Sage Foundation, undertook a study of truancy in Chicago.[1] As one phase of this study we became interested in the problem of the children between fourteen and sixteen. In Chicago during a single year 7978 boys and 4560 girls under sixteen years of age were granted working certificates; of these children 8985 were only fourteen years of age, and 1557 had not yet reached the fifth grade.

It has already been pointed out that in Illinois these children are required by the Compulsory Education Law to be either at work or in school, but that there is no provision for helping children to find work and no institution to which they can be sent if they refuse to return to school. Attention has also been called to the fact that the Parental School, an admirable institution maintained by the Board of Education for truant boys,[2] cannot legally receive any boy over fourteen nor retain any boy already committed to the school after he reaches the legal working age. Here, however, as in the ordinary school, nothing is done to help the boy find suitable work or to make the transition from school to work easy for the child. The plight of the boy discharged from the institution merely because he is fourteen and therefore a legal wage earner is apparent. Boys are sent to the Parental School only when they are in special need of the training and of the disciplinary life which that school is so well equipped to provide. The boy so released when he has no job in sight and no one at home able or interested to find him one, is in grave danger of losing all that the school may have done for him.

These Parental School boys are, therefore, in much greater need of supervision than the majority of children who leave school to go to work. They have been uncontrollable at school, and they

[1] This study was undertaken as part of the Juvenile Court inquiry on which the department had been engaged for several years. The first volume dealing with the results of this inquiry, "The Delinquent Child and the Home," is now in press and will shortly be issued by the Charities Publication Committee for the Russell Sage Foundation.

[2] It may be well to call attention here to urgent need for a similar institution for truant girls or girls who are incorrigible at school.

come for the most part from homes that are, to say the least, unfavorable to their right development. In some cases they come from homes in which the father drinks or in which the mother is shiftless and incompetent; in a few cases the mother herself is a drinking woman or worse; when there are degraded conditions in the home the degradation is accompanied by poverty; and in still other cases there is poverty alone, poverty which is honest and respectable but which means pressing need for what the child can earn. It was found, for example, in a study of truant cases last year, that out of 579 boys who were brought to court for the first time on a truancy charge, 157 belonged to families which had at some time been on the records of the United Charities. It is obvious that to return to these homes children released from all effective control on the part of the school authorities and unaided by any sympathetic, firm, and intelligent guidance, is to run the risk of undoing all that has been gained by sending them away. On the other hand, if the boy can be persuaded voluntarily to return to school, or if he can be found the right job and persuaded to stick to it, if misunderstandings with the foreman can be explained and adjusted, if there is someone at hand to give him encouraging and sturdy advice when he wants to "chuck the job and try something new" or "loaf for a bit," the succeeding months may continue the discipline and right development begun in the Parental School.

These children, then, who according to the statute must be released on their fourteenth birthday from the Parental School, have again after their return home the alternative under the law of returning to school or of finding a job. To undertake to advise these children with regard to their choice of work and to assist them in finding jobs if they were unwilling to return to school opened an interesting opportunity to combine investigational with practical work. To attempt to understand the problem of employment as they faced it seemed to be not only germane to our truancy inquiry but likely to be of some immediate practical value. We attempted to serve, in short, as a sort of employment agency for these boys, believing this to be one of the best methods of understanding the questions connected with their finding work, the kind of positions open to them, the ease or difficulty of finding " vacant jobs," their treatment by the employer, and their conduct in work after they were placed.

In other words, to get directly from and with them the employment experience of these boys dismissed from the Parental School solely because of their age seemed relevant to an inquiry into the adequacy of the Compulsory Education Law, the effectiveness of the court as a device for strengthening the school, and the reasonableness of accepting " lawful employment " as a substitute for schooling during these two important years of the child's life.

To try to assist boys or girls in finding work is a task not to be lightly undertaken. It means not only a thoroughgoing investigation into opportunities of employment open to children under sixteen but a careful study of the particular child. On the one hand, it means interviews with employers and foremen and, on the other, interviews with the child before he leaves school, with his teachers, and with parents in the home—interviews which give as complete information as can be gained of what the boy wants to do and thinks he can do, of what his teachers believe him to be fitted for physically and mentally, and, most important of all, the judgment of his parents, their hopes and fears if they will share them, and such light as his home circumstances and relationships throw on the possibilities of his working career. This is, of course, only half the battle. There is also the selection from among all of the available jobs that can be found, the one to which the boy seems best adapted, and then frequently the difficult task of persuading the boy to give up being a messenger boy or some other wasteful occupation on which he may have set his heart, convincing the parents perhaps to take a lower wage at the start in a job which is going to mean learning as well as earning, and, finally, constant communication with the boy after he is placed. For watching the child after a job has been found is as important as finding the job. The temptation to leave one employer and " try another " is in the air. Boys give up their jobs on the most trivial pretexts and often without telling the employer they intend to leave. One boy left a good job with a good firm and became a telegraph messenger because

he did not like the shape of the packages he was asked to carry ;
a Bohemian boy left a shop where he was being taught a trade
and went into a large factory which offered only unskilled work for
either men or boys, because he resented having a Polish boy in the
shop and said it was nicer when he was "the only boy." Other
boys leave because they like a change and can usually "pick up
some kind of work." In such cases it is often possible to persuade
the employer to give the boy another trial, to show the boy how
much he may gain by working steadily for the same firm, and to
explain to the parents the dangers of casual habits. The task is
not a simple task. It involves often many interviews, much firm
but gentle dealing with boy and parents, and close coöperation with
employer ; but it also means a knowledge of the chaos by which
fourteen-year-old children are allowed to enter the wage-earning
market unguarded and unguided, which is worth all it costs. The
effort to find good places for boys or girls who leave school to go
to work shows, as nothing but direct practical experience can show,
the great dearth of educational or disciplinary work for children
under sixteen. It shows in the most unmistakable terms that the
serious study of this question is the duty of the schools, unless
they are willing to sit by and take no notice as the child goes
forth to unlearn what the school has taught.

It was realized, of course, that the same problem presented itself
to the fourteen-year-old girls who are leaving school to go to work,
and that the same method would be of even greater value in the
case of girls than of boys because, few as are the opportunities of
an industrially promising kind for boys, they are fewer for girls,
since most employments for women to-day are in fact "blind-alley,"
or "dead end," employments. Moreover the problem of school
attendance for girls is one to which much less attention has been
given. The number of girls whose attendance is so irregular or
whose conduct so bad as to call for action on the part of the Compulsory Education Department is almost negligible, and these are
not brought into the Juvenile Court. There is no Parental School
for girls. We therefore had no opportunity to undertake in connection with our Juvenile Court inquiry the same investigational
experiment for girls which we undertook for the Parental School

boys. But by the intelligent coöperation of three women's organizations, the Chicago Woman's Club, the Chicago Association of Collegiate Alumnæ, and the Woman's City Club, this work was made possible. Through their joint gift we were enabled to obtain for four months the service of a special investigator who was peculiarly fitted for the work. Miss Davis had been engaged with the department in an earlier study of the delinquent wards of the court, and had been especially skillful and successful in obtaining data concerning delinquent girls and in understanding the needs and difficulties of those girls. She had more recently been for two years in the Illinois Children's Home and Aid Society, in charge of the work for homeless girls, and she came directly from that position to this undertaking. She seemed to have the training, sympathy, experience, and resourcefulness needed in this work; and the results of her brief inquiry will, we believe, justify the confidence placed in the department by the three coöperating organizations and, in turn, the confidence of the department in her.

Toward the end of the school year, as the knowledge of trade conditions accumulated and the connection with good employers became gradually established, we were able to take care of a very considerable number of children sent to us by the settlements who knew of our experimental work, and by the United Charities and some other organizations. In particular, especially handicapped children were sent to us — a one-armed girl, a lame boy, a deaf-and-dumb girl, and undersized or delicate children who were in work that was too hard for them or unsuitable for other reasons.

A few illustrations will perhaps be of interest in showing that the "better job" did not always mean lower wages, though whenever possible it meant a chance to learn and a chance of promotion as a result of steady, faithful work:

Emma C——, a girl of fifteen, who had finished the seventh grade, had been employed in a department store as "inspector" earning $2.50 a week. She was a capable, promising girl, and employment was found for her in a braiding and embroidery shop where she is learning hand and machine embroidering and where she earns $5 a week. Her sister, a bright girl of sixteen and an eighth-grade graduate, who had been working in a department store for nine months as "wrapper" and earning $4.50 a week, was placed in an office position where she is earning $6 a week.

Lena S——, a little girl of fourteen, who had finished the sixth grade and who knew how to sew, had found a job for herself in a tailor shop "finishing pants" at $2.50 a week. She was placed in a Michigan Avenue shop where good needlewomen are in demand, at an initial wage of $4 a week.

Elizabeth B——, a bright little girl of fourteen, had "done well" in the seventh grade and should have gone on to the eighth, but her father was an epileptic and she was the eldest of eight children. On the day she was fourteen, therefore, she became the "sole support of the family." She was sent to us by the United Charities from a place where she had been earning $3.50 a week folding circulars, and she was placed in the filing department of a large commercial agency where she was paid in the beginning $4 a week. In six months she was earning $5 a week, and the forewoman reports that she is learning typewriting in her "spare time" and is going to make a good office assistant.

Steve H——, who was sent by the United Charities, was an eighth-grade graduate and another "sole support" of a family of eight, in this case deserted by the father. The boy was sixteen years old, extremely small for his age, and was "carrying boards" in a box factory, earning $6 a week. He was a very eager, ambitious boy, and as he was sixteen years old it was not difficult to find a chance for him as a compositor's apprentice with a good printing firm. His initial wages in this case were only $4, but it was not difficult to raise a small fund to pay the family the difference between his apprenticeship wage and his box-factory wage until he had been "raised." He has been in the shop nearly a year now, his wages have been raised three times, he enjoys his work, and his foreman speaks well of him.

Albert Z——, who is fifteen and had finished sixth grade, worked for a year in a box factory "carrying boards" and earned $4 a week. Fortunately he was laid off when the work became slack. Employment was found for him in a printing shop where he has an opportunity to learn the trade and where his initial wage was $4.50 a week.

James R——, a bright Bohemian boy of fifteen, who had finished the seventh grade, worked in a department store nearly two years as messenger boy. He had begun at $4 a week, and his wages had not been raised during that time. He left because he "wanted to learn something." He was placed in a printing shop where he is learning the trade and where his initial wage was $4.50 a week.

Salvatore, an Italian boy of fourteen, the "sole support" of a fatherless family of six, was sent to us because he was "working too hard" and often "fell asleep at his work." He was working in a department store as a "cash boy," earning $2.50 a week, and earning an extra $2 by working on a milk wagon from three to six in the morning. It was possible to place him with an engraving company where the prospects to learn the trade were good and where his wages were $4.50 a week at the start.

In the month of June we undertook to interview and to place all of the children who were planning to go to work at the end of the school year in the Washburne School, one of the largest schools on the West Side. Office hours were kept in a neighboring settlement, the Henry Booth House, which generously offered space, and the principal, Mr. Thompson, was glad to coöperate by sending the children to us and by giving his personal advice. Besides interviewing the children, the homes were all visited, and when the parents seemed able to keep the child in school longer, they were strongly urged to do so.

By way of summary a few brief tables are presented to show the practical results of this very humble attempt of the department to serve as an informal employment agency for these boys and girls. During the year 254 children, 80 girls and 174 boys, were interviewed.[1] Of the boys 50 were still in the Parental School but about to be discharged when interviewed. The following tables summarize the actual work done.

WORK FOR BOYS WHO WERE INTERVIEWED OCTOBER 1, 1910, TO OCTOBER 1, 1911

Number of boys placed 59
Number who secured work themselves or through parents or friends 29
Number returned to school . . . . 43°
Number for whom nothing could be done 6
Number who moved away and were lost 3
Number now waiting for positions 34
    Total number of boys interviewed 174

The ages of these boys were as follows:

Age	Number of Boys
14 years	105
15 years	31
16 years	18
Over 16 years	20
Total	174

[1] Miss Davis was assisted in this work by Miss Edith Foster. Further assistance in the preparation of the report has been given by Miss Grace P. Norton and Miss Maud E. Lavely.

LIST OF INDUSTRIES OR OCCUPATIONS IN WHICH 59 BOYS WERE PLACED

Commercial engraving	14
Printing	13
Bookbinding	6
Metal trades	9
Electrical work	3
Commercial lithography	2
Jewelry work or manufacturing	1
Box factory	2
Woodworking	1
Farm work	4
Office work	3
Clipping bureau	1
Total	59

WORK FOR GIRLS WHO WERE INTERVIEWED OCTOBER 1, 1910, TO OCTOBER 1, 1911

Number of girls placed	49
Number who secured work themselves or through parents or friends	4
Number returned to school	7
Number for whom nothing could be done	5
Number now waiting for positions	15
Total number of girls interviewed	80

The ages of these girls were as follows:

AGE	NUMBER OF GIRLS
14 years	23
15 years	21
16 years	23
Over 16 years	13
Total	80

LIST OF INDUSTRIES OR OCCUPATIONS IN WHICH 49 GIRLS WERE PLACED

Sewing trades	5
Engraving	9
Bookbinding	18
Office work	10
Millinery	2
Weaving	3
Sample work	2
Total	49

It should, perhaps, be pointed out that we have never been willing to assume the responsibility of placing girls in offices where only one or two girls were employed. We have used large commercial houses where there were a large number of girls, where the dangers of isolated employment were avoided, and where there was at the same time greater opportunity for a bright girl to "work up."

In connection with the problem of girl employment which has been of special interest to the members of the organizations which provided for the appointment of Miss Davis and the special investigation into girls' trades, it may be pointed out that in addition to the information obtained and the experience gained there have been results of a definitely practical kind: first, the data gathered by Miss Davis were placed at the service of Miss Wells, principal of the new Lucy L. Flower Technical High School, so that various questions connected with the curriculum of that school could be determined with reference to trade opportunities for girls; and second, at the request of Mrs. Young, the superintendent of schools, Miss Davis has been authorized by the School Management Committee of the Board of Education to hold office hours in the school building in order to advise the girls who have entered upon a course of technical training there with reference to their more intelligent and deliberate selection of a trade and their more advantageous placing at the end of their course.

The results of the investigation which Miss Davis has carried on are presented here in a separate report. It is hoped that the information which is published will be valuable in many practical ways. Details given regarding wages, hours, possibilities of training, and prospects of advancement should prove useful not only to teachers but to the directors of girls' clubs in settlements, to district visitors in the offices of the United Charities, and to other persons who come in close contact with girls whose home conditions force them to leave school early and go to work. Information is also given as to shop conditions, the kind of girls who go into the trade, their nationality and age, and such practical details as could be obtained.

Some word should perhaps be said with regard to the limited scope of Miss Davis's report. It is in every respect very incomplete ; it covers only a small number of trades, and in most cases the reports for these trades are based on a relatively small number of interviews. A complete report on the opportunities of employment open to girls would mean an investigation into all trades in which women are employed. The report which Miss Davis submits represents the work of a single investigator for four months only. If it is possible to continue her work, we look forward to the publication of a more complete report at a later date. It seemed worth while, however, to publish a preliminary report in order that such information as had been gained might be of immediate service. It should be pointed out too that further investigation will make possible not only an increase in the number of trades for which information is available but more complete and detailed reports of the trades which have already been covered in this preliminary investigation.

A word should perhaps be said with regard to the basis on which the trades included in this report were selected. It will be remembered that this investigation went hand in hand with a search for actual places for girls who wanted work. Since we could not cover the entire field, we started with trades which seemed to promise fairly good openings, trades which we had reason to believe offered some skilled work and opportunities of advancement. In general, we omitted the large factory industries, such as box or candy making, where girls easily found work for themselves and where the work for girls seemed to be largely unskilled. Some trades were selected because of a definite application from a girl who wanted that special kind of work. For example, when a girl who wanted to learn hairdressing was sent to us, we found it necessary, in trying to find a shop where we could place her, to visit thirty-eight different hairdressing establishments.

We have, as the report shows, interviewed 80 girls, 44 of whom were under sixteen years of age. The question that we had to face was what was the best that could be done for the girl, considering her school grade, her health, and her general ability. In many cases — one might almost say the majority of cases — the girls under sixteen seemed hopelessly unfitted for any good place. They needed to be taught and trained, and yet we were asking employers to pay for their labor. At the time this investigation was made, there were no day trade classes in Chicago for girls of this sort. In order to find out what the possible value of a day trade school might be, the question was definitely put to each employer or employer's representative who was interviewed, "How far would a trade school be of value in the industry you represent?" We have published the answers to this question in some detail because there is sure to be in the near future a larger provision in the way of day trade classes for girls, and any information relating to the subject will be useful. The opening of the new Lucy L. Flower Technical High School will undoubtedly serve as a pioneer and guide to those interested in industrial training for girls. Hull House is about to offer a day class in trade dressmaking, which will be open to girls who are too ill equipped to enter the Technical High School. It is for girls of this sort that a special appeal must be made — girls who have left school from the lower grades, who are not fit to go to work, but whose parents need to utilize their slight wage-earning capacity at the earliest possible moment. While the parents of such girls are unwilling to let them go back to school unless they are given some definite preparation for work, permission could often be obtained for them to attend a day trade class which would give in six months a definitely better chance of entering a trade and of earning more money than they would otherwise have. In large settlements where the girls would also have the benefit of day classes in cooking, gymnastics, or dancing, which would give them discipline and training of another sort, the girl would undoubtedly have a much better chance in the industrial world.

A study of Miss Davis's report shows that even in the best trades there is very little educational work for girls under sixteen. Employers do not like to be bothered with an arrangement which means having part of the force on a different time-shift. The thorough study of this question will, we believe, demonstrate the fact that machinery is taking the place of the unskilled work of children in modern industrial and business organization, and that it will be much better for industry in the long run if children spend the years between fourteen and sixteen in definite preparation for their industrial life. If there is so little work that is good for them to do, is it not the duty of the community to face the fact and make some provision for these two years that are being wasted in the lives of thousands of children who are every year going into unprofitable work? This is not the place to discuss the questions connected with trade or industrial training for girls. It may be worth while, however, since it is so closely connected with questions before us here in Chicago, to quote from a very remarkable report of the Education Committee of the London County Council submitting some reports on women's trades compiled by the late Mrs. Oakeshott when she was inspector of women's trade and technical classes for the London County Council. In considering opportunities which a girl had of learning a trade in the workroom, the need of trade classes for girls became apparent. Entirely apart from the fact that it was difficult to find suitable apprenticeships for girls, it was pointed out that the trade school had certain definite advantages.

"The trade school," Mrs. Oakeshott explained, "aims at making a worker of a kind such as the workroom rarely if ever can make. By means of its carefully selected trade teacher and Advisory Committee of Experts, it gives the child a thorough all-round rudimentary knowledge of the industry she is to enter. That is the basis of the trade school. And if this were all, a carefully arranged apprenticeship might be as good. The trade school has other objects in view. The girl who enters such a school spends two years more in all the wholesome influences of school life. The child of fourteen is not at once placed in a workroom where hours of work are from 8.30 A.M. to 7.30 P.M. She spends these two years gaining strength morally and physically while her industrial training is secured. The whole spirit of the school is intended to encourage the esprit de corps, which is lacking in women engaged in industrial work. General education is continued and the subjects chosen are those which are calculated to quicken the intelligence and interest of the girl in the active life she is to enter. Artistic training in relation to each trade is given, and the young worker has an opportunity of experimenting, planning, and trying to produce original work. In the trade school it does not matter if the material is spoiled, provided a lesson has been learned. Lastly, it gives a hint that when the drudgery has been mastered there is responsible work to come. And this is where workroom training often deadens keenness and interest. It does not exist to teach; it exists to get work turned out as quickly and as cheaply as possible. Therefore the worker is often kept to the one process that she can perform quickly and well; thereby originality and interest are frequently killed."

Other countries are considering this problem with greater seriousness; and trade and technical schools, continuation schools, juvenile-labor exchanges, juvenile advisory committees, apprenticeship and skilled-employment committees have been successfully organized. In order that the opportunity before us in Chicago may be more evident, a report upon the experiments now under way in Germany and England is included in this report.

In conclusion we may perhaps repeat that the fourteen- or fifteen-year-old child is very helpless and ill equipped to enter alone and unguarded upon her wage-earning life; the parent is unable to advise or guide; the private employment office is a wholly unsuitable agency; and up to the present the school has been inactive. This means that there is a rich opportunity for constructive work and a clear field of service. We feel ourselves most fortunate in having been allowed to suggest, through this investigation, the great need of undertaking the delicate task of employment supervision; the fact that it is a proper function of the school; and the method which we believe to be the right method, involving as it does close coöperation with the parents, the employers, and the other agencies which have been concerned in the problems of the individual family and based on accurate knowledge of the wage-earning opportunities and industrial possibilities for children of this group.

WHAT WE NEED TO KNOW ABOUT OCCUPATIONS

By Dr. Charles R. Richards, Director, Cooper Union,
New York

(An Address delivered at the Second National Conference on Vocational
Guidance, New York, 1913)

The points which I want to emphasize represent simply an attempt to bring out what seem to me to be the fundamentals necessary in studying the industries, the fundamental data which we must know in order to move forward in this matter of vocational guidance. The data that I have here are arranged in these main headings: the economic data; what might be called the physical data, concerning the occupation and the influence of the occupation upon character; then, separately considered, the opportunities presented by an occupation for beginners; and finally the relation of the occupation to school training.

Let me take these up serially with you, first on the side of the economic data. One of the things that we need to know is the size of the industry as represented in the country and its importance. On the other hand we have to know the size of the occupation in the locality. Oftentimes very large occupations and industries are purely local, and in the matter of guidance, as well as the matter of education, we must take in such a fact. We have here in the city of New York tremendous concentration of the clothing industry! We have in various cities of this state and New England a like concentration of the textile industries. We have such things as the manufacture of paper boxes and the manufacture of books, which are to a very large extent localized industries.

A further point: Is this industry a growing or a diminishing field? Is it something that is passing out, or is it growing? This point has been referred to by the chairman. There are many industries that in the last twenty-five years have been entirely transformed through machinery from the handwork stage to the mill and factory stage. (I must draw my illustrations mainly from industries rather than from other large fields of occupations.) It was n't many years ago that there were a great many cabinet-makers' shops in New York City, very largely carried on by Germans. There are very few to-day. The cabinetmaking business has become almost entirely a mill industry. Carriage building is another instance where the occupation is changing from a skilled trade to a factory industry. Blacksmithing and carpentry in the old sense are becoming of much less importance. Of course, on the other hand, there are many things which are increasing rapidly; the whole field of electric manufacture, printing, construction in iron and steel, etc.

Is the occupation overcrowded, or is there a scarcity of workers, particularly of high-grade workers? Of course this point means a good deal in regard to opportunity. Jewelry, for instance, appears to be a very desirable trade. And yet, when we look into it, we find there is generally a scarcity not only of high-grade workers in jewelry but of ordinary workers, the reason being that jewelry to a considerable extent is a seasonal trade. We find that in trades like engraving there is always a scarcity of high-grade workers, due to the fact of the very long period of training required.

Is the occupation stable, or is it tending to frequent change? I have already touched upon the changing nature of our industries to-day. Cooperage, for instance, only a few years ago was a matter entirely of handwork. To-day barrels are not made by hand. Their manufacture has become entirely a matter of machinery, almost automatic in its character. Millinery and the making of dress and fur goods are constantly changing in the methods and character of work.

The hours per day enter into the situation. Also the question of whether overtime is a large feature, as it is in many trades in this city, notably in the clothing trade.

Is the payment by time-work or piece-work? Is the trade seasonal or steady — another point that has been touched upon by the chairman. This last consideration, of course, affects many of the trades, especially the trades of the large cities, the great metropolitan centers, and is affecting us here, especially in the whole field of the clothing trades.

The next point, the different grades or kinds of work represented in an occupation. That is the thing that some day or other we have got to know very much more about than we know to-day. We roughly classify occupations as we look at them. We think of machine work as a high-grade occupation, representing one of the highest degrees of skill, one of the most desirable occupations, paying very good wages. But machine work to-day is not an occupation representing one kind of work. It is an occupation or industry tremendously subdivided, so that there are grades and grades of work, and in almost any machine-operated establishment there are to-day comparatively few high-grade and high-paid workers and a large number of comparatively low-paid and low-grade workers. This set of facts is going to be one of the hardest for us to obtain to the point that they become common knowledge and that we may understand the economic opportunities of an industry in a more discriminating fashion than we can to-day. Shoe manufacture is one of the classical instances of a subdivided industry. There are, they say, about one hundred and one different operations through which the shoe passes, and there are consequently one hundred and one different branches and different grades of workers in the shoe-manufacturing industry. A department store, on the other hand, represents another grade of vocation tremendously subdivided. We must know the names of these different branches, the kind of work that is performed in each, and the average wages paid in it. We ought to know something about the relative numbers that are in the different lines of work, to be able to judge how much is represented by the high-grade and desirable positions, and how much by the undesirable.

And in this connection we need to know something that we know very little about to-day, we need to know the qualities that are necessary for success in a particular occupation: whether strength and endurance are the things that are needed, whether intelligence, mental alertness, quickness, accuracy, dexterity of hand, nimbleness and carefulness, or artistic feeling are demanded; what, in other words, are the things that mean success and efficiency.

So much for the economic side. Of course this whole economic division might be greatly amplified. I have tried to touch here only upon what seems to be some of the basic points in this data; and I shall return to that field when taking up the opportunities for beginners.

As to the physical and hygienic conditions of the occupation, the chairman has referred to these conditions as being a vital element for our consideration. The question whether the work is performed inside or outside of doors is an item on this side. The building trades and the work of transportation represent, of course, outside work, as compared with the great bulk of the industries of to-day which are performed inside factories and stores, and which are sedentary in their nature.

Does the worker sit or stand for long periods without shifting, or does the work involve moving about? In this connection often arises the question whether the strength and health of a particular individual are adjusted to things like clerical work, things like brush making, which involve sitting at the bench continually.

Is the occupation conducted in close, crowded, or basement rooms, or in airy, well-ventilated rooms with windows? No one who is not well fortified on the side of strength and health can continue in that condition very long and maintain strength and health when working under the conditions in which at least part of the clothing and machine-operating trades in this city are conducted, where the work is often performed in very crowded and in very close quarters.

Does the work involve exposure to heat or cold, or sudden changes in temperature? Of course the question of laundries and many industrial operations come in there.

Is time allowed for dinner? Are there opportunities for obtaining warm meals? Does the work involve eye strain? And does the work involve severe nervous strain? Miss Josephine Goldmark has brought to us in that remarkable book of hers the effect of certain of the modern types of industry on this matter of eye strain and the matter of nervous strain, and their relation to fatigue and their relation to efficiency. The work of the telephone operator, the work of fine needlework, and the work of fine machine work, like watchmaking, all are involved in this question.

Does the work involve special dangers from machinery? Of course our factory laws to-day are increasingly taking care of this side, and there is less cause for anxiety. ·And yet, even to-day, there still exist marked dangers from machinery in certain trades; as in rubber mills, where the rolls represent that great danger, and in sawmills, as well as in rolling mills for iron and steel.

Is the work carried on in an atmosphere with much dust in it? Flour mills and grinding and polishing establishments, of course, represent dangerous possibilities in this direction, although, especially in flour mills, the matter of dust is being taken care of and removed by machinery in a way that was unthought of a few years ago.

Are there special unhealthy conditions, such as constant wetting of hands or contact with poisonous materials, such as lead paint? The number of unhealthy employments is much smaller to-day than in former times, but the report of the Illinois State Commission on Occupational Diseases indicates how serious are the dangers in this direction.

Influence of the occupation upon the character and the growth of workers. This consideration, which has also been touched upon by the chairman, is a matter that we are only beginning to think of these last few years. Is the occupation stimulating to growth, or is it deadening in its effect? Is the worker surrounded by conditions that are stimulating to ambition, stimulating to mental alertness, or are the conditions such that he stands still? Is the task monotonous and dreary, or is it something which is quickening and educating in its daily influence? Of course the whole field of industry differentiates very markedly in this respect. Trades like printing and high-grade machine work present stimulating, quickening influences. Many other occupations where the work involves simply the feeding of an automatic machine, like many of the stamping factories; some of the lower-grade work in the textile mills, especially in cotton mills; candy dipping; and paper-box making — of course represent the other extreme. I think we are probably going to think more and more of this side as we continue to study occupations, and to see whether the conditions present influences favorable or unfavorable for the growth of the worker.

Are the influences surrounding the work morally deteriorating ? That point has been touched on also by the chairman. We in New York City have seen in the last few years the investigation of the messenger service, and consequent legislative action which has resulted in an entire change in the city of New York of the night messenger service.

Next to the last division of my paper is the analysis of the opportunities for beginners in occupations, questions concerning which it is particularly desirable to study and inform ourselves about in this matter of vocational guidance.

First, the different ways in which beginners enter the occupation. I had the opportunity this noon of a conference with half a dozen gentlemen representing the clothing trades of New York City. One of the remarks made at that conference by one of these gentlemen was the fact that there is no regular way of entering the clothing trades of this city. Young men, young women, girls enter the clothing establishments, and the whole field of machine operating, with no definite status and very little training. They come into no definite position, but they shortly obtain the work which their own ability entitles them to. They find themselves, and the employer finds where they belong. This condition of things is of course tremendously characteristic of the whole bulk of American labor, of American industry. We have very little of the orderly procedure of Germany or France or of England in regard to the matter of entering the industries. The great mass of young people come into it year after year in miscellaneous fashion as beginners and find themselves. They come in, to a large extent, as helpers or tenders of machines. Take the whole field of commercial work. What a great variety of conditions of entrance are presented there. Beginners come in as office boys, with working papers, they come in as high-school graduates, they come in as college graduates. There is no one way, but an infinite variety of the ways, in which occupations are entered upon.

Are untrained beginners wanted by employers ? That is a question that reacts very decidedly upon the question of schooling. In any city we find in quite a number of trades that the employer is much disinclined to taking untrained beginners. In many trades the whole supply of workers is fed from outside of the city. Their training is obtained in the small towns and cities of the state, and they come to New York with some degree of industrial training and obtain employment because of that fact. In some branches of the clothing trade it is impossible for untrained beginners to obtain a foothold. Even in the electrical workers, it is not easy for a boy to get a position without any practical experience or some knowledge of electricity obtained in school.

Average age at which beginners enter the occupation ; preferred age from employers' standpoint. Occupations, of course, vary considerably in this matter, but here in America we are coming pretty much to the age of sixteen as the minimum age for entrance to the desirable and the high-grade occupations. Not that a great many boys and girls of fourteen are not going into work, and not, of course, that there are not many that must go to work at this age. There are, on the other hand, a few instances where beginners cannot enter the trades until considerably later. In foundry work there are practically no beginners taken under eighteen years of age. Practically no one goes into cigar making in New York City that is under twenty-one years of age. In steam and hot-water fitting, on account of the strength required in the work, eighteen to nineteen is the minimum age at which beginners enter.

The wages at entrance. This is, of course, one of our necessary facts. Are the wages small at first, increasing slowly to high wages, or are they comparatively large at first, but with a small rate of increase ? Where there is a systematic provision inside of the trade for teaching and learning, as in apprenticeship, the beginning wage is always extremely small, $4 or $5 a week ; but there is the opportunity for gradual increase up to high wages. On the other hand, the highly specialized industry, based on piecework and much automatic machinery, is the occupation where the wages are relatively high at first, or very near the first, but where the ultimate opportunity is relatively small, where the opportunity of increase is exhausted in a year, two years, or three years.

The next three points — the per cent of beginners leaving in space of one year, the per cent remaining in low-paid work at the end of six years, and the per cent advanced to more skilled or responsible work at higher wages — represent the kind of data that we must know to tell us accurately the degree of economic opportunity presented by this or that occupation.

Referring again to the machine industry, as I have said, we think of it as a high-grade industry, presenting a fair rate of return at skilled work. But until we know better how to answer some of these three questions, we really know very little as to the chance of a boy who goes into the machine industry arriving at the stage of the skilled worker. So the percentage of those that remain and the percentage that arrive at more skilled and advanced work at higher wages are very important elements in the data that we need. Take such trades as lithography, for instance. We think of this as a high-grade trade. And yet over 50 per cent of the operatives employed in lithographic establishments in New York City are engaged in low-grade work, bringing less than $10 a week for the men and less than $9 a week for the women. Yet that is one of the trades we are apt to hold up as a high-grade industry, and one offering the best of opportunities.

Have all beginners opportunity to learn more than one operation or kind of work? That, of course, is closely associated with the question of the extent of opportunities presented to the adult worker.

Are there opportunities later on for those showing ability to change from one department to another? That is one of the main questions that face us in the study of an industry like the shoe industry. Upon such a question depends largely the breadth of opportunity and surety of steady employment at times of trade fluctuation in such an industry.

Is the occupation open at the top for all beginners with requisite ability? How are skilled or high-grade workers recruited? Does the worker receive any instruction or training from the employer? Is there an apprenticeship system? What percentage of all young beginners are apprenticed? Even in those industries which are thought of as industries with a well-organized apprenticeship system, we find that the actual proportion of apprentices is extremely small to the number of beginners. Take, for instance, the case of one of our large electrical corporations, where they have an admirable school for the training of apprentices. Some six years ago when I asked the director of the school how many entered during the year, I was told about sixty. It is probable that the number is larger now, as the school has been increased. When I asked how many young persons entered the factory in unskilled and low-grade work during the period of a year, I was told about fifteen hundred. This illustrated the percentage of apprentices, those that were going to be trained for high-grade work as compared with the total number of young persons entering that industry.

What are the trade-union restrictions as to apprenticeship or helpers? These also involve data that we need to know.

But beyond all these questions we ought to know the relations of the occupation to school facilities, and any study of an occupation, it seems to me, should necessarily be bound up and connected with some study of the relation of school facilities to that occupation. Such a question as whether this industry — this particular occupation that is being studied — is hampered by the lack of knowledge or training on the part of beginners, is a question we have got to ask of industry to know where we stand in the matter.

Is school training beyond the " working-paper " grade of value for success in the occupation? Is school training beyond the graduation from grammar schools of advantage? Is a complete high-school education of advantage? Is vocational-school training, in any form, an advantage? If either general or vocational training is an advantage, just what kind of training is most necessary for efficiency? (a) General knowledge. (b) Industrial and economic intelligence. (c) Specialized technical knowledge. (d) Manipulative skill. Would such instruction be most helpful if obtained before entrance upon the occupation, or after? Is there need for vocational training before entering the occupation? What institutions exist to furnish such training? Is supplementary (evening) instruction desirable to complete the equipment of workers in the occupation? Is there provision in existing institutions for such instruction? Is there need for a part-time school, vocational or otherwise, for boys and girls at work in the occupation? Would employers be willing to allow young employees to attend such a school — half a day — whole day — without reduction in wages? This last set of questions represent but some of those that must be asked of an occupation to find out just what relation school facilities present regarding that particular occupation. Those questions, you will note, are not questions which start from the school side. I have not asked, Have we schools which provide for industry? It seems to me we must approach the question from the other side. We must ask specifically of a particular occupation, " Have we the schools that adequately and properly equip people for entering or for advancing in your occupation?" Only by making the approach in this way to the occupations will we ever be able to find out whether we are adjusted on the school side to the needs of practical life.

It is evident that if we are to carry out any scheme of vocational guidance, we need besides this sort of information data that are obtained on the inside of the schools. We need data as to the aptitudes and ability of the children that are gained by sympathetic and discriminating observers. But all that is outside of my field to-day.

The collection of the data to which I have specifically referred is evidently a pretty big task.

It is also very evident that unless this information is accurate it has very little use. In fact, it is worse than useless, because it is misleading.

It is evident also that to gather data of this kind means a great undertaking, because a large number of establishments must be studied to cover the great differences in practice and in method and in organization that obtain in American conditions.

It is evident also that the people who collect information of this kind should be people with a large amount of industrial and social intelligence.

This kind of data, on the other hand, is a kind that we need not alone for vocational guidance. It is data that we must have that society may the better understand itself and interpret itself. This sort of data would be of fully as much value for purely educational purposes as for vocational guidance. We absolutely need it for reaction upon the whole school problem. We are never going to be able to make a satisfactory adjustment of school instruction to the needs of practical life until we understand more of the conditions under which young people enter the vocations.

It is evident, too, it seems to me, that data of this kind should be made a real social asset. It needs to be put in terms that can be used by all kinds and conditions of people. Data of this sort is something that, in its elements at least, ought to be known and understood by parents and the public in general; and this means that it should be made available in very simple and popular form.

Whether such a task as this is going to be undertaken or going to be performed by the national or state government, or by private initiative, it is very difficult to say. It seems to me very clear that we must have this data and that in the nature of things we are going to have it some way or other in the future.

On the other hand, it is very clear that the work of vocational guidance does not need to stop until this data is collected in an absolutely comprehensive fashion. What we need for vocational guidance is sound, accurate information; not necessarily comprehensive information. Data that is far less comprehensive than the outline I have mentioned here may be extremely valuable for these purposes. Out of data of this kind we shall know, at least, very definitely what are the specially harmful trades or occupations; what are harmful on account of physical, sanitary, or moral dangers; or what are simply brutalizing, as the work of the rolling mills. We should know also what vocations are beneficial, or which give generous opportunities, because of their economic advantages, or because of the educational influences surrounding them and because of the fact that they permit continuity of growth. And, perhaps most important of all, we should know better with such data where to place the emphasis in our educational work, and we should know much better than we do to-day how far and in what direction we should counsel pupils toward further schooling, and how much toward the industries.

PART III. EXAMPLES OF VOCATIONAL INFORMATION

THE ARCHITECT

(From " Vocations for Boys," issued by the Vocation Bureau of Boston)

THE PROFESSION: ITS NATURE, CONDITIONS, AND FUTURE

Architecture is the art of building or the art of designing appropriate construction. It deals with the design and working drawings for buildings and the superintendence of their execution. There are two sides to the profession, — the artistic and the practical, — which are quite inseparable in preparation and in practice, and both demand a general knowledge of construction. The successful architect is one who has decided capacity either for designing buildings and accessories or for getting work done expeditiously, properly, and with economy.

The chief work of the architect is indoors, planning and designing, with some outside work when superintending construction. The physical conditions found in this occupation are of the best. A possible danger is injury to the eyesight. The hours required are short compared to those of most occupations, usually from nine to five, though there is always opportunity for occasional work outside of one's regular employment. Students in architecture in the higher-grade institutions can generally find summer employment, either without pay or at a low rate.

While the hours are short the work of the draftsman is very exacting, and the responsibilities of the practicing architect very great. He has not only to supervise construction but also to direct the expenditure, often, of large sums of money in the interests of a client who trusts in his professional and business abilities and standards. He may have, also, to harmonize the conflicting interests of the various people concerned in the construction of a building.

Closely allied to architecture are the various branches of engineering: structural engineering, connected with the use of iron in construction, either by itself or with concrete; civil engineering, as connected with surveying; domestic engineering, which covers matters concerned in heating, ventilating, electric light and power, and plumbing. The tendency to specialization is increasing in these lines, and there is a growing demand for the architectural engineer and for the mechanical engineer. Such are found in all large offices. In addition to the engineering there is the work connected with the grading, planting, and decoration of grounds, and this again touches on horticulture, agriculture, and forestry. This is the special work of the landscape gardener or landscape architect. All of these occupations require draftsmen, and all require special training and experience. With all of these branches of architecture the architect is so closely connected as to make it desirable, if not necessary, that he should have some fundamental knowledge of all. On this account the profession of architecture is becoming more and more complex, and offices tend to become larger and more thoroughly organized and specialized, so that the complex problems involved in almost any modern building, with its accessories and surroundings, may receive proper study.

There is, therefore, in the whole field of architecture a very wide range, with very great opportunities for young men of varying talents and abilities. It is a profession of the highest standing, and has the future of an important occupation.

PAY, POSITIONS, AND OPPORTUNITIES

Wages are paid to the learner, but varying from $3 a week to $6, according to age, fitness, and ability. The rate of increase is generally $1, $1.50, and $2 a week yearly until one reaches permanent employment as draftsman or designer. These earn on an average from $800 to $1500 a year, though exceptional men earn more, up to $2000 or $3000. Men holding high positions in a firm, though not members of it, often have a share in the profits.

The majority entering the profession remain draftsmen permanently, at pay varying from $20 to $35 a week. Graduates from advanced college courses may earn $40 a week or more in permanent employment as draftsmen, after spending two or three years in an office. The draftsman is sometimes called the architect's assistant. Boston offices employ from two or three to twenty-five or more draftsmen in each.

The earnings of the practicing architect, who is not working on a salary, are variable, ranging from $1000 to $5000 or $10,000 a year. A small number·of American architects with a national reputation earn greater sums, but comparatively few in the profession receive more than moderate incomes. Architectural receipts depend upon the conditions of the building business, and this in turn upon the state of general business. Again, the class of contracts rather than their number is to be taken into consideration. An architect sometimes devotes a year or even more to the designing of a single building, of which he usually superintends the erection. The minimum fee, named as professional and binding by the American Institute of Architects, for plans, specifications, and superintendence is 6 per cent of the total cost of the building, and on buildings costing less than $10,000 a higher rate is usually charged. The fee for the architect's services on small buildings is seldom less than $100, and the architect of a city block, hotel, or public building may receive from $3000 to $25,000 or more.

Many of the best architects find it of great advantage to work under partnership arrangements, as firms. The firm gets a wider range of clients when it can offer expert service in each of the various lines of the profession.

Besides draftsmen architects require expert stenographers and bookkeepers, and one of these is often an office manager, attending to the administration of the office routine. Such a position does not require professional education or training but business knowledge and executive ability. In a large office of from twenty to one hundred men this position is a responsible and well-paid one.

Pursuits allied to architecture, and in a sense supplementary to it, are the designing and manufacture of furniture, rugs, interiors, and stained glass, mural painting, and landscape architecture. In recent years the architect has found a new and important field in town and city planning. Members of the profession are usually included in building commissions, as in the Boston Schoolhouse Commission.

The outside superintendent is often merely a capable draftsman with thorough knowledge of construction in all trades and ability to handle men. Such a man need have no especial training in design, although experience will have given him some judgment in such matters. The clerk of the works, or superintendent of construction, is paid by the owner, but is under the control of the architect. Such men receive from $1500 to $2500 a year.

Architecture is a profession that centers in cities and towns, and the unprecedented growth of large cities in this country has given the American architect a constantly enlarging field of activity and service.   •

THE BOY: QUALITIES AND TRAINING REQUIRED

A boy fourteen years old may find a place in office work in this profession with some opportunity for learning. Usually, however, a boy must be at least sixteen years of age, and he is not likely to become exclusively a draftsman until he is twenty. One must have imagination, structural sense, skill in designing and drafting, a mechanical or artistic cast of mind, and judgment. Good health and habits and good eyesight are essential. Some architects prefer city boys on account of their acquaintance with streets and buildings.

There are two natural divisions in this profession, demanding two kinds of men. First is the artist. He is a designer, and works indoors on plans for construction. He must have creative ability, artistic feeling, and power to sketch. He must constantly study art and architecture. He may, however, have but a minimum of mathematical knowledge.

The second is the construction man indoors and out, the superintendent of outdoor work. He must acquire a comprehensive working knowledge of construction, of the writing of specifications, and of superintending work. He may have a minimum of artistic feeling and ability, but he must have a maximum of mathematical and technical knowledge and of administrative ability.

As a rule architects are trained in a professional school, after having obtained a college degree, and this study is supplemented by travel and study abroad; but many boys become good draftsmen, and some few good architects, with no other school education but that of the high school, and no other professional education but that acquired in an office and through the various evening classes and university extension work.

In all cases high-school training is required, yet this may only make one a draftsman; for advancement beyond this position, technical education is necessary, except in cases of especial ability. Designers and practicing architects are nearly all graduates of technical schools or colleges, such as the Massachusetts Institute of Technology or the Graduate School of Applied Science at Harvard. Many young men in architects' offices, especially those who have not had a college training, study in evening classes in the Y.M.C.A. Institute or in the Architectural Club. It is a profession demanding constant study and concentration of thought and endeavor.

There are many scholarships in the colleges and in connection with architectural societies for draftsmen of marked ability. These afford opportunities for education with tuition fees paid or one or two years of foreign travel and study with all expenses paid.

A liberal education is of the greatest value. Architects owe many of their ideas to foreign examples, and the more one is educated the more he will profit by travel and study. Nevertheless, in this country the capacity to organize and direct an office is essential for him who would have charge of large work. A knowledge of French is an advantage, as many books on architecture are written in that language; yet one needs above all a thorough knowledge of the English language. Draftsmen will need a working knowledge of ordinary construction or else of historic ornament, and skilled work alone will often not suffice. A student of architecture should keep in touch with new books and magazines, and study the kinds and uses of material. This knowledge is especially important now when so many new kinds of material are coming into use. Terra cotta in architectural work has an increasing interest. Concrete, also, is a material whose structural and ornamental possibilities are only beginning to be understood. With this multiplying of kinds of material, the student cannot afford to neglect the subject. The conditions of practice in which the client often disregards time make it necessary for the student to learn to work quickly, yet he must take care that his work appear finished rather than crude, and that it show character rather than copying.

COMMENTS OF PEOPLE IN THE PROFESSION

There is but little change in the personnel of a firm from year to year, and the profession is a life occupation for those going into it.

Professional education is by far the best; one cannot well educate one's self for an occupation having such high requirements.

The complexity of modern life as echoed in modern buildings is so great that the work of the conscientious architect is arduous and wearing in the extreme, and its best appreciation comes largely from other architects and artists.

The architect has an unusual opportunity to be helpful in civic advance. He is recognized by the public as a professional man as well as an artist, and consequently has a hearing which as an artist alone he would lack. Though he cannot afford to do much real work without fees, still by his attitude he can in a very marked way direct public taste toward the principles of good design in city planning and in civic art. The architect can direct men's eyes so that they too can " dream dreams " of things which may be brought to pass.

SUGGESTIONS FROM AN ARCHITECT TO A BOY WHO WISHES TO ENTER THE PROFESSION

A boy must have creative ability to become an architect, but the boy who loves sketching or modeling, or work with tools, may have the making of one. The capacity to think for one's self, to plan work ahead and get it done on schedule time, to be prompt, explicit, and thorough, these are qualifications of prime importance in architectural work. It is sometimes said that the client more readily appreciates good business methods than good design; yet competition among the best designers is always keen.

The architect must be an administrator as well as an artist. This is a recent outgrowth, but under present conditions the student must look forward to becoming a partner in or part of a large concern. For this he receives no training in school, so if your bent is for designing and not for handling men, try to put through some actual work while studying. You will learn much from your relations with a client, and from the trades that go into the work. If it be only an ell to a house or an outbuilding, so long as the responsibility rests on you, do it. Have interests outside of architecture. Design such things as interior decoration, draperies, and light fixtures, or other accessories.

There is no recipe for getting clients. The best way to get clients is to deserve them.

It is not hard for a bright boy to get into an architect's office as messenger or office boy, with a chance to make tracings. This is the beginning of the average draftsmanship, and its relation to actual work will be learned in the office and by going out into the work itself. Part time in an architect's office and part time in a technical school will help a boy to a thorough education in the profession; but unless his heart is in his work from the first, he had better seek another occupation.

CENSUS REPORTS

A. Massachusetts, 1905, Selected Occupations, Age Periods for Architects, Designers, Draftsmen, etc.

	Males	Females	Totals
Under 16 years	—	—	—
16 to 24 years, inclusive	690	9	699
25 to 44 years, inclusive	1619	33	1652
45 to 64 years, inclusive	476	3	479
65 years and over, and unknown	74	1	75
Aggregate number	2859	46	2905

B. United States, 1900, Occupations, Total Persons Ten Years of Age and over, Architects, Designers, Draftsmen, etc.

	Male	Female	Totals
Of native parentage	14,890	524	15,414
Of foreign parentage	13,628	518	14,146
Aggregate number	28,518	1042	29,560

Bibliography

To gain an idea of architecture as a profession, read first some good history of architecture, such as Sturgis, Hamlin, Mathews, Waterhouse, or the chapters on architecture in some good history of art, such as Reinach or Luebke; then look over the photographs and drawings of buildings described by the books you have read.

On the modern practice of architecture the latest edition of T. M. Clark's " Building Superintendence " is very valuable for a beginner, and such books as Chandler's or Snyder's " Details of Building Construction " give an idea of what is required by office drawings.

Besides these, it is advisable to go over the articles in the cyclopedia on architecture and also on building, especially in the Encyclopedia Britannica.

Read books on allied pursuits, such as furniture designing and manufacturing, rugs, interior furnishing, landscape architecture, mural painting, tile work, stained glass, steel construction, building materials, carpentry, masonry, sanitation, and town planning.

CLARK, T. M. Building Superintendence (A Manual for Young Architects). The Macmillan Company, New York.

Cyclopedia of Architecture and Building. American Technical Society, Chicago, 1907.

HAMLIN, A. D. F. History of Architecture. Longmans, Green, & Co., New York, 1897.

LUEBKE. Outlines of the History of Art, edited by Russell Sturgis, 2 vols. Smith, Paul Elder and Company, New York and London.

STURGIS, RUSSELL, and FROTHINGHAM, A. L. History of Architecture, 3 vols. Batsford, London, 1910.

WATERHOUSE, P. L. Story of the Art of Building (Library of Useful Stories). D. Appleton and Company, New York, 1901.

Journals of the Profession

The Architectural Review, Boston.

The Brickbuilder, an architectural monthly, Boston.

The American Architect, New York.

Architecture, New York.

The Architectural Record, New York.

The Technology Architectural Record, Massachusetts Institute of Technology Architectural Society.

· THE GROCER

(From " Vocations for Boys," issued by the Vocation Bureau of Boston)

THE BUSINESS: ITS NATURE, DIVISIONS, AND FUTURE

The grocer is a merchant who deals in groceries and provisions, or household food supplies. He stands between the producer and consumer, buying from the one and selling to the other the food staples of the people.

The occupation, as a business, has two broad divisions, wholesaling and retailing. The wholesaler buys from the producer or manufacturer and sells to the retail dealer. The large retailer, however, often buys directly from the producer. The wholesaler who sells to smaller wholesale dealers is usually called a jobber, while one who does business on a commission is styled a commission merchant. A large percentage of the business of the market district of Boston is done on a commission basis. The wholesaler or the large retail dealer may also be an importer. The large dealer is usually called a merchant, and the small dealer a storekeeper, as in other lines of mercantile business.

Formerly most grocery stores, wholesale and retail, dealt in groceries only. Now an increasing number carry also what are called provisions, such as fresh meats and fresh vegetables or fish. While this makes a larger general business, it entails the loss incident to handling perishable goods, such as fruits, and the uncertainty of the meat trade. The duties, also, of the employee are more exacting and onerous in the grocery and provision trade and his average earnings slightly less, as will appear in the census reports quoted in this bulletin.

The grocery and provision trade is one of the great divisions of merchandising. Its magnitude is shown by the place it holds in the total cost of living. In a census taken by the government in 1903, of 1189 representative families in Massachusetts, it was found that food constituted 40.9 per cent of the total living expenses. Again, by the twelfth census of the United States it appears that the business had increased over 36 per cent in the decade between 1890 and 1900.

On the other hand, it is not so easy for a person with small capital to go into this business as it was twenty years ago, except possibly in a small city or town. The grocery trade of the department store, the modern chain system of grocery stores, and the large retail grocery store with capital enough to conduct a cash business, all bring great competition into the field, with excessive advertising and cutting of prices, and imperil the business of the small dealer, lessening it or driving him out altogether, unless he has control of some special line of goods.

Two conditions have worked against the retail business in the past, often causing financial failure. First, the former widespread system of selling on credit has resulted in a constant loss from poor accounts, and dealers with small capital have frequently had to go out of business. Modern methods of doing business, with the cutting of prices to small margins in staple lines, are resulting in the general establishment of the cash system in the grocery trade. Secondly, in many cases men have come from other occupations in middle life into the grocery business, thus entering it from the top, and lacking the necessary knowledge that would have resulted from growing up in it. As a consequence there have been many failures from this cause. The increasing difficulties of entering the occupation late in life and as a proprietor with small capital are likely to lessen the number of such failures.

The larger business, affording employment to a large number of persons at pay about equaling that of most unskilled occupations, is that of the retail grocer. It offers a variety of opportunity, and to many people proves an interesting and fairly remunerative pursuit.

The wholesale-grocery trade offers to a smaller number of men of fair education, business ability, and mercantile tastes and training more permanent employment and a larger opportunity for earnings and advancement.

The near future will show a fuller development of the cash system, larger stores, an increasing need of full knowledge of all conditions from the bottom up, and a larger opportunity and demand for expert buying, management, and salesmanship in a constantly widening field.

CONDITIONS OF EMPLOYMENT

In this occupation there are some objectionable conditions to be met, and many arduous duties to be performed by boys. The hours of service are from 7 in the morning until 6 or to 6.30 at night, and until 10 o'clock or later on Saturday evening. The hours, however, are lessening, from improved means of cold storage and modern methods of conducting business. Suburban stores close on Wednesday afternoon, giving a half holiday to their employees. Pay is low considering the work to be done, and the large number of employees under twenty-one in most stores makes the average wages of the employee seem small, less than $11 a week in the state, but somewhat larger in Boston. It is an occupation demanding few special requirements, and for the most part little training, so that the position of the average employee is less certain than in an occupation that is entered by a regular course of preparation.

A more serious condition still is that the occupation in most lines calls for physical activity, and employers dismiss many employees in middle life and fill their places with young men. So that unless one becomes a member of a firm, or proves especially valuable to a house in some line of service, or because of certain personal qualities, he cannot be sure of employment in the later years of life.

The boy must do all the less agreeable work, such as sweeping and cleaning refrigerators. He is sometimes tried out purposely by the harder duties. He must take care of goods and handle heavy cases, and bags and boxes of provisions in the provision trade. Though work on the wagon is hard, most boys are attracted to it. The use of the grocery wagon, however, is decreasing because of the cost of maintaining routes, the difficulties of collecting accounts, and the advantages of cash trade at the store itself.

The boy in a grocery store is on his feet through a long and busy day, and his work lightens in the city only in the summer season and in the smaller store. The larger store may still supply its customers who go out of town in the summer, so that mail-order trade is increased.

The occupation of the grocer is a healthful one because of the prevailing conditions of open air and physical exercise.

POSITIONS IN THE SMALL RETAIL STORE

The division of labor in stores carrying groceries and provisions is becoming more definite each year, especially in large establishments in which a high state of organization is necessary for the best financial results. In a small store the positions are few. They are as follows: The errand or chore boy; the clerk behind the counter, who is concerned mainly in selling goods or waiting upon customers; the order clerk, who takes orders upon the wagon and usually delivers them; the head man, who has general charge of the other employees; the proprietor, who, as a rule, acts as his own manager and buyer. In addition there may be an expert meat cutter. The places of bookkeeper and cashier are usually filled by girls or women.

POSITIONS IN THE LARGE RETAIL STORE

A wide variety of employment is afforded by the large, modern retail store, which may combine a wholesale business with its retail trade. There are very many positions, mainly as follows: the errand boy; the helper on a wagon or driver on a wagon; the order clerk, who assembles orders; the checker, who checks orders before they are packed or delivered; the packer; the card writer, who addresses shipping cards or tags; the shipper; the salesman behind the counter; the route salesman, who calls at residences for orders; the receiving clerk, who attends to the receiving of all merchandise; the stockman, who has the care of merchandise carried in stock, opens cases, and keeps the salesroom supplied; the window dresser; the investigator of complaints; the clerk in the telephone and mail-order department; the manager or foreman of a department;

the floor manager, who has charge of the salesroom and sales-men; the buyer in a department; the collector, who goes out to collect delinquent accounts; the credit man, who passes upon and has oversight of charge accounts; the bookkeeper and accountant, stenographer, operator of the typewriter, and cashier, who may be men in the large store; the clerk in the foreign department; the advertising manager; clerk in manager's office, who handles correspondence and records; the manager's assistant; the manager, usually separate from the ownership; and the proprietor.

POSITIONS IN THE WHOLESALE STORE

There are necessarily fewer places in the wholesale business on account of the less detail involved and the magnitude of individual sales. First is a division called the outside help: the elevator boy, who brings out goods to fill orders; the receiver of merchandise; the packer; and the shipper. Then come four groups of salesmen, whose place is very important in the business: the store salesman, the city salesman, the suburban salesman, and the country sales-man. The third division is that of the buyers and assistants in various departments, chiefly these: canned goods; teas and coffee; sugar, molasses, and rice; dried fruits; flour; and cigars. There are floormen for each floor, and finally the manager and proprietor.

In the wholesale provision trade, carried on largely by small commission houses, the important positions are those of manager, buyer, and store salesman.

PAY AND OPPORTUNITIES

In a small store a boy of fourteen or fifteen years of age may receive $3 or $4 a week at first, as errand boy and helper. In an average store a boy of seventeen or eighteen years would receive from $5 to $8. In a large retail or wholesale store a young man of nineteen or twenty years would enter at $10 or $12. Increase in pay is small, possibly averaging $1 a week yearly, until one reaches the average or maximum in a department. With some stores, especially in the provision line of the market district, there is opportunity for Saturday employment, at pay ranging from $1.50

to $3 for the day and evening. In the case of many boys and young men this Saturday employment leads to permanent work in the occupation.

Boys serve as general helpers, deliver packages, help on wagons, assist in shipping, have the care of goods, fill shelves, learn prices, and in general fit themselves to act as selling clerks. They do little selling, however, before six months' or a year's employment. By the end of a year's service, or when the average boy would become a clerk, a permanent choice is likely to be made between the selling side and the merchandise side of the business.

There are open all the opportunities of the many positions already enumerated in the retail and wholesale stores. Above the boy, the average employee, with not much difference between departments or divisions of labor, earns from $12 to $15 a week. With some stores pay above $12 depends upon the amount of daily or weekly sales made by a clerk on a practical commission basis. Bookkeepers and accountants and clerks who fill places demanding some special training or experience receive a little more, up to $20 a week for ordinary houses, and $25 or $30 with very large firms. Traveling salesmen, head-store salesmen, floorwalkers, buyers, and managers of departments, or, in general, men filling places which call for special business abilities, receive from $20 to $50 in the larger stores in Boston.

With the large houses expert buyers and traveling salesmen are most in demand.

THE BOY: QUALITIES AND TRAINING REQUIRED

While one may enter this occupation at the age of fourteen, many stores selling groceries and provisions do not take boys under sixteen or eighteen years of age. Aside from errands and simple duties, boys should have age and strength for handling quantities of goods and for long hours of work. City grocers often prefer the country boy, who has become accustomed to long hours and steady application.

A boy should have at least a grammar-school education and be able to make simple computations, such as invoices and sales, quickly and accurately. A high-school course or a business course would be a great advantage. For bookkeeping and accounting one should be well equipped in the keeping of accounts and in commercial arithmetic. Some employers, however, prefer to take a boy directly from school, without especial training in accounting, and teach him their own system. Office clerks and secretaries should know commercial law and in some cases commercial geography. There is an increasing demand for young men as stenographers and operators of typewriters in the large stores, and in the large wholesale and retail houses college graduates are frequently found in the higher positions.

COMMENTS OF PEOPLE IN THE OCCUPATION

Almost any boy of average ability and of good habits who is willing to work and is faithful to reasonable duties can become a successful employee in a grocery store.

As substantially all merchants and storekeepers were at one time salesmen, we must draw the conclusion that the selling department of business offers the greatest opportunities for advancement to the boy who wishes to enter a mercantile business life.

The young man who goes into this business for himself should be a natural trader and master of detail. He should be able to economize where others waste.

The storekeeper comes into direct contact with most of his customers. He knows them socially as well as in a business way. His personality counts as much as does his store. We need more men in business for themselves and masters of themselves.

EXTRACTS FROM CENSUS OF MASSACHUSETTS, 1905

A. MANUFACTURE AND TRADE

	GROCERIES	GROCERIES AND PROVISIONS
Number of establishments	4306	2761
Partners and stockholders	8137	9109
Capital invested	$17,418,740	$8,646,118
Value of goods sold	$101,092,078	$67,052,908
Number of wage earners	8608	8908
Amount paid in weekly wages	$90,180	$90,664
Average weekly earnings	$10.48	$10.18
Number of salaried persons	639	218
Amount paid in weekly salaries	$14,957	$2949
Average weekly salaries	$23.41	$13.53

B. Classified Weekly Wages, by Kinds of Business

	Males	Females	Both Sexes
Groceries	7211	1397	8608
Under $3	133	27	160
$3 but under $4	125	51	176
$4 but under $5	178	68	246
$5 but under $6	230	214	444
$6 but under $7	350	290	640
$7 but under $8	362	195	557
$8 but under $9	336	182	518
$9 but under $10	682	102	784
$10 but under $12	1413	164	1577
$12 but under $15	2220	84	2304
$15 but under $20	911	18	929
$20 and over	271	2	273
Groceries, provisions, etc.	7708	1200	8908
Under $3	251	25	276
$3 but under $4	169	30	199
$4 but under $5	174	41	215
$5 but under $6	266	160	426
$6 but under $7	407	267	674
$7 but under $8	316	204	520
$8 but under $9	464	170	634
$9 but under $10	500	102	602
$10 but under $12	1455	131	1586
$12 but under $15	2544	60	2604
$15 but under $20	1039	10	1049
$20 and over	123	—	123

C. Classified Weekly Salaries, by Kinds of Business

	Males	Females	Both Sexes
Groceries	568	71	639
Under $5	7	6	13
$5 but under $6	6	8	14
$6 but under $7	13	11	24
$7 but under $8	3	8	11
$8 but under $9	20	7	27
$9 but under $10	11	8	19
$10 but under $12	41	9	50
$12 but under $15	83	11	94
$15 but under $20	79	3	82
$20 and over	305	—	305
Groceries, provisions, etc.	178	40	218
Under $5	11	1	12

$5 but under $6	9	6	15
$6 but under $7	5	10	15
$7 but under $8	9	5	14
$8 but under $9	7	8	15
$9 but under $10	6	4	10
$10 but under $12	19	2	21
$12 but under $15	46	3	49
$15 but under $20	34	1	35
$20 and over	32	—	32

D. Manner of selling Goods, by Kinds of Business

	Number of Establish- ments	Amount of Capital Invested	Total Value of Goods sold	Amount paid weekly in Wages	Amount paid weekly in Salaries
Food and Food Products . .	14,224	$71,708,282	$448,082,405	$507,490	$67,121
Retail	12,441	30,968,451	181,258,332	319,437	15,327
Wholesale . .	1,401	30,217,112	161,783,929	144,715	37,542
Jobbing . . .	112	2,278,321	15,387,709	8,829	2,736
Commission . .	234	5,850,056	78,479,132	29,962	7,519
Exporting . . .	4	65,000	248,630	130	80
Importing . .	28	2,070,145	8,476,266	3,080	3,280
Exporting and importing . .	4	259,197	2,448,407	1,337	637

Food and Drug Laws of Massachusetts

Reprinted from Manual of Health Laws, January, 1911.
Sale of Adulterated Foods and Drugs forbidden

Section 16. No person shall manufacture, offer for sale, or sell, within this commonwealth, any drug or article of food which is adulterated within the meaning of section eighteen; but no employee, other than a manager or superintendent, shall be punished for a violation of this section unless such violation was intentional on the part of the said employee.

Section 18 (in part). *Adulteration defined :*

Food shall be deemed to be adulterated: 1. If any substance has been mixed with it so as to reduce, depreciate, or injuriously affect its quality, strength, or purity. 2. If an inferior or cheaper substance has been substituted for it wholly or in part. 3. If any valuable or necessary constituents or ingredients have been wholly or in part taken from it. 4. If it is in imitation of or is sold under the name of another article. 5. If it consists wholly or in part of a diseased, decomposed, putrid, tainted, or rotten animal or vegetable substance or article, whether manufactured or not, or in case of milk, if it is produced by a diseased animal. 6. If it is colored, coated, polished, or powdered in such a manner as to conceal its damaged or inferior condition, or if by any means it is made to appear better or of greater value than it is. 7. If it contains any added substance or ingredient which is poisonous or injurious to health. 8. If it contains any added antiseptic or preservative substance, except common table salt, saltpetre, cane sugar, alcohol, vinegar, spices, or, in smoked food, the natural products of the smoking process; but this paragraph shall not be construed as permitting the use of cane sugar in maple syrup, maple sugar, honey, cocoa, or any other food product in which the presence of cane sugar as a preservative is unnecessary. Furthermore, the provisions of this definition shall not apply to any such article if it bears a label on which the presence and the percentage of every such antiseptic or preservative substance are clearly indicated, nor shall it apply to such portions of suitable preservative substances as are used as a surface application for preserving dried fish or meat, or as exist in animal or vegetable tissues as a natural component thereof, but it shall apply to additional quantities. The provisions of this and the two preceding sections relative to food shall not apply to mixtures or compounds not injurious to health and which are recognized as ordinary articles or ingredients of articles of food, if every package sold or offered for sale is distinctly labeled as a mixture or compound with the name and per cent of each ingredient therein.

Section 24. Penalties :

Whoever falsely stamps or labels any cans, jars, or other packages containing fruit or food of any kind, or knowingly permits such stamping or labeling, or, except as hereinafter provided, violates any of the provisions of sections sixteen to twenty-seven, inclusive, shall be punished by a fine of not less than twenty-five nor more than five hundred dollars; and whoever sells such goods so falsely stamped or labeled shall be punished by a fine of not less than ten nor more than one hundred dollars.

Section 55. Sale of adulterated, diseased, or skimmed milk ; penalties :

Whoever, himself or by his servant or agent, or as the servant or agent of another person, sells, exchanges, or delivers, or has in his custody or possession with intent to sell, exchange, or deliver, or exposes or offers for sale or exchange, adulterated milk or milk to which water or any foreign substance has been added, or milk produced from cows which have been fed on the refuse of distilleries, or from sick or diseased cows, or, as pure milk, milk from which the cream or a part thereof has been removed, and whoever sells, exchanges, or delivers, or has in his custody or possession with intent to sell, exchange, or deliver, skimmed milk containing less than nine and three-tenths per cent of milk solids exclusive of fat, shall for a first offence be punished by a fine of not less than fifty nor more than two hundred dollars, for a second offence by a fine of not less than one hundred nor more than three hundred dollars, and for a subsequent offence by a fine of fifty dollars and by imprisonment for not less than sixty nor more than ninety days.

BIBLIOGRAPHY

HIGGINBOTHAM, HARLOW N. The Making of a Merchant. Forbes & Company, Chicago, 1906.

Business Periodicals

The Grocers' Magazine, Boston.
The New England Grocer and Tradesman, Boston.

THE MACHINIST

(From " Vocations for Boys," issued by the Vocation Bureau of Boston)

THE TRADE: ITS DIVISIONS, DANGERS, CONDITIONS, AND FUTURE

The trade of the machinist consists in the manufacture, installing, and repair of machinery; or, "A machinist is a constructor of machines and engines, or one versed in the principles of machines; in the general sense, one who invents or constructs mechanical devices of any kind."

The two grand divisions of the occupation are general machine work and tool making. The manufacturing branch of the industry, which is almost entirely shop work, has the following specialized lines or divisions: the all-round machinist, only a very small per cent of those engaged in the occupation; the lathe hand; the planer hand; the milling-machine hand; the drill-press hand; the erecting- and assembling-shop hand; the tool, jig, and die hand (a division itself highly specialized); the automatic-machine operator, who is hardly a machinist; and the outside erecting and assembling hand, who must have good judgment and often expert knowledge of the machine to be erected. Another division in the industry, in some cases quite separate, in others not, is that of the machine repairer, who ranks with the erector and assembler.

Pattern and model making is connected with most branches of the machine trade. Patterns and models are made both in metal and in wood. The worker in metal is usually a machinist or a person of natural ability in the use of machinery; the worker in wood is merely a skilled mechanic.

Many machinists engage in several of the divisions of the industry or pass readily from one to another. Employees of the government generally remain fixed in one.

The four divisions of persons connected with the occupation,

534

receiving wages or salary, are the apprentice boy, the journeyman, the foreman, and the superintendent.

The chief danger of the occupation is from dust in cutting and grinding metals, especially in brass working. There is danger from machinery, with hard labor and strain in handling heavy materials or working on heavy products. There is considerable monotony, also, in working on automatic machines. On the other hand, some shops manufacture such a variety of products — one shop visited manufacturing 3800 different kinds of tools — that the workman's interest is steadily maintained.

There is keen competition in the general lines of the industry. Many machine shops manufacture special machines, tools, or articles, some of which are under patent control and are thereby less affected by competition. The field of the machinist has been enlarged in recent years by the growth of the automobile industry.

The high specialization of processes at the present time and constant improvements in the machinery used in the modern shops affect the number of employees, making it comparatively less in the individual shop in most cases year by year, while the entire industry enlarges.

There is an ever-widening field for the expert machinist, and the future of the industry will be good in all lines because of the constantly increasing demands of the industrial world.

PAY, POSITIONS, AND OPPORTUNITIES

Pay at the beginning ranges from $3 to $8 a week, according to age, conditions of apprenticeship, or shop entered. Outside of the apprenticeship system, it varies generally from $4 to $6 a week. The average yearly increase for boys is small, being usually $1 a week each year.

Boys do errands, act as messengers or as assistants to machinists, do drilling, milling, lathe work, planing, shaping, and run light machines. A young man, after a period of learning such processes, earns from $12 to $15 a week in most shops. In the general trade the wages paid are as follows: in lathe and planer work, erecting and assembling, and operating automatic machines, from $1.50 to $2.50 a day; in milling and drill-press work, $1.25

to $2 a day; in tool, jig, and die making, from $2.50 to $4.50 a day; in outdoor erecting and assembling, from $2.50 to $4.50, with traveling or personal expenses added in some cases; in the repair shop, $2.50 to $4; the journeyman who has finished his apprenticeship or period of learning earns $2.50 or $2.75 a day; a foreman earns from $21 to $25 a week. The salary of a superintendent depends mainly on the man, ranging from some hundreds of dollars a year in the small shop to many thousand in the great corporation. The average machinist in Boston earns about $16 a week, in the state about $600 a year, and the average workman in the trade in the United States about $400 a year, taking into consideration the conditions of unemployment usually existing. Anyone earning less than $2 is sometimes ranked as a helper; one getting over $2.50, an expert.

In repair shops very few boys are employed, trained machinists being regularly drawn from other branches of the industry.

Firms which conduct an apprenticeship system do not generally desire boys on any other basis, and give to the few taken outside of the system only unimportant duties, as errand and messenger service, which afford little chance to learn and advance in the occupation.

Outside of the trade of the machinist, boys who have had some business training do office work in machine shops, as bookkeepers, accountants, and stock-ledger keepers, at about the same pay as such service brings in other industries.

Outside of any single, easy process, it takes at least three years to make a boy worth much to an employer in a machine shop. Advancement is slow to the age of twenty or twenty-one.

APPRENTICESHIP IN THE TRADE

Apprenticeship is as old as the trade itself. In earlier times the boy learned by observing and assisting the master machinist for a longer or shorter period. The result was usually a workman along narrowly specialized lines. The later method involves broad lines of general instruction, for long periods, in training schools or systems connected with large establishments and under the oversight of men of the highest skill in the trade.

The modern apprenticeship system in the various trades in this country had its beginning in the years from 1860 to 1872; and from the latest statistics available forty-three states have laws relating to the employment of apprentices. Thirty-eight states provide that in addition to the trade the apprentice shall be taught the common English branches of education in some public or other school, or through such means as the employer may provide.

The older and larger machine shops in Boston and vicinity have some full or partial apprenticeship system, and the general conditions connected with it are as follows:

1. There is an indenture or agreement of apprenticeship.
2. The age preferred for entering is sixteen or seventeen, and the age limits are fifteen and eighteen.
3. The usual length of time required is four years, with a probationary period of two months.
4. The pay is generally 8 cents an hour the first year, 10 cents the second year, $12\frac{1}{2}$ cents the third year, and 15 cents the fourth year.
5. There is usually a bonus of $100 payable at the end of the period of apprenticeship. Against this bonus each apprentice may be charged for tools, technical books, drafting equipment, etc.
6. Time used in study counts as actual service in the shop.
7. Wages are paid weekly, for fifty-four hours in the winter, and fifty-five in summer.

In the apprenticeship system of one large corporation, for machinists, work is given during the first six months on the bolt and milling machines and on small tools; on general bench work for the second six months, as shaping and filing; for the third six months boys work under the direction of various machinists, on drills, planers, grinders, lathes, and boring mills; the fourth six months they are given more difficult work, on slotters, planers, and shapers. At the beginning of the third year the apprentice is placed at whatever tool he has shown himself to be most efficient with and is given work which will develop his special ability. After the first six months, school work is required of the apprentice, unless he shows that he is already proficient therein. During the period of probation, apprentices are required to serve as messengers, in office duties, or in any miscellaneous service.

The system of another large corporation is here given in full, by permission:

APPRENTICE COURSES FOR MACHINISTS, DIE AND TOOL MAKERS, AND PATTERN MAKERS

These courses are open to boys of at least fifteen years of age who have had a grammar-school education or its equivalent, and who are physically strong enough to undertake the prescribed work.

The courses last four years (including the trial period).

Apprentices are paid a compensation of:

Eight (8) cents for each hour of actual service for the first half year;

Ten (10) cents for each hour of actual service for the second half year;

Twelve (12) cents for each hour of actual service for the second year;

Fourteen (14) cents for each hour of actual service for the third year;

Sixteen and one half (16½) cents for each hour of actual service for the fourth year.

The regular working hours are fifty-five per week, so that the weekly wages, even at the beginning, are sufficient for self-support.

The completion of the full term of apprenticeship entitles the graduated apprentice to a "Certificate of Apprenticeship" and a cash bonus of one hundred dollars ($100).

The classroom instruction is based on a grammar-school education, and includes arithmetic, algebra, geometry, and plane trigonometry, physics as it concerns simple machines, power transmission, strength of materials, machine design, magnetism and electricity, mechanical drawing and jig and fixture design. For pattern-maker apprentices an extended course in mechanical drawing is substituted for jig and fixture design and for part of the physics instruction.

While only a small percentage of machinists serve an apprenticeship, this system helps make the all-round machinist and a fair proportion of the most skillful workmen in the various branches of the trade.

In the first corporation mentioned about five per cent of all employees at the present time are serving in some part of the apprenticeship system.

Union shops allow one apprentice for the shop and one for each five machinists.

THE BOY: QUALITIES AND TRAINING REQUIRED

In this occupation a boy is rarely taken under fifteen years of age. From sixteen to eighteen is the age very generally preferred.

Only the larger firms have a regular apprenticeship system, since young men after learning the trade pass so readily from one shop to another or from one branch of the trade to another.

Boys should have a grammar-school education. In the occupation are found many high-school and technical-school graduates, these quite generally becoming foremen or superintendents. It is an advantage for young men in machine shops to continue their studies in mathematics and drawing in evening schools or classes.

A boy should have natural mechanical skill or adaptability to tool work and handwork. He should be strong, energetic, and of good physique.

Three important factors in advancement in this trade are : first, mastery of the work in hand; second, the ability, the health, and the energy to master the related studies bearing on the trade, such as shop mathematics, shop English, shop drawing, and shop science and practice; third, the development of the qualities of management.

COMMENTS OF PEOPLE IN THE TRADE

It is a detriment to a boy to specialize. The constant repetition of a process dulls ambition and narrows interest and power.

We will not hire the indifferent, street-corner boy. Some parts of the year it is very difficult to find any suitable ones. We want the best out of the schools, and offer them a good future.

The chief trouble with boys in this industry is their inclination to go from shop to shop, while yet practically learners only.

The repair shop is a place for expert workmen only, masters of the machines which they have to repair.

Boys naturally want to earn more than is possible in learning a trade, and it is not always easy to maintain an apprenticeship system in this country. The present high industrial organization calls for short cuts and time-saving methods. The machinist, however, should serve several years to become an expert workman.

The chances of a boy to learn are better in a small shop, where he can have the constant personal attention of an employer or foreman.

Machinists are quite generally satisfied with their vocation, coming into it after some deliberation and sometimes through a system of apprenticeship.

The past in this occupation has been good, and the future has a fair outlook. There is a lack still of skilled machinists.

COMMENTS FROM THE MASSACHUSETTS BOARD OF HEALTH REPORT,
DANGEROUS OCCUPATIONS, 1907

Manufacture of Machinery, Machine Parts, and Metal Supplies

In the manufacture of machinery and metal supplies there are several operations which involve exposure to dust, fumes, vapors, or extreme heat. These include making castings, cleaning and smoothing, grinding and polishing, and scaling.

While the nature of some of the processes is such as to warrant classification of this industry with the dangerous trades, the conditions under which the work is done are very largely responsible for the injurious effects on the health of the employees, and these conditions are to a considerable extent avoidable or at least susceptible of improvement.

STATISTICS OF MANUFACTURE, MASSACHUSETTS, 1908

FOUNDRY AND MACHINE-SHOP PRODUCTS

	THE STATE	BOSTON
Number of establishments	519	106
Capital devoted to production	$60,525,711	$11,152,410
Value of stock and materials used	$20,791,813	$2,976,147
Amount of wages paid during the year	$18,699,125	$2,200,481
Average yearly earnings	$601.03	$681.47
Value of product	$56,208,811	$7,171,175
Males employed	30,661	3190
Females employed	451	39
Both sexes	31,112	3229
Smallest number	25,874	2576
Greatest number	37,863	4045

THE STATE CENSUS, MASSACHUSETTS, 1885–1905

GROWTH OF THE INDUSTRY BY DECADES

	1885	1895	1905	PER CENT OF INCREASE 1885–1905
Number of establishments . . .	622	660	709	12.38
Capital invested	$24,743,677	$39,254,244	$75,797,145	200.63
Value of product	$20,635,970	$31,858,110	$59,621,469	188.92
Average number of employees .	14,644	21,598	33,182	126.59
Total amount paid in wages . .	$7,249,855	$11,624,673	$19,271,846	164.44
Average yearly earnings . . .	$495.07	$538.23	$580.79	17.31
Population of the state	1,942,141	2,500,183	3,003,680	54.66

NOTE. The small increase in the number of establishments is due in part to the method of census enumeration in 1905, which included only those establishments whose yearly output in goods amounted to at least $500, and in part to the tendency toward large-scale enterprise.

SELECTED OCCUPATIONS, MASSACHUSETTS, 1905

AGE PERIODS FOR MACHINISTS IN EMPLOYMENT

	AGGREGATE			MACHINISTS			MACHIN- ISTS'
	Males	Females	Totals	Males	Females	Totals	HELPERS
Under 16 years	110		110	32		32	78
16 to 24 years, inclusive . .	6,835	2	6,837	4,986	2	4,988	1,849
25 to 44 years, inclusive . .	15,810	1	15,811	15,278	1	15,279	532
45 to 64 years, inclusive . .	6,069		6,069	5,882		5,882	187
65 years and over, and unknown	782		782	767		767	15
Aggregate number	29,606	3	29,609	26,945	3	26,948	2,661

UNITED CENSUS, MANUFACTURES, MASSACHUSETTS, 1905

MACHINES AND MACHINERY

Number of establishments	709
Private firms	479
Corporations	222
Industrial combinations	8
Partners and stockholders	7512
Amount of capital invested	$75,797,145
Value of stock used	$22,273,370
Value of goods made	$59,621,469
Persons employed	
Average number	33,182
Men 16 years and over	32,395
Women 16 years and over	539
Children under 16 years	248
Smallest number	27,736
Greatest number	38,984
Excess of greatest over smallest	11,248
Total amount paid in wages	$19,271,846
Average yearly earnings	$580.79
Number of salaried persons	2836
Total amount paid in salaries	$3,814,114
Average salaries	$1,344.89
Average proportion of business done (per cent)	61.96
Average number of days in operation	290.82

BIBLIOGRAPHY

COMPTON, ARTHUR G. First Lessons in Metal Working. John Wiley & Sons, New York, 1908.

Cyclopedia of Modern Shop Practice, edited by H. M. Raymond, American Technical Society, Chicago, 1907.

JAMIESON, ANDREW. Applied Mechanics. Charles Griffin & Co., London, 1905.

MASON, OTIS S. The Origins of Invention. Charles Scribner's Sons, New York, 1907.

Trade Periodicals

Machinery.
The American Machinist.
The Scientific American.

OCCUPATIONS AND INDUSTRIES OPEN TO CHILDREN BETWEEN FOURTEEN AND SIXTEEN YEARS OF AGE

By Anne Davis

(Published by the Board of Education, Chicago, 1914)

THE KINDS OF INDUSTRIES OPEN TO CHILDREN

Each year in Chicago from twelve to fifteen thousand children between the ages of fourteen and sixteen years leave school to go to work. The opportunities offered to these children are few. Not only does the Child Labor Law of Illinois forbid children to operate dangerous machinery, or to be engaged in any employment that might be "dangerous to life or limb" but several other factors prohibit children from entering into desirable occupations. For instance, in dressmaking, millinery, and other skilled trades for girls the demand is more and more for the older girl, with some maturity and reliability and, if possible, with some training. The union rules prohibit boys from entering the skilled trades until they are sixteen. Both boys and girls are considered too careless and immature for clerical work, so we find only a few so young in offices. In brief, practically the only work open to the children who leave school at the legal age of fourteen is the most unskilled and poorly paid.

Most of the employment open to these young wage earners is offered by box factories, candy factories, tailor shops, and department stores. Even some individual establishments in this group have raised the minimum age of all their employees to sixteen because the younger boys or girls are too "childish," and they have found it "an economic waste to bother with them." Outside of this group of child-employing industries there is the errand work and messenger work for boys, which, however, seldom leads to anything.

542

Other industries and occupations than those mentioned employ a relatively small number of children under sixteen and thus deserve a brief treatment. The principal industries in this last-named group are the following: engraving (p. 6); boot and shoe manufacturing (p. 6); molding and picture-frame manufacturing (p. 6); knitting (p. 6); laundry work (p. 7); office work (p. 7); bookbinding (p. 7); press clipping (p. 8); novelty work (p. 8); and bakery work (p. 8).

Engraving. Most engraving houses employ young girls to lay the card on the copper plate, since the printer who inks and polishes the plate cannot touch the card without soiling it. There is no chance for advancement in this work for the girl under sixteen, and the wages seldom exceed $4.

Boot and shoe manufacturing. In boot and shoe factories boys and girls tie and cut threads, polish and clean shoes, tag and lace and assemble parts of shoes, and do light packing. The usual wage is $3.50. Though the work for the boy or girl under sixteen requires no skill, the machine operating offers fairly good opportunities to those older. The usual wage for an experienced operator is $12, though those who are more expert can earn from $14 to $20. On account of the monotony of the beginner's work, however, few children remain in the industry until they are old enough for the more skilled processes.

Molding and picture-frame manufacturing. In molding and picture-frame factories boys are employed to wrap frames in paper and sawdust before packing in crates, to carry moldings to different parts of the factory, and to take moldings from machines which apply whiting. Girls wrap moldings and glue ornaments on the frames. For this work the boys and girls are paid from $3.50 to $5 a week. The boys, if they stay until they are sixteen, may be taught the more skilled parts of the trade, such as gold and silver gilding, hand carving, veneering, sizing and graining, engraving, and lacquering. The older girls apply whiting to the frames before they are gilded and also do some gilding. The maximum wage in picture-frame making is $30 a week. The usual wage is from $15 to $20. The maximum wage for girls is $10, but few earn more than $7 or $8.

Knitting. In knitting mills, girls cut threads, sort, count, wrap and label, tie tags on gloves, and run errands in the factory. There is no chance for advancement until the girl is old enough to learn to operate a machine. Girls under sixteen earn from $2.50 to $4 a week. The average wage for experienced operators runs from $9 to $12, few ever earning as high as $15.

Laundry work. Laundries employ a few young girls to "shake" and mark clothes. Occasionally they wrap the laundry for delivery. They earn from $3.50 to $4. The outlook for the fourteen-to-sixteen-year-old girl is poor. No girl should be encouraged to enter work of this sort until she is eighteen years of age and is strong enough to endure the constant standing.

Office work. In office work there are varying opportunities offered. A fourteen-year-old boy or girl may succeed in obtaining an office position that will lead to something, but ordinarily, even where the child from fourteen to sixteen has had a business-college training, he has not sufficient education back of him to advance very far. Moreover, employers are unwilling to employ children for office positions, because they are too immature for the work. Practically the only office work open to the child under sixteen is such mechanical labor as pasting, filing, folding, inserting, and addressing and opening mail. Of this, the circular work and addressing is often temporary. The wages vary from $3.50 to $6 per week, and in no case is there likely to be much "future."

Bookbinding. A few binderies employ girls under sixteen to fold by hand printed sheets to the size of the pages and to feed wire-stitching machines. The work of the fourteen-year girl is mechanical and often temporary; consequently it is better for girls to enter the trade at sixteen. The introduction of machinery has displaced some of the skilled handwork, but still there is a fairly good opportunity in the trade for the older girl.

Girls under sixteen generally earn only $3.50 or $4 a week — seldom more than $5 a week. Much of the work is paid on a piece basis, and experienced girls earn as high as $18 and $20 a week during the busy season. The usual wage is from $9 to $14 a week. Since bookbinding is considered a fairly good trade for girls, it will be treated more fully in another pamphlet.

Novelty work. Novelty work includes metal, paper, celluloid, jewelry, and leather novelties, and postal cards and calendars. More girls than boys are employed at this work. They do such simple processes as gluing stones in rings; carding jewelry; tying ribbons and strings on invitations and calendars; stringing bags; pasting; mounting; putting leather in watch fobs; assembling, sorting, counting, and coloring postal cards. The beginner generally earns from $3 to $5. There is no opportunity for advancement either in wage or manual skill, and the work is seasonal. The best-paid workers seldom receive more than $7 or $8 a week.

Press clipping. Press-clipping bureaus employ girls under sixteen to clip articles from newspapers, paying them $3.50 and $4 a week. "Clipping" is mechanical work and requires more speed than intelligence. If a girl is quick and fairly bright she may be promoted to the position of "reader," who reads and marks articles to be clipped. The best readers never earn more than $9 a week. Not only is there no future in the work, but it prepares a girl for no other line of work.

Bakeries. Both boys and girls are employed in smaller bakeries to pack and wrap, ice cakes, and carry trays. In the large biscuit and cracker factories a few children pack and label, but older girls are preferred.

Besides the trades mentioned, soap, ink, seed and spice, druggist-supplies, extract, and preserved-fruit manufacturing establishments employ children to pack, bottle, and label. The work is very unskilled and seasonal. The wages seldom exceed $6 or $7.

It can readily be seen that all of this miscellaneous work open to the child under sixteen is of an unskilled nature and furnishes little or no training that may later prove valuable. Children are likely to get into the rut of factory work, losing all incentive and ambition to progress, or to acquire the habit of continual shifting from one job to another. Even where a position may broaden out into something better after the age of sixteen is reached, the child, with a child's restlessness and lack of foresight, often changes to something that appeals simply on account of its novelty. In every case the years between fourteen and sixteen spent at work afford little gain either in money or training and mean much actual loss in strength and mental development. This is true not only of the work already briefly discussed but of the five trades mentioned above, which employ the greatest number of children just leaving school. These trades it seems necessary to discuss more fully.

PAPER–BOX MAKING

Paper-box manufacturing is an industry in which a comparatively large number of girls and a few boys under sixteen are employed. The industry includes the making of paper boxes of all sizes and for all purposes, from the small drug box to the jewelry box, which requires a fair amount of skill and deftness in the making. Some factories make only folding boxes, such as suit boxes, charlotte-russe boxes, oyster and ice-cream boxes. No skill is required in this work. Many large manufacturing establishments make in their own factories the boxes in which their own goods are packed. Some establishments, in which only large boxes are made, do not employ girls under sixteen. Boys from fourteen to sixteen are employed as errand boys, from which they may advance after they are six-teen to the cornering machines and later to the scoring machines. The trade is, however, preëminently for women and girls.

Processes. The young girl just beginning the work may do four processes — bending up, pony covering, turning in, and closing and tying of the boxes. The pony-covering machine is a hand machine, consisting of a reel which holds the paper, a glue pot in which a copper roller revolves, and a wooden form onto which the box fits. The form turns as the girl at the machine draws the covering paper over the roller and glues it to the box, rubbing it smooth until all four sides are covered. After the box is covered, the paper which protrudes over the edges is folded in. The girl who operates the covering machine generally does this "turning in," as it is called, if the box is small. If she has large boxes to cover, she is usually supplied with a helper, who turns in the edges. The last process consists of putting on the covers and tying the finished boxes into bundles for shipping.

Girls over sixteen are generally put on "covering machines," "staying machines," or "table work." The covering machine is practically the same as a pony-covering machine, only it is larger and is run by power. The operator of this machine always has a "turning-in," girl to assist her.

The process of "staying" consists of fastening the corners of the box together with a gummed strip of manila paper which runs over a wheel and through a trough of water. After this paper is adjusted, a heavy iron form, which fits over the form on which the box rests, presses it into place. The staying machine is the only dangerous machine operated by girls. The operators wear steel finger tips to protect their fingers.

The handwork, or table work, is divided into several classes. Beginners paste labels on boxes, such as drug boxes. The more skilled workers do "bingeing"—the joining of the bottom and top of the box at one side—or "necking," which consists of gluing to the inside of boxes projecting rims over which the lid fits. Some of this work requires the use of hot glue and represents the most skilled process of box making, necessitating a quick and delicate touch.

Wages. The beginning wage for girls under sixteen varies from $2.50 in some factories to $3.50 in others. The girl is paid on a piece basis as soon as she can earn more than the guaranteed wage. Girls under sixteen seldom earn more than $5 at any time.

The covering- and staying-machine operators earn from $6 to $11, piecework. The handworkers, after they have become experienced, earn $8 to $12.

The boys under sixteen generally receive $3.50 a week. Boys over sixteen employed on the cornering machines earn from $6 to $8. Operators of scoring machines earn from $14 to $21 on a piece basis.

Hours. Girls under sixteen work from 7.30 to 4 o'clock with one-half hour for lunch. Girls over sixteen who are pieceworkers generally work from 7.30 to 5 P.M., with one-half hour for lunch, and on Saturdays from 7 to 4. In June, July, and August the factories close at 1 P.M. on Saturdays.

Seasons. The seasons in box manufacturing vary somewhat in different shops, depending upon the product. The busy season in most factories begins in September and lasts until Christmas.

January and a part of February are generally slack months. Business picks up until Easter or a little later, and again June and July are slack.

Paper-box making is not a highly skilled trade, and the processes are easily learned. Except in the best work there is little scope for intelligence, and a mechanical quickness and a delicacy of touch are all that is required.

Though the girl who is employed in a box factory is generally poorly paid, working conditions are on the whole favorable. The work is light, and the air is free from dust or fumes. The odor from the glue, though disagreeable at first, is not harmful. Nearly all of the girls sit at their work and in a fairly upright position. Both the hand and machine work, however, are monotonous and afford no opportunity for mental development.

The work of the fourteen-to-sixteen-year-old girl is particularly mechanical. Nearly all of the processes which she now performs can be done by machinery. There is a power machine into which the cardboard after it is "scored" and "cornered" may be fed, and come out a finished product; the "bending up," "covering," and "turning in" may all be completed in one process. The machine turns out about sixty boxes a minute. The girl under sixteen is paid five cents a gross for making this same box, and it takes her all day to do the work that the machine can turn out in less than one hour. With the introduction of machinery fewer girls under sixteen would be employed, since by law they cannot operate power machines; accordingly it may be seen that there would be less handwork for the girl over sixteen. The presence of the fourteen-year-old girl in the box industry undoubtedly keeps the wages from rising to a higher level.

DEPARTMENT STORES

Though the department stores employ a large number of boys and girls fourteen and fifteen years of age, it is difficult to obtain any definite or accurate information with regard to wages and opportunities. On the whole, the work seems unpromising for the young child. Indeed, two of the largest stores in the city prefer not to employ children under sixteen years of age.

Boy beginners are employed as errand and cash boys. From these positions they may work into office or stock work. The stock boy has unlimited opportunity to become acquainted with the various commodities offered for sale and may in time be promoted to the position of junior salesman, then to that of salesman, and finally to that of buyer; or he may pass to the advertising office or retail office.

The girls fourteen and fifteen years of age are stock and errand girls. They may be advanced from these positions to the office, or they may become inspectors. The inspectors are promoted to cashiers and then saleswomen. The exceptional girl may become head of a department, a buyer, or an assistant buyer.

Wages. Girls under sixteen earn from $3 to $4 as stock, errand, and office girls. The usual wage of salesgirls is about $7. After years of selling, the maximum is generally $10 or $12. In some stores, where the girls are paid on a commission basis, the exceptional girl earns as high as $15 and $18. Buyers receive from $1000 to $5000 in very exceptional cases.

Boys under sixteen years of age earn from $3 to $4.50. Boys of sixteen earn from $6 to $8, depending upon the nature of the work. The salesmen earn from $10 to $20, except in rare cases of ability. The buyer's and assistant buyer's salaries are variable according to the ability of the person. The buyers receive from $1000 or $2000 to several thousand dollars a year.

Hours. The hours are from 8 or 8.30 A.M. to 5.30 or 6 P.M., with one hour for lunch. The hours vary in the different stores. During the holidays and when stock is being taken, there is some night work. A few stores close at 1 o'clock on Saturdays during the summer months.

Seasons. In some department stores, trade is in a degree seasonal. During the holiday season and at the time of special sales extra help is usually taken on, to be laid off again after the rush. Business is usually slack during the summer months. This seasonal increase does not affect the regular employees.

Chances for advancement. The chances for advancement are rather doubtful for the boy or girl who begins to work at fourteen with less than a grammar-school education and with little desire to get ahead. A child must be bright, alert, neat, and must have some initiative, tact, and ambition, to work up to the more promising positions. The opportunities for boys who possess these qualities and who are interested in their line of work are unlimited. Only a few, however, succeed in reaching the higher positions which call for marked ability. The majority drop out when they are clerks or before, because they are not capable of further advancement.

With regard to girls the chances for advancement are no less uncertain, although 65 or 70 per cent of all employees are girls. It is usually from two to five years before the girl who begins to work at fourteen becomes a salesgirl. As the work offers a great many temptations to the young and inexperienced girl, only the mature girl of strong character should be encouraged to enter the department stores, and then, if she is intelligent and discriminating.

CANDY MANUFACTURING

Candy manufacturing in Chicago includes the making of hard candies, such as stick candy, and of chocolates and bonbons. There are a number of rather low-grade factories that employ a good many girls under sixteen, paying them low wages. Some of the better candy factories, however, are refusing to employ children.

Processes. The mixing, kneading, and pouring the fondant into molds, all the heavy work and the operating of machinery, is done by men. Candy making is not a good industry for boys to enter, since there is little chance for advancement, the work is unskilled, and the wages low. The majority of boys and men who enter the candy industry are foreigners who are willing to work for low wages. Very few boys under sixteen are employed.

The girls pack and wrap, and dip chocolates and bonbons. The beginner — the girl of fourteen — does the less careful packing and wraps chocolates and bar candy in oiled, glazed, or tinfoil paper. She may be advanced from this work to the fancy packing or to chocolate and bonbon dipping.

The chocolate dipping is the most skilled work in the manufacturing of candy. There are three processes of dipping. The " hand dipper" tosses the molded fondant into a kettle of melted chocolate, twisting it about with her hand until it is completely covered. Then she places it on oiled paper at her side and with a quick movement she finishes it off on top with an extra twirl of chocolate. This requires some deftness and skill, though it is necessarily low-grade work.

"Fork dipping" is used in the dipping of bonbons and is very much the same as hand dipping except that the fondant is held on a two-pronged fork. "Machine dipping," used only in the making of cheaper grades of candies, is done by men.

The fancy packing requires a little skill, and the girl must exercise some taste in arranging the candy in layers and finishing the top layer to look attractive.

Wages. Much of the work is paid on a piece basis as well as a time basis. The beginners, who usually do the less-skilled packing, receive from $2.50 to $6.

The fancy packers, who are generally paid on a piece basis, earn as high as $10 or $12 in some factories during the busy season. The usual wage is from $6 to $8. Chocolate and bonbon dippers earn from $8 to $10 in some factories and as high as $12 in others. In the busy season just before Christmas, expert dippers have been known to earn from $18 to $25 in some factories. This means, however, that the girls have to work at a higher rate of speed.

Seasons. The busy season in the candy industry is from September until Christmas. There is a dull season from January until shortly before Easter, when the work picks up again. The summer months are slack.

Hours. Though the hours vary a little in different candy factories, they are, for the most part, from 7.30 to 4.30 or 5.30, with one-half hour for lunch.

Conditions. The work does not offer much opportunity for the bright or ambitious girl, for it is uninteresting as well as unskilled. The only requirements are speed and dexterity. In some factories, moreover, low-grade girls are employed and the general conditions are poor. There are, however, factories that offer pleasant and sanitary surroundings, and work is at least not harmful. The packing is light and clean work, and the dipping, while not clean, is by no means difficult.

READY-MADE CLOTHING

The manufacturing of ready-made clothing in Chicago is a large and growing industry and is the largest field for child labor in Chicago. It includes the manufacturing of women's coats and skirts, men's ready-made suits, house dresses, kimonos, aprons, neckwear, gloves, children's clothes, overalls, men's shirts, petticoats, corsets, ladies' underwear, nightdresses, knit goods, laces, embroideries, garters, and suspenders. In the factories where lingerie, women's waists and dresses, and lighter clothing are made, however, very few girls under sixteen are employed. Those who do find work in these factories clip threads, sew on buttons, cut the goods under the lace, prepare the trimming for the operator, inspect the finished garments, and do light packing. If the girls remain until they are sixteen, they are taught to operate the power machine. The majority of shops, however, prefer to employ experienced machine operators. The conditions in these shops are generally better than in tailor shops; the work is lighter and offers better opportunities.

Processes. The greater number of children under sixteen are found in the shops where men's clothing is made. The work which these children do is unskilled and offers little if any opportunity to learn the trade. A few do finishing, that is, all the handwork on a garment. The majority, however, do not do any form of needlework but are employed as sorters, errand boys and girls, bottom trimmers, basting pullers, label and ticket sewers, check girls, and strap and belt trimmers. Girls often brush clothes, which requires standing all day. The largest number of children employed in any one occupation pull bastings. Boys' work is generally confined to errand work and to nonsewing occupations, such as pulling bastings. Since all this work is merely incidental to the manufacturer, he is not interested in training the children for any of the more skilled processes or in keeping them until they are old enough to work on power machines.

Girls at sixteen years are occasionally advanced to the power-machine work, which requires accuracy and a degree of intelligence, and which pays a fairly high wage. Generally, however, they become "finishers." The boys over sixteen may be advanced to power-machine work. They may become edge basters or pressers. Pressing requires considerable physical strength. The machine operating is the most skilled branch of the trade for both men and women.

Hours, seasons, wages. The hours and seasons vary in different establishments according to the nature of the work. In some shops, where the "special-order" trade is carried on, there is a good deal of rush work involving long hours for a time, followed by shorter hours and a period of unemployment. The busy season of the "ready-made" trade comes when the "special-order" work is slack.

The slack seasons generally extend over a period from four to six months. In a number of establishments the employees are not laid off during this time, but they are often forced to seek other employment, since there is seldom enough work to keep them busy a full week.

The hours during the rush seasons are generally nine and one half a day. During the slack season the hours vary.

The children under sixteen generally earn from $2 to $5 a week, though many earn less than $2 a week. The majority do not earn more than $4 a week. Nearly all the workers in tailor shops are paid on a piece basis, and the wages vary according to the nature of the work. The handworkers may earn from $8 to $12 during the busy season, and in exceptional cases, as high as $16. Machine operators, after a few months' experience, earn $12 or $13 if they are very skillful, and occasionally as high as $20 a week. In some instances men operators earn as high as $25 and $30. In all branches of the trade the wages drop considerably during the slack season.

The unskilled and monotonous nature of the work for the child under sixteen, the constant standing in some processes and the constant sitting and bending over the work in others, the confinement in close rooms, the eyestrain, the speeding, the often low wage, and the fact that it is possible to have garment shops in tenements where the conditions are unsanitary are disadvantages in the trade which make it especially bad for children who enter it.

ERRAND AND MESSENGER WORK

The majority of boys under sixteen years of age are employed as errand boys in various offices, shops, and factories, such as printing, engraving, electrical, and machine shops; tailoring, dressmaking, and millinery establishments; drug stores, confectionery stores, and florist shops. In nearly every factory from one to several boys are employed to run errands. Aside from this a large number of boys are employed as telegraph messengers.

In very few instances does the errand boy work into a position offering permanency and advancement. Generally the employer has no intention of keeping him after he has passed beyond the errand-boy age and is unwilling to accept the low wage offered for this work. Many establishments, such as printing and engraving shops, employ more errand boys than they can possibly apprentice to the trades at sixteen, and it is only the occasional boy who has the perseverance to "stick" until he is advanced to the shop work.

In electrical and machine shops the errand work is often too heavy for a younger boy, and only a few under sixteen are employed. Here too there is little chance to learn a trade. In one large shop in the city a few boys under sixteen are employed to run errands within the plant, where they have a chance to learn a little by observation. The boys sign a contract that they will stay with the firm until they are sixteen, when they may enter the shop or the office. Here there is a definite arrangement between the employer and the boy and his parents that the boy will have an opportunity to learn a skilled trade. This is the only shop that offers this opportunity to boys under sixteen.

If the trades offer but little hope for advancement to boys who begin as errand boys, other lines of work offer still less. In some establishments there is absolutely nothing for the boy to do when he is too old for errand work. For instance, dressmaking, millinery, florists, confectionery, and tailor shops seldom have anything to offer the boy at sixteen. In wholesale millinery houses the errand boy occasionally advances to stock boy, but only in rare instances. There is scarcely a drug store that does not employ one or two boys, but few of them are apprenticed at sixteen.

That errand work affords no practical training is not its chief detriment. It is deteriorating and makes the boy unfit for any steady employment. The life on the streets encourages idleness and loafing. As a result a great majority of errand boys begin a process of aimless drifting from one job to another. By the time they are sixteen, or shortly after, many of them have become casual laborers. Employers in the better and more skilled lines of work prefer boys who have never worked to boys who have run errands for a year or two and thus have formed unsteady habits.

Aside from its unwholesome influence on a boy's mental and moral development, errand work is often bad for him physically. Sometimes he is required to push or carry heavy weights far in excess of his strength. While it may seem that the errand boy is engaged in a healthy, outdoor occupation, he is exposed to wet and cold weather, often with insufficient clothing.

Though boys under sixteen are allowed by law to work only eight hours a day, the errand boy often has to work overtime. Frequently employers send them out just before closing time on errands which require them to go long distances, so that they reach home at a late hour.

The wages which errand boys receive are as low as $3 in some instances and as high as $6 in others, though in a majority of cases they rarely exceed $5. The higher wage often means that the employer has no inducement to offer the boy besides the wage itself.

The telegraph messenger has the least chance for advancement of all the boys engaged in errand work. He seldom has any prospect with the telegraph company itself. One company in the city offers to send the messenger boys in its employ to the school of telegraphy one hour a day. Out of 337 boys employed, however, only 25 attend the school, since they are not paid for the time spent in training. Except for this one opportunity, there is absolutely no chance for the messenger boy to learn anything. Since much time is spent in loafing between messages, the moral effect upon the boy is not good. Some employers are unwilling to engage boys who have been in the messenger service, because they idle away their time and many of them have fallen into bad company as the results of being on the streets.

Messenger boys are paid on a commission basis, receiving one and one-half cents for each message delivered. The boy who is quick can earn about $5 a week. The majority earn between $4 and $5. Each boy has a certain amount deducted from his wages each week to pay for his uniform.

Altogether a boy cannot be urged too strongly to keep out of errand work. Though the wages offered may in many cases seem high to the fourteen-year-old boy, the years between fourteen and sixteen, if spent in school, will do much more toward increasing his future capacity than any of the aimless work which is open to him at fourteen. To both boys and girls the schools offer many practical advantages which will help to fit them for the more skilled and higher-paid branches of work.

TELEPHONE OPERATING

(Issued by the Girls' Trade Education League, Boston, Massachusetts)

NATURE OF THE WORK

In telephone operating, two or more lines in a network of innumerable wires are brought into connection with each other. This connection is made by girls in operating rooms of central offices, or "exchanges," where by their skillful management of a piece of apparatus called a switchboard they enable people at a distance apart to talk with each other. Exchanges are both public and private, the public exchanges being those of the telephone company, while the others are really branch exchanges of the same system, installed in such places as hotels and large mercantile establishments in order to create a quicker and more efficient mode of communication for those within.

In order to understand the work of a telephone operator as clearly as possible in its simpler elements, let us imagine ourselves entering one of the metropolitan exchanges. We find ourselves in a large room where our first impression is the low hum of numerous voices, then, in a large horseshoe curve around three sides of the room, the row of one hundred or more girls, seated on high revolving chairs, back to the center. Almost at the same time we notice the continuous stretch of switchboard which they face and at which they are closely engaged. Each girl has over her head light steel bands, worn like a fillet. These bands hold a receiver to her ear, while suspended from her neck is a light, horn-shaped transmitter, into which she talks.

Examination of the switchboard shows that it consists of two planes. The one more noticeable on entering the exchange is upright, extending above the heads of the operators. The other is horizontal, joining the former at right angles. It is about a foot wide and extends in front of the girls like a narrow table.

The upright portion of the switchboard is divided into vertical sections about six feet wide, and each section is divided again into panels. In the lowest panel is a series of round holes, or " jacks," and directly over each jack is a miniature electric lamp, glass covered. It is in this panel that the group of subscribers' lines for which the individual operator is responsible terminates. In the uppermost panel there are no lamps, but a myriad of jacks in numerical order, one for every line in the exchange. Beside each jack are tiny figures, indicating the line numbers. The equipment in this panel is called a "multiple," because it is repeated in every section of the switchboard. On a middle panel, where there are more jacks, the "trunk lines" of other exchanges terminate.

On the tablelike portion of the switchboard, in order from back to front and extending lengthwise of the table, are (1) two rows of metal plugs, opposite in pairs; (2) two rows of small lamps of the same number and arrangement as the plugs and associated with them; (3) a row of levers, or ringing keys, each one of which corresponds in position to a pair of lamps and plugs. At the left of these is a group of fifty or more push buttons, each bearing the name of an exchange.

Such is the apparatus with which the telephone operator works. Each section of the switchboard is divided into three operators' "positions." While one girl is primarily responsible for a single position, yet she is required to do "teamwork" with the girls on either side of her, particularly when they are busier than she is. When a subscriber takes his receiver off the hook to call "central," one of the tiny lamps on the low panel of the upright part of the switchboard glows to indicate the fact that he is calling. The operator picks up a cord and inserts one plug in the jack over which the light is burning; at the same time she throws forward the corresponding lever. This puts her in communication with the subscriber, and the signal light goes out. She makes the familiar inquiry, "Number?" and repeats it when given. If the number called for is in her own exchange, she takes the second of the pair of plugs in use and, on the "multiple" above, plugs into the jack beside which is printed in small figures the number that has been called. At the same time she presses the proper lever. By so doing she rings the person desired, and one of the two lamps on the table, opposite the cords in use, glows. If there is a response to the ring the light goes out, and as either of the subscribers hangs up his receiver at the end of the conversation one of the lamps glows again. When both are burning it is a signal for the operator to take down the cords, or " disconnect."

At a busy time, while an operator is making one connection, lights on the upright section flash before her in succession, signaling that there are other subscribers desiring her attention. She must observe these and, so far as possible, take each in order as soon as the previous connection is completed. At the same time she must watch every connection already made, to see that there are no " cut-offs " and to be ready to disconnect so soon as the conversation is finished.

If the number called for is in another exchange, in addition to signals and movements like those already described, the process of making connection involves the use of one of the push buttons at the operator's left, by which she communicates with an operator in the exchange called for, through whose assistance a desired connection is made.

THE GIRL: QUALIFICATIONS REQUIRED

From the nature of the work and from the fact that the satisfaction of an exacting public depends directly upon the type of girl who serves, it is obvious that telephone operating calls for a superior force of workers.

To gain entrance to the work, a girl must be between seventeen and twenty-five years of age. She must be possessed of good health and normal hearing, she should have a voice which is ordinarily clear, and she must have good eyesight. Perfect connections on the switchboard depend upon the constantly accurate vision of the operator; a girl who is obliged to wear glasses for a defect of vision, therefore, will not be accepted unless the glasses correct the defect. Again, in working at the switchboard, if her sitting height and arm reach are below normal, she is handicapped on account of a required average reach. She should be able to write a legible hand in order to make satisfactory records of telephone calls. An applicant should be one who is careful of her personal appearance. Girls are barred from the work if they are noticeably lacking in neatness and refinement of person.

Not only do the regular calls demand mental alertness and self-restraint, but these are sometimes varied by emergency calls. A girl must be ready to respond to hurried appeals for doctor, hospital, fire department, or police; and on her thorough knowledge, cool judgment, and quick wit oftentimes depends speedy aid or rescue in cases of suffering and danger.

Both training and experienced practice afterwards mean painstaking and exacting work and require above all else concentration, quickness of thought and movement, accuracy, patience, and self-control. In this there is a real demand on a girl's nerve energy, and she must possess health and endurance and an even disposition to meet it.

Because a would-be telephone operator must be intelligent, alert, and dependable, the more education she has had to bring out these qualifications the better chance she has of being accepted for the work. In 1912 there were but 13 per cent of all the girls taken into the service who had not received some high-school training, and these were able to offer special qualifications, such as natural ability above the average, development through previous employment, through intelligent reading, or through attending evening classes. Of the 87 per cent who had had some high-school training, 11 per cent were graduates.

It may be helpful to vocational counselors to know the system by which applicants for entrance to the telephone school where girls are trained for the work are graded by the principal, who interviews them.

Candidates are classed A, B, C, and "Rejected." The A group represents perfect physique, marked intelligence, graduation from high school, or commercial or college education, along with good personal appearance.

The B group represents the average girl who, although possibly deficient in one or more points, has other favorable qualifications which, with the opportunity for training afforded by the school, secure her entrance to the work without serious difficulty.

The C group includes those who have not had high-school education and those who, although having attended high school, in making out their application blanks and in personal interview do not appear to measure up to standards expected of high-school candidates. This group sometimes includes also those who offer satisfactory qualifications in point of education but are deficient on the point of personal appearance. Girls are never drawn from the C group so long as A or B girls are available.

Those rejected (from 44 to 45 per cent) are not considered beyond the first interview, because they are obviously lacking in most of the requirements.

Of all who are admitted to the school about 25 per cent are dropped afterwards because of deficiencies, especially in application and grasp of thought as students, in accuracy and concentration in practice work, and ability to master the mechanics of the switchboard.

TRAINING REQUIRED

Any girl who wishes to enter one of the central offices of the telephone company in greater Boston must attend the telephone school. The length of apprenticeship is from one to two months, the first month being spent in the school and the remainder of the time in an exchange. In her school course the student is taught the manual operation of a switchboard and instructed, by means of lectures illustrated by charts and various parts of apparatus, in the general duties she will be called upon to perform and in the rules and etiquette which must be observed. Her speaking voice is trained, particularly in enunciating, and her power of concentration is developed. Throughout the course the student is tested carefully in the lectures and classroom as to her ability to become a successful operator, especially on the point of quickness of perception.

The school operating room in appearance and equipment is like an actual exchange. No girl deals with subscribers, that is, the telephone-using public, but with teachers who sit at desks in the center of the room and who pass the students typical calls and so produce, by manipulation of the apparatus, the same conditions on the switchboard as those which the girls would meet in dealing with the public.

At the end of the school period the student is assigned to an exchange, where she has from two to four weeks of further training, this being actual practice work with subscribers under special supervision before she becomes a regular operator.

POSITIONS AND PAY; OPPORTUNITIES FOR ADVANCEMENT

During the student period a girl is paid $5 a week. At the end of this time she is placed in an exchange, and her pay remains the same during a continued period of apprenticeship which is never longer than four weeks after leaving the telephone school. She is then assigned to a regular operator's position, where she receives $6 a week. At the end of a year from the date of entrance to the school, through increases at regular intervals, the $6 wage is raised to $8, and at the end of one and a half years to $9. At the end of two and a half years the wage received is $10, at the end of four years $11 ; at the end of six years the maximum for general operators, $12, is reached. These rates of pay apply only to operators on day positions. Those on evening work receive one dollar more, and those on night work two dollars more, per week than day operators of corresponding rank.

Possibility for advancement to positions above that of operator depends again upon the ability of the individual and upon the character of her work as estimated by her superiors. Above the position of operator are those of :

Senior operator. Promotion to this position is secured not by seniority in length of service but by manifest ability. Senior operators are not only the most expert operators but also the ones who are being tried out for greater responsibilities later. They are usually considered as standing in direct line for the position of supervisor. The salary paid is slightly higher than that of operators.

Supervisor. The name indicates the chief duty of a girl in this position, that is, supervising the work of the operators, although she is essentially an instructor. The supervisor also gives them her aid if there is any special difficulty in operating. The salary paid is from $12 to $15.

Chief operator. A person in this position has entire charge of the operating room and is responsible for the character of the service rendered by her working force and for the arrangement of hours and assignment of wages. The salaries of chief operators vary, according to the size of the exchange, from $15 to $25.[1]

With the exception of chief operators, all girls of the operating force employed on evening work receive one dollar more, and on night work two dollars more, per week than those on day work.

A girl's retention in the service and promotion to the higher positions are dependent upon the number of calls she can handle and the quality of service she gives, her regularity and punctuality in attendance, and her willingness to serve, as well as her disposition as shown in her relations with her fellow employees, her superiors, and the public.

Besides the positions given in order of promotion there are positions on toll or long-distance operating and at the information desk. Subscribers are referred to the latter when desiring special information. The work in these positions varies considerably from that in regular operating, but the pay is the same. There are possibilities for experienced telephone operators in private branch exchanges. In such exchanges large business houses find it advantageous to employ their own operators. Here a girl's experience may lead to a broader field of work, for it is necessary that she should know not only the routine of operating but also in a general way the business of the concern. In such positions the wages vary according to the responsibility required.

CONDITIONS OF THE WORK

Hours. To meet the public demand, telephone service must be given at every moment of every day, including Sundays and holidays, not only during the morning and afternoon but during the evening and the night. Moreover there is a very great variation in the number of calls at different times of the day; for example,

[1] Wages as given, effective June 1, 1913.

in a central office located in the heart of the business district the number of calls may be exceedingly great from ten to eleven in the morning and from three to four in the afternoon, falling and rising between these busiest hours, decreasing markedly during the evening, dropping to a low minimum during the night, and then beginning to increase again in the early business hours in the morning.

Therefore different groups of girls come on at various hours of the day. To illustrate, some may come on at 7, some at 7.45, others at 8.30, 9.15, and 9.45 A.M., and still others at 12.30, 2.30, 6.30, and 10 P.M., but all may be classed in three general groups : (1) those on day service, whose hours of work, eight in number, are consecutive and end not later than 7 P.M.; (2) those on evening service, whose hours, but seven in number, are in some cases consecutive, in others not—that is, the working day for some girls is divided with a gap of five hours between a number of hours in the forenoon and a number in the late afternoon and evening, for others it is continuous, beginning in the afternoon and ending in the evening; (3) those on night service, whose hours begin at 10 P.M. and end at 7 A.M.

In connection with these hours several facts should be noted :

1. It is not found necessary to require night work of any girl, as the number willing to take it is sufficient to meet it. This is due chiefly to the lightness of the work, the higher pay, the small number of girls required, and, in some instances, to special home conditions which make it desirable to the individual girl. It is the policy of the company to place on the night work no girl under twenty-one years of age.

2. Evening work is given to beginners who enter the telephone school with the understanding that they are liable to be given evening hours at first. A girl so placed is transferred to more desirable hours as opportunity occurs, until she finally receives straight day work if she prefers it.

3. A girl on evening work serves a smaller number of hours, and on either evening or night work she receives the extra pay already stated. If she serves on "divided hour" work and goes home between her two work periods, she is allowed car fare.

4. Great care is taken for the protection of girls while on evening and night duty, and on the night work the number is always more than one in an exchange.

5. The frequency with which a girl must work on Sundays and holidays varies in the different exchanges according to the difference in decrease of calls on these days. As a rule, therefore, a girl in an exchange located in a residential district has to serve oftener at such times. Whenever a girl is called upon for work on these days, however, she is paid at the rate of time and one half, and if she is employed Sunday she has a day off during the same week.

6. Girls on both day and evening duty are given two relief periods of fifteen minutes each and a lunch hour of forty-five minutes or an hour. Those on night duty are given an hour for lunch and rest.

Steadiness of employment. Although the work fluctuates at different times of the year, no girls are laid off.

Vacations. During slack periods vacations are given, two weeks in length, with pay, each girl receiving one such vacation each year.

Physical conditions. The physical conditions under which a telephone operator works are of the best. In every exchange, provided by the telephone company, are rest rooms worthy of the name in the comfort which they afford and in the taste with which they are furnished. Here the girls have opportunity for rest, sociability, and reading, in their relief and lunch periods. Individual lockers, excellent toilet rooms, and hospital rooms add to the girls' health and comfort. A matron is in charge, whose duty is to care for the girls' welfare. In the larger exchanges there are well-equipped and attractive lunch rooms, where lunch is served at cost. A woman physician, serving permanently, examines the girls as to their physical qualifications on entrance to the telephone school and is constantly studying the working conditions from the human side. After the girls are placed in an exchange it is the duty of the chief operator to watch them in regard to health and to refer them to the physician when they appear to need her care or advice.

Benefit fund. A liberal plan for the payment of sickness benefits to employees, of life insurance to their dependents at death, and pensions became effective January 1, 1913.

SUGGESTIONS FOR THE GIRL

1. A girl who wishes to take up telephone operating and who thinks she has the necessary qualifications should apply in person at the telephone school, 50 Oliver Street, from 2.30 to 3.30 P.M., except on Saturdays. When she does so she will be given an application blank, on which she will be asked to state her name and address and the names of her parents and their place of residence; where she last attended school and the grade and year in which she left it; any previous places of work, positions held, length of time in each, and wages received; and the names of responsible persons, not her relatives, which shall serve as references.

2. If she is under seventeen and still in school but thinks she would like to take up telephone operating later, she should continue her schooling at least until she is old enough to enter the telephone school and until graduation from high school if possible. The continued education will be of direct benefit to her in her work. Then again, a girl who seeks telephone operating directly from school succeeds as a rule more easily than one who has been engaged in some occupation which called for none of the faculties demanded in telephone operating, even though previously she had attended high school.

3. The girl who has been actually obliged to leave school early to go to work but who has real ambition to become a telephone operator should supplement her schooling by evening classes and by good general reading done under competent direction.

SUMMARY OF THE VOCATION

Disadvantages. 1. Most of the girls who enter telephone operating are given, for a time at least, evening hours which carry the work up to ten and, in rare instances, to eleven o'clock; and some girls go home at these hours without protection. Others work during the night hours, which is not, of course, an ideal situation, although the ones who serve are older girls, taking these hours voluntarily, and being well protected while on duty.

2. Every operator must take her turn in working on Sundays and holidays. As already stated, this is much more frequent for some than for others.

3. There is a considerable degree of nerve strain in the work due to the necessary concentration and alertness of mind and correlated action of eye, ear, and hands; to rigid requirements in respect to phraseology, articulation, courtesy of reply, and speed; to inconsiderateness on the part of subscribers; due also to the closeness with which the work must be supervised. Not only are the operators corrected and guided by the supervisors, who are by them constantly at the switchboard, but at a time unknown to them, their work is checked up also by an observer, who, seated at a desk, "listens in" to different operators to test the type of service which they are rendering. Service tests are made also from outside the exchange. These observations are made with a view to correcting weaknesses in the service and giving the supervisors an opportunity to instruct the operators how to work most efficiently. Obviously a girl of a decidedly nervous, sensitive temperament is unsuited for the work.

Advantages. 1. To the right type of girl telephone operating affords self-development. The necessary concentration of mind, quickness of perception, accuracy, and self-control contribute towards a responsible womanliness. Instead of being monotonous, girls declare that there is something "interesting," "fascinating," about it, and their enjoyment in the work seems to lie particularly in the play of human nature over the wire, never exactly the same any two days or two hours of the day — a continued variation in tone of voice, speech, and places called for. Then again, the girl of ability and ambition finds a keen interest in her effort to prove herself equal to the difficult task of "clearing her board" when large numbers of calls come over the switchboard rapidly in succession.

In special positions, such as "toll" and "information," operators acquire special knowledge. The toll operators, for example, learn much of geography and acquire mathematical ability in very practical fashion.

2. Girls of intelligence and more than grammar-school education find congenial coworkers. Their physical welfare is carefully

regarded. It is undoubtedly true also that there is no other occupation in which young girls are employed where their moral welfare is so safeguarded by their environment as in the telephone exchange.

3. The wages paid compare favorably with those of other kinds of work employing girls of the same age and schooling, and from the first there is opportunity for advancement in point both of wage and position.

4. Employment is absolutely steady, in contrast to the irregularity of employment found in nearly if not every other kind of work that girls enter.

BOARD OF HEALTH AND CENSUS REPORTS

. There are no statistics from either source which are of value for the present bulletin.

STATISTICS FOR BOSTON FROM THE NEW ENGLAND TELEPHONE AND TELEGRAPH COMPANY

Within the limits of the "Metropolitan District" are some 50 telephone central offices, serving nearly 160,000 subscribers' stations, from which originate some 850,000 calls per day.

To handle the traffic in these offices a force of over 2500 young women is employed. Given below is the distribution of this force in the different positions. All positions except those designated as operators are positions carrying higher pay than the maximum salary of operators and to which positions promotions are made from the operating force, selection being in accordance with ability displayed.

	Nos.	Totals	Precentages
Operators	2100	2100	83.2
Senior operators	94		
Supervisors	156		
Chief clerks	12		
Chief operators and assistants . . .	72		
School principal and instructors . .	11		
Private branch exchange supervisors .	5		
Clerks in department offices	73	423	16.8
		2523	

In addition to the positions in the employ of the company, there are some 1200 private branch exchange operators in the city. Wherever possible, the telephone company endeavors to furnish experienced employees to operate the private branch exchanges in such places as hotels and business offices, as it is obviously to the advantage of both subscribers and the company to have only experienced employees participating in such an important part of the telephone service. The work of these operators is supervised by a force of experienced young women, designated in the above list as private branch exchange supervisors, who constantly travel about among the private branch exchanges, instructing the employees as to proper methods and inspecting their work.

REFERENCES

TAYLOR, GRAHAM. The Telephone Girl. *The Survey*, Vol. XXIV, April 2, 1910, pp. 60–64.

BAXTER, SYLVESTER. The Telephone Girl. *The Outlook*, Vol. LXXXIII, May 26, 1906, pp. 231–239.

HARRINGTON, MISS M. E., Principal Boston School for Operators. The Training of Operators in Boston. *Telephone Topics*, Vol. IV, June, 1910, pp. 18–19.

The Selection and Development of a Supervisor. *Telephone Topics*, Vol. IV, July, 1910, pp. 16–17.

A paper read at a meeting of Boston chief operators by Miss G. M. Taylor, Richmond chief operator.

RICHARDSON, ANNA STEESE. The Girl who earns her Own Living, Chapter X, " Telephone Operating." New York, Dodge, 1909.

Written from the standpoint of New York conditions.

" Investigation of Telephone Companies," United States Senate Report, 1910, Document No. 380.

This investigation was made by the Bureau of Labor in response to a Senate resolution of May 28, 1908, calling for an investigation into telephone companies engaged in the conduct of interstate business. The report is a valuable contribution to a clearer understanding of conditions, both local and general, in the telephone business. In Chapter I, pp. 9–113, are presented such subjects as Housing of Exchanges and Equipment, Training Schools, Application and Entrance Examinations, Working Shifts or Tricks and Hours of Labor for Operators, Description of Telephone Work, Length of Service of Operators, Supervision, The Public and the Operator, Wages, Care for the Health of Operatives, and Welfare Work.

GOLDMARK, JOSEPHINE. Fatigue and Efficiency, pp. 43–53, " The Telephone Service." New York, Charities Publication Committee, Russell Sage Foundation, 1912.

The Company and the Employee. Boston, New England Telephone and Telegraph Company, 1913.

A small booklet, primarily designed for the perusal of employees, and stating clearly and concisely the regulations and policy of the company in their relations with the former. The specific information which it contains under such heads as The Performance of your Duties, Your Future, Promotion, Wages, Amount of Work, Quality of Work, etc., is of such a nature that it would be directly helpful to a vocational counselor.

Current Literature

Telephone Topics, issued monthly by the New England Telephone and Telegraph Company. Edited by employees.

SURVEY OF OCCUPATIONS OPEN TO THE GIRL OF FOURTEEN TO SIXTEEN YEARS

By Harriet Hazen Dodge

(Published by the Girls' Trade Education League, Boston, Massachusetts)

I

THE FIELD OF WORK AND ITS CONDITIONS

The field of work. More than 4000 girls in Boston of the age of fourteen to sixteen years are working for wages. Opportunity is afforded them chiefly by the department stores, the candy factories, and the shoe factories, which secure about 60 per cent of the total number, the department stores leading with about one third of all employed.

Outside this group the number of these young girls in any individual industry is small, those industries which take the next greatest numbers being knitting mills, paper-box factories, bookbinderies, 'laundries, and shops producing machine-made clothing, along with those where the cheaper tailoring is done. The number entering millinery and dressmaking appears to be constantly decreasing, and the kind of work offered to be chiefly that of errand girl.

A remainder of 20 to 24 per cent are distributed among miscellaneous industries, in which, with the exception of some cases where the girls are engaged in packing and labeling, the number in each industry is small, the range being something like two to thirty. These industries include among others so great a variety as addressing and mailing, featherwork, engraving, electric work, leather work; braid and ornament, brush, buffing-wheel, carpet, cigar, cork, druggists'-supplies, elastic and rubber goods, extract, hardware, nail, novelty, preserved-fruit, and tin-can manufacturing.

In this miscellaneous group young girls are found in the cigar industry employed in stripping the midrib from the tobacco leaves,

571

"branding" or stamping the name on the cigars by a machine operated by a foot lever, and labeling the boxes after they have been packed; in the manufacture of carpets they "set" the colors for the printer, who calls these out by numbers, to which the color setters must quickly respond by rolling along its track the right box of dye to the spot where it is needed in coloring the design; in buffing-wheel manufacture they unfold bolts of flannel and refold them again in layers, then when circular pieces have been cut from these they place them one on top of the other, preparatory to their being stitched many times around on a machine to form the buffing wheel; in brush making they insert handles in ferrules, fasten ferrules to handles, weigh and insert bristles, and when the brush is finished wrap the bristles with paper before packing; in novelty manufacture they fold, inspect, erase soiled spots from, and count Christmas and Easter cards and valentines, and do simple pasting on these and on calendars, and collate the calendar leaves; in engraving they lay the cards one at a time on the copper plate for the engraver, whose hands, covered with ink, are too soiled to touch them; in featherwork they tie ends of ostrich feathers to fashion willow plumes, and assemble pieces of marabou on a series of iron teeth or prongs, preparatory to the making of boas; in electric work they wind wire and assemble pieces of apparatus; in leather work, such as the making of pocketbooks, bags, and belts, they assemble parts, do simple pasting, and turn the edges of the leather; in thread and twine factories they "doff," that is, remove the bobbins from their spindles when they are filled with the spun yarn and replace them with empty ones; in addressing and mailing they insert circulars in envelopes and address them in longhand.

With the exception of cigar making, carpet manufacture, and leather work, the usual wage in these occupations, even after consecutive years of employment, is $5 to $7, and there is almost no opportunity for advancement either in wage or manual skill, while in the novelty-card manufacture and addressing and mailing the work is nearly always temporary.

In the cigar manufacture, which is strongly unionized, the beginner in stripping tobacco leaves serves an apprenticeship of two weeks at $3.50, at the end of which time she receives the regular wage of $7. After gaining experience and skill, she may advance on piecework to the maximum of $10 to $11. Labeling and stamping are paid by the week from $5 to $7.

In the carpet industry young girls start on a low wage and in work which is very disagreeable because of the chemical action of the dye on clothing, nails, and skin, but there is the possibility of advancement to filling, or winding the drums of yarn, and to printing the design in colors by a set pattern, with practically steady employment and a comparatively fair wage.

The leather work offers the possibility of increase in wages above the $5-to-$6 wage, and for a small number of older workers the opportunity of operating power sewing machines.

In the remainder of these miscellaneous industries girls are for the most part packing, bottling, and labeling, for example, in biscuit, preserved-fruit, druggists'-supplies, extract, and nail manufacturing; or "finishing," that is, "trimming" or cutting threads on a machine-stitched product, as in the case of elastic and rubber goods; or doing rude sewing, as that of tags on garments and braid ornaments on cards. In all these cases the usual wage is $4 to $5, and very rarely exceeds $6.

The limited range of choice. Such is the occupational field open to the fourteen-to-sixteen-year-old girl. Seldom, because of her immaturity, can she secure general office work, even though she be an accurate speller and bright in arithmetic; naturally, she is considered by her parents as too young to go away from home to the responsibilities of domestic service, and for like reason personal service, such as that of nursery maid, is all but barred, while the minimum-age requirement of the infants' hospitals which train girls for this work is seventeen years. To become a telephone operator she must also be at least seventeen years of age, and the Telephone Company gives preference always to those girls who have had high-school education, almost never taking a girl who has had only the grammar-school course. The highly skilled trades of millinery and dressmaking have practically closed their doors on the fourteen-to-sixteen-year-old apprentice, although there is constant demand for older girls who have real ability or who have had training before entering the shops.

Range of choice for the untrained fourteen-to-sixteen-year-old girl, therefore, lies almost absolutely between the factory and the department store, and even within these restricted boundaries possibilities are lessening. One of the largest department stores in Boston has recently set the minimum age of all female employees at seventeen, including stock and bundle girls.

Many individual establishments in the factoryized industries offering work which she can perform will not employ the fourteen-to-sixteen-year-old girl because she is "too immature," "thoughtless," "childish," "undersized and slow to grasp details," "careless," "frivolous," "irresponsible," "full of kinks"; and, as one far-sighted employer said, "the firm is looking for dividends and it cannot afford the economic waste." In the minds of many employers just the two years' more maturity is a decided asset, while some in the same industry in which others are employing the fourteen-to-sixteen-year-old girl will not take girls under eighteen. Employers who express approval of the child-worker do so because "her fingers are nimble," because she is "more easily taught their ways," or because, when there is a lack of supply of experienced and mature workers, they resort to "taking her on and training her." It may be said here that in establishments where the standard is higher in regard to age requirements it is nearly always above the average in other respects.

In the group of occupations employing the greatest number of fourteen-to-sixteen-year-old girls — namely, the candy factory, the department store, and the shoe factory — the last two hold opportunities for advancement to a high wage. In the stitching room of the shoe factory are workers excellently paid who started at the age of fourteen, and in the department stores there are assistant buyers and buyers who have risen to their present position from that of cash girl and are receiving salaries well into the thousands. Bookbinding, paper-box making, clothing-machine operating, the knitting mills, and the laundries include work which is semiskilled and which affords to some a living wage. That opportunity for advancement is wholly lacking in many of the occupations which the fourteen-to-sixteen-year-old girl enters has already been pointed out. But where opportunity does exist for advancement to more desirable positions, even in the first possible steps, whether it be from bundling to selling on the bargain table in the department store, or from the totally unskilled task of the factory to the task which is slightly skilled, the sifting process for the mass of young girl-workers is a merciless one, and is based upon perseverance and capability noticeably above the average, upon a tactful aggressiveness, and upon the existence of a vacancy above. Dropped into the monotonous, unskilled, though manually active, tasks of the factory, or the more attractive but continuously low-paid tasks of the department store, the average young girl-worker lacks the control, the perseverance, the far-sightedness, and the patience to stick to and perform her present task with an eye to a position beyond.

One of two things often happens therefore — she shifts from one place to another looking vainly for something more satisfactory, or her sensitiveness gives way to dull resignation, and small flames of initiative and ambition easily die out. In the factory she frequently remains year after year at the same low-paid work, which develops neither manual skill nor intelligence. In the department store studies of the situation thus far make it apparent that the great majority of cash and bundle girls do not reach selling, but, discouraged by the low wage and the keenness of competition in getting ahead, they drift instead into other occupations, obviously those of the factory, with the hope, sometimes realized, sometimes not, of " doing better " elsewhere, in wages at least.

The girl's handicap in schooling. Often when the fourteen-year-old girl enters industry the amount of mental training which she has gained from school is but the minimum required by law. The department store lays more emphasis upon schooling than the factory, where the requirement in this respect is usually the legal one only, but in the former a full grammar-school education is not necessary, only one store in Boston requiring it. The mass of our fourteen-to-sixteen-year-old wage earners have received far less than the full grammar schooling, and very many whose associations in their home life are constantly with those of foreign birth and foreign language enter upon their vocational careers able merely to pass the letter of the law — " to read at sight and write legibly simple sentences in the English language. "

And yet almost every employer in factories, describing the type of girl he desires, specifies the "bright" girl. This means the girl who is naturally bright, who understands the directions of her forewoman easily, and who uses judgment, even in doing unskilled work. But it is easy to imagine the handicap in meeting this qualification for the foreign-born girl whose school life ends with the educational requirement by law in Massachusetts for the girl who would seek work at fourteen.

The girl's handicap in health. In early wage earning, not only does the girl's mentality tend to become warped, but frequently her health becomes impaired also. Her work usually requires constant sitting or constant standing. It takes her suddenly from some sunshine, some out-of-doors, and some play at least, confining her for an eight- or nine-hour day at a set task indoors, too often under workroom conditions which, in matters of ventilation, spacing, and light, are directly opposed to her physical welfare. For these reasons, when range of choice for the girl is limited to store or factory, other things being equal, it is preferable for her to find a place near enough her own home so that she can secure out-of-door air in walking to and from her work, go home for a warm lunch, and save car fares.

The problem for the educator. The wage-earning world affords the untrained fourteen-to-sixteen-year-old girl meager opportunities, and it necessarily places a low valuation on her earning capacity. Because of the unskilled work which it gives her to perform, it has an influence upon her efficiency as a future worker and upon her future worth as a human being, which is nearly always a destructive one. Added to this stands the now well-established fact that the majority of girls do not leave school early for work because of financial conditions of the home. Instead, they leave because "other girls are leaving," because they are "too big for their class," because they "don't get on well in their studies," or because they are "tired of school and would rather go to work."

The situation, therefore, presents a serious problem to educators, for the solution of which they have begun earnestly to strive. This is particularly true in Boston. Here the public trade school appeals to many girls who would otherwise have left school at the earliest possible moment, but who now obtain further schooling and special training in the trades of millinery, dressmaking, and clothing-machine operating.

At the North Bennet Street Industrial School experimental work is being done under private enterprise but subject to the supervision and approval of the Board of Superintendents of the Boston Public Schools, looking towards a possible modification of the upper grammar school which shall be especially adapted to pupils who leave school early to enter industrial pursuits. The girls are taught sewing, cooking, and housekeeping, learn something of textiles, and receive instruction in academic subjects particularly helpful in wage earning, such as arithmetic and English.

The public continuation classes in preparatory salesmanship enable girls employed in such positions as cash, bundle, and stock girls to become better prepared for advancement in their work, and more intelligent generally. They are allowed by their employers to attend these classes without loss of pay for the time taken.

Through a public continuation school recently established in the North End for the girls working in the candy factories, an experiment is being made in furnishing educational opportunities to those who have left school unfitted for successful and happy lives. A certain number of these girls are allowed by their employers to attend the school for a specified number of hours a week, without decrease in wages. They are given a course in household arts, which aims to give them greater efficiency and more healthful ideals in respect to the service which they may render in industry or in the home.

The whole problem raised by the young girl in industry is the development and conservation of worthy womanhood in spite of conditions which tend to suppress and destroy it. Its solution can be effected only through the coöperation of educators and employers, of teachers and parents, through a more intimate knowledge of individual girls in the schoolroom and of the experience of girl wage earners; and through an adaptation of schools and classes to the real needs of individual girls as future wage earners and home makers.

II

OUTLINES OF PRINCIPAL OCCUPATIONS

DEPARTMENT-STORE WORK

	EMPLOYMENT OF THE 14–16-YEAR-OLD GIRL
Approximate percentage of all employed	33%. More than in any other occupation.
Kinds of work	Cash girl; bundle girl.
Beginning wage	$2.50–$4 in the majority of stores.
First steps of advancement	Cash girl to bundle girl; bundle girl may advance to cashiering and office work, or to stock girl and selling.
Qualifications	Brightness, alertness. Ability in spelling, penmanship, arithmetic, and good conversational English. Practical knowledge of fractions in making out sale slips is especially important.
Outlook for the girl in respect to:	THE OCCUPATION
A. *Wage*	Doubtful in the majority of stores. Advancement to selling depends upon the adaptability, alertness, and stature of the girl, upon initiative and capability above the average. If a girl starts at fourteen, it is usually from three to five years before she can become a sales girl. Cashiers receive $4–$6, and general office girls $4–$7. The wage of stock girls is $4–$6, and the average wage of sales girls is about $7. The maximum in

A. Wage (continued)	selling after long service and in a few cases is $10–$12. In the "room at the very top," however, buyers receive $1000–$5000, and in rare cases much more.
B. Manual skill	None.
C. Mental development	Poor for a young girl lacking in healthy ideals. Her mind tends to become stunted because of false standards, based upon the artificialities of life, which are chiefly and constantly before her view. Good for an older girl with strong character and power of discrimination. Even the work of cash and bundle girls affords mental exercise, and the selling calls for keen observation and tact. Constant contact with people tends towards breadth of view.
Disadvantages or dangers	Constant running to and fro of the cash girls; constant standing of the sales girls; poor ventilation, especially in bargain basements, and exposure to drafts. For the young girl, unsteadiness of employment and extravagant desire for dress induced by her surroundings.
Seasons	Rush, months previous to Christmas. Dull, January, February, and the summer months.
Hours (usual)	8–5.30 or 6, with a half hour to an hour for lunch. During summer months, closing at 1 on Saturdays and at 5 on other days.
Location of establishments	Center of the city; Roxbury, South Boston.
Opportunities for training	Classes held in stores; continuation classes of public schools, and of Women's Educational and Industrial Union.

CANDY MANUFACTURE

	EMPLOYMENT OF THE 14–16-YEAR-OLD GIRL
Approximate percentage of all employed	16%. Only the department stores employ more.
Kinds of work	Floor girls, carrying trays from one department to another; wrapping; packing.
Beginning wage	$3–$4.50.
First steps of advancement	Floor girl to wrapping pieces of candy in tin or gilt foil and packing candy in boxes; or to dipping, that is, immersing the cream candy molds (usually with the hand) in melted chocolate.
Qualifications	Cleanliness; manual dexterity.
Outlook for the girl in respect to: ·*A. Wage*	THE OCCUPATION Very poor. Average wage, $5–$6. Maximum for wrappers and packers, $7; for dippers, $8. Payment usually on the time basis.

B. Manual skill	Poor. Dipping requires skill of a low grade and all the other kinds of work are unskilled.
C. Mental development	None.
Disadvantages or dangers	Temperature of the dipping rooms above or below normal; tendency of new workers to overindulge in candy eating.
Seasons	Busiest, September to Christmas. Busy, before Easter and until early summer. Dull, January and July.
Hours (usual)	Fifty-four hours a week in a few establishments; in others, usually the largest factories, 48–50 hours a week, with a half holiday Saturday. 7.30 or 8 to 5.30 or 6, with a half hour to an hour for lunch.
Location of establishments	North End chiefly; South Boston.
Opportunities for training	None outside the factory.

BOOT AND SHOE MANUFACTURE

	EMPLOYMENT OF THE 14–16-YEAR-OLD GIRL
Approximate percentage of all employed	14%.
Kinds of work	Floor girls, doing miscellaneous work, especially running errands between different departments; tagging; blacking; lacing; sorting and assembling parts of shoe; trimming threads; cementing bows and ornaments on to shoes; applying cement to edges of leather; turning and pressing these edges by hand. The small young girl is most often placed as floor girl, and at sorting and assembling.
Beginning wage	$3–$5.
First steps of advancement	From the miscellaneous processes given above, to stitching, in which the first process is stitching linings.
Qualifications	Manual dexterity; speed; good eyesight.

Outlook for the girl in respect to: *A. Wage*	THE OCCUPATION
	
	Good because of the opportunities in the stitching room. The kinds of work here are:
	   1. Stitching on linings. Range of wage, $6–$15; usual wage, $7–$9.
	   2. Top stitching. Range of wage, $8–$18; usual wage, $10–$12.
	   3. Tip stitching and vamping. Range of wage, $8–$25; usual wage, $12–$15.
	Stitchers are paid by the piece. Seasonal fluctuation lowers the average wage for the year,

A. Wage (continued)	which remains, however, above that in clothing-machine operating. (See Clothing Industry.)
B. Manual skill	Fair. The work in the stitching room calls for skill of much the same order as that in clothing-machine operating.
C. Mental development	Poor.
Disadvantages or dangers	On the work in the stitching room, eyestrain; tense application and overspeeding on account of piecework; noise and jar of machines. In some processes, dirtiness of work.
Seasons	Busy, summer and winter months. Dull, late spring and late fall.
Hours (usual)	7.30–5.30, with an hour or a half hour for lunch, and a half day on Saturday in the summer.
Location of establishments	Jamaica Plain, South Boston, East Boston.
Opportunities for training	None outside the factory.

DRESSMAKING

	EMPLOYMENT OF THE 14–16-YEAR-OLD GIRL
Approximate percentage of all employed	1½%–2%. Almost none as apprentices; chiefly as errand girls.
Kinds of work	When doing apprentice work, sewing on hooks and eyes, overcasting, seam binding.
Beginning wage	$1.50–$3.
First steps of advancement	Assisting in waist and skirt finishing.
Qualifications	A real liking to sew; a desire to fashion things from materials; ability to use the hands readily; good eyesight; ability to apply oneself steadily; quickness of movement; good general education.
Outlook for the girl in respect to: A. *Wage*	THE OCCUPATION Poor for the untrained fourteen-to-sixteen-year-old girl, as she is nearly always used for errands rather than in apprenticeship. Good for the older girl with marked ability or with trade training. The average dressmaker's assistant gets $6–$9. Wages range from the apprentice's fee to the $30–$40 week wage of head waist drapers in dressmaking shops. A person who becomes head

A. Wage (continued)	of her own establishment may secure $1000–$5000 or more income. The dressmaker who goes out by the day receives $1.50–$3.50, according to her ability.
B. Manual skill	Good.
C. Mental development	Good. The work demands intelligence, it offers a stimulus to the imaginative and creative sense, and enables the girl to apply what she learns to the making of her own clothes.
Disadvantages or dangers	Eyestrain; constant sitting; overtime in rush seasons; hurried lunch hours; danger in the large dressmaking shops that a girl remain on a subdivision of the work and so fail to master the trade; in some establishments irregularity in receipt of wages, due to delay of customers in paying bills.
Hours (usual)	Work is steady for nine to ten months of the year, with two dull months in summer and sometimes one in winter.
Seasons	8.30–5.30 or 6, with a half hour to an hour for lunch, the entire six days in the week.
Location of establishments	Large shops, chiefly Boylston and Tremont streets; others scattered over the city.
Opportunities for training	Boston Trade School for Girls. High School of Practical Arts.

MILLINERY

	EMPLOYMENT OF THE 14–16-YEAR-OLD GIRL
Approximate percentage of all employed	1 %–1½%.
Kinds of work	In apprenticeship, doing simple work in the making of hats. This includes making bandeaux, making and sewing in linings, making frames, and putting on facings.
Beginning wage	Apprenticeship is usually without pay, both spring and fall seasons. Then, $3–$4.
First steps of advancement	From apprenticeship to assistant maker, receiving $3–$4 at first, and $5–$6 within a year or two.
Qualifications	Liking to sew; artistic sense; originality; resourcefulness, not only in the trade but in ability to tide over the dull season with other work; dry hands; ability to use one's fingers quickly; good eyesight; good general education.
Outlook for the girl in respect to:	
A. Wage	THE OCCUPATION

Same as dressmaking. Steps of advance from assistant maker are:

1. Maker at $8–$12, who covers as well as makes frames and is responsible for seeing that the hats are prepared for the trimmer.
2. Trimmer, $15–$25 or more, demanding originality and artistic ability.
3. Possibility of owning one's own establishment, with an income varying according to one's business ability.

B. Manual skill	Good. Same as dressmaking.
C. Mental development	Good. Same as dressmaking.
Disadvantages or dangers	Tensity and unsteadiness of work and overtime resulting from the short rush season; eyestrain; constant sitting; hurried lunch hours.
Seasons	Twelve to fourteen weeks in the spring and again in the fall. This short season, added to the low wage of the first two or three years, should be looked squarely in the face by a girl who must earn her own living.
Hours (usual)	Long. In the busy season as long as the law permits.
Location of establishments	Same as dressmaking.
Opportunities for training	Boston Trade School for Girls. High School of Practical Arts.

ERRAND GIRL

	EMPLOYMENT OF THE 14–16-YEAR-OLD GIRL
Approximate percentage of all employed	Percentages given for dressmaking, millinery, and the clothing industry include errand girls. From one to several employed in different dressmaking, millinery, and tailoring establishments.
Kinds of work	Delivering hats and gowns to customers; going to the stores for trimmings and materials to match samples.
Beginning wage	$3–$5 when errand girl only.
First steps of advancement	
Qualifications	Brightness and carefulness, and responsibility in receiving and executing directions.
Outlook for the girl in respect to: A. *Wage*	THE OCCUPATION None, unless a girl does errands incidentally to apprenticeship, which but very seldom happens. In such a case she may gradually be taught the trade, and her wage ranges from car fares to $2.50 the first year. It should be carefully noted that if an untrained girl receives the higher wage in a millinery or dressmaking establishment the first year, the chances are that she is *not* being taught the trade. This is particularly true of millinery.

B. Manual skill	None, unless accompanied by apprenticeship.
C. Mental development	None, except that in connection with apprenticeship the errand work is of value in familiarizing the girl with the various materials used in the trade and their relative prices.
Disadvantages or dangers	Lack of outlook. Weariness engendered by running hither and thither at beck and call, oftentimes carrying large parcels. Exposure to temptations which may present themselves to a young girl going about in a large city alone and unprotected.
Seasons	Demand for her employment comes chiefly in the spring and fall.
Hours (usual)	From eight to ten hours a day. Uncertain, and varying with the need for the girl's services.
Location of establishments	
Opportunities for training	The occupation requires none.

CLOTHING INDUSTRY

	EMPLOYMENT OF THE 14–16-YEAR-OLD GIRL
Approximate percentage of all employed	(Products, ready-made and cheaper tailored garments.) 4%–6%.
Kinds of work	For the untrained girl, unskilled handwork, or "hand finishing": sewing on hooks and eyes and buttons; cutting threads; pinning; folding; packing.
Beginning wage	$3–$5.
First steps of advancement	The untrained fourteen-to-sixteen-year-old girl is only in rare instances transferred to sewing on the power machines. Ordinarily she remains on hand finishing.
Qualifications	Good eyesight, carefulness, application, speed.
Outlook for the girl in respect to: *A. Wage*	THE OCCUPATION Poor in hand finishing. Maximum wage, $6–$7. (Paid by the week.) Fair in machine work. A girl advances to more difficult processes and higher wage as her skill and speed increase. Usual wage, $7–$9. Maximum, $10–$11. (Paid by the piece.) Figures given are the estimated averages for the year, allowing for unsteadiness of employment.

B. Manual skill	Fair. The machine work calls for intelligent control of hand and finger movements, fine, quick, and accurate.
C. Mental development	Doubtful. It is possible, when a girl has the opportunity to handle an entire garment, to gain suggestions for the making of her own clothes.
Disadvantages or dangers	Eyestrain; tense application and overspeeding on account of piecework; constant sitting; noise and jar of machinery.
Seasons	Seasons fluctuating, according to public demand for product. In general: Busy, September–December, March–June. Slack, January–February, July–August.
Hours (usual)	8–6, with a half hour to an hour for lunch. In some cases, shortened day Saturday.
Location of establishments	Factories producing machine-made clothing, chiefly Bedford Street district. Tailoring shops, chiefly North and West Ends.
Opportunities for training	Boston Trade School for Girls. Hebrew Industrial School. These schools train girls in clothing-machine operating.

KNIT-GOODS MAKING

	EMPLOYMENT OF THE 14–16-YEAR-OLD GIRL
Approximate percentage of all employed	3%–4%.
Kinds of work	Tagging, packing, putting on buttons and fasteners, and, in the hosiery mill, looping (operating a machine which knits the stocking toe) and topping (with fingers placing the stitches which "top" the foot of the stocking carefully on metallic points arranged on a ring, preparatory to the knitting of the foot).
Beginning wage	$3–$5.
First steps of advancement	From the small jobs, such as tagging, to hand finishing (where sweaters are made) or to the knitting machines, and from time-work to piece-work.
Qualifications	Good health, especially strong lungs and good eyesight; keen observation; quick motions; carefulness.
Outlook for the girl in respect to: *A. Wage*	THE OCCUPATION Fair. The wage for the work on the knitting machines ranges from $6–$14. Usual wage, $7–$9.

B. *Manual skill*	Doubtful.
C. *Mental development*	None.
Disadvantages or dangers	Constant sitting or constant standing during long hours; eyestrain · lint in the atmosphere; noise of machinery.
Seasons	Comparatively steady, what fluctuations there are varying in different years.
Hours (usual)	7.30–12, and from 1–6. Establishments giving Saturday afternoons usually have a shorter lunch hour.
Location of establishments	South Boston, Bedford and Albany streets districts, and West Roxbury.
Opportunities for training	None outside the factory.

LAUNDRY WORK

	EMPLOYMENT OF THE 14–16-YEAR-OLD GIRL
Approximate percentage of all employed	2%–2½%.
Kinds of work	" Shaking," which consists of vigorously shaking the damp and crumpled pieces into a smoother state and piling them one on top of another ready for the mangles; wrapping laundry for delivery.
Beginning wage	$3.50–$4.
First steps of advancement	From shaking to receiving from or feeding the mangle. Feeding the mangle means placing the pieces smoothly and accurately on moving metal "aprons " which carry them under heated rollers, by which they are dried and pressed. Receiving means folding the clothes rapidly and neatly as they come out smooth and dry. Wage, $4.50–$5.
Qualifications	Physical strength; endurance; quickness of movement.
Outlook for the girl in respect to : _A. Wage_	THE OCCUPATION Poor for the fourteen-to-sixteen-year-old girl. It is only in a very exceptional case that she is possessed of the necessary strength and the perseverance to remain in the work long enough to reach the starching and ironing room. The processes of starching and ironing are paid by the piece, with a wage in the one case of $6–$12 ; in the other, $8–$12. But these processes are performed only by the older girls and by women.

B. Manual skill	Poor in most of the processes. Fair in fancy ironing.
C. Mental development	None.
Disadvantages or dangers	Constant standing; in the shaking, strain on the shoulders and back. Oftentimes dampness and poor ventilation; danger, in spite of the guard required by law, of an injured hand on the mangling machine if a worker is careless.
Seasons	Busiest, summer. Slack, winter.
Hours (usual)	52–54 hours per week. Daily hours vary with the different days of the week.
Location of establishments	Chiefly in South End. Some in Dorchester and North End.
Opportunities for training	None outside the laundries.

PAPER-BOX MAKING

	EMPLOYMENT OF THE 14–16-YEAR-OLD GIRL
Approximate percentage of all employed	2%–2½%.
Kinds of work	As helpers or " strikers " moistening paper with glue; turning up the sides and ends of boxes ready to be " stayed " or fastened at the corners; slipping the covers on to completed boxes; piling; carrying; packing.
Beginning wage	$3.50–$4.
First steps of advancement	From " striking " to machine work, which includes the operating of covering, banding, staying, and lacing machines.
Qualifications	Accuracy of hand and eye; deftness; neatness; speed.
Outlook for the girl in respect to : *A. Wage*	THE OCCUPATION Doubtful in the factories making plain boxes. Wages range from $7–$12. Usual wage, $7–$8. Paid by the piece. Fair in factories making fancy candy boxes, where in bench work the box is made by hand. Wages in this work range from $8–$14. Usual wage, $10–$12. Paid by the piece.

B. Manual skill	None in "striking" and little on the machine work; fair on the bench work, which requires the exercise of a skillful hand, and while it does not demand originality, does give the opportunity for fashioning a thing in its wholeness.
C. Mental development	None.
Disadvantages or dangers	Odor and handling of glue, disagreeable to some girls, especially at first; danger of serious injury to the hands in operating the staying machine if a girl fails to make use of the guards which are provided by law.
Seasons	Vary according to the product. In nearly every factory, however, dull through January, after Easter, and in midsummer.
Hours (usual)	Somewhat less than 54 a week in most of the factories. 8–5.30, with a half hour for lunch; or 7.30–5.30, with an hour for lunch.
Location of establishments	North Station district.
Opportunities for training	None outside the factory.

BOOKBINDING

	EMPLOYMENT OF THE 14–16-YEAR-OLD GIRL
Approximate percentage of all employed	1%–2%.
Kinds of work	The less difficult folding by hand of printed sheets for book forms; feeding folding machines; inserting pamphlets in envelopes for mailing.
Beginning wage	$3–$4.
First steps of advancement	Transfer from the simpler to the more difficult processes, such as more difficult hand folding; pasting; laying of gold leaf on book covers; machine sewing.
Qualifications	Neatness; accuracy; speed.
Outlook for the girl in respect to: *A. Wage*	THE OCCUPATION Poor for the fourteen-to-sixteen-year-old girl because of the temporary and unskilled work which is so often given her when she is employed. Doubtful for others because of the increasing number of machines which are gradually displacing handwork in almost every process. Usual wage of experienced workers, $7–$8. Most of the work is paid by the piece. (Figures given are the estimated average wages for the year, allowing for unsteadiness of employment.) Maximum, $10–$12.

B. Manual skill	Doubtful. The handwork which is done by girls and women to-day is for the most part mechanical.
C. Mental development	Doubtful. In some of the binderies a variety of interesting printed and illustrative matter passes through the worker's hands, which, in spite of the required speed, may give to an intelligent person some play of imagination.
Disadvantages or dangers	In gold laying there is a very serious lack of ventilation, due to the fact that the slightest stir of air interferes with the proper laying of the thin gold leaf.
Seasons	Vary greatly with the different binderies; for example, those which handle school books are busiest during the weeks of summer vacation; those putting out fiction are the busiest in the months preceding Christmas.
Hours (usual)	8.30–12; 1–5.30. Saturday afternoons free throughout the year.
Location of establishments	Chiefly Summer, Federal, and Purchase streets.
Opportunities for training	None outside the bindery except the U. S. Grant School in East Boston, a public prevocational center.

PACKING AND LABELING

	EMPLOYMENT OF THE 14–16-YEAR-OLD GIRL
Approximate percentage of all employed	Impossible to determine. A great many engaged in this occupation in connection with various industries.
Kinds of work	Packing in boxes all sorts of goods, according to the industry, from nails to bonbons; pasting labels on boxes.
Beginning wage	$4–$5.
First steps of advancement	
Qualifications	Speed, and in the labeling a certain degree of neatness and accuracy.
Outlook for the girl in respect to: *A. Wage*	THE OCCUPATION Very poor. Maximum, $5–$6.

B. Manual skill	Poor.
C. Mental development	None.
Disadvantages or dangers	Lack of outlook.
Seasons	Vary according to the industry.
Hours (usual)	Vary according to the industry.
Location of establishments	All over the city.
Opportunities for training	The occupation requires none.

JUVENILE EMPLOYMENT IN THE BUILDING TRADES

By Ernest Aves

(From a Report of an Inquiry into the Conditions of Juvenile Employment in London)

THE POSITION IN THE BUILDING TRADES

The area of the inquiry into the conditions affecting juvenile employment in the London building trades was limited almost entirely to the county. The names of the employers seen were derived mainly from various available registers, but, in a few districts, through local inquiry at the labor exchanges and elsewhere, as to whom it would be most useful to see. In addition, a few trade unionists, foremen and others, have been interviewed.

In the building and allied trades something over 400 employers of all grades were seen in the few weeks in February and March, 1911, during which this inquiry, as well as that into the leather-working industries, was in most active progress. During the whole or part of this period four investigators were engaged in the work.

Although the inquiry has been made primarily with reference to juvenile labor in connection with the building trades, the subject matter may be conveniently split up into three main divisions:

1. The economic characteristics of the group of trades investigated.
2. The prevailing conditions as regards wages, etc.
3. The more personal elements involved, especially the outlook and degree of responsibility accepted or felt by the main classes concerned, including parents, juveniles, employers, and journeymen.

A. *The Group as a Whole*

The occupations grouped under the building and allied trades are highly complex, and modern tendencies are making them increasingly so, with the.result that generalizations, never very easy to make with regard to this group, are becoming still more insecure. Before proceeding to any analysis of the building trades according to occupation, certain broad features may, however, be indicated :

1. The building trades are free, on the whole, from the competition of products introduced from external sources of supply, and thus to a great extent from external competition in any form.

2. They form the largest group of industries in London, and are connected with the supply, whether in the form of dwelling or business accommodation, of that which ranks among the primary requirements of life, in connection with which, moreover, partly through legislation and municipal administration and partly through more general causes, the demand is tending constantly to change and to rise.

3. Most of the separate occupations demand a considerable amount of skill, while those that rank as skilled at all require, at least in their highest branches, much skill, and thus for their mastery thorough training.

4. As a group the occupations rank among those which are the more highly organized, and in which, speaking generally, recognized and relatively favorable conditions as regards wages and hours of labor prevail.

5. The trades provide almost exclusively occupations for males and for the most part require not less than an average standard of strength and soundness of constitution.

In addition it may be mentioned :

6. That experience gained in some of the most important branches of the building trades, including carpentry, joinery, bricklaying, and plumbing, is, next to that of agriculture, most likely to be of use to those who may emigrate.

The above are considerations that make roughly for the economic strength and thus for the advantageousness of this group of occupations. There are, however, other considerations which tell in the opposite direction, and among these the following may be mentioned:

1. Employment in some branches of the trade is apt to be unusually precarious owing largely to a normal seasonal irregularity in the aggregate demand and also to the rapidity with which the amount of work in hand by the individual employer, be he master builder or specialist, tends to change in volume. It is thus an occupation in which special vigilance is apt to be required to secure continuous employment.

2. Although rarely in any sudden and unusual degree, building occupations are, nevertheless, in some cases, liable to displacement by the use of new material in construction; by the fresh uses to which old materials are put, or by fresh combinations adopted; by machinery; and by changes in fashion.

3. Over wide areas in the county of London building extension has finished and with it much of that particular kind of demand which is peculiar to a young and expanding center of population.

4. The great activity and prosperity of the building trades during the closing years of the last century, culminating in 1900, when the number of operatives in the building trades rapidly increased, has been followed by a period of comparative slackness, if not of positive depression, during which it has been difficult for the new members of the trade to be satisfactorily absorbed, and during which, therefore, there has been an unusually small number of openings for fresh learners.

5. A large supply of provincially trained labor is apt to be available at any time when London conditions create fresh openings.

6. The kind of labor that the London building trades require, largely because of the quick work and the specialized skill that are demanded in the metropolis, tends to make it difficult for the London boy to start in most of them.

Such considerations as those just enumerated may be said to weaken the economic position of these trades either as affecting all grades or, as in the case of numbers 5 and 6, especially from the point of view of the juvenile.

It is impossible to strike a balance between these advantages and disadvantages, but it is convenient to place on record in summarized form some of the general considerations that have to be borne in mind in any endeavor to appreciate the claims of the building trades in London as a field of employment for the young.

For the most part the features mentioned above refer to skilled branches of the trade, although some of them, both on the side of advantage and of disadvantage, refer to the trade as a whole and are thus relevant to certain occupations, such as laborers, excavators, scaffolders, roof tilers, and others with whom this inquiry has no direct concern, either because no industrial training is required for the occupations in question or because there is no scope or suitability in them for boy labor.

B. *The Principal Branches*

The following notes refer to some of the more important occupations in the building trades, and are inserted to indicate in a general way the position which they appear to occupy within the group:

Bricklaying. The bricklayer is still one of the most widely and variously requisitioned classes of worker in the building trades, and in some branches of his craft London still requires the highest examples of his skill. Relatively to the total volume of building enterprise it is, however, not improbable that the demand for the services of the bricklayer is destined to diminish owing to the use of iron and steel in building construction, of machine-dressed stone, and of reënforced concrete.

Reënforced brickwork has also been experimented with successfully, and inasmuch as, if adopted, it would diminish the need for some of the more skilled portions of the bricklayer's art, as in the gauged brickwork of arches, its introduction, although using the bricklayer's own particular medium, would not be calculated to improve his position.

At the moment, however, the most important substitutes for solid brickwork are iron and steel in construction; stone for facing the metal framework; and occasionally reënforced concrete.

On the other hand, the extent to which such frameworks are faced with brick has to be borne in mind, while the extended use of inside tiling also somewhat increases the demand for the bricklayer. This work is, however, shared with the plasterers, by whom it is also claimed, and with specialists, who may have been either bricklayers or plasterers, but who are now often engaged solely on this kind of work. With regard to dwelling houses in which fireproof construction is not regarded as necessary and in which exceptional strength and simplicity of form are not essentials, fashion rather than new methods of construction are probably the most important influences likely to affect at all speedily the demand for any particular class of worker. At the present moment, for instance, the fashion of having stone frontages when they can be afforded is in vogue, but there is no certainty that this will continue, and a revival of the fashion for brick frontages might be followed by an actual shortage of bricklayers able to execute the more highly skilled branches of their calling.

In spite, therefore, of certain changes which (especially on large buildings involving straightforward work) threaten the bricklayer's trade, and although, as stated, his share in the aggregate of building operations is likely slightly to diminish, there is no reason to anticipate any speedy radical change in the extent to which he will be required in the building trade.

Masonry. The demand for masons is, like that for bricklayers, somewhat affected by the increasing extent to which, in certain classes of buildings, iron and steel are used in construction; but, as in the case of the other trade, the effect on demand is diminished by the common practice of facing with stone, although in the form of veneering frontages rather than of solid constructive work. The use of machinery for dressing the stone and the use in London of stone prepared and dressed at the quarries are two other important facts to be noted in connection with this trade.

The extent to which stone that is used on buildings in London has been prepared in the quarries has reached very large dimensions, but is stated not to have increased appreciably during the last nine or ten years, the real introduction of stone thus prepared having taken place during the previous ten years. Twenty years ago the use of such stone in London was the exception; but at that period, although the innovation was resisted, the rates of wages paid to masons at the quarries were much lower than those paid in London, and the advantage to the contractor of having his stone dressed at the quarries was then so appreciable that the amount thus prepared steadily increased in volume for several years. At the present time, however, London and provincial wages are more nearly alike, and the tendency for more of the stone used in London to be cut and dressed at the quarry thus operates with less force. The advantage of avoiding the transport of waste material by working the stones at the quarry remains, but it is not so great as is sometimes assumed, because the railway rates for worked stone are higher than those for the undressed material.

Perhaps more important as an active influence in the trade than the use on London buildings of stone worked in the provinces is the increasing use of machinery in the preparation of stone. Although this tends to diminish the demand for hand labor, two compensating effects may be noted, one affecting primarily the quarryman and the other the mason himself. Both are traceable to the fact that the use of stone in building construction is greatly stimulated by the use of machinery itself. Not only is the quantity of stone thus increased, but more hard stone is also said to be used and more labor is thus apt to be required in getting it. As regards the London mason, the more frequent use of stone on buildings stimulates demand for his labor both through the supplementary work that has necessarily to be done by hand even when machinery is used, and also through the additional work involved in the actual fixing of the stone on the building. In at least two ways, therefore, the use of machinery in the preparation of stone sets at work certain compensating influences. On the whole it is probable that the character of the work of the mason has changed and is likely to change more than the aggregate demand for his services. In stone carving the demand remains to a great extent unaffected by mechanical inventions, and is subject mainly to the dictates of fashion.

Marble masonry. As regards the increasing use of machinery the position of the marble mason is very similar to that of other stonemasons, but the extent to which the raw material is in this case imported renders him liable to a certain amount of foreign, as distinct from provincial, competition and a considerable quantity of finished work, especially in stock sizes, is imported, mainly from Belgium and Italy.

Some protection from this form of competition is afforded by the conditions of London work to which reference has been already made, namely, to the speed with which contracts have frequently to be executed; but when there is time there is an increasing tendency to send architects' drawings with the specifications abroad. Although this competiton has been felt more seriously in recent years, it is said not to have reached an acute stage. The character of the work imported is of a good as well as a cheap class, and it is stated that in England men able to undertake the higher class of work, and especially carving work, are more rarely found than in Italy.

Plastering. Plasterers are divided roughly into the solid or "outside" workers (that is, those whose work is done on the building) and the comparatively new class of fibrous or "inside" workers (that is, those whose work, apart from fixing, is done in the shops); and the latter is the more expanding branch of the trade. It is expanding not only as representing a process that is being more widely adopted, but also because of the increasing richness of the plasterer's work that is more frequently attempted, because more easily executed and repeated. The work, apart from the designing, involves modeling (largely done by foreigners), making the molds, casting, and fixing; and while in some of the simpler processes a lower grade of labor approximating to that of the unskilled laborer himself suffices, competent plasterers, especially if they know the solid as well as the fibrous work, have probably a more certain prospect of employment in the future than any other important class of the building trades.[1]

[1] It should be observed that the demand for plasterers has been somewhat exaggerated during the present year owing to the numbers required for temporary work at the Crystal Palace in connection with the Festival of Empire, at the White City, and in decorative work for the Coronation.

Such loss of solid work on the buildings as has been incurred through the extended use of fibrous plastering, of concrete floors, and of partitions of various kinds that dispense with either the whole or a great part of the plasterer's labor, is to some extent compensated by the greater scope for his work on exteriors in the shape of stucco or rough cast.

The change in the character of much of the plasterer's work renders less important than formerly the stoppage of the supply of learners that used to be derived from the " hawk " boys who served the plasterer with his material and from whom the ranks of the trade were mainly recruited up to about twenty-five or more years ago.

The place of the hawk boys was taken by that of laborers owing to the preference on the part of builders for having men on the job who could be turned more rapidly to other kinds of work than simply serving the plasterer. In its ordinary forms plastering is not a very highly skilled trade, but the shortage of plasterers in the past appears to afford an illustration in the recent experience of the building trades in which the neglect of the responsibility of training learners on the part of employers led to conditions that for a few years greatly handicapped the trade.

Painters. The ease with which the cruder forms of the painter's craft can be acquired probably explains in part the frequent complaint of the scarcity of men who are fully trained, while the exceptionally seasonal character of the demand also diminishes the attractions of this trade. Moreover certain styles of painting, graining, marbling, stenciling, and gilding, that used to demand skill in decorative work have largely gone out of fashion, and the simpler style now in vogue — especially the plain white groundwork, often with an enamel finish — requires comparatively little training.

For such higher branches of decorative work as are in demand, although opinion is somewhat conflicting on this matter, there appears to be a fairly sufficient supply of the necessary labor. It is said, however, that there is shortage of good brush hands, that is, of those who (although without special knowledge of their craft, including the mixing of paints) are able to put a good finish on painting work, and of men who are in all ways dependable — but it is said, also, that the learner, so far as the actual technique of the trade is concerned, could master all that is necessary for most work at the present time in vogue in a year.

It is probable that character is relatively an especially valuable asset in this trade.

For the boy, however, the trade is not very healthy, and this fact, combined with its precariousness and the numerous channels of entry from the ranks of laborers or even from outside the building trades altogether, makes it an occupation of doubtful attractiveness. The demand, altered somewhat in character, is likely to be maintained and even to increase in volume, but the other considerations mentioned still leave the general economic position of the trade somewhat insecure.

Sign writing is a subsidiary branch of the trade of minor importance, but is comparatively stable in character.

Carpentry and joinery. Few branches of the building trades are being more affected by changes that are in progress, to some of which reference has been already made, than are those of the carpenter and joiner. As workers in wood the position of these is apt to be assailed by every increase in the demand for or obligation to provide fireproof constructions, and the use of iron and steel, concrete, and terra cotta has been certainly hastened by this consideration. On the buildings the chief ways in which the demand for the carpenter has been weakened has been through the use of metal girders and concrete, either for floors or roofs, and of artificial stone and of ironwork for staircases, while iron doors and other metal fitments, formerly of wood, are threatened. In connection with the use of reënforced concrete, on which a few smiths and more "concreters" (the latter a special class of laborer that is being created) are mainly employed, a compensating demand of some importance for the carpenter makes itself felt in the construction of the wooden molds, or "shuttering," which are required for the concrete. But when all is said, the modern substitutes for timber are weakening the demand for the carpenter, especially in much of the heavier woodwork formerly used on certain classes of large buildings.

In joinery by far the most important influence is the extending use of machine-made joinery and the increasing precision of the machines themselves; but in this case, although the character of much of the work in the shops is being altered very fundamentally and the demand for the fully qualified joiner being seriously weakened, there is, again, a twofold compensating influence:

1. More joinery, including for instance more paneling, is apt to be included in the specifications, while much of the joinery also tends to be more elaborate in character; and
2. Hardwood, which can be worked by the machines almost as easily as the softer varieties, is apt to be more widely used. From both these causes some compensation is found, more work, both in hand finishing and especially in fixing, being made for the joiner. These twofold influences — on the one hand an extended use of machinery and on the other an increasing demand — apply also to wooden shop-fittings and cases, for which London firms have a high reputation.

Wood carving, only in the cruder surface-cutting forms of which can machinery be used, is not unlikely to be stimulated by the increasing extent to which other forms of woodwork can be done by machinery. The demand for wood carving is mainly determined by taste and by prosperity; but, given prosperity, the demand for the wood carver is likely to increase and one leading London builder has singled this out as the branch of the trade in which there was not only a real shortage but also at the moment most scope.

Plumbing. Two main considerations demand notice in connection with this trade, one pointing to a weakening and the other to a strengthening of its position.

The former effect is being brought about by the extending use of iron, instead of lead, piping, bringing the fitter into direct competition, and of ready-made plumbers' fittings, while a somewhat similar tendency accompanies the substitution of concrete or asphalt for the older type of flat roofing with its covering of lead.

On the other hand, the greater volume of sanitary work required and the higher standard of plumbing that, partly in the interests of public convenience but mainly in that of the public health, is demanded point to a more active demand for the services of the plumber.[1]

Thus, while the aggregate demand for his work is probably tending to diminish in quantity, the demand for proficiency is increasing and, in consequence, the openings for fully trained and competent men. It may be noted that the plumber, as such, claims work on iron piping in connection with sanitary work and with the distribution of cold water. To hot-water fitting the plumber makes no claim as of right, but, receiving his somewhat higher rate of pay, competes with the hot-water fitter on the ordinary industrial basis of comparative efficiency, and on this basis a certain amount of this work is being won back.

Electrical working. The electrical industry is concerned with all work on current-carrying apparatus and is thus differentiated from mechanical engineering, which in some of its branches is concerned with the making of such apparatus. The principal services which the electrical workers attached to the building trades render are those of installation and repair, chiefly in connection with electrical lighting. Some of the tasks thus involved are simple in character, and a considerable number of men and young men are engaged on them with no knowledge of the science of their calling. The minimum of manual skill required is, it is true, not difficult to acquire, but competent men in this trade must master at least its rudimentary principles. Thus, although a somewhat undiscriminating movement into the trade has reached large proportions, its importance and the scope which it offers for the utilization of special knowledge still leave it as one of the expanding and promising subsidiary branches of the building trades.

Structural ironworking. Structural ironworkers are really smiths or fitters engaged upon a particular branch of constructional work that is unsuited for the employment of boys and upon which they are in practice not engaged.

---

[1] In this connection a new process may be noted that dispenses with the usual wiped joint and for which other advantages are claimed in addition to those of economy in time and material. If widely adopted, the process will effect a very considerable alteration in plumbing practice.

Other branches. Various other branches of the building trades are not so well defined as most of those to which reference has been already made, and among these may be mentioned hot-water fitting, gas fitting, paper hanging, and glazing, the two last being often executed by painters.

On the other hand, some minor and inferior crafts are apt to be specialized, such as parquet flooring and stone and marble mosaic work. In neither of these, except in the more artistic forms of mosaic work, is there much scope for training. Certain occupations, again, overlap with the metal trades and have no exclusive connection with building, such as zinc workers, coppersmiths, smiths and fitters other than those mentioned above, and art-metal workers. Much smiths' work is a provincial rather than a London industry, including practically the whole of the metal work used in the reënforcement of concrete.

C. *A Period of Transition*

In connection with various branches of the building trade, notably bricklayers, carpenters, and plasterers on solid work, the importance of the use of new materials and of new combinations of materials in building construction has been mentioned, but attention has been drawn to some of the ways in which the displacement of labor in one direction has been accompanied by an increased demand elsewhere, and by the ways in which labor actually displaced is itself sometimes compensated or partly compensated by a demand for new services. It may be noted, however, that the changes in building methods to which reference has been made are in few cases entirely modern, and the long period during which both metal and concrete have to some extent been used in constructive work is a reminder of the general truth that changes in building methods nearly always come about very gradually. Partial explanations of this are found in the fact that architects do not readily specify for new materials unless they are assured not only that they are of proved advantage over the old but also that contractors (who, like the architects, are chary of adopting new materials and new methods) will tender at a sufficiently low figure; and this, the more novel the material and processes are to them, the less likely they are to do. A main explanation of the conservative attitude tending to prevail in the building trades is, moreover, to be found in the fact that, apart from the flimsiest of speculative cottage building, they generally operate for the fairly distant, as well as for the more immediate, future. This consideration is of special moment in connection with the large type of construction that so far has been found most suitable for the use of concrete, since, in order to insure its durability when dependent upon the metal reënforcements, exceptional care has to be exercised alike in the selection of materials and in all subsequent processes. This is especially the case when surfaces are exposed to the action of water or damp air, in order that all possible safeguards may be taken against the risks of a gradual rusting of the metal inside its concrete covering and of a perhaps remote, but eventual, collapse.

Thus, for various reasons, no changes of fundamental importance leading to an extensive displacement of labor are likely to occur rapidly. The present is, however, a time of transitional development in the building trades, and although there may be no great likelihood of a sudden and extensive loss of their employment by any class of journeyman, even a slow weakening of their positions would greatly affect and greatly complicate the problem from the point of view of the juvenile. To the latter it will make all the difference in ten or twenty years' time whether demand has been tending to diminish in the trade of his choice even at the rate of only 1 or 2 per cent per annum, or has been tending to increase at a similar rate, or even to remain stationary ; and even if, after a few years, the juvenile should be able to insure his footing in a declining trade, it is apt to be at the cost of the journeyman of to-day, who may find himself prematurely displaced. It is in connection with this question as to whether they do or do not offer reasonable chances of an assured industrial future that several branches of the building trades create a problem of such great perplexity.

It may be noted, however, that when any new process or material is used great advantages are looked for, either in a direct or indirect saving in the cost of construction or in increased safety from fire, in a greater durability, in economy of space, or it may be in greater beauty. Should, therefore, one or more of these advantages be secured at any time in any markedly increased way, it is a fair presumption that the demand for new building construction would respond, and the building and rebuilding (for which there is great scope in London) be stimulated. It is, as has been indicated, improbable that any such considerable changes in process, and thus in demand, will occur at all speedily; and it is also true that, should this happen, the position of some grades, perhaps bricklayers or carpenters, would not improbably be still further relatively weakened. But, as has been seen, other branches might gain, and it is desirable to emphasize this general fact that, although any given change of process may tend to weaken the economic position of some particular class of operative, it generally tends not only to represent, at any rate as indicated by the demand of a period, a gain to the community, but not infrequently to benefit directly some other section or sections of wage earners. The other point to which reference has been also made is of perhaps even greater significance, namely, the latent but potential demand for new buildings that exists in a great and wealthy community such as London, which, although to a great extent built over, contains such large numbers of ill-constructed dwellings, offices, and shops. There is special need to give due weight to such a consideration as the foregoing in estimating the prospects that seem to be afforded by the building trades because of the normal tendency of the mind to exaggerate the permanency of existing buildings and thus not to give their proper importance to the forces that are making and may make for reconstruction.

Particulars respecting Different Occupations

On the following pages various salient particulars have been summarized with regard to the principal branches of the building trades, and a rough and tentative attempt has been also made to classify the different occupations from the point of view of their advantageousness, mainly with reference to the prospects which they seem to offer as callings for London boys.

The paragraphs that follow immediately refer to matters concerning which the same particulars apply to several or all branches.

Term of engagement. Except for boys on a weekly wage, one hour's notice on either side is the general rule.

The working week. A working week of fifty hours for summer (thirty-nine weeks) and forty-four hours for winter (thirteen weeks from the second Monday in November) is usual.

Hours: summer. From Monday to Friday, 6.30 to 8 ; 8.30 to 12 noon ; 1 to 5. Saturdays, 6.30 to 8 A.M.; 8.30 to 12 noon. *Winter.* Monday to Friday, 8 to 12 noon ; 12.30 P.M. to 4.30 P.M. Saturdays, 8 to 12 noon.

In the shops the hours are as above, with one hour for dinner in winter, the leaving-off time being 5 P.M. instead of 4.30.

The above conditions apply to bricklayers, carpenters, and joiners, stonemasons and plasterers, and, with slight variations, to plumbers, general smiths and fitters, and wood-cutting machinists. The most important standing difference is that plumbers have one hour for dinner throughout the winter.

Provision for meals. It is agreed that employers shall provide, where practicable and reasonable, a suitable place for the workmen to have their meals on the works, with a laborer to assist in preparing them, and shall open the same one hour before starting time in winter, with similar attendance.

Provision in accordance with this general understanding appears to be usually made.

Holidays. The most usual holidays are Bank holidays with, as a rule, the following day — a relic, as one employer described it, "of days when drinking was more rife." When occasionally apprentices are taken, an additional holiday of one or two weeks is sometimes given, generally with pay.

Periods of probation. When boys are occasionally taken on from the outside with a view to apprenticeship, or even definitely as learners from the outset, there is generally a period of trial, ranging from a fortnight to three months, the most usual being one month. An informal period of probation is under existing conditions much more frequent, boys being often employed on indefinite nontechnical work for a year or so to begin with ; those who by their behavior have then proved themselves "likely boys" being sometimes selected for actual craft training at the bench or in the yard. Throughout every branch of the trade formal apprenticeship is the exception.

Premium. Premiums average from nothing to £50. The larger amounts may be accompanied by special training and the assumption of a special responsibility for the boy, but, without any guarantee that this will follow, are mainly paid to the occasional firms of good standing that are willing to take one or more apprentices and by custom have put their premium at a high figure. In such cases an asset of value in after life is, however, generally obtained, a genuine apprenticeship passed under certain firms being an initial guarantee of competency.

The higher premiums are rarely paid by parents themselves, and, whatever the scale of payments adopted, it is generally lower in the case of the boys who are sons of employees of the apprenticing firm.

It is probable that the scale of premiums, when these are paid at all, is somewhat inflated owing to the funds and endowments available in London for apprenticeship purposes, and it appears to be not infrequently the case that boys who are inmates of charitable institutions of one kind or another obtain an advantage as regards the chance of being apprenticed that is sometimes disheartening to parents who have brought their own children up. Boys who have undergone some special handicap in life demand, it is true, some special backing; but a system that makes it possible for a parent to feel, as one man who had tried unsuccessfully to place his son expressed it, that "the best way to get a boy apprenticed is to neglect him" is clearly not entirely satisfactory. On the other hand, it must be remembered that the extent to which boys are obtained "through charities" is partly explained by the ease with which the formal bond can be arranged with these agencies and by their command of or access to the necessary funds, as contrasted with the frequent tendency of parents themselves, as also of their children, to shrink from the more formal tie of apprenticeship even when this is occasionally opened to them.

Attendance at classes. In several branches of the trade, but especially as regards joiners, plumbers, electrical workers, some branches of plastering and decorative design, attendance at trade classes is approved by many employers ; but the practice of giving time off during the day for attendance thereat is very rarely either granted or, under existing conditions, required.

District notes. Other things being equal, the entry of the boy into any branch of the building trades is likely to be most difficult in those parts of London where working room is most valuable, as in the City of London ; or in firms whose work is most uniformly of the highest grade, as in the case of decorators with an exclusively West End connection.

Accidents. The deaths attributed to building operations in London during 1908 numbered fifty-one, or somewhat fewer than those caused by railways, and sevenfold less than those caused by horses and vehicles. It is only in comparison with occupations that are practically free from danger to life that the building trades, although including within their scope many operations involving considerable risk, can as a group be classed as dangerous.

The eye is liable to injury in those occupations involving the cutting of stone ; that is, in bricklaying and masonry.

A few particulars are added with reference to individual occupations.

Bricklayers

Wages. A starting wage for a boy from fifteen to sixteen years of age ranges from 5 s. to 8 s. per week, but the more usual appears to be 6 s. Customary finishing wages for apprentices, reached in from four to five years, may be put at 18 s. per week. The rate for journeymen is $10\frac{1}{2}$ d. per hour, unless they are engaged on work demanding special skill or responsibility, when it may be from $\frac{1}{2}$ d. to $1\frac{1}{2}$ d. per hour higher.

Age of entry. The usual age of entry for boys is from fifteen to sixteen.

Special qualifications. Great muscular strength is not required, but a good constitution is necessary, much of the work being exposed. The higher branches of the trade require good natural abilities.

Disadvantages. The trade is seasonal and more than usually affected by the weather. Places of work shift, and time is thus apt to be lost and expense incurred. The number entering the trade during the decade 1891–1901 was very large, and the potential provincial supply of labor is also large, many entering the trade in London as improvers. London training can be excellent, but it is difficult to get all-round experience in the metropolis, which in this, as in some other branches of the building trades, is better as a finishing school than as a training ground.

Advantages. The trade is fairly well organized, and a large aggregate demand is still maintained.

General Classification

1. *As regards health.* (See under *Masonry*.)

2. *Economic.* The present demand for the ordinary bricklayer, able only to execute the more straightforward work, is inactive, and the expansion of the demand for this class of man in the future is uncertain.

General prospects are moderate[1] save for the first-class mechanic, for whom, especially if qualified to take the position of leading hand or foreman, they are good.

Stonemasons

Wages. The starting wage ranges from 4 s. to 8 s., and the finishing wage for apprentices, reached in from four to five years, is from 15 s. to 21 s. The trade-union rate of wages is 10½ d. per hour, and for fixing, 11¼ d. per hour.

Age of entry. The usual age of entry is from fifteen to sixteen, and, considerable strength being required, sixteen appears to be the better age.

Special qualifications. Muscular strength and, even under modern conditions, the moral qualities of patience and persistence. (See also under *Bricklaying*.)

Disadvantages. As in the case of bricklaying, the fixing work is more than usually affected by the weather; the places of work shift; and the provincial supply of labor is large. Stonecutting is being especially affected by the use of machinery, and great

---

[1] In this section the classification "good," "fair," "moderate," and "bad" is used.

quantities of the stone fixed in London have been prepared at the quarries.

General Classification

1. *As regards health.* Masons' phthisis is a recognized complaint, and both masons and bricklayers are specially liable, as following dusty occupations, to phthisis and to diseases of the respiratory system. Masons, classed with bricklayers and "builders" in the returns (England and Wales) of the Registrar-General of occupational mortality of males aged twenty-five to sixty-five, form, however, a group with a death rate about 10 per cent lower than the average for all occupations, and the special risk of phthisis does not leave this group, therefore, as a whole, an unhealthy occupation. But it should not be entered by boys with weak chests. The chances of life of those engaged in it are sharing in the widespread improvement in this respect.

2. *Economic.* Prospects moderate.

Marble Masons

Wages. The starting wage is from 4 s. to 8 s., and the ultimate wage for apprentices at the end of five years should be not less than 20 s. Adult wages are often somewhat lower than those of stonemasons, ranging from $8\frac{1}{2}$ d. per hour upwards.

Usual age of entry. From fifteen to sixteen.

Special qualifications. In every branch of the building trades obedience and diligence, coupled with the ability and willingness to do what one is told, rank at the outset as the elementary industrial virtues. But for a young marble mason who is going to succeed at his calling, and qualify at least as a leading hand, a sense of color is a special qualification of value.

Disadvantages. In addition to the extending use of machinery the distinctive disadvantage, which is said, however, not as yet to have reached an acute stage, is the extent to which marble used in London has been prepared abroad.

General Classification

1. *As regards health.* (Cf. *Masonry.*)
2. *Economic.* Prospects fair.

Plasterers

Wages. Starting wages for boys range from 5 s. to 7 s., and the ultimate wage for apprentices, generally reached in five years, may be put at from 15 s. to 20 s. per week, but the more common class of improvers is paid 6 d. and 7 d. per hour. The trade-union rate for adult labor is 11 d. per hour.

Age of entry. The usual age at which the boys enter the trade is from fourteen to sixteen.

Special qualifications. For most branches of the trade a good constitution is necessary, much of the work being damp and often done under exposed conditions. Fixing fibrous plasterwork is sometimes heavy work, and skillful manipulation as well as strength are apt to be required. More distinctive qualifications are now concerned rather with the earlier processes of the work done in the shops, and may involve, according to the scale and character of the work attempted, a knowledge of drawing and design.

Disadvantages. Special care should still be exercised so as to select a foreman or employer under whom the tone is satisfactory. The work is dirty.

Advantages. The increasing and very varied use that is being made of plasterwork and the scope offered by the trade are two of its marked features. Labor is drawn from the provinces to a less extent than in the case of bricklayers, masons, and carpenters, and as regards its products the trade is practically free from all forms of outside competition, both provincial and foreign.

General Classification

1. *As regards health.* Classed with paper hangers and white-washers, the comparative mortality of the group thus composed is very slightly (1 per cent) higher than the standard of all occupied males in England and Wales aged twenty-five to sixty-five. The mortality from alcoholism and liver complaints, from phthisis, and respiratory diseases are among the cases in which the standard rate is slightly exceeded.

2. *Economic.* Prospects good.

Carpenters and Joiners

Wages. The starting weekly wage for boys may range from 5 s.
to 8 s., and the ultimate wage of apprentices, usually reached in
four or five years, ranges from about 16 s. to 20 s. A common
wage as improvers is from 6 d. to 7 d. per hour. The trade-union
rate for journeymen is $10\frac{1}{2}$ d. per hour.

Age of entry. The usual age at which boys enter the trade is
from fourteen to sixteen, a larger proportion entering at fourteen
and fifteen than in some of the branches in which the work is
heavier and in which there is less opportunity for boys to start
by doing miscellaneous nontechnical work.

Special qualifications. As in most other branches of the building trades, for its average members no special qualifications are
necessary, and a general qualification, to the effect that a boy has
to be useful to the man he is working with, is of wide application.
But in this trade a knowledge of drawing and ability to interpret
drawings, a liking for tools, with a natural handiness in their use,
are special advantages ; and for those boys who are competent to
qualify as leading hands or foremen there is more than the average scope for the exercise of special gifts, not only such as the
mastery of the technical requirements of the trade, but for the
moral qualities of tact, patience, and the capacity to manage men.
Most of the positions as foremen of works come ultimately to
members of this particular occupation. In the machine shops
quickness in the manipulation of the material rather than in that
of tools is especially useful ; but the best use of machinery will
still involve a knowledge of the qualities of the timber that is
being ·used. ·

Disadvantages. The substitution of machine joinery for handwork and thus the tendency for the inside joiner to become a fitter
rather than a maker ; the unsuitability of wood in fireproof constructions ; the partial displacement of the carpenter on some
classes of buildings ; the general superiority of the provinces as
a training ground ; the cost of the outfit of tools, estimated at
from about £3 to £10 according to the place and character of

the work undertaken;[1] and the considerable influx into the trade during the decade 1891–1901.

Advantages. The general character of the trade and the clean and wholesome nature of the material upon which the operative works; the scope for initiative and the relatively greater chance of promotion to the position of foreman of works; a fairly effective organization and the diminished chance of irregular entry into the trade owing to the necessity of having an outfit of tools; and a wider provision of technical classes in London than in any other branches of the building trades.

General Classification

1. *As regards health.* These trades, ranking as the healthiest in the building-trade group, have a mortality rate 12 per cent below that of the group as a whole and 18 per cent below that of the standard rate for all classes occupied between the ages of twenty-five and sixty-five. The relative immunity from alcoholism and liver disease, respiratory diseases, and accidents is marked, and the general mortality figure between the above ages, like that of almost all other groups, is tending to decline. It is probable, however, that employment in a machine-joinery shop is less healthy than in other shops, owing to the greater prevalence in them of dust; but of this there is as yet no statistical proof.

2. *Economic.* Prospects seem to be moderate, except for the well-trained and competent worker, and especially for higher-grade carpenters able to deal with panelings and moldings of a delicate character. For these, prospects are good, as also in the allied trade of wood carvers, but the demand for these is relatively small.

Painters and Decorators

Wages. The starting wage of boys ranges from 5 s. to 8 s., and the ultimate wage of apprentices, reached in about five years, may be put at about 18 s. The wages of journeymen range from $8\frac{1}{2}$ d.

---

[1] Under modern conditions less money is apt to be spent for tools than formerly, when a complete kit might come to £20 or £25.

to 10½d. per hour, or in the case of trained decorators, to something over this maximum.

Age of entry. A customary age at which boys enter the trade is about fifteen, but for plain painting a feature of the trade is the ease with which it can be entered at almost any age. The position is reflected in the saying that "every sailor is a painter."

Special qualifications. For plain painting no special qualifications are required, but for decorative interior work they range upwards until the operative becomes merged in the decorative artist. For the high-grade painter ability to paint freely in the historic styles of ornament and an appreciation for beauty of form and color are required.

Disadvantages. The seasonal character of the trade and the indefiniteness of its technical qualifications; the consequent ease with which the lower grades of the trade can be entered, especially perhaps as regards outside painting; and the changes of fashion as regards styles, increasing a normal irregularity of demand.

Advantages. The great aggregate demand and the scope in its higher branches for originality of treatment and for the play of the artistic temperament.

General Classification

1. *As regards health.* In the Registrar-General's returns of England and Wales painters are classified with plumbers and glaziers, and in the group thus formed the comparative mortality figure is 11 per cent above the standard of occupied males between the ages of twenty-five and sixty-five. The excessive mortality is most marked under the headings plumbism and diseases of the urinary system. The mortality from alcoholism and liver diseases is low, and the group is less liable than the average to fatal accidents. During the ten years from 1892 to 1902 the general mortality for the above ages declined at almost every stage of life, but the high mortality from plumbism and Bright's disease did not fall.

2. *Economic.* Excepting for those who are well trained and exceptionally qualified for the trade, prospects are moderate and the standing drawback of the trade is its normally seasonal character. In the subsidiary occupation of sign writing the merit of its comparative stability may be noted.

Plumbers

Wages. The starting wage is from 5 s. to 8 s. per week, and the ultimate wage for apprentices, usually reached in five years, may be put at from 14 s. to 18 s. The trade-union rate is 11 d. per hour. Many youths enter the trade who begin as mates (or laborers) attending the skilled man, and learners not infrequently rank for a time as improvers at 6 d. to 7 d. an hour. Formal apprenticeship, as in all other branches of the building trades, is quite exceptional.

Age of entry. Those who enter the trade as boys generally do so at from fifteen to sixteen years of age, and the character of the work and the weight of the tools make it an unsuitable trade for the boy to enter earlier.

Disadvantages. Some displacement of plumbers is being caused, mainly by the use of materials other than lead.

Advantages. Through its Registration Council this trade has a completer machinery for securing some degree of standardization than any other ; and although the proportion of the trade that, either as masters or operatives, does register is small, the craft principle recognized, of registration under a body representative of both sections of the trade, is one of its special advantages.

To set against the displacement mentioned above is the great aggregate demand for the services of the plumber and, as affecting public health, the high standard of workmanship that is often exacted.

General Classification
   1. *As regards health.* (Cf. under *Painting.*)
   2. *Economic.* Prospects fair.

Smiths and Fitters, including Gas and Hot-Water Fitters

Wages. Wages of apprentices or learners range from 2 s. 6 d. to 8 s., and the usual rate is from 5 s. to 6 s. per week. An ultimate wage reached in from four to five years may be put at from 12 s. 6 d. to a guinea. The usual adult wage is from $9\frac{1}{2}$ d. to 11 d. per hour.

Age of entry. The usual age at which boys enter these trades is from fifteen to sixteen.

Disadvantages. The increasing volume of casting diminishes the demand for smiths, while the greater precision in this process lessens the importance of the fitter. Gas-fitting, except possibly in connection with heating and cooking, is in itself not an expanding trade.

Advantages. The increasing use of iron and steel in building, both in the main structures and in various minor fitments, increases the demand for smiths and fitters. A rising standard of demand for baths and hot-water supply in dwellings increases the demand for hot-water fitters.

General Classification

1. *As regards health.* No statistics are available for this group of occupations, but its components enjoy average conditions.

2. *Economic.* Prospects fair.

Electrical Workers

Wages. The usual starting wage for boys is from 5 s. to 6 s. per week, and a rate of 14 s. to 15 s. should be reached in three or four years. For journeymen 8½ d. per hour is sometimes paid, but the trade-union rate is 9½ d., except for plumber jointers, for whom it is 11 d.

Hours of labor. The working week recognized by the trade union is one of fifty-three hours, but fifty-four hours in shops is frequent. On buildings the usual number of hours is fifty.

Usual age of entry. For those who enter the trade as boys, fifteen is a common age.

Disadvantages. The indefiniteness of the necessary qualifications and the somewhat chaotic conditions of a rapidly expanding trade.

Advantages. The scope offered by the trade for a high degree of efficiency; its growth; its intrinsic interest; and the facilities for technical training provided in London.

General Classification

1. *As regards health.* Something above the average standard.

2. *Economic.* Prospects for trained men are good, and for others fair.

The Personal Elements involved

Out of 431 returns from employers in the building trades obtained for the purposes of the present inquiry and analyzed, less than half included any boys. In different occupations the proportion of boys to adults varies, there being more juveniles, for instance, among joiners and plumbers than among bricklayers and masons; but London employers in the building and allied trades as a whole absorb far less than their proportionate share of boy labor.[1] The chief and perhaps the only exception is found in the case of plumbers.

The London master builder falls into four main classes, affording a rough indication of the direction in which the opportunities required for the satisfactory learning of a trade are or are not likely to be found. The classes are as follows:

1. The builder and contractor of good standing mainly or largely engaged on new contract work.

[1] Apart from plumbers, the Census enumeration rarely makes a comparison possible, save in the case of carpenters and joiners, as between the age groups in the building trades in London and in the provinces. When comparison is possible the figures refer in respect to the earlier periods of life only to those under fifteen years of age, where the numbers are always small, and to those of fifteen and under twenty-five years of age, a period which, for London, includes, for most occupations, many improvers who have been trained in the provinces.

The age period for which a comparison would be most instructive would be that between fifteen and under twenty years of age — that is, for the years during which the largest numbers are learning their trade and when the migration to London or elsewhere, although it may have begun, is not in full operation. A comparison for these years is, however, not available from the published returns.

For those periods with which comparison is possible the following figures are given by way of illustration:

CARPENTERS AND JOINERS, 1901 — MALES

Town	All Ages Total	Under Fifteen		Fifteen and under Twenty-Five	
		Number	Per Cent of Total	Number	Per Cent of Total
London	32,934	224	.68	7,763	23.5
Leeds	3,560	69	1.93	1,186	33.3
Bradford	1,839	20	1.08	544	29.5
Leicester	1,620	20	1.23	551	34.0
Lincoln	607	3	.49	185	30.6
Lincoln (rural districts) . .	1,481	32	2.16	501	33.8

2. The builder of good standing mainly engaged on the work of repairs and renewals. This class will include the better grades of jobbing builders.
3. The builder and contractor mainly engaged on new work of a speculative character.
4. Small jobbing builders.

The firms most likely to be suitable for training boys will fall almost entirely in either class 1 or class 2 ; but the firms with the largest plant or those undertaking in some branches of the trade the highest class of work do not for various reasons necessarily provide the best or most hopeful training ground.

Class 3, rarely found in the county of London north of the Thames, because of the comparative exhaustion there of vacant building areas, is ruled out for the most part, partly because of the character of much of the work undertaken by this class of employer and of the conditions under which it is executed. In class 4, again, which includes a very large number of employers, those suitable for taking apprentices and learners are exceptional, mainly because operations are apt to be on too small and modest a scale to provide the variety and continuity necessary for satisfactory craft training.

In special branches of the trade many employers are found, the most important being electric-lighting firms, master masons, master plasterers, master plumbers, and master decorators.

In this class machine-joinery shops working for builders may be also included.

As regards standing and class of work undertaken, the above, with the exception of the builders' joiners, fall into classes corresponding roughly with those of the master builders themselves, and their suitability as regards the employment of juvenile labor would thus involve roughly a similar discrimination.

Apart from any question of the suitability or unsuitability of any class of firms for the employment of boys, or the attitude adopted by employers towards these, the most important general reasons for the shortage of boys in the London building trades are found in the character of much of the work and the prevailing rental conditions.

The rents of many London shops and yards are themselves high, and employers are thus inclined to desire that space and bench room should be occupied in as far as possible by labor that is at any given time most suited to the work in hand. Thus the learner, as representing relatively inefficient labor, is apt on this account to be eliminated.

Moreover, in the case of new work the sites, and in that of repairs, renewals, and alterations the sites and existing buildings combined, are also apt to have high market value, and while out of use to represent to an exceptional degree the locking up of capital and the loss of convenience. Building work in London is thus not only apt to demand a high standard of skill but exceptional speed in its execution, and on this score again the scope for the learner is apt to be unusually restricted.

In this connection may be mentioned the degree of responsibility often put upon the foreman engaged on contract work for keeping down costs to a profitable figure ; and since the foreman is often the person who engages the labor he requires, his position and duties are further elements that tend to keep the boy and the learner outside as representing relatively unremunerative labor.

The floating character of the great mass of labor outside the shops, with a term of engagement nominally at one hour's notice, and often practically limited to something less than that for which a man's particular branch of the trade may be required for some individual contract, again handicaps the learner, whose term of service should as an elementary condition be continuous.

The difficulty of the juvenile in certain trades, notably in plastering, plumbing, and masonry, has also been increased by the tendency in recent years for the work to be executed by subcontract and for the master builder less frequently and less completely than before to maintain a permanent inside staff in his own shops or yard. Thus, in many directions, a devolution of responsibility by the employer, be it to manager, foreman, or subcontractor, that appears to secure the greatest efficiency of the moment, is creating conditions that weaken seriously those elements in the organization of the trade which most conduce to the revival of good and systematic training of the juveniles. To an unusual degree the provinces and the uncalculated chances of the future are relied upon in London to provide for the labor requirements of this great industry.

There are thus various personal motives and economic conditions that go far towards explaining the common view adopted with regard to boy labor which finds expression in the reiterated statement that "only adults are employed," not infrequently with the further admission that there is an unwillingness to employ labor of any other kind. There are many exceptions, of course, but the above reflects a very usual point of view.

We are told, for example, that a manager "constantly refuses to take either learners or apprentices." The reason is mentioned : "the speed with which their contracts have to be executed renders it impracticable for either foreman or workmen to spare any time in training boys."

In this case, however, the unsatisfactoriness of the position adopted is admitted.

"At the same time," it is stated, "he feels there is a necessity in the trade generally for the proper training of boys, there being too many inefficient workmen at the present time."

How boys are obtained. Such boys as are at present employed are obtained, whether as apprentices or learners, in a great variety of ways ; and it is a natural result of the comparatively small numbers required that on the whole the existing sources of actual supply are considered fairly adequate, although more completely so in respect of quantity than of quality. These sources are mainly as follows, and may be divided, on the one hand, into those which imply a personal recommendation or introduction of some description, — sometimes without the intervention of any organization, as in the case of the sons of employees, and sometimes with, as when boys are obtained through a school or polytechnic, — and, on the other, into those which are apt to be entirely impersonal, as in the case of advertisement.

The following is an enumeration of the various channels utilized :

    1. Involving some kind of personal introduction, through
        a. Parents in the trade, whether employees or others ;
        b. The recommendation of friends, clients, or tenants.

2. Involving the use of some kind of organization, as when boys are obtained through
   a. Neighboring schools or polytechnics;
   b. Sunday schools, Bands of Hope, Bible classes, Church Lads' brigades, etc., or on the recommendation of the clergy;
   c. Apprenticeship associations;
   d. City companies and other charities, including the Jewish Board of Guardians;
   e. The labor exchanges or, as is occasionally mentioned, through a trade-union secretary.
3. Entirely impersonal channels, as through
   a. Advertisement, either through the press or through a notice exposed in the window;
   b. The chance personal application apt to result from the adoption of the previous method, boys being frequently sent out by their parents to look for work.

As a rule, when boys are taken on they are really wanted; but the general attitude of employers in these trades with regard to boys is reflected in the fact that they are also not infrequently taken on to oblige someone, often an employee or client, and this form of quasi-economic engagement characteristic of a trade in which boys are rather at a discount is thus deserving of notice.

On the whole the existing methods are, as stated, considered, if not satisfactory, adequate or fairly adequate, and under existing conditions an excess of applications is frequently mentioned.

Many of these methods are, it may be noted, not only intrinsically satisfactory but also inevitable, and even their variety may be not without its advantages. Thus the practical problem of the moment is not so much to introduce a uniform method of placing and training boys as to improve existing machinery, and as far as possible to provide such guidance and means of coördination as will minimize the risk in the future of an ignorant and unbalanced movement into such occupations as may seem (and, indeed, may be at any moment) advantageous, but the character of which is easily and quickly weakened by an uninformed drift into them, such as characterized the movement into the building trades during the closing years of last century, and, to some extent, the movement into the electrical industry more recently.

The greatest defect consciously recognized by the ·better class of employers in some of the present methods of finding and engaging boys is, however, the ignorance in which they are apt to be left, if not as to the boy's immediate antecedents, as to his real personal record.

It is true that occasionally a reputable employer may prefer to rely on his own judgment and experience in getting this knowledge, and to maintain that comparatively free hand in dismissing or retaining the boy which is possessed when he comes without any kind of introduction or outside recognition whatever.

But this attitude is more exceptional, and, on the whole, with a good deal of indifference on the question, those methods of securing boys are preferred which carry with them that kind of knowledge which throws light on the chances that the boy will prove suitable, diligent, and trustworthy.

The actual introduction of the boy to the employer by the parent, if not an employee himself, is clearly very exceptional, and the extent to which parents are often handicapped by lack of knowledge alike of employers and of trade conditions, however careful they may wish to be, is well known. From various causes, therefore, the assumption of parental responsibility for the boy in industry does not appear to be a very active influence. Thus the best available alternatives for this are often welcomed; and in the minds of a fair number of employers the adoption of a definite scheme by which, whatever other details it might embody, an active responsibility and care for the welfare of the boy should be shown commends itself to their judgment, always provided that in the exercise of that care no intrusion on the proper sphere of the responsibilities of the employer is incurred.

It is thus very significant of the view held with regard to juvenile labor in the building trades and to the supply of adequately trained labor in the future that in a group of trades in which the practice of apprenticeship has, so far as London is concerned, been almost abandoned, and in which, up to a point, metropolitan requirements have been and can be met by provincially trained labor, two apprenticeship schemes should have been recently prepared by those who in a very partially organized industry have the best right to speak on behalf of the employers as a whole; namely, the Master Builders' and, with special reference to decorators, the Master Decorators' associations.

In their general aim these schemes are identical, and, according to the former of the two mentioned, it is recommended that for boys commencing their apprenticeship at fourteen, fifteen, or sixteen the school age should end at seventeen;[1] that, combined with workshop or trade experience, time off, equivalent to two afternoons weekly, should be allowed for studying the theoretical side of their trade; that the continued employment of apprentices should be subject to good behavior and satisfactory progress; and — a clause especially relevant to the question of influence and responsibility — that steps should be taken to see that the conditions of apprenticeship are being reasonably fulfilled on both sides.

It is and must remain an open question as to how far the practice of fully indentured apprenticeship as is contemplated in the proposals of the master builders is likely to be revived in the building trades in London; but when the various considerations bearing on this point are taken into account, including the very divergent view held both by employers and parents as to the merits and suitability of full apprenticeship, it is certain that other channels of entry to most operative branches of the trade will have to be taken into account, not only as those which will probably, but will inevitably, be used.

In spite of the views expressed in favor of indentured apprenticeship and of the testimony to the guarantee of thoroughness that can be best insured by that method, there is also abundant evidence

---

[1] These proposals to raise the school age for certain classes of boys, although with a more limited application, conform in this respect, and thus in a broad general principle, with the Education (School and Continuation Class Attendance) Bill now before Parliament. According to this bill, if children are exempted from attendance at school up to the age operative in any locality, on the grounds that they are about to enter beneficial employment, they must in that case, up to the age of sixteen and in the absence of some reasonable excuse, attend continuation classes, as specified in the local by-laws, for a period not exceeding 150 hours in the year. If provision were made in the bill to give power to include day trade classes in the classes to be thus specified, the agreement in their general principles between the proposals of the master builders and the government as regards age conditions and compulsory attendance would be very marked.

that the chances that a boy will learn his trade are always slight, whether he be apprenticed or not,' if he is himself indifferent; and it is equally clear that those boys who mean to learn their trade can generally do so, in spite of the modern risks of specialization, in the absence of any formal undertaking. The formal bond between the employer and lad appears indeed to be a much less important consideration than the character of the latter and the way in which the former interprets his responsibilities. It is to be noted, moreover, that in a great majority of cases an apprentice or learner when once accepted is apt to pass out of the purview of the employer himself, and to a still greater extent his chances of learning a trade will then be in direct ratio to his quickness and usefulness, since trouble is apt to be taken — be it by the foreman or by the journeyman made responsible for the lad — only in the case of those boys who give little trouble, and to be withheld in the case of those from whom no *quid pro quo* can be expected. Unsatisfactory and incomplete though the present method of training is apt to be, and difficult though it is to find suitable substitutes even for a method of apprenticeship that often carries with it no guarantee of adequate training, the changed conditions in some trades and the desirability of supplementing workshop experience with the training of the school seem to point to the necessity of an extensive modification of the older forms of apprenticeship for the great majority of lads — perhaps for all.

In this connection the different grades of competency that are required in the various trades have to be recognized as well as the correlative fact that, on the side of the boy as of the adult operative, intelligence, aptitude, and diligence show corresponding differences. Thus grades of training as well as grades of skilled requirements have perhaps to be recognized more frankly in practice. The attempt, even in a single occupation, to adopt a uniform system of placing and training for all lads would overlook those differences of aptitude, character, and upbringing which are perhaps as important in connection with occupations that rank as manual as they are in respect to employers and professional men.

To some extent this classification of the young will proceed automatically : the best and most suitable firms will tend to attract the best lads, and, again, the best of these will tend to use most effectively the trade school and the trade class when these are provided and are suitable. Those who thus obtain the best experience in the shops or yards and the most scientific training of the schools will, so far as the London trained operative is concerned, furnish the future aristocracy of the trade and those from among whom leading hands and foremen and to some extent employers are most likely to be found.

The automatic sifting of the best and the uncertain training that is at present provided for the rank and file are, however, inadequate ; and while it is useless to expect a change of practice that will place all in the initial years of their industrial life on the same level of opportunity, it is perfectly reasonable and even essential to consider by what means an improvement of method can be widely adopted so as to shift to a somewhat higher level the training of perhaps every skilled grade.

The chief, but not the sole, agents in securing this will be the employers themselves, since it is only by their consent and good will that the training ground of the shops and yards can be made to play their necessary part. And as has been seen, many of the employers, even of the highest grade, are unwilling to adopt any line of action the effects of which do not seem to yield a direct and manifest advantage to themselves. It is this point of view that will apparently have, in many cases, to give way to a wider and, it may be added, a more farsighted recognition of the claims of a great industry and thus of the community of which it forms an essential part.

As regards the frequent attitude of employers towards this question of juvenile employment, it may be observed that since certain economic reasons — such as the character and organization of London work and the pressure and keenness of the internal competition — tend to prejudice the position of the London boy in the building trades, it is necessary to appraise somewhat carefully the opinions frequently expressed adverse to the boys themselves. As a class these are clearly necessary to the trade, so that towards them there is apt to be a latent feeling of obligation, which in its turn involves the danger of a hasty condemnation, even as a justification for a line of conduct that, if adopted by all employers everywhere, would lead in a few years to a crisis in at least some branches of the trade. Although some allowance has thus to be made when boys are condemned as on the score of conduct, lack of discipline, lack of interest in their work, or absorption in games, the repetition of such and similar complaints is so constant that a good deal of weight has to be attached to it; and, even though as a class boys in an inquiry of this kind are an unheard party, the conclusion has to be reached that some share of the responsibility for the present position has to be borne by the boys themselves, and that the impatience, lack of consideration, and shortsightedness often manifested by the employer have evidently their counterpart frequently in the impatience, want of discipline, and other shortcomings on the part of the boy. Thus, while on the one side there would appear to be need of a wider outlook, on the other there is abundant indication of the scope for bringing a new series of influences to bear — not only in respect of their industrial and general training but also through a friendly guardianship and, if need be, control — on those who are beginning their industrial life. To the recognition of this necessity there is much striking testimony.

The constant reference to the need of competent tradesmen and to the shortage of those who can be placed in positions of responsibility points significantly to the necessity of providing more adequately for, at least, some of the genuine labor requirements of the trade.

It may be pointed out that the more systematic and efficient training of a number proportionate to the calculated requirements of a trade would not weaken the competitive position of its present members, although an ill-regulated influx, as has been experienced in the past, would undoubtedly tend to have that effect. It must be remembered, moreover, that an understocked labor market tends not infrequently to have the same weakening influence, although more gradually and in ways less easily distinguished.

Thus it is well known that within the range of the building trades an internal competition of process and occasionally of craft is constantly making itself felt; and it is a general truth that, when the balance of strength is turned at any given period disproportionately in what appears to be the favor of some particular section, competing processes come more quickly into use, and not infre- quently the competition of new processes — either in the shape of alternative materials or of fresh inventions — may be engendered. The history of the building trades affords more than one example of the truth of this statement.

But a labor supply that is ill suited to the elastic requirements of the community, either because of an actual shortage and a dis- proportionate costliness or because of inferior training and unde- veloped skill, and thus of inferior work, checks the demand in a much more fundamental way than that just indicated; namely, by diminishing the demand for its services.

It is a commonplace that the contractor who is not trusted to that extent finds his position prejudiced, and exactly the same truth holds good of the journeyman, for, as in commerce, so in the build- ing trades, that confidence which the operative no less than the contractor has to take his share in creating is the basis upon which every healthy manifestation of its activity rests. The conclusion is thus reached that up to the point that is in accord with the require- ments every unit, whatever his particular grade may be, that enters a trade duly qualified technically and fearless in his integrity, so far from weakening the position of the members of the trade which he joins strengthens it, mainly because of the confidence that he helps to inspire. Thus at the bench or the yard or on the job, not less than in the classroom, the claim of the qualified learner to be taught the best of which he is capable is not only a simple and direct moral obligation but is also in accordance with the dictates of an intelligent and farsighted self-interest. As a leading trade- unionist remarked: " It is better for a trade to have its members ' full ' and not ' half ' mechanics." And another: " In the inter- ests of the trade union competent membership is regarded as essen- tial, since the way in which their work is done tells directly upon the demand on the part of the public for their services."

On the other hand, it must be observed that as a counterpart of the organization of a trade in which efficiency is apt to be inter- preted in terms of speed, a good deal is heard of the difficulty of combining thoroughness with the requisite quickness and of the danger of dismissal should work, through being "too good," take too long. The danger is greatest in connection with parts of the work that are least open to observation, but it is apt to become more marked in an industry situated as are the building trades to-day, when fresh combinations of new and old materials are so often specified, with the result that the latter, associated in the public mind with strength, are often introduced rather for effect than for structural purposes. The extent to which work is concealed on a building and to which work that is visible is intended to deceive the eye as to the part which it is really playing in construction are practical considerations that weaken the uniformity of the demand for good work and that, in tending to lower the ethical constructive standard of a great industry, tend also inevitably to complicate the problems of industrial training.

It is outside the scope of this report to endeavor to indicate the best methods of training (and these will indeed, as has been implied, differ with the trade and with the individual), as also is the attempt to indicate the proper or most practicable relationship between the trade school or class and the workshop, or, again, the extent to which the practical experience of the latter is essential if the greatest use of the more theoretical training of the former is to be insured.

It may be noted, however, that even as regards those occupations in which the trade school or the trade class is likely to be of the greatest service, as for joiners, plumbers, electrical workers, and fibrous plaster workers, there is almost a consensus of opinion that the practice of the school tends to differ to an important, although in a somewhat indefinable, way from that of the workshop. To a great extent this difference appears to be traceable to the inability of the former to give the learner what is regarded as a commercial aptitude in the handling of tools and material and thus the command of commercial efficiency. In those cases, therefore, in which learners have not had the opportunity of combining the twofold experience, the task of adaptation to the requirements of the workshop is sometimes at first made more difficult, rather than less, by the training of the schools, although ultimately the value of the latter, if it has been properly assimilated, secures its advantage. In as far as possible, however, the best arrangement appears to be that the double experience should be gained concurrently, to the end that the maximum advantage from both may be secured.

So far the necessity for the temporary absence of the lad during working hours has hardly been raised, but many employers would clearly be opposed to it, on the ground that work would be too greatly disorganized. In the view of others, however, this difficulty is apt to be exaggerated and as applying to most branches of the trade, in which the apprentice or learner does not or need not work directly with the trained man, the difficulty is said not to exist. It would probably be most real in the case of young plumbers, but in respect to suitable classes in all branches of the trade the view appears to be a sound one that, in workshop organization, sooner or later the question of absence for industrial training, and perhaps more general education, will have to be taken into completer account. Even assuming that effective attendance in the evening ought to be expected, the expectation is not likely to be realized as regards most boys, either because they would be unwilling to give the time or too tired to profit by the teaching if they did.

In conclusion, reference may be made again to what has been described as the suitable proportion of learners and the possibility of securing such a proportion in accordance with some organized plan.

It is obvious that the numbers thus required for the various trades can never be laid down with exactitude.

The elements of the problem are too obscure — such as the allowance which it would be necessary to make for trade fluctuation, for migration from the country, and for the movement away from London to the provinces or to other parts of the empire, and for the effect of inventions, changes in trade custom, and in fashion. But there are certain data which give some basis of rough calculation, such as the census figures, indicating, albeit very defectively, the decennial expansion or contraction of trades;[1] the average working life of the individual; the conditions set out in several trades as to the proportion of juvenile to adult workers; and the census of wages figures of adults and juveniles in London.

---

[1] The comparison of the figures for 1911, when published, with those for 1901 will have greater usefulness than any earlier returns, since comparable figures for the county occupational-age periods will be for the first time available.

On such bases, conflicting though the elements of the problem are, it is not unreasonable to conclude that an approximately safe figure could be arrived at by those with a knowledge of the various trades, at least as to the minimum number that ought year by year to be admitted to them in London for training there.

On this point a suggestion that, for some trades, conferences between representatives of employers and workers might prove of use appears worth consideration, both sides being intimately concerned in any proposals that might be made.

It is evident that, in order to act on such recommendations, a greater degree of cohesion in the trade would be required than at present exists, if only because the proposals themselves and the action taken on them ought to be accompanied by as complete knowledge as possible of the number and ages of existing apprentices or learners. It is possible that in the future useful information bearing on this point will be made available through the new National Insurance Bill; but, should official returns be insufficient, there is no apparent reason why such information should not be furnished by responsible employers to any central organization admitted to be acting in the best interests of the trade.

When an estimate has been formed of the shortage of learners or apprentices in any given trade, and of its special needs, — which would probably at present be for more careful selection and training of recruits rather than for any great increase in their numbers, — a deliberate effort would have to be made to secure such vacancies and such an allocation of vacancies as would meet the requirements.

In this portion of the task also the guidance of the trade itself would be of great value, owing largely to the completer knowledge that could thus be made available than by any other means, of such firms as would be not only willing to train boys but suitable for the task.

In this connection it may be observed that the returns from employers obtained for the present investigation provide a considerable amount of evidence bearing directly upon the above point. There are great difficulties, however, in the way of securing this information widely and reliably other than indirectly through those possessing a wide knowledge and an intimate experience of the trade. Outside its ranks cumulative experience can provide much of the necessary guidance, but internal changes in personnel and in the character of the management, be it at the top or in the workshop, will always be very difficult to trace. Other things being equal, it may be observed that in all cases the most suitable firms are likely to be those of which the heads have a first-hand appreciation of trade craftsmanship in at least some branches of the trade and whose qualifications are not simply organizing capacity, command of capital, and commercial insight.

In view of the condition of the trade it may well be that in some of its branches there is at the present time no demonstrable need for any additional learners or apprentices, but even at the moment this is not the case right through the trade. It is desirable, however, as much for the future as for the present, to look forward to the inception of a scheme in which those representing the trade would be combined in an attempt to estimate its personal needs; and to stimulate the trade so that those needs might be met, in as far as possible, steadily and continuously and not spasmodically as in the past.

As compared with such a movement, inspired by a concern for the welfare of the building trades as a whole, the question as to the particular conditions of training which it may be best to adopt — whether with or without premium, whether with indentured apprenticeship or as learners under agreement, or merely as learners — would be of comparative unimportance and, as has been already indicated, the best would probably vary not only as between occupation and occupation but also as between firm and firm.

The whole problem, apart from its more purely social character, is, on the one hand, educational and, on the other, industrial. As regards education and the training that can be given outside the workshop or the yard, it is clear that this will have to be as elastic as possible, lending itself to a ready adaptation, as need may arise, to changing industrial conditions, since these, although they can be influenced by the training of the classroom, cannot be determined by it.

On the other hand, the industrial problem is itself complicated by those conditions which are tending constantly to give new and often lower values to technical qualifications. While, therefore, new elements of uncertainty and deterioration are being introduced into some of the older occupations, it may be observed that at the same time in some directions the importance of resourcefulness and adaptability, and perhaps character, is increasing, and training will have to take this into account.

∴ Under modern conditions, however, in which the elements of change and uncertainty have been seen to enter so conspicuously, no part of the practical task either of school or shop training or of placing the lad in industry can be stereotyped; and in the latter task the most intimate knowledge possible will be required alike of the boys, of the employers, and of the industry as a whole. It is in the last two respects that the knowledge and accumulated experience of the labor exchanges should become increasingly valuable, as complementary to any personal knowledge that such a body as the Juvenile Advisory Committee may have at its disposal as to the career of the boy himself and as to his own wishes and that of his parents as to what his future occupation is to be.

In respect to the juvenile, the most important outcome of the experience of the labor exchanges, aided, it may be hoped, by the active assistance of the trades concerned, will be a certain power to judge as to the relative advantages which available vacancies appear to offer, and gradually this judgment, especially in respect to lads seeking to enter occupations to which they have no hereditary claim, will probably be the best that the juvenile, or those acting on his behalf, can obtain. But it is expedient that its inevitable limitations should be recognized, and that the guidance which it may make possible, whatever the authority or body that gives it may be, should be clearly interpreted as being rather the provision of an opportunity to make the best choice possible than the acceptance of any responsibility as regards both parents and boys for the satisfactoriness and stability of any particular occupation chosen. At the inception of a machinery that, should it expand, will necessarily tend to affect the outlook and habits of the rising generation in a very definite way, it is permissible to emphasize the importance of these points, in order that care may be taken at the outset to dissociate in the public mind the function of giving advice and the exercise of a friendly care from the assumption of a responsibility that cannot in any large sense, under existing conditions, be borne.

APPENDIX

I

· The following extracts have been chosen from the material collected for the present inquiry as being either representative or suggestive in character:

(37) Large Builders and Contractors in Southeast London

Learners in all branches begin at 2 d. an hour, and reach 6 d. at the end of four years, equivalent to a rise of 1 d. per week each year.

Boys who are going to work in branches where there is machinery, if taken at an earlier age, are kept in the foreman's office until they are sixteen. Apprenticeship, though preferable, is dying out, as men oppose it and boys do not like to be tied. Apprentices, moreover, sometimes take advantage of their position. Exchanges for juveniles would be superfluous in this district as there is a large supply of boys available, skilled and otherwise.

(31) A Firm of Builders and Contractors in West London

From 30 to 100 employed.

Boys are taught by workmen under supervision of foreman. Quite satisfactory, as man is supervised by employers also. The men themselves are not usually well disposed towards boys, whom they consider competitors. The boy has, therefore, to use his wits and pick up what he can himself. Boys are not in much request unless they are so good as to be worth their bench room, which is valuable now, owing to rates and rents.

(218A) An Old-Established and Important Firm of Builders in South London

Employing from 250 to 550.

Wage scale for plumber, bricklayer, and plasterer apprentices for five years: 5 s., 8 s., 12 s., 15 s., 20 s.

The scale for joiners for six years: 5 s., 8 s., 10 s., 12 s., 15 s., 20 s.

Afterwards, if they stay on, they work as improvers for a year or two at 8 d. per hour.

The usual age is fifteen to sixteen, boys younger than this not being strong enough.

Boys are recommended personally by the vicar of the neighboring church, by clients, friends, etc., or are sons of employees. Firm attaches importance to personal recommendations, and is unable to accept all who are recommended even now.

(215) A Firm of about Fifty Years' Standing in South London

Employing from about 40 to 110 persons, according to state of trade. The employer is keenly interested in the whole question of training boys and has taken considerable pains personally to give those in his employ a first-class training, finding it good policy. His most efficient workers are those trained by himself, and their mutual relations are all the more harmonious.

An arrangement has been made with the foreman to form a class in the evenings for training a few of his boys in first-class painting and decorating, including graining, sign writing, and enameling.

∴ The large majority of efficient men in London is said to be over forty years of age and trained under the old apprenticeship system. The boys are started at $1\frac{1}{2}$ d. per hour and rise $\frac{1}{2}$ d. per hour according to progress made until they attain journeymen's rates. Three boys are learning electrical work (wiring, etc.), three are plumbers' mates, none at present in joiners' shop. Boys are also taken for joinery work, painting, and decorating.

∴ Plumbers' boys start at $1\frac{1}{2}$ d. and in three or four years (according to ability) rise to 3 d. or $3\frac{1}{2}$ d. per hour. Afterwards they go with plumbers as mates at 6 d. to 7 d. per hour.

Boys learning wiring, etc., rise to 3 d. or 4 d. per hour in three to four years, and then frequently go to other firms as assistant wiremen at 8 d. per hour.

Most of the boys now with firm commenced at age of sixteen to seventeen. The firm, however, is willing to take them younger. In the painting and decorating work, the employer himself assists in training boys and watches their progress closely. In the other trades boys assist men under supervision of foremen.

(24) A Large South London Firm of Builders and Contractors

Employing from 400 to 900.

Four apprentices (indentured) (sixteen to eighteen years), in joiners' shop; no other juveniles.

$\left.\begin{array}{l} 2\text{ d. per hour first year} \\ 4\frac{1}{2}\text{ d. per hour last year} \end{array}\right\} 2\text{ d., } 2\frac{1}{2}\text{ d., } 3\text{ d., } 3\frac{1}{2}\text{ d., } 4\frac{1}{2}\text{ d.}$

Wages usually amount to premium and sometimes exceed this.

Usual age at which boys are taken, from fifteen to sixteen years. Apprenticeship in some cases extends over three years only.

No special qualifications required, but willingness and average intelligence.

Kept on by firm as improvers for two years after apprenticeship, and then paid full wages.

Probation of one month.

Term: from three to five years; ends at age of twenty-one.

Premium £50.

Employees' sons are given preference; more applications than can be entertained.

Abundant supply of skilled men in most branches; fast work in bricklaying makes it unprofitable to employ apprentices in this work.

(27) A Large Firm of Builders and Contractors in Northwest London

Numbers employed ranging from 250 to 500.

This firm employs boys in joiners' shop only. Boys are learners, neither indentures nor any form of agreement being used.

Employed two years as *shop boys* (that is, wait on men generally) and receive 4s. to 5s. weekly. Afterwards begin bench work and commence at 3d. per hour, rising to 5d. and 6d. per hour according to their work. Fully qualified joiners are paid 10½d. per hour. Shop boys are taken on at fourteen to fifteen years. Any smart boy is eligible. Training under foreman. Boys advised to attend local technical institute. Boys are not discharged in slack seasons, but hours are shortened, no deduction made from *shop boys'* wages; bench boys are paid by the hour. When boys are wanted foreman gives preference to sons of workmen. No scarcity of applicants experienced up to the present. Workmen often recommend sons of friends or acquaintances. Supply of skilled men pretty constant from the country.

(443) An Old-Established Firm of Jobbing Builders in North-west London

The number of men they employ varies from 30 to 100. Among these there are only two juveniles. The latter are office boys or messenger boys, who, after "finding their feet" during a year or two, take to some trade and learn it as they go along. This generally happens when they are sixteen or seventeen years old. The firm has had no apprentice for twelve years. The following objections to apprenticeship were mentioned:

If a boy can get on as apprentice, he can get on without being apprenticed.

Lads take advantage of the fact that they are bound for five years, and cannot be got rid of.

Again, boys grow impatient and dissatisfied during their term. Many want to be off to Canada.

Finally, the old system rather made for overspecialization. Boys were compelled to stick to one kind of job and learned nothing else.

As to whether the building trade holds out prospects of permanent employment, it was said that there is not now the same continuous work that was once provided for the men when masters were more scrupulous and did not let men go if they could possibly help it. The prospects of permanent employment are, however, fair. A jobbing carpenter is always in demand; but many things — sashes, doors, etc. — are now manufactured by machinery, and that limits the field of employment. It also narrows the boy's opportunity of learning his business thoroughly.

CONDITIONS OF JUVENILE EMPLOYMENT IN THE READY-MADE WOMEN'S CLOTHING TRADES IN LONDON, IN THE SPRING OF 1911

By Miss Collet, Senior Investigator for Women's Industries

(Report on Inquiry communicated by the Board of Trade to the London Juvenile Advisory Committee for use in connection with the Juvenile Section of the London Labor Exchanges, July, 1911)

Firms visited and numbers employed by firms giving information. Visits have been paid to 965 firms entered in the London directory as engaged in the manufacture of costumes, blouses, mantles, skirts, millinery, underclothing, corsets, and embroidery.

Detailed reports of every visit have been supplied to the secretary of the London Juvenile Advisory Committee.

Of these 965 firms, 259 were found to have warehouses only, with no factories or workshops of their own in the area visited; 42 had retail shops employing no one in manufacture unless on alterations; 69 employed no juvenile labor and gave only vague information or were working for private customers only; 13 employed no one outside their family; 46 had left the address given; and 23 refused information.

The remaining 513 firms employed approximately 30,600 persons at the time of inquiry. The table on page 648 shows the distribution of the firms in trades and districts.

Although many firms were entered in the directory as manufacturers in only one branch of these trades, investigation showed that no hard-and-fast line could be drawn between costume makers, coat and skirt makers, mantle makers, blouse makers, and skirt makers. The blouse makers in several cases were blouse makers only if under that term the "blouse suit," or robe, be included. Mantle makers and ladies' tailors were manufacturers of costumes, the latter name being assumed in workrooms where men were largely employed. The number solely employed on the premises of these firms in making ladies' mantles for outdoor wear was small. Few firms confine themselves to making skirts only, and the underskirt makers had in general suffered so severely from the "hobble skirt" fashion that some of them were abandoning this branch altogether.

TABLE SHOWING THE NUMBER OF FIRMS GIVING INFORMATION, GROUPED ACCORDING TO TRADE IN EACH LABOR-EXCHANGE AREA VISITED

TRADE	NUMBER OF FIRMS												
	Bethnal Green	Camden Town	City	Elephant	Finsbury	Hackney	Islington	Kilburn	Rotherhithe	Shepherd's Bush	Stepney	Walham Green	Total[1]
Costumes, blouses, mantles, skirts	15	5	95	8	61	13	18	73	—	1	25	5	319
Infants' millinery	1	—	8	—	4	—	3	—	—	—	—	—	16
Underclothing	1	—	7	—	7	1	1	2	—	—	8	·	27
Corsets	—	1	5	5	1	5	1	3	2	—	7	—	30
Embroidery	—	2	14	—	11	1	2	12	—	—	1	2	45
Ladies' millinery	2	1	45	—	16	—	3	8	—	—	1	—	76
Total	19	9	174	13	100	20	28	98	2	1	42	7	513

In the West End group have been included a considerable number employed by firms doing the highest class of work for private customers but included in the inquiry because they are engaged to a great extent in making models for sale to other firms.

Learners. It is only in such firms manufacturing the highest class of goods and hardly using a sewing machine that apprenticeship is at all customary. Even in those branches of the trades in which handwork is of great importance, there are few cases in which any binding agreement is entered on. In all branches (and they are the majority in the ready-made trades) where piecework

[1] The exchange areas of Clapham Junction, New Cross, Camberwell, Woolwich, and Lewisham were not visited, the numbers employed in these trades being shown by the factory returns to be relatively small in those districts.

is adopted the earnings of the cleverer girls so greatly exceed those of the slowest that after a few months as learners on a time wage they are put on piece rates and earn what they can. After a year they cease to be regarded as learners. This is especially the case with machinists. In other cases they may be learners on a time wage for a much longer period. Any attempt to define the period of time during which a girl was regarded as a learner was generally met by the reply that everything depended so much upon the girl.

With such a vague definition of the period during which a girl remained a learner, the following table, showing the number of learners employed, can convey little exact information. Still it may be taken as presenting the maximum number of girls required as learners in any one year, and if we assume that the proportion employed by the firms who did not state the number of learners employed by them was the same as in the firms giving the information, we get a maximum demand of about 3000 girls as learners in the firms visited.

The following table shows the number of workpeople employed by firms with no learners and by firms with learners :

Trade	Total Number of Workpeople Employed by Firms Giving Information	Number of Workpeople Employed by Firms with no Learners	Number employed by Firms with Stated Number of Workers		Number of Workpeople Employed by Firms with Learners whose Number was not stated
			Workpeople	Learners	
Costumes, blouses, mantles, skirts .	21,927	3316	15,165	1764	3446
Infants' millinery .	1,374	215	1,099	78	60
Underclothing . .	2,199	230	1,233	138	736
Corsets	733	49	532	29	152
Embroidery . . .	1,287	160	1,047	159	80
Ladies' millinery .	3,043	393	2,239	301	411
Total	30,563	4363	21,315	2469	4885

Wages of learners. Firms employing 25,000 workpeople gave particulars of the weekly wages given to learners while on time wage. Disregarding a first week's trial for nothing required by some firms:

Firms employing 13½ per cent paid nothing at first to learners
Firms employing 16 per cent paid 2 s. or less
Firms employing 27 per cent paid 2 s. 6 d.
Firms employing 26 per cent paid 3 s.
Firms employing   9 per cent paid 3 s. 6 d., 4 s., or 4 s. 6 d.
Firms employing   8½ per cent paid 5 s.
      Total . . . 100

A rise of 6 d. a week at the end of three months or of 1 s. at the end of six months was common; full particulars have been given in the detailed reports.

At the beginning of the second year time wages were no longer paid by many firms, their learners then earning varying amounts on piecework. Firms employing about 11,800 workpeople gave particulars of the wages earned at the beginning of the second year, referring to hand workers in most cases. From these it appears that at the beginning of the second year

Firms employing 3 per cent paid 2 s. or 2 s. 6 d.
Firms employing 24 per cent paid 3 s. or 3 s. 6 d.
Firms employing 8 per cent paid 4 s. or 4 s. 6 d.
Firms employing 33 per cent paid 5 s. or 5 s. 6 d.
Firms employing 24 per cent paid 6 s.
Firms employing 3 per cent paid 6 s. 6 d. and under 10 s.
Firms employing 5 per cent paid 10 s.

Wages in third and fourth year. With so much variety in the earnings of machinists in their second year, it followed naturally that employers could give no definite information with regard to wages at the end of a third year. There was a tendency to remember the wages of some clever girl whose performances had especially struck her employer's attention.

The Board of Trade report on Earnings and Hours of Labor in 1906 gives the wages earned in a full week for girls under eighteen years of age, and interpreting these returns by the light of information given by employers to the investigators, a girl of seventeen of good capacity, without exceptional ability, after three years' experience in these trades would be earning on piecework from 9 s. to 12 s. a week.

Range of earnings of adult workers. From the Board of Trade returns the following estimate has also been formed of the ordinary range of earnings of women of eighteen years and upwards in these trades, the best paid and the worst paid being omitted in each group :

ORDINARy RANGE OF EARNINGS FOR A FULL WEEK OF
WOMEN OF EIGHTEEN yEARS AND UPWARDS

Forewomen	20 s. to 30 s.
Cutters	14 s. to 20 s.
Machine sewers, hand or foot	
Time	12 s. to 17 s.
Piece	12 s. to 19 s. 6 d.
Machine sewers, power	
Time	12 s. to 17 s.
Piece	11 s. to 19 s.
Hand sewers	
Time	10 s. to 16 s.
Piece	10 s. 6 d. to 20 s.

Hours and mealtimes. Although on their factory schedules the employers as a rule enter their hours as being the full number permitted by law, namely, from 8 A.M. to 8 P.M. on ordinary days, with only one and one-half hours' interval for meals, and 8 to 4 on Saturdays, with one half hour's interval, the full legal time is practically never worked unless at times of pressure, except in workshops employing men, more especially in the Jewish workshops.

The hours of labor were stated by firms employing 26,000 workpeople, and it will be seen from the table given below that only 9 per cent began work at 8 A.M., 39 per cent at 8.30, 13 per cent at 8.45 to 8.55, and 39 per cent at 9 A.M.

The law permits a breakfast interval to be fixed from 8 A.M. to 8.30 A.M., so that if workers begin work at 8.30 it is not obligatory on employers to allow more than one hour's further interval before 8 P.M. Those beginning at 8.30 might legally, therefore, be employed 60 hours in the week. Only 8 in 10,000 beginning at this hour worked as much as 57½ hours, and only 4 per cent worked as many as 55 hours.

The law permits workpeople in these trades to be employed for five hours continuously, and it would therefore be legal for an employer to make his workpeople work from 2 P.M. to 7 P.M. without an interval for tea. No employer in the ready-made women's clothing trades has been found who conducts his business on such lines; even those who leave off work at 6 o'clock are nearly always allowed an interval for tea during the afternoon. The employers usually stated that the girls were allowed one hour for dinner and half an hour for tea. As, however, no legal obligation rests upon them to give this tea interval when the half hour for breakfast and the hour for dinner have been entered on their schedule (unless the period of work after dinner lasts more than five hours), it is possible that in practice the tea interval would vary with the pressure of work. The table showing the weekly hours of work practically allows for this possibility by giving a range of $2\frac{1}{2}$ hours in each group. It seems that of the 26,000 workpeople employed by firms giving information as to hours, 16 per cent were employed 45 and under $47\frac{1}{2}$ hours a week, 31 per cent were employed $47\frac{1}{2}$ and under 50 hours, 31 per cent were employed 50 and under $52\frac{1}{2}$ hours, 17 per cent were employed $52\frac{1}{2}$ and under 55 hours, 2 per cent were employed 55 and under $57\frac{1}{2}$ hours, and 3 per cent were employed $57\frac{1}{2}$ hours and upwards. As a considerable proportion of the last group were men, the hours could in their case, if they chose, exceed the limit of 60 hours imposed on women and young persons.

It will be seen from the accompanying table that on the whole the later the work begins the shorter the hours that are worked.

In the E.C. district 8 per cent of the workpeople began work at 8 o'clock; 27 per cent at 8.30; 5 per cent at 8.45; and 60 per cent at 9 o'clock.

In the W. and S.W. district 1 per cent began work at 8 o'clock; 49 per cent began at 8.30; 29 per cent at 8.45; and 21 per cent at 9 o'clock.

In the N.E. and N. district 24 per cent began work at 8 o'clock; 52 per cent at 8.30; 2 per cent at 8.45; and 22 per cent at 9 o'clock.

In East London 47 per cent began at 8 o'clock; 41 per cent at 8.30; and 12 per cent at 9 o'clock.

TABLE SHOWING (*A*) THE NUMBER AND (*B*) THE PERCENTAGE OF WORKPEOPLE BEGINNING WORK AT DIFFERENT HOURS, AND THE NUMBER OF HOURS WORKED BY THEM PER WEEK

WORKING HOURS PER WEEK (EXCLUDING MEALTIMES)	NUMBER EMPLOYED BEGINNING WORK AT				
	8	8.30	8.45 to 8.55	9	Total
Under 45	—	30	9	7	57[1]
45 and under 47½	—	1,287	250	2,587	4,224[2]
47½ and under 50	394	3,005	809	3,893	8,101
50 and under 52½	712	3,430	1789	1,990	7,921
52½ and under 55	192	1,932	489	1,692	4,305
55 and under 57½	279	329	—	—	608
57½ and upwards	780	8	—	—	788
Total	2357	10,021	3346	10,169	26,004[1,2]

WORKING HOURS PER WEEK (EXCLUDING MEALTIMES)	PERCENTAGE WORKING DIFFERENT PERIODS PER WEEK BEGINNING WORK AT				
	8	8.30	8.45 to 8.55	9	Total
Under 45	—	—	—	—	—
45 and under 47½	—	13	8	25	16
47½ and under 50	17	30	24	38	31
50 and under 52½	30	34	53	20	31
52½ and under 55	8	19	15	17	17
55 and under 57½	12	4	—	—	2
57½ and upwards	33	—	—	—	3
Total	100	100	100	100	100
Percentage beginning Work at the Different Times .	9	39	13	39	100

The number of hours worked per week was on the whole less in the E.C. district than elsewhere.

In the E.C. district 64 per cent worked less than fifty hours per week; in the N.E. and N. district 44 per cent; in the W. and S.W. district 32½ per cent; in the E. district 8 per cent; in the other districts 49 per cent.

Only 5 per cent worked more than fifty-five hours in the E.C. district; less than ½ per cent in the W. and S.W. district; 7 per

[1] Including 11 beginning at 9.30.
[2] Including 100 beginning at 9 in winter and earlier in summer.

TABLE SHOWING THE NUMBER OF HOURS WORKED PER WEEK
IN DIFFERENT DISTRICTS

Hours worked per Week (excluding Mealtimes)	Number of Workpeople employed in District by Firms giving Information					
	E.C.	W. & S.W.	N.E. & N.	E.	Other Districts	Total
Under 45 . . .	7	50	—	—	—	57
45 and under 47½	2,228	804	1092	—	100	4,224
47½ and under 50	5,115	2201	375	64	346	8,101
50 and under 52½	2,222	3969	1347	95	288	7,921
52½ and under 55	1,342	2341	308	194	120	4,305
55 and under 57½	136	27	220	175	50	608
57½ and upwards	467	6	11	293	11	788
Total . .	11,517	9398	3353	821	915	26,004

cent in the N.E. and N. district; 57 per cent in the E. district;
7 per cent in the other districts. As already stated, those employed for so large a number of hours included a considerable
proportion of men.

The underclothing and infants' millinery trades show the short-
est hours worked per week.

A considerable number of workpeople employed in the embroidery firms are engaged on other work than embroidery, military
tailoring accounting for the number employed more than fifty-five

TABLE SHOWING THE PERCENTAGE OF WORKPEOPLE IN THE
TRADES WORKING DIFFERENT AMOUNTS PER WEEK

Number of Hours worked per Week (excluding Mealtimes)	Costumes, Blouses, Skirts and Mantles	Under-clothing and Infants' Millinery	Corsets	Embroidery	Ladies' Millinery
Under 47½	15	33	10	10	12
47½ and under 50 . . .	29	37	8	44	40
50 and under 52½ . . .	32	25	78	19	22
52½ and under 55 . . .	18	5	4	13	26
55 and under 57½ . . .	2	—	—	14	—
57½ and upwards . . .	4	—	—	—	—
Total	100	100	100	100	100

hours. The inquiry was not intended to cover any branches of men's clothing, but it was impossible to judge beforehand whether the embroidery done was restricted to one branch or the other, or was even connected with clothing at all. All firms visited employing embroiderers have been included in the table.

Overtime. Young persons under eighteen years of age are not permitted in any circumstances to work beyond the ordinary period allowed by law.

In all cases the employers stated that if young persons during the busy seasons were detained for the full legal period, they were paid for overtime if time workers.

Seasonal fluctuations. The women's clothing trades are, of course, liable to seasonal fluctuations, but the ready-made branches are less affected by these than the private-custom trade, in which the fluctuations are also accentuated by changes of fashion and by special events. The use of machinery, besides necessitating a larger capital and therefore bringing into the trade a different class of employer, is an incentive towards regular production. The manufacturers do not acquiesce in the waste of capital arising from the standstill of their machinery, and they therefore aim more and more at filling up the slack season of one branch by manufacturing other kinds of clothing in demand at different seasons.

Fluctuations of employment on the employer's premises are also much reduced by the common custom of giving out work to be done by home workers during the busy season. These home workers are frequently married women who have previously worked in the factory or workshop.

Except in the ladies' millinery branch, in which employers in many cases frankly admit that their works are closed for considerable periods, there was a tendency on their part to minimize the amount of slackness. Employers with 100 workpeople at one period and 65 at another would say that they never dismissed anyone and that they always tried to retain competent workers. The explanation of the discrepancy between this statement of fact and the figures was generally that pieceworkers in slack times went of their own accord, being unable to earn enough to make it worth while attending.

The following table shows the percentage in each trade employed by firms admitting slackness in certain months:

PERCENTAGE OF THE TOTAL NUMBER WHO WERE EMPLOYED BY FIRMS AFFECTED BY SLACKNESS DURING THE WHOLE OR PART OF A SPECIFIED MONTH

Month	Costumes, Blouses, Mantles, and Skirts		Under-clothing	Infants' Millinery	Embroidery	Ladies' Millinery
	Firms manufacturing for wholesale or retail firms	Retail firms manufacturing for themselves				
January	22	65	—	15	5	22
February	10	54	—	3	5	1
March	4	11	—	—	1	—
April	2	1	—	2	2	4
May	5	1	—	5	—	12
June	19	1	2	29	· 16	57
July	16	4	—	19	33	69
August	23	93	52	5	22	29
September	7	15	15	5	6	3
October	6	—	15	50	—	16
November	16	—	15	56	1	55
December	31	51	2	35	9	77
Not affected by seasonal slackness	47	—	45	8	56	1
Total employed by firms giving definite information as to slack periods	10,075	6420	1611	767	855	2137

These figures give a rough indication of the months in which inefficient workers in these trades may be earning little or nothing, but of course give no information as to the extent to which they are affected.

During 1909 and 1910, wholesale firms in the costume, blouse, mantle, and skirt trades, employing on the average 2353 workpeople in 1910, supplied particulars of the numbers employed at the end of each month to the Board of Trade. Retail firms, employing on the average 1837 workpeople in 1910, supplied similar particulars. Five firms in the underclothing and infants' millinery trades, employing 468 workpeople on the average in 1910, and seven in the ladies' millinery trades, employing 328 workpeople on the average in 1910, have also made returns, and although the numbers employed by them are small, they may be useful as indications of seasonal effects.

In the following table the average number employed in the twelve weeks in each year for which returns were made is represented by 100 :

TABLE SHOWING THE NUMBER OF WORKPEOPLE PAID WAGES IN THE LAST PAY WEEK OR OTHER ORDINARY WEEK IN EACH MONTH OF 1909 AND 1910 BY FIRMS FURNISHING RETURNS, EXPRESSED AS PERCENTAGES OF THE AVERAGE WEEKLY NUMBER EMPLOYED

| Month | Costumes, Blouses, Mantles, and Skirts | | | | Undercloth-ing and Infants' Millinery | | Ladies' Millinery | |
| | Wholesale firms | | Retail firms | | | | | |
	1909	1910	1909	1910	1909	1910	1909	1910
January	93	97	91	95	94	107	117	116
February	104	109	91	90	96	92	123	135
March	107	108	98	103	95	94	120	133
April	105	105	103	110	90	93	123	127
May	108	105	106	110	98	98	126	82
June	101	100	107	110	105	99	87	62
July	90	89	106	103	99	97	85	64
August	92	93	61	56	104	101	98	110
September	106	101	103	102	103	106	126	126
October	104	99	113	106	99	103	84	117
November	96	98	114	111	106	103	57	70
December	94	96	107	104	110	105	54	59
Average weekly number . .	100	100	100	100	100	100	100	100
Percentage increase or decrease in average in 1910 on average number employed in 1909	—	+2.9	—	+2.6	—	+28.9	—	—4.2

If these monthly returns be compared with the preceding table showing months in which firms were affected by slackness, it will be seen that they tally very closely in the costume, blouse, mantle, and skirt trades in both branches; such discrepancies as appear at first sight are explained by the facts that the first table refers to "some period of the month" and the latter to either the third or fourth week of the month, and that employers do not dismiss at once when a decline begins and must take on workpeople in preparation for an expected pressure.

There is no such agreement in the case of the underclothing and infants' millinery trades, and this is no doubt due to the fact that these trades are far less affected by the seasons than by peculiarities in the trade of each firm.

In the case of the ladies' millinery trade the two tables confirm each other when the facts noted in the case of the costume etc. trades are remembered. In May, 1910, there was an unusual slackness due to the death of the late king.

It will be seen that in the ladies' millinery trade for five months in the year the numbers employed are less than three fourths of the numbers employed in the busy season, and that in some months they are much lower still. A mediocre worker in this trade must expect to be "given holidays" for about three to five months in the year.

These returns only indicate the fluctuations in *numbers* employed; the fluctuations in the *amounts of wages* paid would vary considerably more in those trades where the greater proportion are on piecework.

The Board of Trade report on Earnings and Hours of Labor in 1906 gives tables bringing out this fact. The fluctuations in numbers and amounts of wages of workpeople employed on "Dress, Millinery, etc. (Factory)" and "Shirts, Blouses, Underclothing, etc." in London in that year are given below. Except in the ladies' millinery trade, employers generally stated that learners were always retained and paid their full-time wage during the slack season.

No special reference has been made in this report to the conditions of employment in the corset trade. The ready-made corset is manufactured mainly in certain provincial towns. One large firm in London nevers employs learners and was not included in the list of firms giving information. With the exception of one firm employing a considerable number the information relating to corset makers was found to deal very largely with firms manufacturing for private customers. This was especially the case in East London and South London.

TOTAL NUMBER OF WORKPEOPLE PAID WAGES, AND AMOUNT OF WAGES PAID, IN THE LAST PAY WEEK OR OTHER ORDINARY WEEK IN EACH MONTH OF 1906 BY LONDON FIRMS FURNISHING RETURNS, EXPRESSED AS PERCENTAGES OF THE AVERAGE WEEKLY NUMBER EMPLOYED AND THE AVERAGE WEEKLY WAGES BILL RESPECTIVELY

MONTH	DRESS, MILLINERY, ETC. (FACTORY)		SHIRTS, BLOUSES, UNDER-CLOTHING, ETC.	
	Number employed	Wages paid	Number employed	Wages paid
		£		£
January	98.4	93.4	99.6	98.2
February	107.3	113.6	101.9	103.5
March	110.4	115.2	102.6	105.6
April	107.4	111.5	101.9	104.8
May	101.7	100.9	101.5	105.6
June	92.4	89.2	100.2	99.5
July	88.1	89.8	97.0	96.8
August	94.0	91.9	97.6	96.8
September	110.1	119.6	100.4	101.8
October	105.7	109.5	100.3	97.5
November	94.0	87.1	99.3	93.8
December	90.5	78.3	97.7	96.1
Weekly average expressed as	100	100	100	100
Actual weekly average . . .	2389	1800	8066	6004

Prospects of promotion in the trades. In the preceding sections attention has been paid to the prospects of the girl of middling ability, the question of wages and regularity of employment being of the most importance in her case. But another point of view must be considered in choosing a trade for girls with marked ability or individuality or capacity for leadership. The women's clothing trades offer more prospect to women in mature years than any other carried on on a large scale. The ready-made branch needs women with the capacity for organizing the work of large numbers, to a greater extent than is required in the smaller firms manufacturing for private customers, where greater artistic ability may generally be necessary but less attention need be paid to economy of production. The woman who makes girls enthusiastic over their work has a place in these industries not readily if at all obtainable in industries in which the management of the workrooms is generally in men's hands. It is only in · industries supplying women's needs that women are to be found in considerable numbers as employers, managers, or head overlookers of workrooms.

In order to compare the prospects of women of mature years in the ready-made women's clothing trades we may note that in the Board of Trade returns for the former group [1] for the United Kingdom there were 211 foremen and 1021 forewomen. In the ready-made tailoring group there were 411 foremen and 187 forewomen. In the ready-made women's clothing group there were 1075 men cutters and 919 women cutters; in the ready-made tailoring group there were no women cutters at all. The women cutters do not earn high rates compared with the men, being employed on lighter work, but any girl who has any special gift for design or management can pass on to higher paid work.

Although the ready-made women's clothing trades offer few great prizes compared with the West End private custom dressmaking and millinery trades, to the rank and file it offers better conditions in the first eight or nine years after leaving the elementary schools; more wages can be earned and work is more regular. The hours of work in the city are, on the whole, shorter than those in the West End private dressmaker's workshop, and the. workroom accommodation is often better. Moreover, mediocrity finds a more secure place in the ready-made trades in later life than it does in the private-custom trade.

Besides the tendency already mentioned for owners of power-driven machinery to endeavor to utilize their plant in the slack season of one branch by adopting another with a different season, it should also be noted that the ready-made trades catering for the middle and working classes are liable to much less violent fluctuations of fashion than the West End private-custom trades; and

[1] Including also men's shirt making.

that whereas the upper classes have more clothing than they need, the working classes have not yet· reached a satisfactory minimum in this respect. Everything therefore points to an increased development in the ready-made branches of the trade.

Trade schools and trade classes. The detailed reports contain particulars of the methods adopted by different firms of training learners. In some cases learners are taught by someone especially in charge of a "learners' table "; sometimes by the forewoman; sometimes by an experienced time-worker; sometimes by a pieceworker who is allowed a certain share of the piece-rate value of the learner's work; sometimes a learner is left to pick up experience with the aid of an experienced pieceworker sitting next to her, who receives no remuneration for the trouble so far as the employer is concerned.

Many employers will take no machinists who have not already had experience elsewhere. Several employers who have taught girls machining complain that as soon as they have become skilled, they have been attracted to employers who offer higher wages but have not gone to the trouble and expense of training.

In many cases machinery was standing idle, not for want of orders but for want of skilled machinists. There was great complaining that many of the machinists who had to be engaged in the season were incompetent.

The employers were unanimous in placing cleanliness and general intelligence first as the essential requisites for a good machinist.

But barely 3 per cent attached any value to trade schools or trade teaching, or seemed to be aware that general intelligence cannot receive much development from a purely specialized and mechanical experience.

The indifference to the teaching offered in the trade schools must not be mistaken for a criticism of this teaching. Hardly any of the employers had any personal knowledge of it, and as there is only one London County Council trade school which has given trade teaching specially intended for girls entering the ready-made women's clothing trade, this is not surprising. During the five years that the Shoreditch Technical Institute has given this training, 73 girls have gone into these trades. One employer stated that she would not use the labor exchanges, as she obtained all her learners from the Shoreditch Institute and found them most satisfactory.

As nearly all the employers were ignorant of the advantages possible from good trade teaching, it followed as a matter of course that very few expressed a willingness to give time off for attendance. But it must also be noted that the few employers who had given time off had not found the experiment a success.

Slack-season classes. During the latter part of the inquiry employers were asked whether they thought slack-season classes would be useful. The suggestion was received more favorably than the proposal that girls should be allowed time off, doubts, however, being expressed as to the willingness of girls to spend their slack time in this manner.

The provision of courses of teaching given during the day and lasting for about four weeks, for girls already in the trade, might possibly show better results than are possible in evening classes held once or twice a week for a whole session. The workshop experience would enable the girl to acquire rapidity of execution, and the change to the classroom might be mentally recreative. The incompetent worker who is dismissed when slackness sets in could improve herself while looking for work, and if the slack-season classes were connected with the Labor Exchange, she could give all her attention to becoming competent instead of looking for work.

Apart from the provision of trade teaching, another aspect of this question is of public importance. A large number of women in these trades employ one or two young girls as learners to assist them in their homes in making up work given out to them by the larger manufacturers or on private-custom work. In many cases the women are employed on a low class of work on which a learner can receive little experience of a thorough kind. Some system is needed by which anyone who employs juvenile labor at a learner's rate of pay should have to give evidence of competence to teach. Much of the inefficiency of girls in the clothing trades is due to their having been trained by incompetent employers.

Arrangements for meals. The question of the arrangements made for meals is an important one when girls are to be placed in employment.

The following table shows the provision made by employers for their workpeople in this respect in the E.C. and West End districts:

NUMBER OF WORKPEOPLE GROUPED ACCORDING TO THE ARRANGEMENTS FOR MEALS

DISTRICT	MEALS PUR-CHASABLE ON PREMISES	PROVISION MADE FOR HEATING FOOD	MAY HAVE MEALS IN WORKROOM	MUST HAVE MEALS OUTSIDE	VAGUE OR NO IN-FORMATION	TOTAL
E.C.	1473	5490	1673	2817	2118	13,571
W. and S.W. .	1982	6560	509	840	659	10,550

More than one fifth of those employed in the E.C. district must go out for meals, and if to these we add those for whom no provision is made for heating food, we find one third obliged to go out for it. In the E.C. district 11 per cent are catered for by their employers, and in the West End 19 per cent. But according to the employers the majority of their workpeople prefer to bring their own food and heat it on the premises to buying the food provided for them by the firm. In the E.C. district 40 per cent and in the West End 62 per cent can adopt this plan in preference to going out for dinner.

In the other districts a much larger proportion of the workpeople live near their work, and the absence of provision for them is of less importance.

Number employed in the trades in London. The Factory Returns for Nontextile Factories in London, 1907, giving details for each borough, have been kindly furnished by the Home Office. The trades under review are included in three groups: (1) Millinery, mantle, corset, and dressmaking; (2) Aprons, pinafores, and blouses; and (3) "Other articles of clothing," which includes miscellaneous articles of men's clothing not separately classified.

The returns for workshops cannot distinguish between those engaged on private-custom work and those engaged on ready-made work except in the group for "Aprons, pinafores, blouses."

NUMBER OF PERSONS EMPLOYED IN WOMEN'S CLOTHING
FACTORIES (LONDON, 1907)

TRADE	FEMALES				MALES			
	Under 16	16 and under 18	18 and up-wards	TOTAL	Under 16	16 and under 18	18 and up-wards	TOTAL
All Districts								
Millinery, mantle, corset, and dressmaking . . .	780	995	6,064	7,839	28	35	767	830
Aprons, pinafores, blouses	304	393	2,027	2,724	6	21	135	162
"Other clothing trades"[1]	445	558	2,829	3,832	49	49	559	657
Total	1529	1946	10,920	14,395	83	105	1461	1649
DISTRICT	MILLINERY, MANTLE, CORSET, AND DRESSMAKING, APRONS, PINAFORES, BLOUSES, AND "OTHER CLOTHING"[1]							
City	247	396	2,595	3,238	21	32	434	487
Finsbury	309	364	2,393	3,066	15	28	291	334
Rest of North London .	311	352	1,770	2,433	12	19	305	336
South London	114	154	722	990	5	1	95	101
West London	314	331	1,922	2,567	2	3	87	92
East London	234	349	1,518	2,101	28	22	249	299
Total	1529	1946	10,920	14,395	83	105	1461	1649

NUMBER OF PERSONS EMPLOYED IN WORKSHOPS IN 1907 ON
APRONS, PINAFORES, BLOUSES

DISTRICT	FEMALES				MALES			
	Under 16	16 and under 18	18 and up-wards	TOTAL	Under 16	16 and under 18	18 and up-wards	TOTAL
City	100	127	1123	1350	2	9	65	76
Finsbury	92	100	473	665	—	3	45	48
Rest of North London .	44	49	236	329	1	—	—	1
South London	96	111	300	507	1	—	1	2
West London	83	134	560	777	—	—	1	1
East London	22	30	125	177	—	1	3	4
London	437	551	2817	3805	4	13	115	132

[1] Excluding tailoring, boots and shoes, hats and caps, shirts and linen collars, and *including* miscellaneous articles of men's clothing not separately classified.

The factories in 1907 employed, therefore, about 16,000 work-people; and although in the three years which have elapsed since the return was made there must have been a considerable increase in the number of factories and a corresponding decline in the number employed in workshops on the lower class of work, it is obvious that a large proportion of the 30,000 employed by the firms visited are employed in workshops where power is not used. In the West End high-class-trade handwork is, to a great extent, the rule.

CONDITIONS OF JUVENILE EMPLOYMENT IN THE BOOKBINDING AND STATIONERY TRADES (GIRLS) IN LONDON, OCTOBER, 1911 — MARCH, 1912

BY MISS COLLET, SENIOR INVESTIGATOR FOR WOMEN'S INDUSTRIES

(Report on inquiry communicated by the Board of Trade to the London Advisory Committee for Juvenile Employment for use in connection with the Juvenile Section of the London Labor Exchanges, November, 1912)

The numbers of persons employed in the County of London, according to the factory and workshop returns made for 1907, in the various trades connected with paper and printing are shown in the table on page 667.

Of these trades the various branches of the stationery trades, the bookbinding trades, and the printing trades were selected for inquiry. This report only deals with women and girls in the stationery and bookbinding trades, the information with regard to boys being reserved for a report on the printing and bookbinding trades. Workshops were not included in the inquiry.

Of the 2587 returns from factories, many related to branches only of works for which two or more separate returns were made, and the great majority of the returns for bookbinding and machine ruling were returns for very small branches of works making other returns and included in the printing trades.

Information was obtained from 100 firms engaged in bookbinding or stationery manufacture, and these 100 firms employed over 17,000 persons out of the 27,000 persons included in returns for 697 works or departments in 1907. Two or three large bookbinding works were visited by the investigators for the printing trade, two or three large stationery works were not visited for special reasons, and five firms refused information. With these exceptions the bookbinding and stationery works left unvisited employed less than twenty persons in 1907.

PAPER, PRINTING, AND STATIONERY TRADES
(COUNTY OF LONDON)

WORKS OF DE-PART-MENTS	BRANCH OF TRADE	MALE PERSONS EMPLOYED				FEMALE PERSONS EMPLOYED			
		Under 16	16 and under 18	18 and upwards	Total (males)	Under 16	16 and under 18	18 and upwards	Total (females)
	A. IN FACTORIES								
3	Paper making	1	—	28	29	—	—	32	32
490	Bookbinding and ma-chine ruling	560	677	6,648	7,885	1,384	1,503	7,621	10,508
1,264	Letterpress printing .	2,484	2,669	29,567	34,720	493	560	2,841	3,894
227	Lithographic printing .	253	329	2,801	3,383	251	329	829	1,409
142	Engraving and photo-graphic processes . .	243	299	2,149	2,691	127	289	525	941
25	Diesinking	7	24	174	205	10	3	18	31
130	Type and stereotype founding	98	123	1,514	1,735	11	46	61	118
25	Paper staining, coloring, and enameling . . .	251	125	835	1,211	16	16	81	113
15	Cardboard	57	68	323	448	106	98	302	506
42	Envelope making . .	43	37	444	524	298	215	1,481	1,994
71	Cardboard-box making .	36	53	457	546	332	368	1,798	2,498
31	Paper-bag making . .	12	20	130	162	62	63	406	531
122	Other articles of station-ery, etc.	203	121	1,130	1,454	609	462	1,806	2,877
2,587	Total	4,248	4,545	46,200	54,993	3,699	3,952	17,801	25,452
	B. IN WORKSHOPS								
—	Paper making	—	—	—	—	—	—	—	—
23	Bookbinding and ma-chine ruling	30	22	61	113	35	7	36	78
—	Letterpress printing .	—	—	—	—	—	—	—	—
9	Lithographic printing .	14	8	98	120	—	3	21	24
131	Engraving and photo-graphic processes . .	101	103	623	827	35	65	297	397
3	Diesinking	2	—	4	6	—	—	9	9
—	Type and stereotype founding	—	—	—	—	—	—	—	—
1	Paper staining, color-ing, and enameling .	—	—	—	—	—	—	2	2
2	Cardboard	3	1	8	12	1	—	2	3
4	Envelope making . .	—	—	8	8	1	4	38	43
43	Cardboard-box making .	10	21	118	149	61	69	472	602
10	Paper-bag making . .	7	2	15	24	7	31	107	145
133	Other articles of station-ery, etc.	76	74	467	617	134	214	785	1133
359	Total	243	231	1402	1876	274	393	1769	2436

In nearly every case the personal investigation was carried out by Miss Gladys M. Broughton, and her detailed reports of her interviews with employers and managers have been supplied to the secretary of the London Juvenile Advisory Committee.

Of the 100 firms giving information 43 were engaged in bookbinding, 17 in stationery manufacture, and 40 in both bookbinding and stationery manufacture.

The numbers employed by the firms giving information in the different labor exchange areas are shown below.

Labor-Exchange Area	Number of Persons employed by Firms giving Information	Percentage of Total
Finsbury	4,576	26.5
City	3,901	22.6
Elephant	2,512	14.5
Hackney and Leyton[1]	1,460	8.4
Camden Town	1,085	6.3
Islington	1,020	5.9
Clapham Junction	1,000	5.8
Bethnal Green and Stepney	979	5.7
Walham Green and Kilburn	530	3.1
Other areas	220	1.2
Total	17,283[2]	100.0

If from the factory returns we take the figures for bookbinding and machine ruling, envelope making, and " other articles of stationery, etc.," we have :

COUNTY OF LONDON, 1907

	Males	Females	Total
Under 16	806	2,291	3,097
16 and under 18	835	2,180	3,015
18 and upwards	8,222	10,908	19,130
Total	9,863	15,379	25,242

Here the boys under 16 are about 8 per cent of the total men and boys, and the girls under 16 are about 15 per cent of the total women and girls.

[1] Return made from offices in the city and included in County of London figures.
[2] Of these about 10,500 were women and girls.

Firms employing 8030 women and girls and 4779 men and boys giving information as to the number of learners employed by them showed that 969 girls (or 12 per cent of the women and girls) and 606 boys (or 13 per cent of the men and boys) were described as learners.

From this it is apparent that a girl has passed the learner stage by the time she is sixteen, while boys continue in it to a much later period.

The County of London demand in these trades for girls on leaving school may be estimated, judging from the factory returns for 1907, at over 1000 per annum. The demand for boys on leaving school would probably be not more than 450 per annum.

But notwithstanding this much larger number of girls who enter these trades, the number of women who remain in them is much smaller than the number of men. The census returns for 1911 are not yet available, but those for 1901 sufficiently show this fact. The information obtained during this inquiry shows that in this respect little change has taken place.

COUNTY OF LONDON, CENSUS 1901

NUMBER OF PERSONS OCCUPIED AT THREE AGE PERIODS

AGE PERIOD	STATIONERY MANUFACTURE		ENVELOPE MAKERS		BOOKBINDING		TOTAL			
	Number		Number		Number		Number		Percentage	
	M	F	M	F	M	F	M	F	M	F
Under 20	368	1,341	52	971	1,033	4,178	1,453	6,490	17.5	42.6
20 and under 25 . . .	301	814	27	391	905	2,449	1,233	3,654	14.9	24.0
25 and upwards . . .	1,267	725	125	575	4,203	3,777	5,595	5,077	67.6	33.4
Total	1,936	2,880	204	1,937	6,141	10,404	8,281	15,221	100	100

A certain number of errand boys should no doubt be added to these figures, which, in consequence of their exclusion from this group in the census returns, understate the proportion of boys who enter these trades and leave them, but in the main the facts are correctly represented. These trades, more particularly the bookbinding trade, can give permanent employment to the boys who enter them, and require skilled men for the bulk of the men's work. The women's work can be done as well by young women between eighteen and twenty-five as by older women.

The principal processes in which women and girls are employed are :

In bookbinding
    Folding (hand and machine)
    Gathering and collating
    Numbering
    Sewing (hand and power)
    Stitching
    Gold laying-on
    Flush binding
  Machine ruling
In stationery manufacture
    Folding
    Gumming or cementing
    Black bordering
    Relief stamping
    Packing

In one large stationery factory learners were first employed as errand girls in many cases, and then taught one or other of the following processes : cementing, hand folding, relief stamping, printing envelopes, machine folding, envelope banding and packing, label making, boxing stationery, and black bordering.

Learners. The work, whether done by hand or machine, is all of a simple nature, requiring regularity and steadiness rather than dexterity and quick-mindedness, although quick fingers are necessary for most of the processes.

In answering the question as to special qualifications required with girls, respectability was more frequently mentioned than any other ; whereas boys in the bookbinding trade were often required to have passed the Seventh Standard, it was often stated that "average intelligence" was all that was required from girls.

A girl learner in these trades is, therefore, after the first two or three months not learning new work in her branch, but merely becoming accustomed to her work. In bookbinding firms girls learning folding, sewing, or stitching are frequently paid time wages for six or twelve months and then put on piece rates, receiving only half ordinary rates for another three, or six, or twelve months, according to the employer's discretion and the custom of the house.

Those who begin as errand girls are, as a rule, paid more at the start than those who at once begin to practice a branch of the trade. But apart from this the determination of the initial wage seems to be more a question of custom in the firm than of any exact calculation of the value of the child to the employer.

Wages of girl learners. Firms employing 9852 women and girls gave particulars of the weekly wages given to learners while on a time wage. Disregarding a first week's trial for nothing required by some firms:

Firms employing 3.4 per cent paid nothing at first to learners
Firms employing 9.9 per cent paid 2s.
Firms employing 8.0 per cent paid 2s. 6d.
Firms employing 9.3 per cent paid 3s.
Firms employing 1.1 per cent paid 3s. 6d.
Firms employing 29.4 per cent paid 4s.
Firms employing 1.6 per cent paid 4s. 6d.
Firms employing 21.5 per cent paid 5s.
Firms employing 15.8 per cent paid 6s. and over
        Total   100

These rates may be contrasted with those paid in the ready-made women's clothing trades already reported on, in which firms employing only $17\frac{1}{2}$ per cent of the total women and girls paid more than 3s. to beginners compared with firms employing 69.4 in the bookbinding and stationery trades.

This difference is explained by the fact that in the former trades, more skill and intelligence being required, the beginner requires more teaching to be of use than in the trades now under consideration.

Wages in second and third years. As a rule only vague information could be obtained as to earnings in the intermediate period between the first year and the attainment of full efficiency.

In the bookbinding branch folders, sewers, and stitchers in the second year usually were paid one half to three quarters of the piece rates, an indication that some skill and experience are necessary in those branches; those paid by time earned generally only about 5s. to 6s. in the second year. In the stationery branches 6s., or more often 7s., a week was paid in the second year. At the end of the third year a girl apparently should be earning 8 s. or 9 s. on time wages.

Range of earnings of competent adult workers. The information given by employers in an interview would naturally omit those whom they do not consider competent workers and would include the rates earned by the best workers.

In the following table are given the percentage employed by employers stating certain rates of wages as the minimum, and the percentage employed by employers stating certain rates of wages as the maximum :

PERCENTAGE OF WOMEN AND GIRLS EMPLOYED BY FIRMS PAYING TO COMPETENT ADULT WOMEN THE UNDERMENTIONED MINIMUM, MAXIMUM, AND MEAN RATES

WEEKLY RATES	MINIMUM RATE	MAXIMUM RATE	MIDDLE POINT[1] OF RANGES STATED BY EMPLOYERS
8s.	0.5	—	—
9s.	—	—	
10s.	39.5	—	—
11s.	1.9	—	2.0
12s.	20.9	2.5	2.3
13s.	0.9	—	7.6
14s.	8.8	1.2	5.3
15s.	14.9	6.5	42.0
16s.	7.1	2.0	16.6
17s.	5.5	6.4	9.2
18s.	—	19.8	8.2
19s.	—	0.2	6.0
20s.	—	41.9	—
21s.	—	7.6	
22s.	—	0.5	
23s.	—	—	—
24s.	—	1.1	—
25s.	—	9.3	0.8
Over 25s.	—	1.0	—
Total	100	100	100
Number of women and girls employed by firms giving information	7295	7295	9225[2]

[1] The middle point in some cases lay between the rate given in the table and the rate above it.

[2] Including numbers employed by firms stating the average earned by competent workers and not stating a range.

This table is not a table of wages but a statement of the importance, with regard to numbers employed, of employers making statements as to wages earned by competent adult workers. It is not comparable with the table compiled from the Board of Trade returns included in the report for the ready-made women's clothing trades, which gives the wages actually earned in an ordinary week by the " middling " workers, omitting the highest and lowest paid.

From this summary it appears that only exceptional women employed in a few exceptional factories earn over 20s. in these trades. Nor do forewomen earn much more. Firms employing close on 60 per cent of the women and girls included in the inquiry gave the average as 15 s. or less.

The lowest maximum is that attained by ruling-machine feeders. The wages of a competent ruling-machine feeder were variously stated as " 8 s. 6 d.," " 7 s. to 10 s.," " 9 s· to 11 s.," " 10 s.," " 7 s. to 9 s. 6 d.," " 9 s· to 10 s.," " 7 s. to 8 s.," " 8 s." The initial wage of ruling-machine feeders during the first year is higher than that paid in most other branches. While there is no reason why girls should not begin work at these machines, those interested in them should see that they are passed on to one or other of the more remunerative and less mechanical branches after the first year or two.

In a very few cases women were employed as ruling-machine operators, the range of their earnings extending to 25 s.

Women earning over 20s. were found amongst folders, sewers, numberers, gold layers-on, relief stampers, and black borderers. Only a very small proportion of folders and sewers reached this limit, and the numbers employed as gold layers-on and black borderers appeared to be very small.

On the whole there seemed to be little difference between the profitableness of one branch compared with that of another. Nothing resembling real apprenticeship among the girls was found except among gold layers-on who at one firm signed an agreement for two years, paid no premium, received payment at once, and earned 6 s. in the third half-year, 8 s. in the fourth, and (if exceptionally good) 10 s. at the end of the two years.

In a few instances girls were found who had been apprenticed (without indentures) for a small premium, but this seemed due to some special arrangements which charitable persons desired to make.

Hours of work. Firms employing 8691 women and girls and 4154 men and boys gave information as to hours and periods of work. The information with regard to women and girls is summarized in the following table for the bookbinding and stationery trades together:

TABLE SHOWING THE NUMBER AND PERCENTAGE OF WOMEN
AND GIRLS BEGINNING WORK AT SPECIFIED HOURS AND THE
NUMBER OF HOURS WORKED BY THEM PER WEEK

Working Hours per Week (excluding Mealtimes)	Percentage working Different Periods per Week beginning Work at —					Number working Different Periods per Week
	8.0	8.15	8.30	9.0	Total	
Under 45	0.6	—	—	—	0.4	35
45 and under 47½	6.5	—	51.2	46.3	18.6	1618
47½ and under 50	6.9	100	35.0	47.7	17.1	1484
50 and under 52½	10.0	—	12.2		9.6	832
52½ and under 55	61.6	—	1.6	6.0	44.2	3839
55 and under 57½	3.8	—	—	—	2.6	232
57½ and upwards	10.6	—	—	—	7.5	651
Total	100	100	100	100	100	8691
Percentage beginning work at specified times . . .	70.5	1.4	20.4	7.7	100	—
Number beginning work at specified times	6128	120	1773	670	8691	—

The hours of beginning work appear to be later in the bookbinding trade than in the stationery trade.

	Percentage of Women and Girls beginning Work at					Number employed by Firms giving Information
	8.0	8.15	8.30	9.0	Total	
Bookbinding	53.3	—	29.2	17.5	100	3535
Stationery	90.2	—	9.8	—	100	2645
Stationery and bookbinding .	73.9	4.8	19.3	2.0	100	2511
Total	70.5	1.4	20.4	7.7	100	8691

The total hours ordinarily worked during the week are also less in the bookbinding trade than in the stationery trade.

Working Hours per Week (excluding Mealtimes)	Percentage of Women and Girls working Different Periods per Week			
	Bookbinding	Stationery	Bookbinding and stationery	All firms giving information
Under 45	1.0	—	—	0.4
45 and under 47½	22.7	6.9	25.1	18.6
47½ and under 50	27.6	—	20.2	17.1
50 and under 52½	11.7	6.7	9.7	9.6
52½ and under 55	13.4	84.5	45.0	44.2
55 and under 57½	6.6	—	—	2.6
57½ and upwards	17.0	1.9	—	7.5
Total	100	100	100	100
Number employed by firms giving information	3535	2645	2511	8691

As a general rule, therefore, the weekly hours of work are at least five less than those permitted by law, and in the case of one third of the women and girls are at least ten hours less.

The hours are on the whole longer than the usual hours in the ready-made women's clothing trades, where 78 per cent worked less than fifty-two and one-half hours compared with only 45.7 per cent in the trades under review.

Seasonal fluctuations. On the other hand, these trades compare very favorably with the clothing trades in regularity of employment. A large percentage are employed by firms stating that they experience no seasonal slackness. Other firms state that they are never slack but have a busy season, when they take on season hands, these occasional workers being frequently married women who have left the trade. No young persons may work more than the ordinary sixty hours a week permitted by law, but the margin between the ordinary hours worked and the full time permitted, together with the overtime permitted for adult women, make it possible for some firms to get through the busy autumn season without employing casual labor.

Firms employing 7162 women and girls gave definite information about slack periods, and firms employing 2221 women and girls gave definite information as to busy seasons and not as to slackness. The information given by this second group has been tabulated, and is given as supplementing and, to a great extent, confirming that given by the first group.

The following table shows for each month the percentage of 7162 women and girls employed by firms affected by slackness and of 2221 women and girls employed by firms affected by extra pressure.

	PERCENTAGE OF 7162 WOMEN AND GIRLS AFFECTED BY SLACKNESS	PERCENTAGE OF 2221 WOMEN AND GIRLS AFFECTED BY PRESSURE
January	6.1	29.9
February	10.8	20.0
March	4.9	25.7
April	1.6	8.1
May	1.0	9.9
June	7.9	9.9
July	17.9	15.8
August	19.8	20.3
September	4.6	73.6
October	1.9	81.3
November	—	89.0
December	—	86.5
No slack months	64.6	—

Both columns of the above table show that there is extra pressure in these trades in September, October, November, and December. April and May show no slackness in the first group of firms, but also show little pressure in the second group.

But although the seasonal fluctuations are neither so numerous nor so severe as in the clothing trades, the large number of small firms competing with each other are not in a position to guarantee full employment through the year. Several small firms do nothing but machine-ruling work, and this work, although paid better at the start than most other processes, leads to nothing and will never yield a fit wage for an adult woman. On the other hand, it sometimes happens that in a very small firm a girl may have a chance of doing many processes which she would never be required to learn in a large one.

Prospects of promotion. A few of the women engaged in the trade become forewomen, but the position does not appear to be much coveted, and the forewoman's pay rarely exceeds 25 s. a week and is frequently less. Having attained her maximum degree of efficiency by the time she is twenty-one, a woman might work at the trade for another thirty years without any prospect of improving her position.

Arrangements for meals. The arrangements for meals for women and girls in these trades in the firms visited were on the whole more satisfactory than in the factories and workshops in the ready-made women's clothing trades in the E.C. district. In many firms the men and boys were expected to go outside for meals, but provision of some kind was nearly always made for the women and girls.

NUMBER AND PERCENTAGE OF WOMEN AND GIRLS EMPLOYED BY FIRMS GIVING INFORMATION GROUPED ACCORDING TO THE ARRANGEMENTS FOR MEALS

	Stationery and Bookbinding		Women's Clothing, E.C. District
	Number	Percentage	Percentage
Meals purchasable on premises . .	1,707	16.3	*10.9*
Provision made for heating food . .	7,515	71.7	*40.4*
May have meals on premises . . .	512	4.9	*12.3*
Must have meals outside	318	3.0	*20.8*
Vague or no information	422	4.1	*15.6*
Total	10,474	100	*100*

In nearly all firms beginning as early as 8 A.M. and working as late as 7 P.M., the full one and a half hours were allowed for meals although not legally compulsory.

Trade classes. There does not appear to be any branch in these trades in which girls would derive any trade benefit by attending trade classes. In bookbinding proper they have no part. A few women with capital have succeeded in obtaining training and have shown a high standard of taste and skill in the bookbinding craft.

But however fitted girls may be for such a trade, there seems to be no desire on either the side of the employer or of the girl that apprenticeship in bookbinding should be thrown open to girls.

It should, however, be remembered that although one department of work generally offers no better opening than any other in these trades for women, nevertheless it is an advantage for a girl to be expert in every branch so that slackness of orders in one branch may be balanced by transference to another branch where there may be a pressure. In so far as fixed agreements with employers are desirable in placing girls in these trades, it would appear to be mainly in this connection, with the object of securing that the girls should acquire skill in several branches.

Advantages and disadvantages. So far as wages are concerned the average girl with no special bent in any direction, but of careful and methodical habits, can earn as much in the ten years after leaving an elementary school as she could earn in other trades. If she obtains employment in a large firm she may suffer a little through trade slackness, but not much from seasonal slackness. The demand for stationery and account books (the latter being a branch of the bookbinding trades in which many women are employed) is likely to increase steadily. The hours of work are less than the full time permitted by law. The girls in the bookbinding works are frequently relatives of the men engaged as printers or bookbinders in the same firm. The social advantages of working along with skilled workmen earning about $2\frac{1}{2}$ times as much as themselves, if not more, are probably not ignored by the parents of girls entering the trade.

On the other hand, the work offers few attractions to an imaginative or constructive mind. It gives no scope for industrial ambition, and gives no practice in any craft useful later on in domestic life. To a girl with a taste for reading, music, social work, or any other unremunerative occupation the comparatively small demand on her intelligence exacted by the daily work may be a recommendation.

PART IV. SOME PRACTICAL ASPECTS OF VOCATIONAL GUIDANCE

VOCATIONAL GUIDANCE AND EMPLOYMENT IN BIRMINGHAM

By Meyer Bloomfield

(From " The School and the Start in Life," *United States Bureau of Education Bulletin*, 1914)

Nowhere in England will be found a more intelligently executed plan of helping children start in life than in the city of Birmingham. The education committee through its central care committee has built up an organization of school care committees which now covers nearly the whole of the city. The scheme operates under the Choice of Employment Act and was approved by the board of education in consultation with the Board of Trade in July, 1911. An integral part of the Birmingham scheme is the chain of juvenile labor exchanges distributed at central points throughout the city, in the management of which there is the closest coöperation between the school and Board of Trade officials. A corps of nearly 1500 men and women, called helpers, undertake to interest themselves in the individual children and their parents who use the labor exchanges. During the first seventeen months nearly 11,000 applications were received from employers, and 7000 children under seventeen years of age were placed, besides numbers of other cases in which the helpers themselves undertook to counsel and place the children.

Birmingham is fortunate in the variety of its skilled occupations. Although there is a vast amount of unskilled work, likely to increase with constant improvement in labor-saving machinery, yet the metal trades, the printing trade, and other industries offer satisfactory opportunities to a large number of workers. To some degree, therefore, the problem of starting young workers in Birmingham is less severe than in Liverpool or London. Notwithstanding these relative advantages, however, a study of the Birmingham enterprise only strengthens the conviction which comes to every student of vocational-guidance work anywhere; namely, that placement for children under eighteen is at best a makeshift so long as the public neglects to put in force certain fundamental social policies through legislation, which policies will be discussed in the closing chapters.

These fundamentals, it should be said, are keenly appreciated by the men and the women who are devoting themselves to the youth of Birmingham. About 13,000 boys and girls leave the elementary schools in that city each year; most of them are absorbed by offices, factories, workshops, and warehouses. The need of guidance and training is apparent as soon as the careers of these children are scrutinized. To meet this need the following plan, in active operation for more than two years, is in charge of the central care committee, which devotes its attention to the industrial problems of boys and girls from the time they leave school until they are seventeen years of age. This committee consists of six members of the education committee, four representatives of teachers, three of employers, three of workmen, four social workers, the school medical officer, and others. The committee carries on its work through two sets of agencies: (1) the juvenile employment exchanges and (2) school care committees.

1. THE CENTRAL JUVENILE EMPLOYMENT EXCHANGE

This is in charge of an officer specially appointed by the Board of Trade on account of his knowledge, training, and fitness for dealing with the employment of juveniles. He attends the meetings of the central care committee and acts in consultation with their officer.

The chief work of the exchange is:

(1) To receive and register applicants for employment from youths and girls under seventeen years of age.

(2) To receive and register applications from employers for juvenile employees.

(3) To endeavor to place the applicants for employment in the situations for which they are best suited and in which they are likely to be most successful.

The exchange is in a good position to select the applicant, because both the exchange and the central care committee have accumulated an immense amount of information about the various trades of the city, and so can advise as to wages, prospects, and conditions in any trade. It knows what trades lead to regular and improving work, and can caution against bad conditions and prospects.

By the time a child applies for a post, the officials above mentioned will have in their possession a report concerning it from the head teacher of its school, from the school medical officer, and from the school care-committee helper. In the first twelve months 7180 applicants were received from employers, and 4907 were filled.

For the convenience of parents and juvenile applicants five branch exchanges have been opened in various parts of the city.

2. SCHOOL CARE COMMITTEES

The scheme provides for the appointment of a school care committee for each elementary school in the city. Many schools thus have their own care committees. In a number of cases it has been found advisable to group several neighboring schools under one care committee. These committees consist of school managers, teachers, and others who are prepared to interest themselves actively in boys and girls. The members are assigned as " helpers " to a small number of children each. The helper is put in touch with the boys or girls about three months before they leave school, and at once tries to set up a friendly relation with the parents as well as with the children by visits to the home or by other means. The children are encouraged to talk about what they would like to be, the parents about what they have in view. When there are vague or unsuitable proposals for a child's employment, or no plans at all, the parents and the child are urged to attend at the juvenile employment exchange, and thereby to find the best available post for which the child is suited. To rouse the sense of parental responsibility, to lead the well-meaning but uninformed parents to industrial knowledge and right action, to encourage the choice of skilled employment rather than employment with no prospect of advancement for the boy — these are among the helper's aims on the industrial side, while the employment exchanges provide the means of giving effect to the school care-committee's work.

The helper endeavors to keep in touch with the boy or girl for about three years. This, as regards employment, is necessary to counteract the aimless drifting or the capricious change from job to job, to give encouragement to face and overcome difficulties, to see that, if changes are advisable, they are made for the youth's benefit and do not give rise to intervals of disastrous unemployment.

The conditions under which boys and girls are employed are in many places quite unsatisfactory and have a bad effect morally or physically, or both. Information is gathered by the central care committee and the juvenile employment exchanges, which some day doubtless will be used to improve these conditions.

FURTHER EDUCATION AND KINDRED INFLUENCES

The helper takes an interest and stimulates the parents' interests too in further education of the boys and girls. They are urged, where the hours of work allow, to join classes at the technical schools, schools of art, evening continuation schools, or at such institutions as may be most suitable to the individual cases.

Some school care committees concern themselves with the means of recreation and assist with boys' or girls' clubs.

Again, meetings of parents are held from time to time, such as have already been organized by several school care committees; also meetings of boys and girls about to leave school or who have recently left. These meetings are found to be valuable means of rousing interest in the future well-being of the children.

The helper's notebook is an interesting device for keeping track not only of the children but of the helper's effectiveness as well. These notebooks when carefully employed are a veritable store of social information. The inside of the cover of each book is printed in the manner indicated on pages 684 and 685. Blank pages are inserted for the helper's notes, the width of which is such that the edges reach the vertical line. The ruled lines for the notes continue the horizontal printed lines of the cover. It is thus unnecessary to print the "headings" on each page, and the "fillers," or blank pages, may be easily renewed.

The duties outlined by the Birmingham education committee for the school care committees are given in full, as they clearly indicate the nature of the work expected of each committee.

DUTIES OF SCHOOL CARE COMMITTEES

1. Members of school care committees should do their best to influence the industrial history and character of the children under their care by insuring that more account be taken of the needs of individual cases and of the general conditions of industry than is possible at present. They should also encourage the wider use of educational institutions of all sorts after the age of compulsory attendance has been passed. Further, they should not only try to influence the child, but also the parents, whose coöperation and support is in the long run absolutely essential.

2. Any person who is already taking an interest in boys or girls between the ages of thirteen and seventeen, or who is otherwise in close touch with families with children of that age, will become *ipso facto* members of the care committee of the school to which the child belongs or belonged.

3. Three months before a child leaves school the responsible helper and the head teacher will confer together as to the child's future, and then consult with and advise the child and its parents. Should a further interview be thought advisable, it would be held one month before the child leaves school. These interviews can take place wherever most convenient.

4. When a child has left school and started work the helper shall keep in effective touch with him and his home and shall continue to advise and encourage him and his parents in every way. (The frequency of his visits or interviews will, of course, vary with the troublesomeness or ignorance of the case.)

5. It is most important that the helper should take care to keep himself informed of all changes in the work and of the home conditions of the child, and report immediately to the secretary of the school care committee (where a child has left work) the date and cause of leaving ; (where a child has started work) the employer's name and trade, nature of work done by the child, wages (piece or day), hours (short time, casual, extra long hours).

It is also desirable to have a general report on the child's progress in work and character twice a year.

6. The helper should give every encouragement to the child to use the juvenile employment exchange to which his school is attached.

7. When the helper needs information about a child under his care he may apply to the secretary of the school care committee for access to the confidential records.

(1) Child's name.   (2) No. . .

Address . . . .

School . . . .

(1) Standard . . . . . }
(2) Date of leaving . . }

Home conditions . . . . .

Father's occupation . . .

Mother's occupation (if any)

No. in family (1) over 14; }
    (2) under 14 . . . . }

Social or other organization

Evening school or classes }
    child promises to attend }

(1) Promise or (2) plans for }
    employment . . . . }

Will application be made }
    to the J. L. Exchange . }

Dates of visits . . . . .

REMARKS AND NOTES

SUGGESTIONS TO SCHOOL CARE COMMITTEES AND HELPERS FOR FILLING UP HELPERS' REPORTS

[The ... is in these suggestions ... to the ...]

1. ... of school ... that friction ...

2. The ... as to "School," ...

3. With ... to "Date of leaving," ... before the ... of legal ...

4. The ... children, ...

5. Under No. 4 on the ... tional, or ...

6. As to No. 5, it is ... will give the ... of the evening school or other ...

7. If the child has a ... If the child has no ... and then give particular as ...

8. With ... to 8, it is ... to register at the ... view, and this ... exchange whether something

COVER OF NOTEBOOK; LEFT

FURTHER EDUCATION

{ Evening school or class attended by child . . .

{ Date of (1) entering . . . (2) leaving . . . . .

Subjects or course . . . . .

{ Progress or reason for leaving . . . .

EMPLOYMENT

Name of employer . . . . .

Address of employer . . .

{ Date of (1) commencing (2) leaving

Trade and nature of work .

{ (1) Weekly wage . . . . . (2) Daily hours . . . . . .

How employment obtained .

{ Progress or reason for leaving . . . . . .

REMARKS, NOTES, AND INFORMATION ON CHANGES OF EMPLOYMENT, ETC.

COVER OF NOTEBOOK; RIGHT

8. The helper should attend his school care committee meetings, when he may bring up individual cases in which he has difficulty in deciding what to advise. Helpers will *not* be expected to bring up ordinary cases.

9. Where a helper is brought into touch with unsuitable conditions in any trade or with any other problems connected with child labor, he may bring the matter up for discussion at the next school care committee meeting. If considered advisable, the school care committee will send up a report on the matter to the branch committee, who shall in turn forward it, with their comments, to the central care committee. Until branch care committees are formed the report would be sent direct to the central care committee.

At the inception of the Birmingham work the coöperation of the chamber of commerce was secured for the purpose of inquiring among the employers representing the leading trades of the city as to the conditions, requirements of different trades, and the possibilities of further training for the young workpeople. The questionnaire used in that inquiry deserves re-publication and is here given :

INDUSTRIAL TRAINING INQUIRY

Name of firm_____

Address of firm_____

Trade_____

Branches of trade carried on or particulars of goods manufactured_____

_____

_____

1. *Employers' requirements*
   (1) Is there a sufficient supply of trained workmen, or do you have difficulty in getting them?

   _____

   (2) (*a*) For what different branches of work do you employ boys in your trade?

   _____

   (*b*) How long would it take an average boy to learn each branch?

   _____

   (*c*) At what age should he begin?

   _____

   (*d*) What special characteristics are most needed?

   _____

   (3) (*a*) Do you want general capacity and training depending on dexterity, powers of observation, self-reliance, initiative, and adaptability?

(*b*) Or do you require only mechanical skill?

(4) (*a*) Would there be any opening for youths if given all-round training in your trade?

(*b*) Or do you want only specialization in parts of it, or in single processes?

2. *Supply of boys*

(1) Do you have any difficulty in getting boys?

(2) How do you get boys — through the labor exchange, by newspaper advertisement, or by window or works notice?

(3) (*a*) About how long do boys stay with you on the average?

(*b*) Is it long enough to learn the trade?

(*c*) What hold have you over the boys, or what means of control?

(4) (*a*) Are the boys you get satisfactory?

(*b*) If not, in what way are they unsatisfactory?

(5) Do you suffer from the frequent changes of jobs common amongst Birmingham boys? What do you consider to be the cause of the frequent changes?

(6) Is there anything objectionable to boys in your trade? If so, have you any suggestions for removing objections or making the trade more attractive?

3. *Schemes of training*

(1) Is there apprenticeship? Or any other definite agreed scheme for training?

(2) If so, give details — premium (if any), commencing wages, raises (amount and time), indentures (if any) or other agreement.

(3) Give criticisms or suggestions for amendment.

(4) Is there any subsequent improvers' stage? If so, give particulars.

(5) (a) Is technical instruction of any use?

(b) Have you any scheme of coöperation with any technical school, evening schools, or other educational institutions?

(c) Give general statement of what is wanted and criticisms of existing classes.

(6) What modification (if any) of the present elementary-school curriculum would you suggest to fit boys to enter your trade?

4. *Prospects of boys*
(1) What number of boys and youths (say 14 to 18) does your firm employ?

(2) What number of men?

(3) (a) Can your trade absorb all the boys you employ when they become men?

(b) If so, at what?

(4) (a) If not, what percentage (or proportion) is absorbed?

(b) At what age do the others drop out?

(c) Do you know what becomes of them?

(5) From what other sources are your men recruited, if not from boys who have been in the trade?

(6) (a) What becomes of machine minders?

(b) What is the class of boy doing this work?

(c) How long on the same machine and what arrangements for acquiring progressive experience of machines?

(7) If any special interest is taken by the management in the boys, what form does it take; for example, treatment in the works, helping them to learn the trade, continuative education, and generally

taking account of the doings and progress? Are there any special instructions to foremen on this?

---

5. *Hours and wages*
  (1) Hours —
    (*a*) What is the usual number of hours worked per week?

    (*b*) What are the ordinary daily hours? From   to
    (*c*) What, if any, seasonal variation of hours?

---

  (2) Wages —
    (*a*) What are the commencing wages of boys (apart from apprentices already dealt with in 3 (2))?

    (*b*) What are the usual subsequent raises (state amounts and periods or ages)?

    (*c*) Does piecework apply at all to boys and youths? If so, please give average earnings in piecework at different ages.

    (*d*) Does "subcontracting" affect the boys and youths? If so, give particulars.

---

6. *General observations*

The following documents give a good insight into the workings of the school care committees :

CENTRAL CARE COMMITTEE

Report of the Conference between Members of the Central Care Committee and Honorary Officers of School Care Committees

The second half yearly conference between members of the central care committee and the honorary officers of school care committees took place at the Education Offices, Margaret Street, on Tuesday, November 26, 1912.

There were present 69 ladies and gentlemen representing the central care committee, two branch care committees, and 40 school care committees and subcommittees. Eighteen school care committees and subcommittees were not represented.

Councilor Norman Chamberlain, chairman of the central care committee, presided.

The agenda of 12 items consisted, with two exceptions, of matters submitted by school care committees themselves for discussion. The following notes and recommendations are given on the items seriatim.

1. *Old scholars' clubs.* (Farm Street, etc., school care committee.)

After the usefulness of old scholars' clubs in the work of the school care committees and the desirability of the central care committee providing facilities for meeting had been briefly advocated, the chairman announced that rooms in schools could be used free of rent, but subject to payment by the clubs of the caretaker's fee. The central care committee had tried to secure the reduction of that fee, or the power to pay it, but the present had been shown to be an unsuitable time to press for this concession.

2. *Apprenticeship.* (Farm Street, etc., school care committee.)

In reply to inquiries, the chairman announced that the central care committee was about to begin an inquiry into the whole question of industrial training, including apprenticeship, in Birmingham.

3. *Clerical work.* (St. Thomas's school care committee.)

Mr. Birch and other speakers said that the amount of clerical work falling upon honorary secretaries was very heavy, and that unless it could be reduced, or at least its increase arrested, it would become impossible for honorary secretaries to cope with it. It was agreed that several forms recently supplied had appreciably reduced clerical work in certain directions. The following suggestions were made:

(1) That the heading of the helpers' reports should be filled in at the office before issue.

(2) That where a committee deals with more than one school, a registrar be appointed for each school or department.

(3) That the cards for summoning meetings be sent from the office.

4. *Return of helpers' reports.* (Bournville and Stirchley school care committee.)

The discussion showed that the difficulty of getting in the helpers' reports is very great and a serious problem. Helpers who have taken cards or to whom cards have been sent have in numbers of cases failed to attend meetings or to send in their reports, even after repeated requests. One honorary secretary had been able to obtain the return of only 20 reports from 93 cases.

Suggestions

(1) Councilor Lord urged the necessity of holding meetings monthly on a recognized day, of handing out new cases then, and calling for reports on cases taken out at the previous meeting. This had proved useful in establishing the habit of attendance in the Sparkbrook district.

(2) That on the next issue of helpers' report cards a note should be printed requesting the return of the report by a specified time. (The chairman stated that this had been done.)

(3) That helpers should be supplied, where the honorary secretary deems it necessary, with stamped envelopes for the return of the reports by post.

(4) That head teachers be requested to use every possible means to obtain and give the correct name of the organization to which a child belongs.

(5) That honorary secretaries send to the central care department the name of any organization which does not return the helpers' reports.

5. *Second reports.* (Sparkbrook school care committee.)

Mrs. Jesper urged the necessity of the helper being in close touch with the child at the actual time of leaving school and commencing work, and of submitting a second report as soon as the child is placed at work. This is the critical time.

6 and 7. *Branch care committees.* (Sparkbrook school care committee.)

The formation of branch care committees was advocated, so that school care committees should coöperate and not work as separate units possibly in some matters in competition with one another. It was further advanced that it was a good arrangement to hold all meetings in a district on the same evening in the week but in different weeks for different committees. The chairman said the policy of the central care committee had so far been to set up branch care committees as soon as the demand for one arose in a district, and to leave school care committees freedom to make their own arrangements as to meetings.

8. *Periodical bulletin.* (Camden Street, etc., school care committee.)

Mr. Mackenzie moved that the central care committee be recommended to issue a quarterly bulletin to helpers, giving instructions, notes, and information concerning the school care committees and their work throughout the city. Many helpers are unable to attend meetings regularly, and either they lost touch with the work, or the honorary secretary had to send out periodically his own bulletin compiled from various communications, circulars, etc., received from the central care department.

The opinion was expressed that the bulletin, if issued, should be supplied gratis and sent direct by post from the central care department. It would relieve the honorary secretaries considerably and would keep the interest of helpers alive.

Recommendation (carried by 11 votes to 8, the majority not voting): "That the central care committee be asked to issue such a bulletin quarterly."

9. *Head teachers and the Juvenile Employment Exchange.* (Camden Street, etc., school care committee.)

Mr. J. T. Booth, on behalf of his committee, raised the question whether the time had not now arrived when all applications from employers for boys and girls should be referred to the exchange. He stated that in numbers of schools very few, if any, children were placed through the exchange. Some head teachers would like to be relieved of the responsibility of sending children to work on request from employers, and also many children did not get the advantages the exchange might give them. Several head teachers spoke against the suggestion, and the feeling of the conference being against such a step at present, the matter dropped.

10. *School-leaving age.*

The conference closed with announcements by the chairman concerning forthcoming lectures to helpers, the first by Mr. C. E. B. Russell, of Manchester. There was not time to deal with the concluding item of the agenda; namely, the present state of the central care committee's work.

CENTRAL CARE COMMITTEE

Juvenile Employment Exchanges and Domestic Service for Girls

Report of the special committee appointed to consider the draft scheme for the appointment of a domestic-service subcommittee of the central care committee, to act with the Juvenile Employment Exchange in placing girls between fourteen and seventeen years of age in domestic service.

Your committee met on February 5, 1913. . . .

The subcommittee were unanimously of opinion that full advantage should be taken of the permission now granted by the Board of Trade to juvenile employment exchanges to undertake, under certain conditions, the placing of girls in domestic service, and they accordingly recommend that measures be taken to commence such work as soon as possible. This recommendation is made on the following grounds:

(1) The local education authority has, through the medium of the exchange, been able to give guidance and assistance to girls leaving school in taking up every class of employment except domestic service, yet domestic service is a suitable occupation and one to be encouraged under proper conditions.

Both head teachers' and helpers' reports indicate domestic service as desired and desirable in a number of cases. It is inconsistent to refuse the helper and the child the same assistance as is available in every other occupation.

(2) The existing means and organizations for bringing employers and young girls desiring domestic service into touch with each other are inadequate.

(3) Judicious after care is desirable in the case of many girls placed in domestic service.

(4) Such a subcommittee would be able to ascertain what exactly are the facilities in the city for training girls for domestic service, and to make suggestions for extension and improvement from time to time.

Your committee examined the draft scheme, which in its general lines has already been approved by the central care committee, and are of opinion that but little alteration is necessary. They recommend that the subcommittee should consist of 20 members, instead of 12 to 16 as previously suggested, and that its constitution should be:

4 Members of the central care committee
4 Representatives of the Girls' Friendly Society
2 Representatives of the Young Women's Christian Association
2 Representatives of Roman Catholics
1 Representative of Graham Street School
1 Representative of the ladies' committee of the Sunday School Union
7 Representatives of branch care committees and school care committees, one to represent each existing branch care committee, and one to be appointed from each of four other districts of the city.

Additions to the draft scheme, as referred to the subcommittee, are recommended to make clear (1) that the subcommittee shall have power to appoint or approve visitors, and (2) that in cases of girls placed by the Juvenile Employment Exchange who belong to or may join certain organizations, for example, the Girls' Friendly Society or the Young Women's Christian Association, the supervision or after care shall be referred to the organization concerned, subject to such reports being made as the subcommittee may deem advisable.

The scheme embodying the suggested amendments would be as follows:

1. That a domestic-service subcommittee be appointed, consisting of 4 members of the central care committee, 4 representatives of the Girls' Friendly Society, 2 representatives of the Young Women's Christian Association, 2 representatives of Roman Catholics, 1 representative of Graham Street School, 1 representative of the ladies' committee of the Sunday School Union, 7 representatives of branch care committees and school care committees (one to represent each existing branch care committee and one to be appointed from each of four other districts of the city); and that the subcommittee have power to appoint or approve visitors.

2. That the functions of the subcommittee be as follows: (1) To make recommendations from time to time to the central care committee on matters of general policy. (2) To establish a rota, one member to be present at the exchange at such times as shall be arranged for the purpose of advising upon the placing of domestic servants.

3. The duties of the member present will be: (1) To discuss the vacancies notified to the exchange. (2) To offer such advice as she may deem desirable to the exchange officer. (3) To report on the work done to the next meeting of the committee. (4) To report to the committee any cases requiring special investigation.

4. The duties of the committee at its weekly meeting will be: (1) To receive a report as to the week's work. (2) To receive notifications from the rota members as to vacancies of which they have advised acceptance on their own responsibility. (3) To consider the vacancies referred to them for further investigation. (4) To arrange for any investigation that may be necessary with regard to these vacancies, and for the result of such investigations to be reported at once to the exchange. (5) To receive and consider reports on such vacancies as have been specially investigated. (6) To arrange for such supervision as may be necessary of the girls placed by the exchange, referring girls who belong or may become attached to the Girls' Friendly Society and Young Women's Christian Association and similar organizations to these organizations for supervision and report. (7) To receive the reports from the helpers who have undertaken such supervision.

5. To confer twice yearly with the ladies acting as helpers in the case of girls placed in domestic service by the exchange, and with others specially interested in the question of domestic service as an occupation for girls and in the training necessary for it.

Report of the Executive Committee to the Central Care Committee

To be presented at a meeting of the central care committee to be held on Monday, April 7, 1913, at 5 P.M.

1. *Domestic-service subcommittee.* The five organizations which were invited to coöperate with the central care committee in placing young girls in domestic service through the Juvenile Employment Exchange have all intimated their willingness to do so, and to nominate representatives on the subcommittee. . . .

2. *Health week.* It is the desire of the " health week " committee that the central care committee and the school care committees should assist in any way open to them in the propaganda of " health week," which commences on April 27. Your chairman has invited the honorary secretaries of school care committees to take part in a conference on the 11th instant, and to discuss the most effective means of helping in the work.

3. *Head teachers' reports — health section.* The hygiene subcommittee have considered the resolution of the central care committee asking whether arrangements could be made for the final medical examination of school children to take place sufficiently long before the date of leaving to allow entries by the medical officers to be made on all head teachers' reports, which are forwarded to the office about four months before the children leave school. In response the hygiene subcommittee have passed the following resolution :

That the central care committee be informed that this subcommittee will place at their disposal the schedules of all children who have been examined prior to their leaving school, but that the examinations will have extended over the whole year and will not necessarily have taken place four months before the children leave school.

Your committee consider that the proposed alteration would give approximately only the same result as before, and would involve a much greater amount of work in the central care department than the present arrangement gives the medical staff. They therefore recommend that the hygiene subcommittee be informed that the central care committee would prefer the continuance of the present system.

4. *Free admission to evening schools.* The attention of the technical education and evening schools subcommittee was invited to the recommendation of several school care committees to the effect that there should be means available to school care committees to obtain free admission to evening schools for children in cases where the investigations of the committees showed that children were actually prevented from attending such schools by inability to pay the fees. The technical education and evening schools subcommittee on the 10th of March resolved as follows :

That the central care committee be informed that this subcommittee are submitting to the education committee at its meeting on the 19th March an amended scheme of free admission to the evening and technical schools of the city.

This scheme has now been approved by the education committee, and empowers head teachers of day schools to award a certain number of free admissions to evening schools. There is also provision for award to scholars already in evening schools of free admissions to subsequent sessions of evening schools and to technical schools. Your committee recommend that a communication be sent to head teachers requesting that in making their award of free admissions they will have due regard to the recommendations of school care committees.

5. *Industrial arrangements in East Birmingham.* The East Birmingham branch care committee have been successful in getting into touch with several of the large firms in the locality and securing their representation on the branch care committee, and on several school care committees. This action prepared the way for arrangements which have been provisionally completed with the Metropolitan Carriage & Wagon Building Co. (Ltd.) and the Wolseley Tool & Motor Car Co. (Ltd.), according to which these firms will engage all their juvenile employees through the Juvenile Employment Exchange, giving preference to those recommended through the school care-committee system of the district. Both firms will give facilities for the boys to attend evening schools and classes, and will encourage them to do so.

6. *Gathering of helpers at Uffculme.* Through the kindness of Mr. Barrow Cadbury the application for the use of Uffculme for a gathering of helpers on September 6 next has been successful. Your committee have appointed Miss Barrow, Councilor Chamberlain, and the Rev. H. S. Pelham to make the necessary arrangements in due course.

7. *Trades for physically defective children.* In response to a request from the special school after-care employment subcommittee your committee recommend that in the pamphlets on local trades now in course of preparation an appendix be inserted giving advice in regard to suitable employment for deaf and physically defective children. The subcommittee mentioned will so far as possible furnish the matter for the appendix.

8. *Receipt of grant from board of education.* The board of education have paid to the education committee the sum of £236 7s. 3d., being the board's contribution toward the salaries of the executive officers, from the approval of the scheme in July, 1911, to December 31, 1912.

9. *Assistant caretakers.* It will be remembered that some time ago the central care committee made representations to the sites and buildings subcommittee concerning the position of assistant school caretakers, recommending that the practice of discontinuing their services at the age of twenty-one years should be abandoned, and that if suitable they should be employed until they could be absorbed as caretakers. The sites and buildings subcommittee were unable to see their way to make the arrangement suggested. Your committee have now learned that the subcommittee have decided to make such appointments in future subject to termination at nineteen years of age.

10. *Pamphlets on trades for boys.* Your committee have had before them a complete set of penny guides to trades and handicrafts for youths and girls

leaving school, issued by George Phillip & Son (Ltd.), of which about twenty have been published. They feel that a set comprising the books on each of the local trades would be of much value to the school care committees, and they therefore recommend that sufficient sets be purchased to furnish one set to each school care committee.

11. *Return based on head teachers' reports.* The following is a statement compiled from the head teachers' reports received during February in respect of children due to leave school before the end of June:

	ALL SCHOOLS				SCHOOLS WITH CARE COMMITTEES			
	Boys	Girls	Total	Per cent	Boys	Girls	Total	Per cent
Number of cards received . .	516	514	1030	—	359	331	690	67.0 .
Number of children attached to some organization . . .	337	360	697	67.7	242	247	489	78.7
Number of children who promised to attend some evening school	279	154	433	42.0	199	110	309	44.8
Number of medical reports appearing on head teachers' reports	192	210	402	39.0	135	138	273	39.6
Number of those examined requiring medical attention .	26	46	72	19.9	21	28	49	18.0

Number of cards marked with discriminatory letter . . . 937, or 91 per cent
Number of cards marked A . . . . 183, or 19.5 per cent
Number of cards marked B . . . . 384, or 41 per cent
Number of cards marked C . . . . 370, or 39.5 per cent
Number of cards not marked . . . . 93, or 9 per cent

SCHOOL STANDARD ATTAINED BY CHILDREN EXPECTED TO . LEAVE SCHOOL DURING JUNE, 1913

Number of cards marked, 954, or 92.6 per cent of total cards sent in

Number of children in

Per cent of total

Ex-seventh standard . . . . 51, or 5.3
Seventh standard . . . . 332, or 34.8
Sixth standard . . . . 288, or 30.2
Fifth standard . . . . 176, or 18.4
Fourth standard . . . . 81, or 8.5
Third standard . . . . 20, or 2.1
Second standard . . . . 6, or .7

12. *Return of employment obtained during February*. The following is a statement concerning employment obtained during the month of February:

School Children obtaining Employment	Total	Per-centage
Number of children reported as having obtained employment on leaving school	752	—
Reported by head teachers as having obtained employment through medium of the school	57	7.5
Obtained employment through the Juvenile Employment Exchange	190	25.3
Reported by head teachers as having obtained employment by their own or their parents' efforts	505	67.2

13. *Juvenile Employment Exchange return*. The following figures have been supplied by the Juvenile Employment Exchange in respect of the four weeks ended Friday, March 28, 1913, namely:

	Applications by Boys and Girls			Vacancies notified by Employers		
	Boys	Girls	Total	Boys	Girls	Total
Central exchange	206	53	259	279	87	366
Jewelers' exchange	33	42	75	40	92	132
Aston exchange	39	45	84	39	34	73
Handsworth exchange	36	10	46	15	24	39
Selly Oak exchange	41	45	86	20	37	57
Sparkhill exchange	28	23	51	5	14	19
Total (4 weeks)	383	218	601	398	288	686
Corresponding totals for February, 1913 (4 weeks)	509	384	863	466	367	833
Corresponding totals for March, 1912 (5 weeks)	601	320	921	496	235	731

The relation of the Birmingham teachers to the scheme herein outlined is real and active. Many head teachers use commendable care in the reports on the children who leave school. These reports indicate the groups of children which in the teacher's judgment need a good deal of after care, those which need only a moderate amount, and those which need no after care except perhaps as to continued education. For the first eight months during

VACANCIES FILLED BY EMPLOYMENT EXCHANGES

	Vacancies filled			Vacancies filled by Children direct from School		
	Boys	Girls	Total	Boys	Girls	Total
Central exchange	173	44	217	50	22	72
Jewelers' exchange	25	19	44	10	9	19
Aston exchange	18	34	52	4	6	10
Handsworth exchange	2	17	19	—	7	7
Selly Oak exchange	19	35	54	8	22	30
Sparkhill exchange	5	4	9	—	—	—
Total (4 weeks)	242	153	395	72	66	138
Corresponding totals for February, 1913 (4 weeks)	308	253	561	98	92	190
Corresponding totals for March, 1912 (5 weeks)	304	153	457	—	—	84

14. *Helpers' reports.* The number of helpers' reports received from school care committees during each of the last six months is as follows:

	First Reports	Second Reports	Total
October, 1912.	316	—	316
November, 1912	702	141	843
December, 1912	403	107	510
January, 1913	278	19	297
February, 1913	449	28	477
March, 1913	513	95	608
Total	2661	390	3051

which these records were kept, nearly half of about 9000 cases were referred to the school care committees, which in turn called upon the helpers for assistance. Many organizations in Birmingham, particularly those interested in boys, have been enlisted in the scheme. Here social workers and teachers, as is the case in Boston, New York, Cincinnati, and other cities, have been giving their time and their energy generously to the work. Parents' meetings are carried on by many school care committees. Employers are often the speakers at such meetings.

It should be borne in mind that the Birmingham experiment coincides with an unusual state of industrial prosperity. There are more vacancies than there are boys. Such trades as the engineering, brass, jewelry, and silversmiths cannot secure enough apprentices. They are glad to have the Juvenile Employment Exchange select workers, even for the more advanced positions. This is due somewhat to the improved quality of the applicants who come to these labor exchanges. It has been the practice of teachers even in cities where labor exchanges are maintained to look after the brightest children themselves, or the favorites of the school, and leave to the labor exchange the difficult children. Obviously this is not coöperation. In Birmingham, on the other hand, many of the schools make a point of advising all the children who leave school to go with their parents to the exchanges. There is still a good deal of placement by the schools, and it is greatly to be hoped that this will in time diminish, if not wholly disappear.

With reference to girl labor, Birmingham presents the problem characteristic of our own American cities. The girls desire office work, and too many take courses in shorthand and typewriting. The start in life for these girls is difficult indeed and the outcome quite unsatisfactory. The market for stenographers and office workers is overstocked. The element amongst whom the exchange renders its most useful service is that group of girls who, desiring a manual occupation, have been guided into the better trades, such as bookbinding, leather stitching, etc. As in the case of the boys, there is a great demand for girl labor. The city has not adequately faced, and few cities have faced, the problem of vocational training for girls. Two useful handbooks have been issued by the central care committee as part of a series on the principal trades and occupations in Birmingham. One deals with the various trades for women and girls; the other on printing and allied trades. There is much effort to secure continued training in evening schools for the children placed.

An idea of the occupations for boys and girls and the number placed from June 1, 1911, to October 31, 1912, may be gained from the tables which follow, but it should be explained that the figures with reference to the messengers, stable boys, etc., apply mostly to

JUVENILE EMPLOYMENT EXCHANGE RETURN SHOWING THE NUMBER OF VACANCIES NOTIFIED AND THE NUMBER OF VACANCIES FILLED, CLASSIFIED UNDER DIFFERENT TRADES OR OCCUPATIONS[1]

TRADES AND OCCUPATIONS	VACANCIES NOTIFIED	VACANCIES FILLED	TRADES AND OCCUPATIONS	VACANCIES NOTIFIED	VACANCIES FILLED
OCCUPATIONS FOR BOYS			OCCUPATIONS FOR BOYS (CONTINUED)		
Telegraph messenger service .	83	80	Laboring	239	122
Art, music	26	18	Miscellaneous employments[2]	175	80
Hotel service	151	104			
Business clerks' work . . .	481	346		6270	3965
Van boys, stable and groom work	170	115			
Warehouse	384	235	OCCUPATIONS FOR GIRLS		
Messenger and porter service	581	434			
Rolling mills	115	90	Domestic service (daily girls)	21	10
Tube manufacture	42	34	Laundry	50	24
Pattern making	11	7	Daily service	135	70
Iron-foundry work	47	18	Clerking	118	96
Brass-foundry work . . .	554	286	Warehouse	724	511
Blacksmithing	42	7	Errand-girl service	83	17
Engineering (general) . . .	323	269	Core making	21	20
Polishing (metal)	270	183	Polishing, brass	26	19
Drilling, milling	374	302	Press, drill, and capstan work	629	456
Tool making	148	119	Screw working	15	8
Gun manufacturing . . .	24	22	White-metal working . . .	94	43
Wire drawing	25	14	Lacquering	125	91
Miscellaneous metal work . .	328	181	Soldering	30	18
Cycle manufacture . . .	71	37	Cycle making	65	45
Motor-car manufacture . .	24	14	Jewelry working	148	64
Goldsmith, silversmith, and jeweler work	383	168	General factory working . .	58	12
Electrical apparatus making .	40	29	Electrical working	39	21
Carpentering and joining . .	143	76	Weighing apparatus making .	15	18
Painting and decorating . .	55	20	French polishing	45	20
Plumbing and gas fitting . .	139	49	Upholstering	22	17
Cabinetmaking	45	23	Cartridge making	270	267
Upholstering	26	9	Candle making	13	11
Wood carving and engraving .	19	11	Soap making	16	15
Other work in wood . . .	29	11	Rubber work	53	50
Glass manufacture	75	43	Leather work	69	50
Soap manufacture	21	18	Paper-bag making	50	33
Rubber work	33	23	Printing	128	70
Leather-goods work . . .	28	11	Bookbinding	15	10
Printing and bookbinding . .	175	92	Draping	15	10
Tailoring	22	7	Tailoring	47	13
Bootmaking	23	8	Dressmaking	35	18
Baking and biscuit manufacture	33	16	Machinists' trade	36	25
Greengrocery	27	8	Button making	68	67
Cocoa and chocolate manufacture	151	150	Cocoa and chocolate making	667	638
Butchering	25	9	Japanning	23	15
Brewing	28	19	Shop service	73	23
Electrical engineering . . .	62	48	Factory work	280	85
			Miscellaneous employments[3]	171	83
			Total	4492	3063

[1] The numbers refer to all children placed from fourteen to seventeen years of age in the period June 1, 1911, to October 31, 1912.

[2] Under this heading have been included all trades and occupations in each of which less than seven boys were placed. They include architecture, photography, gardening, assistant caretakers, railway service, colliery workers, diesinking, lamp making, motor and carriage building, ironmongers, scientific, surgical, weighing, and electrical instrument making, bricklaying and plastering, brick and tile manufacture, French polishing, manufacturing chemists, candle and grease manufacture, paper, envelope, and cardboard-box manufacture, drapery and clothing trades, japanning, pawnbroking, and various dealers.

boys over sixteen, and that many of the employers have placed the boys in these positions after an understanding with the labor-exchange officials that advancement was fairly certain after a few months.

RETURNS SHOWING THE VACANCIES FILLED BY CHILDREN DIRECT FROM SCHOOL THROUGH THE EXCHANGE[1]

BOYS

Telegraph messenger service . .	80
Drawing offices	10
Hotel service	10
Office work	114
Van-boy and stableboy work, etc.	3
Warehouse	32
Messenger (preliminary to various trades)	84
Gardening	2
Tube mills	2
Rolling mill	3
Brass working	28
Blacksmithing	1
Engineering (mechanical) . . .	54
Polishing (metal)	6
Tool making	46
Gun making	5
Miscellaneous metal trades . . .	23
Cycle trade	5
Motor trade	9
Jewelry, silversmiths, etc. . . .	55
Electrical fittings manufacture .	12
Carpentering and joining . . .	13
Plumbing and gas fitting	8

BOYS (CONTINUED)

Furniture, cabinetmaking, etc. .	10
Glass trade	3
Rubber manufacture	8
Leather manufacture	3
Brush trade	1
Printing, bookbinding, etc. . . .	30
Tailoring	3
Boot trade	2
Cocoa and chocolate manufacture	85
Grocery work	2
Electrical engineering	12
Laboring in factories	9
Total	683

GIRLS

Pupil-teacher work	1
Theater service	1
Laundry-maid service	2
Day-servant work	21
Clerk work	50
Warehouse-girl service	104
Errand service	6
Florist service	1

The following circulars issued by the central care committee are of interest:

CITY OF BIRMINGHAM EDUCATION COMMITTEE

CENTRAL CARE COMMITTEE

To boys about to leave school:

1. You will be leaving school very soon — in a few months probably. It is most important that you should carefully choose the kind of work you want to do.

[8] Under this heading have been included all trades and occupations in each of which less than seven girls were placed. They include pupil teacher, theater service, telephone service, pen makers, wireworkers, opticians, shroud makers, glassworkers, brush makers, rope and canvas workers, milliners, mineral-water manufacture, restaurant workers, pawnbrokers, etc.

[1] The numbers are given in respect of the various trades and occupations, and cover the period January 1 to November 30, 1912.

2. Talk over *now* with your parents and your teacher what sort of work you would like, and what would suit you best.

3. Think of the future. There are many well-paid jobs for boys which end when you are seventeen or eighteen years old, and which do not train you for anything else. If you go to work of this kind, you will find it very hard to make a fresh start at eighteen. You will probably be out of work a good deal and have low wages when you are a man.

4. Try to become a skilled workman. Learn a trade if you get the chance. Your wages will very likely be less while you are learning the trade, but you will be much better off later on. Aim at being a first-class workman, and do not be satisfied to become only half-skilled.

5. If you or your parents want to know more about different trades and occupations, go to the Employment Exchange for Boys at 168 Corporation Street, or to the exchange nearest to you. If you want help in getting a suitable situation, call at the exchange a week or two before you leave school and get your name put on the register. Ask your parents to go with you.

6. Someone from the school care committee will very likely call at your home to talk over your future with you and your parents, and to help you in any way he can.

7. Stay at the day school as long as you can. When you leave, join some evening school or class, and choose those classes which will help you in your work. What you learn will be a great help to you.

8. If your situation is a good one with a promising future, stick to it through thick and thin. Even if you think it is not a good one, do not leave it until you have got something really better.

9. Before leaving ask advice from your parents, your old schoolmaster, or your care-committee friend. Also go to the exchange some Friday evening between 6 and 7 P.M.

10. If you are out of work, go to the exchange any morning. The manager will be glad to see you and to help you to get a suitable situation. But beware of moving from place to place without good reason. It is sure to be a bad thing for you in the end if you do this.[1]

City of Birmingham Education Committee

CENTRAL CARE COMMITTEE

Juvenile employment — A word to parents

To what work do you intend to put your children when they leave school? What trade or other calling have you in view for your boy, what employment for your girl? What are they best fitted for, and likely to succeed in? Have you carefully thought the matter out, and made the best possible plans? These questions are of the greatest importance to you and your children.

Many of you are probably undecided. Some of you perhaps do not fully

[1] A list of exchanges follows with the hours when open.

know what the commerce and industries of the city have to offer in the way of employment for juveniles.

The education committee, acting with the Board of Trade, have adopted a big scheme for giving you information and for helping you to place your children in situations to the greatest advantage.

A central juvenile employment exchange has been opened in Corporation Street, with branches in different parts of the city. Your boys and girls up to seventeen years of age are cordially invited to call at the exchanges when in want of a situation. You and they should go there when in need of information and advice about employment. Especially should you consult the exchange if you have a child who will be leaving school soon, and it is best to go some weeks before the child is due to leave.

You may ask why there is any need to change the present way in which children find work, that is, by their friends or relations speaking for them, by looking in the papers, or by walking round the different factories in the district.

It is quite clear that you will have a larger number of situations from which to choose at our exchanges, as most of the good employers all over the town will be getting their workers from them. Your child will thus be more certain to get there a situation suited to its health, its powers, and its personal ambitions. If a child gets a job for which it is fitted and which it likes, it will do better and be happier than if it has to take a job in the casual and uncertain way which is now usual. Nor will it take so long or mean as much tramping about and so many useless inquiries as now.

You will also be able to find out more correctly and more fully the conditions and prospects in any trade, for the ladies or gentlemen in charge of the exchanges will always be glad to give you advice if you care to ask them.

In many of the schools we are also starting care committees, whose members will take a personal interest in the child during the first three or four anxious years of its working life. They will take especial trouble with children when they are about to leave the day school for good. Just before this happens some member of the care committee, perhaps already known to you, will be only too glad to talk over with you and your child the plans for the future; the teachers, too, have very kindly promised their help. This will be very useful to you, as they have great opportunities of finding out the sort of work at which the child will be happiest and do best.

We are also hoping that the care committee will be able to arrange for meetings of parents, when the different trades can be discussed and questions asked.

Everyone realizes that the way a child starts on its working life will settle its whole career, and that the time is the most important in its whole life. Unless a child starts at the work for which it is best suited from the point of view of health, character, and ability, it will suffer throughout its life, and will be deprived of a real chance of success. Unless a child begins to learn a trade young, it will never learn it well. It is to help those parents who realize this, and to arouse those few who do not yet realize it, that we are starting this scheme, and we hope very much that you will support it in every way you can.

MEDICAL INSPECTION AT THE START IN LIFE

By Meyer Bloomfield

(From " The School and the Start in Life," *United States Bureau of Education Bulletin*, 1914)

Every part of the United Kingdom has its certifying factory surgeons, so called, appointed by the chief inspector of factories. There are altogether 2000 of these officers, who are frequently also medical officers of health, and, most unfortunately, are paid for the examination of children by fees from the employers. The duties of the factory surgeons, under the Factory and Workshops Act of 1901 and 1907, and the order of the Secretary of State are :

1. To examine every child or young person under the age of sixteen within seven days (or thirteen days in the rare cases where the surgeon's residence is more than 3 miles from the place of work) of his commencement of work in a factory or in any workshop where one or more of the following processes are carried on : file cutting, carriage building, rope and twine making; brick and tile making; making of iron and steel cables, chains, anchors, grapnels, and cart gear; making of nails, screws, rivets; baking bread, biscuits, or confectionery; fruit preserving; making, altering, ornamenting, finishing, or repairing wearing apparel by the aid of the treadle sewing machines.

2. To make certain examinations and inquiries in connection with accidents, workmen's compensation cases and dangerous trades.

It should be noted that, under the Factory and Workshops Act, a worker under the age of sixteen must be reëxamined each time he changes his place of employment. " Half-timers," that most pitiful class of spent children, must also be reëxamined when they commence employment as " full-timers." Something like 500,000 examinations are made annually. In 1910 nearly 8500 children were rejected as being physically unfit for employment. In about 6000 cases the surgeons exercised their powers with more or less care under the Factory and Workshops Act (1901) to grant " conditional certificates " ; for example, pass the child for employment subject to exclusion from certain processes entailing danger. In 1911 the number of young persons rejected from employment amounted to 10,000. Some juvenile advisory committees have undertaken to follow up cases of boys and girls rejected by the certifying surgeons and to find them suitable employment if any employment is desirable. There is very great need of coördinating the activities of factory surgeons, medical officers, and the advisory committees. No one more keenly appreciates the present unsatisfactory situation than does Sir George Newman, the chief medical officer of the Board of Education. In the United Kingdom, as in the United States, there has been little intelligent effort to correlate the work of employment health inspection with the social needs of the children.

Coöperation is essential from every viewpoint. There is nothing to prevent the child rejected at the factory gate by the factory surgeon from obtaining employment in an occupation outside the factory act and removed from any legal scrutiny, employment often infinitely more harmful physically than that from which he has been rejected. Because the home and the school figure so little in the present methods of medical factory inspection, the rejected child is frequently unable to explain to the parent the physician's reason for rejection. The factory act stipulates that a written explanation of the reason for rejection shall be given, but this provision is a dead letter. An exceptional illustration of the coöperation here suggested may be found in the efficient work of the medical officer (school) for Dewsbury. In this instance there is the fortunate fact that the medical officer is also the certifying factory surgeon, a situation which gives him the opportunity to see the child in school before employment, and in the places of employment at the time of being engaged.

This physician has made it his business, wholly on his own initiative, to notify the Dewsbury advisory committee for juvenile employment of the rejections made which needed the attention of the committee. The committee's secretary or some member visits the parent until the children obtain suitable employment or medical treatment. In addition to giving information of rejected cases, another group of children are also reported to the advisory

committee. A certifying factory surgeon meets with certain children who may have some defect which careful treatment can
remedy and thus prevent later and more serious obstacles to
passing a medical inspection.

The following table shows the cases of all kinds reported by the
Dewsbury certifying factory surgeon to the advisory committee
and dealt with during the year 1911 to April, 1912 :

> Cases notified as rejected from employment 52
> Cases where conditions have improved and the children are
>   now in suitable employment 19
> Cases where children have received medical treatment and are
>   now in suitable employment 31
> Cases of children unfit for employment 2
> Cases of delicate children in employment notified 24
> Total number of cases rejected and delicate visited and re-
>   ported on 76

On the following page is an interesting table of cases in connection with the Dewsbury work, interesting because of the comments recorded on the conditional certificates.

The Dewsbury advisory committee has made an investigation
not only of working-children, but also of school children who work
out of hours, an evil which does not as a rule come to the notice
of the medical or any other officers.

These surveys of the range of employments in which children
are found, and of the working hours of children whose energies
are presumed to be dedicated to the state in the work of growth
and self-improvement, are suggestive of the possible disclosures,
once advisory committees, schools, and medical officers unite, as
they should, in a comprehensive policy of protecting youth. There
have been not a few investigations into the physical condition of
working school children. While differences in the health of such
children' have been found to be dependent in part upon the nature
of the occupation, the strain, confinement, etc., all indications
point to beginning work at too early an age as a prime source of
breakdown and later incapacity. There is a wealth of suggestive
material to be found in the reports and investigation of a number
of school medical officers. One of them will be briefly summarized.

Year	Reason	Work allowed	Work forbidden
1908	1. Lateral curvature of spine	Attend loom	Not to lift heavy baskets, etc.
	2. Defective vision . . .	Folding blankets	Machine work
1909	1. Defective vision, lateral nystagmus (congenital)	Simple handwork, and general errand work in patent-glazing factory	Work with machinery
1910	1. Mentally somewhat dull	Paper-box making by hand	Anything to do with cutting or machinery of any kind
	2. Too young	Making firewood into bundles	Not to chop wood, work at machinery, or carry heavy weights
	3. Small stature	Errand boy	Not to chop wood, work at machinery, or carry heavy weights
	4. Small stature	Errand boy	Not to chop wood, work at machinery, or carry heavy weights
1911	1. Left knock-knee	Fringing machine, as this allows sitting	Work necessitating prolonged standing
	2. Operation for hernia years ago	Ordinary work	No lifting or carrying weights
	3. Small stature	Giving in	No weight lifting or work with machinery in motion
	4. Knock-knee	Sew buttons on blouses .	Not to use machines
	5. Heart disease	Sew buttons on blouses .	Not to use machines
1912	1. Small stature	Giving in	Nothing else in connection with weaving
	2. Small stature	Winding	Nothing entailing overreaching or weight lifting
	3. Post laparotomy scar .	Light work in connection with printing	Prolonged standing or machine work

1. Paper boys, 89. Get up between 5.30 and 6 A.M.; usually have a piece of bread and perhaps some tea before they leave home; hasten to the station or news-agent's shop, which may be as much as 2 miles away from their homes, for bundles of papers, take the papers to various houses; length of round varies; time taken varies accordingly from one to two and one-half hours; then a hasty breakfast at home before going to school. Many of the boys have an evening round also. The average wage is 2 s. 6 d. per week; some of the boys who sell papers, in addition to delivering them to regular customers, get a commission on the number sold, and earn from 4 d. to 6 d. per week. Their corrected average height was 1 inch, and weight 2½ pounds, less than those of the 383 boys not employed out of school hours. Slight spinal curvature was found to be more frequent among these boys than among those employed otherwise, owing to the heavy bundles of papers carried.

2. Milk boys, 37. Get up between 4.30 and 5.30 A.M.; have a morsel of food before leaving home, rounds generally take three hours or longer, afterwards

a hurried breakfast, often eaten on the way to school. Some of these boys go around again during the dinner hour, some when afternoon school is over. Their average wage is 2s. 6d. per week. The corrected average height of these boys was 1 inch, and weight ½ pound, less than those of the 383 boys not employed. Those who had worked for two years or more were found to be 2 inches and 3 pounds below the average.

3. Errand boys, 66. These boys spend most of their spare time in the dinner hour and in the evening in delivering parcels or baskets of provisions; they often carry heavy weights, and are apt to take very hurried meals. They generally earn 2s. or 2s. 6d. a week. Their average height and weight were not found to differ much from the normal, but some who had worked for two years or more were found to be as much as 1¼ inches and 5 pounds below normal.

4. House boys, 77. Employed in the early mornings to clean boots and knives, carry coals, and so forth, in private houses. Get up about 6.30 A.M.; work for one or two hours before school; are often provided with breakfast by their employers. They earn about 2s. a week. These are picked boys who work under good conditions. Those examined were found to be on the average ½ inch taller and 2 pounds heavier than the nonemployed boys.

5. Boys employed in miscellaneous occupations; for example, garden boys and barber's boys, 41. Little or no difference was found between these and the nonemployed boys.

6. Boys employed on Saturdays, and sometimes Sundays, as golf caddies or as errand boys (38) were found to be of normal height and weight for their age.

The success of the experiment in Dewsbury has led the advisory committees in other places to seek the coöperation of certifying surgeons. Some sort of coöperation has been secured or promised in Huddersfield, Leeds, Halifax, Nottingham, Northampton, and in other towns. In Huddersfield the education committee passed a resolution authorizing the school nurses to assist the secretary of the juvenile employment advisory committee in following up cases.

The relation of medical supervision to the right start in vocation is clear enough. Inspection at the leaving stage is indispensable. All vocational counseling, labor-exchange service, and after care must take their cue from the physician's report. Examination at this stage reveals the results of school life, home environment, incidental employment, and the inheritance of the candidate for a calling. This examination, furthermore, is of peculiar interest to the English people, because the children of this age are nearing the insurable age under the Insurance Act. At no other period in a youth's life is medical supervision more necessary, and from a public viewpoint more urgent. The prevailing practice in all the countries studied, as with our own, shows a too slight regard for this vital matter. The whole scheme of factory legislation, vocational schools, and social legislation in general, rests on insecure foundations if the medical supervision of adolescent workers is inefficient. Medical investigations in England have shown that physically unfit children are liable to a high degree of accident in the course of their work. An intrinsic value in medical supervision is that it supplies a method of individual selection of the worker, something no general provisions, such as factory acts, can as well accomplish.

The Employment of Children Act, 1903, contains the following provisions :

A child shall not be employed to lift, carry, or move anything so heavy as to be likely to cause injury to the child.

A child shall not be employed in any occupation likely to be injurious to his life, limb, health, or education, regard being had to his physical condition.

If the local authority send to the employer of any child a certificate signed by a registered medical practitioner that the lifting, carrying, or moving of any specified weight is likely to cause injury to the child, or that any specified occupation is likely to be injurious to the life, limb, health, or education of the child, the certificate shall be admissible as evidence in any subsequent proceedings against the employer in respect of the employment of the child.

The local authority is thus given ample power medically to guide the young work seeker. Instances are unfortunately too few where the physician has thoroughly exercised this power.

What may yet be accepted as a necessity in the English scheme of vocational assistance is the appointment of special medical officers for the advisory committees, who shall act in a coördinate capacity with the school medical officer and the factory surgeon. These medical advisers would probably be assigned to work in connection with all the various types of schools, such as evening schools and trade schools, and with the children who use the labor exchanges.

Inspection at the place or time of employment goes only part way. The child-helping schemes so extensive throughout England and Scotland need above all else the reënforcement of a medical department with full powers to investigate occupations in their relation to a sound physical development. The absence of a medical-research and health-guidance department in almost all vocational-assistance enterprises is responsible for much of their ineffectiveness.

SCHOOL AND EMPLOYMENT

By Meyer Bloomfield

(From "The School and the Start in Life," *United States Bureau of Education Bulletin*, 1914)

This discussion will attempt to suggest an outline for an American school policy with respect to the relation of our schools to the start in life of their children, profiting so far as possible by the lessons and cautions of foreign experience. In the absence thus far in this country of considerable experience in connecting schools with employment and in organizing safeguards for the start in life, it is of course obvious that little more than a tentative draft of a policy and of the possible next-steps can be ventured; yet for all that actual practice may suggest in the way of detail, machinery, and administration, there are certain principles fundamental to any service connected with the start in life. Experienced social workers, educators who make their school work function as social service, and efficient workers connected with the movements for vocational guidance and education are in no doubt as to the need of taking the next steps and as to what at least one or two of these steps should be.

To competent students of the problems considered in this study, it is clear that a thorough scheme of vocational advising and of training necessarily involves provisions for placement, for supervision, and for methods of organized study which are calculated to yield material for enlightening public opinion and for legislative action. Vocational service of any kind is so large an undertaking that specialized phases of it may well occupy the whole time of any organization, but it is submitted that any scheme of vocational service which does not in some way come in direct contact with the problems connected with the actual start in life of youth is in danger of finding itself an unreal undertaking, busied with lifeless abstractions regarding shadowy beings instead of men, women, and children.

Participation, then, is here advocated as fundamental to any successful scheme of vocational service ; such participation as we know to be the best feature of the neighborhood worker's activities. Contact with the practical world insures that salutary concreteness of criticism and appraisal which sound growth requires. Some personal touch with boys and girls and men and women and the trying out of one's theories and capacities as a vocational counselor in real experience are the key to successful vocational assistance.

KNOWLEDGE OF CONDITIONS, AND STRUGGLE FOR AN IDEAL

Workers in the field of vocational education and guidance, therefore, whether they be in vocational schools, labor exchanges, advisory committees, or vocational-guidance enterprises, are expected to face their task from two standpoints when helping young people to a start in life. They are forced, necessarily, to deal with the working world as they find it, and they are equally obligated to illumine their work with an ideal of what ought to be the conditions. A knowledge of existing conditions is the foundation of the daily, personal service which a vocational agency is called upon to render ; but without the corrective of a social vision any vocational scheme, whatever may be its immediate practical benefits, can hardly be regarded as an important instrument of human conservation. The knowledge here suggested cannot be based on mere fragmentary accumulation of many kinds of occupational details, gathered in the course of visits to work places ; it must be knowledge founded on organized data gathered by the specialist trained in the technic of vocational investigation. The vision and ideal here suggested must not be a vague and futile longing for something different, but an intelligent purpose founded on clear sight of a goal, and expressing itself in aggressive and telling ways.

It is now trite to say that school life is sharply ended at the option of children who go to work as soon as the law will let them. Likewise is it now a truism that this leaving time has been mostly neglected and the children exposed to peculiar dangers. The child's entry into working life has not been on the whole looked upon as a special concern of the school. Individual teachers and school principals have always, doubtless, taken an interest in individual children, or even in entire classes. But, outside a few cities in this country, one will not find any systematic and worth-while effort to compile and interpret the work histories of children who have left school for employment; and few indeed are the agencies which concern themselves with the transition problems of youth in the abyss between school and work. There are, to be sure, the vocational schools and vocational departments of our high schools, which, as a matter of course, are more or less active in securing employment for those whom they have trained. Not many a school has gone beyond the mere placement stage for its pupils, and not many have scrutinized the occupations sufficiently to influence their own curriculum. But if the vocational schools, close to work conditions though they presumably are, and more pressingly required than other types of schools to concern themselves with the start in life, have, on the whole, so little organized the machinery and formulated the principles of service in helping young people during the transition period, what shall we say as to the public schools generally?

The children who leave the schools of our country, whether they graduate or drop out, are obliged to find themselves, somehow or other, as workers. The schools have done little, specifically, to point the way. In a sense, the schools deserve much praise for the little they have been doing toward a vocational start in life; for with no resources, time, or preparation, their efforts in this difficult field could only have been absurdly inadequate and possibly harmful. Several causes account for the failure on the part of the public to support the schools in organizing the much-needed start in life service. In the first place, the schools have been kept so busy with what is called preparing for life that the teachers have been given no leisure for more active contact with that life. On the whole, the American public has not called too vigorously for such vital participation on the part of the teachers. In fact, the situation has not been greatly encouraging to that growing number of teachers who are disheartened over much of the present lifeless routine of fitting for life. The community has been, on the whole, too little alive to the moral hazards and the hard perplexities which the young job seeker experiences. Finally, a persistent idea regards work seeking and employment as a private concern of the individual, and the employment bargain and all that follows it as nothing more than the personal affair of the bargaining parties.

INCREASING INTEREST IN YOUTHFUL WORKERS

Now our best practice and belief continually belie this obsolete notion. That society feels its vital stake in all that attaches to the employment contract, particularly of minors, is abundantly demonstrated by the great variety of protective measures going forward, such as school working certificates, health and factory inspection, licensing rules for employment agencies, and the increasing number of child-labor laws and of state-aided vocational-training opportunities.

The English system of juvenile advisory committees rests on a clear recognition of society's duty to protect and befriend its young work beginners. The increasing importance of school people in the work of these committees is suggestive of the place which the schools will occupy in the near future as guardians of the adolescent.

From two directions the schools are compelled more and more to consider their relations to the start in vocation. On the one hand, the movements for vocational training and guidance bring the school face to face with the occupational world; on the other, the organization of the labor market through public employment offices, a field in which we have been thus far lamentably backward, will oblige the schools to work out a policy with respect to these agencies. As yet few states maintain public employment offices; but, doubtless, there will be many more, as the wastefulness of present work-seeking methods is realized. Nevertheless not many schools will be satisfied merely to refer their leaving children to a near-by public employment office, with no voice, oversight, or power.

To a considerable degree the success of vocational guidance and training efforts is conditioned by the thoroughness of their articulation with working conditions and with social movements. Within a well-defined sphere of its own in the school system, vocational service is of the utmost value. It endeavors to help pupils to self-knowledge, and to reconstruct school programs in order that they may more sensitively minister to the self-discovery and economic needs of different pupils. Vocational service — both guidance and training are here included — is an instrument for talent saving and for interpreting school life in terms of career building. In its larger relationships, however, vocational service is only one phase of the social organization of school and vocation. It introduces into education the motive of the life-career and the idea of fitness of the individual, apart from class or group; it introduces into employment the idea of fitness of the task, and appraises the occupations in terms of career values as well as social worth.

The passing of the labor exchanges act was facilitated by the belief that a personal advisory service in connection with work seeking would help lessen the waste due both to job hunting and to misemployment. No little addition to the volume of unemployment comes from what W. H. Beveridge, director of the labor exchanges, calls "qualitative maladjustment." No more promising institution than the public school exists to undertake the task of qualitative vocational adjustment. The question arises as to whether the public-school system would best undertake alone to deal with the start in vocation, or leave it to other agencies, while reserving for itself the task of providing for needs which arise in the course of employment, such as further training opportunities. It is submitted that the schools will have to concern themselves actively and dominantly with every phase of the vocational start in life. Is the average school system ready to undertake this new and enormously difficult business? It is not. Indeed, so little is it prepared to do this work at the present time that a hasty undertaking of it would probably indicate a lack of understanding. It is doubtful, in the first place, if a school department can alone effectively organize the labor market for young workers. The pronouncements on this subject by Scotch and English authorities are convincing. On the whole, experience seems to support the proposition that the school system is not the most suitable agency to attempt the organization of the labor market for the young and the correlative proposition, that the carrying on of juvenile employment agencies without control over them by the school is not in the best interests of the children.

It is assumed that work seeking in this country will more and more be under the direction of the public through state or possibly municipal agencies; for we are almost the only advanced industrial country to continue the present demoralizing chaos of an unorganized labor market. Public labor bureaus, when rightly managed and properly understood, are capable of considerably larger services than labor registration, important though this is. Developments in the best of these bureaus in England and in Germany promise a new type of civic center and agency for industrial betterment. Everywhere the best practice is to separate the juvenile from the adult departments of these bureaus, and the girls' from the boys' departments. More and more the young work seekers' problems are being treated as something distinctly different from those of adults. We are confronted, then, with the need of not only organizing placement provisions for the young, but, in addition, a comprehensive instrument of social and educational protection.

RELATION OF THE PUBLIC SCHOOL TO THE EMPLOYMENT AGENCY

The public school must remember the fact that it is, primarily, an educational institution with social aims. What a century of child-welfare effort and experience has taught the friends of working-children, the schools can, least of all, afford to ignore. More than any other institution, the school must stand for a high minimum of protection for all children. It is not to the credit of our schools that, on the whole, they have been unaware of a situation which many an employer has known for some time, and this is, the economic uselessness of children from fourteen to sixteen. Schools have sometimes been willing to plunge into small or large employment schemes as if full-time work were the right thing for growing children.

Of the public schools, more than of any other institution, public or private, we have the right to expect a clear vision and a determined stand with respect to the interests of childhood and youth. Private societies do and may, by way of experiment, make concessions and compromises in order to carry out their various purposes, but in the practice of the public-school system, we look for exemplification of the permanent principles which should control all the activities in which young people find themselves.

There are three distinct aspects of the problem of adolescent employment: the educational, economic, and social. Through extension of vocational-training opportunities, and especially through the provision for prevocational schools which, when their purposes are better understood, will become *self-discovery schools* and, as such, afford young people and their teachers a most important basis for vocational guidance, the schools are beginning to deal with the first of the three aspects named.

As public labor offices grow in number, the economic side of the problem will be given at least a preliminary treatment. This will be not more than preliminary, however, for a juvenile employment department is, notwithstanding general opinion, a placement agency only secondarily. It is in facing the third or social aspect of the entire problem that we find the basis for satisfactory organization.

IMPORTANCE OF DEVELOPING RIGHT ATTITUDE

This proposed social basis for juvenile labor organization is intended not so much to protect the boy worker or girl worker under eighteen against employers as against themselves. The greatest difficulty in dealing with the boy who is about to leave school for work lies in the fact that he regards himself as a worker who has outgrown the learner. Not until disastrous experience has overtaken many of these children do they begin to realize how much a learning attitude would have meant in building a career. A large part of this difficulty is due to leaving the question of the boy's future unconsidered until school-leaving time.

As we do things piecemeal in this country, we are likely to find in a number of places a vocation bureau in the schools, with perhaps a number of vocational-training classes; a separate employment bureau of the city or state to which boys are sent or drift; and perhaps a private or semipublic advisory body with no real power, making futile efforts to help the troubled children with a disorganized machinery of service.

We need to write into the law-establishing labor offices that a juvenile department shall be managed by a central executive committee appointed by the school system; which committee shall be made up of school people, employers, social workers, and employees, to advise as to the school vocational-guidance and training activities, on the one hand, and manage the occupational research and placement supervision activities of the labor bureau, on the other. This committee should be empowered, through health officers and other trained specialists, to study children; to take them out of work places, if need be; and through scientific investigations to list occupations from the viewpoint of opportunity as well as their manifold reactions on the worker. Children under sixteen are to be under training, part time at least, until the public is ready to care for their entire fourteen-to-sixteen-year period.

From what has been said regarding the duties of a juvenile employment agency, with its suggested twofold powers, namely, close supervision of the vocational activities of the school system and control over placement and its associated features, it is clear that "employment agency" is a misnomer. Perhaps a better name for such a body and agency would be the "vocational-service bureau." Service, intelligent, deliberate, and coördinated with the work of all existing upbuilding agencies, is indeed the main business of an employment office for minors. There are problems connected with such employment of the greatest importance to the public and on these we have little or no information. These are the amount of juvenile underemployment, misemployment, and unemployment; the causes of maladjustment, and how far training and what kind of training can lessen these causes; and the specific, thoroughly analyzed, requirements of the occupations. To enlighten the public as to these matters and secure such constructive legislation as may be necessary is perhaps the most far-reaching work which such a service bureau can do. It is not difficult to conceive that a public enterprise which combines help to groping youth with social planning will in time have laid foundations of a service which will safeguard, strengthen, equip, and inspire boys and girls for their appropriate work to an extent nowhere as yet to be found.

INDEX

Lightning Source UK Ltd.
Milton Keynes UK
UKHW010233070119
334855UK00011B/2007/P